DATE DUE

Handbook of
WORK STRESS

*To Sam and Lilly, Rhoda and Aubrey, Paye and Morris,
and Max, who never had to support me but always did.*

Julian Barling

For Debra, who continues to turn my distress into eustress.

E. Kevin Kelloway

To my wife, Joan, for all of her encouragement and support.

Michael R. Frone

Handbook of WORK STRESS

Editors

Julian Barling
Queen's University

E. Kevin Kelloway
St. Mary's University

Michael R. Frone
State University of New York at Buffalo

SAGE Publications
Thousand Oaks ▪ London ▪ New Delhi

For information:

Sage Publications, Inc.
2455 Teller Road
Thousand Oaks, California 91320
E-mail: order@sagepub.com

Sage Publications Ltd.
1 Oliver's Yard
55 City Road
London EC1Y 1SP
United Kingdom

Sage Publications India Pvt. Ltd.
B-42, Panchsheel Enclave
Post Box 4109
New Delhi 110 017 India

Printed in the United States of America

Library of Congress Cataloging-in-Publication Data

Handbook of work stress / [edited by] Julian Barling, E. Kevin Kelloway, Michael R. Frone.
    p. cm.
Includes bibliographical references and index.
ISBN 0-7619-2949-5 (cloth)
  1. Job stress—Handbooks, manuals, etc. I. Barling, Julian. II. Kelloway, E. Kevin. III. Frone, Michael Robert.
HF5548.85.H363 2004
158.7′2—dc22

                         2004008543

This book is printed on acid-free paper.

04   05   06   07   10 9 8 7 6 5 4 3 2 1

Acquisitions Editor:	Al Bruckner
Editorial Assistant:	MaryAnn Vail
Production Editor:	Diane S. Foster
Copy Editor:	Robert Holm
Typesetter:	C&M Digitals (P) Ltd.
Proofreader:	Scott Oney
Indexer:	Molly Hall
Cover Designer:	Ravi Balasuriya
Graphic Designer:	Janet Foulger

Contents

PART I

Sources of Work Stress

1

Editors' Overview: Sources of Work Stress

In one way or another, the questions of the causes or sources of work stress have attracted considerable empirical attention and public fascination for several decades. This interest has coalesced around several fundamental questions: Are some jobs inherently more stressful than others? Are some individuals more prone to stress than others? In this first section of this handbook, the contributors identify and discuss different sources of work stress.

Terry Beehr and Sharon Glazer's chapter starts this section with their focus on one of the most widely studied stressors, namely organizational role stressors. Research on role stressors has been conducted for at least 40 years (Kahn, Wolfe, Quinn, Snoek, & Rosenthal, 1964) with two meta-analyses having been published two decades ago (Fisher & Gitelson, 1983; Jackson & Schuler, 1985). Beehr and Glazer, therefore, summarize some 40 years of research in their chapter. Gina Bellavia and Mike Frone address the work-family conflict, an issue that has also attracted much scientific and lay interest for several decades because of the widespread assumption that balancing the oft-conflicting demands of work and family must surely be stressful.

To some extent at least—and in some cases to a great extent—the rest of the chapters in this section confront something of a different challenge. Specifically, the authors of the remaining chapters have all addressed topics of considerable interest to organizations and employees alike that have not yet been addressed adequately from a "work stress perspective." Some topics have yet to receive any sustained empirical attention. A prime example of this is Michelle Inness and Julian Barling's focus on terrorism. It is reasonable to assume that prior to the attacks in the United States on September 11, 2001, not many people (at least in North America) would have been concerned about terrorism coming to the workplace; since then, it is doubtful that this assumption holds. Inness and Barling speculate theoretically on the reasons the fear of terrorism is experienced as a significant workplace stressor.

The topics of the remaining chapters have all been addressed in the organizational psychology/behavior and management literatures, but they have not yet received sustained empirical attention from a stress perspective. Some of the issues covered are widespread: For example, technology is ubiquitous in today's workplaces, and Michael Coovert, Lori Foster Thompson, and Philip Craiger provide a model for understanding why technology is experienced as a work stressor. In a similar vein, very few people working in an organizational context would be immune from experiencing workplace politics, and Ken Harris and Micki Kacmar provide a conceptual template for understanding the stressors inherent in workplace politics. Although most people will gladly tell horror stories about poor leadership and its personal or organizational effects, it too has yet to be cast conceptually within a work stress framework. Kevin Kelloway, Niro Sivanathan, Lori Francis, and Julian Barling provide a framework in which poor leadership can be seen as a workplace stress issue. Although there is widespread concern about the financial strain resulting from layoffs, job insecurity, and underemployment, there has not been a sustained empirical focus on this issue. Tahira Probst integrates these different areas in providing a model of the stressful experience of economic stressors. Last, there is an extensive focus on the issue of harassment at work, both in general and to some extent from a stress perspective. Kathleen Rospenda and Judith Richman extend this by incorporating the experience of discrimination, thereby providing a stress-based framework for integrating workplace harassment and discrimination.

Two chapters in this first section on the sources of work stress deal with substantive issues that have generated a substantial level of general interest in the management and organizational psychology/behavior literatures. Russell Cropanzano, Barry Goldman, and Lehman Benson III take the vast literature on workplace injustice and provide a framework for understanding just why it could be experienced as stressful. There is a large body of literature on the predictors of workplace aggression (and much less on the psychological consequences); Aaron Schat and Kevin Kelloway provide a work stress perspective for understanding workplace aggression.

The remaining issues covered in this section have attracted empirical attention in the past but in areas other than organizational psychology/behavior or management in general. Peter Totterdell reviews the voluminous research literature on work schedules, not all of which emanates from a psychological or behavioral basis, and provides an understanding of the psychological nature and effects on work scheduling. Workplace safety has typically been conceptualized as an outcome variable more likely to have been studied in areas such as ergonomics, industrial relations, and the law; Leanne Barlow and Rick Iverson show how workplace safety can be conceptualized as a psychological workplace stressor with its own unique outcomes. Similarly, there has been scant attention to the stressful nature of industrial relations for both management and employees—a bona fide field of interest, despite the few studies that have pointed to the potentially stressful experience, for example, of labor disputes and strikes. Drawing from the literature on industrial relations, Lori Francis and Kevin Kelloway generate a model of the stressful experience of labor relations. Last, most theories of job design and work stress largely ignore the role of physical working conditions (e.g., Karasek & Theorell, 1990; Sauter, Murphy, & Hurrell, 1990). Yet recent research shows how physical working conditions and subjective work experiences and stressors interact (e.g., Melamed, Fried, & Froom, 2001), and Janetta Mitchell McCoy and Gary Evans relate what is known about physical working conditions to workplace stress.

Consistent across the chapters are discussions by the authors of the nature of stress pertaining to their specific focus and methodological issues in the area, as well as questions that can be asked to direct future research.

References

Fisher, C. D., & Gitelson, R. (1983). A meta-analysis of the correlates of role conflict and ambiguity. *Journal of Applied Psychology, 68,* 320–333.

Jackson, S., & Schuler, R. (1985). A meta-analysis and conceptual critique of research on role ambiguity and role conflict in work settings. *Organizational Behavior and Human Decision Processes, 36,* 16–78.

Kahn, R. L., Wolfe, D. M., Quinn, R. P., Snoek, J. D., & Rosenthal, R. A. (1964). *Organizational stress: Studies in role conflict and ambiguity.* New York: Wiley.

Karasek, R., & Theorell, T. (1990). *Health work: Stress, productivity and the reconstruction of working life.* New York: Basic Books.

Melamed, S., Fried, Y., & Froom, P. (2001). The interactive effects of chronic exposure to noise and job complexity on changes in blood pressure and job satisfaction: A longitudinal study of industrial employees. *Journal of Occupational Health Psychology, 6,* 182–195.

Sauter, S. L., Murphy, L. R., & Hurrell, J. J. (1990). Prevention of work-related psychological disorders: A national strategy proposed by the National Institute for Occupational Safety and Health (NIOSH). *American Psychologist, 45,* 1146–1158.

2

Organizational Role Stress

Terry A. Beehr

Sharon Glazer

All the world's a stage,

And all the men and women merely players.

They have their exits and their entrances;

And one man in his time plays many parts,

His acts being seven ages.

William Shakespeare (1564–1616)
As You Like It, act 2 scene 7

The study of role stress perhaps really began before or during the time of Shakespeare when Shakespeare's Jacques so poignantly noted, prior to Orlando's entrance onto the stage with Adam, that we are all mere actors playing multiple roles on the stages of life. On our various stages, we take upon ourselves different roles to play, and it is the expectations of others around us (e.g., supervisors and coworkers) rather than those of a playwright and audience that guide our behaviors on the stage set of the workplace. Even Shakespeare's Macbeth states that "life's but a walking shadow, a poor player that struts and frets his hour upon the stage." Here, Macbeth is concerned with the finality of life and death, and although role stressors do not have to lead to death, stress on the work stage costs as much as $145 billion annually in injuries alone (National Institute for Occupational Safety and Health [NIOSH], 2000). Many of these "accidents" could have been prevented through clear, unconflicting, and timely communications from those who help direct the play and are demanding of those performing in a work role.

Definition of Role
Stress as Construct and Domain

Beehr and McGrath (1992; McGrath & Beehr, 1990) wrote that stressors are stress-producing environmental circumstances or stress-producing events and conditions (SPECs). In other words, events and conditions in the environment, whether the environment entails physical or psychosocial stimuli, create a motivation to react. If stressors or SPECs are not readily coped with, negative reactions ensue, and these reactions are referred to as strains. Researchers have classified stressors in numerous ways. For example, West and West (1989) classified stressors into four "location" categories ranging from the environment to the organization to the environment internal to one's self. These components include (a) stressors that exist outside the organization (extraorganizational stressors; e.g., traffic to and from work); (b) stressors that come from within the organization (organizational stressors; e.g., job security); (c) stressors that relate to the duties and responsibilities of work (task-related stressors; e.g., traveling for work); and (d) stressors that relate to various work roles (individual role stressors). Davidson and Cooper (1983) listed numerous stressors that include stressors inherent to the job (e.g., the role one plays in the organization, interpersonal relationships, and organizational structure and climate) and those brought in from the external environment (e.g., home or social environments). Role stressors are distinguished from other types of stressors in that they relate to the role one plays.

Role Stress as Stressor

There are numerous types of stressors, as addressed above; however, role stress consists of stressors that have been defined as environmental demands, constraints, and events that affect an individual's *role* fulfillment (Parasuraman & Alutto, 1984). They emanate from the perceived expectations that others have for one's behaviors or even one's own expectations for appropriate behaviors. Role stressors fall into the sociopsychological domain of stress as the stressors are the perceived characteristics of the expectations of others who have a stake in one's activities. By sociopsychological, we mean that the social environment consisting of "role senders" (people who have expectations for the focal person's actions) defines one's role. Like actors on a stage, we perceive what the audience or others on stage with us expect of us, and if these expectations are perceived to be unduly taxing, they will lead to strains. If they are perceived as manageable, then strains will not occur.

People take on many roles in life. The two major life domains are nonwork and work. In the nonwork domain, people take on roles related to kinship such as daughter or son, brother or sister, mother or father, uncle or aunt, spouse, friend, and so forth. One might even take on a more specific role than "friend," for example, social coordinator. In the work domain, people take on the roles of employee, subordinate, supervisor, coworker, or sometimes customer. In every role we play, there are others who have expectations of us. Their expectations can be—or at least can be perceived to be—unclear, conflicting with other expectations, and/or too taxing (overloading).

Demands (Expectations) as Part of Role Stressors

The idea of expectations as demands stemming from our roles invokes the concept of communications whereby someone has a message to send that is supposed to communicate expectations (regarding our action or inaction). When recipients of the communication interpret (or decode) the message, their perceived expectations are developed. The key word here is "perceived." Regardless of whether the communicated demand was decoded correctly, the perception of demand determines the nature of the potential role stressors. In occupational stress, discovering that job incumbents perceive role messages or demands as unclear or ambiguous indicates a need to clarify role expectations. In fact, when Schaubroeck, Ganster, Sime, and Ditman (1993) had managers clarify their roles with subordinates, satisfaction with subordinates' supervisors increased 3 months after the intervention.

Prevalence of Role Stress in the Workforce

It is difficult to know the amount of role stress in the workforce. National statistics about health cannot indicate the degree to which poor health is caused by stress or work stress, let alone role stressors specifically. A national survey of male workers in the 1960s (Kahn, Wolfe, Quinn, Snoek, & Rosenthal, 1964) found that the stressors role ambiguity, role conflict, and role overload (considered an identifiable type of role conflict in that study) are quite widely experienced in the American workplace. About a third of the workers in the sample indicated that they experienced role ambiguity. This was based on questions asking the extent to which employees were "disturbed," "distressed," "bothered," or "under tension" due to ambiguities about the expectations for their jobs. Using similar question wording, over 40% indicated they experienced various types of role conflict and quantitative role overload. Only about 20% indicated that they experienced qualitative role overload (being in jobs requiring skills they did not possess), however.

Although one could propose that either more or less role stress than that exists today, there is little solid evidence to go on. We examined five recent empirical articles reported by different researchers at different locations involving different samples (Day & Livingstone, 2001; Iverson, Olekalns, & Erwin, 1998; Jex & Elacqua, 1999; Jimmieson, 2000; Posig & Kickul, 2003) that provided relevant self-reported survey data about their measures of role stressors. They are studies of role stress in samples of customer service representatives, hospital employees, and military personnel, as well as two samples of a variety of service and nonservice jobs. Means and standard deviations reported in the studies suggest that there probably still exist a substantial number of these role stressors in the workplace. The mean role stressor scores in these studies were consistently at or above the scales' midpoints, with people even one standard deviation above the sample mean reporting scores substantially above the scales' midpoints. Overall, therefore, it seems likely that at least a large minority of workers experience role stress today.

Role Theory

Roles in Social Networks, Including Work Organizations

Roles are socially acceptable forms of behaviors within a given context. People learn to "act" in their roles through communications with others. People who have a stake in another's work role (the role senders), such as supervisors, managers, coworkers, subordinates, and any others who interact with the role receiver (the focal person or incumbent of the role) regarding work, communicate to the person in the given "role" about their expectations for appropriate role behavior. Thus, even one's family members might be part of a worker's role set by communicating expectations for achieving higher status in the workplace, bringing home a paycheck, or providing medical benefits for the family as a result of maintaining membership in the organization. These communications (or lack thereof) then are interpreted by the role receiver. The way the role expectations are interpreted can lead to a perception of demands, constraints, or even opportunities to engage in certain behaviors.

As implied above, a role can be defined as the social character one "plays" in an organization. Roles are potential attitudes and behaviors expected of someone by other influential figures (Jex & Beehr, 1991; Terborg, 1985). People who have impact on the "role player" have expectations about the nature of the task performed and the kinds of behaviors expected from the role player (Sloan & Cooper, 1986). Roles represent "patterns of interpersonal connectedness" (McGrath, 1976, p. 1384). Behavior on a given assignment and in a given setting is contingent upon the ongoing relationship shared with peers, who both directly and indirectly affect the assigned task. A role is, therefore, a result of assumed influence and expectations others have about how one ought to behave on an assignment in a given setting. These expectations and influences usually have been reinforced through past communications or role messages sent by others, not necessarily to the target person, and implied by the actions taken by those who have had similar roles (McGrath, 1976). Hence, a person's role is based on inferences made from others' expectations for attitudes and behaviors.

For some psychologists, the concept of role stressors may be perceived as an individual difference variable. It might be construed as a person's inability to interpret expectations. However, in occupational stress research, role stressors are more often considered to be characteristics of the social system (Jex & Beehr, 1991). In other words, the social system, or people's role sets (those who have a stake in the incumbent's role), communicate demands, constraints, or opportunities that might or might not be achievable. Whether the incumbent of the role has the resources to cope with those stressors is where the individual differences lie. Stressors emanating from one's role often require one to cope with the expectations (or lack of expectations) communicated.

According to Beehr (1995) and Robertson, Cooper, and Williams (1990), role conflict (including both intra- and interrole conflict), role ambiguity, and role overload are the most widely studied occupational stressors. Often people use Kahn et al.'s (1964) job-related tensions scale to measure these role stressors; however, this measure more likely assesses strains as the items relate to aspects of work that "bother" one (Beehr, 1995). When someone reports that something is bothering him or her, that bothering is arguably a psychological strain the person is feeling. As a result, a number of researchers (e.g., Beehr, Walsh, & Taber, 1976; Rizzo, House, & Lirtzman, 1970) have created role stressor scales that phrase the stressors in terms of demands and constraints produced from social interactions apart from the person's reactions to them.

Role Sets and Expectations for Focal Person

According to role theory, a "sender" is one who communicates messages or places demands on an employee (Beehr, 1985). Sometimes, the "receivers" of the role message perceive it as overly demanding of their time and skills, vague, and/or excessively challenging. When workers perceive messages in a negative light, a person's role at work is often studied as a source of job-related strains (Sloan & Cooper, 1986).

Role ambiguity. Kahn et al. (1964) were among the first researchers to define these role stressors as an explanation of role-based strain. They, Beehr (1976), and Schuler (1980) conceptualize role ambiguity as the lack of specificity and predictability concerning an employee's job or role functions and responsibilities. Others (Beehr, 1985; Cooper, 1981; Terborg, 1985) subsequently added that role ambiguity is an objective situation at work in which there is insufficient, misleading, or restricted flow of information pertaining to one's work role (Pearce, 1981), but it should not be operationalized in terms of the person's reaction of uncertainty regarding what actions are to be taken (Beehr & Bhagat, 1985). Ideally, environmental role ambiguity differs from the individual's uncertainty in that uncertainty has to do with the inability to predict what is expected of oneself and ambiguity has to do with a lack of information in the environment (Beehr, 1995). Therefore, role ambiguity is the lack of clarity about duties, objectives, and responsibilities needed to fulfill one's role—often due to an inadequate understanding of colleagues' work expectations of job behaviors (Cooper, Cooper, & Eaker, 1988; Peterson et al., 1995). Role ambiguity is often perceived when there are changes in technology, social structures, new personnel entering the organization (McGrath, 1976), changes in jobs (e.g., new job, transfer, or promotion), new supervisor, or new workplace (Cooper et al., 1988; Ivancevich & Matteson, 1980). Some of these changes occur due to events in the environment outside the organization (e.g., shifts in nationwide economic stability or security threats) that affect work-related role ambiguity inside the organization. In essence, role ambiguity is a situation in which there is lack of clearly defined role expectations (Kemery, 1991).

Role conflict. Role conflict has been defined as two or more sets of incompatible demands concerning work issues (Bacharach, Bamberger, & Conley, 1990; Beehr, 1995; Kahn et al., 1964; Katz & Kahn, 1978; Kemery, 1991). Specifically, incompatible demands may be between the expectations placed on a worker by concerned parties or by the interface between two or more roles of the same person (Cooper et al., 1988; Peterson et al., 1995). The latter is referred to as interrole conflict (Beehr, 1995; Cooper et al., 1988). Rizzo et al. (1970) maintain that role conflict also exists when organizational requirements clash with personal values and obligations to others. Kahn et al. (1964), Cooper et al. (1988), and Beehr (1995) would refer to this as person-role conflict. Role conflict can be experienced as one tries to fulfill one set of expectations when to do so it is necessary to deviate from performing or behaving according to the same role sender's other set of expectations. This depicts intrasender role conflict (Beehr, 1995; Cooper et al., 1988). However, role conflict is most prevalent when two or more people or groups expect or demand of the message receiver different kinds of behaviors. This is referred to as intersender role conflict (Beehr, 1995; Cooper et al., 1988; Kahn et al., 1964). This can even occur because the person simultaneously holds multiple roles; interrole conflict occurs, for example, when the parental role demands that the parent pick up a child from the babysitter's at 5 P.M., but the boss expects the employee to work past 5 P.M. to finish a task. Baruch, Biener, and Barnett (1987) imagine role conflict as feeling torn by these pressures; that is, differing expectations placed on the employee cause the employee to feel divided in having to choose between, or to deal with, the varying demands or expectations.

A commonly studied type of interrole conflict deals with work and family roles. Gupta and Jenkins (1985) wrote that people in such relationships can experience many types of conflicts, depending on whether the conflicts are with one's spouse (or family role), one's work role, or between the two. Interrole conflict between work and family goes under other names as well including (lack of) work-family balance (Frone, 2003) and "crossover" stress (Etzion & Westman, 2001; Westman, 2001, 2002; Westman & Etzion, 1995; Westman, Etzion, & Danon, 2001).

According to Frone's (2003) review, family dissatisfaction, absence of workers from their families' lives, and poor performance in one's family role are caused when work problems "spill over" to the family domain. When family problems spill over to one's work domain, there are work role–related problems, including withdrawal behaviors (except for quitting, because that would create a host of other family-role problems) and poor performance. Both work-to-family conflict and family-to-work conflict have been studied as having an effect on psychological distress, abuse of alcohol, and poor physical health (for further review of literature, see Frone, 2003). Crossover literature shows that burnout in husbands affected their wives' burnout (Westman & Etzion, 1995; Westman et al., 2001), that burnout in wives affected their husbands' burnout (Westman & Etzion, 1995), and that such "crossover" would likely occur more in stressful conditions (Etzion & Westman, 2001).

Role overload. Role overload can be conceived either as imbedded in role conflict (Beehr, 1995; Cooper et al., 1988; Kahn et al., 1964; Rizzo et al., 1970) or as separate from role conflict (Bacharach et al., 1990; Beehr et al., 1976; Caplan, 1971; Glazer, 1995; Kahn, 1980). As a distinct construct, role overload is considered to be caused by too much work, time pressures and deadlines (Sofer, 1970), and lack of personal resources needed to fulfill duties, commitments, and responsibilities (Peterson et al., 1995). In other words, it is an incompatibility between work demands and time available to satisfy the demands (Bacharach et al., 1990; French & Caplan, 1973). Role overload is usually defined as the inability to fulfill organizational expectations (assigned tasks) in the time available (Kahn, 1980). This is the definition for *quantitative* overload, which relates to time-based demands or limitations (Newton & Keenan, 1987; see Beehr, 1985, for further discussion on quantitative overload).

Researchers also believe that role overload comes in a qualitative form. Qualitative overload occurs when employees do not have the qualifications (qualities) to do the tasks well regardless of how much time they have (Beehr, 1985; French & Caplan, 1973). That is, regardless of the amount of time available, the worker does not have the necessary knowledge, skills, and abilities to accomplish the task (Beehr, 1985). This should be rare if employees are selected into their roles based on their technical qualifications, but it does occur nevertheless. An example might be a manager whose training and background are in general management (whose education might be an MBA, for example) but who is hired or promoted into a position requiring supervision of a technical engineering function. The manager might feel the need to pressure the subordinates (engineers) to complete a job within certain time and cost parameters, but if the engineers report that the parameters are unrealistic, then the supervisor is not qualified to decide whether to go ahead with the product as it is, on time, or to be late and miss the time goal so that the product will be better.

According to McGrath (1976), quantitative role overload inflicts less strain than the other role stressors. The emergence of role overload, according to McGrath (1976), may be a coping strategy used by employees. Employees would allegedly complain of too much work or too little time in order to defray difficult tasks or additional role demands that may actually be unenjoyable as opposed to time-consuming. Some may even claim to be overloaded as an excuse for their lowered performance. Regardless of which stressor has greater impact, role overload, role conflict, and role ambiguity preclude people from managing their roles in accomplishing or completing tasks well (Schuler, 1980), thereby having immediate influence on job strain (Bacharach, Bamberger, & Conley, 1991).

Nontraditional role stressors. A number of other role stressors have been found in the business expatriate literature. By *expatriate,* we refer to people who are sent abroad on an international assignment by a parent company (where the person is employed) to work in a foreign country, generally for a period of more than 1 year. Expatriate assignment is "considered . . . a special case of work role transition" (Aryee & Stone, 1996, p. 151). Going on an international assignment not only changes the general environments but also changes the people who would normally be in one's role set. Therefore, in the expatriate stress literature, a number of stressors not normally studied when role stressors are discussed actually fit nicely into the concept of role stressors. These include role discretion, role novelty, role innovation, and job (or role) feedback.

Role discretion is described as the extent to which employees can "adapt their work role and setting to themselves rather than adapting themselves to the situation" (Black & Gregersen, 1991, p. 501). In other words, workers have discretion to decide how they perform their jobs and how they mold their work environment in order to perform or delegate work (Aryee & Stone, 1996). This is particularly important for international assignees as it provides the worker with the opportunity to perform in ways that are "normal" for that individual, thus reducing ambiguity and increasing adjustment to the company in the host country. Black and Gregersen (1991) showed that 34% of variance in expatriate adjustment to the host country could be accounted for by role discretion and interaction with home nationals and (negatively accounted for) by role ambiguity and role conflict. Role discretion was also found to positively predict work adjustment, job satisfaction, and quality of life (Aryee & Stone, 1996); and job autonomy (similar to role discretion) related positively to job satisfaction and organizational commitment among 504 expatriates working in Saudi Arabia (Bhuian, Al-Shammari, & Jefri, 1996).

Role novelty refers to the extent to which an expatriate's new work role involves tasks, skills, and methods for engaging in work that differ from previous work roles (Aryee & Stone, 1996). This potential role stressor did not significantly correlate with or predict work adjustment, job satisfaction, marital satisfaction, or quality of life among 184 American and Australian expatriate employees in Hong Kong, however.

Another potential stressor particular to the international assignee is *role innovation*, defined as "adjusting to the transition by changing the new role expectations and requirements" (Black, 1992, p. 173). Related to role discretion, role innovation means international assignees or role incumbents modify their work roles. Unlike most studies that look at role stressors as antecedents, Black (1992) studied the socialization tactics used that would predict role innovation. Socialization tactics that were collective (i.e., experiencing common events together with others in similar situations) related positively with role innovation, but socialization tactics that were serial (i.e., experienced organizational members serve as mentors) and fixed (i.e., sequences of events are specified, including assignment duration) were negatively related with role innovation. In other words, expatriates adjust to their jobs via cues from members of their role set and do not make major changes without determining what is expected of them by others and when. This exhibits very well the principles of role theory.

Black and Gregersen's (1991) results were partially supported by Stroh, Dennis, and Cramer (1994) through their study on the effects of role clarity (role ambiguity), role discretion, role conflict, and role novelty on work adjustment among 190 expatriates working on assignment for five multinational corporations. Stroh et al. (1994) found that role discretion and role clarity were positively correlated with work adjustment; however, role conflict also positively correlated with work adjustment. Also, role novelty was negatively correlated with expatriates' adjustment.

Aryee and Stone (1996) examined the extent to which role discretion, role conflict, role support, role novelty, and role ambiguity affected the overall adjustment and job satisfaction of 184 American and Australian expatriate employees in Hong Kong. Consistent with other studies, role discretion positively related with job satisfaction, and both role conflict and role ambiguity negatively related with job satisfaction.

Potential Moderators

There has been a long, intensive search for moderators of the role stressor-strain relationships. As with many empirical searches for interaction effects, some of the results are inconsistent, but some themes are nevertheless prominent. The idea of moderation or moderator effects is that there is a statistical interaction between role stressors and a moderator variable that predicts strains. The characteristics of some sorts of people or some sorts of situations moderate or alter the effects of stressors on strains so that sometimes role stressors lead to strains more strongly than at other times. Moderators can be considered in two broad categories: environment characteristics and person characteristics.

Environmental moderators. The two most commonly tested environmental moderators of the effects of role stress are probably social support and job control. The idea that social support, sometimes under other labels, could moderate the relationships between role stressors and strains has been around for a long time (e.g., see Kahn et al., 1964, regarding interpersonal moderators). The proposition of control as a moderator of job stressor-strain relationships, although not always in regard to role stressors specifically, is probably best known from demand-control theory (e.g., for an early proposal see Karasek, 1979). Perhaps one of the earliest empirical tests of both of these environmental variables as moderators in the presence of role stress was conducted nearly 30 years ago (Beehr, 1976). Both of these environmental variables are commonly recommended as potential moderators regarding almost any kind of organizational stressors, not just role stressors. Tests of the current version of demand-control theory (now more commonly called demand-control-support theory), for example, explicitly account for potential moderating effects of both of these environmental variables (e.g., Parkes, Mendham, & von Rabenau, 1994; Rodriguez, Bravo, Peiro, & Schaufeli, 2001; Searle, Bright, & Bochner, 2001).

Social support is a natural topic for role stress researchers because role stress itself is inherently social. Role stressors are due to other people—their expectations, demands, and role messages (Kahn et al., 1964). Social support has been defined and operationalized in a wide variety of ways (Beehr, 1995; Cohen & Wills, 1985; Vaux, 1988). Indeed, it seems to be a metaconstruct (Beehr, 1985; Vaux, 1985); the term is used to explain potential effects of many different interpersonal variables. One set of categories is structural versus functional support (Cohen & Wills, 1985). Structural social support exists when one is embedded in a social structure. If an employee is a member of an organization, however, he or she is always embedded in the organizational structure, which is a social structure. If the employee is married, he or she is embedded in a family, another social structure. Therefore, nearly all employees can be said to "obtain" structural support, making it almost a given or constant in most samples of workers. Perhaps for that reason, research on role stress and social support in the workplace rarely studies this type of support. In order to study structural social support as a variable rather than a constant, researchers could focus on people in isolated jobs (such as a lone consultant) versus jobs that are not isolated. Of course, these jobs might also vary in many other ways, confounding the research efforts. Another alternative would be to measure degrees of structural support (e.g., how many people are in the employee's immediate part of the social structure).

Functional support depends on what the other people (potential supporters) do, and it is frequently studied in role stress research. The issue is whether supporters perform some function for the stressed person, and these functions are commonly divided into two categories: emotional and instrumental functions. Emotional support is the kind many of us think of when we consider the concept of social support. It consists of showing caring and sympathy and generally sharing or empathizing with the emotions and situations of the stressed person.

A meta-analysis calculated the average corrected correlation between social support and strains as −.21 (Viswesvaran, Sanchez, & Fisher, 1999). This estimate, however, combines all types of stressors (role stressors as well as others), all sources of support (who provides it), all types (e.g., emotional and instrumental) of social support, and all types of strains (e.g., psychological, physical complaints, and physical illness). Both the types of social support and the types of strains are so varied that there can be very large variations in the relationship between them. Although it is important to know the degree to which social support might affect strains, for present purposes we would like to know about the effects of social support specifically in conjunction with *role* stressors. Two meta-analyses (Beehr, 1994; Viswesvaran et al., 1999) concluded that the average change in R-square for the interaction of stressors with social support is about .02, but again this was not specific only to role stressors. In our own studies specifically on role stressors, however, the strength of the R-square change has been about the same (Beehr & Drexler, 1986; Beehr, Farmer, Glazer, Gudanowski, & Nair, 2003; Beehr, Jex, Stacy, & Murray, 2000; Beehr, King, & King, 1990; Dunseath, Beehr, & King, 1995; Fenlason & Beehr, 1994; Kaufmann & Beehr, 1986, 1989). This consistency suggests that the strength of the moderating effect of social support on the effects of role stressors is probably quite weak.

Of course, it is assumed that social support moderates by reducing the impact of stressors on strains, but that is not always the case. Instead, there are frequent instances of "reverse buffering," in which the presence of social support strengthens the relationship between stressors and strains instead of weakening it (e.g., Glaser, Tatum, Nebeker, Sorenson, & Aiello, 1999; Kaufmann & Beehr, 1986). This unexpected result makes social support an enigmatic moderator variable (Beehr et al., 2003). When it moderates, it is usually in a favorable way, but occasionally it is not! We (Beehr & Glazer, 2001) have since tried to look at the cultural context of support as a potential explanation for the mixed results. There appears to be some preliminary support for cultural differences in reports of supervisor support, with Asians perceiving less supervisor support than western Europeans and Anglos (Glazer & Bell, 2003).

Job control is the degree to which people have some control over their own work or have input into the functioning of their workplaces. It has often been suggested as a moderator of the stressor-strain relationship (Spector, 2002). The best known examples of research on stress and control are probably in relation to demand-control-support theory of occupational stress, and by comparison, much less research has been done on control specifically in relation to role stress in the workplace. It should be noted that the concept of control is probably relevant to several popular variables in the organizational sciences, including autonomy, participation, participative decision making, and empowerment. Each of these implies some degree of control for the person in the workplace.

Almost three decades ago, it was shown that autonomy could moderate the relationship between role ambiguity and depression (Beehr, 1976). Role ambiguity was not as strongly related to depression for employees with more job autonomy as for those with less of it. In more recent studies, however, job control did not moderate the relationship between role stressors and psychological strains in one study (O'Driscoll & Beehr, 2000), and it only moderated the relationship between overload and the organizational level variable, health care costs, in another (Ganster, Fox, & Dwyer, 2001).

It is also possible that control has a stronger moderating effect for some people than for others. Having jobs that allow control and using control are two different phenomena. People with high self-efficacy believe they can perform well in general or at least in their specific situation (e.g., Bandura, 1982). Relevant to the present discussion, environmental control should be more useful and used more by individuals who are high in self-efficacy, and therefore these two conditions in combination might be more important than either one alone. Jimmieson (2000) found a three-way interaction between role conflict (but not role overload), self-efficacy, and job control predicting one element of burnout (depersonalization) but not predicting other psychological or physical strains.

Individual difference moderators. Some individual differences that might moderate the role stressor-strain relationships are specific to the stressor, but others appear to be theoretically useful moderators for any combination of stressors and strains. An example of an individual characteristic that should have moderator effects primarily with a specific stressor is need for clarity. It is intuitively obvious that need for clarity should moderate the relationship between a particular stressor, role ambiguity, and strains. This was found in the early days of research on occupational stress in a study of nurses (Lyons, 1971). We primarily found in the research literature, however, tests of individual difference moderators that have been proposed as broadly effective moderators and not proposed for specific role stressors.

Hardiness is a term used to indicate personality characteristics of someone who is stress resistant, and elements of hardiness usually include a sense of control over one's own life, a sense of commitment to something important in one's life, and a sense of being challenged by change (rather than being threatened by it) and wanting to meet that challenge (Kobasa, 1979). These are individual differences that might moderate the relationship between any stressors, including role stressors, and strains. The literature on hardiness has especially looked at life stressors rather than job stressors; but overall, previous reviewers often concluded that there is a general lack of evidence for the buffering effect of this operationalization of hardiness—or that the evidence at best is mixed (Beehr & Bowling, in press; Funk &

Houston, 1987; Hull, Van Treuren, & Virnelli, 1987). Nevertheless, there might be some individual difference variables that could consistently moderate the relationship between role stressors and strains. Self-efficacy, locus of control, negative affectivity, and type A are considered here.

Self-efficacy has been recommended for study as a moderator of stressor-strain relationships (e.g., Hastings & Bham, 2003), including in relation to role stress. Self-efficacy consists of cognitive evaluations people make of their abilities to perform a specific task. One possible mechanism for this effect would occur if people who believe in their own self-efficacy are prone to initiate and persist at coping efforts. The more people try to cope, the better the odds are that they will succeed in reducing their own strains. A study of female office workers in Japan (Matsui & Onglatco, 1992) showed that a specific kind of self-efficacy, career self-efficacy, moderated the effects of role overload as expected. In studies of military personnel, Jex and his colleagues (Jex & Bliese, 1999; Jex, Bliese, Buzzell, & Primeau, 2001) found that self-efficacy moderated the relationships of role ambiguity and role overload with some psychological strains including anxiety and tension, but in a study of educational employees, self-efficacy did not moderate role stressor-strain relationships (Jex & Gudanowski, 1992). Consistent with the coping explanation, self-efficacy was part of a three-way interaction with coping style predicting outcomes. This points up the likely complexity of any moderating effect of self-efficacy.

Internal *locus of control* is an individual difference variable that indicates the extent to which employees believe their own voluntary actions influence outcomes (rewards and punishments) that they will receive. Like job control as an environmental job characteristic, described previously, dispositional beliefs about control might also buffer or moderate the aversive effects of role stressors. As noted earlier, control is usually considered one of the elements of the individual difference referred to as "hardiness," which is supposed to moderate the relationship between all types of stressors and strains. Hardiness has been a popular individual difference variable to examine for moderating effects on stress in general, but reviews have questioned its effectiveness as a moderator (Semmer, 2003). Beehr and Bowling (in press) recently concluded, "In sum, the notion that hardiness acts as a buffer of the deleterious effects of stressors has received at best only mixed support. The general lack of evidence for the buffering effect of hardiness was noted in the early years of hardiness research by other authors (Funk & Houston, 1987; Hull et al., 1987)."

Aside from the larger construct of hardiness, to what extent does locus of control moderate stressor-strain relationships? Regarding job stress in general, Semmer (2003) concluded tentatively that locus of control might buffer job stress effects on strain although longitudinal evidence is less convincing than evidence from cross-sectional studies. Regarding role stressors specifically, Noor (2002) found that locus of control moderated the relationship between work-family interrole conflict and job satisfaction, but it was not a moderator when the criterion was strain. It is sometimes argued that job satisfaction is an important attitude but is not actually strain or psychological health (e.g., Beehr, Glaser, Canali, & Wallwey, 2001). Therefore, the Noor study actually did not support locus of control as a moderator of role stressor-strain relationships. A study by Rahim and Psenicka (1996) found that locus of control did moderate the relationships between role stressors and psychiatric symptoms, and earlier studies by Keenan and McBain (1979) and by Fusilier, Ganster, and Mayes (1987) also indicated that it might moderate role stressor-strain relationships. Overall, there is enough evidence to conclude that locus of control has promise as a moderator of the relationship between role stressors and employee strains.

Type A behavior pattern, as the name implies, was conceived as a set of *behaviors,* but it is usually treated in research as if it is relatively stable, like a trait (Beehr, 1995). Type A was proposed originally as a direct cause of coronary heart disease (Friedman & Rosenman, 1974), but in this chapter we are primarily concerned with its potential to interact with role stressors to predict any kind of strain (coronary heart disease or any other potential strain). It consists of a set of behaviors indicating a concern with time, competition, and status and is often characterized by aggression or hostility. Many researchers now believe that hostility might be the component that best predicts cardiovascular problems (Adler & Matthews, 1994; Ganster, Schaubroeck, Sime, & Mayes, 1991), but that may not mean anything regarding its moderating effects on the relationships between role stressors and strains. There is some evidence that type A people may cope differently than type B people, and it is therefore possible that this would predict and explain any moderator effects (Havlovic & Keenan, 1991; Kirmeyer & Diamond, 1985).

So, do type A people react more strongly to role stressors than type B people do? One early study found that type A moderated the relationship between role ambiguity and psychological strain but did not moderate relationships for other role stressors (role conflict and role overload; Keenan & McBain, 1979). Another found a moderating effect between workload and anxiety among students experiencing stress working with computers but no moderating effect regarding other role stressors or other psychological or physical strains (Caplan & Jones, 1975). A study in Japan found that type A moderated the relationships between some role stressors and psychological strain, but this interaction effect seemed to be part of higher-order interactions, depending on other variables such as gender and job position (Iwata, Suzuki, Sato, & Abe, 1992). One study did not find that type A moderated the relationships between role conflict stressors and physical indices such as blood pressure and heart rate, but it did moderate the relationships of role conflict with self-reported physical strains or with psychological strains; furthermore, there were no moderating effects in relation to role ambiguity and role overload (Orpen, 1982). Type A did not moderate the relationships of role ambiguity and role conflict with psychological and psychosomatic strains in a sample of managers either (Gavin & Axelrod, 1977). Finally, one study found that type A seemed to moderate in an unexpected way; type A people actually seemed to experience less psychological strain than type B people over time when role stressors were increasing (Newton & Keenan, 1990).

Overall, the results of studies specifically of role stressors' effects as moderated by type A behavior pattern seem mixed; they tend to be old; they are somewhat promising for future research; and modern type A researchers might suggest looking at subparts of type A instead of the entire construct for role stress moderating effects.

Negative affectivity (NA) is a relatively stable trait entailing a tendency to experience negative perceptions, thoughts, and feelings. There has been considerable controversy about the role of NA in occupational stress experiences. For example, in survey research, the stable NA trait might be the cause of increased self-reports about what are assumed to be temporary psychological strains and even about perceptions of environmental stressors. Researchers sometimes therefore argue that research should hold NA constant statistically to remove its effect. Some have argued either for or against this tactic (e.g., Brief, Burke, George, Robinson, & Webster, 1988; Spector, Zapf, Chen, & Frese, 2000). Whether NA is a nuisance variable to control or whether that action would amount to removing some valid prediction of strains by role stressors is unanswerable here, but in any event, we are interested in whether NA can have moderator effects. Although NA might artificially inflate the strength of zero-order correlations between stressors and strains, it is unlikely to artificially aid the finding of significant interactions between NA and role stressors to predict strains. Instead, correlations between NA and the role stressors might have a conservative effect (i.e., it might reduce the ability to find interactions).

Although there seems to be no stated reason, stressors resembling role overload have been a particular focus of studies of NA as a moderator and role stress. One study did not find NA to moderate the relationship between role overload and psychological strain (Moyle, 1995), whereas three others did (Houkes, Janssen, de Jonge, & Bakker, 2003; Zellars, Perrewé, & Hochwarter, 1999; Parkes, 1990). Another study found that NA moderated the relationships of overload and role ambiguity with depression for women but not for men (Heinisch & Jex, 1997). Overall, NA appears to be promising as an individual difference moderator, especially concerning role overload.

Outcomes

The effects of role stressors can be either positive or negative, though generally occupational stress literature focuses on the negative outcomes of stressors. If the effect of role stressors is positive (e.g., improved productivity), then the stressor might have been an opportunity for attaining a goal (e.g., promotion and, thus, responsibility) or the individual coped with the demanding situation (e.g., overload coped with by good delegation) such that the results were favorable. If the effect of role stressors is negative (e.g., anxiety or depression), then the stressor was not coped with well. When negative individual or group reactions occur as a result of stressors, then it is said that strains are experienced (Beehr & Newman, 1978; Jex & Beehr, 1991).

Strains are often divided into three categories: psychological, physiological, and behavioral strains. Psychological strains include reactions that are mentally experienced by the individual, for example, depression, anxiety, and burnout—even though some of these are thought to have physiological or neurological components. Physical strains are reactions of the body due to the reception of stressors, for example, coronary heart or artery disease, twitching of muscles, sweating/perspiration, high blood pressure, and general aches and pains felt in various parts of the body. Finally, behavioral strains are depicted in terms of a person's negative reactions to a stressor that are harmful to him- or herself. Behavioral strains include, for example, excessive alcohol consumption, tobacco smoking, or planning suicide.

Organizational outcomes can also occur due to role stressors or to the resulting strains or other employee reactions to the stressors. These include employee reactions such as behaviors and attitudes of commitment or good citizenship to the organization or withdrawal behaviors, violence, and effects on performance. The distinction here is that they have serious, direct, immediate consequences for the welfare of the organization.

Individual Strains

For the most part, role stressors are more strongly related to psychological strains than to physiological and behavioral strains (Jex & Beehr, 1991). It is possible that the reaction to role stressors is generally psychological first and then later physiological and/or behavioral. Someone who perceives a great deal of role overload might feel anxious (psychological strain), and the anxiety might then cause one to lose sleep (physical strain) thinking about the overload. When one loses sleep for an extended period of time, the individual might resort to taking extra sleeping pills (behavioral strain). Anxiety, loss of sleep, and taking sleeping pills have an effect on one's overall performance, which can create more role stressors (e.g., reduced performance one day might mean overload the next).

Psychological. Psychological strains occur when stressors lead to impaired cognitive functioning or disturbed affect (Gross, 1970). One of the most commonly studied psychological strains is burnout. Burnout is a psychological condition that is the result of job stress for which one's ability to cope with stressors and manage strains has been expended. Research has repeatedly shown that role stressors are related to burnout (Anderson, 1991; Peiro, Gonzalez-Roma, Tordera, & Manes, 2001; Schaufeli & Janczur, 1994; Shirom, 2003). Other psychological strains resulting from role stressors include lower job satisfaction (Fisher & Gitelson, 1983; Jackson & Schuler, 1985) and higher anxiety (Glazer & Beehr, in review; Srivastava, Hagtvet, & Sen, 1994). According to Beehr (1995), role ambiguity (lack of information) might lead to dissatisfaction with work but not necessarily a general sense of job stress, except if ambiguity leads to uncertainty (lack of predictability).

Physical. A physiological strain is one in which there is a change in the body (Gross, 1970) as a result of stressors. Although relatively few studies have been published linking role stressors to physiological strains, on the average, workers are absent due to feeling ill or stressed at least 20 days per year, and this costs U.S. organizations over $100 billion in lost production and disability compensation claims (Quick, Quick, Nelson, & Hurrell, 1997). Surely, some of the stressors causing ill health are role related. Examples of physiological strains include coronary artery or heart disease, high blood pressure, hypertension, (maybe) cancer (indirectly through smoking or alcohol abuse), diabetes, weight gain or loss, back pain, arthritis, headaches, vision problems, gastrointestinal problems, sleeplessness, susceptibility to influenza and colds, heart palpitations, ulcers, thrombosis, stroke, and heart attacks. Most likely, 50% of these physiological strains are a result of lifestyle (Quick et al., 1997) including how one engages in work. A few studies have shown weak relationships of role stressors with physical or somatic complaints (Caplan, Cobb, French, Harrison, & Pinneau, 1975; Ganster, Fusilier, & Mayes, 1986; Osipow & Davis, 1988), and one (e.g., Kaufmann & Beehr, 1986) found no relationship with blood pressure.

Ghadially and Kumar (1989), in a cross-cultural study of stressors, coping mechanisms, and strains, reported that for their U.S. sample, interpersonal conflict was a major stressor. Among their Taiwanese sample, however, overload and home-job conflict were major stressors. Indians did not report any significant stressors. Although stressors were different, the strains most reported and agreed on between the three cultures were physical, including tension, fatigue, and physical complaints. In Hurrell and Lindstrom's studies (1992; Lindstrom & Hurrell, 1992), a Finnish sample had significantly fewer job demands (workload, hours worked per week, lack of job clarity, intragroup and intergroup conflict, and limited promotion opportunities) than the Americans, but they reported more heart symptoms and stomach trouble. Americans, however, had more headaches and sleep problems (Lindstrom & Hurrell, 1992).

Behavioral. Behavioral strains are negative ways of reacting to stressors that cause harm to one (Beehr, 1995). Some of the unhealthy ways people might react to stressors are by drinking alcohol, consuming an excess amount of drugs, committing suicide, engaging in violent behaviors, smoking, over- or undereating, engaging in unsafe, risky behaviors, snapping at coworkers or family members, and even overexercising (as this too can be harmful to the body). Few research studies have demonstrated a relationship between role stressors and such behavioral strains. Adriaanse, Van Reek, Zandbelt, and Evers (1991) purported that nurses, in comparison to teachers, physicians, nonhealth professionals, and the general population, form a heavy smoking (i.e., cigarette consumption) profession, possibly because of the high task-oriented work assignments placed on them in a male-dominated organization and the low social support they receive. A study by Steffy and Laker (1991) found that the correlation between role ambiguity and alcohol consumption for relaxation purposes or quantity of alcohol intake was positive, but small (.09 and .03, respectively, $p < .05$; $N = 8,640$). These results echo those of Jex and Beehr (1991) who indicated a low correlation between stressors and behavioral strains.

Organizational Outcomes

Organizational outcomes are employee behaviors that have a more direct negative effect on the organization than on the individual (Beehr, 1995). As far back as the 1920s, Eric Trist began working on the Quality of Worklife Movement by focusing on the health and well-being of workers and the effects on achieving organizational goals. As noted earlier, all immediate outcomes of stressors are individual reactions, but when the individual's reactions are more directly harmful to the organization than to the individual, we designate these as organizational outcomes (outcomes to the organization). For example, a person's (lack of) psychological commitment to the workplace can result in organizational costs such as turnover. If the behavior of turnover occurs or changes in performance occur due to role stress, the organization is affected directly. Therefore, use of the terms psychological, physiological, and behavioral organizational strains, in essence, refers to individuals' negative reactions that directly affect the organization.

Psychological. Examples of employees' psychological reactions to stress that are deemed organizational consequences include organizational commitment, turnover intention, psychological contract, and organizational justice. These have effects on the organization mainly due to the employee behaviors they are likely to cause. The most widely studied organizational consequence of role stressors has been organizational commitment. Organizational commitment consists of three dimensions or components (Allen & Meyer, 1990): affective, continuance, and normative commitment. In brief, affective organizational commitment is an emotional attachment to, identification with, and involvement in one's organization. Continuance commitment is the need to stay in an organization because of lack of alternatives or fear of losing accrued benefits by leaving the organization. Normative commitment has to do with one's sense of obligation to remain with the employing organization, often due to agreement with the organization's values, norms, or goals. Meyer, Stanley, Herscovitch, and Topolnytsky's

(2002) meta-analysis revealed that work-family interrole conflict most strongly correlated with affective commitment. Also, role conflict and role ambiguity have been negatively correlated with both affective and normative commitment. Role stressors do not seem to be related to continuance commitment, however (Glazer & Beehr, in review; Meyer et al., 2002), and one study of salespeople found no overall relationship between role stressors and organizational commitment (Singh, 1998). Little research has examined normative commitment in relation to role stressors making it difficult to reach conclusions on this component.

It appears that role stressors are related to turnover intentions (e.g., Bedeian, Mossholder, & Armenakis, 1983; Grandey & Cropanzano, 1999; Singh, 1998). Obviously, if these intentions are carried out, the resulting turnover can be a cost to the organization. An early meta-analysis indicated the correlation between role stressors and turnover intentions might be only around .20 (Jackson & Schuler, 1985).

Behavioral. Most of the research on behavioral organizational strains has focused on performance (in terms of quality and quantity of productivity, and goal achievement) and withdrawal (e.g., absenteeism frequency and duration, and turnover) (Beehr, 1995), though grievances and injuries have also been addressed as performance strains (Quick et al., 1997). Quick et al. also review health care costs and compensation awards as organizational strains. The extent to which role stressors relate to health care costs and compensation awards cannot readily be determined from the available literature. It is highly likely, however, that many of the grievances stem from interpersonal conflict including overloading subordinates with work assignments and workplace harassment.

It would, of course, be very important to organizations if role stressors strongly influenced job performance. A book by Jex (1998) reviewing research on all types of occupational stress and job performance found little or no clear, systematic evidence of the effects of role stressors on performance, however. Other reviews (e.g., Beehr, 1995) and meta-analyses (e.g., Jackson & Schuler, 1985) have also found little consistent relationship, linear or nonlinear, between role stressors and job performance.

Absenteeism is costly to organizations, and stress could easily affect it either because people stay away due to the unpleasantness of the stressor or because the strains are basically illnesses that make it hard to work. Kaufmann and Beehr (1986) found some relationship between role stressors and absenteeism but mostly in interaction with (the lack of) social support.

Turnover intention is related to role stressors, as noted earlier, but actual turnover has a weaker and less consistent relationship as some studies find positive results and others do not (e.g., Gupta & Beehr, 1979; Vredenburgh & Trinkaus, 1983). Turnover has been studied in relation to role stressors much less than turnover intentions have, however.

Epilogue

As noted at the beginning of this chapter, our lives are composed of many roles that we play. The work role, by itself and in conjunction (or in conflict) with other roles, can be an important stress producer. Rather than being defined and scripted by a master playwright, our work roles are defined by the more plebeian sources of ourselves and our contemporaries inside and outside of our work organizations. The nature of their expectations and the way that we understand them can cause us to feel good or bad, and role stress is usually considered to be evidenced by some of the bad feelings and accompanying physical and behavioral consequences of role characteristics. It seems clear that role stressors can directly affect our own selves as well as our employing organizations.

Among the organizational outcomes, poor organizational citizenship behavior seems to be a particularly strong possibility that needs more research. People often engage in extraorganizational behaviors in times when they feel close with the organization and appreciated by it or by people representing it. However, when role stressors are perceived, people might retract from engaging in extrarole behaviors, especially if the behaviors involve people in one's role set who are also reasons for the individual's role stressor to begin with. Our roles being defined by the people about us rather than by a master writer has consequences for our relationships with those people.

Role stressors were some of the first occupational stressors investigated in organizational psychology, and we now know quite a bit about them. Research is still needed on more job-specific role stressors and on intensity, frequency, and duration of the role stressors. Further, future research is still needed to examine some of the less studied outcomes (perhaps especially the behavioral consequences to both the individual and the organization). In addition, the usual call for more longitudinal research is relevant to the role stress area, although some of the studies reviewed did have longitudinal elements to them. As noted elsewhere, the search for complete understanding of work-role stress is an unfinished enterprise (Beehr, 1998).

References

Adler, N., & Matthews, K. (1994). Health psychology: Why do some people get sick and some stay well? *Annual Review of Psychology, 45,* 229–259.

Adriaanse, H., Van Reek, J., Zandbelt, L., & Evers, G. (1991). Nurses' smoking worldwide: A review of 73 surveys on nurses' tobacco consumption in 21 countries in the period 1959–1988. *International Journal of Nursing Studies, 28,* 361–375.

Allen, N. J., & Meyer, J. P. (1990). The measurement and antecedents of affective, continuance, and normative commitment to the organization. *Journal of Occupational Psychology, 63,* 1–18.

Anderson, J. G. (1991). Stress and burnout among nurses: A social network approach. *Journal of Social Behavior and Personality, 6,* 251–272.

Aryee, S., & Stone, R. J. (1996). Work experiences, work adjustment, and psychological well-being of expatriate employees in Hong Kong. *The International Journal of Human Resource Management, 7,* 150–164.

Bacharach, S. B., Bamberger, P., & Conley, S. (1990). Work processes, role conflict, and role overload: The case of nurses and engineers in the public sector. *Work and Occupations, 17,* 199–228.

Bacharach, S. B., Bamberger, P., & Conley, S. (1991). Work-home conflict among nurses and engineers: Mediating the impact of role stress on burnout and satisfaction at work. *Journal of Organizational Behavior, 12,* 39–53.

Bandura, A. (1982). Self-efficacy mechanism in human agency. *American Psychologist, 37,* 122–147.

Baruch, G. K., Biener, L., & Barnett, R. C. (1987). Women and gender in research on work and family stress. *The American Psychologist, 42,* 130–136.

Bedeian, A. G., Mossholder, K. W., & Armenakis, A. A. (1983). Role perception-outcome relationships: Moderating effects of situational variables. *Human Relations, 36,* 167–183.

Beehr, T. A. (1976). Perceived situational moderators of the relationship between subjective role ambiguity and role strain. *Journal of Applied Psychology, 61,* 35–40.

Beehr, T. A. (1985). Organizational stress and employee effectiveness. In T. A. Beehr & R. S. Bhagat (Eds.), *Human stress and cognition in organizations: An integrated perspective* (pp. 57–81). New York: Wiley.

Beehr, T. A. (1994, May). *Meta-analysis of occupational stress and social support.* Paper presented at the annual meeting of the Midwestern Psychological Association, Chicago.

Beehr, T. A. (1995). *Psychological stress in the workplace.* London: Routledge.

Beehr, T. A. (1998). Research on occupational stress: An unfinished enterprise. *Personnel Psychology, 51,* 835–844.

Beehr, T. A., & Bhagat, R. S. (1985). *Human stress and cognition in organizations: An integrated perspective* (pp. 57–81). New York: Wiley.

Beehr, T. A., & Bowling, N. A. (in press). Hardy personality, stress, and health. In C. L. Cooper (Ed.), *Handbook of stress medicine and health* (2nd ed.). New York: CRC Press.

Beehr, T. A., & Drexler, J. A., Jr. (1986). Social support, autonomy, and hierarchical level as moderators of the role characteristics-outcomes relationship. *Journal of Occupational Behaviour, 7,* 207–214.

Beehr, T. A., Farmer, S. J., Glazer, S., Gudanowski, D. M., & Nair, V. N. (2003). The enigma of social support and occupational stress: Source congruence and gender role effects. *Journal of Occupational Health Psychology, 8,* 220–231.

Beehr, T. A., Glaser, K. M., Canali, K. G., & Wallwey, D. A. (2001). Back to basics: Re-examination of demand-control theory of occupational stress. *Work & Stress, 15,* 115–130.

Beehr, T. A., & Glazer, S. (2001). A cultural perspective of social support in relation to occupational stress. In P. Perrewé, D. C. Ganster, & J. Moran (Eds.), *Research in occupational stress and well-being* (pp. 97–142). Greenwich, CT: JAI.

Beehr, T. A., Jex, S. M., Stacy, B. A., & Murray, M. A. (2000). Work stressors and coworker support as predictors of individual strain and job performance. *Journal of Organizational Behavior, 21,* 391–405.

Beehr, T. A., King, L. A., & King, D. W. (1990). Social support and occupational stress: Talking to supervisors. *Journal of Vocational Behavior, 36*, 61–81.

Beehr, T. A., & McGrath, J. E. (1992). Social support, occupational stress, and anxiety. *Anxiety, Stress, and Coping, 5*, 7–19.

Beehr, T. A., & Newman, J. E. (1978). Job stress, employee health, and organizational effectiveness: A facet analysis, model, and literature review. *Personnel Psychology, 31*, 665–699.

Beehr, T., Walsh, J., & Taber, T. (1976). Relationship of stress to individually and organizationally valued states: Higher order needs as a moderator. *Journal of Applied Psychology, 61*, 41–47.

Bhuian, S. N., Al-Shammari, E. S., & Jefri, O. A. (1996). Organizational commitment, job satisfaction, and job characteristics: An empirical study of expatriates in Saudi Arabia. *International Journal of Commerce and Management, 6*, 57–80.

Black, J. S. (1992). Socializing American expatriate managers overseas. *Group and Organization Management, 17*, 171–192.

Black, J. S., & Gregersen, H. B. (1991). Antecedents to cross-cultural adjustment for expatriates in Pacific Rim assignments. *Human Relations, 44*, 497–513.

Brief, A. P., Burke, M. J., George, J. M., Robinson, B., & Webster, J. (1988). Should negative affectivity remain an unmeasured variable in the study of job stress? *Journal of Applied Psychology, 73*, 193–198.

Caplan, R. D. (1971). *Organizational stress and individual strain: A social-psychological study of risk factors in coronary heart disease among administrators, engineers, and scientists.* Unpublished doctoral dissertation, University of Michigan, Ann Arbor.

Caplan, R. D., Cobb, S., French, J. R. P., Jr., Harrison, R. V., & Pinneau, S. R. (1975). *Job demands and worker health: Main effects and occupational differences.* Washington, DC: U.S. Government Printing Office.

Caplan, R. D., & Jones, K. W. (1975). Effects of workload, role ambiguity, and type A personality on anxiety, depression, and heart rate. *Journal of Applied Psychology, 60*, 713–719.

Cohen, S., & Wills, T. A. (1985). Stress, social support, and the buffering hypothesis. *Psychological Bulletin, 98*, 310–357.

Cooper, C. L. (1981). *The stress check: Coping with stress of life and work.* Englewood Cliffs, NJ: Prentice Hall.

Cooper, C. L., Cooper, R. D., & Eaker, L. H. (1988). *Living with stress.* London: Penguin.

Davidson, M. J., & Cooper, C. L. (1983). Working women in the European community—The future prospect. *Long Range Planning, 16*, 49–55.

Day, A. L., & Livingstone, H. A. (2001). Chronic and acute stressors among military personnel: Do coping styles buffer their negative impact on health? *Journal of Occupational Health Psychology, 6*, 348–360.

Dunseath, J., Beehr, T. A., & King, D. W. (1995). Job stress–social support buffering effects across gender, education, and occupational groups in a municipal workforce. *Review of Public Personnel Administration, 15*, 60–83.

Etzion, D., & Westman, M. (2001). Job stress, vacation, and the crossover of strain between spouses—Stopping the vicious cycle. *Man and Work, 11*, 118–126.

Fenlason, K. J., & Beehr, T. A. (1994). Social support and occupational stress: Effects of talking to others. *Journal of Organizational Behavior, 15*, 157–175.

Fisher, C. D., & Gitelson, R. (1983). A meta-analysis of the correlates of role conflict and ambiguity. *Journal of Applied Psychology, 68,* 320–333.

French, J. R. P., Jr., & Caplan, R. D. (1973). Organizational stress and individual strain. In A. J. Marrow (Ed.), *The failure of success.* New York: AMACOM.

Friedman, M., & Rosenman, R. H. (1974). *Type A behavior and your heart.* New York: Knopf.

Frone, M. R. (2003). Work-family balance. In J. C. Quick & L. E. Tetrick (Eds.), *Handbook of occupational health psychology* (pp. 143–162). Washington, DC: American Psychological Association.

Funk, S. C., & Houston, B. K. (1987). A critical analysis of the hardiness scale's validity and utility. *Journal of Personality and Social Psychology, 53,* 572–578.

Fusilier, M. R., Ganster, D. C., & Mayes, B. T. (1987). Effects of social support, role stress, and locus of control on health. *Journal of Management, 13,* 517–528.

Ganster, D. C., Fox, M. L., & Dwyer, D. J. (2001). Explaining employees' health care costs: A prospective examination of stressful job demands, personal control, and physiological reactivity. *Journal of Applied Psychology, 86,* 954–964.

Ganster, D. C., Fusilier, M. R., & Mayes, B. T. (1986). Role of social support in the experience of stress at work. *Journal of Applied Psychology, 71,* 102–110.

Ganster, D. C., Schaubroeck, J., Sime, W. E., & Mayes, B. T. (1991). The nomological validity of the type A personality among employed adults. *Journal of Applied Psychology, 76,* 143–168.

Gavin, J. F., & Axelrod, W. L. (1977). Managerial stress and strain in a mining organization. *Journal of Vocational Behavior, 11,* 66–74.

Ghadially, R., & Kumar, P. (1989). Stress, strain and coping styles of female professionals. *Indian Journal of Applied Psychology, 26,* 1–8.

Glaser, D. N., Tatum, C. B., Nebeker, D. M., Sorenson, R. C., & Aiello, J. R. (1999). Workload and social support: Effects on performance and stress. *Human Performance, 12,* 155–176.

Glazer, S. (1995). *Antecedents and consequences of job stress among Israeli registered nurses: A structural equations model.* Unpublished master's thesis, University of Baltimore, Baltimore, Maryland.

Glazer, S., & Beehr, T. A. (in review). Toward a universal theory of occupational stress: A four-country study.

Glazer, S., & Bell, L. (2003, February). *A cross-cultural study of supervisor emotional social support.* Paper presented at the annual meeting of the Society for Cross-Cultural Research, Charleston, South Carolina.

Grandey, A. A., & Cropanzano, R. (1999). The conservation of resources model applied to work-family conflict and strain. *Journal of Vocational Behavior, 54,* 350–370.

Gross, E. (1970). Work, organization, and stress. In S. Levine & N. A. Scotch (Eds.), *Social stress* (pp. 54–110). Chicago: Aldine.

Gupta, N., & Beehr, T. A. (1979). Job stress and employee behaviors. *Organizational Behavior and Human Decision Processes, 23,* 373–387.

Gupta, N., & Jenkins, G. D., Jr. (1985). Dual-career couples: Stressors, strains, and strategies. In T. A. Beehr & R. S. Bhagat (Eds.), *Human stress and cognition in organizations* (pp. 141–176). New York: Wiley.

Hastings, R. P., & Bham, M. S. (2003). The relationship between student behaviour patterns and teacher burnout. *School Psychology International, 24,* 115–127.

Havlovic, S. J., & Keenan, J. P. (1991). Coping with work stress: The influence of individual differences. *Journal of Social Behavior and Personality, 6,* 199–212.

Heinisch, D. A., & Jex, S. M. (1997). Negative affectivity and gender as moderators of the relationship between work-related stressors and depressed mood at work. *Work & Stress, 11,* 46–57.

Houkes, I., Janssen, P. P. M., de Jonge, J., & Bakker, A. B. (2003). Personality, work characteristics and employee well-being: A longitudinal analysis of additive and moderating effects. *Journal of Occupational Health Psychology, 8,* 20–38.

Hull, J. G., Van Treuren, R. R., & Virnelli, S. (1987). Hardiness and health: A critique and alternative approach. *Journal of Personality and Social Psychology, 53,* 518–530.

Hurrell, J. J., & Lindstrom, K. (1992). Comparison of job demands, control, and psychosomatic complaints at different career stages of managers in Finland and the United States. *Scandinavian Journal of Work, Environment, & Health, 18,* 11–13.

Ivancevich, J. M., & Matteson, M. T. (1980). *Stress and work.* Glenview, IL: Scott, Foresman.

Iverson, R. D., Olekalns, M., & Erwin, P. J. (1998). Affectivity, organizational stressors, and absenteeism: A causal model of burnout and its consequences. *Journal of Vocational Behavior, 52,* 1–23.

Iwata, N., Suzuki, K., Sato, K., & Abe, K. (1992). Type A personality, work stress, and psychological distress in Japanese adult employees. *Stress Medicine, 8,* 11–21.

Jackson, S., & Schuler, R. (1985). A meta-analysis and conceptual critique of research on role ambiguity and role conflict in work settings. *Organizational Behavior and Human Decision Processes, 36,* 16–78.

Jex, S. M. (1998). *Stress and job performance: Theory, research, and implications for managerial practice.* Thousand Oaks, CA: Sage.

Jex, S. M., & Beehr, T. A. (1991). Emerging theoretical and methodological issues in the study of work-related stress. *Research in Personnel and Human Resources Management, 9,* 311–365.

Jex, S. M., & Bliese, P. D. (1999). Efficacy beliefs as a moderator of the impact of work-related stressors: A multilevel study. *Journal of Applied Psychology, 84,* 349–361.

Jex, S. M., Bliese, P. D., Buzzell, S., & Primeau, J. (2001). The impact of self-efficacy on stressor-strain relations: Coping style as an explanatory mechanism. *Journal of Applied Psychology, 86,* 401–409.

Jex, S. M., & Elacqua, T. C. (1999). Time management as a moderator of relations between stressors and employee strain. *Work & Stress, 13,* 182–191.

Jex, S. M., & Gudanowski, D. M. (1992). Efficacy beliefs and work stress: An exploratory study. *Journal of Organizational Behavior, 13,* 509–517.

Jimmieson, N. L. (2000). Employee reactions to behavioural control under conditions of stress: The moderating role of self-efficacy. *Work & Stress, 14,* 262–280.

Kahn, R. (1980). Conflict, ambiguity, and overload: Three elements in job stress. In D. Katz, R. Kahn, & J. Adams (Eds.), *The study of organizations* (pp. 418–428). San Francisco: Jossey-Bass.

Kahn, R. L., Wolfe, D. M., Quinn, R. P., Snoek, J. D., & Rosenthal, R. A. (1964). *Organizational stress: Studies in role conflict and ambiguity.* New York: Wiley.

Karasek, R. A. (1979). Job demands, job decision latitude, and mental strain: Implications for job redesign. *Administrative Science Quarterly, 24,* 285–308.

Katz, D., & Kahn, R. (1978). *The social psychology of organizations*. New York: Wiley.

Kaufmann, G. M., & Beehr, T. A. (1986). Interactions between job stressors and social support: Some counterintuitive results. *Journal of Applied Psychology, 71*, 522–526.

Kaufmann, G. M., & Beehr, T. A. (1989). Occupational stressors, individual strains, and social support among police officers. *Human Relations, 42*, 185–197.

Keenan, A., & McBain, G. D. (1979). Effects of type A behaviour, intolerance of ambiguity, and locus of control on the relationships between role stress and work-related outcomes. *Journal of Occupational Psychology, 52*, 277–285.

Kemery, E. R. (1991). Affective disposition, role stress, and job withdrawal. In P. L. Perrewé (Ed.), *Handbook on job stress* [Special issue]. *Journal of Behavior and Personality, 6*, 331–347.

Kirmeyer, S. L., & Diamond, A. (1985). Coping by police officers: A study of role stress and type A and type B behavior patterns. *Journal of Occupational Behavior, 6*, 183–195.

Kobasa, S. C. (1979). Stressful life events, personality and health: An inquiry into hardiness. *Journal of Personality and Social Psychology, 37*, 1–11.

Lindstrom, K., & Hurrell, J. J. (1992). Coping with jobs stress by managers at different career stages in Finland and the U.S. *Scandinavian Journal of Work, Environment & Health, 18*, 14–17.

Lyons, T. F. (1971). Role clarity, need for clarity, satisfaction, tension, and withdrawal. *Organizational Behavior and Human Performance, 6*, 99–110.

Matsui, T., & Onglatco, M. (1992). Career self-efficacy as a moderator of the relation between occupational stress and strain. *Journal of Vocational Behavior, 41*, 79–88.

McGrath, J. E. (1976). Stress and behavior in organizations. In M. D. Dunnette (Ed.), *Handbook of industrial and organizational psychology* (pp. 1351–1395). Chicago: Rand McNally College.

McGrath, J. E., & Beehr, T. A. (1990). Time and the stress process: Some temporal issues in the conceptualization and measurement of stress. *Stress Medicine, 6*, 93–104.

Meyer, J. P., Stanley, D. J., Herscovitch, L., & Topolnytsky, L. (2002). Affective, continuance, and normative commitment to the organization: A meta-analysis of antecedents, correlates, and consequences. *Journal of Vocational Behavior, 61*, 20–52.

Moyle, P. (1995). The role of negative affectivity in the stress process: Tests of alternative models. *Journal of Organizational Behavior, 16*, 647–668.

National Institute for Occupational Safety and Health. (2000, July 28). *National occupation research agenda: 21 Priorities for the 21st century*. Retrieved March 15, 2003, from www.cdc.gov/niosh/00-143g.html

Newton, T. J., & Keenan, A. (1987). Role stress reexamined: An investigation of role stress predictors. *Organizational Behavior and Human Decision Processes, 40*, 346–368.

Newton, T. J., & Keenan, T. (1990). The moderating effect of the type A behavior pattern and locus of control on the relationship between change in job demands and change in psychological strain. *Human Relations, 43*, 1229–1255.

Noor, N. M. (2002). Work-family conflict, locus of control, and women's well-being: Tests of alternative pathways. *Journal of Social Psychology, 142*, 645–662.

O'Driscoll, M. P., & Beehr, T. A. (2000). Moderating effects of perceived control and need for clarity on the relationship between role stressors and employee affective reactions. *Journal of Social Psychology, 140,* 151–159.

Orpen, C. (1982). Type A personality as a moderator for the effects of role conflict, role ambiguity, and role overload on individual strain. *Journal of Human Stress, 8,* 8–14.

Osipow, S. H., & Davis, A. S. (1988). The relationship of coping resources to occupational stress and strain. *Journal of Vocational Behavior, 32,* 1–15.

Parasuraman, S., & Alutto, J. A. (1984). Sources and outcomes of stress in organizational settings: Toward the development of a structural model. *Academy of Management Journal, 27,* 330–350.

Parkes, K. R. (1990). Coping, negative affectivity, and the work environment: Additive and interaction predictors of mental health. *Journal of Applied Psychology, 75,* 399–409.

Parkes, K. R., Mendham, C. A., & von Rabenau, C. (1994). Social support and the demand-discretion model of job stress: Tests of additive and interactive effects in two samples. *Journal of Vocational Behavior, 44,* 91–113.

Pearce, J. L. (1981). Bringing some clarity to the role ambiguity research. *Academy of Management Review, 6,* 665–674.

Peiro, J. M., Gonzalez-Roma, V., Tordera, N., & Manas, M. A. (2001). Does role stress predict burnout over time among health care professionals? *Psychology and Health, 16,* 511–525.

Peterson, M. F., Smith, P. B., Akande, A., Ayestaran, S., Bochner, S., Callan, V., et al. (1995). Role conflict, ambiguity, and overload: A 21-nation study. *Academy of Management Journal, 38,* 429–452.

Posig, M., & Kickul, J. (2003). Extending our understanding of burnout: Test of an integrated model in nonservice occupations. *Journal of Occupational Health Psychology, 8,* 3–19.

Quick, J. C., Quick, J. D., Nelson, D. L., & Hurrell, J. J. (1997). *Preventive stress management in organizations.* Washington, DC: American Psychological Association.

Quick, J. C., & Tetrick, L. E. (2003). *Handbook of occupational health psychology* (pp. 143–162). Washington, DC: American Psychological Association.

Rahim, M. A., & Psenicka, C. (1996). A structural equations model of stress, locus of control, social support, psychiatric symptoms, and propensity to leave a job. *Journal of Social Psychology, 136,* 69–84.

Rizzo, J. R., House, R. J., & Lirtzman, S. I. (1970). Role conflict and ambiguity in complex organizations. *Administrative Science Quarterly, 15,* 150–163.

Robertson, I. T., Cooper, C. L., & Williams, J. (1990). The validity of the occupational stress indicator. *Work & Stress, 4,* 29–39.

Rodriguez, I., Bravo, M. J., Peiro, J. M., & Schaufeli, W. (2001). The demands-control-support model, locus of control and job dissatisfaction: A longitudinal study. *Work & Stress, 15,* 97–114.

Schaubroeck, J., Ganster, D. C., Sime, W. E., & Ditman, D. (1993). A field experiment testing supervisory role clarification. *Personnel Psychology, 46,* 1–25.

Schaufeli, W. B., & Janczur, B. (1994). Burnout among nurses: A Polish-Dutch comparison. *Journal of Cross-Cultural Psychology, 25,* 95–113.

Schuler, R. S. (1980). Definition and conceptualization of stress in organizations. *Organizational Behavior and Human Performance, 25,* 184–215.

Searle, B., Bright, J. E. H., & Bochner, S. (2001). Helping people sort it out: The role of social support in the job strain model. *Work & Stress, 15,* 328–346.

Semmer, N. K. (2003). Individual differences, work stress and health. In M. J. Schabracq, J. A. M. Winnubst, & C. L. Cooper (Eds.), *The handbook of work and health psychology* (2nd ed., pp. 83–120). Chichester, UK: Wiley.

Shirom, A. (2003). Job-related burnout: A review. In J. C. Quick & L. E. Tetrick (Eds.), *Handbook of occupational health psychology* (pp. 245–264). Washington, DC: American Psychological Association.

Singh, J. (1998). Striking a balance in boundary-spanning positions: An investigation of some unconventional influences on role stressors and job characteristics on job outcomes of salespeople. *Journal of Marketing, 62,* 69–86.

Sloan, S. J., & Cooper, C. L. (1986). *Pilots under stress.* London: Routledge & Kegan Paul.

Sofer, C. (1970). *Men in mid-career.* London: Cambridge University Press.

Spector, P. E. (2002). Employee control and occupational stress. *Current Directions in Psychological Science, 11,* 133–136.

Spector, P. E., Zapf, D., Chen, P. Y., & Frese, M. (2000). Why negative affectivity should not be controlled in job stress research: Don't throw out the baby with the bath water. *Journal of Organizational Behavior, 21,* 79–95.

Srivastava, S., Hagtvet, K. A., & Sen, A. K. (1994). A study of role stress and job anxiety among three groups of employees in a private sector organization. *Social Science International, 10,* 25–30.

Steffy, B. D., & Laker, D. R. (1991). Workplace and personal stresses antecedent to employees' alcohol use. *Journal of Social Behavior and Personality, 6,* 115–126.

Stroh, L. K., Dennis, L. E., & Cramer, T. C. (1994). Predictors of expatriate adjustment. *International Journal of Organizational Analysis, 2,* 176–192.

Terborg, J. R. (1985). Working women and stress. In T. A. Beehr & R. S. Bhagat (Eds.), *Human stress and cognition in organizations: An integrated perspective* (pp. 245–286). New York: Wiley.

Vaux, A. (1988). *Social support: Theory, research, and intervention.* New York: Praeger.

Viswesvaran, C., Sanchez, J. I., & Fisher, J. (1999). The role of social support in the process of work stress: A meta-analysis. *Journal of Vocational Behavior, 54,* 314–334.

Vredenburgh, D. U., & Trinkaus, R. J. (1983). An analysis of role stress among hospital nurses. *Journal of Vocational Behavior, 22,* 82–95.

West, J. P., & West, C. M. (1989). Job stress and public sector occupations: Implications for personnel managers. *Review of Public Personnel Administration, 9,* 46–65.

Westman, M. (2001). Stress and strain crossover. *Human Relations, 54,* 717–752.

Westman, M. (2002). Gender asymmetry in crossover research. In D. L. Nelson & R. J. Burke (Eds.), *Gender, work stress, and health* (pp. 129–149). Washington, DC: American Psychological Association.

Westman, M., & Etzion, D. (1995). Crossover of stress, strain and resources from one spouse to another. *Journal of Organizational Behavior, 16,* 169–181.

Westman, M., Etzion, D., & Danon, E. (2001). Job insecurity and crossover of burnout in married couples. *Journal of Organizational Behavior, 22,* 467–481.

Zellars, K. L., Perrewé, P. L., & Hochwarter, W. A. (1999). Mitigating burnout among high-NA employees in health care: What can organizations do? *Journal of Applied Social Psychology, 29,* 2250–2271.

3 Work Schedules

Peter Totterdell

The mental and physical health of workers depends not only on what they do at work but also on when they work and for how long they work. This chapter will therefore describe some of the temporal characteristics of work and examine their impact on workers. Understanding the psychological effects of work schedules is important because an increasing number of people work on schedules that do not conform to the standard "9-to-5," Monday to Friday workweek.

Although this chapter will consider various forms of work schedule, it will focus on two main topics: shift work and long work hours. These topics have been chosen because they appear to pose the greatest problems for organizations and workers, they have attracted the most research attention, and they illustrate the dual importance of the arrangement and length of work time. The chapter will cover issues such as international changes in use of shift work and weekly work hours, the application of chronobiological and stress models, the reasons for alternative work schedules, comparisons between different forms of work schedule, differences in how individuals respond to work schedules, effects on physical and mental health, and possible societal, organizational, and individual interventions for minimizing schedule-related problems.

Definition of Stressor

Organizations make use of a wide range of work schedules by varying the times of day at which employees start work, the number of hours they work each day, and the days of the week and the weeks of the year they work. Examples of commonly used types of work schedule include shift work, compressed work (fitting the workweek into fewer days by extending daily hours), overtime, part-time, flexible hours (allowing workers to fix their own daily start and end times outside core hours), annual hours/hours averaging (cumulative work hours calculated over an extended period), staggered hours (starting work at slightly different fixed times), time-autonomous (work time is shaped by tasks), special leave (e.g., parental, educational), and on-call (see International Labour Organization [ILO], 1995, for further details). Any schedule, including a standard workweek, can act as a stressor if it does not conform to the needs of the individual worker. However, the nature of some work schedules means that they have an increased likelihood of causing problems. Working at night or for extended hours, for example, can incur fatigue-related problems that are not associated with some of the other schedules.

Like most of the other types of work schedule, shift work encompasses a variety of different work patterns. Shift work refers to a system of working in which one group of workers replaces another during the workday so that the number of operating hours exceeds the work hours of any particular individual. A shift worker, however, is normally defined as someone who regularly starts or ends work outside of daytime hours (e.g., 7 A.M. to 7 P.M.). Shift systems that operate 24 hours a day, 7 days a week are known as continuous; those that stop at the weekend are semicontinuous; and those that stop for a period during weekdays as well as at the weekend are discontinuous. A distinction is also made between rotating systems in which workers periodically change from one shift (e.g., morning shift) to another (e.g., night shift) and permanent systems in which workers only work one type of shift (e.g., a morning shift or a night shift). The other main characteristics that distinguish between shift systems are the start times of shifts, length of shifts, speed of rotation (i.e., how many consecutive shifts of one type are worked before rotation), direction of rotation (in forward/delaying rotating systems, workers switch to a shift that begins later; and in backward/advancing rotating systems, they switch to an earlier shift), rest periods between shifts, and regularity or flexibility of shifts (which refers to the extent to which the pattern of shifts is fixed or the amount of choice workers have over which shifts they work).

In relation to the topic of length of work hours, there is no agreed definition of what constitutes long work hours. In looking at the effects of work hours, many researchers have treated weekly work hours as a continuum whereas others have set a threshold such as 48 hours and have examined the effects of working longer. Other research has instead concentrated on the effects of the number of consecutive hours worked (e.g., extended shifts).

Prevalence of Exposure to
Different Work Schedules in the Workforce _____

Data from a 1991 population survey in America revealed that only 31.5% of employed workers over 18 regularly worked a standard daytime weekday schedule of 35 to 40 hours a week, and only 55% worked a fixed daytime weekday schedule of any number of hours (Presser, 1995). The figures also showed that 20.1% of people worked nonstandard hours and 40.1% worked nonstandard days. These proportions were similar for men and women. A similar survey conducted in 2001 found that 14.5% of full-time workers worked a shift other than a daytime one, which was 3.5% less than 10 years earlier (Bureau of Labor Statistics [BLS], 2002). This figure included 4.8% working evening shifts, 3.3% working night shifts, 2.8% on irregular shifts, and 2.3% on rotating shifts. Among part-time workers (< 35 hrs.), who constitute about one fifth of the American workforce, about 36% work a shift other than a regular daytime shift (Beers, 2000).

By way of comparison, the Third European Survey of Working Conditions conducted in 2000 found that 22% of the workforce was involved in shift work across 15 European Union member countries (Boisard, Cartron, Gollac, & Valeyre, 2003). The number of workers on rotating shifts had increased by 1.7% since 1995 to 16.8%, and the numbers working at least one night shift per month had increased by 1% to 18.4%. Although the proportion of shift workers was similar for men and women, 24% of men worked at least one night per month compared with 12% of women.

The number of hours that people work, both weekly and lifetime, has decreased around the world since the start of the twentieth century, but the decrease began to slow in the 1990s (ILO, 1995). By the end of the century, working weeks had become shorter (especially in countries that have high average weekly hours such as Japan), amount of allowable leave had increased, and workers entered the workforce later and left earlier. However, the global trend disguised some underlying changes and large variations between countries, occupations, and individuals. For example, the increase in the number of women in the workforce caused an increase in both the number of dual earners and the number of hours worked in dual-earner households (Clarkberg & Moen, 2001). The distribution of work hours also changed so that greater proportions worked short hours or long hours. For instance, between 1973 and 1994 part-time work increased in all industrialized countries except Italy (ILO, 1995).

In 2000, average weekly work hours in the European Union were 36.7 hours (40 hrs. for men, 32.5 hrs. for women, and 39.9 hrs. for full-time workers) (Boisard et al., 2003). Among different professional categories, managers had the highest average weekly hours at 44 hours per week. Comparable U.S. figures for 1999 (BLS, 2001) showed an average workweek of 38.4 hours (42 hrs. for men, 36 hrs. for women, and 42.7 hrs. for full-time workers), and 43.9 hours for managers. U.S. managers' average work hours and the proportion of them working more than 48 hours per week did not change much during the last decade, but nearly 30% worked more than 48 hours per week in 1999 (BLS, 2000). Indeed, Jacobs and Gerson (1998) reported that more than 25% of men and 10% of women in the United States currently worked in excess of 50 hours compared with 20% and 5% respectively in 1970. The proportion of full-time Australian workers working more than 48 hours per week similarly increased from 19% in the late 1970s to 32% in the late 1990s (Pocock, 2001). Boisard et al. (2003) reported that 20.7% of full-time workers in the European Union worked more than 45 hours per week, but this proportion varied greatly from 10.6% in Belgium to 31.8% in the United Kingdom.

Another trend in working hours that has occurred in recent years is the increase in the use of flexible work schedules in which workers can vary the times at which they start and end work. The proportion of U.S. workers on flexible schedules increased from 15% in 1991 to 28.8% in 2001 (BLS, 2002). This trend has occurred across all occupations (Beers, 2000). However, flexible schedules are more common for workers in service-producing (35.3%) than goods-producing industries (23.1%), more common for managers and professionals (45.5%) than other occupations, and more common for men than women (30% vs. 27.4%) (BLS, 2002).

Major Theoretical Models

The study of work schedules has associated both shift work and long hours of work with a range of deleterious effects on mental and physical health. This section examines some of the theoretical models that have been proposed to account for the relationships between work schedules and health outcomes. The range and nature of those outcomes are described in a later section of the chapter.

Shift work. A unique feature of shift work models is that they usually incorporate the notion of disturbed biological rhythms caused by working at night or in the early morning. Humans have evolved as a diurnal species that is normally awake during the day and asleep at night. Internal anticipation of the Earth's 24-hour cycle of light and dark is reflected in 24-hour rhythmic fluctuations in many physical and mental functions known as circadian rhythms. These rhythms—such as those involving body temperature, melatonin synthesis, urinary electrolyte production, blood pressure, short-term memory performance, and alertness—peak at different times of day but are normally higher during the day and lower during the night. The circadian system appears to be made up of at least two processes: a strong endogenous body clock and a weaker exogenous process that is more susceptible to external influence (see Folkard & Hill, 2002). Some rhythms, such as the sleep-wake cycle, are less strongly coupled to the body clock and in certain circumstances can "break out" from the body clock to run with their own natural periodicities. Studies in which people have been isolated from time cues have shown that the natural period of the body clock is closer to 25 hours than 24 hours (e.g., Wever, 1979), but it is normally entrained to run at 24 hours by zeitgebers such as the light-dark cycle and social cues (e.g., mealtimes).

The circadian system is therefore not adapted for night work because the rhythms prepare workers for rest when they have to work and for activity when they have to sleep. There is therefore a mismatch between the circadian system and the work schedule. Over a number of consecutive nights of work, the circadian system begins to adjust to the altered activity pattern, but the individual rhythms adjust at different rates depending on the extent to which they are controlled by the body clock. This produces internal dissociation between the rhythms and may account for some of the problems caused by shift work. It is also possible that the rhythms may never fully adjust to a nocturnal routine (Knauth & Ilmarinen, 1975) because (unlike jet lag) the external cues encourage the circadian system to remain on a diurnal pattern. For this reason, the rhythms also adjust more quickly back to a diurnal routine when a worker has days off (Knauth, Emde, & Rutenfranz, 1981).

As well as circadian rhythm disturbance, models of shift work also regularly feature sleep disturbance and social disturbance as likely causes of problems for workers. Curtailed and poor quality sleep are common experiences for shift workers (e.g., Akerstedt, 1985). Although environmental factors such as light and noise probably play a part in making daytime sleep difficult for night shift workers, the body clock is also responsible. Experiments have shown that ease of falling asleep and duration of sleep depend on the time of day at which sleep is initiated (Lavie, 1986; Zulley, Wever, & Aschoff, 1981). Social disturbance also features in models of shift work because the work schedule often means that workers can only partake in domestic and leisure activities at times that are mismatched with those of the people around them such as family and friends (Colligan & Rosa, 1990).

To give a flavor of models of shift work and health, some example models will be described briefly in chronological order of publication. For more detailed overviews of these models see Taylor, Briner, and Folkard (1997) and Smith et al. (1999). The stress-strain model proposed by Rutenfranz, Knauth, and Angersbach (1981) was one of the first shift work models. In this model, the stress of altering work and sleep hours produces strain in the form of complaints and diseases. This pathway is influenced by intervening variables such as physiological adaptability, personality, family situation, and housing conditions. The destabilization model of shift work (Haider, Kundi, & Koller, 1981; Kundi, 1989) proposes that shift work causes health problems by interfering with the dynamic equilibrium that holds between work, sleep, and family. For example, shift workers may sacrifice sleep in order to spend more time with their family, and this may reduce their capacity to function effectively at work. Personality, social environment, and work situation moderate the destabilization process. The model also proposes that the shift worker's destabilization moves through stages of adaptation (first 5 yrs. of shift work), sensitization, and accumulation (after 15–20 yrs.), so that major health changes are only manifest during the last stage.

Models by Monk (1988) and Olsson, Kandolin, and Kaupinnen-Toropainen (1990) view the shift worker's ability to cope with shift work as critical in determining whether the schedule will lead to health problems. Monk proposes that the ability to cope with shift work depends on interference from three interrelated domains: the biological clock, sleep, and social/domestic factors. Olsson and colleagues, in contrast, see shift work as just one of several occupational stressors whose effects depend on the appraisal and coping strategies of the worker.

In reviewing these and similar models of shift work, Taylor et al. (1997) observe a move from simple models that portray linear relationships to more complex models characterized by dynamic relationships based on multiple pathways and interrelationships between problems. These more complex models rely more heavily on concepts from stress theory. Nomothetic models (such as the stress-strain model) characterize stress in terms of features of the shift worker's environment, and idiographic models (such as coping models) characterize stress in terms of the transaction between the shift worker and his or her environment. According to Taylor et al. (1997), the trend toward using general stress concepts has increased diversity in shift work research but at the cost of a lack of clarity and falsifiability. Most of the models serve as heuristic frameworks rather than descriptions of data. Most shift work research has not been concerned with theory testing.

Taylor and colleagues have called for midrange theories that specify which shift features are related to which symptoms under which circumstances. The process model of shift work (Smith et al., 1999) is an example of this type of theory. The model is based on a framework originally proposed by Folkard and colleagues (Barton et al., 1995; Folkard, 1993) in which shift system features lead to disturbed biological rhythms, sleep, and family/social life. These disturbances result in acute effects on mood and performance and eventually chronic effects on mental and physical health. Individual and situational differences and coping strategies modify this process. Smith et al. (1999) tested a modified version of this model using survey data from three groups of shift workers. In support of the model, they found that individual (e.g., inflexible sleep habits) and situational (e.g., workload) factors resulted in sleep and social disturbances that triggered different types of coping behavior leading to acute (e.g., fatigue) and chronic outcomes (e.g., digestive and cardiovascular symptoms).

Finally, with respect to shift work, there are also a number of chronobiologic models that make specific predictions concerning levels of sleepiness, alertness, and performance on different shift schedules based on the sleep times of shift workers. The most developed of these models, the three process model, was first described by Folkard and Akerstedt in 1987 and has since been further refined and validated (e.g., Akerstedt & Folkard, 1997; Folkard, Akerstedt, Macdonald, Tucker, & Spencer, 1999). The model incorporates processes C, S, and W. C is a circadian sinusoidal component, S is a homeostatic component that falls during wakefulness and is reversed during sleep, and W is a short-lived wake-up process. Predicted alertness is the sum of these three components. Validation of the model using subjective alertness ratings from shift workers has identified the need to additionally incorporate a first night shift compensation effect (shift workers are more alert on the first night shift and less alert on the second night shift than would be expected) and a time on shift effect (alertness decreases over the course of a shift).

Long hours. The time on shift effect also fits with the next topic, which is the theoretical basis of the relationship between long work hours and health. As with shift work research, the emphasis in this area has been on finding empirical evidence for the relationship rather than theory development. The main pathways that have been implicated in the relationship between work hours and health are increased fatigue, reduced motivation, prolonged exposure to work stressors, and the use of poor lifestyle habits such as smoking, lack of exercise, and inadequate diet (Sparks, Cooper, Fried, & Shirom, 1997; Spurgeon, Harrington, & Cooper, 1997). However, fatigue has proved difficult to define and can cover a range of physical and psychological functions, such as muscular, perceptual, and cognitive fatigue (White & Beswick, 2003). Fatigue has been viewed as one aspect of a general stress response (see Craig & Cooper, 1992). White and Beswick (2003) distinguish between acute fatigue, such as that incurred by a long workday, and cumulative fatigue, such as that incurred by a long workweek. Major factors that contribute to fatigue because of long work hours include high workload, insufficient sleep, and insufficient time for recovery.

One view is that the time required to recover from a stressor such as long work hours may be a better predictor of the severity of stress and the likelihood of chronic effects than the immediate response (e.g., Depue & Monroe, 1986). Recovery models that have been applied to work hours include the adaptive-cost hypothesis (e.g., Totterdell, Spelten, Smith, Barton, & Folkard, 1995), which proposes that the severity of aftereffects is a function of the effort required to adapt to aversive events, and the effort-recovery model, which proposes that sufficient recovery time is needed to offset the costs of work effort (e.g., Van der Hulst & Geurts, 2001). Increased fatigue and irritability in and outside work are seen as indicators of lack of adaptation or insufficient recovery from work.

Other researchers have used more general theories of work behavior to guide their studies of work schedules. Baltes, Briggs, Huff, Wright, and Neuman (1999), for example, used the work adjustment model and job characteristics theory to formulate their hypotheses on the effects of compressed workweeks and flextime. Nomothetic and idiographic models of job stress have also been applied to the issue of work hours. Bliese and Halverson (1996), for example, found that the relationship between work hours and well-being was best modeled from a nomothetic perspective. In other words, there was a stronger relationship between work hours and well-being at a group than at an individual level. This may suggest that long work hours act as a stressor when imposed on a group of workers but not when individuals choose to work long hours.

Related to the issue of individual preferences, Holton, Lee, and Tidd (2002) recently applied a discrepancy/congruency model to explain workers' response to work schedules. The model predicts that employees will be more satisfied and perform more effectively when they work the number of hours they prefer on schedules that fit their needs. In line with this model, Holton et al. (2002) found that work status congruence (the match between workers' preferences and organizational practices) was associated with job satisfaction, organizational commitment, retention, and performance.

Causes and Predictors for the Stressor

There are a variety of reasons why nonstandard work schedules are used by organizations. In some cases, the requirement to use such a schedule is a necessity. For example, some form of shift work schedule is necessary to provide 24-hour capability in a range of essential services such as fire protection, police, health care, transport, telecommunications, power, and water utilities. Some production industries also require extended operating times to sustain continual production processes (e.g., chemical industry). In other cases, the reason for using nonstandard schedules is economic. Manufacturing organizations, for example, may choose to maximize their return on investment in expensive machinery by operating it continually (e.g., production lines). New technology has also made extended operations possible in some jobs. Data processing centers and call centers, for example, are commonly used around the clock seven days a week. The demand for nonessential services outside regular daytime hours and weekdays has also increased. Provision of extended hours of access to shops, restaurants, entertainment, fuel, broadcasting, and cleaning services is now more common. Changing patterns of work, such as greater participation of women in the workforce, has partly fueled the demand for extended services.

Beers (2000) reported that job gains in service occupations in the United States were largely responsible for keeping the proportion of shift workers relatively static between 1985 and 1997. In 2000, night work in Europe (Boisard et al., 2003) was most common for industrial workers (35.7%) and service/sales workers (23.4%) and least common for office staff (5.2%) and agriculture and fisheries workers (13.9%). In 2001, shift work in the United States (BLS, 2002) was most common in protective services such as police and firefighting (49.0%) and food services (40.4%) and least common among managers and professionals (6.7%) and farming, forestry, and fishing occupations (5.6%).

There is a higher proportion of shift workers among full-time workers under 24 years of age (22.5%) than after that age (13.5%) (BLS, 2002). The same data show that men are more likely to work a nondaytime shift than are women (16.4% vs. 12.1%), partly because they are more likely to choose occupations in which shift work is more common (Beers, 2000). Men are more likely to work both weekdays and weekends than are women (21.8%

vs. 14.7%) (Presser, 1995). Presser (1995) also demonstrated that marriage discourages shift work among women but not men and that having children affects women's but not men's likelihood of working shifts. Specifically, women with children ages 5 to 13 are less likely to work shifts than women with children under 5 or without children. This fits with women's reported reasons for working shifts. Women with preschool-age children are more likely to report child care as their main reason for working shifts. The most common reasons that shift workers in general give for why they work shifts are that it is the nature of the job (53.3%), personal preference (13.3%), better arrangements for family or child care (8.9%), and better pay (6.9%) (BLS, 2002). Night workers more commonly report personal preference as their reason for working shifts (21.5%).

Separate from shift work, there is a global trend toward using more flexible forms of work schedule in order to enhance economic efficiency by matching the demand for labor with supply (ILO, 1995). As well as responding to economic pressures, flexibility also enables organizations to take greater account of workers' preferences, needs, and capabilities (Martens, Nijhuis, Van Boxtel, & Knottnerus, 1999). However, according to the ILO (1995), organizations are also using longer time intervals for calculating average hours worked per week, and collectively agreed deviations from work time legislation are common. These trends makes long hours of work more likely for certain individuals at certain times. Schemes involving average hours enable employers to balance weeks of high and low volume by expanding and contracting work hours without incurring overtime costs. Use of overtime (or extended hours) usually increases during the initial stages of economic recovery when employers are unsure of the strength of recovery. Extending work hours can also be a more attractive option to employers than hiring and training new recruits who may prove surplus to requirements during recession. In the United Kingdom, workweeks exceeding 48 hours are more common for men (19%) than women (4%), for middle age (31% of 30–39-year-olds) than younger workers (5% of 20–24-year-olds), and in managerial positions (22%) (see White & Beswick, 2003).

At the same time as extending the work hours of some individuals, organizations are also reducing the work hours of others (see ILO, 1995). Sometimes work hours are reduced to obtain greater flexibility in order to extend operating time. Use of part-time work has also increased, partly because of the increase in the size of service industries and partly to accommodate the child care requirements of women. However, involuntary part-time work has also increased, and a study of European part-time workers found that 37% would prefer full-time work (ILO, 1995). Organizations also make greater use of contingent workers, and an increasing number of individuals have more than one job (Golden & Applebaum, 1992).

Allied to these trends is the increase in employees' desire for sovereignty over their time. A European survey found that, in return for more leisure time or money, 61% of people would work an early shift, 22% would work a night shift, 44% would work on Saturday, and 21% would work on Sunday (ILO, 1995). However, these figures varied greatly between countries. Jacobs and Gerson (1998) reported that about half of employees would prefer to work fewer hours, rising to over 80% of those who work more than 50 hours per week. Twenty-five percent of workers said they would take a pay cut to reduce their hours of work, but 17% would increase their work hours for more money. Indeed, there is evidence of a time divide in which employees working long hours would prefer shorter hours and employees working short hours would prefer longer hours (Drago, 2000). In a study of over 4,000 couples, Clarkberg and Moen (2001) found that under half of wives and husbands were working a preferred schedule, and of these, two thirds felt they were working too much. Six years later, in the same study, 60% of individuals who wanted to reduce their work hours had done so, and those who wanted to reduce to zero work were most successful in doing so.

Known Moderators

Research has found that the relationship between work schedules and health depends on a wide range of factors, many of which are amenable to intervention. These factors include characteristics of the work schedule, characteristics of the work environment and job, individual differences and behaviors, and workers' control or influence over their schedule. This section will briefly describe current knowledge concerning some of these factors.

Shift system. One of the most important influences on the experience of shift work is the design of the shift system. For example, there is a long-standing debate about whether shift systems should be designed so that workers rotate between different shifts and, if so, how fast the rotation should be. Wilkinson (1992), for example, argued that permanent night shift systems are preferable because they allow the circadian system to adjust. In contrast, Folkard (1992) argued that, except for safety critical operations, it is better to use rapidly rotating systems to minimize circadian disturbance, reduce cumulative sleep deficit, and allow workers some normal social time. There seems to be some agreement that slowly rotating shift systems (e.g., weekly changes) are least desirable (Knauth, 1996), but a recent meta-analysis found that such systems have a less negative effect on sleep than rapid rotation (Pilcher, Lambert, & Huffcutt, 2000). The order of shifts in a rotating shift system is also important. Comparisons between systems have generally favored delaying systems (e.g., Barton & Folkard, 1993) because they encourage a sleep pattern more in line with the body clock and they avoid quick changeovers between shifts, but the evidence is not conclusive (Tucker, Smith, Macdonald, & Folkard, 2000). The start times of work shifts also have an impact, and research suggests that an early start to the morning shift should be avoided (e.g., Kecklund, Akerstedt, & Lowden, 1997).

Another shift system characteristic that has received considerable research attention and is relevant to the issue of length of work hours is the duration of work shifts and, relatedly, the compression of workweeks. Much of the research has focused on the use of 12-hour shifts compared with 8-hour shifts. Following a comprehensive review of research on the relative effects of 8-hour and 12-hour shifts, Smith, Folkard, Tucker, and Macdonald (1998) concluded that the evidence shows few differences between them. Schedules involving 12-hour shifts appear to have some advantages in terms of workers' satisfaction with their job, family, and social life but may cause fatigue-related problems particularly at the end of shifts (e.g., Mitchell & Williamson, 2000). More generally, a meta-analysis of compressed workweek schedules showed that they have positive effects on job and schedule satisfaction and performance ratings but no effects on absenteeism or productivity (Baltes et al., 1999).

Job-related factors. A number of other job-related factors such as work environment and job content can also modify the response to work schedules. For example, in relation to work environment, Parkes (2002) demonstrated that offshore workers reported better sleep quality and longer sleep durations than their onshore counterparts. Costa (1996) also points out that exposure and susceptibility to toxicological agents can vary over the course of 24 hours. Concerning job content, the impact of long hours may be greater for jobs requiring sustained attention and for sedentary jobs (Sparks et al., 1997). There is also limited evidence that social support in the workplace, especially from supervisors, can buffer the impact of shift work on job strain (Schmieder & Smith, 1996).

Individual differences. Individuals differ in their tolerance to shift work, and researchers have investigated a number of characteristics that might predict tolerance. Questionnaire measures based on circadian rhythm concepts have been somewhat more successful in predicting shift work tolerance than circadian rhythm characteristics themselves (e.g., Vidacek et al., 1995). For example, individuals who are categorized as evening rather than morning types, because they tend to wake up and go to sleep later and prefer activities later in the day, appear to adjust better to night work (see Harma, 1993). There is also evidence that shift work tolerance is greater for individuals who are more flexible in their sleeping habits or who can overcome drowsiness more easily (e.g., Costa, Lievore, Casaletti, Gaffuri, & Folkard, 1989). The predictive powers of these measures for shift work tolerance are small but greater than those of other individual difference measures (Kaliterna, Vidacek, Prizmic, & Radosevic-Vidacek, 1995). Neuroticism has also been linked to poor shift work tolerance (e.g., Parkes, 2002), but it may be a consequence rather than a predictor of poor tolerance (see Harma, 1993). In relation to age, older shift workers experience more problems than younger shift workers because circadian adjustment becomes more difficult with age (see Parkes, 2002).

Studies comparing male and female shift workers have generally found few differences in tolerance (Singer, 1989). Menstrual cycle phase can influence women's experience of different shifts such that problems caused by the night shift may be exacerbated during the premenstrual phase (Totterdell, Spelten, & Pokorski, 1995). However, outcomes are more likely to be influenced by differences in domestic workload than biological differences (Harma, 1993). For instance, some studies have found that women with children experience more fatigue-related problems than either women without children or men with or without children (Estryn-Behar, Gadbois, Peigne, Masson, & Le Gall, 1990). There is some evidence that women are more likely than men to show a positive relationship between long work hours and ill health, but this may also be due to differences in nonwork roles (Sparks et al., 1997). Men may also be more vulnerable to strain when their wives work long hours than vice versa (Galambos & Walters, 1992).

Mental and behavioral strategies adopted by shift workers also appear to influence their adjustment to the schedule. For example, use of effective coping strategies, commitment to shift work, and physical fitness have all been associated with less disturbance (Harma, 1993; Smith et al., 1999).

Control over schedule. One factor that appears to facilitate workers' reactions to schedules is the level of control or influence that they have over their schedule. Different forms of work schedule control have shown benefits. For example, shift work tolerance can be enhanced by participation in the design of the schedule (Kogi, 1996), choice of working on a particular schedule such as permanent night shifts (Barton, 1994), and ongoing influence over which shifts are worked (Barton, Smith, Totterdell, Spelten, & Folkard, 1993). Hours worked may be less influential on outcomes than schedule control and the extent to which schedules fit individuals' needs (Fenwick & Tausig, 2001; Gareis & Barnett, 2002). Similarly, for workers who reduce their work hours, the tradeoff of activities and job-role quality may be better predictors of distress than work hours (Barnett & Gareis, 2000a, 2000b). In relation to control over daytime work hours, a meta-analysis of flexible schedules found that the positive effects of flextime schemes diminish over time, are lower in jobs that are high in autonomy, and reduce with increasing flexibility (Baltes et al., 1999).

Key Measurement Issues

Many of the issues concerning measurement in the study of work schedules are shared by research on other sources of work stress and will therefore be described in the chapter on methodological issues. This section, however, will highlight some issues that are highly salient or unique to the study of work schedules. See Boggild and Knutsson (1999) for more detailed discussion of some of these issues.

The first issue concerns the problem of who to include in the target sample. Shift work, for example, encompasses a wide range of different schedules, and the amount of exposure to night work in particular varies greatly depending on the schedule and on the individual worker. Comparisons of working hours are also hampered by the fact that working hours can be calculated in many different ways. For example, working hours are measured through payroll records, self-reports of annual or weekly hours, retrospective self-reports of work during a target week, calculated workweeks, and time-use diaries. These different methods can produce different results (Herman, 1999; Jacobs, 1998). The problem of obtaining accurate figures is also likely to increase as people work more flexible schedules, take on additional jobs, travel more, and do more work at home.

Identification of appropriate comparison groups is also difficult. For example, shift work is more common for certain types of occupation, so discovered differences between shift workers and day workers may reflect occupational differences. Shift workers also tend to have lower socioeconomic status, but controlling for this factor is problematic because it is related to having an unhealthy lifestyle, which may be one of the mechanisms by which shift work causes problems. Comparing workers who do the same job may be one answer, but even then work conditions (e.g., smoke and noise) and job demands may be different at night than by day.

Primary selection into and secondary selection out of study groups may also bias results. People who apply to do shift work may have different personality characteristics and lifestyles, and they may be selected based on an assessment of particular capabilities such as an ability to cope with shift work. However, demonstration of a change in disturbance with increased exposure to shift work can counter a primary selection interpretation. A sizable proportion of shift workers (between 10 and 20% according to Kivimaki, Kuisma, Virtanen, & Elovainio, 2001) also switch back to day work, commonly due to health problems. This leads to a biasing effect known as healthy survivors. The bias is compounded by the fact that former shift workers, who typically have greater health problems than shift workers, make up part of the comparison group. A comparison group made up of individuals who have never done shift work may therefore be more appropriate. The healthy survivor effect also applies to long work hours because individuals who cannot cope with long hours sometimes switch to shorter hours. Individuals working long hours because of work demands (who may therefore be most likely to suffer problems) may also exclude themselves from studies due to lack of time.

Timing of measurement administration is another important consideration in work schedules research. Circadian rhythms can account for large amounts of variation in many physiological and mental processes. Hence, for example, taking measurements only during duty periods would mean that night workers were more likely to be sampled at the lowest point in their rhythms.

Finally, the assessment of work schedules is multidisciplinary, multimethod, and multifactorial. Shift work research, for example, includes studies involving laboratory, field, survey, intervention, archival, and epidemiological methods. Measures used include physiological parameters, polysomnographic indexes, cognitive performance, work performance, health and safety records, and self-reported attitudes, behaviors, and well-being. In relation to survey research, the Standard Shiftwork Index (and its shortened version) is probably the most widely used battery of self-report measures for assessing shift work schedules (Barton et al., 1995; Kaliterna & Prizmic, 1998).

Outcomes of the Stressor

Shift work and long work hours have been connected with a wide range of negative outcomes. This section of the chapter will describe some of these. It should be borne in mind, however, that although research may have shown that the risk of these outcomes is significantly higher than for standard work schedules, this does not mean that the risk is necessarily high in absolute terms. Some of the outcomes may also require many years of exposure to the schedule stressor before they materialize.

In broad terms, research supports a link between both shift work and long work hours and ill health. For example, a study of a patient population (Martens et al., 1999) found that patients working rotating shifts, compressed workweeks, and irregular hours had greater physical and psychological complaints than a control group. Concerning long hours, a meta-analysis of 21 study samples found a small, significant trend of increased health symptoms with increasing work hours (Sparks et al., 1997). Psychological effects of longer work hours were shown to be greater than physiological effects. Another recent review of the literature (Van der Hulst, 2003) also found that there was evidence of a relationship between long work hours and adverse health. Although there was evidence of both physiological changes and changes in health behavior resulting from long work hours, Van der Hulst concluded that there was greater support for a physiological recovery mechanism than a lifestyle mechanism.

Sleep and fatigue. Two studies involving very large sample sizes have linked work hours to sleep disturbance. Ribet and Derrienic (1999) found from interviews with 21,000 French workers that shift work and long work hours were two of the four main risk factors for sleep disturbance. Similarly, using interviews with a Swedish population sample of 58,000 individuals, Akerstedt, Fredlund, Gillberg, and Jansson (2002) found that shift work was a predictor for sleep disturbance and that overtime work was a predictor for fatigue. There is widespread agreement that shift work can disturb the duration and quality of sleep (e.g., Tepas & Carvalhais, 1990). In a review of long working hours, White and Beswick (2003) reached the conclusion that the evidence supports a link between long work hours and fatigue.

Gastrointestinal disorders. A number of studies have reported increased incidence of gastrointestinal disorders (including appetite disturbance, abdominal pains, and peptic ulcer) in shift workers (Costa, 1996). There are a number of possible explanations including changes to neuroendocrine functions due to altered sleep patterns, changes to meal times (which can act as circadian synchronizers), and changed content of meals (including increased carbohydrate intake).

Cardiovascular diseases. Shift work and long work hours have also been linked with increased risk of cardiovascular diseases (Costa, 1996; White & Beswick, 2003). Based on an assessment of 17 studies that have examined the risk for shift workers, Boggild and Knutsson (1999) estimated that male and female shift workers have a 40% increase in cardiovascular disease risk. However, not all of the large-scale studies in that review found an association, and the results concerning dose response were mixed. A number of possible mechanisms have been proposed to explain the heightened risk of cardiovascular disease for shift workers including circadian disruption, social disruption, health behaviors (e.g., diet, smoking, alcohol use, exercise), and biochemical changes (e.g., cholesterol). Research concerning these mechanisms is limited, but there is some support for explanations based on dietary differences and increased smoking in shift workers (Boggild & Knutsson, 1999; Kivimaki et al., 2001). Concerning long work hours, a number of studies have found an increased risk of coronary heart disease and acute myocardial infarction in workers who worked long days or long weeks (see Liu & Tanaka, 2002).

Cancer. A number of recent studies have also linked night work to increased risk of breast cancer (e.g., Davis, Mirick, & Stevens, 2001; Hansen, 2001; Schernhammer et al., 2001) and colorectal cancer (Schernhammer et al., 2003). In relation to breast cancer, the research has found that the increase in risk for night workers may be as high as 50 to 60% and that the risk depends on dosage of night work (in terms of both number of night shifts worked per week and years of employment on night work). The explanation for the link is thought to be that melatonin production is suppressed by exposure to light during night work, and the suppressed melatonin level enhances tumor development.

Menstrual and pregnancy problems. Further, in relation to women's health, shift work has been linked to higher rates of menstrual problems (e.g., Uehata & Sasakawa, 1982) and, in some but not all relevant studies, to higher risk of adverse pregnancy outcome such as preterm birth, low birth weight, and miscarriage (see Costa, 1996; Infante-Rivard, David, Gauthier, & Rivard, 1993). A meta-analysis of working conditions and pregnancy outcome (Mozurkewich, Luke, Avni, & Wolf, 2000) found that shift work was a risk factor for preterm birth. The researchers put this risk into perspective by stating that one preterm birth might be avoided for each 23 to 171 women who discontinue shift work. Long work hours were not associated with preterm birth.

Other health problems. Musculoskeletal disorders, such as back problems, have also been associated with shift work and working long hours, especially in occupations requiring strenuous physical work such as nursing (Guo, 2002; Lipscomb, Trinkoff, Geiger-Brown, & Brady, 2002). Shift work has been associated with a number of other minor and major health outcomes. For example, compared with day workers, shift workers are at higher risk for common infections such as colds and flu (Mohren et al., 2002). Mohren and colleagues found in their study that controlling for health behaviors, sleep, and job demands reduced the association. It is likely that increases in infection are due to depressed immune functioning caused by shift work.

Mental health. As well as being linked to problems of physical health, shift work has also been linked to mental health problems (see Cole, Loving, & Kripke, 1990; Costa, 1996; Koller, Haider, & Kundi, 1981). Studies have found increased acute psychological and somatic symptoms such as job strain and irritability among shift workers. Shift workers may also be at greater risk for a number of chronic psychological problems including chronic fatigue, persistent anxiety, neurotic disorders, and depression. Indeed, it has been observed that shift work maladaptation and depression share a number of core complaints, possibly because they have circadian disturbance in common (Healy, Minors, & Waterhouse, 1993). Long work hours have also been associated with poor psychological health and depression (White & Beswick, 2003), but there is a paucity of research on chronic effects.

Absence. One indicator of health outcomes is absenteeism. Although there is some evidence that workers on rotating shifts have more sick leaves (e.g., Ohayon, Lemoine, Arnaud-Briant, & Dreyfus, 2002), it has also been reported that rotating shift workers are less inclined to stay absent from work (Costa, 1996). In fact, the picture is somewhat more complex in that absence rates vary across the shift cycle (Nicholson, Jackson, & Howes, 1978). For example, absences are likely to be higher on morning shifts because of difficulties in awakening and at weekends because of the social value of this time. One study found that the introduction of flextime reduced absenteeism (Dalton & Mesch, 1990). Absenteeism has not commonly been included in studies of long hours.

Mortality. Few studies have examined whether shift work or long hours are associated with mortality. A study by Nylen, Voss, and Floderus (2001), however, examined this issue using Swedish mortality data for more than 9,000 women and 11,000 men between 1973 and 1996. The results indicated that shift work was not associated with mortality. There was, however, an increased mortality risk for men and women who reported working more than 5 hours per week on an extra job. Overtime work in excess of 5 hours per week had a weak positive association with mortality, but less than 5 hours overtime was protective for men. Part-time work was also associated with increased mortality risk in men.

Performance and safety. Apart from health disorders, there is also the influence of work schedules on performance and safety to consider. Although different types of performance peak at different times of day, a composite view of 24-hour work performance based on data from a number of studies has shown that speed and accuracy decline reaching a trough during the night (Monk, Folkard, & Wedderburn, 1996). Comparing incident risk (which includes both accidents and injuries) on different shifts is difficult because work conditions usually differ, but a few studies have overcome the problem (e.g., Smith, Folkard, & Poole, 1994). Pooling the available data for incident risk on shifts, Folkard and Tucker (2003) have found that risk is higher on afternoon shifts and highest on night shifts compared with morning shifts; increases over the course of a shift, but falls after the second hour of a night shift; increases over consecutive shifts of any kind, but increases more on night shifts; and increases between rest breaks within a shift. Concerning long work hours, White and Beswick (2003) concluded that there is a link with the likelihood of accidents (especially in occupations involving driving), but the link with performance was considered less conclusive. Studies have, however, shown that overtime can lower productivity (Shepard & Clifton, 2000) and impair cognitive performance (Proctor, White, Robins, Echeverria, & Rocskay, 1996). One difficulty in this research area is that workers may exert compensatory effort to overcome fatigue-related deficits.

Family outcomes. Finally for this section on outcomes, work schedules can also have an impact on the families of workers. Although shift work has some advantages for scheduling nonwork activities, it has been related to a number of adverse effects including greater marital dissatisfaction, more family conflict, and greater emotional problems and lower school achievement in children (Barton, Aldridge, & Smith, 1998; Staines & Pleck, 1983; Wedderburn, 1993). Fenwick and Tausig (2001), however, found that only non-Monday to Friday schedules were associated with greater family conflict. Findings concerning the impact of long work hours on family-related outcomes are not clear-cut but suggest an association with increased family conflict. In a study of 190 dual-earner families, Crouter, Bumpus, Head, and McHale (2001) found that long work hours for men were not associated with marital quality; but when long hours were combined with work overload, they were associated with poor relationships with adolescent children.

Major Empirical Studies

Whereas the theoretical development of the understanding of work schedules has been limited to a relatively small number of models, there have been many hundreds of empirical studies conducted on the topic. These studies range from small-scale experimental studies conducted in sleep laboratories to large-scale population surveys. Although the research varies in quality, it is difficult to identify a small number of studies that stand as hallmarks within the field. Many of the best studies have already been discussed (and some are still to be discussed) in relation to their individual contributions within the wide range of topics. Rather than present these studies again, this section will therefore be curtailed to leave space for other substantive issues.

Future Research Needs

Although international research on working time is flourishing, a number of research needs are apparent. First, there is an obvious need for more theoretical development and theory testing. In particular, more attention is required to elucidate the precise biological, psychological, and social pathways by which work schedules produce particular effects. It is by no means clear, for example, how acute effects become transformed into chronic effects. Another question concerns whether some individuals are at greater risk of health disorders than are others (Boggild & Knutsson, 1999).

As in many other areas of work stress, there is also a need for more longitudinal studies that can both tease out causal relations and investigate how individuals adapt to work schedules over weeks, months, and years. Empirical studies also need to take greater heed of potential nonlinear effects and the effects of combinations of work schedule (and individual) characteristics. For example, Lipscomb et al. (2002) found that musculoskeletal problems were predicted by the combination of nondaytime shifts and weekend work and by the combination of long workdays and long workweeks.

Controlled studies to evaluate the potential benefits of interventions such as diet modification, fitness training, and use of bright light treatment (see next section) for shift workers are also required. For example, most current studies of bright light involve simulated night work rather than actual night work. There are also unanswered questions about the health effects of continually phase shifting circadian rhythms using bright light (Eastman et al., 1995).

Researchers have begun to develop models that can simulate the likely impact on alertness and fatigue of shift workers' sleep patterns (e.g., Akerstedt, 1998; Folkard et al., 1999) and work schedules (e.g., Dawson & Fletcher, 2001; Kostreva, McNelis, & Clemens, 2002). Further development of these models is required including additional validation of results against actual work schedules. For example, current models are unable to account for some known trends in safety risk (Folkard & Tucker, 2003) and take no account of individual differences such as morningness and sleep flexibility. Future computer-aided design of shift schedules (e.g., Nachreiner, Qin, Grzech-Sukalo, & Hedden, 1993) will also need to take account of the personal preferences of workers because of the trend toward flexible schedules and the positive benefits of worker choice. On this issue, there will also need to be an assessment of the potential tradeoff between the positive influence of worker choice and the potential negative influence of workers who choose work hours that maximize short-term social benefits to the long-term detriment of health.

There is also a need for more evidence-based research that can be used to support the development and implementation of working time regulations. At present, many of the parameters used in such regulations are based on indirect or slim evidence. In relation to this issue, the recent increase in the application of meta-analysis to work schedule issues is a welcome development because it represents a move away from idiosyncratic use of evidence from single studies. However, in order for meta-analysis to be viable, researchers will have to be more stringent in reporting the exact characteristics of the work schedules that they have studied. One final point here is that further research is needed on cultural differences in reactions to work schedules. The majority of research on work schedules takes place in a few countries, yet working time practices from one culture may not travel well to another.

Implications for Practice, Policy, and Intervention

There are a variety of ways in which the problems induced by work schedules can be reduced. Interventions are possible at three levels: societal, organizational, and individual. Examples of interventions at each level will be described. However, Kogi (1996) describes the importance of using multifaceted interventions based on consensus building at all levels.

Societal interventions. Most countries have national or local regulations concerning hours of work for night and shift workers. Agreements on hours of work also exist between countries. For example, the International Labor Organization has adopted many conventions and recommendations on hours of work and shift work (see Kogi & Thurman, 1993). The European Community Directive on Working Time also contains legislation pertaining to shift work. The directive includes a limit of an average of 48 hours work a week (but workers can choose to work more), a limit of an average of 8 hours work in 24 hours for night workers, a right to a minimum daily rest period of 11 hours, a right to a day off each week, a right to 4 weeks paid leave each year, a right to a rest break if the workday is longer than 6 hours, and a right for night workers to receive free health assessments.

Organizational interventions. The most obvious intervention for an organization to take is to change the work schedule. In relation to shift work, this can involve changing the way the night shift is covered, changing the speed and direction of rotation between shifts, changing the timing of shifts, and changing the duration of shifts. Research evidence concerning such changes has been collated into principles for designing and evaluating shift schedules (e.g., Knauth, 1996; Kundi, 2003). Computer models incorporating principles of shift schedule design (see section on future research) offer organizations the possibility of examining the likely consequences of different schedules.

Researchers (e.g., Kogi, 1996; Jeppesen, 2003) have advocated the importance of adopting a participatory approach that involves all stakeholders during the planning and implementation of new shift systems.

A more radical solution to the design of shift schedules, which may be appropriate for some types of work, is to adopt a "follow the sun" approach in which work is moved between groups of workers located in different time zones around the world so that each group of workers remains on a daytime schedule. This kind of global shift work scheme has been used for customer service operations and software development (e.g., Carmel, 1999), but it may cause its own kind of problems such as task coordination and intercultural difficulties.

Other potential organizational interventions include selection of workers who can tolerate nonstandard schedules and provision of appropriate occupational health services. There is currently insufficient basis for selecting shift workers because the predictive validity of most individual difference measures for shift work tolerance is low and desirable scores are easily faked (Monk et al., 1996). However, preventive medical consultations are warranted, in which workers are advised against shift work if they have specified medical conditions and informed if they meet criteria that are predictive of shift work intolerance (Koller, 1996). Occupational health services should also offer shift workers regular health assessments, counseling, maternity protection, and the option to transfer to day work (Koller, 1996). Improvements in health care and treatment of disease can enable workers to participate in work schedules from which they would otherwise have been excluded. For example, insulin-dependent diabetes is now easier to control during night work (Costa, 2003).

Individual interventions. A wide range of interventions for helping individual employees adjust to shift work have been investigated, including naps, fitness, drugs, phototherapy, and behavior modification. Taking a nap before (e.g., Harma, Knauth, & Ilmarinen, 1989) or during a night shift (e.g., Smith & Wilson, 1990) may have beneficial effects for alertness and performance although negative effects have also been found (e.g., Rosa, 1993). Naps may compensate for sleep loss, but they may also increase drowsiness immediately following the nap and may slow circadian adaptation. There is some evidence that improving fitness can improve adaptation to night work. For example, Harma, Ilmarinen, Knauth, Rutenfranz, & Hanninen (1986) found that a group of nurses who undertook a fitness-training program for 4 months were more alert and performed better on memory tests than a control group, especially on the night shift.

A number of "alertness-enhancing" drugs have been considered as possible countermeasures to fatigue induced by work schedules, including amphetamine, caffeine, modafinil, and pemoline. In a review of use of these drugs, Akerstedt and Ficca (1997) ruled out amphetamine because of its side effects, deemed caffeine appropriate for ad hoc use, and judged that modafinil and pemoline were promising but required more testing in applied settings. Another drug under consideration is orexin, a hypothalamic peptide whose production is impaired in narcolepsy (Siegel, Moore, Thannickal, & Nienhuis, 2001).

There is also promise of interventions that can adjust shift workers' circadian systems to suit their work schedule. For example, oral ingestion of melatonin has been found to induce phase shifts of endogenous melatonin (which is normally secreted at night by the pineal gland). Taking melatonin at the desired bedtime has been found to improve the sleep and alertness but not the performance of shift workers (Folkard, Arendt, & Clark, 1993).

Lewy, Wehr, Goodwin, Newsome, and Markey (1980) discovered that very bright light (about 2,500 lux) could suppress the secretion of melatonin at night. Subsequent research has shown that appropriate timing and magnitude of bright light can advance, delay, and even suppress circadian rhythmicity (e.g., Jewett, Kronauer, & Czeisler, 1991). Studies of bright light treatment during simulated night shifts have demonstrated large circadian phase shifts and enhanced alertness and performance (e.g., Campbell & Dawson, 1990; Czeisler et al., 1990; Eastman, 1992; Martin & Eastman, 1998). However, more research on the health effects and practical feasibility of these interventions is required (Eastman et al., 1995).

Shift workers may also benefit from behavioral and cognitive techniques such as sleep hygiene programs (that encourage shift workers to adopt particular sleep habits) and counseling programs (see Penn & Bootzin, 1990; Rosa et al., 1990). There have also been various initiatives to produce and evaluate educational programs and guidelines for shift workers (e.g., Tepas, 1993; Wedderburn & Scholarios, 1993).

Conclusion

The variety of work schedules used by organizations is probably greater now than it has ever been. This variety provides employers and employees with the necessary flexibility to meet diverse requirements. Unfortunately, some work schedules can seriously compromise the health and productivity of employees. Problems are most likely to arise when work schedules are unsympathetic to the body clock, do not allow sufficient time for physiological and psychological recovery, and do not take account of employees' preferences. Current trends toward a 24-hour society and toward a time divide between households that work long hours and households that work short hours threaten to increase the prevalence of schedule-related problems. Wider recognition and understanding of the links between the temporal nature of work and well-being will be essential in preventing or minimizing these problems.

References

Akerstedt, T. (1985). Adjustment of physiological circadian rhythms and the sleep wake cycle to shiftwork. In S. Folkard & T. H. Monk (Eds.), *Hours of work— Temporal factors in work scheduling* (pp. 185–198). New York: Wiley.

Akerstedt, T. (1998). Is there an optimal sleep-wake pattern in shift work? *Scandinavian Journal of Work, Environment & Health, 24,* 18–27.

Akerstedt, T., & Ficca, G. (1997). Alertness-enhancing drugs as a countermeasure to fatigue in irregular work hours. *Chronobiology International, 14,* 145–158.

Akerstedt, T., & Folkard, S. (1997). The three-process model of alertness and its extension to performance, sleep latency, and sleep length. *Chronobiology International, 14,* 115–123.

Akerstedt, T., Fredlund, P., Gillberg, M., & Jansson, B. (2002). Work load and work hours in relation to disturbed sleep and fatigue in a large representative sample. *Journal of Psychosomatic Research, 53,* 585–588.

Baltes, B. B., Briggs, T. E., Huff, J. W., Wright, J. A., & Neuman, G. A. (1999). Flexible and compressed workweek schedules: A meta-analysis of their effects on work-related criteria. *Journal of Applied Psychology, 84,* 496–513.

Barnett, R. C., & Gareis, K. C. (2000a). Reduced-hours employment—The relationship between difficulty of trade-offs and quality of life. *Work and Occupations, 27,* 168–187.

Barnett, R. C., & Gareis, K. C. (2000b). Reduced-hours job-role quality and life satisfaction among married women physicians with children. *Psychology of Women Quarterly, 24,* 358–364.

Barton, J. (1994). Choosing to work at night—A moderating influence on individual tolerance to shift work. *Journal of Applied Psychology, 79,* 449–454.

Barton, J., Aldridge, J., & Smith, P. (1998). The emotional impact of shiftwork on the children of shiftworkers. *Scandinavian Journal of Work, Environment & Health, 24,* 146–150.

Barton, J., & Folkard, S. (1993). Advancing versus delaying systems. *Ergonomics, 36,* 59–64.

Barton, J., Smith, L., Totterdell, P., Spelten, E., & Folkard, S. (1993). Does individual choice determine shift system acceptability? *Ergonomics, 36,* 93–100.

Barton, J., Spelten, E., Totterdell, P., Smith, L., Folkard, S., & Costa, G. (1995). The Standard Shiftwork Index: A battery of questionnaires for assessing shiftwork-related problems. *Work & Stress, 9,* 4–30.

Beers, T. (2000, June). Flexible schedules and shift work: Replacing the "9-to-5" workday? *Monthly Labor Review.*

Bliese, P. D., & Halverson, R. R. (1996). Individual and nomothetic models of job stress: An examination of work hours, cohesion, and well-being. *Journal of Applied Social Psychology, 26,* 1171–1189.

Boggild, H., & Knutsson, A. (1999). Shift work, risk factors and cardiovascular disease. *Scandinavian Journal of Work, Environment & Health, 25,* 85–99.

Boisard, P., Cartron, D., Gollac, M., & Valeyre, A. (2003). *Time and work: Duration of work.* Dublin: European Foundation for the Improvement of Living and Working Conditions.

Bureau of Labor Statistics. (2000). *Are managers and professionals really working more?* (Summary 00-12). U.S. Department of Labor, Washington, DC.

Bureau of Labor Statistics. (2001). *Geographical profile of employment and unemployment, 1999* (Bulletin 2537). U.S. Department of Labor, Washington, DC.

Bureau of Labor Statistics. (2002). *Workers on flexible and shift schedules in 2001 summary.* U.S. Department of Labor, Washington, DC.

Campbell, S. S., & Dawson, D. (1990). Enhancement of nighttime alertness and performance with bright ambient light. *Physiology and Behaviour, 48,* 317–320.

Carmel, E. (1999). *Global software teams: Collaborating across borders and time zones*. Englewood Cliffs, NJ: Prentice Hall.

Clarkberg, M., & Moen, P. (2001). Understanding the time-squeeze—Married couples' preferred and actual work-hour strategies. *American Behavioral Scientist, 44*, 1115–1136.

Cole, R. J., Loving, R. T., & Kripke, D. F. (1990). Psychiatric aspects of shiftwork. In A. J. Scott (Ed.), *Occupational medicine: Shiftwork* (pp. 301–314). Philadelphia: Hanley & Belfus.

Colligan, M. J., & Rosa, R. R. (1990). Shiftwork effects on social and family life. In A. J. Scott (Ed.), *Occupational medicine: Shiftwork* (pp. 315–322). Philadelphia: Hanley & Belfus.

Costa, G. (1996). The impact of shift and night work on health. *Applied Ergonomics, 27*, 9–16.

Costa, G. (2003). Factors influencing health of workers and tolerance to shift work. *Theoretical Issues in Ergonomics Science, 4*, 263–288.

Costa, G., Lievore, F., Casaletti, G., Gaffuri, E., & Folkard, S. (1989). Circadian characteristics influencing interindividual differences in tolerance and adjustment to shiftwork. *Ergonomics, 32*, 373–385.

Craig, A., & Cooper, R. E. (1992). Symptoms of acute and chronic fatigue. In A. P. Smith & D. M. Jones (Eds.), *Handbook of human performance* (Vol. 3, pp. 289–339). London: Harcourt Brace Jovanovich.

Crouter, A. C., Bumpus, M. F., Head, M. R., & McHale, S. M. (2001). Implications of overwork and overload for the quality of men's family relationships. *Journal of Marriage and the Family, 63*, 404–416.

Czeisler, C. A., Johnson, M. P., Duffy, J. F., Brown, E. N., Ronda, J. M., & Kronauer, R. E. (1990). Exposure to bright light and darkness to treat physiologic maladaptation to night work. *New England Journal of Medicine, 322*, 1253–1259.

Dalton, D. R., & Mesch, D. J. (1990). The impact of flexible scheduling on employee attendance and turnover. *Administrative Science Quarterly, 35*, 370–387.

Davis, S., Mirick, D. K., & Stevens, R. G. (2001). Night shift work, light at night, and risk of breast cancer. *Journal of the National Cancer Institute, 93*, 1557–1562.

Dawson, D., & Fletcher, A. (2001). A quantitative model of work-related fatigue: Background and definition. *Ergonomics, 44*, 144–163.

Depue, R. A., & Monroe, S. M. (1986). Conceptualization and measurement of human disorder in life stress research: The problem of chronic disturbance. *Psychological Bulletin, 99*, 36–51.

Drago, R. (2000). Trends in working time in the U.S.: A policy perspective. *Labor Law Journal, 51*, 212–218.

Eastman, C. I. (1992). High intensity light for circadian adaptation to a 12-hour shift of the sleep schedule. *American Journal of Physiology, 263*, 428–436.

Eastman, C. I., Boulos, Z., Terman, M., Campbell, S. S., Dijk, D. J., & Lewy, A. J. (1995). Light treatment for sleep disorders: Consensus report 6. Shift work. *Journal of Biological Rhythms, 10*, 157–164.

Estryn-Behar, M., Gadbois, C., Peigne, E., Masson, A., & Le Gall, V. (1990). Impact of nightshifts on male and female hospital staff. In G. Costa, G. Cesana, K. Kogi, & A. Wedderburn (Eds.), *Shiftwork: Health, sleep and performance* (pp. 89–95). Frankfurt am Main, Germany: Verlag Peter Lang.

Fenwick, R., & Tausig, M. (2001). Scheduling stress—Family and health outcomes of shift work and schedule control. *American Behavioral Scientist, 44*, 1179–1198.

Folkard, S. (1992). Is there a best compromise shift system? *Ergonomics, 35,* 1453–1463.

Folkard, S. (1993). Editorial: Special issue on night and shiftwork. *Ergonomics, 36,* 1–2.

Folkard, S., Akerstedt, T., Macdonald, I., Tucker, P., & Spencer, M. B. (1999). Beyond the three-process model of alertness: Estimating phase, time on shift, and successive night effects. *Journal of Biological Rhythms, 14,* 577–587.

Folkard, S., Arendt, J., & Clark, M. (1993). Can melatonin improve shift workers' tolerance of the night shift? Some preliminary findings. *Chronobiology International, 10,* 315–320.

Folkard, S., & Hill, J. (2002). Shiftwork: Body rhythm and social factors. In P. Warr (Ed.), *Psychology at work* (5th ed., pp. 51–76). London: Penguin Books.

Folkard, S., & Tucker, P. (2003). Shift work, safety and productivity. *Occupational Medicine-Oxford, 53,* 95–101.

Galambos, N. L., & Walters, B. J. (1992). Work hours, schedule flexibility and stress in dual-earner spouses. *Canadian Journal of Behavioral Science, 24,* 290–302.

Gareis, K. C., & Barnett, R. C. (2002). Under what conditions do long work hours affect psychological distress? A study of full-time and reduced-hours female doctors. *Work and Occupations, 29,* 483–497.

Golden, L., & Applebaum, E. (1992). What is driving the boom in temporary employment? *American Journal of Economics and Sociology, 51,* 473–492.

Guo, H. R. (2002). Working hours spent on repeated activities and prevalence of back pain. *Occupational and Environmental Medicine, 59,* 680–688.

Haider, M., Kundi, M., & Koller, M. (1981). Methodological issues and problems in shiftwork research. In L. Johnson, D. Tepas, W. P. Colquhoun, & M. J. Colligan (Eds.), *Biological rhythms, sleep, and shiftwork* (pp. 145–163). Jamaica, NY: Spectrum.

Hansen, J. (2001). Increased breast cancer risk among women who work predominantly at night. *Epidemiology, 12,* 74–77.

Harma, M. (1993). Individual differences in tolerance to shiftwork: A review. *Ergonomics, 36,* 101–110.

Harma, M. J., Ilmarinen, I., Knauth, P., Rutenfranz, J., & Hanninen, O. (1986). The effect of physical fitness intervention on adaptation to shiftwork. In M. Haider, M. Koller, & R. Cervinka (Eds.), *Night and shiftwork: Longterm effects and their prevention* (pp. 221–229). Frankfurt am Main, Germany: Verlag Peter Lang.

Harma, M., Knauth, P., & Ilmarinen, J. (1989). Daytime napping and its effects on alertness and short-term memory performance in shiftworkers. *International Archives of Occupational and Environmental Health, 61,* 341–345.

Healy, D., Minors, D. S., & Waterhouse, J. M. (1993). Shiftwork, helplessness and depression. *Journal of Affective Disorders, 29,* 17–25.

Herman, A. M. (1999). *Report on the American Workforce.* U.S. Department of Labor, Washington, DC.

Holton, B. C., Lee, T. W., & Tidd, S. T. (2002). The relationship between work status congruence and work-related attitudes and behaviors. *Journal of Applied Psychology, 87,* 903–915.

Infante-Rivard, C., David, M., Gauthier, R., & Rivard, G. (1993). Pregnancy loss and work schedule during pregnancy. *Epidemiology, 4,* 73–75.

International Labour Organization. (1995). Working time around the world. *Conditions of Work Digest (Geneva), 14.*

Jacobs, J. A. (1998, December). Measuring time at work: Are self-reports accurate? *Monthly Labor Review.*

Jacobs, J. A., & Gerson, K. (1998). Who are the overworked Americans? *Review of Social Economy, 56,* 442–460.

Jeppesen, H. J. (2003). Participatory approaches to strategy and research in shift work intervention. *Theoretical Issues in Ergonomics Science, 4,* 289–301.

Jewett, M. E., Kronauer, R. E., & Czeisler, C. A. (1991). Light-induced suppression of endogenous circadian amplitude in humans. *Nature, 350,* 59–62.

Kaliterna, L., & Prizmic, Z. (1998). Evaluation of the survey of shiftworkers (SOS) short version of the standard shiftwork index. *International Journal of Industrial Ergonomics, 21,* 259–265.

Kaliterna, L., Vidacek, S., Prizmic, Z., & Radosevic-Vidacek, B. (1995). Is tolerance to shiftwork predictable from individual difference measures? *Work & Stress, 9,* 140–147.

Kecklund, G., Akerstedt, T., & Lowden, A. (1997). Morning work: Effects of early rising on sleep and alertness. *Sleep, 20,* 215–233.

Kivimaki, M., Kuisma, P., Virtanen, M., & Elovainio, M. (2001). Does shift work lead to poorer health habits? A comparison between women who had always done shift work with those who had never done shift work. *Work & Stress, 15,* 3–13.

Knauth, P. (1996). Designing better shift systems. *Applied Ergonomics, 27,* 39–44.

Knauth, P., Emde, E., & Rutenfranz, J. (1981). Re-entrainment of body temperature in field studies of shift work. *International Archives of Occupational and Environmental Health, 49,* 137–149.

Knauth, P., & Ilmarinen, J. (1975). Continuous measurement of body temperature during a 3-week experiment with inverted working and sleeping hours. In P. Colquhoun, S. Folkard, P. Knauth, & J. Rutenfranz (Eds.), *Proceedings of the 3rd International Symposium on Night and Shiftwork,* Westdeutscher Verlag, Germany, 66–74.

Kogi, K. (1996). Improving shift workers' health and tolerance to shiftwork: Recent advances. *Applied Ergonomics, 27,* 5–8.

Kogi, K., & Thurman, J. E. (1993). Trends in approaches to night and shiftwork and new international standards. *Ergonomics, 36,* 3–13.

Koller, M. (1996). Occupational health services for shift and night workers. *Applied Ergonomics, 27,* 31–37.

Koller, M., Haider, M., & Kundi, M. (1981). Possible relations of irregular working hours to psychiatric psychosomatic disorders. In A. Reinberg, N. Vieux, & P. Andlauer (Eds.), *Night and shift work: Biological and social aspects* (pp. 465–472). Oxford: Pergamon.

Kostreva, M., McNelis, E., & Clemens, E. (2002). Using a circadian rhythm model to evaluate shift schedules. *Ergonomics, 45,* 739–763.

Kundi, M. (1989). A destabilization theory on health impairments by night- and shift work—Some tests about its predictive value. *Zentralblatt für Hygiene und Umweltmedizin, 189,* 248–265.

Kundi, M. (2003). Ergonomic criteria for the evaluation of shift schedules. *Theoretical Issues in Ergonomics Science, 4,* 302–318.

Lavie, P. (1986). Ultrashort sleep-waking schedule. "Gates" and "forbidden zones" for sleep. *Electroencephalography and Clinical Neurophysiology, 63,* 414–425.

Lewy, A. J., Wehr, T. A., Goodwin, F. K., Newsome, D. A., & Markey, S. P. (1980). Light suppresses melatonin secretion in humans. *Science, 210,* 1267–1269.

Lipscomb, J. A., Trinkoff, A. M., Geiger-Brown, J., & Brady, B. (2002). Work-schedule characteristics and reported musculoskeletal disorders of registered nurses. *Scandinavian Journal of Work, Environment & Health, 28*, 394–401.

Liu, Y., & Tanaka, H. (2002). Overtime work, insufficient sleep, and risk of non-fatal acute myocardial infarction in Japanese men. *Occupational and Environmental Medicine, 59*, 447–451.

Martens, M. F. J., Nijhuis, F. G. N., Van Boxtel, M. P. J., & Knottnerus, J. A. (1999). Flexible work schedules and mental and physical health. A study of a working population with non-traditional working hours. *Journal of Organizational Behavior, 20*, 35–46.

Martin, S. L., & Eastman, C. I. (1998). Medium-intensity light produces circadian rhythm adaptation to simulated night-shift work. *Sleep, 21*, 154–165.

Mitchell, R. J., & Williamson, A. M. (2000). Evaluation of an 8-hour versus a 12-hour shift roster on employees at a power station. *Applied Ergonomics, 31*, 83–93.

Mohren, D. C. L., Jansen, N. W. H., Kant, I., Galama, J. M. D., van den Brandt, P. A., & Swaen, G. M. H. (2002). Prevalence of common infections among employees in different work schedules. *Journal of Occupational and Environmental Medicine, 44*, 1003–1011.

Monk, T. H. (1988). Coping with the stress of shiftwork. *Work & Stress, 2*, 169–172.

Monk, T. H., Folkard, S., & Wedderburn, A. I. (1996). Maintaining safety and high performance on shiftwork. *Applied Ergonomics, 27*, 17–23.

Mozurkewich, E. L., Luke, B., Avni, M., & Wolf, F. M. (2000). Working conditions and adverse pregnancy outcome: A meta-analysis. *Obstetrics and Gynecology, 95*, 623–635.

Nachreiner, F., Qin, L., Grzech-Sukalo, H., & Hedden, I. (1993). Computer aided design of shift schedules. *Ergonomics, 36*, 77–84.

Nicholson, N., Jackson, P., & Howes, G. (1978). Shiftwork and absence: An analysis of temporal trends. *Journal of Occupational Psychology, 51*, 127–137.

Nylen, L., Voss, M., & Floderus, B. (2001). Mortality among women and men relative to unemployment, part time work, overtime work, and extra work: A study based on data from the Swedish twin registry. *Occupational and Environmental Medicine, 58*, 52–57.

Ohayon, M. M., Lemoine, P., Arnaud-Briant, V., & Dreyfus, M. (2002). Prevalence and consequences of sleep disorders in a shift worker population. *Journal of Psychosomatic Research, 53*, 577–583.

Olsson, K., Kandolin, I., & Kauppinen-Toropainen, K. (1990). Stress and coping strategies of three-shift workers. *Le Travail Humain, 53*, 175–188.

Parkes, K. (2002). Age, smoking, and negative affectivity as predictors of sleep patterns among shiftworkers in two environments. *Journal of Occupational Health Psychology, 7*, 156–173.

Penn, P. E., & Bootzin, R. R. (1990). Behavioural techniques for enhancing alertness and performance in shift work. *Work & Stress, 4*, 213–226.

Pilcher, J. J., Lambert, B. J., & Huffcutt, A. I. (2000). Differential effects of permanent and rotating shifts on self-report sleep length: A meta-analytic review. *Sleep, 23*, 155–163.

Pocock, B. (2001). *The effect of long hours on family and community life.* Queensland Department of Industrial Relations, Brisbane.

Presser, H. B. (1995). Job, family, and gender: Determinants of nonstandard work schedules among employed Americans in 1991. *Demography, 32,* 577–598.

Proctor, S. P., White, R. F., Robins, T. G., Echeverria, D., & Rocskay, A. Z. (1996). Effect of overtime work on cognitive function in automotive workers. *Scandinavian Journal of Work, Environment & Health, 22,* 124–132.

Ribet, C., & Derriennic, F. (1999). Age, working conditions, and sleep disorders: A longitudinal analysis in the French cohort ESTEV. *Sleep, 22,* 491–504.

Rosa, R. (1993). Napping at home and alertness on the job in rotating shift workers. *Sleep, 16,* 727–735.

Rosa, R. R., Bonnet, M., Bootzin, R. R., Eastman, C. I., Monk, T., Penn, P. E., Tepas, D. I., & Walsh, J. K. (1990). Intervention factors for promoting adjustment to nightwork and shiftwork. In A. J. Scott (Ed.), *Occupational medicine: Shiftwork* (pp. 391–415). Philadelphia: Hanley & Belfus.

Rutenfranz, J., Knauth, P., & Angersbach, D. (1981). Shiftwork research issues. In L. Johnson, D. Tepas, W. P. Colquhoun, & M. J. Colligan (Eds.), *Biological rhythms, sleep, and shiftwork* (pp. 165–195). Jamaica, NY: Spectrum.

Schernhammer, E. S., Laden, F., Speizer, F. E., Willett, W. C., Hunter, D. J., Kawachi, I., & Colditz, G. A. (2001). Rotating night shifts and risk of breast cancer in women participating in the Nurses' Health Study. *Journal of the National Cancer Institute, 93,* 1563–1568.

Schernhammer, E. S., Laden, F., Speizer, F. E., Willett, W. C., Hunter, D. J., Kawachi, I., et al. (2003). Night-shift work and risk of colorectal cancer in the Nurses' Health Study. *Journal of the National Cancer Institute, 95,* 825–828.

Schmieder, R. A., & Smith, C. S. (1996). Moderating effects of social support in shiftworking and non-shiftworking nurses. *Work & Stress, 10,* 128–140.

Shepard, E., & Clifton, T. (2000). Are longer hours reducing productivity in manufacturing. *International Journal of Manpower, 21,* 540–552.

Siegel, J. M., Moore, R., Thannickal, T., & Nienhuis, R. (2001). A brief history of hypocretin/orexin and narcolepsy. *Neuropsychopharmacology, 25,* 14–20.

Singer, G. (1989). Women and shiftwork. In M. Wallace (Ed.), *Managing shiftwork* (pp. 25–48). Bundoora, Australia: Brain Behaviour Research Institute, La Trobe University.

Smith, A. P., & Wilson, M. (1990). The effects of naps during night duty on the performance and mood of female nurses working in an intensive care unit. In G. Costa, G. Cesana, K. Kogi, & A. Wedderburn (Eds.), *Shiftwork: Health, sleep and performance* (pp. 147–153). Frankfurt am Main, Germany: Verlag Peter Lang.

Smith, C. S., Robie, C., Folkard, S., Barton, J., Macdonald, I., Smith, L., Spelten, E., Totterdell, P., & Costa, G. (1999). A process model of shiftwork and health. *Journal of Occupational Health Psychology, 4,* 207–218.

Smith, L., Folkard, S., & Poole, C. J. M. (1994). Increased injuries on night shift. *The Lancet, 344,* 1137–1139.

Smith, L., Folkard, S., Tucker, P., & Macdonald, I. (1998). Work shift duration: A review comparing eight hour and 12 hour shift systems. *Occupational and Environmental Medicine, 55,* 217–229.

Sparks, K., Cooper, C., Fried, Y., & Shirom, A. (1997). The effects of hours of work on health: A meta-analytic review. *Journal of Occupational and Organizational Psychology, 70,* 391–408.

Spurgeon, A., Harrington, J. M., & Cooper, C. L. (1997). Health and safety problems associated with long working hours: A review of the current position. *Occupational and Environmental Medicine, 54,* 367–375.

Staines, G. L., & Pleck, J. H. (1983). *The impact of work schedules on the family.* Ann Arbor, MI: Institute for Social Research.

Taylor, E., Briner, R. B., & Folkard, S. (1997). Models of shiftwork and health: An examination of the influence of stress on shiftwork theory. *Human Factors, 39,* 67–82.

Tepas, D. I. (1993). Educational programmes for shiftworkers, their families, and prospective shiftworkers. *Ergonomics, 36,* 199–210.

Tepas, D. I., & Carvalhais, A. B. (1990). Sleep patterns of shiftworkers. In A. J. Scott (Ed.), *Occupational medicine: Shiftwork* (pp. 199–208). Philadelphia: Hanley & Belfus.

Totterdell, P., Spelten, E. R., & Pokorski, J. (1995). The effects of nightwork on psychological changes during the menstrual cycle. *Journal of Advanced Nursing, 21,* 996–1005.

Totterdell, P., Spelten, E. R., Smith, L. R., Barton, J., & Folkard, S. (1995). Recovery from work shifts: How long does it take? *Journal of Applied Psychology, 80,* 43–57.

Tucker, P., Smith, L., Macdonald, I., & Folkard, S. (2000). Effects of direction of rotation in continuous and discontinuous 8-hour shift systems. *Occupational and Environmental Medicine, 57,* 678–684.

Uehata, T., & Sasakawa, N. (1982). The fatigue and maternity disturbances of night work women. *Journal of Human Ergology, 11 Suppl.,* 465–474.

Van der Hulst, M. (2003). Long workhours and health. *Scandinavian Journal of Work, Environment & Health, 29,* 171–188.

Van der Hulst, M., & Geurts, S. (2001). Associations between overtime and psychological health in high and low reward jobs. *Work & Stress, 15,* 227–240.

Vidacek, S., Prizmic, Z., Kaliterna, L., Radosevic-Vidacek, B., Cabrajec-Grbac, S., Fornazar-Knezevic, B., et al. (1995). Shiftwork tolerance and circadian rhythms in oral temperature and heart rate. *Work & Stress, 9,* 335–341.

Wedderburn, A. (Ed.). (1993). *Social and family factors in shift design.* Dublin: European Foundation for the Improvement of Living and Working Conditions.

Wedderburn, A., & Scholarios, D. (1993). Guidelines for shiftworkers: Trial and errors? *Ergonomics, 36,* 211–218.

Wever, R. A. (1979). *The circadian system of man: Results of experiments under temporal isolation.* New York: Springer.

White, J., & Beswick, J. (2003). *Working long hours* (WPS/02/10). Health and Safety Laboratory, Sheffield, UK.

Wilkinson, R. T. (1992). How fast should the night shift rotate? *Ergonomics, 35,* 1425–1446.

Zulley, J., Wever, R. A., & Aschoff, J. (1981). The dependence of onset and duration of sleep on the circadian rhythm of rectal temperature. *Pflugers Archiv, 391,* 314–318.

4

Organizational Justice

Russell Cropanzano

Barry M. Goldman

Lehman Benson III

H uman beings have long reflected on the nature of fairness. Aristotle presented a model of equity that bears more than a little resemblance to current thinking (Homans, 1961). Plato wrote about justice in his *Republic*. Likewise, both Herodotus's *History* and Plutarch's *Lives* extolled the just Athenian government of Solon (c. 638–559 B.C.). As ancient as these writings are, interest in fairness is even older. For example, concerns over fairness are manifested in the Torah and in Hammurabi's code.

Such philosophical and legal writings are *prescriptive* or *normative* theories of justice because they attempt to specify what people *should* do. Although the sort of justice described in this chapter shares much of the same cultural and intellectual foundation, there is an important difference. When we use the terms *justice* or *fairness* in this chapter, we are referring to a subjective or phenomenological appraisal of a given stimulus. That is, the theories considered here are *descriptive* because they articulate how people react to a given outcome, process, or interpersonal interaction. Something is "fair" or "just" not because it should be so but because some person or persons believe it to be (for more on this distinction, see Cohen & Greenberg, 1982; Greenberg & Bies, 1992). In other words, this chapter is about employees' systematic *perceptions* of (in)justice and how these perceptions affect experienced strain.

With all this in mind, our goal in this chapter is to squarely confront the implications that organizational justice has for the experience of employee

Authors' Note: The authors wish to thank Carolina Moliner for her helpful comments on an earlier draft of this chapter.

stress and well-being at work. We will argue that injustice is a potentially destructive process. Our presentation will proceed in three broad sections. First, we discuss the nature of workplace fairness. This should provide a brief overview for readers who are not entirely familiar with the major concepts and central measurement issues. Second, we review empirical research documenting the relationship of injustice to felt strain in a general way. Third, we take a closer look at the "why?" question by considering three different theoretical frameworks for studying the linkage between injustice and well-being. Finally, we discuss some things managers can do to manage workplace fairness in a way that reduces employees' felt strain.

What Is Injustice? Definition of a Stressor Domain

Research has shown justice perceptions can be classified into at least three broad families: distributive justice (the fairness of the outcomes), procedural justice (the fairness of the process by which outcomes are assigned), and interactional justice (the fairness of the interpersonal transaction). We will briefly review below these three types of justice.

Distributive Justice

Distributive justice involves an individual's subjective assessment of the fairness of an outcome distribution. Much distributive justice research has focused on equity as the relevant standard by which fairness is determined (Sheppard, Lewicki, & Minton, 1992). By this standard, employees ought to receive outcomes consistent with the quantity and quality of results they produce. For example, a compensation plan could pay the most to the highest performers, or the first employees terminated in a layoff should be the lowest performers. As we shall soon discuss, equity theory has been especially important for understanding employee burnout.

Under equity theory, the employee is proposed to engage in an internal balancing of his or her perceived inputs (e.g., effort, experience, and education) and outcomes (e.g., rewards, punishments, and allocations) with a chosen "referent other's" perceived inputs and outcomes. The choice of the "other" is usually based on characteristics such as similarity (in terms of jobs, education, or background), proximity (e.g., people in the next office), and salience (with respect to people who come quickly to mind for whatever reason, e.g., role models) (Kulik & Ambrose, 1992; Sheppard et al., 1992). The employee's perception of fairness depends on the results of this comparison of the employee's perceived inputs and outputs with that of the other, with individuals tending to be much more sensitive to comparisons when they feel that they do not receive as much as the referent as opposed to when they receive more than the referent (Sweeney, McFarlin, & Inderrieden, 1990). We emphasize that the focus of distributive justice is not directly with the perceived *favorableness* of an outcome but with the perceived *fairness* of an outcome. As a consequence, strictly speaking, distributive justice does not apply in situations in which someone is unhappy with a particular outcome they receive unless that person can point to some standard of fairness that is violated by the outcome (Cropanzano & Greenberg, 1997). We shall return to the issue of standards when we discuss injustice-stress theory later in this chapter.

Procedural Justice

Procedural justice is generally defined as the perceived fairness of the process used to determine outcomes. Following an unfavorable outcome, employees will respond more favorably if they believe the procedures that resulted in the unfavorable outcome were fair (Thibaut & Walker, 1975, 1978; Tyler & Lind, 1992). Leventhal (1980) further developed these ideas by identifying six justice rules (accuracy, representativeness, bias suppression, consistency, ethicality, and correctability) that are thought to be useful in judging the fairness of the formal or structural elements of procedures.

Interactional Justice

Bies and Moag (1986) first introduced the idea that people also look at interpersonal treatment received during enactment of procedures, especially those aspects that concentrate on the relationship between the authority and those subject to his or her decision, as part of their assessment of fairness. They termed this interactional justice and distinguished it from the structural aspects of procedural justice. Generally speaking, there are two broad categories of interactional justice. The first type refers to the respect and dignity with which employees are treated; the second type refers to the adequacy and completeness of the information provided to workers (Bies, 1987; Sitkin & Bies, 1993). Subsequent research has revealed strong support for interactional justice as a separate dimension (Masterson, Lewis, Goldman, & Taylor, 2000; Goldman, 2003).

Before moving on, we should note that some scholars have subdivided interactional justice into two components. These include interpersonal justice (the extent to which one is treated with politeness and esteem) and informational justice (the extent to which one receives social accounts and explanations about events and process) (e.g., Greenberg, 1993). Evidence is beginning to support this model (e.g., Colquitt, 2001). However, because the research discussed herein tends not to separate interactional justice into these two component parts, our present review will not do so either. We emphasize, however, that this should be an important consideration for future research.

Summary

So far we have learned two important things about organizational justice. First, the term refers to perceptual or subjective phenomena. In this sense, when we study "justice," we are studying how people form justice judgments and how these judgments affect subsequent responses. Second, we have seen that there are at least three families of justice perceptions—outcomes, processes, and interpersonal interactions—with each corresponding to a different aspect of the work environment. What remains is for us to examine the linkages between these different types of justice and worker stress.

An Overview of the Research

As Kahn and Byosiere (1992) have noted, the term *stress* has been defined in sundry ways, each definition somewhat distinct from others. In this chapter, and consistent with one of the usages suggested by Kahn and Byosiere, we use the word *stress* to indicate a process whereby environmental events called "stressors" induce consequences for individuals. These consequences are referred to collectively as "strain." In order for stressors to induce strain, they need to be interpreted by individuals (Lazarus & Folkman, 1984). For instance, one might see that an important goal is threatened by his or her inability to meet a performance standard. This sense of being overwhelmed is stressful. In any case, these cognitive interpretations are mediators in that they lay between the environmentally induced stressors and the psychological experience of strain.

When this brief analysis of stress is considered in light of our earlier comments on the nature of justice, we can immediately see different ways to conceptualize fairness as part of the stress process. We have illustrated some of these possibilities in Figure 4.1. Let us begin with Panel A. First and most simply, *workplace fairness* can be defined as a stressor (a suitably interpreted environmental event that evokes an aversive response). In this straightforward approach, injustice is one's reaction to an event. It takes its place beside other stressors such as workload or role conflict, though it does not necessarily change our understanding of these variables.

Panel B of Figure 4.1 displays a second possibility. In this framework, workplace fairness takes place further "downstream" in the causal flow. That is, once a stressor is recognized, the fact that such negative events are themselves present in the environment is seen as unfair. In other words, justice is a response to other stressors. In this regard, justice is part of the cognitive interpretation, presumably a secondary cognitive interpretation, that carries the impact of the stressors so that they create strain. Justice, therefore, is a mediator.

Another type of relationship is shown in Figure 4.2. It is probably the case that there are important moderated relationships that need to be considered

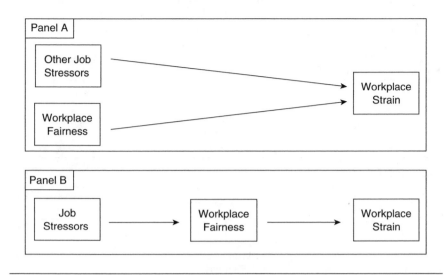

Figure 4.1   Two Prototypical Models of Organizational Justice and Workplace
Stress

along with the additive effects described earlier. Figure 4.2 illustrates two possibilities. In Panel A we see that the impact of workplace fairness may be moderated by other variables. That is, injustice may strongly affect felt strain under some conditions but only weakly affect strain under others. As we shall soon review, this is the type of theory discussed by most scholars (e.g., Schmitt & Dörfel, 1999; VanYperen, Buunk, & Schaufeli, 1992). However, there is another possibility.

Figure 4.2, Panel B, presents an alternative. It could be that stressors at work hurt more if they are also unfair but less if they are fair. In other words, workplace fairness could be viewed as a moderator of the relationship between stressors and job strain. In this view, levels of justice (i.e., justice or injustice) can buffer or inflame the effects of other stressors. Perhaps stressors may be most likely to produce strain if they are unjust. Unfortunately, tests of this model have yielded, at best, mixed results (cf. Tepper, 2001; Zohar, 1995).

Of course, one need not select a one-size-fits-all conceptual model. Injustice may carry the impact of some stressors although others show direct effects. Likewise, justice may moderate some stressors while not affecting others. Unfortunately, the research to date is too limited for us to disentangle all of these possibilities. The key point is that different scholars have conceptualized justice in different fashions. To illustrate, let us now consider a few empirical examples.

Studies That Do Not Test for Justice as a Mediator

A longitudinal study by De Boer, Bakker, Syroit, and Schaufeli (2002) provides a good example of a study that does not treat justice as a mediator. These scholars examined absenteeism among 514 security guards. DeBoer

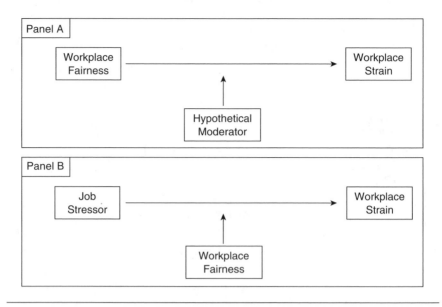

Figure 4.2   Two Types of Potential Moderator Effects Involving Organizational
                 Injustice

and his colleagues found that both distributive and procedural injustice
predicted physical symptoms. These symptoms, in turn, predicted absenteeism. These findings held even when other stressors were controlled.

Another example of a study that takes a similar approach is that conducted by Elovainio, Kivimäki, and Vahtera (2002). In this study, Elovainio
and his colleagues assess the procedural and interactional (these authors
used the term *relational*) justice of over 4,000 hospital employees.
Interactional injustice proved to be an effective predictor of self-reported
health, psychiatric morbidity, and absenteeism. Procedural injustice predicted absenteeism. Elovainio et al. did not test a mediated effect for justice.
However, they covaried out other stressors such as workload and job control. Hence, these authors concluded that justice is an important predictor of
strain above and beyond other stressors. This is very close to Panel A in our
Figure 4.1.

A similar approach was taken in a longitudinal study of 3,373 hospital
workers conducted by Kivimäki, Elovainio, Vahtera, and Ferrie (2002). This
follow-up study found generally consistent results. After controlling for baseline health and various demographic variables, procedural injustice was associated with psychiatric symptoms, self-reported health, and absenteeism. (The
procedural justice/absenteeism effect was only found for men, however).
Interactional injustice was associated with self-reported health and absenteeism. The longitudinal nature of this study allowed Kivimäki et al. to assess
the possibility of reverse causality. Perhaps good health causes justice perceptions rather than the other way around. The authors found no evidence for
this, thereby buttressing their contention that injustice produces strain.

Treating Justice as a Mediator

An excellent example of a study that treats justice as a mediator is presented by Elovainio, Kivimäki, and Helkama (2001). Using a sample of 688 Finnish municipal workers, Elovainio and his colleagues tested a model that is very similar to that presented in Panel B of Figure 4.1. In particular, Elovainio et al. argued that job control (a stressor) engenders a sense of procedural and interactional justice. Perceptions of these two types of injustice, in turn, reduced feelings of psychological strain. The authors found support for their mediated model. As we shall see, other studies have also found support for the proposition that strain at work mediates the impact of injustice (e.g., Moliner, Martínez-Tur, Peiró, Ramos, & Cropanzano, 2003). This work will be discussed in the appropriate sections below.

Treating Justice as a Moderator

Earlier we observed that some scholars see justice as a potential moderator of the stressor/strain relationship (e.g., Zohar, 1995) whereas others see justice as the stressor in need of moderation (e.g., VanYperen et al., 1992). At least one study treated justice both ways. Tepper (2001) maintained that distributive injustice and procedural injustice interacted to predict psychological strain. In particular, the relationship between procedural unfairness and strain should be greater when distributive justice is low and weaker when distributive justice is high. In the terminology we were using earlier, distributive justice buffers the adverse effects of procedural injustice. Tepper found supportive results in two independent tests of this model. From Tepper's model we can see the effects of each type of justice (procedural or distributive) depend on the level of the other. In the case of Tepper's study, we could say that the deleterious effects of a procedural injustice are allayed by a fair outcome. Later in the paper we will review various studies that test moderators of the injustice/stress relationship. As we shall see, some of these were supportive (Schmitt & Dörfel, 1999; VanYperen et al., 1992), but at least one was not (Zohar, 1995). Clearly, this is a topic in need of additional research inquiry.

Theories of Justice and Worker Well-Being

We have shown that scholars sometimes treat injustice as a mediator between more commonly studied stressors and at other times treat injustice as simply a predictor in its own right. In the former case, justice carries or transmits the effects of other stressors. In the latter case, it does not. Both the mediated and unmediated approaches are reasonable (pending empirical investigation, of course!), though researchers should be specific as to their theory and plan their data collection and analyses accordingly. In the next section, we take a closer look at three theoretical perspectives that have been used to understand justice in the context of workplace stress. They include role stress theory, injustice-stress theory, and burnout. Along the way, we will discuss additional empirical evidence pertaining to each model.

Role Stress Theory

An initial approach to integrating organizational justice with worker health was taken by Zohar (1995). Zohar's model was a straightforward extension of the classic research on role dynamics theory (e.g., Goode, 1960; Katz & Kahn, 1966; Kahn, Wolf, Quinn, Snoek, & Rosenthal, 1964). According to role dynamics theory, "role senders" are organizational members who communicate expectations to employees. Often, though not necessarily, these role senders are managers who convey demands (Teas, 1983). In the earliest versions of the model, these demands were said to create role conflict (two or more requirements that work against each other) and role ambiguity (requirements that are not clear). Research suggested that conflict and ambiguity engendered dissatisfaction, anxiety, and a desire to leave the organization (e.g., Rizzo, House, & Lirtzman, 1970). Later work added new dimensions. According to Peterson et al. (1995), role overload refers to having too many requirements. Likewise, Karasek (1979) and Zohar (1995) added the notion of restricted latitude (too little control over requirements).

Although interest in role dynamics theory seems to have waned in recent years, it did inspire a good deal of research during the 1970s and 1980s (e.g., Bedeian & Armenakis, 1981; Behrman & Perreault, 1984; House & Rizzo, 1972), with work continuing into the 1990s (Netemeyer, Johnston, & Burton, 1990; Peterson et al., 1995). Though we consider some limitations of role dynamics theory in a moment, it should be emphasized that by using this framework, Zohar (1995) was analyzing justice though the lens of a widely studied model of worker stress. He argued that the four role dynamics—conflict, ambiguity, overload, and lack of control—could adversely affect worker health. However, he added a fifth role stressor, role justice.

Some Ambiguity

There is some ambiguity in the relationship of role justice to the other role demands. Let us refer back to the two prototypical models presented in Figure 4.1. Zohar (1995, p. 488) seems to be arguing that the four role stressors *cause* role justice (the latter or mediated model): "In the remainder of this paper we shall refer to justice perceptions provoked by role stress conditions as Role Justice (RJ)." Likewise, Zohar's measure of justice (see pp. 489–490) seems to refer specifically to role stress. These considerations would imply that role stress (overload, conflict, ambiguity, lack of control) create a sense of injustice. This injustice, in turn, causes diminished worker well-being. However, Zohar did not analyze the data in this fashion. As Vermunt and Steensma (2001) observe, Zohar did not test for mediation. Hence, the model is tested as if role justice is a fifth type of role stress that is correlated with, though not caused by, the other four stressors (the former or unmediated model in Figure 4.1).

Zohar's (1995) Findings

Zohar (1995) investigated his model among a sample of 213 Canadian hospital nurses. He found that nurses who reported lower levels of role justice experienced more physical symptoms and higher turnover intentions than did their colleagues who reported greater role justice. Moreover, these findings held even after controlling for all of the aforementioned role stressors. Zohar also tested the possibility that justice acts as a *moderator* of role strain perceptions. In particular, he argued that when conflict or ambiguity is dealt with in an unfair fashion, "one is likely to overestimate their prevalence" (p. 488). Notice how this idea fits with our illustration in Figure 4.2, Panel B. However, when this moderator effect was tested, it was found to be nonsignificant (pp. 491–493).

Problems With the Role Stress Approach

In explicitly integrating workplace justice with a model of organizational stress, Zohar (1995) has made a significant contribution to our understanding. However, the strength of this integration may also hide a potential weakness because any limitations of the role dynamics model could be transferred into Zohar's framework. One notable problem is the level of empirical support. Although much of the literature supports role dynamics theory, other research has been less conclusive. Two meta-analyses, one by Fisher and Gitelson (1983) and another by Jackson and Schuler (1985), found substantial but incomplete support for role dynamic theory's predictions. That having been said, an optimist might plausibly see this situation as an opportunity for organizational justice. Perhaps the inclusion of new constructs, such as role justice, could lead to stronger empirical results. After all, if support for role dynamics theory were perfect, then there would be far less justification to add a new variable (role justice) to the model.

Injustice-Stress Theory

Another promising framework integrating worker stress with organizational justice is Vermunt and Steensma's (2001) *injustice-stress theory*. The authors build their model from theories of worker stress as well as theories of workplace injustice. In particular, Vermunt and Steensma begin with a consideration of *multiple discrepancies theory*. Loosely speaking (more detail in a moment), this analysis specifies that individuals have certain things that they are actively seeking in their work lives. To the extent that these objectives are not met, individuals experience diminished satisfaction, reduced life satisfaction, heightened strain, and so on (cf. Campbell, Converse, & Rogers, 1976; Michalos, 1986; Vermunt, Spaans, & Zorge, 1989). Gaps between what is desired and what is obtained are deleterious to healthy psychological and physical functioning, at least if these gaps are excessively large. In broad outline, the analysis offered by multiple discrepancies theory is highly similar to that offered by other models of work stress (e.g., Edwards, 1992; Kahn & Byosiere, 1992) as well as some theories of job satisfaction (e.g., Hulin, 1991; Locke, 1976; Weiss & Cropanzano, 1996).

Of course, different theories emphasize types of discrepancies. Building on the work of Michalos (1985), Vermunt and Steensma (2001, pp. 33–34) list six types of gaps that have been examined in previous research. We quote their titles directly:

- Goal-achievement gap
- Ideal-real gap
- Expectation-reality gap
- Previous-best comparison
- Social comparison
- Person-environment fit

According to the model, individuals experience a discrepancy between the demands of the environment and their capability to meet those demands. When their capacity is overwhelmed, the worker experiences stress, unhappiness, and dissatisfaction. Interestingly, although recognizing the conceptual existence of six possible gaps, research reviewed by Michalos (1985) has found that three of these discrepancies are especially important for explaining variance in satisfaction and well-being: (a) goal-achievement, (b) previous-best, and (c) social comparison.

Three Discrepancies That Produce Injustice

None of these ideas would strike a stress researcher as especially surprising. However, injustice-stress theory takes the matter a bit further. To illustrate, we diagram the model in Figure 4.3. As can be seen, Vermunt and Steensma (2001) argue that at least some of the discrepancy can be attributed to the allocation decisions by one's supervisor or another organizational authority. Qualitative research reported by Vermunt (2002, Study 1) is consistent with this notion. When these actions violate a standard of justice, they add to the strain experienced by the worker. Notice, therefore, that the stress is "externally imposed," in the narrow sense of being triggered by an outside event. This is, of course, similar to what one would expect in a model of workplace stress.

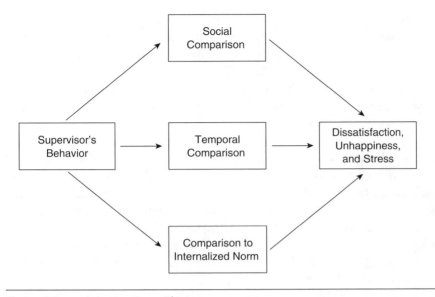

Figure 4.3   Injustice-Stress Theory

The next step in the model is the evaluation of the supervisor's behavior with respect to certain standards. Building on the aforementioned work on discrepancies, Vermunt and Steensma (2001) emphasize three types of discrepancies that can engender stress: social comparison, temporal comparison, and internalized norms. As can be seen in our figure, these three discrepancies are the proximal determinants of happiness, satisfaction, and strain. In other words, they are critical to the psychological etiology of the stress response. Given the newness of the theory, evidence to date remains limited. However, the model does have some support. For example, in a role-playing study reported by Vermunt (2002, Study 2), respondents indicated that unfair treatment could act as a workplace stressor even beyond the effects of workload. In particular, Vermunt found evidence that justice provides a direct main effect on perceived strain. Given this, we shall discuss the pivotal discrepancies in more detail below.

Social comparison. The first is social comparison. Individuals attempt to assess the fairness of what they receive and how they were treated in reference to other people. As we noted earlier, the idea of a social comparison has long been familiar to justice researchers (e.g., Folger, 1986; Stouffer, Suchman, DeVinney, Star, & Williams, 1949). In fact, these types of discrepancies were the principal conceptual driver in such venerable frameworks as equity theory (Adams, 1963, 1965), social evaluation theory (Pettigrew, 1967), and relative deprivation theory (Crosby, 1976, 1984). However, the historic models tended to emphasize distributive justice (e.g., Martin, 1981), for instance, what one received relative to that received by a similar other (for a classic example, see Homans, 1961).

Although acknowledging this, injustice-stress theory adds that social comparisons can be used to ascertain the justice of procedures as well. Evidence is supportive. A laboratory study by Grienberger, Rutte, and van Knippenberg (1997) found that individuals compared the amount of task control they received with that allowed to other experimental participants. When they received less control than others, respondents were more likely to experience a sense of injustice.

Temporal comparison. According to Vermunt and Steensma (2001), a second standard used by employees to assess fairness is what they have received in the past. Unfavorable departures from a past agreement are likely to be seen as unfair. There is good evidence that individuals respond more strongly when something is taken away than when something fails to occur (cf. Levin, Schneider, & Gaeth, 1998). For instance, we would anticipate that a person receiving a pay cut would be more upset than one who failed to receive an equivalently sized pay raise. Although this phenomenon has been well-documented in the literature, it has only rarely been applied within the organizational justice literature. Fortunately, there is some evidence that workers dislike losing things of value. Interestingly, and also consistent with injustice-stress theory, procedural justice may moderate these outcome effects (Brockner, Wiesenfeld, & Martin, 1995).

Internalized norms. Social and temporal comparisons require the employees to ascertain their treatment with respect to some external standard—either the receipts of others or their own receipts at a previous time. Although these mechanisms are important to the model, injustice-stress theory does not require an external frame of reference. In fact, consistent with other research (e.g., Folger, 1998, 2001), Vermunt and Steensma (2001) maintain that fairness can be ascertained directly by employing an internalized norm. That is, justice can be deduced by comparing an action to some moral standard.

There is direct evidence for this important prediction. In a study of 295 automobile workers, Schmitt and Dörfel (1999) measured perceptions of procedural justice, justice sensitivity (i.e., the extent to which a worker is concerned with or cares about justice), job satisfaction, and psychosomatic well-being (basically, the number of days the worker had been sick in the previous 6 months). Consistent with injustice-stress theory, justice sensitivity moderated the impact of procedural justice on job satisfaction and psychosomatic well-being.

Schmitt and Dörfel (1999) are not alone in demonstrating the importance of internalized standards. When we discuss burnout (see below), we shall review a study by VanYperen et al. (1992) that also supports the inclusion of normative standards as mechanisms for ascertaining (in)justice. These are important findings. Such standards add an explicitly moral motive to the model. In effect, Vermunt (2002) and Vermunt and Steensma (2001) are maintaining that immorality is a stressful thing for people to endure. Folger

(1998, 2001) has referred to these effects as *deontic*, as they are based on internalized moral duties rather than on tangible external benefits such as pay (for additional evidence see Kahneman, Knetsch, & Thaler, 1986; Turillo, Folger, Lavelle, Umphress, & Gee, 2002).

Injustice by Degree

Another implication of injustice-stress theory is that employees are cognizant of the *degree of injustice*. Generally speaking, we might say that a big injustice (discrepancy) hurts more than a small injustice (discrepancy). Only preliminary research is available on this point. However, it does seem supportive of the model. For example, Vermunt, Wit, van den Bos, and Lind (1996) found that a highly inaccurate procedure was seen as less fair than a slightly inaccurate one. Likewise, a slight injustice only lowered state self-esteem by a small amount; a larger injustice lowered it by a larger amount.

Despite this supportive evidence, it is important to inject one caveat. The evidence reviewed thus far is based on justice *judgments*. This is an evaluation made by an individual with respect to the fairness of a particular event. However, injustice often spurs behavior, and it is important to ascertain how individuals *decide* which course of action to take. Experimental research by Gilliland, Benson, and Schepers (1998) suggests that justice *decisions* (choices) are arrived at via a different mechanism than are justice *judgments*. The judgments are made via an additive mechanism like the one described by Vermunt and Steensma (2001). The greater these violations (either in size or in number), the greater the injustice. The relationship between the size of the discrepancy and injustice judgments, therefore, exhibits a linear function. Justice decisions, on the other hand, may exhibit the quality of a threshold. That is, it takes a certain number of violations before one crosses a boundary that primes action. The relationship between the size of the discrepancy and justice decisions, therefore, exhibits a "step function." A small violation, or small number of violations, can have no effect. However, once a boundary is exceeded, the decision to act is made. Further violations should have little if any additional effects.

Comparison to Zohar (1995)

Although Vermunt and Steensma's (2001) injustice-stress theory and Zohar's (1995) extension of role dynamics theory differ in certain details, they also share notable consistencies. For one thing, both models see supervisory behavior as producing much of the stress experienced by workers. In role dynamics theory, the individual's coping ability is overwhelmed by the demands of role senders. The boss plays a pivotal role in Vermunt's (2002) model as well, though Vermunt also emphasizes that managers can take steps to reduce their ill effects on workers. Another point of agreement is that both models found that injustice produces only additive main effects on stress (compare Zohar, 1995, with Vermunt, 2002, Study 2). Neither researcher found that injustice interacted with other stressors.

For all of this, there is at least one difference between these two models. Both frameworks see a gap between demands and coping ability as producing stress. However, they differ in the way that they conceptualize these concerns. In role dynamics theory, the principal stressors are classified based on the type of problem the employee is facing. For example, there is too much to do (overload), it isn't clear what to do (ambiguity), and so on. Zohar (1995) argues that these stressors could produce a sense of injustice. Additionally, Zohar argues that this sense of injustice increases felt strain beyond the effects of other role stressors. But, and this is critical, Zohar does not specify how individuals decide that the four role stressors are *unfair* rather than just frustrating.

Injustice-stress theory, on the other hand, focuses on how workers think about *fairness*. That is, Vermunt (2002) emphasizes the criteria used to make a fairness judgment: social comparisons, temporal comparisons, and internalized norms. This information is used to ascertain whether or not something is *unfair* rather than simply uncomfortable. In this regard, injustice-stress theory explicitly makes the important leap from "stressful-and-difficult" to "stressful-and-unfair."

Burnout and Justice

A third approach to integrating research on organizational justice with worker well-being has focused on employee burnout. Burnout can be succinctly defined as "a prolonged response to chronic emotional and interpersonal stressors on the job" (Maslach, Schaufeli, & Leiter, 2001, p. 397). Generally speaking, burnout has pernicious consequences for individuals, including reduced organizational commitment, heightened turnover, and lower job performance (Cropanzano, Rupp, & Byrne, 2003; Wright & Cropanzano, 1998). As a result of these ill effects, burnout has long been a major concern for organizational scientists, and several excellent reviews are available (e.g., Cordes & Dougherty, 1993; Kahill, 1988; Lee & Ashforth, 1996; Maslach & Leiter, 1997; Shirom, 1989). In their seminal work, Maslach and Jackson (1981) argued that burnout had three dimensions: (a) emotional exhaustion (a sense of being depleted and overextended), (b) depersonalization (detachment or withdrawal from others), and (c) diminished personal accomplishment (lower self-efficacy for one's performance). These three dimensions were codified into the Maslach Burnout Inventory (MBI) and inspired a considerable amount of research (cf. Lee & Ashforth, 1996). Although other models of burnout have been proposed (e.g., Demerouti, Bakker, Nachreiner, & Schaufeli, 2001; Maslach & Leiter, 1997; Pines & Aronson, 1988), the original three-factor model has been most widely used in research on workplace fairness. Therefore, this model is emphasized in our review.

Burnout and Inequity: The Research Evidence

In a theoretical paper, Buunk and Schaufeli (1993) discuss how social comparisons can lead to a sense of burnout among people in helping professions. These authors explicitly mention that "the lack of equity" (p. 56) may be one contributor to workplace stress. This sense of distributive injustice should adversely contribute to professional burnout. Generally speaking, the results support Buunk and Schaufeli's (1993) model. When caregivers perceive a lack of reciprocity, they tend to experience more burnout than when reciprocity is present (e.g., Schaufeli & Janczur, 1994; VanYperen, 1996, 1998).

Similar findings were obtained in another field study by Van Dierendonck, Schaufeli, and Sixma (1994). As was true for VanYperen et al. (1992), this study also employed professional caregivers (567 general practitioners) as respondents. Notably, Van Dierendonck et al. (1994) used a two-factor model of burnout. Although emotional exhaustion was retained, the correlated variables of depersonalization and diminished personal accomplishment were collapsed into a single dimension termed "negative attitudes" (see also Schaufeli & Van Dierendonck, 1993). Generally speaking, their model stated that (a) harassment from patients causes feelings of inequity, (b) inequity heightens emotional exhaustion, and (c) emotional exhaustion in turn increases negative attitudes. Though the data were cross-sectional, linear structural analysis suggested that the data were largely consistent with the proposed model.

Of course, all workers are not affected in precisely the same fashion. To illustrate, consider a cross-section field study by VanYperen et al. (1992). These authors examined burnout among 194 nurses. Burnout was measured with all three Maslach (1982) dimensions—emotional exhaustion, depersonalization, and diminished personal accomplishment—though these were aggregated into a single scale. When nurses felt that they gave more to their patients than they received in return, they tended to report higher levels of burnout. Interestingly, and consistent with predictions, this effect was moderated by communal orientation. The authors state that "communal orientation refers to the desire to give and receive benefits in response to the needs of and out of concern for others" (p. 173). Therefore, when communal orientation was high, an imbalance was less likely to predict burnout. Among nurses with a lower communal orientation, the imbalance was more likely to predict burnout.

VanYperen et al.'s (1992) findings are consistent with injustice-stress theory and with the Schmitt and Dörfel (1999) study reviewed earlier. In particular, VanYperen and his colleagues seem to have identified a good example of what Vermunt and Steensma (2001) refer to as an "internalized standard." Specifically, if a nurse has internalized the norm of helping others (i.e., has a high communal orientation), then he or she is less reactive to an imbalance in inputs to outcomes. When a nurse lacks such an internalized standard, then imbalances have a more adverse impact.

Extending the Model #1: Other Occupations

Buunk and Schaufeli's (1993) model was originally formulated within the context of professional caregivers (e.g., nurses and general practitioners). For this reason, the imbalance they are referring to is between what one provides others and what one gets in return. The burnout literature has long emphasized the caregivers (e.g., Maslach, 1982). Although this vital population remains the target of much research, it is important to recognize that the basic burnout concepts tend to generalize well to other populations of workers (Shirom, 1989). Given this, one would anticipate that the inequity discussed by Buunk and Schaufeli could be just as potent if it took place within other professions. Suffice it to say, evidence strongly supports this conclusion. For instance, Van Horn, Schaufeli, and Enzmann (1999) found that a lack of reciprocity promotes stress among teachers, and Kop, Euwema, and Schaufeli (1999) documented similar effects among police officers.

Extending the Model #2: Other Sources of Inequity

As we have seen, the "inequity" described by Buunk and Schaufeli (1993) referred to perceived ill treatment of a caregiver by a patient. Hence, their model is about injustice within the context caregiver/patient relationships and not worker/management relationships as is true of, say, injustice-stress theory. Of course, there are other sources of injustice as well. Although retaining the notion of patient/caregiver inequity, Schaufeli, Van Dierendonck, and Van Gorp (1996) added that an imbalance can also occur between the individual and the organization. In particular, Schaufeli and his colleagues (1996) maintained that inequity from both sources can contribute to employee burnout, but only inequity from the organization contributes to (diminished) organizational commitment. The model was tested and supported on a sample of 220 student nurses. It was then successfully cross-validated on a second sample that was similar to, but independent of, the first. Findings from both samples supported predictions strongly suggesting that inequity from either patients or the employing organization can create burnout among workers.

That having been said, the data here are not perfectly consistent. In a cross-sectional field study, Hendrix and Spencer (1989) attempted to predict absenteeism among 443 government employees in the United States. Their detailed model included a host of traditional job stressors as predictors (e.g., role conflict, role ambiguity, job autonomy, etc.). Among these was pay equity. Notice, of course, that this is a different sort of equity than that measured in other research of this kind. Generally speaking, Hendrix and Spencer then proposed that these stressors would predict various indicators of strain including burnout, cold/flu episodes, and alcohol involvement, among others. Finally, Hendrix and Spencer anticipated that the amount of strain would predict absenteeism. Though pay equity had a significant zero-order correlation with burnout ($r = -.19$), this relationship was not significantly in the final path model, which controlled for the impact of other stressors. However, pay equity did predict cold/flu episodes, and these episodes in turn predicted absenteeism.

Extending the Model #3: Curvilinear Relationships

There is a counterintuitive implication of using inequity to predict burnout. According to equity theory, both underreward (getting less than one deserves) and overreward (getting more than one deserves) can create discomfort. By extension, being disadvantaged and being overly advantaged should both engender burnout. In other words, the relationship between equity and burnout is curvilinear. Individuals should experience the least burnout at moderate levels, and burnout should increase at the extremes. Just such a model was proposed and tested in two cross-section field studies reported by Van Dierendonck, Schaufeli, and Buunk (1996). Results were supportive.

In order to rule out potential alternative explanations, Van Dierendonck, Schaufeli, and Buunk (2001) followed up their 1996 effort with a longitudinal study of 245 human service professionals. As one would expect given our review thus far, inequity correlated with emotional exhaustion even though the two measures were taken 1 year apart. More critical here, the relationship between inequity and emotional exhaustion was nonlinear. Under conditions of both underreward and overreward, these human resource professionals showed heightened levels of emotional exhaustion. The least emotional exhaustion appeared when there were intermediate levels of reported equity.

Extending the Model #4: Procedural and Interactional Justice

As we have seen thus far, most of the research on justice and burnout has emphasized the predictive value of distributive justice (operationalized as inequity) and de-emphasized procedural and interactional justice. In a recent paper, Moliner et al. (2003) have attempted to remedy this problem. Moliner and her colleagues were primarily interested in understanding extra-role customer service behaviors (ERCS). In the course of this, these authors build an integrative model that draws on both the justice and the burnout literatures. The model is displayed in Figure 4.4. According to Moliner et al., employees' judgments of their outcomes (i.e., whether or not they are fair) partially influence their judgments of the process and the interaction. For this reason, distributive fairness is one, though by no means the only, cause of procedural and interactional justice. Procedural and interactional justice in turn affects burnout (operationalized by Moliner et al. as emotional exhaustion and cynicism together) and psychological engagement. Finally, burnout and engagement were expected to affect ERCS.

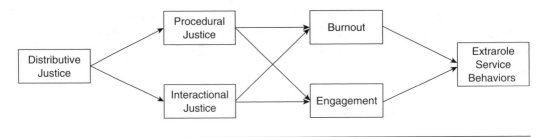

Figure 4.4   Moliner's Integrated Model of Injustice and Well-Being at Work

To test her model, Moliner and her colleagues (2003) surveyed 317 contract employees of 59 Spanish hotels. Generally speaking, results were consistent with her model. The one notable exception was that burnout did not predict ERCS. In fact, extrarole customer service behavior was directly predicted by engagement. Otherwise, findings were strongly supportive. Significantly, the impact of distributive justice was mediated by procedural and interactional justice. Likewise, the impact of procedural and interactional justice was accounted for by engagement.

Comparison With Other Theories

When compared with the other models reviewed in this section of our chapter, the evidence linking injustice (or at least inequity) to burnout is by far the most extensive. There are now several studies, some of them longitudinal, that demonstrate a tie between a lack of reciprocity and burnout. Moreover, Buunk and Schaufeli's (1993) model has proven quite dynamic. As we have reviewed, it has been extended multiple times so as to add new occupations, different sources of inequity, and even curvilinear relationships.

For all this empirical support, Buunk and Schaufeli's (1993) framework seems to have a curiously different flavor than that possessed by the work of Zohar (1995). In the Buunk and Schaufeli model, perceived injustice creates stress. That is, when one senses unfairness (usually understood as inequity), burnout is likely to result. In the role justice theory, on the other hand, stressful working conditions are perceived as unfair. Hence, the stressful working conditions are experienced first. Perceptions of (in)justice come later as a consequence of workplace stress.

In this regard, the causal order seems a bit different for the two models, at least at first glance. Upon further reflection, however, this seeming inconsistency becomes more apparent and less real. Vermunt and Steensma's (2001) injustice-stress theory might provide a means of analyzing these issues. As described earlier, injustice-stress theory maintains that individuals experience certain types of discrepancies as stressors. Exposure to these stressors may, under certain conditions, be viewed as unfair. Unfairness then exacerbates employee stress levels. Therefore, if Zohar's (1995) four role stressors (conflict, ambiguity, overload, and lack of decision latitude) are seen as stressors and burnout is viewed as a stress response, then the different models become intelligible. In effect, justice is a variable that partially mediates between stressors and strain. More work is needed to directly test these ideas, but they are consistent with research to date.

Implications for Managers

In this chapter we have paid special attention to the problematic aspects of organizational justice. When fairness is not present, mangers and employees are in a "lose-lose" situation where neither benefits. However, this point implies a happier converse. Providing justice places all parties into a "win-win" situation. Employees who are fairly treated are less stressed, have better attitudes, and are more productive (Wright & Cropanzano, 1998; Cropanzano et al., 2003). The benefits of this can accrue to everyone.

A threshold implication of this focus on justice is that the attention and concern that a manager has in diagnosing stress may send justice signals to employees. For example, the willingness to acknowledge the level of stress in an organization may signal a level of concern for employees that they appreciate or interpret as involving just treatment. Conversely, the unwillingness to engage in a stress diagnostic or the lack of seriousness associated with a lax stress diagnostic may send signals of injustice, particularly interactional injustice (i.e., that the manager is unconcerned or does not respect the interests of the employees).

Another managerial implication of justice and worker well-being is that justice should be incorporated in any comprehensive stress reduction strategies. For example, an obvious technique to reduce stress is to avoid circumstances that cause distress. Justice can be a moderator of a number of circumstances at work that can affect whether those circumstances are perceived to be stressful or not. Consequently, the manager has a large degree of control over whether or not those same circumstances will be perceived to be stressful by treating his or her employees in a fair manner.

Planning can be another important element in stress avoidance, and this also has implications for justice. A number of otherwise stressful situations at work (e.g., performance appraisal, compensation reviews) can be made more fair (and therefore less unjust) by careful managerial planning. This planning should include a shift in perspective so that the manager is forced to take the employee's perspective and, in this way, hopefully anticipate (and thereby avoid) potential "trouble spots" in relations with employees. Some of these "trouble spots" can include entering or exiting a job, performance appraisals, competitive promotions, or hiring.

Epilogue

In his classic analysis, Cannon (1935; see also Cannon, 1932) metaphorically explained stress as a physical process. When, say, enough force is exerted on one end of a stationary steel rod, the rod bends. Stress causes distortion to the original shape. In a like fashion, employees can also be distorted by workplace stress. This is an elegant and compelling analogy, but we should keep in mind that like all metaphors it has its limits. Human beings are not inanimate objects. Workplace stress is not simply a mechanical response to impersonal physical forces. Instead, we try to make sense out of the myriad events and demands around us. Part of this sense-making process includes an assessment of social justice. "Was that *fair?*" is a basic question asked by workers. An answer of "no," should that occur, is hurtful. It endangers our health and our sense of psychological well-being. The literature on stress and well-being has documented many things that can affect the health of employees—too much work, ambiguous assignments, conflicting demands, environment toxins, and many others. However, the work reviewed here suggests that at least one other stressor should be added to the list—fairness. Having to confront unfairness takes its toll on employee well-being. We are all happier and healthier working with others who affirm our dignity through fair outcomes, procedures, and interpersonal transactions.

References

Adams, J. S. (1963). Toward an understanding of inequity. *Journal of Abnormal and Social Psychology, 47,* 422–436.

Adams, J. S. (1965). Inequity in social exchange. In L. Berkowitz (Ed.), *Advances in experimental social psychology* (Vol. 2, pp. 267–299). New York: Academic.

Bedeian, A. G., & Armenakis, A. A. (1981). A path analytic study of the consequences of role conflict and ambiguity. *Academy of Management Journal, 24,* 417–424.

Behrman, D., & Perreault, W. D., Jr. (1984). A role stress model of the performance and satisfaction of industrial salespersons. *Journal of Marketing, 48,* 9–21.

Bies, R. J. (1987). The predicament of injustice: The management of moral outrage. In L. L. Cummings & B. M. Staw (Eds.), *Research in organizational behavior* (Vol. 9, pp. 289–319). Greenwich, CT: JAI.

Bies, R. J., & Moag, J. S. (1986). Interactional justice: Communication criteria of fairness. In R. J. Lewicki, B. H. Sheppard, & M. H. Bazerman (Eds.), *Research in organizational behavior* (Vol. 9, pp. 289–319). Greenwich, CT: JAI.

Brockner, J., Wiesenfeld, B. M., & Martin, C. L. (1995). Decision frame, procedural justice, and survivors' reactions to job layoffs. *Organizational Behavior and Human Decision Processes, 63,* 59–68.

Buunk, B. P., & Schaufeli, W. B. (1993). Burnout: A perspective from social comparison theory. In W. B. Schaufeli, C. Maslach, & T. Marek (Eds.), *Professional burnout: Recent developments in theory and research* (pp. 53–69). New York: Hemisphere.

Campbell, A., Converse, P. E., & Rogers, W. L. (1976). *The quality of American life.* New York: Russell Sage.

Cannon, W. B. (1932). *This wisdom of the body.* New York: W.W. Norton.

Cannon, W. B. (1935). Stresses and strains of homoeostasis. *American Journal of Medical Science, 189,* 1.

Cohen, R. L., & Greenberg, J. (1982). The justice concept in social psychology. In J. Greenberg & R. L. Cohen (Eds.), *Equity and justice in social behavior* (pp. 1–41). New York: Academic Press.

Colquitt, J. A. (2001). On the dimensionality of organizational justice: A construct validation of a measure. *Journal of Applied Psychology, 86,* 425–446.

Cordes, C. L., & Dougherty, T. W. (1993). A review and an integration of research on job burnout. *Academy of Management Review, 18,* 621–656.

Cropanzano, R., & Greenberg, J. (1997). Progress in organizational justice: Tunneling through the maze. In C. L. Cooper & I. T. Robertson (Eds.), *International Review of Industrial and Organizational Psychology.* New York: Wiley.

Cropanzano, R., Rupp, D. E., & Byrne, Z. S. (2003). The relationship of emotional exhaustion to work attitudes, job performance, and organizational citizenship behaviors. *Journal of Applied Psychology, 88,* 160–169.

Crosby, F. (1976). A model of egoistical relative deprivation. *Psychological Bulletin, 83,* 85–113.

Crosby, F. (1984). Relative deprivation in organizational settings. In B. M. Staw & L. L. Cummings (Eds.), *Research in organizational behavior* (Vol. 6, pp. 51–93). Greenwich, CT: JAI.

De Boer, E. M., Bakker, A. B., Syroit, J. E., & Schaufeli, W. B. (2002). Unfairness at work as a predictor of absenteeism. *Journal of Organizational Behavior, 23,* 181–197.

Demerouti, E., Bakker, A. B., Nachreiner, F., & Schaufeli, W. B. (2001). The job demands-resources model of burnout. *Journal of Applied Psychology, 86,* 499–512.

Edwards, J. R. (1992). A cybernetic theory of stress, coping, and well-being in organizations. *Academy of Management Review, 17,* 238–274.

Elovainio, M., Kivimäki, M., & Helkama, K. (2001). Organizational justice evaluations, job control, and occupational strain. *Journal of Applied Psychology, 86,* 418–424.

Elovainio, M., Kivimäki, M., & Vahtera, J. (2002). Organizational justice: Evidence of a new psychosocial predictor of health. *American Journal of Public Health, 92,* 105–108.

Fisher, C. D., & Gitelson, R. (1983). A meta-analysis of the correlates of role conflict and ambiguity. *Journal of Applied Psychology, 68,* 320–333.

Folger, R. (1986). Rethinking equity theory: A referent cognitions model. In H. W. Beirhoff, R. L. Cohen, & J. Greenberg (Eds.), *Justice in social relations* (pp. 145–162). New York: Plenum.

Folger, R. (1998). Fairness as a moral virtue. In M. Schminke (Ed.), *Managerial ethics: Moral management of people and processes* (pp. 13–34). Mahwah, NJ: Lawrence Erlbaum.

Folger, R. (2001). Fairness as deonance. In S. W. Gilliland, D. D. Steiner, & D. P. Skarlicki (Eds.), *Research in social issues in management* (Vol. 1, pp. 3–33). New York: Information Age.

Gilliland, S. W., Benson, L., III, & Schepers, D. H. (1998). A rejection threshold in justice evaluations: Effects on judgment and decision making. *Organizational Behavior and Human Decision Processes, 76,* 113–131.

Goldman, B. M. (2003). The application of referent cognitions theory to legal-claiming by terminated workers: The role of organizational justice and anger. *Journal of Management, 29,* 705–728.

Goode, W. J. (1960). A theory of role strain. *American Sociological Review, 25,* 483–496.

Greenberg, J. (1993). The social side of fairness: Interpersonal and informational classes of organizational justice. In R. Cropanzano (Ed.), *Justice in the workplace: Approaching fairness in human resource management* (pp. 79–103). Hillsdale, NJ: Lawrence Erlbaum.

Greenberg, J., & Bies, R. J. (1992). Establishing the role of empirical studies of organizational justice in philosophical inquiries into business ethics. *Journal of Business Ethics, 11,* 433–444.

Grienberger, I. V., Rutte, C. G., & van Knippenberg, A. F. M. (1997). Influence of social comparisons of outcomes and procedures on fairness judgments. *Journal of Applied Psychology, 82,* 913–919.

Hendrix, W. H., & Spencer, B. A. (1989). Development and test of a multivariate model of absenteeism. *Psychological Reports, 64,* 923–938.

Homans, G. C. (1961). *Social behavior: Its elementary forms.* New York: Harcourt Brace Jovanovich.

House, R. J., & Rizzo, J. R. (1972). Role conflict and role ambiguity as critical variables in a model of organizational behavior. *Organizational Behavior and Human Performance, 7,* 467–505.

Hulin, C. (1991). Adaptation, persistence, and commitment in organizations. In M. D. Dunnette & L. M. Hough (Eds.), *Handbook of industrial and organizational psychology* (2nd ed., Vol. 2, pp. 445–505). Palo Alto, CA: Consulting Psychologists Press.

Jackson, S. E., & Schuler, R. S. (1985). A meta-analysis and conceptual critique of research on role ambiguity and role conflict in work settings. *Organizational Behavior and Human Decision Processes, 36,* 16–78.

Kahill, S. (1988). Symptoms of professional burnout: A review of the empirical evidence. *Canadian Psychology, 29,* 284–297.

Kahn, R. L., & Byosiere, P. (1992). Stress in organizations. In M. D. Dunnette & L. M. Hough (Eds.), *Handbook of industrial and organizational psychology* (2nd ed., Vol. 3, pp. 571–650). Palo Alto, CA: Consulting Psychologists Press.

Kahn, R. L., Wolfe, D. H., Quinn, R. P., Snoek, J. D., & Rosenthal, R. A. (1964). *Organizational stress: Studies in role conflict and ambiguity.* New York: Wiley.

Kahneman, D., Knetsch, J. L., & Thaler, R. H. (1986). Fairness and the assumptions of economics. *Journal of Business, 59,* S285–S300.

Karasek, R. A. (1979). Job demands, job decision-latitude, and mental strain: Implications for job redesign. *Administrative Science Quarterly, 24,* 285–308.

Katz, D., & Kahn, R. L. (1966). *The social psychology of organizations.* New York: Wiley.

Kivimäki, M., Elovainio, M., Vahtera, J., & Ferrie, J. E. (2002). Organisational justice and health of employees: Prospective cohort study. *Occupational and Environmental Medicine, 60,* 27–34.

Kop, N., Euwema, M., & Schaufeli, W. B. (1999). Burnout in police officers. *Work & Stress, 13*, 326–340.

Kulik, C. T., & Ambrose, M. L. (1992). Personal and situational determinants of referent choice. *Academy of Management Journal, 17*, 212–237.

Lazarus, R. S., & Folkman, S. (1984). *Stress, appraisal, and coping.* New York: Springer.

Lee, R. T., & Ashforth, B. E. (1996). A meta-analytic examination of the correlates of the three dimensions of job burnout. *Journal of Applied Psychology, 81*, 123–133.

Leventhal, G. S. (1976). Fairness in social relationships. In J. W. Thibaut, J. T. Spence, & R. C. Carson (Eds.), *Contemporary topics in social psychology* (pp. 212–239). Morristown, NJ: General Learning Press.

Leventhal, G. S. (1980). What should be done with equity theory? In K. J. Gergen, M. S. Greenberg, & R. H. Willis (Eds), *Social exchange: Advances in theory and research* (pp. 27–55). New York: Plenum.

Levin, I. P., Schneider, S. L., & Gaeth, G. J. (1998). All frames are not created equal: A typology and critical analysis of framing effects. *Organizational Behavior and Human Decision Processes, 76*, 149–188.

Locke, E. A. (1976). The nature and causes of job satisfaction. In M. D. Dunnette (Ed.), *Handbook of industrial and organizational psychology* (1st ed., pp. 1297–1349). Chicago: Rand McNally.

Martin, J. (1981). Relative deprivation: A theory of distributive justice for an era of shrinking resources. In L. L. Cummings & B. M. Staw (Eds.), *Research in organizational behavior* (Vol. 3, pp. 53–107). Greenwich, CT: JAI.

Maslach, C. (1982). *Burnout: The cost of caring.* Englewood Cliffs, NJ: Prentice Hall.

Maslach, C., & Jackson, S. E. (1981). The measurement of experienced burnout. *Journal of Occupational Behavior, 2*, 99–113.

Maslach, C., & Leiter, M. P. (1997). *The truth about burnout: How organizations cause personal stress and what to do about it.* San Francisco: Jossey-Bass.

Maslach, C., Schaufeli, W. B., & Leiter, M. P. (2001). Job burnout. In S. T. Fiske, D. L. Schacter, & C. Zahn-Waxler (Eds.), *Annual review of psychology* (Vol. 52, pp. 397–422). Palo Alto, CA: Annual Reviews.

Masterson, S., Lewis, K., Goldman, B., & Taylor, S. (2000). Integrating justice and social exchange: The differing effects of fair procedures and treatment on work relationships. *Academy of Management Journal, 43*, 738–746.

Michalos, A. C. (1985). Multiple discrepancies theory (MDT). *Social Indicators Research, 16*, 347–413.

Michalos, A. C. (1986). Job satisfaction, marital satisfaction, and the quality of life: A review and a preview. In F. M. Andrews (Ed.), *Research on the quality of life* (pp. 57–83). Ann Arbor: Institute for Social Research, University of Michigan.

Moliner, C., Martínez-Tur, V., Peiró, J. M., Ramos, J., & Cropanzano, R. (2003). *Linking justice to extra-role customer service: Does well-being at work mediate?* Manuscript in preparation.

Netemeyer, R. G., Johnston, M. W., & Burton, S. (1990). Analysis of role conflict and role ambiguity in a structural equations framework. *Journal of Applied Psychology, 75*, 148–157.

Peterson, M. F., Smith, J. P. B., Akande, A., Ayestran, S., Bochner, S., Callan, V., et al. (1995). Role conflict, ambiguity, and overload: A 21-nation study. *Academy of Management Journal, 38*, 429–452.

Pettigrew, T. (1967). Social evaluation theory. In D. Levine (Ed.), *Nebraska symposium on motivation* (Vol. 15). Lincoln: University of Nebraska Press.

Pines, T. L., & Aronson, E. (1988). *Career burnout: Causes and cures.* New York: Free Press.

Rizzo, J. R., House, R. J., & Lirtzman, S. I. (1970). Role conflict and ambiguity in complex organizations. *Administrative Science Quarterly, 15,* 150–163.

Schaufeli, W. B., & Janczur, B. (1994). Burnout among nurses: A Polish-Dutch comparison. *Journal of Cross-Cultural Psychology, 25,* 95–113.

Schaufeli, W. B., & Van Dierendonck, D. (1993). The construct validity of two burnout measures. *Journal of Organizational Behavior, 14,* 631–647.

Schaufeli, W. B., Van Dierendonck, D., & Van Gorp, K. (1996). Burnout and reciprocity: Towards a dual-level social exchange model. *Work & Stress, 10,* 225–237.

Schmitt, M., & Dörfel, M. (1999). Procedural injustice at work, justice sensitivity, job satisfaction and psychosomatic well-being. *European Journal of Social Psychology, 29,* 443–453.

Sheppard, B. H., Lewicki, R. J., & Minton, J. W. (1992). *Organizational Justice.* New York: Lexington Books.

Shirom, A. (1989). Burnout in work organizations. In C. L. Cooper & I. T. Robertson (Eds.), *International review of industrial and organizational psychology: 1989* (pp. 25–48). New York: Wiley.

Sitkin, S. B., & Bies, R. J. (1993). Social accounts in conflict settings: Using explanations to manage conflict. *Human Relations, 46,* 349–370.

Stouffer, S. A., Suchman, E. A., DeVinney, L. C., Star, S. A., & Williams, R. M., Jr. (1949). *The American soldier: Adjustment during army life* (Vol. 1). New Jersey: Princeton University Press.

Sweeney, P. D., McFarlin, D. B., & Inderrieden, E. J. (1990). Using relative deprivation theory to explain satisfaction with income and pay level: A multistudy examination. *Academy of Management Journal, 33,* 423–436.

Teas, K. R. (1983). Supervisory behavior, role stress, and the job satisfaction of industrial salespeople. *Journal of Marketing Research, 20,* 84–91.

Tepper, B. J. (2001). Health consequences of organizational injustice: Tests of main and interactive effects. *Organizational Behavior and Human Decision Processes, 86,* 197–215.

Thibaut, J., & Walker, L. (1975). *Procedural justice.* Hillsdale, NJ: Lawrence Erlbaum.

Thibaut, J., & Walker, L. (1978). A theory of procedure. *California Law Review, 66,* 541–566.

Turillo, C. J., Folger, R., Lavelle, J. J., Umphress, E. E., & Gee, J. O. (2002). Is virtue its own reward? Self-sacrificial decisions for the sake of fairness. *Organizational Behavior and Human Decision Processes, 89,* 839–865.

Tyler, T. R., & Lind, E. A. (1992). A relational model of authority in groups. In M. Zanna (Ed.), *Advances in experimental social psychology* (Vol. 25, pp. 115–191). San Diego, CA: Academic.

Van Dierendonck, D., Schaufeli, W. B., & Buunk, B. P. (1996). Inequity among human service professionals: Measurement and relation to burnout. *Basic and Applied Social Psychology, 18,* 429–451.

Van Dierendonck, D., Schaufeli, W. B., & Buunk, B. P. (2001). Burnout and inequity among human service professionals: A longitudinal study. *Journal of Occupational Health Psychology, 6,* 43–52.

Van Dierendonck, D., Schaufeli, W. B., & Sixma, H. J. (1994). Burnout among general practitioners: A perspective from equity theory. *Journal of Social and Clinical Psychology, 13,* 86–100.

Van Horn, J. E., Schaufeli, W. B., & Enzmann, D. (1999). Teacher burnout and lack of reciprocity. *Journal of Applied Social Psychology, 29,* 91–108.

VanYperen, N. W. (1996). Communal orientation and the burnout syndrome among nurses: A replication and extension. *Journal of Applied Social Psychology, 26,* 338–354.

VanYperen, N. W. (1998). Information support, equity and burnout: The moderating effect of self-efficacy. *Journal of Organizational and Occupational Psychology, 71,* 29–33.

VanYperen, N. W., Buunk, B. P., & Schaufeli, W. B. (1992). Imbalance, communal orientation, and the burnout syndrome among nurses. *Journal of Applied Social Psychology, 22,* 173–189.

Vermunt, R. (2002). Employee stress, injustice and the dual position of the boss. In S. W. Gilliland, D. D. Steiner, & D. P. Skarlicki (Eds.), *Emerging perspectives on managing organizational justice* (pp. 159–176). Greenwich, CT: Information Age.

Vermunt, R., Spaans, E., & Zorge, F. (1989). Satisfaction, happiness and well-being of Dutch students. *Social Indicators Research, 21,* 1–33.

Vermunt, R., & Steensma, H. (2001). Stress and justice in organizations: An exploration into justice processes with the aim to find mechanisms to reduce stress. In R. Cropanzano (Ed.), *From theory to practice: Vol. 2. Justice in the workplace* (pp. 27–48). Mahwah, NJ: Lawrence Erlbaum.

Vermunt, R., Wit, A., van den Bos, K., & Lind, E. A. (1996). The effects of unfair procedures on negative affect and protest. *Social Justice Research, 9,* 109–120.

Weiss, H., & Cropanzano, R. (1996). An affective events approach to job satisfaction. In B. M. Staw & L. L. Cummings (Eds.), *Research in organizational behavior* (Vol. 18, pp. 1–74). Greenwich, CT: JAI.

Wright, T. A., & Cropanzano, R. (1998). Emotional exhaustion as a predictor of job performance. *Journal of Applied Psychology, 83,* 486–493.

Zohar, D. (1995). The justice perspective on job stress. *Journal of Organizational Behavior, 16,* 487–495.

5

Poor Leadership

E. Kevin Kelloway
Niro Sivanathan
Lori Francis
Julian Barling

An aggressive, bullying boss I used to work for would build himself up into a state of rage at least three times a week. He once became so enraged that he actually threw the office kettle out of the window shouting, "You're not drinking my tea and coffee!" as staff looked on in disbelief.

My boss really drove me up the wall to a point where I started developing stomach problems, which my doctor linked to stress.

My husband worked for the NHS and became the target of the department bully. When he stood up for himself, the manager stood behind his desk waiving his fists and saying my husband was mentally impaired and had lost all his friends.

Employees shared these stories and others on the British Broadcasting Company (BBC) Web site following a news story on menacing bosses and their role in workplace stress (BBC, 2003). Although these stories are extreme, they help bring to light the vital role leaders play in organizations and the profound impact they have on the stress and well-being of those they lead.

Authors' Note: Preparation of this chapter was supported by funding from the Nova Scotia Health Research Foundation to the first and third authors and from the Social Sciences and Humanities Research Council of Canada to the first and fourth authors.

The notion that poor-quality leadership has negative effects for individuals is not new (Day & Hamblin, 1964), and the research that has been conducted on the link between leadership and mental health has invariably focused on the potentially negative effects of poor-quality leadership. Poor leadership also has been associated with increased levels of employee stress (Offermann & Hellmann, 1996) and retaliation (Townsend, Phillips, & Elkins, 2000). Ashforth (1997) found that when abusive supervisors used noncontingent punishment, employees felt a sense of helplessness and alienation from work. Furthermore, Atwater, Dionne, Camobreco, Avolio, and Lau (1998) reported that leadership effectiveness of supervisors in the military is negatively affected when supervisors resort to noncontingent punishment. Richman, Flaherty, Rospenda, and Chistensen (1992) found heightened levels of psychological distress among medical residents who reported to abusive supervisors.

Generally, employees who perceive their supervisors to be abusive experience low levels of job and life satisfaction, lower levels of affective commitment, increased work-family conflict, and psychological distress (Tepper, 2000) as well as psychosomatic symptoms, anxiety, and depression (Hoel, Rayner, & Cooper, 1999). Additionally, Dupre, Inness, Connelly, Barling, and Hoption (2003) found a relationship between teenagers' experience of abusive supervision and their own aggression directed toward their supervisors.

The stress of poor supervision also manifests in physical outcomes. Wager, Fieldman, and Hussey (2003) reported that on days when a sample of nurses worked for a supervisor they did not like, they experienced a 15-mm increase in systolic blood pressure and a 7-mm increase in diastolic blood pressure when compared with days when they worked for a supervisor they did like. Changes of this magnitude result in a 16% increased risk of a coronary failure and a 38% increased risk of stroke. Moreover, the findings are consistent with the observation that exposure to aggressive behavior at work (i.e., bullying) is associated with increased risk for both depression and cardiovascular disease (Kivimäki, Virtanen, Vartia, Elovainio, Vahtera, & Keltikangas-Järvinen, 2003).

Despite these consistent findings and a wealth of anecdotal evidence, surprisingly little research has concentrated on identifying what constitutes poor leadership or on the mechanisms through which poor leadership affects workplace stress. In this chapter, we attempt to explain the nature of poor leadership and highlight some of the potential mechanisms through which poor leaders contribute to employee stress. First, we identify poor leadership as a source of stress (i.e., a stressor) in and of itself. At least two aspects of leadership may be stressors: leaders who are abusive or punitive and leaders who simply evidence inadequate leadership abilities for a given context. Second, we suggest that poor leadership may be a "root cause" that gives rise to other well-documented workplace stressors. In this sense, we suggest that existing models of organizational stress are deficient in their lack of consideration of organizational context; we suggest that leadership is a critical element of context that needs to be considered in understanding organizational stressors. Finally, we note the possibility that leadership might moderate stressor-strain relationships. Leaders are, of course, a potent source of social support in the workplace, and such support is documented as a stress buffer. We suggest that poor leadership may serve to isolate individuals and deny access to social support and thereby exacerbate the negative effects of workplace stressors.

Poor Leadership: Definition and Prevalence

Leadership is undoubtedly one of the most ubiquitous potential stressors in the workplace. Although most stressors are specific to a given workplace, virtually everyone has a formal leader to whom they report. Throughout our discussion we shall be using the term "leader" to reference individuals in organizations who have assumed a formal leadership role (e.g., supervisors, managers, etc.). Although leadership theorists typically have focused on leadership as a process rather than leadership as a role (Yukl, 1998), our focus is on individuals who by virtue of their organizational position have legitimate reward and coercive power (French & Raven, 1959).

How might such individuals evidence poor leadership? At least two possibilities are apparent: Leaders may be abusive, aggressive, or punitive, and leaders may simply lack appropriate leadership skills. We suggest that both conditions lead to increased employee stress.

Abusive Leadership

Abusive leadership occurs when individuals in a formal leadership role engage in aggressive or punitive behaviors toward their employees. These behaviors can vary widely from leaders degrading their employees by yelling, ridiculing, and name-calling to terrorizing employees by withholding information or threatening employees with job loss and pay cuts. Such behaviors have been variously termed "workplace harassment" (e.g., Rospenda, 2002), "emotional abuse" (e.g., Keashly, 1998, 2001), "bullying" (e.g., Einarsen, 1999; Hoel et al., 1999), or simply "workplace aggression" (for a review, see Schat & Kelloway, Chapter 8, this volume). Although conceptually abusive supervision includes acts of physical violence, empirically the incidence of coworker violence (including leader-follower violence) is very low (LeBlanc & Kelloway, 2002; U.S. Postal Service [USPS], 2000). Indeed, in their study, LeBlanc & Kelloway (2002) found no reported incidents of physical violence between coworkers. Acts of nonphysical aggression are relatively more common. Pizzino (2002) reported that supervisors accounted for 20% of aggressive behaviors reported by unionized respondents whereas members of the public were responsible for 38% of respondents' reports of aggressive behavior.

However, we suggest that the impact of such behaviors is exaggerated by the position of the perpetrator. That is, aggressive acts by supervisors might have more deleterious effects on employee outcomes than do similar acts committed by members of the public or other coworkers. Although we know of no data that directly test this suggestion, indirect support emerges from several sources.

First, LeBlanc and Kelloway (2002) examined the impact of aggression from members of the public and coworkers. They found that any effects of public aggression/violence on outcomes were indirect, being mediated by fear of future violence (see also Barling, Rogers, & Kelloway, 2001; Rogers & Kelloway, 1997; Schat & Kelloway, 2000, 2003). However the effects of coworker aggression on personal and organizational outcomes were direct. These data suggest that the actions of coworkers, including leaders, have a stronger impact on personal well-being than do the actions of members of the public.

Second, the data reported by LeBlanc and Kelloway (2002) are consistent with a body of evidence suggesting that organizational context plays a crucial role in understanding the effects of workplace violence and sexual harassment (see for example, Barling et al., 2001; Fitzgerald, Drasgow, Hulin, Gelfand, & Magley, 1997). We suggest that the organizational position of the perpetrator is one such critical contextual factor. As a result of their organizational position and their power in the organization, leaders may be more prone to engage in abusive behaviors (see, for example, Keashly, Trott, & MacLean, 1994) perhaps because of a sense of invulnerability (Dekker & Barling, 1998). Moreover, these actions may be more salient to the target because of the aggressor's ability to control organizational sanctions and rewards.

Passive Leadership

Although the foregoing discussion focused on the notion of abusive leadership, we also recognize that a lack of leadership skills may be a source of stress for individuals. We term this lack of skills "passive leadership." We define passive leadership as comprising elements from both the laissez-faire and management-by-exception (passive) styles articulated in the theory of transformational leadership (Bass & Avolio, 1997). Leaders engaging in the management-by-exception (passive) style do not intervene until problems are either brought to their attention or become serious enough to demand action (Bass, 1990). Leaders who rely on the laissez-faire style avoid decision making and the responsibilities associated with their position (Bass, 1990; Hater & Bass, 1988).

There is now a great deal of data supporting the effectiveness of transformational leadership behaviors. Transformational leaders exhibit four characteristics in their interactions with employees; idealized influence, inspirational motivation, intellectual stimulation, and individualized consideration

(Bass, 1990). Via these characteristics, transformational leaders positively affect a number of important outcomes. Although a review of this literature is beyond our current scope, it is clear that managers' transformational leadership style is positively associated with employee commitment to the organization (Barling, Weber, & Kelloway, 1996; Bycio, Hackett, & Allen, 1995; Koh, Steers, & Terborg, 1995), trust in the leader (Podsakoff, MacKenzie, & Bommer, 1996), lower levels of role stress (Podsakoff et al., 1996), and both job satisfaction (Hater & Bass, 1988) and satisfaction with the leader (Hater & Bass, 1988; Koh et al., 1995). Transformational leadership is also associated with higher performance in laboratory studies (e.g., Howell & Frost, 1989; Kirkpatrick & Locke, 1996) as well as field studies. In the latter, transformational leadership has been associated with performance outcomes such as organizational citizenship (Koh et al., 1995; Podsakoff et al., 1996), employee performance (Hater & Bass, 1988), group level financial performance (Barling et al., 1996; Howell & Avolio, 1993), and project performance (Keller, 1992). Adding external validity to these findings, shop stewards' transformational leadership is associated with their rank-and-file members' commitment to and participation in the union (Fullagar, McCoy, & Schull, 1992; Kelloway & Barling, 1993).

In contrast to transformational leadership, passive leadership is generally considered to be ineffective. For instance, Howell and Avolio (1993) reported that passive management by exception is negatively related to business unit performance, and laissez-faire leadership is generally accounted to be the least effective style (Bass & Avolio, 1994). Perhaps most important, there are both conceptual and empirical grounds on which to suggest that passive leadership (a) is distinct from and (b) has negative effects beyond those attributable to a lack of transformational leadership skills.

Several existing studies support the distinction between transformational and passive leadership (e.g., Bycio et al., 1995). Bass (1985) distinguished "active" and "passive" leadership as separate higher-order factors underlying his leadership measure. Researchers have since investigated this distinction, often combining Bass and Avolio's (1990) management-by-exception/passive and laissez-faire dimensions into a single higher-order passive leadership dimension (e.g., Den Hartog, Van Muijen, & Koopman, 1997). In general, these studies have supported the usefulness of this distinction. For instance, Garman, Davis-Lenane, and Corrigan (2003) found that management by exception (passive), although positively correlated with the laissez-faire style, is negatively correlated with transformational leadership. Similarly, they reported that active and passive management by exception are independent constructs, thereby furthering the empirical support for the distinction between active and passive leadership.

It is generally accepted that passive leadership correlates negatively, and transformational leadership positively, with numerous organizational outcomes (Den Hartog et al., 1997; Howell & Avolio, 1993). However, although the laissez-faire or management-by-exception (passive) styles are regarded as ineffective approaches to leadership (Bass & Avolio, 1994), few studies have considered the extent of the impact that these styles have on negative organizational consequences (for an exception see Zohar, 2002). Rather, the existing research has focused on the positive organizational impact of more active forms of leadership.

Perhaps because of the consistency of these findings, it has become common to speak of "transformational" leaders as a category; that is, a leader is considered to be transformational or not. Although positive effects are obtained when one is a transformational leader, the presumption is that the absence of transformational leadership simply results in the absence of these positive effects. In contrast, we suggest that passive leadership may create negative effects that go beyond those attributable to a lack of transformational leadership skills.

First, we note that transformational leadership is not a category, and it is incorrect to hold that there are transformational and nontransformational leaders. Interestingly, it is possible for elements of transformational and passive leadership to be present in a single individual. That is, leaders are not differentiated by whether or not they are transformational leaders but rather on the frequency with which they demonstrate various transformational and passive behaviors (Bass, 1985). The Multifactor Leadership Questionnaire (MLQ), the most common measure of leader behavior, assesses the frequency of transformational and passive leadership actions. An implication of this approach to measurement is that the labels "transformational" and "passive" leadership actually represent the degree to which an individual engages in various actions (Bass, 1985; Bass & Avolio, 1990). They do not reflect separate categories of leadership. The implications of this relationship have been largely overlooked in the existing leadership literature.

In a recent study, Kelloway, Mullen, and Francis (2004) examined the impact of transformational and passive safety leadership on safety outcomes. Replicating Barling, Loughlin, and Kelloway's (2002) earlier analysis, they found that transformational leadership was positively associated with safety outcomes. Passive safety leadership, however, was empirically distinct from both transformational leadership and negatively predicted safety outcomes. Moreover, passive leadership offered an incremental prediction of outcome variance (i.e., over and above that attributable to transformational leadership). Kelloway et al. (2004) suggested that passive leadership may explain variance beyond that attributable to transformational leadership for other leadership-related outcomes. One such outcome is employee stress.

Thus, both abusive and passive leadership are exemplars of poor leadership that are plausibly linked to employee stress. One remaining question concerns the mechanisms that sustain this link. That is, how is leadership related to employee stress? We now turn our analysis to this question.

Leadership as a Root Cause

Models of job stress typically begin by distinguishing between the stressor (i.e., the objective source of stress; Pratt & Barling, 1988) and stress or strain (i.e., employee reactions to the stressor). Within this context, models of how individual well-being is affected by workplace conditions have focused on establishing relationships between job characteristics/stressors and either mental (e.g., Kelloway & Barling, 1991) or physiological (e.g., Barling & Kelloway, 1996) health. Theorists and researchers have proposed a variety of mechanisms to explain how these associations occur. Models vary in their "breadth" (i.e., the number of organizational conditions considered) as well as the functional relationships specified between stressors and outcomes.

Although models vary considerably, what they share in common is that they take as a starting point the specification of a list of environmental conditions, labeled stressors. For example, Karasek's (1979; Karasek & Theorell, 1990) demand-control-support model is perhaps the best known of all models relating job characteristics to well-being. In brief, the demand-control-support model is based on two hypotheses relating to the main effects and interactions of the constituent variables. That is, the model proposes the following:

1. High demands, lack of control, and lack of social support predict strain outcomes.

2. Demands, control, and support interact to predict strain (such that high control and high social support buffer the effects of demands on strain outcomes).

Warr (1987) identified a broader array of environmental conditions as a source of workplace stress than Karasek's demand-support-control model. Warr's vitamin model listed nine environmental conditions as sources of stress in the workplace: the opportunity for control, the opportunity for skill use, externally generated goals, task variety, environmental clarity, the availability of money, physical security (freedom from physical threat or danger), the opportunity for interpersonal contact, and valued social position.

Both models, and indeed most models of workplace stress, take as their starting point the existence of job stressors. In considering the potential for poor leadership to affect workplace stress, we suggest that poor leadership might be a root cause of workplace stressors. That is, the presence, absence, or intensity of particular stressors may be determined by the quality of leadership in the workplace. To evaluate how leadership might act as a root cause, we consider the National Institute for Occupational Safety and Health (NIOSH) model of workplace stress (Sauter, Murphy, & Hurrell, 1990). We focus on the NIOSH model because it is a simple taxonomy of workplace stressors based on extensive review of the empirical literature. Using this model as a framework, we consider how leadership might play a role in creating workplace stress. The workplace stressors identified in the NIOSH model are outlined in the sections that follow. In each case, we consider how leaders may affect the prevalence and impact of the stressor in the workplace.

Workload and Work Pace

The experience of being overworked is not new, and, if anything, some would suggest that it is increasing within particular sectors (Cartwright & Cooper, 1997). The strains associated with being overworked have been found to be uniformly negative across behavioral, psychological, and physiological outcome domains (e.g., Jex & Beehr, 1991). Measures of role overload are empirically linked to assessments of both context-free (e.g., Kelloway & Barling, 1991) and context-specific mental health (see, for example, Frone, Russell, & Cooper, 1992; Posig & Kickul, 2003). Issues of workload and work pace become increasingly important in an environment in which hours of work are increasing. The data suggest that working couples have seen their average work year increase by nearly 700 hours in the past two decades and that up to 30% of the workforce is exhausted by the end of the workday (NIOSH, 2002).

Organizational leadership is clearly linked to workload and pace in most organizations. By establishing the pace of work and the amount of work that is required, and by specifying deadlines, organizational leaders effectively establish workloads and work pace for most individuals. Thus, when leaders set tight deadlines or assign extra tasks without considering existing workloads, they become a source of workplace stress through the experience of overload. To the extent that passive leaders are unaware of the concerns of their employees, they may be less attuned to the amount of work that their employees can reasonably manage and thus endorse a heavy workload or unmanageable work pace. Similarly, abusive leaders who in their actions display little concern for the welfare of their employees may also be more likely to set unreasonable deadlines and workloads than highly effective leaders.

Role Stressors (Conflict, Ambiguity, and Interrole Conflict)

Role conflict exists whenever individuals face incompatible demands from two or more sources. Role ambiguity reflects the uncertainty employees experience about what is expected of them in their jobs; the opposite of role ambiguity would be role clarity. Interrole conflict exists when employees face incompatible demands from two or more roles. The most common form of interrole conflict is work-family conflict in which the demands of work conflict with the roles of parent or spouse. Kelloway and Barling (1991) found that the experience of role stressors at work predicted mental health in the workplace. Considerable research has also now emerged documenting the stressors associated with interrole conflict and, more specifically, work-family conflict (see, for example, Kelloway, Gottlieb, & Barham, 1999; Gignac, Kelloway, & Gottlieb, 1996; Gottlieb, Kelloway, & Martin-Matthews, 1996).

Because organizational leaders are tasked with establishing the expectations for employees, they are a potent source of role expectations for individuals in organizations. Thus, supervisors who fail to establish clear expectations or who promote conflicting goals actively promote increased role stress. Supervisors who establish expectations for long hours in the office may promote work-family conflict. Researchers have long believed managers play a key role in the presence of role ambiguity. Certainly, passive leaders may neither take the time to assure that their employees have clear role descriptions nor even realize that their employees are experiencing any type of role conflict. In many instances, however, researchers have argued that role ambiguity is the variable that might be most readily influenced by managers. Singh and Rhoads (1991) have argued that role ambiguity is most susceptible to managerial intervention in attempts to reduce stress in the workplace.

With respect to abusive leadership, research by Monat, Averill, and Lazarus (1972) suggests that a hostile situation is even more stressful if one does not know when exactly it will occur (i.e., role ambiguity). Temporal uncertainty is yet another avenue by which abusive leaders affect the stress levels of those they lead. Temporal uncertainty refers to an individual's inability to know when a given event or action is likely to occur. Within the context of this discussion, temporal uncertainty refers to the unpredictability of the leader's behavior. This suggests that abusive bosses who have bursts of aggression not only have a direct psychological impact on individuals but also produce a chronic state of stress in workers as workers find themselves always needing to be on guard, not knowing when another outburst will be directed their way. As highlighted by the example at the start of this chapter, the worker is not shocked by his or her boss's escalation in anger but by the unpredictability of the boss's actions during his state of chaos (i.e., throwing a coffee pot out the window).

Career Concerns

Career-related factors such as job insecurity, fear of job obsolescence, under- and overpromotion, and, more generally, concerns about career development have been identified as stressful. For example, in their study of South African miners, Barling and Kelloway (1996) found that job insecurity was associated with both negative affective reactions and raised blood pressure. The importance of job insecurity as a stressor in the workplace is highlighted by observations that the temporary or contingent labor force is rapidly increasing and that job tenure has declined for many workers (NIOSH, 2002).

Recently, the development of the effort-reward imbalance model has focused research attention on the role of organizational rewards as a psychosocial stressor. Siegrist (1996) proposed the effort-reward imbalance model that essentially suggests that strain results when rewards are not consistent with efforts in work environments. In this view, efforts are described as the strivings of the individual to meet the demands and obligations of the job. Rewards are conceptualized as encompassing financial rewards, esteem rewards, and career rewards, including job security. Similar to its intellectual forebearer, equity theory (Adams, 1965), the effort-reward imbalance theory is based on the notion that individuals attempt to maintain a state of equilibrium and cannot maintain an imbalance between effort and rewards over an extended period of time. Siegrist does, however, involve an individual variable (i.e., overcommitment) to explain potential discrepancies. That is, individuals who are overcommitted to their work may maintain a high-effort, low-reward environment. Eventually, however, this condition will result in ill health (Siegriest, 1996). Initial results using cardiovascular risk as the outcome generally support the model propositions (Peter & Siegrist, 1999). The relative recency of the effort-reward imbalance theory has resulted in a lack of formal evaluation of the theory, although these initial results seem promising.

Organizational leaders are, of course, the primary gatekeepers of organizational reward structures. Indeed the legitimate power (e.g., French & Raven, 1959) of supervisors is closely linked to reward power. Managers have the power to reward subordinates (Yukl & Falbe, 1991) or, alternatively, to deny such rewards. For example, bonuses, merit pay, and career decisions are frequently based on annual performance reviews conducted by organizational leaders (Murphy & Cleveland, 1995; Milliman, Nason, Zhu, & De Cieri, 2002). The empirical data suggest that such ratings are often a function of whether or not supervisors like their subordinates (Lefkowitz, 2000). For example, Scullen, Mount, & Goff (2000) found that over 50% of the variance in performance ratings was attributable to idiosyncratic rating errors—more than twice as much as was attributable to true variation in employee performance.

Work Scheduling

Working rotating shifts or permanent night work results in a disruption of physiological circadian rhythms as well as disrupted social activities and has been identified as a work-related stressor. For example, employees who work nights or overtime report that this affects their mental and physical health outcomes (Ettner & Grzywacz, 2001), and there is a great deal of literature on how to schedule shifts so as to minimize these effects (e.g., Tucker, MacDonald, Folkard, & Smith, 1998). These effects are sufficiently well established to provide the basis for labor law in the European Union that regulates the scheduling of shifts and rest days (International Labour Office, 1988, 1990). On a more macro scale, researchers have examined the effect of scheduling of vacation time (Westman & Eden, 1997) on well-being. Related to issues of workload and pace, there has been concern expressed about the absolute number of hours required of some employees, particularly trainees and interns who may be required to work excessively long hours during the course of their training (e.g., Bartle & Rodolfa, 1999).

Again, in many organizations, shift schedules are drawn up by those in organizational leadership roles, and supervisors can create or minimize stress by adjusting how they schedule shifts. Decisions as to when to require over-time or who is required to work overtime are also frequently left to managers and supervisors. To that extent, individuals who report to passive or abusive leaders may not receive optimal work scheduling options, as these leaders are likely less aware of or concerned about the importance of work scheduling for the well-being of individual employees.

Interpersonal Relations

Poor interpersonal relations in the workplace are consistently identified as a source of stress. Conversely, having well-established sources of social support (i.e., receiving support from coworkers and supervisors) may actually reduce the effects of other workplace stressors (House, 1981). As we previously reviewed, leaders who are abusive, aggressive, or punitive are a clear source of stress for individuals in the workplace. However, such behaviors by a supervisor may also lead to individuals becoming isolated or rejected by the work group. That is, in order to win favor with, or avoid being a victim of, an abusive supervisor, coworkers may harass, exclude, or engage in "mobbing" (Schuster, 1996) coworkers.

Supervisors may also affect well-being through their impact on interactional injustice. Interactional injustice refers to the perceptions of low-quality interpersonal treatment experienced by individuals within a work environment (Bies, 2001). A sample of behaviors exhibited by a supervisor that could be perceived as interactional injustice may include not paying attention to subordinates' concerns, not displaying any empathy for an employee's quandary, not treating employees in a fair manner, betraying confidences, and not interacting with employees in a civil manner. These examples are by no means exhaustive but are examples of forms of injustice that share the common thread of being interpersonal in nature and at the dyadic level. Although the other two forms of injustice (procedural and distributive) have received more empirical scrutiny, Mikula, Petrik, and Tanzer (1990) report findings that a large portion of perceived injustices concern the manner in which people were treated interpersonally rather than the procedural or distributive elements in a job.

Organizational scholars have empirically linked justice evaluations to a host of organizational outcomes such as organizational citizenship (Skarlicki & Latham, 1996), job satisfaction (Parker, Baltes, & Christiansen, 1997), and retaliation (Skarlicki, Folger, & Tesluk, 1999). However, research into the relationship between interactional justice and employee health variables is lacking (Elovainio, Kivimaki, & Helkama, 2001). Articles do exist, however, that link these two variables through indirect mechanisms. Thus, drawing on this thin literature, we reason supervisor interactional injustice to have negative impact on employee stress. More specifically, we propose that abusive supervisors through unjust interactions negatively affect employees' pride and self-esteem, which serially affects the level of stress they encounter at work.

Subordinates who experience interactional justice come to trust and respect their leaders. We argue that this, in turn, is likely to result in high-quality relationships with their supervisors, which will have positive effects on employees' psychological well-being and performance on the job. A meta-analysis exploring this proposition found high-quality relationships between supervisor and follower to be positively correlated to job performance, satisfaction with supervision, overall satisfaction, commitment, lack of role conflict, and low turnover intentions (Gerstner & Day, 1997). Conversely, when passive or abusive supervisors behave in an unjust manner, employees may deem these interactional injustices to be a breach of the psychological contract. These employees, in turn, are more likely to feel stress and anger and be moved to retaliate (see Rousseau, 1995).

Job Content and Control

As phrased by Sauter et al. (1990, p. 1153), "narrow, fragmented, invariant and short-cycle tasks that provide little stimulation, allow little use of skills or expression of creativity and have little intrinsic meaning for workers" are considered as stress provokers in the NIOSH content model of workplace stressors. There is now substantial evidence that job characteristics such as skill use, skill variety, and autonomy are associated with both motivation and individual mental health (Fried & Ferris, 1987; Hackman & Oldham, 1980; Kelloway & Barling, 1991; Parker & Wall, 1998). Because organizational leaders are responsible for job design and task assignment, they have the potential to influence the content of jobs. Perhaps most significantly, supervisors and managers directly affect the amount of control experienced by employees.

The notion that personal control is beneficial to psychological and physiological well-being is not new. Organizational scholars have confirmed repeatedly the convincing relationship between job control and health and lack of job control and ill health (e.g., Bosma, Stransfeld, & Marmot, 1998; Shirom, Melamed, & Nir-Dotan, 2000; Tetrick, Slack, DaSilva, & Sinclair, 2000).

Control, autonomy, and decision latitude are increasingly referred to, often interchangeably, as organizational practices that promote job performance. Within research circles, control has long been regarded as a critical element in job redesign research to promote performance (Hackman & Oldham, 1980) and worker mental health (Wall & Clegg, 1981). Not surprisingly, the role of job control in stress-strain process has been receiving increased investigation. The primary impetus for this line of research has largely been a result of Karasek's (1979) demand-control-support model. Karasek and Theorell (1990) argue that a healthy workplace is one where the worker's level of demand on the job is met with appropriate levels of control, promoting growth and development on the job. Conversely, a job in which demands are high and control is low is posited to result in job strain and burnout. Empirical findings, however, have not supported a moderating pattern between job control and employee health (Pomaki & Maes, 2002). Nonetheless, increasing empirical evidence accumulates in the literature on the importance of job control in promoting well-being (see Karasek & Theorell, 1990).

Although certain organizational level policies restrain the amount of control one has on the job (Thomas & Ganster, 1995), following Karasek and Theorell's (1990) model, we argue that an employee's immediate supervisor, given behavioral and psychological proximity to his or her followers, has a vast influence on an employee's perceived level of job control. Given that passive leaders either avoid the responsibilities of their position or only step in during crisis situations, it is unlikely that they will take the necessary time to engage in a stress prevention strategy such as attempting to positively influence an employee's perception of control. With respect to abusive supervisors who occupy an immediate leadership role, we suggest that their unique position may enable them to significantly limit employees' job control across two areas—*environmental control* and *perceived control*.

Environmental control refers to the measure of alternatives the employee is given by the supervisor, the organization, or the immediate work environment (Spector, 1998). In most instances, the specified amount of control remains at the discretion of the employee's immediate supervisor. For instance, Johansson, Aronsson, and Lindstrom (1978) found that jobs that taxed employees' cognitive ability while giving employees little control of the pace of work (machine controlled) resulted in increased health disorders, job strain, and job dissatisfaction. Abusive leaders exert tight control over their environment (Offermann & Hellmann, 1996), and by controlling their environment, they are able to control the people within it. It is this control these types of leaders mobilize in abusing their power. Environments in which leaders are granted the power to control work demands present an ideal situation for abusive supervisors to exercise their power. Perceived control is a measure of the alternatives individuals believe they have (Spector, 1998). It is possible, even with control, for the individual to perceive the situation to be out of control. For instance, Steers and Rhodes (1978) have shown a small degree of absenteeism to be healthy for an organization as it allowed employees to temporarily escape the stressful conditions. Many organizations subscribe to this notion and have set policies that allow employees to be absent from work when they feel it is needed, for example, for family or personal responsibilities. Nonetheless, individuals may not trust management (Kramer, 1999) enough to exercise their control, instead fearing that they might be disciplined or punished. In a relationship that is already characterized by power and status differences, employees who have to deal with abusive supervisors may, out of distrust or fear, choose not to approach them.

In addition, individuals may also feel low job control when they lack self-efficacy. Self-efficacy (a form of perceived control) refers to a person's conviction that he or she can accomplish a certain task successfully (Bandura, 1997). Given the ability to change the pace of work, work environment, or resources, an individual with low self-efficacy will likely feel incapable of accomplishing the work. This problem is compounded when this same individual reports to an abusive or passive supervisor. Given that an individual's self-efficacy can be influenced by words and actions directed at the individual (Bandura, 1997), verbally abusive supervisors who constantly put down their workers are most likely to have an adverse effect on their employees' self-efficacy. Passive leaders, relative to transformational leaders, are often out of touch with the needs of their employees. To that extent, they will be less likely to engage in encouraging conversations and provide the type of positive feedback that may elevate an employee's self-esteem. In either case, when employees are faced with a job-related setback and must take control, their run-down self-efficacy will make this an arduous task.

Parkes, Mendham, and von Rabenau (1994) found that a job that entails high demands but low control prompts ill health in employees only when support is low. This suggests that in jobs where there is an inherently high level of demands and low control and in jobs where supervisors have little influence on job demands or control, the amount of support extended by the supervisor to the employees has the potential to help cushion the psychological and physiological impact of the work environment. Thus, it is not hard to imagine an unskilled leader in this situation (a) failing to recognize employees' struggle in coping with a high-demand, low-control job, and consequently (b) failing to extend the necessary support for the employees in such jobs. Drawing on past research (Tepper, 2000), it is also conceivable that abusive supervisors, recognizing employees' struggle with the work conditions, intentionally withdraw support for their employees as a form of passive aggression toward them (Neuman & Baron, 1998).

Lack of Supervisor Social Support

A plethora of studies have repeatedly illustrated that individuals who have a network of family and friends for psychological or material support show evidence of greater physical and psychological well-being than those who lack this network (Gottleib, 1981). Moreover, social support has been established to be a causal agent in the well-being of individuals (House, 1981). Although the importance of social support has been established in the literature, the process by which it influences psychological well-being remains to be clarified. One proposition argues that social support "buffers" individuals from the damaging effects of stress. Thus, the ability to rely on social resources helps individuals gird themselves for life's stressful events (Cohen & McKay, 1984). The alternate proposition argues that irrespective of stressful events, a rich social support network provides individuals with regular positive interactions, stability, and relational rewards. These positive experiences collectively help individuals avoid many of the negative experiences that could result in increased stress (Wills, 1985). Review of the literature suggests that both models are accurate in varying degrees (Cohen & Wills, 1985).

Similar interpersonal relational networks that individuals rely on for social support are also evident within a work arena. The social relationships that occur within a workplace have far-reaching impact on the individual's mental and physical well-being. For many, the importance of this social support is not appreciated until retirement. The findings of Bosse, Aldwin, Levenson, Workman-Daniels, & Ekerdt (1990) suggest that for many workers the most meaningful friendships they look to for social support are those formed at work; and the importance of workplace-based social support extends into periods of unemployment (Jackson, 1986). Not surprisingly, an abundance of empirical studies have highlighted the importance of social support within a work environment (Armeli, Eisenberger, Fasolo, & Lynch, 1998; Dignam, Barrera, & West, 1986; Dormann & Zapf, 2002). Although the evidence for a low degree of social support having a direct effect on stress is more convincing within an organizational context than that of a buffering effect of a high degree of support, a leader's social support (or the lack thereof) will have both a direct and indirect effect on followers. The assumption that leaders exert both direct and indirect effects seems reasonable given the meta-analysis findings by Viswesvaran, Sanchez, and Fisher (1999) that suggest social support has both a direct and an indirect effect on the stressor-strain relationship.

Although we acknowledge the continuing discourse among researchers on what exactly constitutes "social support" (Payne & Jones, 1987), given the short length of this chapter and our focus on leadership, we use one frequent definition of social support in explaining how leaders extend social support to their followers. Using House's (1981) classification, we argue that leaders have the responsibility for providing instrumental support (task-specific help), emotional support (empathy, affect, and comfort), informational support (awareness, advice, and directives), and appraisal support (feedback, suggestions, and encouragement). Abusive leaders not only fail to provide social support to buffer stressful conditions but neglect to provide the bare amount of support that followers desire to function without stress. For example, an abusive leader may fail to help an overworked follower by reducing the task load (instrumental support). Similarly, this same leader may fail to provide much needed empathy for an employee coping with bereavement (emotional support), fail to provide the necessary safety directives to carry out tasks in a safe manner (informational support), and fail to motivate and engage followers in their jobs (appraisal support). Passive leaders are also unlikely to provide adequate social support for their employees. Given that they avoid the responsibilities of their role until serious issues come to their attention, it is conceivable that they will often be unaware that their employees need social support, be it emotional, informational, instrumental, or appraisal in nature. For instance, consider the case of a passive supervisor who does not provide instrumental help to an overworked employee because that leader is not paying attention to the demands in the workplace. This lack of social support, either individually or collectively, has far-reaching effects on the levels of employee stress.

Cummings (1990) provided early evidence of the importance of supervisory social support. Examining employed graduate and undergraduate students, Cummings (1990) found that supervisory social support buffered the effects of occupational stress and its effects on job dissatisfaction. This effect was even more pronounced in supervisor-employee relationships in which the employee valued the relationship. Extending this further, accumulating evidence suggests that supervisor social support is potentially most vital in occupations that are inherently stressful. Karlin, Brondolo, and Schwartz (2003) studied New York City traffic enforcement agents, individuals who have the stressful job of issuing parking violations to motorists, who often greet agents with insults and threats. In such a stress-provoking job, the study found that immediate supervisor support to be negatively correlated with systolic blood pressure.

Additionally, and also discouraging to workers, abusive leaders pose a double threat to employee stress. Barling, Bluen, and Fain's (1987) findings suggest that the support extended to employees is most effective when the source of support originates from within the same realm as the stressor. Barling and colleagues found social support from immediate supervisors to be more effective than family support following an acute disaster. That is, if the source of stressor is the work environment, supervisors are in a favorable position to have the largest positive impact on this stressor through their supervisory social support. However, support received from a supervisor may not be beneficial when the supervisor is perceived to be the source of the stress (e.g., MacEwen & Barling, 1988), and the presence of abusive supervision or tyrannical leadership may thus be expected to exert significant negative effects on employee well-being.

Thus, with longer working hours, shorter contracts, and a culture of downsizing (Tetrick & Barling, 1995) all adding to job-related stress, the need for efficient leaders who can afford their followers the necessary social support to confront their work environments is critical.

Epilogue

Consistent evidence has now accumulated on the weight of key variables in the promotion of employee stress. Interpersonal relations, job scheduling, job control and content, lack of supervisor social support, career concerns, workload and pace, and role stressors magnify the presence or degree of stress among workers (Sauter et al., 1990). Leaders in their central roles are granted the power to influence all these variables. This power and resulting influence on employees is often underestimated by leaders (Offermann & Hellmann, 1996) and has often resulted in detrimental effects on employee well-being. The management of employees and their well-being is more crucial in our workplace since 9/11 (Dutton, Frost, Worline, Lilius, & Kanov, 2002; Frost, 2003).

In this chapter, we have outlined the ways in which poor leadership is related to workplace stress. In doing so, we first engaged in a discussion of what constitutes poor leadership. In particular, we concluded that leaders who are passive or abusive may have a negative impact on the health and well-being of their employees. Abusive leaders are those who act in an overly punitive or aggressive manner. Passive leaders are those individuals who do not demonstrate the necessary abilities for a leadership role and often fail to live up to their responsibilities. We suggest that poor leaders contribute to the experience of stress among their employees in two main ways. First, poor leadership by itself is likely a source of stress for the individuals who report to them. Additionally, poor leaders are likely to create a work environment that is rife with other work stressors such as lack of control and heavy workloads. Taken together, these points suggest that leadership has a pervasive effect on stress and well-being in the workplace.

In light of the direct connections we have drawn between the qualities of organizational leaders and the prevalence of stressors in the workplace, we encourage both researchers and practitioners to explore more fully the nature of the relationship between leadership and stress. Clearly, leaders influence the amount of stress that employees experience. Given that stress is a pervasive and expensive organizational problem, with some estimates suggesting that employee stress costs organizations $150 billion per year, we encourage a program of work that investigates leadership training as a primary stress-prevention strategy. For example, research suggests individuals can be successfully trained in transformational leadership (Barling et al., 1996). If individuals can acquire more active and appropriate leadership behaviors, we suggest that employee stress will be lessened and employee well-being improved.

References

Adams, J. S. (1965). Inequity in social exchange. In L. Berkowitz (Ed.), *Advances in experimental social psychology* (Vol. 2, pp. 267–299). New York: Academic.

Armeli, S., Eisenberger, R., Fasolo, P., & Lynch, P. (1998). Perceived organizational support and police performance: The moderating influence of socioemotional needs. *Journal of Applied Psychology, 83*(2), 288–297.

Ashforth, B. (1997). Petty tyranny in organizations: A preliminary examination of antecedents and consequences. *Canadian Journal of Administrative Sciences, 14*, 1173–1182.

Atwater, L. E., Dionne, S. D., Camobreco, J. F., Avolio, B. J., & Lau, A. (1998). Individual attributes and leadership style: Predicting the use of punishment and its effects. *Journal of Organizational Behavior, 19, 559–576*.

Bandura, A. (1997). *Self-efficacy: The exercise of control*. New York: W. H. Freeman.

Barling, J., Bluen, S. D., & Fain, R. (1987). Psychological functioning following an acute disaster. *Journal of Applied Psychology, 72, 683–690*.

Barling, J., & Kelloway, E. K. (1996). Job insecurity and health: The moderating role of workplace control. *Stress Medicine, 12, 253–260*.

Barling, J., Loughlin, C., & Kelloway, E. K. (2002). Development and test of a model linking safety-specific transformational leadership and occupational safety. *Journal of Applied Psychology, 87, 488–496*.

Barling, J., Rogers, A. G., & Kelloway, E. K. (2001). Behind closed doors: In-home workers' experience of sexual harassment and workplace violence. *Journal of Occupational Health Psychology, 6, 255–269*.

Barling, J., Weber, T., & Kelloway, E. K. (1996). Effects of transformational leadership training on attitudinal and financial outcomes: A field experiment. *Journal of Applied Psychology, 81, 827–832*.

Bartle, D. D., & Rodolfa, E. R. (1999). Internship hours: Proposing a national standard. *Professional Psychology: Research and Practice, 30, 420–422*.

Bass, B. M. (1985). *Leadership and performance beyond expectations*. New York: Free Press.

Bass, B. M. (1990). From transactional to transformational leadership: Learning to share the vision. *Organizational Dynamics, 18*(3), 19–31.

Bass, B. M., & Avolio, B. J. (1990). *Transformational leadership development: Manual for the Multifactor Leadership Questionnaire*. Palo Alto, CA: Consulting Psychologists Press.

Bass, B. M., & Avolio, B. J. (1994). *Improving organizational effectiveness through transformational leadership*. Thousand Oaks, CA: Sage.

Bass, B. M., & Avolio, B. J. (1997). *Full range leadership development: Manual for the Multifactor Leadership Questionnaire*. Palo Alto, CA: Mind Garden.

Bies, R. J. (2001). Interactional (in)justice: The sacred and the profane. In J. Greenberg & R. Cropanzano (Eds.), *Advances in organizational justice* (pp. 89–118). Palo Alto, CA: Stanford University Press.

Bosma, H., Stansfeld, S. A., & Marmot, M. G. (1998). Job control, personal characteristics, and heart disease. *Journal of Occupational Health Psychology, 3, 402–409*.

Bosse, R., Aldwin, C. M., Levenson, M. R., Workman-Daniels, K., & Ekerdt, D. (1990). Differences in social support among retirees and workers: Findings from the normative aging study. *Psychology and Aging, 5, 41–47*.

British Broadcasting Company (BBC). (2003, June 23). Unfair bosses raise blood pressure. Retrieved June 2003 from http://news.bbc.co.uk/1/hi/ health/3012546.stm

Bycio, P., Hackett, R. D., & Allen, S. J. (1995). Further assessment of Bass' (1985) conceptualization of transactional and transformational leadership. *Journal of Applied Psychology, 80, 468–478*.

Cartwright, S., & Cooper, C. L. (1997). *Managing workplace stress*. Thousand Oaks, CA: Sage.

Cohen, S., & McKay, G. (1984). Social support, stress and the buffering hypothesis: A theoretical analysis. In A. Baum, J. E. Singer, & S. E. Taylor (Eds.), *Handbook of psychology and health* (Vol. 4, pp. 253–267). Hillsdale, NJ: Lawrence Erlbaum.

Cohen, S., & Wills, T. A. (1985). Stress, social support, and buffering hypothesis. *Psychological Bulletin, 98,* 310–357.

Cummings, R. C. (1990). Job stress and the buffering effect of supervisory support. *Group and Organizational Studies, 15,* 92–104.

Day, R. C., & Hamblin, R. L. (1964). Some effects of close and punitive styles of supervision. *American Journal of Sociology, 69,* 499–510.

Dekker, I., & Barling, J. (1998). Personal and organizational predictors of workplace sexual harassment of women by men. *Journal of Occupational Health Psychology, 3,* 7–18.

Den Hartog, D. N., Van Muijen, J. J., & Koopman, P. (1997). Transactional versus transformational leadership: An analysis of the MLQ. *Journal of Occupational and Organizational Psychology, 70,* 19–34.

Dignam, J. T., Barrera, M., & West, S. G. (1986). Occupational stress, social support, and burnout among correctional officers. *American Journal of Community Psychology, 14*(2), 177–193.

Dormann, C., & Zapf, D. (2002). Social stressors at work, irritation, and depressive symptoms: Accounting for unmeasured third variables in a multi-wave study. *Journal of Occupational and Organizational Psychology, 75*(1), 33–58.

Dupre, K., Inness, M., Connelly, C., Barling, J., & Hoption, C. (2003). *Predicting teenagers' workplace aggression.* Manuscript submitted for publication.

Dutton, J. E., Frost, P. J., Worline, M. C., Lilius, J. M., & Kanov, J. M. (2002, January). Leadership in times of trauma. *Harvard Business Review,* 55–61.

Einarsen, S. (1999). The nature and causes of bullying at work. *International Journal of Manpower, 20,* 16–27.

Elovainio, M., Kivimaki, M., & Helkama, K. (2001). Organizational justice valuations, job control, and occupational strain. *Journal of Applied Psychology, 86,* 418–424.

Ettner, S. L., & Grzywacz, J. G. (2001). Workers' perceptions of how jobs affect health: A social ecological perspective. *Journal of Occupational Health Psychology, 6,* 101–113.

Fitzgerald, L. F., Drasgow, F., Hulin, C. L., Gelfand, M. J., & Magley, V. J. (1997). Antecedents and consequences of sexual harassment in organizations: A test of an integrated model. *Journal of Applied Psychology, 82,* 578–589.

French, J. R. P., & Raven, B. (1959). The bases of social power. In D. Cartwright (Ed.), *Studies in social power.* Ann Arbor, MI: Institute for Social Research.

Fried, Y., & Ferris, G. R. (1987). The validity of the job characteristics model: A review and meta-analysis. *Personnel Psychology, 40,* 287–322.

Frone, M. F., Russell, M., & Cooper, M. L. (1992). Antecedents and outcomes of work-family conflict: Testing a model of the work-family interface. *Journal of Applied Psychology, 77,* 65–78.

Frost, P. J. (2003). *Toxic emotions at work: How compassionate managers handle pain and conflict.* Cambridge, MA: Harvard Business School Press.

Fullagar, C., McCoy, D., & Schull, C. (1992). The socialization of union loyalty. *Journal of Organizational Behavior, 13,* 13–26.

Garman, A. N., Davis-Lenane, D., & Corrigan, P. W. (2003). Factor structure of the transformational leadership model in human service teams. *Journal of Organizational Behavior, 24,* 803–812.

Gerstner, C. R., & Day, D. V. (1997). Meta-analytic review of leader-member exchange theory: Correlates and construct issues. *Journal of Applied Psychology, 82*(6), 827–844.

Gignac, M. A., Kelloway, E. K., & Gottlieb, B. (1996). The impact of caregiving on employment: A mediational model of work-family conflict. *Canadian Journal of Aging, 15,* 514–524.

Gottleib, B. H. (Ed.). (1981). *Social networks and social support.* Beverly Hills, CA: Sage.

Gottlieb, B., Kelloway, E. K., & Martin-Matthews, A. (1996). Predictors of work-family conflict, stress, and job satisfaction among nurses. *Canadian Journal of Nursing Research, 28,* 99–118.

Hackman, J. R., & Oldham, G. R. (1980). *Work redesign.* Reading, MA: Addison-Wesley.

Hater, J. J., & Bass, B. M. (1988). Superiors' evaluations and subordinates' perceptions of transformational and transactional leadership. *Journal of Applied Psychology, 73,* 695–702.

Hoel, H., Rayner, C., & Cooper, C. L. (1999). Workplace bullying. In C. L. Cooper & I. T. Robertson (Eds.), *International review of industrial and organizational psychology* (Vol. 14). Chichester, UK: Wiley.

House, J. S. (1981). *Work stress and social support.* Reading, MA: Addison-Wesley.

Howell, J. M., & Avolio, B. J. (1993). Transformational leadership, transactional leadership, locus of control and support for innovation: Key predictors of consolidated business-unit performance. *Journal of Applied Psychology, 78,* 891–902.

Howell, J. M., & Frost, P. J. (1989). A laboratory study of charismatic leadership. *Organizational Behavior and Human Decision Processes, 43,* 243–269.

International Labour Office. (1988). Night work. *International Labour Conference 76th session, Geneva, Switzerland, Report 5*(1).

International Labour Office. (1990). Night work. *International Labour Conference 77th Session, Geneva, Switzerland, Report 4*(1).

Jackson, P. R. (1986). Personal networks, support mobilisation and unemployment. *Psychosomatic Medicine, 18,* 397–404.

Jex, S. M., & Beehr, T. A. (1991). Emerging theoretical and methodological issues in the study of work-related stress. In K. M. Rowland & G. R. Ferris (Eds.), *Research in personnel and human resources management* (Vol. 9, pp. 311–365). Greenwich, CT: JAI Press.

Johansson, G., Aronsson, G., & Lindstrom, B. O. (1978). Social psychological and neuroendocrine stress reactions in highly mechanized work. *Ergonomics, 21,* 583–599.

Karasek, R. A. (1979). Job demands, jobs decision latitude, and mental strain: Implications for job redesign. *Administrative Science Quarterly, 24,* 258–308.

Karasek, R., & Theorell, T. (1990). *Healthy work: Stress, productivity and the reconstruction of working life.* New York: Basic Books.

Karlin, W. A., Brondolo, E., & Schwartz, J. (2003). Workplace social support and ambulatory cardiovascular activity in New York City traffic agents. *Psychosomatic Medicine, 65,* 167–176.

Keashly, L. (1998). Emotional abuse in the workplace: Conceptual and empirical issues. *Journal of Emotional Abuse, 1,* 85–115.

Keashly, L. (2001). Interpersonal and systemic aspects of emotional abuse at work: The target's perspective. *Violence and Victims, 16,* 233–268.

Keashly, L., Trott, V., & MacLean, L. M. (1994). Abusive behavior in the workplace: A preliminary investigation. *Violence and Victims, 9,* 341–357.

Keller, R. T. (1992). Transformational leadership and the performance of research and development project groups. *Journal of Management, 18,* 489–501.

Kelloway, E. K., & Barling, J. (1991). Job characteristics, role stress and mental health. *Journal of Occupational Psychology, 64,* 291–304.

Kelloway, E. K., & Barling, J. (1993). Members' participation in local union activities: Measurement, prediction and replication. *Journal of Applied Psychology, 78,* 262–279.

Kelloway, E. K., Gottlieb, B. H., & Barham, L. (1999). The source, nature, and direction of work and family conflict: A longitudinal investigation. *Journal of Occupational Health Psychology, 4,* 337–346.

Kelloway, E. K., Mullen, J., & Francis, L. (2004). *Divergent effects of transformational and passive leadership on employee safety.* Manuscript submitted for publication.

Kirkpatrick, S. A., & Locke, E. A. (1996). Direct and indirect effects of three core charismatic leadership components on performance and attitudes. *Journal of Applied Psychology, 81,* 36–51.

Kivimäki, M., Virtanen, M., Vartia, M., Elovainio, M., Vahtera, J., & Keltikangas-Järvinen, L. (2003). Workplace bullying and the risk of cardiovascular disease and depression. *Occupational and Environmental Medicine, 60,* 779–783.

Koh, W. L., Steers, R. M., & Terborg, J. R. (1995). The effects of transformational leadership on teacher attitudes and student performance in Singapore. *Journal of Organizational Behavior, 16,* 319–333.

Kramer, R. A. (1999). Trust and distrust in organizations: Emerging perspectives, enduring questions. *Annual Review of Psychology, 50,* 569–598.

LeBlanc, M. M., & Kelloway, E. K. (2002). Predictors and outcomes of workplace violence and aggression. *Journal of Applied Psychology, 87,* 444–453.

Lefkowitz, J. (2000). The role of interpersonal affective regard in supervisory performance ratings: A literature review and proposed causal model. *Journal of Occupational and Organizational Psychology, 73,* 67–85.

MacEwen, K. E., & Barling, J. (1988). Interrole conflict, family support and marital adjustment of employed mothers: A short-term, longitudinal study. *Journal of Organizational Behaviour, 9,* 241–250.

Mikula, G., Petrik, B., & Tanzer, N. (1990). What people regard as unjust: Types and structures of everyday experiences of injustice. *European Journal of Social Psychology, 20,* 133–149.

Milliman, J., Nason, S., Zhu, C., & De Cieri, H. (2002). An exploratory assessment of the purposes of performance appraisals in North and Central America and the Pacific Rim. *Human Resource Management, 41,* 87–102.

Monat, A., Averill, J. R., & Lazarus, R. S. (1972). Anticipatory stress and coping reactions under various conditions of uncertainty. *Journal of Personality and Social Psychology, 24,* 237–253.

Murphy, K. R., & Cleveland, J. N. (1995). *Understanding performance appraisal: Social, organizational, and goal-based perspectives.* Thousand Oaks, CA: Sage.

National Institute for Occupational Safety and Health (NIOSH). (2002). *The changing organization of work and the safety and health of working people: Knowledge gaps and research directions.* Cincinnati, OH: Author.

Neuman, J. H., & Baron, R. A. (1998). Workplace violence and workplace aggression: Evidence concerning specific forms, potential causes and preferred targets. *Journal of Management, 24,* 391–419.

Offermann, L. R., & Hellmann, P. S. (1996). Leadership behavior and subordinate stress: A 360° view. *Journal of Occupational Health Psychology, 1,* 382–390.

Parker, C. P., Baltes, B. B., & Christiansen, N. D. (1997). Support for affirmative action, justice perceptions, and work attitudes: A study of gender and racial-ethnic group differences. *Journal of Applied Psychology, 83,* 376–389.

Parker, S. K., & Wall, T. D. (1998). *Job and work design: Organizing work to promote well-being and effectiveness.* Thousand Oaks, CA: Sage.

Parkes, K. R., Mendham, C. A., & von Rabenau, C. (1994). Social support and the demand-discretion model of job stress: Tests of additive and interactive effects in two samples. *Journal of Vocational Behavior, 44,* 91–113.

Payne, R. L., & Jones, J. G. (1987). Measurement and methodological issues in social support. In S. V. Kasl & C. L. Cooper (Eds.), *Stress and health: Issues in research methodology* (pp. 167–205). New York: Wiley.

Peter, R., & Siegrist, J. (1999). Chronic psychosocial stress at work and cardiovascular disease: The role of effort-reward imbalance. *International Journal of Law and Psychiatry, 22,* 441–449.

Pizzino, A. (2002). Dealing with violence in the workplace: The experience of Canadian unions. In M. Gill, B. Fisher, & V. Bowie (Eds.), *Violence at work: Causes, patterns, and prevention* (pp. 165–179). Cullompton, UK: Willan.

Podsakoff, P. M., MacKenzie, S. B., & Bommer, W. H. (1996). Transformational leader behaviors and substitutes for leadership as determinants of employee satisfaction, commitment, trust and organizational citizenship behaviors. *Journal of Management, 22,* 259–298.

Pomaki, G., & Maes, S. (2002). Predicting quality of worklife: From work conditions to self-regulation. In E. Gullione & R. A. Cummins (Eds.), *The universality of subjective well-being indicators* (pp. 141–173). Dordrecht, The Netherlands: Kluwer Academic.

Posig, M., & Kickul, J. (2003). Extending our understanding of burnout: Test of an integrated model in nonservice occupations. *Journal of Occupational Health Psychology, 8,* 3–19.

Pratt, L. I., & Barling, J. (1988). Differentiating between daily events, acute and chronic stressors: A framework and its implications. In J. J. Hurrell, L. R. Murphy, S. L. Sauter, & C. L. Cooper (Eds.), *Occupational stress: Issues and developments in research.* London: Taylor & Francis.

Richman, J. A., Flaherty, J. A., Rospenda, K. M., & Christensen, M. (1992). Mental health consequences and correlates of medical student abuse. *Journal of the American Medical Association, 267,* 692–694.

Rogers, K., & Kelloway, E. K. (1997). Violence at work: Personal and organizational outcomes. *Journal of Occupational Health Psychology, 2,* 63–71.

Rospenda, K. M. (2002). Workplace harassment, services utilization, and drinking outcomes. *Journal of Occupational Health Psychology, 7,* 141–155.

Rousseau, D. M. (1995). *Promises in action: Psychological contracts in organizations.* Thousand Oaks, CA: Sage.

Sauter, S. L., Murphy, L. R., & Hurrell, J. J., Jr. (1990). Prevention of work-related psychological disorders: A national strategy proposed by the National Institute for Occupational Safety and Health (NIOSH). *American Psychologist, 45,* 1146–1158.

Schat, A. C. H., & Kelloway, E. K. (2000). The effects of perceived control on the outcomes of workplace aggression and violence. *Journal of Occupational Health Psychology, 4,* 386–402.

Schat, A. C. H., & Kelloway, E. K. (2003). Reducing the adverse consequences of workplace aggression and violence: The buffering effects of organizational support. *Journal of Occupational Health Psychology, 8,* 110–122.

Schuster, B. (1996). Rejection, exclusion, and harassment at work and in schools. *European Psychologist, 1*(4), 293–309.

Scullen, S. E., Mount, M. K., & Goff, M. (2000). Understanding the latent structure of job performance ratings. *Journal of Applied Psychology, 83,* 956–970.

Shirom, A., Melamed, S., & Nir-Dotan, M. (2000). The relationships among objective and subjective environmental stress levels and serum uric acid: The moderating effect of perceived control. *Journal of Occupational Health Psychology, 5,* 374–385.

Siegrist, J. (1996). Adverse health effects of high effort/low reward conditions. *Journal of Occupational Health Psychology, 1,* 27–41.

Singh, J., & Rhoads, G. K. (1991). Boundary role ambiguity in marketing oriented positions: A multidimensional, multifaceted operationalization. *Journal of Marketing Research, 28,* 328–338.

Skarlicki, D. P., Folger, R., & Tesluk, P. (1999). Personality as a moderator in the relationship between fairness and retaliation. *Academy of Management Journal, 42,* 100–108.

Skarlicki, D. P., & Latham, G. P. (1996). Increasing citizenship behavior within a labor union: A test of organizational justice theory. *Journal of Applied Psychology, 2,* 161–169.

Spector, P. E. (1998). A control theory of the job stress process. In C. L. Cooper (Ed.), *Theories of organizational stress.* New York: Oxford University Press.

Steers, R. M., & Rhodes, S. R. (1978). Major influences on employee attendance: A process model. *Journal of Applied Psychology, 63,* 391–407.

Tepper, B. J. (2000). Consequences of abusive supervision. *Academy of Management Journal, 43,* 178–190.

Tetrick, L. E., & Barling, J. (Eds.). (1995). *Changing employment relations: Behavioral and social perspectives.* Washington, DC: American Psychological Association.

Tetrick, L. E., Slack, K. J., DaSilva, N., & Sinclair, R. R. (2000). A comparison of the stress-strain process for business owners and nonowners: Differences in job demands, emotional exhaustion, satisfaction, and social support. *Journal of Occupational Health Psychology, 5,* 464–476.

Thomas, L. T., & Ganster, D. C. (1995). Impact of family-supportive work variables on work-family conflict and strain: A control perspective. *Journal of Applied Psychology, 80,* 6–15.

Totterdell, P., Spelten, E., Smith, L., Barton, J., & Folkard, S. (1995). Recovery from work shifts: How long does it take? *Journal of Applied Psychology, 80,* 43–57.

Townsend, J., Phillips, J. S., & Elkins, T. J. (2000). Employee retaliation: The neglected consequence of poor leader-member exchange relations. *Journal of Occupational Health Psychology, 5,* 457–463.

Tucker, P., MacDonald, I., Folkard, S., & Smith, L. (1998). The impact of early and late shift changeovers on sleep, health, and well-being in 8- and 12-hour shift systems. *Journal of Occupational Health Psychology, 3,* 265–275.

U.S. Postal Service (USPS) Commission on a Safe and Secure Workplace. (2000). *Report of the United States Postal Service Commission on a Safe and Secure Workplace.* New York: National Center on Addiction and Substance Abuse at Columbia University.

Viswesvaran, C., Sanchez, J. I., & Fisher, J. (1999). The role of social support in the process of stress: A meta-analysis. *Journal of Vocational Behavior, 54,* 314–334.

Wager, N., Fieldman, G., & Hussey, T. (2003). The effect on ambulatory blood pressure of working under favourably and unfavourably perceived supervisors. *Occupational and Environmental Medicine, 60,* 468–474.

Wall, T. D., & Clegg, C. W. (1981). A longitudinal field study of group work redesign. *Journal of Occupational Behaviour, 2,* 31–49.

Warr, P. B. (1987). *Work employment and mental health.* Oxford, UK: Oxford University Press.

Westman, M., & Eden, D. (1997). Effects of a respite from work on burnout: Vacation relief and fade-out. *Journal of Applied Psychology, 82,* 516–527.

Wills, T. A. (1985). Supportive functions of interpersonal relationships. In S. Cohen & S. L. Syne (Eds.), *Social support and health* (pp. 61–82). New York: Academic.

Yukl, G. (1998). *Leadership in organizations* (4th ed.). Upper Saddle River, NJ: Prentice Hall.

Yukl, G., & Falbe, C. M. (1991). Importance of different power sources in downward and lateral relations. *Journal of Applied Psychology, 76,* 416–423.

Zohar, D. (2002). The effects of leadership dimensions, safety climate, and assigned priorities on minor injuries in work groups. *Journal of Organizational Behavior, 23,* 75–92.

6

Work-Family Conflict

Gina M. Bellavia

Michael R. Frone

Although conflict between work and family life was undoubtedly a stressor for many people prior to 1970, sociologists have suggested that this issue began to generate substantial interest during recent decades, in large part because families in which all of the adults work for pay have become much more common (e.g., Bianchi & Raley, 2003; Jacobs & Gerson, 1998, 2001). In 1970, just 35.9% of all married couples made up of Americans aged 18 to 64 were composed of two earners, but this figure rose to 59.6% by the year 2000 (Jacobs, 2003). Additionally, the proportion of single-parent households increased from 11.1% in 1970 to 24.3% in 2000, and the proportion of single parents who were employed rose from 53.2% to 71.0% during the same period (Bianchi & Raley, 2003). Prior to these demographic changes, most families had a woman whose primary responsibility was domestic labor and a man whose primary responsibility was economic labor. Now, within a majority of American households headed by married couples, each member of the couple has a paid job, and there is the domestic labor to be done (Jacobs, 2003). Men with working wives average 45.0 hours per week on the job, and women with working husbands average 36.6 hours per week on the job (Jacobs, 2003). Joint domestic labor ranges from 36.8 hours per week for childless married couples to 54.0 hours per week for married couples with children (Sayer, 2002). Consequently, most married couples have a total workload equivalent to approximately three full-time jobs. Among single parents, most find themselves responsible for both bringing in income and doing the domestic labor in their households (Bianchi & Raley, 2003). On average, single fathers work 36.8 hours per week and single mothers work 38.5 hours per week (Jacobs, 2003). Single mothers perform 36.9 hours per week of domestic labor on average (Bianchi & Raley, 2003). Assuming that single fathers do a similar amount of domestic labor, we can conclude that single parents in general have the equivalent of two full-time jobs for which they are solely responsible.

Paid employment can conflict not only with the work that needs to be done at home but also with the leisure aspect of family life. Part of the family role involves spending recreational time with other family members (Daly, 2001). Although this is supposed to be time for relaxation and fun, attempting to fit it in around work and family responsibilities often seems only to add to the stress of trying to balance work and family life (Daly, 2001). A majority of American parents report that they spend too little time with their oldest children (60% of fathers, 55% of mothers) and their spouses (59% of fathers, 66% of mothers). Fifty-four percent of fathers say that they spend too little time with their youngest children and 41% of mothers have the same complaint (Bianchi & Raley, 2003). As these figures suggest, combining work and family has become a relevant issue for a sizable proportion of Americans.

The United States is not the only country where combining work and family is a pertinent issue. Although much of the work-family research has come out of the United States, studies on this topic are being generated all over the world. A search of the PsycInfo database turned up 37 countries that have produced articles on combining work and family roles. Table 6.1 lists these countries and shows that they span all six inhabited continents.

Table 6.1   Countries Where Research on Combining Work and Family Life Is Conducted

North America	South America	Europe	Africa	Asia	Australia/ Oceania
Canada	Brazil	Austria	South Africa	China	Australia
Dominican Republic	Peru	Croatia	Tanzania	Hong Kong	New Zealand
Mexico	Venezuela	Czech Republic		India	
United States		Denmark		Iran	
		Finland		Israel	
		France		Japan	
		Germany		Korea	
		Greece		Malaysia	
		Italy		Pakistan	
		Netherlands		Singapore	
		Norway		Thailand	
		Poland			
		Spain			
		Sweden			
		United Kingdom			

Given the expansiveness of the work-family conflict literature, we cannot review all of it in this chapter. However, we will attempt to cover much of it, focusing on the following subjects in particular: the definition of work-family conflict, the prevalence of work-family conflict in the workforce, the major theoretical models applicable to the issue of work-family conflict, major empirical studies of work-family conflict, the primary causes and outcomes of work-family conflict, relevant moderators of relations involving work-family conflict, key issues in the measurement of work-family conflict, future research needs in the area of work-family conflict, and finally, implications for practice, policy, and intervention. Although work and family also may facilitate each other, we do not cover work-family facilitation in this review both because of the focus of this handbook on stress and because of the scarcity of research on work-family facilitation. For a recent review of research on work-family facilitation, the reader is referred to a chapter by Frone (2003).

Definition of Work-Family Conflict

The widely cited definition of work-family conflict states that it is "a form of interrole conflict in which the role pressures from the work and family domains are mutually incompatible in some respect. That is, participation in the work (family) role is made more difficult by virtue of participation in the family (work) role" (Greenhaus & Beutell, 1985, p. 77). According to this definition, work-family conflict can occur in two directions: family can interfere with work *(family-to-work conflict)* or work can interfere with family *(work-to-family conflict)*. For example, a parent might experience family-to-work conflict when it is necessary to take time off from work to stay home with a sick child. Alternatively, a spouse or parent might experience work-to-family conflict when late work hours make it difficult to arrive home in time to prepare healthy meals for other family members. Factor analyses and empirical research on predictors and outcomes support the idea that family-to-work conflict and work-to-family conflict are two distinct constructs (Frone, Russell, & Cooper, 1992b; Kelloway, Gottlieb, & Barham, 1999; Netemeyer, Boles, & McMurrian, 1996).

Prevalence of Work-Family Conflict

Although the social and demographic changes discussed earlier suggest that families have more to do, does this mean that people actually experience conflict between their work and family lives? Three nationally representative surveys conducted in the United States during the 1990s suggest that they do. The National Survey of Midlife Development in the United States (MIDUS; Brim et al., 2003), the 1997 National Study of the Changing

Workforce (NSCW; Families and Work Institute, 1999), and the National Comorbidity Survey (NCS; Kessler, 2002) all measured work-family conflict, although each used a different scale. (See Appendix A for the scales used in each survey.) Using the data sets from these studies, we examined the prevalence of work-family conflict among adults between the ages of 25 and 54 who worked at least 20 hours per week and had some form of immediate family (i.e., a spouse or live-in partner and/or at least one child under 18 years old). In Table 6.2, we first present the overall percentage of people in each study who reported experiencing work-family conflict at least "sometimes." We then present the prevalence rate according to various demographic characteristics and indicate when the rates differ significantly by demographic subgroups.

Table 6.2   Prevalence of Work-to-Family Conflict (WFC) and Family-to-Work Conflict (FWC) in Three National Surveys of the U.S. Population (Percentages)

Demographic Characteristic	WFC[a]			FWC[b]		
	MIDUS N = 1,195	NSCW N = 1,925	NCS N = 2,378	MIDUS N = 1,195	NSCW N = 1,925	NCS N = 2,378
Overall population	40.2	55.0	26.3	13.6	9.9	11.6
General intraindividual						
Age						
25 – 34	38.3	56.6*	27.4	13.6	10.7	12.9
35 – 44	44.1	57.4	27.8	15.9	11.1	12.4
45 – 54	37.0	50.6	21.3	10.0	7.6	7.2
Gender						
Male	41.5	52.4*	28.3	12.3	9.7	14.8***
Female	38.9	57.9	23.8	15.1	10.1	8.9
Race						
White	41.4	55.3	27.8	13.1	8.8**	11.8
Black	32.5	55.8	17.0	17.5	14.1	8.5
Other	38.1	51.4	22.0	14.3	14.7	14.7
Family role environment						
Family status						
Married, no child < 18[c]	39.7	51.1*	25.6*	7.8***	6.2***	5.5***
Married w/child < 18	39.7	56.1	28.4	15.5	10.6	13.9
Single parent	45.0	59.8	18.8	21.7	15.6	17.2
Age of youngest child						
< 6	40.2	58.9	27.7	18.1	15.4	14.7
6 – 13	42.7	58.1	26.4	17.8	9.0	14.3
14 – 17	35.2	48.7	23.6	9.9	8.5	10.8
No child < 18	40.2	51.1**	25.5	7.9***	6.2***	5.5***

Demographic Characteristic	WFC[a]			FWC[b]		
	MIDUS N = 1,195	NSCW N = 1,925	NCS N = 2,378	MIDUS N = 1,195	NSCW N = 1,925	NCS N = 2,378
Work role environment						
Self-employment status						
Self-employed	42.8	53.5	39.8***	12.8	17.2***	17.0**
Not self-employed	39.7	55.4	24.4	13.8	8.4	10.8
Number of work hours						
20 – 34	31.8***	41.1***	16.0***	19.0	14.1	11.1
35 – 40	34.7	49.8	19.7	11.9	10.4	11.6
> 40	47.5	59.0	36.6	13.6	9.1	11.7
Occupation						
Managerial/ Professional	48.8***	58.2*	34.6***	17.6**	9.7	9.2
Other	36.1	53.2	21.6	11.7	10.0	13.9

NOTE: MIDUS = National Survey of Midlife Development in the United States; NSCW = National Study of the Changing Workforce; NCS = National Comorbidity Survey. In all three studies, the proportions are weighted to take into account the sampling design. In the NCS, the significance tests were adjusted for design effects. Such an adjustment was not necessary in the other two studies. See text for description of the sample.

a. Work-to-family conflict was measured with four items in the MIDUS, four items in the NSCW, and three items in the NCS.
b. Family-to-work conflict was measured with four items in the MIDUS, five items in the NSCW, and three items in the NCS.
c. In the NSCW, variables referring to children counted children as present if they lived with the respondent for at least half of the year.

  * Within columns and demographic characteristics, groups differ at $p < .05$.
 ** Within columns and demographic characteristics, groups differ at $p < .01$.
*** Within columns and demographic characteristics, groups differ at $p < .001$.

What is immediately apparent from Table 6.2 is that the prevalence rates of work-to-family conflict are quite discrepant from study to study. The NCS elicited the lowest rate of work-to-family conflict at 26.3%, which was about half of the NSCW rate of 55.0%. The MIDUS rate fell squarely between the other two at 40.2%. There are a number of possible reasons for these differences in rates. A first possibility is that the discrepancies are due to sampling error. However, because all three studies were based on relatively large national probability samples of the U.S. population, this explanation seems unlikely. A second possible explanation may be that the different work-to-family conflict scales used in each survey elicited different responses from participants. However, differences in scales did not lead to large differences in the rates of family-to-work conflict. A third possibility is that the differences reflect actual changes over time. Because the surveys were conducted during different time periods—the NCS from 1990 to

1992, the MIDUS from 1995 to 1996, and the NSCW in 1997—it is possible that rates of work-to-family conflict rose between those time periods and that the surveys captured these changes. However, changes in employment patterns during the 1990s do not appear to have been drastic enough to warrant such sharp increases in work-to-family conflict. Thus, it is doubtful that this explanation would fully account for the differences in rates, although it may have been a contributing factor. A fourth possible explanation is that reports of work-to-family conflict may have risen (even though the actual experience of it may not have) because the issue of work-to-family conflict received increasing media attention throughout the 1990s. This attention may have raised people's consciousness about work-to-family conflict, which in turn may have led them to perceive it in their own lives when they previously did not. Moreover, this explanation is consistent with the relative similarity in the rates of family-to-work conflict across the three studies because little media attention has been paid to this dimension of work-family conflict.

Despite the discrepancies in the reported rates of work-to-family conflict, we can still obtain useful information from the three national surveys. They at least give us a range of rates so that we can get a sense of approximately what proportion of people are experiencing work-family conflict. Taken together, the surveys suggest that between a quarter and half of the U.S. population aged 25 to 54 that works half-time or more and has some form of immediate family at home experiences work-to-family conflict at least some of the time. The prevalence rates for family-to-work conflict were much lower, ranging from 9.9% to 13.6%. Thus, work-to-family conflict seems to be more prevalent than family-to-work conflict. Said differently, family roles appear to encounter higher levels of cross-role interference than work roles. Other studies have reported similar findings (see Frone, 2003, for a more detailed discussion of this pattern).

Looking at the data according to demographic characteristics, we first note that there is little support for differences across some basic characteristics that are typically examined, such as gender, race, and age. However, other demographic characteristics consistently show statistically significant differences across studies. For example, people who work more hours have higher rates of work-to-family conflict than do people who hold managerial or professional positions. Regarding family-to-work conflict, we find that having younger children in the household is related to higher levels. Furthermore, looking at different combinations of marital and parental status reveals that family-to-work conflict is highest among single parents of children under 18 years old, followed by married parents of children under 18, and finally married people without children under 18. These findings support the contention of Frone and his colleagues (Frone et al., 1992b; Frone, 2003) that work demands generally cause work-to-family conflict and family demands generally cause family-to-work conflict.

Major Theoretical Models
Relevant to Work-Family Conflict

Several theories have been invoked in the study of work-family conflict. We will discuss two theories that have been central to the development of thought and research on work-family conflict and one relatively new theory that has strong potential for guiding research to further explicate how the work and family domains might interact to create conflict. First, we will cover ecological systems theory, which provides a framework for the second and third theories that we will discuss, namely role theory and boundary/border theory.

Ecological systems theory. Ecological systems theory proposes that a person's development is lifelong and is best understood by examining the interaction between the characteristics of that person and the characteristics of his or her environment (Bronfenbrenner, 1989). Thus, ecological systems theory depicts a model of human development that includes feedback loops between the person and his or her environment, with each affecting the other in turn. The environment is described as comprising a hierarchy of four systems: the microsystem, the mesosystem, the exosystem, and the macrosystem. The system most proximal to the individual is the microsystem. This system reflects a "pattern of activities, roles, and interpersonal relations" that a person experiences in a context that has certain characteristics and that includes other people with certain attributes (Bronfenbrenner, 1989, p. 227). For our purposes, the most relevant microsystems are in the home and the workplace. At the second level, the mesosystem is composed of the linkages between two or more microsystems, such as those between the home and the workplace (Bronfenbrenner, 1989). At the third level is the exosystem, which is the same as the mesosystem except that one of the microsystems does not actually contain the individual (Bronfenbrenner, 1989). One example of an exosystem would be the relation between one's home life and one's spouse's work life. The combination of the three types of systems just described creates a distinct pattern within each culture or subculture, and this pattern is referred to as the *macrosystem* (Bronfenbrenner, 1989).

Researchers have used the ecological systems framework to guide the study of work-family conflict (e.g., Grzywacz, 2000; Hammer, Bauer, & Grandey, 2003; Voydanoff, 2002). Most work-family conflict research has been conducted at the level of the mesosystem. That is, the research primarily has examined the effects a person's home life and work life have on each other and how these effects occur. Some research, however, has explored processes at the level of the exosystem. For example, a number of studies have utilized samples of couples or families to look at the effects of one partner's work experiences on the other partner's home experiences (e.g., Chan & Margolin, 1994; Westman & Etzion, 1995) or the effects of parents' work experiences on children's home or school experiences (e.g., Crouter, MacDermid, McHale, & Perry-Jenkins, 1990; Harrison & Ungerer, 2002). A good deal of work-family research has examined the macrosystem level because sociodemographic variables tend to fall into this category. Some research also has examined macrosystem level variables by comparing work-family conflict processes in countries that have very different cultures (e.g., Aryee, Fields, & Luk, 1999).

Role theory. Although work-family conflict research has been strongly influenced by ecological systems theory, its roots lie in role theory. As mentioned earlier, roles make up part of the microsystem level of the ecological systems framework. According to role theorists, a role is a set of activities or behaviors that others expect an individual to perform (Kahn, Wolfe, Quinn, Snoek, & Rosenthal, 1964). Goode (1960) proposed that having multiple roles to fulfill, as most people do, is overly demanding. In his view, once people have multiple roles, it will be impossible for them to meet all the expectations of all the roles because these expectations inevitably will conflict in some way. This type of conflict has been labeled *interrole conflict* (Kahn et al., 1964). It is out of this concept of interrole conflict that Greenhaus and Beutell (1985) developed their definition of work-family conflict that has guided most of the research on interference between work and family life.

Boundary/border theory. Boundary theory (Ashforth, Kreiner, & Fugate, 2000; Nippert-Eng, 1996) and border theory (Clark, 2000; Michaelson & Johnson, 1997) build on role theory and fit nicely within the ecological systems framework. According to boundary/border theory, each of a person's roles takes place within a specific domain of life, and these domains are separated by borders that may be physical, temporal, or psychological (Ashforth et al., 2000; Clark, 2000). Boundary/border theory specifically addresses the issue of "crossing borders" between domains. Although this theory is relevant to all domains of life, its most common application is to the domains of home and work (Ashforth et al., 2000; Clark, 2000; Nippert-Eng, 1996). Because its focus is on how people move back and forth between their work and home lives, this theory has strong potential for further elucidating work-family conflict processes at the mesosystem and exosystem levels of the ecological framework.

According to boundary/border theory, the flexibility and permeability of the boundaries between people's work and family lives will affect the level of integration, the ease of transitions, and the level of conflict between these domains (Ashforth et al., 2000; Clark, 2000; Nippert-Eng, 1996). *Flexibility* is defined as the degree to which the boundaries between domains may shift (Ashforth et al., 2000; Clark, 2000). Said differently, flexibility is the degree to which a role can be performed outside of the typical spatial and temporal boundaries of its domain. For example, can an employee work at home, or is she restricted to the workplace? Can an employee work whichever hours he chooses, or is he limited to regular work hours? *Permeability* is defined as "the degree to which elements from other domains may enter" (Clark, 2000, p. 756). In other words, when one is in a particular domain, how easy is it for people, materials, and thoughts from another domain to enter? According to boundary/border theory, boundaries that are flexible and permeable facilitate integration between work and home domains. When these domains are relatively integrated, transitions should be easier, but work-family conflict should be more likely. Conversely, when these domains are segmented, transitions should be more effortful, but work-family conflict should be less likely. For example, people who work at home and make their own hours can more quickly and easily transition between work and family roles but may be more likely to receive interference from one domain while in the other. However, people who have a separate work environment and a more structured work schedule may require more time and effort to transition between work and family roles but may be less likely to receive interference from one domain while in the other. People have a certain amount of control over how flexible and permeable their boundaries between work and home are. Thus, even when characteristics of a workplace or a home create an opening for flexibility and permeability, an individual may choose to keep the boundary tight. For example, people who have the option of working at home may do so only rarely or may create rules for family members to follow in order to minimize family-to-work conflict. Thus, the flexibility and permeability of boundaries and the experience of conflict between home and work will depend on aspects of the individual as well as those of the two domains (Ashforth et al., 2000; Clark, 2000; Nippert-Eng, 1996).

Major Empirical Studies

Although our understanding of work-family conflict is not the direct outcome of a few key studies, such studies do set the stage for future empirical research. Therefore, we would like to review briefly a few studies that have had an influence on the direction of empirical research on work-family conflict. Looking over past research chronologically, it is evident that there have been two generations of models of work-family conflict. Next, we describe these two generations of models. Later, while discussing future research directions, we highlight what we believe would be the key characteristics of a third-generation model of work-family conflict.

First-generation model. Kopelman, Greenhaus, and Connolly (1983) presented and tested perhaps the first model of work-family conflict that included the antecedents and outcomes of work-family conflict. In general, this model proposed that work and family characteristics affect work-family conflict, which in turn affects job and family satisfaction, which then affect overall life satisfaction. Work characteristics were also expected to directly affect job satisfaction, whereas family characteristics directly affect family satisfaction. At the heart of the model was the notion that work-family conflict represented an important mediating variable that linked antecedents and consequences across the work and family domains. A number of other studies have tested this model either in whole or in part (e.g., Bacharach, Bamberger, & Conley, 1991; Bedeian, Burke, & Moffett, 1988; Higgins & Duxbury, 1992; Rice, Frone, & McFarlin, 1992). A limitation of this first-generation model was that the conceptualization of work-family conflict was general and did not differentiate between work-to-family and family-to-work conflict. Moreover, despite the general conceptualization of work-family conflict, the measures employed often assessed only work-to-family conflict. This created some inconsistencies between the proposed conceptual model and some empirical results. For example, some studies found that work-family conflict was negatively related to family satisfaction (Bedeian et al., 1988), but it was unrelated to job satisfaction (e.g., Bacharach et al., 1991; Bedeian et al., 1988). This result may not be surprising when one understands that in each of these studies work-to-family conflict was actually assessed. In other studies that used a global measure that confounded both directions of work-family conflict, it was found that work-family conflict indeed predicted both job and family satisfaction (Higgins & Duxbury, 1992; Rice et al., 1992). Another overall limitation of the first-generation model was that although it allowed for a crossover effect of antecedents in one role to outcomes in another role, it did not allow for the possibility of a reciprocal relation between the work and family domains.

Second-generation model. In an effort to address the limitations of the first-generation model, Frone et al. (1992b) presented what might be referred to as a second-generation model. At the heart of this model was a distinction between work-to-family conflict and family-to-work conflict. Building from this distinction, it was proposed that work-to-family conflict mediated the relation of work characteristics to family distress/dissatisfaction whereas family-to-work conflict mediated the relation between family characteristics and work distress/dissatisfaction. Like the first-generation model, the second-generation model predicted that job and family distress/dissatisfaction would be related to overall depression, that work characteristics were directly related to job distress/dissatisfaction, and that family characteristics were related to family distress/dissatisfaction. As in the first-generation model, work-family conflict was seen as an important mediating variable that linked the characteristics of one role (work or family) to the outcome of the other role (family or work). However, work-family conflict was conceptualized to have a directional component that led to more specific hypotheses regarding these cross-role relations. Also, by distinguishing between work-to-family and family-to-work conflict, Frone et al.'s (1992b) model incorporated a reciprocal relation between the two directions of conflict, which allowed for a reciprocal relation between the work and family domains. A number of studies have tested this model either in whole or in part (e.g., Aryee et al., 1999; Carlson & Kacmar, 2000; Grandey & Cropanzano, 1999; Stoeva, Chiu, & Greenhaus, 2002; Vinokur, Pierce, & Buck, 1999). More recently, Frone, Yardley, and Markel (1997) refined the earlier model. Specifically, in this revised model, a more detailed attempt is made to model the reciprocal relation between work and family domains, a distinction is drawn between distal and proximal causes of work-to-family and family-to-work conflict, additional role-related outcomes are considered, and the relations between the two directions of work-family conflict and both work- and family-related affect are differentiated into predictive and outcome relations. To date, no other studies have attempted to test this revised model.

Predictors of Work-Family Conflict

Work-family conflict has causes, predictors, and risk factors that come from three general sources: the individual, the family role environment, and the work role environment. Although we may be referring to these variables as causes of work-family conflict, it is important to note that the types of studies that have been conducted generally have not been able to establish causal relations or directions. We can have greater confidence in a hypothesized causal relationship when it has been based on theory, when it has been demonstrated in a longitudinal study, or when other possible confounding influences have been controlled. Unfortunately, all of these conditions are rarely met in any single empirical study. Another issue that has made it difficult to interpret the relationship between work-family conflict and other variables is that work-to-family conflict and family-to-work conflict have not always been measured separately. This problem has plagued many studies, and we will discuss it further in the section entitled "Key Measurement Issues." For now, we should note that in the sections on predictors, outcomes, and moderators, we will only review studies that do not confound the two dimensions of work-family conflict.

General intra-individual predictors. Numerous studies have included demographic characteristics such as sex, age, family status, age of youngest child, and job type, among the predictors of work-family conflict. The results for such demographic predictors generally have been similar to the results found across the three national surveys discussed earlier.

Personality characteristics can be risk factors for work-family conflict or protective factors against work-family conflict. Trait negative affectivity has been found consistently to be positively related to both work-to-family and family-to-work conflict (e.g., Batt & Valcour, 2003; Bruck & Allen, 2003; Grzywacz & Marks, 2000; Stoeva et al., 2002). Few studies have examined other personality characteristics as risk factors for work-family conflict. One exception is a study showing that having a preoccupied attachment style is a risk factor for family-to-work conflict (Sumer & Knight, 2001). Other studies have shown that certain personality characteristics represent protective factors. Specifically, hardiness (Bernas & Major, 2000) seems to protect people from work-to-family conflict, and conscientiousness seems to protect people from family-to-work conflict (Bruck & Allen, 2003).

Other dispositional characteristics also have been explored. For example, Kelloway et al. (1999) found that general stress symptomatology predicted work-to-family conflict over a 6-month time lag. Time management preferences also have been related to work-family conflict (Adams & Jex, 1999). Specifically, preferring to be organized reduces both work-to-family conflict and family-to-work conflict. The latter effect is only indirect through an increased sense of control over time, and the former effect is both direct and indirect through perceived control over time. Interestingly, making lists and schedules seems to increase the perception of both forms of work-family conflict by giving people the sense that they have less control over their time. Research on the planning fallacy has demonstrated that people consistently underestimate the amount of time that it will take them to accomplish a task (Buehler, Griffin, & Ross, 1994). Having written records of what they were *supposed* to get done (in the form of lists and schedules) may make salient to people the fact that they are not able to complete on time the tasks that they have set out for themselves (Macan, 1994). Because people sincerely believe that they can accomplish tasks in the time that they allow (Buehler et al., 1994), they may feel confused and may perceive a lack of control over their time when they are unable to do so. This perception of lack of control over one's time may in turn lead to perceptions of greater work-family conflict (Adams & Jex, 1999).

Family role environment predictors. As Frone and colleagues (Frone et al., 1992b; Frone, 2003) have hypothesized, variables related to the family primarily predict family-to-work conflict as opposed to work-to-family conflict. As might be expected, spending more time on family-related work such as childcare and household chores has been associated with higher levels of family-to-work conflict (Frone, Yardley, et al., 1997; Fu & Shaffer, 2001; Gutek, Searle, & Klepa, 1991). In addition to time involvement, psychological involvement with one's family has been shown to predict family-to-work conflict (Adams, King, & King, 1996; Frone et al., 1992b). Researchers also have examined family stressors as a predictor of family-to-work conflict. They have found that both general family stressors (Bernas & Major, 2000; Frone et al., 1992b; Frone, Yardley, et al., 1997; Stoeva et al., 2002) and specific family stressors such as being criticized or burdened by family members (Grzywacz & Marks, 2000), experiencing family role conflict (Carlson & Kacmar, 2000), and experiencing family role ambiguity (Carlson & Kacmar, 2000) are related to higher levels of family-to-work conflict. The ways in which people deal with the resulting stress further affect their level of family-to-work conflict. Specifically, using an avoidant or resigned coping style in the face of family stress has been associated with a higher level of family-to-work conflict, but using a direct-action or help-seeking coping style has been associated with a lower level of family-to-work conflict (Rotondo, Carlson, & Kincaid, 2003).

Variables concerning relationships with specific family members also predict family-to-work conflict. For example, marital tension has been shown to lead to family-to-work conflict (Aryee et al., 1999; Fox & Dwyer, 1999; Grzywacz & Marks, 2000). Having children is another predictor of family-to-work conflict (Burke & Greenglass, 1999; Grzywacz & Marks, 2000). In addition, factors that increase parental responsibility, such as having younger children, having more children, and living with one's children increase family-to-work conflict (Behson, 2002a; Fu & Shaffer, 2001; Madsen, 2003; Rotondo et al., 2003; Stoeva et al., 2002). Finally, certain problems that have to do with children, such as the unavailability of child care (Fox & Dwyer, 1999) and feeling overloaded by one's parenting duties (Frone, Yardley, et al., 1997) also are associated with higher levels of family-to-work conflict.

Although some aspects of relationships with family members can increase family-to-work conflict, other aspects of those relationships can help to decrease it. Specifically, different kinds of social support can help alleviate family-to-work conflict. Receiving instrumental support such as assistance with childcare or household chores from one's spouse or other family members reduces family-to-work conflict (Adams et al., 1996; Frone, Yardley, et al., 1997; Fu & Shaffer, 2001). Receiving emotional support from one's spouse or other family members can also lessen perceptions of family-to-work conflict (Adams et al., 1996; Bernas & Major, 2000; Grzywacz & Marks, 2000).

Work role environment predictors. Work-related variables primarily predict work-to-family conflict as opposed to family-to-work conflict. It is unsurprising that the amount of time spent working is the most consistent predictor of work-to-family conflict, with higher numbers of work hours predicting higher levels of work-to-family conflict (e.g., Batt & Valcour, 2003; Frone, Yardley, et al., 1997; Fu & Shaffer, 2001; Grzywacz & Marks, 2000; Gutek et al., 1991; Higgins, Duxbury, & Johnson, 2000; Madsen, 2003; Mennino & Brayfield, 2002; O'Driscoll, Ilgen, & Hildreth, 1992; Thompson, Beauvais, & Lyness, 1999). Studies that have examined the relation between psychological involvement in one's job and work-family conflict have generally reported a positive relationship (Adams et al., 1996; Carlson & Kacmar, 2000; Frone et al., 1992b; Major, Klein, & Ehrhart, 2002), although one study failed to find a relationship (Aryee et al., 1999).

Exposure to work stressors consistently predicts higher levels of work-to-family conflict. Specific work stressors related to higher levels of work-to-family conflict include work demands or overload, work-role conflict, work-role ambiguity, and job distress or dissatisfaction (Bernas & Major, 2000; Burke & Greenglass, 1999; Carlson & Kacmar, 2000; Fox & Dwyer, 1999; Frone et al., 1992b; Frone, Yardley, et al., 1997; Fu & Shaffer, 2001; Grzywacz & Marks, 2000; Major et al., 2002; Stoeva et al., 2002). Moreover, using ineffective methods of coping with these work stressors can serve to increase one's work-to-family conflict. Specifically, people who have an avoidant or resigned way of coping with work stressors exhibit greater work-to-family conflict (e.g., Rotondo et al., 2003).

Certain aspects of people's jobs that may not be directly conceived of as stressors can cause work-family conflict. For example, jobs that require coordination with others at work produce higher levels of work-to-family conflict (Batt & Valcour, 2003). In addition, the more forms of technology (e.g., e-mail, laptop computers, etc.) that people use to communicate between the home and work domains or to do work at home, the greater the work-to-family conflict that they experience (Batt & Valcour, 2003). Results have been mixed for the effect of job level on work-family conflict. This may be because researchers have coded job level in different ways. For example, one study characterized job level as a continuous variable ranging from hourly workers to executives (Thompson et al., 1999); another study created one category that included managers and professionals and another category that included everyone else (Higgins et al., 2000); and other studies have dummy-coded for multiple job types (e.g., administrative support vs. all others, technical vs. all others; Batt & Valcour, 2003; Mennino & Brayfield, 2002). Consequently, higher- and lower-level positions have been grouped together at times, making it unclear whether there is a relationship between job level and work-family conflict. Higgins et al. (2000) examined managers and professionals compared with people in lower-level positions and found that job level did not make a difference for work-to-family conflict, but the number of hours worked did. Specifically, those who worked 30 or more hours per week reported more work-to-family conflict regardless of their job level. However, they also found that the proportion of managerial/ professional workers who work part-time is substantially smaller than the proportion of lower-level workers who work part-time. Thus, job level may be confounded with number of hours worked. This could partly account for the discrepancies in findings on job level and work-to-family conflict if different studies used samples with different compositions of people in higher- and lower-level jobs and did not control for number of hours worked.

Other dimensions of work can help ease rather than produce work-family conflict. For example, greater job security is associated with lower levels of work-to-family conflict (Batt & Valcour, 2003). Job security may alleviate the feeling that one has to do everything possible to keep one's job, including allowing work to interfere with family life. Receiving social support from one's supervisor or coworkers also can reduce work-to-family conflict (Fox & Dwyer, 1999; Frone, Yardley, et al., 1997; Grzywacz & Marks, 2000).

As might be expected, characteristics of the workplace specific to the issue of combining work and family life affect work-family conflict. Workplace cultures that encourage balance between employees' work and family lives tend to lessen work-to-family conflict (Behson, 2002b; Thompson et al., 1999), as do specific indicators of such cultures, such as organizational or supervisor support for balancing work and family life (Anderson, Coffey, & Byerly, 2002; Batt & Valcour, 2003; McManus, Korabik, Rosin, & Kelloway, 2002; O'Driscoll et al., 2003), low organizational demands for working outside of regular work hours (Thompson et al., 1999), and the absence of negative career consequences for people who utilize family-friendly policies (Anderson et al., 2002; Thompson et al., 1999). In some studies, people who work for organizations that have a greater number of formal policies aimed at providing balance between work and family life have reported lower levels of work-to-family conflict (Thompson et al., 1999) or family-to-work conflict (McManus et al., 2002, Study 2). Individual family-friendly policies also have been associated with lower levels of work-family conflict. For example, flexible schedules have been shown to reduce work-to-family conflict (Anderson et al., 2002; Major et al., 2002), and telecommuting has been shown to reduce both forms of work-family conflict (Madsen, 2003). However, other studies and other family-friendly policies, such as dependent care policies, have failed to show similar effects (Anderson et al., 2002; Batt & Valcour, 2003; McManus et al., 2002, Study 1; O'Driscoll et al., 2003). Logically, what appears to be more important for reducing work-to-family conflict is the use rather than the availability of family-supportive policies (McManus et al., 2002, Study 1; O'Driscoll et al., 2003).

Outcomes of Work-Family Conflict

Similar to the predictors of work-family conflict, the relevant outcomes can be divided into those that primarily concern the individual, those that primarily concern the family, and those that primarily concern work.

Individual outcomes. Most of the individual-level outcomes involve the mental and physical health and well-being of the person experiencing work-family conflict. Both forms of work-family conflict have been shown to negatively affect mental health and well-being. These effects have been demonstrated for general mental health and well-being (Grzywacz, 2000), dissatisfaction with life (Adams et al., 1996; Aryee et al., 1999; Carlson & Kacmar, 2000; Perrewé, Hochwarter, & Kiewitz, 1999), stress (Anderson et al., 2002; Kelloway et al., 1999), psychosomatic symptoms (Burke & Greenglass, 1999), depression (Frone, Russell, & Barnes, 1996; Frone et al., 1992b; Frone, Russell, & Cooper, 1997; Grzywacz & Bass, 2003), general psychological distress (Frone, Barnes, & Farrell, 1994; Grzywacz, 2000;

O'Driscoll et al., 1992), medication use (Burke & Greenglass, 1999), cigarette use (Frone et al., 1994), drinking problems (Frone et al., 1994; Frone et al., 1996; Frone, Russell, et al., 1997; Grzywacz & Bass, 2003), substance dependence disorders, clinical mood disorders, and clinical anxiety disorders (Frone, 2000; Grzywacz & Bass, 2003). In addition, work-to-family conflict has been demonstrated to lead to emotional exhaustion (Burke & Greenglass, 1999).

Research also has shown that higher levels of work-family conflict are related to worse physical health. Both directions of work-family conflict have been found to predict poor overall physical health (Frone et al., 1996; Frone, Russell, et al., 1997; Grzywacz, 2000) and the co-occurrence of multiple chronic health problems (Grzywacz, 2000). Each direction of work-family conflict also has been related to a more specific health problem. That is, family-to-work conflict has been shown to longitudinally predict the onset of hypertension (Frone, Russell, et al., 1997), and work-to-family conflict has been shown to predict obesity (Grzywacz, 2000).

Work-family conflict likely affects physical health through its influence on both mental health and health-related behaviors. For example, work-family conflict has been shown to cause psychological strain or distress, which has been found to cause physiological effects that can lead to physical health problems such as hypertension and high cholesterol (e.g., Landsbergis et al., 2001; Steptoe, 1991). In addition, distress can lead to unhealthy behaviors such as substance use (e.g., Cooper, Frone, Russell, & Mudar, 1995; Frone, 1999), overeating (Greeno & Wing, 1994), eating a less healthful diet, and skipping meals (Cartwright et al., 2003). Furthermore, one of the ways that work-to-family conflict manifests itself may be that people lack the time or energy to prepare food, especially healthy food, for themselves and their families, which can result in greater frequency of skipping meals and eating restaurant and junk food (Devine, Connors, Sobal, & Bisogni, 2003). Work-family conflict may also deter people from investing time and energy in exercise if they already feel that they lack the time and energy to adequately fulfill their work and family demands. All of the behaviors just discussed may occur as a result of work-family conflict and can have long-term negative consequences for people's health and well-being. Research directly testing these hypothesized indirect paths from work-family conflict to physical health would likely prove fruitful and informative.

Family-related outcomes. The effects of work-family conflict are not specific to realms that affect only the individual. Predictably, work-family conflict affects outcomes that relate to the family as well. Both forms of work-family conflict have been shown to predict lower family satisfaction (Aryee et al., 1999; Burke & Greenglass, 1999; Carlson & Kacmar, 2000; Frone et al., 1994; Frone, Yardley, et al., 1997), though the relation involving family-to-work conflict may be indirect (Frone, Yardley, et al., 1997). In addition, work-to-family conflict predicts decreased performance in the family role, increased family-related absenteeism and tardiness, increased parenting overload, and the receipt of less emotional support and instrumental assistance from family members (Adams et al., 1996; Frone, Yardley, et al., 1997; MacEwen & Barling, 1994).

Work-related outcomes. Work-family conflict also has been shown to affect outcomes in the work domain. Both directions of work-family conflict have a negative influence on affective reactions to one's job. For example, work-to-family conflict and family-to-work conflict predict lower levels of job satisfaction (Anderson et al., 2002; Aryee et al., 1999; Burke & Greenglass, 1999; Frone et al., 1994; Perrewé et al., 1999), ,although the relation involving work-to-family conflict may be indirect (Frone, Yardley, et al., 1997). Also, family-to-work conflict leads to higher levels of job distress (Behson, 2002a; Frone et al., 1992b; Frone, Yardley, et al., 1997). In addition, family-to-work conflict affects outcomes related to how effective people are at their jobs. For example, family-to-work conflict has been related to higher levels of work overload, lower levels of self-reported work performance, and higher rates of absenteeism (Anderson et al., 2002; Burke & Greenglass, 1999; Frone, Yardley, et al., 1997; MacEwen & Barling, 1994).

Work-family conflict also affects people's intentions of leaving their jobs. However, in contrast to the other work outcomes just described, job turnover may be better predicted by work-to-family conflict than family-to-work conflict (see Frone, 2003, for a more detailed discussion of this issue). O'Driscoll et al. (1992) found that higher levels of work-to-family conflict predict lower levels of organizational commitment. In addition, other studies have found that work-to-family conflict, but not family-to-work conflict, predicts intentions to quit one's job or profession (Anderson et al., 2002; Greenhaus, Parasuraman, & Collins, 2001; Kirchmeyer & Cohen, 1999). Regarding actual turnover, Greenhaus et al. (2001) found that accountants who experienced higher levels of work-to-family conflict were more likely to leave their profession if their psychological career involvement was relatively low. Family-to-work conflict was not related to actual turnover.

Finally, as might be expected, employees who experience more family-to-work conflict express a greater need for work flexibility. The experience of family-to-work conflict, but not work-to-family conflict, increases the importance of potential family supportive programs (e.g., flextime, job sharing) for employed parents (Frone & Yardley, 1996). Also, when family-to-work conflict is higher, people are more likely to make informal adjustments to their work schedules so that they can meet family needs that arise during work hours (Behson, 2002a). For example, a parent might leave work early one day to attend a parent-teacher conference but then work late the next day to make up for it.

Known Moderators

As with the predictors and outcomes of work-family conflict, the moderators of relations involving work-family conflict can derive from the individual, the family domain, or the work domain. These moderators may qualify the effects of other variables on work-family conflict or they may qualify the effect of work-family conflict on its various outcomes. We will discuss both types of moderator effects.

General intraindividual moderators. Gender has been examined as a moderator of the predictors and outcomes of work-family conflict in a number of studies (e.g., Anderson et al., 2002; Frone, 2000; Frone, Russell, & Cooper, 1992a; Frone et al., 1992b; Frone et al., 1996; Grzywacz & Marks, 2000; Gutek et al., 1991). Consistent with research on gender differences in the prevalence of work-family conflict, there is little evidence that the relationships between either direction of work-family conflict and its putative antecedents and outcomes differ across men and women. Researchers also have examined trait negative affectivity as a moderator of work-family conflict. Stoeva et al. (2002) found that family stress is a stronger predictor of family-to-work conflict for people who are higher in negative affectivity.

Family-related moderators. Some family-related variables have been shown to moderate relations involving work-family conflict. For example, Fox and Dwyer (1999) reported that work stressors such as workload variability and frequent stressful events were stronger predictors of work-to-family conflict among people who normally spend more time on family work. Similarly, family stressors such as marital tension and unavailability of child care were stronger predictors of family-to-work conflict when a person spent more time on family work. In addition, the personal importance of the family role has been shown to moderate work-family conflict relations. Specifically, higher levels of family role conflict have been related to higher levels of family-to-work conflict when people who place great importance on their work do not also place great importance on their families (Carlson & Kacmar, 2000).

Work-related moderators. Several work-related variables have been shown to moderate work-family conflict relations. Amount of time spent working moderates both directions of work-family conflict. Lower levels of supervisor support lead to higher levels of work-to-family conflict for people who work more hours (Fox & Dwyer, 1999). Also, family stressors such as unavailability of childcare and marital or parental tension result in greater family-to-work conflict for people who work more hours (Fox & Dwyer, 1999). In addition to time involvement, psychological involvement in work also moderates work-family conflict relations. Lower levels of supervisor support lead to higher levels of work-to-family conflict for people who are more psychologically involved in their jobs (Fox & Dwyer, 1999). Also, family stressors such as marital tension, lack of spousal assistance with housework, and family role ambiguity have a stronger positive relationship with family-to-work conflict when one is more psychologically involved in one's job (Carlson & Kacmar, 2000; Fox & Dwyer, 1999). On the other hand, when people do experience work-to-family conflict, high job involvement may deter them from leaving their profession. Greenhaus et al. (2001) found a positive relationship between work-to-family conflict and both intention to withdraw and actual withdrawal from the accounting profession only for people with low job involvement.

Work-related variables that have been shown to help protect people from experiencing work-family conflict or its effects include supervisor support and informal work accommodations to family. Specifically, work role conflict has been found to be positively related to work-to-family conflict for people who have low levels of supervisor support but not for those who have high support (Fu & Shaffer, 2001). In addition, making more frequent adjustments to one's work patterns in order to accommodate family responsibilities attenuates the positive relation between family-to-work conflict and work stress (Behson, 2002a).

Key Measurement Issues

Having briefly reviewed the empirical record on the causes and outcomes of work-family conflict, it is natural to wonder whether the central construct has been measured well. In recent years, there have been several deliberate attempts to develop valid measures of work-family conflict (Carlson, Kacmar, & Williams, 2000; Curbow, McDonnell, Spratt, Griffin, & Agnew, 2003; Kelloway et al., 1999; Mallard & Lance, 1998; Netemeyer et al., 1996). Nonetheless, in this section we will discuss four key issues concerning the measurement of work-family conflict that pose potential problems, either singly or in combination, for the interpretation of past research results. Not all measures or all studies of work-family conflict suffer from each limitation to the same degree, but most work-family conflict research is affected by some of the measurement issues described next.

Directionality of work-family conflict. Researchers have not consistently measured both directions of the work-family conflict construct. Despite the fact that work-family conflict is conceptually bidirectional in nature, most early research on this topic failed to measure the two different directions of conflict (Frone et al., 1992b; Greenhaus & Beutell, 1985). Studies tended to use measures that assessed only work-to-family conflict or that confounded the two types of conflict (Frone et al., 1992b). In 1985, Greenhaus and Beutell noted that the development of work-family conflict scales should include items assessing both work-to-family conflict and family-to-work conflict.

Early research by Gutek et al. (1991) and Frone and his colleagues (1992a, 1992b) provided empirical support for the idea that work-to-family conflict and family-to-work conflict represent two separate dimensions with different rates of prevalence and different role-related antecedents and outcomes. These early findings have been replicated in a number of subsequent studies (e.g., Carlson & Kacmar, 2000; Frone, Yardley, et al., 1997; Kelloway et al., 1999; Netemeyer et al., 1996). Although much work-family conflict research has incorporated this distinction during the past decade, there are still a number of recent exceptions (e.g., Berg, Kalleberg, & Appelbaum, 2003; Carlson, 1999; Carlson & Perrewé, 1999; Senecal, Vallerand, & Guay, 2001). Sometimes, however, the issue is not that a study failed to use items that assess both directions of work-family conflict. Rather, it is that even when items assessing both directions of work-family conflict were used, they were aggregated into an overall measure that confounds the directionality of work-family conflict. Inconsistency in the measurement and operationalization of work-family conflict is problematic because it leads to difficulty in comparing results across studies. Thus, it is important to be aware of this potential inconsistency when comparing the results of different studies. In future studies, it would be advisable for researchers to assess separately and analyze simultaneously both directional dimensions of work-family conflict.

Parallel construction of items. Even when both directions of work-family conflict are measured, items for the two dimensions are not always parallel in construction. This becomes apparent when examining past measures of work-family conflict (e.g., see the newly developed scales noted earlier and the measures for the three national surveys presented in Appendix A). It should be noted that there is variability in the extent to which commensurate items have been developed. For example, using the items from the three national surveys discussed earlier, the studies can be easily rank-ordered on the degree to which parallel items were developed. The NCS used items that are exactly parallel, the MIDUS used items that were somewhat less commensurate, and the NSCW used items that were the least parallel. Moreover, if one looks at the items developed by Carlson et al. (2000), the three items assessing strain-based work-to-family interference collectively assess the extent to which work causes someone to be frazzled, emotionally drained, and stressed at home. In contrast, the three items assessing strain-based family-to-work interference collectively assess the extent to which family causes someone to be preoccupied with family, unable to concentrate, and tense at work. It seems that the items assessing work-to-family conflict primarily refer to affective or emotional reactions whereas the items assessing family-to-work conflict primarily refer to cognitive reactions.

Such lack of substantive equivalence makes it difficult to have confidence in comparisons made across the two directions of work-family conflict within a single study and across multiple studies using different measures. For example, within a single study, comparisons of mean levels or prevalence rates across the two directions of conflict are made more difficult to interpret if the items are assessing different underlying dynamics or processes. Moreover, if different underlying processes are being assessed, it may lead to spurious patterns among the predictors and outcomes of work-to-family and family-to-work conflict. To date, the potential for bias in substantive findings introduced by the use of nonparallel items has received little conceptual or empirical attention. Clearly, this is an issue that needs to be explicitly considered in the development of work-family conflict measures.

Confounding causes and consequences. Another source of potential measurement artifacts is the approach of using measures or items that presumably assess time-based, strain-based, and behavior-based work-family conflict. This approach grew out of a literature review by Greenhaus and Beutell (1985). In that review, Greenhaus and Beutell stated, "the literature suggests three major forms of work-family conflict: (a) time-based conflict, (b) strain-based conflict, and (c) behavior-based conflict" (p. 77). However, our reading of their review suggests that Greenhaus and Beutell did not uncover evidence of three forms of work-family conflict. Rather, what they reviewed and showed was that there are at least three different classes of predictors of conflict between work and family life. There are time-based predictors, strain-based predictors, and behavior-based predictors. This contention is supported by the title of their review, "Sources of Conflict Between Work and Family Roles."

We believe that it is problematic to infer a taxonomy of different forms of work-family conflict from a taxonomy of different types of causal antecedents of work-family conflict. In other words, just because there are different types of causal antecedents of work-family conflict, it does not logically follow that there are different forms of work-family conflict itself. To make this argument clearer, let us put it in a more extreme context by considering the measurement of depression as an alternate example. Past research suggests that there are several classes of putative causal antecedent variables: demographic (gender), personality (neuroticism), and environmental (marital problems). Despite these different types of causes, it would be difficult to make a case for separate measures of demographic-, personality-, and environment-based depression. For example, an item from the Center for Epidemiologic Studies Depression Scale (Radloff, 1977) is "I felt depressed or very unhappy." As will be discussed shortly, it would be problematic to create an environmentally based measure of depression by rewording this item to read, "Because of marital problems, I felt depressed or very unhappy" or "The demands at work have made me feel depressed and very unhappy."

But what is the problem with attempting to measure time-, strain-, and behavior-based work-family conflict? First, although the directional component of work-family conflict follows directly from the conceptual or constitutive definition of work-family conflict provided by Greenhaus and Beutell (1985) that was given earlier, the three forms of work-family conflict do not follow from this definition. Second, although some measures have defined work-family conflict in terms of its antecedents and outcomes without explicitly trying to assess time-, strain-, and behavior-based conflict, we believe that the development of items to assess these three types of conflict creates a situation whereby work-family conflict is even more likely to be assessed in terms of its putative causes or outcomes. This, of course, risks creating a conceptual and measurement confound. As noted by Harrison (2002), defining and assessing a construct in terms of its causes or outcomes makes collecting data on those causes or outcomes meaningless because the cause or outcome is already given. In other words, if one does proceed to assess a relation between a predictor (or outcome) and a measure of work-family conflict that is defined in terms of the predictor (or outcome), the relation is not meaningful because one is correlating what amounts to two measures of the predictor (or outcome) construct. For example, consider an item that has been used to assess strain-based family-to-work conflict: "Because of the demands I face at home, I am tired at work." In essence, this item assesses fatigue experienced during the workday. It would be difficult to imagine that an individual who said *very often* to this work-family conflict item could also say *never* or *seldom* to items measuring level of fatigue while at work. In fact, it could be argued that this work-family conflict item is really a fatigue item that includes a potential causal attribution for one's fatigue while working. Fowler (1995) warns against developing items that build in causal attributions because respondents are often incapable of validly reporting on the reasons for what they do and experience. It is useful to point out that this measurement issue is not unique to the assessment of work-family conflict. For example, similar concerns have been explicitly voiced with regard to the measurement of job involvement (e.g., Kanungo, 1982) and work-related withdrawal behaviors (Harrison, 2002).

A potential outcome of measuring work-family conflict in terms of its putative causes or outcomes is spurious, or at least inflated, relations and potential differential effects that are artifactual rather than having substantive meaning. Therefore, we believe that the wording of work-to-family and family-to-work conflict items should be as general as possible. This way, researchers can see if the three types of predictors are related to the general measures of work-family conflict. In other words, are time-, strain-, and behavior-based work-related predictors related to a general measure of work-to-family conflict? Similarly, are time-, strain-, and behavior-based family-related predictors related to a general measure of family-to-work conflict? There also is a benefit to this approach on the outcome side in that in future research, any documented relations between work-family conflict and a variety of work and family-related outcomes (role withdrawal, role performance) or general health outcomes will be more credible.

Appropriate response anchors. The final measurement issue is the selection of appropriate response anchors for items that assess work-family conflict.

Consider an item that has been used to assess work-to-family conflict: "After work, I come home too tired to do some of the things I'd like to do." Participants are then asked to respond using anchors ranging from *strongly disagree* to *strongly agree*. We believe that most work-family researchers are interested in the frequency of occurrence of work-family conflict. However, agree/disagree response anchors provide no information on the frequency with which individuals experience work-family conflict. If an individual reported *strongly agree* to the above item, we would have no idea if this actually means that he or she comes home from work too tired *very frequently*. A *strongly agree* response might merely represent the respondent's level of certainty that the event occurs at all. In other words, even if someone only rarely comes home from work too tired, they could conceivably respond *strongly agree* because they want to show that they are very certain that this event does occur. Moreover, there is no way to estimate even the prevalence of work-family conflict because such response anchors do not allow for a zero point. In other words, does *strongly disagree* mean *never*? The agree/disagree response format was used in some of the earliest measures of work-family conflict (e.g., Kopelman et al., 1983) and is still being used in several of the most recently developed measures (e.g., Carlson et al., 2000; Mallard & Lance, 1998; Netemeyer et al., 1996).

Despite the current use of agree/disagree response anchors in the assessment of work-family conflict, we believe that it would be better to use a frequency-based response format. The typical frequency-based response format that has been used in the past has the following or similar anchors: *never, seldom, sometimes, often, very often* (e.g., Kelloway et al., 1999; also see Appendix A for the response anchors used in the three national studies). This response scale is an improvement over the agree/disagree format in that one can assess the prevalence of work-family conflict with more confidence. However, it still offers very little useful information regarding the absolute level of the frequency of occurrence. For example, does a response of *very often* mean every day or once a week or once a month? Moreover, does *very often* have the same meaning across respondents? The problems associated with using vague qualifiers as response anchors are well-known (e.g., Schwarz, 1999). There are two potential solutions to this problem. First, using an open-ended response format, one can ask respondents to report the number of times over some specified period (e.g., past week, past month, past year) that they have experienced a given indicator of work-family conflict. Second, one can use a closed-ended response format that more clearly captures the absolute frequency of occurrence. For example, if the reporting time frame was the past 12 months, one might use *never, less than once a month, 1 to 3 days per month, 1 to 2 days per week, 3 to 5 days per week, 6 to 7 days per week*. Either of these two strategies is likely to produce better frequency data and responses that are less biased by the lack of shared meaning that comes with the use of vague qualifiers. Nonetheless, it would be prudent to consult past research on how the design of fixed-frequency response anchors can shape respondents' answers to questions (e.g., Schwarz, 1999).

Summary. Highlighting the four major measurement issues that have affected past and current measures of work-family conflict is not meant to discourage work on this issue. Rather, our intent is to motivate the development of measures of work-family conflict with even stronger construct validity. However, as we point out, there are a number of issues that require more explicit and more serious consideration. In fact, the starting point might be the formulation of a more fully developed and precise conceptual or constitutive definition of work-family conflict (see Harrison, 2002, for a detailed discussion of this issue). In the end, stronger measures of work-family conflict will lead to more valid research findings that then will provide the bedrock for sounder policy recommendations.

Future Research Needs

Due to the focus of this handbook on stress, we have focused on conflict between work and family life. However, combining work and family life can also result in more positive outcomes such as work-family facilitation. Work-family facilitation has been defined as "the extent to which participation at work (or home) is made easier by virtue of the experiences, skills and opportunities gained or developed at home (or work)" (Frone, 2003, p. 145). Like work-family conflict, work-family facilitation is bidirectional in nature, originating in either the work or the family domain. Research showing that work-family facilitation is not simply the absence of work-family conflict but rather a separate construct (e.g., Grzywacz & Marks, 2000) suggests that it may be important to examine the net effect of the advantages and disadvantages of combining work and family roles to obtain a complete picture of the way that they interact. There has been much less research on work-family facilitation than on work-family conflict, and we suggest that our understanding of the work-family interface would be greatly enhanced by decreasing this gap.

It is likely that our understanding of the interaction between work and family life also would be enhanced by expanding the most recent second-generation models of the work-family interface. We believe that a third-generation model would include multiple members of the work and family domains as well as the concept of time. Most of the work-family conflict literature is based on the reports of individual respondents, each of whom represents a single work-family system. However, because the issue of work-family conflict involves two domains that generally include collectives of people—not just the target respondent—it would likely be informative to obtain supplementary measurements from those people. Specifically, we may be able to achieve a more complete picture of work-family conflict if we include other family members and work associates in our research designs. Others' reports of the target respondent's experiences may validate the reports of the target respondent, providing greater confidence in the findings. Alternatively, the particular relationship of a person to the target respondent may give that person a different perspective on the target's work-family conflict. For example, target respondents' perceptions of the frequency and consequences of their work interfering with their family lives may differ from their spouses' and children's perceptions. Likewise, target respondents' perceptions of the frequency and consequences of their family lives interfering with their work may differ from their supervisors' and coworkers' perceptions. Family members and work associates may perceive more or less conflict and greater or lesser consequences than the target respondent, depending on their personalities, their understanding of the demands of the situation, or other factors. Thus, collecting reports from multiple sources would give us the opportunity to test for moderators of work-family conflict that have their source outside of the target respondent. It would also give us a better sense of the experience and outcomes of work-family conflict for the target respondent and for the other people in the work and family systems.

Researchers may have been discouraged from collecting this type of multisource data in the past due to a dearth of statistical techniques that could handle the resulting nonindependence in the data (Raudenbush, Brennan, & Barnett, 1995). Recently, however, multilevel modeling techniques have been developed to allow for nonindependent data (Teachman & Crowder, 2002). Because multilevel models can deal with nonindependent data, they also are appropriate for the analysis of longitudinal data. Longitudinal data can be useful in the study of work-family conflict because levels of work-family conflict undoubtedly fluctuate over time for many people. Research that obtains measurements from the same respondents at different time points would likely add to our knowledge of the circumstances that are associated with work-family conflict and also of personal characteristics that might interact with circumstances to increase or inhibit work-family conflict. Thus, an expanded model of the work-family interface should incorporate time in addition to multiple people from the work and family domains. Such a model will require multilevel conceptualizations, research designs, and data analysis strategies.

We will briefly discuss one final research need that has been mentioned before but that bears repeating. We echo the calls of other researchers for an expansion beyond the study of work-family conflict to the study of conflict between work and nonwork roles other than those involving the nuclear family. Certainly, the nuclear family is the most important nonwork role for most people, but a growing number of people also have demands associated with the care of elderly parents and other elderly family members. Although not as large, a developing literature exists on work-eldercare conflict (e.g., Barling, MacEwen, Kelloway, & Higginbottom, 1994; Hepburn & Barling, 1996). There are also many nonfamily roles that people fulfill, such as the student role, leisure role, citizen role, neighbor role, and religious role, that may be in conflict with the work role. These roles are rarely studied in conflict research, and if they are, they tend to be grouped together as "nonwork roles" as opposed to examined individually (Frone, 2003). Conflict between work and each of these roles can have consequences that are serious, though potentially different from one another. For example, if work interferes with the school role, an individual may experience lower academic achievement (e.g., Markel & Frone, 1998) that may in turn hinder career advancement. Work may interfere with the civic role and lead to a lack of participation in the democratic process because people's work schedules may not allow them to vote or to take the time to learn about political candidates or issues. On the other hand, performing any of the nonwork roles can interfere with one's work role. For example, performing the neighbor role by shoveling the driveway of the elderly person next door may cause one to be late for work. Thus, conflict between work and various nonwork domains can have a variety of consequences for the individual, for other people in the individual's life domains, for organizations, and even for the larger society. It will be important to study each combination of work and nonwork roles to obtain a more complete picture of the consequences of interrole conflict.

Implications for Practice, Policy, and Intervention

The research that has examined the effects of family-supportive workplace policies has shown that these policies can often have an ameliorating effect on employees' work-family conflict. However, these policies seem to be most effective at reducing work-family conflict within a workplace culture that encourages, or at least does not penalize employees for, the use of such policies. Thus, employers who would like to avoid the negative effects of work-family conflict for their employees and their organizations would be wise to offer a variety of family-supportive programs and encourage their employees to utilize them.

In addition, the results reviewed regarding coping styles and work-family conflict suggest that employers may wish to offer their employees some form of stress management training. People who use avoidant or resigned coping styles have been shown to experience higher levels of both work-to-family and family-to-work conflict, but those who use help-seeking or direct-action coping styles have reported lower levels of family-to-work conflict. Thus, training people to use the most effective ways of coping with stress may reduce their work-family conflict.

For their part, individuals can take advantage of policies and programs that organizations offer with the intention of helping them minimize conflict between their work and family lives. In addition, the results of one study reviewed suggest that people who make schedules and lists of things to do may wish to stop these practices in order to reduce perceptions of work-family conflict. However, this recommendation is based on a single study and thus should be taken with caution, especially given that people who multitask may have more success with these practices than people who do not (Bluedorn, Kaufman, & Lane, 1992).

Finally, other members of a domain can help to reduce a person's work-family conflict. Support for balancing one's work and family life from one's supervisor as well as general social support from one's supervisor or coworkers reduces work-to-family conflict. Also, instrumental or emotional support from one's spouse or other family members diminishes family-to-work conflict. Thus, people who see others in their environments struggling with conflict between their work and family lives may be able to make a difference by offering their support.

Epilogue

The information that we have reviewed suggests that work-family conflict is a stressor that affects many people. In fact, work-family conflict affects more than just the individuals experiencing it; it also directly or indirectly affects family members, coworkers, supervisors, organizations, and communities. Work-family conflict often has been seen as a problem for individual workers. However, given the potentially severe consequences and the widespread impact of work-family conflict, it seems to be a problem best tackled with collaboration from organizations, individuals, and governments. With these parties collaborating to find possible solutions and researchers conducting sound studies to test the efficacy of such solutions, we can go a long way toward achieving an optimal balance between work and family life for all.

References

Adams, G. A., & Jex, S. M. (1999). Relationships between time management, control, work-family conflict, and strain. *Journal of Occupational Health Psychology, 4,* 72–77.

Adams, G. A., King, L. A., & King, D. W. (1996). Relationships of job and family involvement, family social support, and work-family conflict with job and life satisfaction. *Journal of Applied Psychology, 81,* 411–420.

Anderson, S. E., Coffey, B. S., & Byerly, R. T. (2002). Formal organizational initiatives and informal workplace practices: Links to work-family conflict and job-related outcomes. *Journal of Management, 28,* 787–810.

Aryee, S., Fields, D., & Luk, V. (1999). A cross-cultural test of a model of the work-family interface. *Journal of Management, 25,* 491–511.

Ashforth, B. E., Kreiner, G. E., & Fugate, M. (2000). All in a day's work: Boundaries and micro role transitions. *Academy of Management Review, 25,* 472–491.

Bacharach, S. B., Bamberger, P., & Conley, S. (1991). Work-home conflict among nurses and engineers: Mediating the impact of role stress on burnout and satisfaction at work. *Journal of Organizational Behavior, 12,* 39–53.

Barling, J., MacEwen, K. E., Kelloway, E. K., & Higginbottom, S. F. (1994). Predictors and outcomes of elder-care-based interrole conflict. *Psychology and Aging, 9,* 391–397.

Batt, R., & Valcour, P. M. (2003). Human resources practices as predictors of work-family outcomes and employee turnover. *Industrial Relations, 42,* 189–220.

Bedeian, A. G., Burke, B. G., & Moffett, R. G. (1988). Outcomes of work-family conflict among married male and female professionals. *Journal of Management, 14,* 475–491.

Behson, S. J. (2002a). Coping with family-to-work conflict: The role of informal work accommodations to family. *Journal of Occupational Health Psychology, 7,* 324–341.

Behson, S. J. (2002b). Which dominates? The relative importance of work-family organizational support and general organizational context on employee outcomes. *Journal of Vocational Behavior, 61,* 53–72.

Berg, P., Kalleberg, A. L., & Appelbaum, E. (2003). Balancing work and family: The role of high-commitment environments. *Industrial Relations, 42,* 168–188.

Bernas, K. H., & Major, D. A. (2000). Contributors to stress resistance: Testing a model of women's work-family conflict. *Psychology of Women Quarterly, 24,* 170–178.

Bianchi, S. M., & Raley, S. (2003, June). *Changing work and family demographics.* Paper presented at the Workplace/Workforce Mismatch: Work, Family, Health, and Wellbeing Conference, Washington, DC.

Bluedorn, A. C., Kaufman, C. F., & Lane, P. M. (1992). How many things do you like to do at once? An introduction to monochronic and polychronic time. *Academy of Management Executive, 6,* 17–26.

Brim, O. G., Baltes, P. B., Bumpass, L. L., Cleary, P. D., Featherman, D. L., Hazzard, W. R., et al. (2003). National survey of midlife development in the United States (MIDUS), 1995–1996 [computer file]. Ann Arbor, MI: Interuniversity Consortium for Political and Social Research.

Bronfenbrenner, U. (1989). Ecological systems theory. *Annals of Child Development, 6,* 187–249.

Bruck, C. S., & Allen, T. D. (2003). The relationship between big five personality traits, negative affectivity, type A behavior, and work-family conflict. *Journal of Vocational Behavior, 63,* 457–472.

Buehler, R., Griffin, D., & Ross, M. (1994). Exploring the "planning fallacy": Why people underestimate their task completion times. *Journal of Personality and Social Psychology, 67,* 366–381.

Burke, R. J., & Greenglass, E. R. (1999). Work-family conflict, spouse support, and nursing staff well-being during organizational restructuring. *Journal of Occupational Health Psychology, 4,* 327–336.

Carlson, D. S. (1999). Personality and role variables as predictors of three forms of work-family conflict. *Journal of Vocational Behavior, 55,* 236–253.

Carlson, D. S., & Kacmar, K. M. (2000). Work-family conflict in the organization: Do life and role values make a difference? *Journal of Management, 26,* 1031–1054.

Carlson, D. S., Kacmar, K. M., & Williams, L. J. (2000). Construction and initial validation of a multidimensional measure of work-family conflict. *Journal of Vocational Behavior, 56,* 249–276.

Carlson, D. S., & Perrewé, P. L. (1999). The role of social support in the stressor-strain relationship: An examination of work-family conflict. *Journal of Management, 25*, 513–540.

Cartwright, M., Wardle, J., Steggles, N., Simon, A. E., Croker, H., & Jarvis, M. J. (2003). Stress and dietary practices in adolescents. *Health Psychology, 22*, 362–369.

Chan, C. J., & Margolin, G. (1994). The relationship between dual-earner couples' daily work mood and home affect. *Journal of Social and Personal Relationships, 11*, 573–586.

Clark, S. C. (2000). Work/family border theory: A new theory of work/family balance. *Human Relations, 53*, 747–770.

Cooper, M. L., Frone, M. R., Russell, M., & Mudar, P. (1995). Drinking to regulate positive and negative emotions: A motivational model of alcohol use. *Journal of Personality and Social Psychology, 69*, 990–1005.

Crouter, A. C., MacDermid, S. M., McHale, S. M., & Perry-Jenkins, M. (1990). Parental monitoring and perceptions of children's school performance and conduct in dual- and single-earner families. *Developmental Psychology, 26*, 649–657.

Curbow, B., McDonnell, K., Spratt, K., Griffin, J., & Agnew, J. (2003). Development of the work-family interface scale. *Early Childhood Research Quarterly, 18*, 310–330.

Daly, K. J. (2001). Deconstructing family time: From ideology to lived experience. *Journal of Marriage and Family, 63*, 283–294.

Devine, C. M., Connors, M. M., Sobal, J., & Bisogni, C. A. (2003). Sandwiching it in: Spillover of work onto food choices and family roles in low- and moderate-income urban households. *Social Science & Medicine, 56*, 617–630.

Families and Work Institute. (1999). The 1997 national study of the changing work force. Unpublished raw data. New York: Author.

Fowler, F. J., Jr. (1995). *Improving survey questions: Design and evaluation.* Thousand Oaks, CA: Sage.

Fox, M. L., & Dwyer, D. J. (1999). An investigation of the effects of time and involvement in the relationship between stressors and work-family conflict. *Journal of Occupational Health Psychology, 4*, 164–174.

Frone, M. R. (1999). Work stress and alcohol use. *Alcohol Research and Health, 23*, 284–291.

Frone, M. R. (2000). Work-family conflict and employee psychiatric disorders: The National Comorbidity Survey. *Journal of Applied Psychology, 85*, 888–895.

Frone, M. R. (2003). Work-family balance. In J. C. Quick & L. E. Tetrick (Eds.), *Handbook of occupational health psychology* (pp. 143–162). Washington, DC: American Psychological Association.

Frone, M. R., Barnes, G. M., & Farrell, M. P. (1994). Relationship of work-family conflict to substance use among employed mothers: The role of negative affect. *Journal of Marriage and the Family, 56*, 1019–1030.

Frone, M. R., Russell, M., & Barnes, G. M. (1996). Work-family conflict, gender, and health-related outcomes: A study of employed parents in two community samples. *Journal of Occupational Health Psychology, 1*, 57–69.

Frone, M. R., Russell, M., & Cooper, M. L. (1992a). Antecedents and outcomes of work-family conflict: Testing a model of the work-family interface. *Journal of Applied Psychology, 77*, 65–78.

Frone, M. R., Russell, M., & Cooper, M. L. (1992b). Prevalence of work-family conflict: Are work and family boundaries asymmetrically permeable? *Journal of Organizational Behavior, 13,* 723–729.

Frone, M. R., Russell, M., & Cooper, M. L. (1997). Relation of work-family conflict to health outcomes: A four-year longitudinal study of employed parents. *Journal of Occupational and Organizational Psychology, 70,* 325–335.

Frone, M. R., & Yardley, J. K. (1996). Workplace family-supportive programmes: Predictors of employed parents' importance ratings. *Journal of Occupational and Organizational Psychology, 69,* 351–366.

Frone, M. R., Yardley, J. K., & Markel, K. S. (1997). Developing and testing an integrative model of the work-family interface. *Journal of Vocational Behavior, 50,* 145–167.

Fu, C. K., & Shaffer, M. A. (2001). The tug of work and family. *Personnel Review, 30,* 502–522.

Goode, W. J. (1960). A theory of role strain. *American Sociological Review, 25,* 483–496.

Grandey, A. A., & Cropanzano, R. (1999). The conservation of resources model applied to work-family conflict and strain. *Journal of Vocational Behavior, 54,* 350–370.

Greenhaus, J. H., & Beutell, N. J. (1985). Sources of conflict between work and family roles. *Academy of Management Review, 10,* 76–88.

Greenhaus, J. H., Parasuraman, S., & Collins, K. M. (2001). Career involvement and family involvement as moderators of relationships between work-family conflict and withdrawal from a profession. *Journal of Occupational Health Psychology, 6,* 91–100.

Greeno, C. G., & Wing, R. R. (1994). Stress-induced eating. *Psychological Bulletin, 115,* 444–464.

Grzywacz, J. G. (2000). Work-family spillover and health during midlife: Is managing conflict everything? *American Journal of Health Promotion, 14,* 236–243.

Grzywacz, J. G., & Bass, B. (2003). Work, family, and mental health: Testing different models of work-family fit. *Journal of Marriage and Family, 65,* 248–262.

Grzywacz, J. G., & Marks, N. F. (2000). Reconceptualizing the work-family interface: An ecological perspective on the correlates of positive and negative spillover between work and family. *Journal of Occupational Health Psychology, 5,* 111–126.

Gutek, B. A., Searle, S., & Klepa, L. (1991). Rational versus gender role explanations for work-family conflict. *Journal of Applied Psychology, 76,* 560–568.

Hammer, L. B., Bauer, T. N., & Grandey, A. A. (2003). Work-family conflict and work-related withdrawal behaviors. *Journal of Business and Psychology, 17,* 419–436.

Harrison, D. A. (2002). Meaning and measurement of work role withdrawal: Current controversies and future fallout from changing information technology. In M. Kozlowski & M. Krausz (Eds.), *Voluntary employee withdrawal and inattendance: A current perspective* (pp. 95–131). New York: Plenum.

Harrison, L. J., & Ungerer, J. A. (2002). Maternal employment and infant-mother attachment security at 12 months postpartum. *Developmental Psychology, 38,* 758–773.

Hepburn, C. G., & Barling, J. (1996). Eldercare responsibilities, interrole conflict, and employee absence: A daily study. *Journal of Occupational Health Psychology, 1,* 311–318.

Higgins, C. A., & Duxbury, L. E. (1992). Work-family conflict: A comparison of dual-career and traditional-career men. *Journal of Organizational Behavior, 13,* 389–411.

Higgins, C. A., Duxbury, L., & Johnson, K. L. (2000). Part-time work for women: Does it really help balance work and family? *Human Resource Management, 39,* 17–32.

Jacobs, J. A. (2003, May). *Changing hours of employment in American families.* Paper presented at the Workplace/Workforce Mismatch: Work, Family, Health, and Wellbeing Conference, Washington, DC.

Jacobs, J. A., & Gerson, K. (1998). Who are the overworked Americans? *Review of Social Economy, 56,* 442–449.

Jacobs, J. A., & Gerson, K. (2001). Overworked individuals or overworked families? *Work and Occupations, 28,* 40–63.

Kahn, R. L., Wolfe, D. M., Quinn, R. P., Snoek, J. D., & Rosenthal, R. A. (1964). *Organizational stress: Studies in role conflict and ambiguity.* New York: Wiley.

Kanungo, R. N. (1982). *Work alienation: An integrative approach.* New York: Praeger.

Kelloway, E. K., Gottlieb, B. H., & Barham, L. (1999). The source, nature, and direction of work and family conflict: A longitudinal investigation. *Journal of Occupational Health Psychology, 4,* 337–346.

Kessler, R. C. (2002). National comorbidity survey, 1990–1992 [Computer file]. Ann Arbor, MI: Inter-university Consortium for Political and Social Research.

Kirchmeyer, C., & Cohen, A. (1999). Different strategies for managing the work/non-work interface: A test for unique pathways to work outcomes. *Work & Stress, 13,* 59–73.

Kopelman, R. E., Greenhaus, J. H., & Connolly, T. F. (1983). A model of work, family, and interrole conflict: A construct validation study. *Organizational Behavior and Human Performance, 32,* 198–215.

Landsbergis, P. A., Schnall, P. L., Belkic, K. L., Schwartz, J., Pickering, T. G., & Baker, D. (2001). Work stressors and cardiovascular disease. *Work, 17,* 191–208.

Macan, T. H. (1994). Time management: Test of a process model. *Journal of Applied Psychology, 79,* 381–391.

MacEwen, K. E., & Barling, J. (1994). Daily consequences of work interference with family and family interference with work. *Work & Stress, 8,* 244–254.

Madsen, S. R. (2003). The effects of home-based teleworking on work-family conflict. *Human Resource Development Quarterly, 14,* 35–58.

Major, V. S., Klein, K. J., & Ehrhart, M. G. (2002). Work time, work interference with family, and psychological distress. *Journal of Applied Psychology, 87,* 427–436.

Mallard, A. G. C., & Lance, C. E. (1998). Development and evaluation of a parent-employee interrole conflict scale. *Social Indicators Research, 45,* 343–370.

Markel, K. S., & Frone, M. R. (1998). Job characteristics, work-school conflict, and school outcomes among adolescents: Testing a structural model. *Journal of Applied Psychology, 83,* 277–287.

McManus, K., Korabik, K., Rosin, H. M., & Kelloway, E. K. (2002). Employed mothers and the work-family interface: Does family structure matter? *Human Relations, 55,* 1–30.

Mennino, S. F., & Brayfield, A. (2002). Job-family trade-offs. *Work and Occupations, 29,* 226–256.

Michaelson, S., & Johnson, D. E. (1997). *Border theory: The limits of cultural politics.* Minneapolis: University of Minnesota Press.

Netemeyer, R. G., Boles, J. S., & McMurrian, R. (1996). Development and validation of work-family conflict and family-work conflict scales. *Journal of Applied Psychology, 81,* 400–410.

Nippert-Eng, C. (1996). Calendars and keys: The classification of "home" and "work." *Sociological Forum, 11,* 563–582.

O'Driscoll, M. P., Ilgen, D. R., & Hildreth, K. (1992). Time devoted to job and off-job activities, interrole conflict, and affective experiences. *Journal of Applied Psychology, 77,* 272–279.

O'Driscoll, M. P., Poelmans, S., Spector, P. E., Kalliath, T., Allen, T. D., Cooper, C. L., et al. (2003). Family-responsive interventions, perceived organizational and supervisor support, work-family conflict and psychological strain. *International Journal of Stress and Management, 10,* 326–344.

Perrewé, P. L., Hochwarter, W. A., & Kiewitz, C. (1999). Value attainment: An explanation for the negative effects of work-family conflict on job and life satisfaction. *Journal of Occupational Health Psychology, 4,* 318–326.

Radloff, L. S. (1977). The CES-D scale: A self-report depression scale for research in the general population. *Applied Psychological Measurement, 1,* 385–401.

Raudenbush, S. W., Brennan, R. T., & Barnett, R. C. (1995). A multivariate hierarchical model for studying psychological change within married couples. *Journal of Family Psychology, 9,* 161–174.

Rice, R. W., Frone, M. R., & McFarlin, D. B. (1992). Work-nonwork conflict and the perceived quality of life. *Journal of Organizational Behavior, 13,* 155–168.

Rotondo, D. M., Carlson, D. S., & Kincaid, J. F. (2003). Coping with multiple dimensions of work-family conflict. *Personnel Review, 32,* 275–296.

Sayer, L. C. (2002, May). *Gender, time and inequality: Trends in women's and men's paid work, unpaid work and free time.* Paper presented at the Annual Meeting of the Population Association of America, Atlanta, GA.

Schwarz, N. (1999). Self-reports: How the questions shape the answers. *American Psychologist, 54,* 93–105.

Senecal, C., Vallerand, R. J., & Guay, F. (2001). Antecedents and outcomes of work-family conflict: Toward a motivational model. *Personality and Social Psychology Bulletin, 27,* 176–186.

Steptoe, A. (1991). The links between stress and illness. *Journal of Psychosomatic Research, 35,* 633–644.

Stoeva, A. Z., Chiu, R. K., & Greenhaus, J. H. (2002). Negative affectivity, role stress, and work-family conflict. *Journal of Vocational Behavior, 60,* 1–16.

Sumer, H. C., & Knight, P. A. (2001). How do people with different attachment styles balance work and family? A personality perspective on work-family linkage. *Journal of Applied Psychology, 86,* 653–663.

Teachman, J., & Crowder, K. (2002). Multilevel models in family research: Some conceptual and methodological issues. *Journal of Marriage and the Family, 64,* 280–294.

Thompson, C. A., Beauvais, L. L., & Lyness, K. S. (1999). When work-family benefits are not enough: The influence of work-family culture on benefit utilization, organizational attachment, and work-family conflict. *Journal of Vocational Behavior, 54,* 392–415.

Vinokur, A. D., Pierce, P. F., & Buck, C. L. (1999). Work-family conflicts of women in the air force: Their influence on mental health and functioning. *Journal of Organizational Behavior, 20,* 865–878.

Voydanoff, P. (2002). Linkages between the work-family interface and work, family, and individual outcomes: An integrative model. *Journal of Family Issues, 23,* 138–164.

Westman, M., & Etzion, D. (1995). Crossover of stress, strain and resources from one spouse to another. *Journal of Organizational Behavior, 16,* 169–181.

Appendix A

National Survey of Midlife Development in the United States (MIDUS)

Response choices

All the time, most of the time, sometimes, rarely, never

Item lead-in

How often have you experienced . . .

Work-to-family conflict items

Your job makes you feel too tired to do the things that need attention at home.

Stress at work makes you irritable at home.

Job worries or problems distract you when you are at home.

Your job reduces the effort you can give to activities at home.

Family-to-work conflict items

Personal or family worries and problems distract you when you are at work.

Stress at home makes you irritable at work.

Activities and chores at home prevent you from getting the amount of sleep you need to do your job well.

Responsibilities at home reduce the effort you can devote to your job.

National Study of the Changing Workforce (NSCW)

Response choices

Very often, often, sometimes, rarely, never

Item lead-in

In the past three months, how often . . .

Work-to-family conflict items

. . . have you NOT had enough time for your family or other important people in your life because of your job?

. . . have you NOT had the energy to do things with your family or other important people in your life because of your job?

. . . have you NOT been able to get everything done at home each day because of your job?

. . . have you NOT been in as good a mood as you would like to be at home because of your job?

Family-to-work conflict items

. . . has your family or personal life kept you from getting work done on time at your job?

. . . has your family or personal life kept you from taking on extra work at your job?

. . . has your family or personal life kept you from doing as good a job at work as you could?

. . . has your family or personal life drained you of the energy you needed to do your job?

. . . has your family or personal life kept you from concentrating on your job?

National Comorbidity Survey (NCS)

Response choices

Often, sometimes, rarely, never

Work-to-family conflict items

How often do things going on at work make you tense and irritable at home?

How often do the demands of your job interfere with your family life?

When you are at home, how often do you think about things going on at work?

Family-to-work conflict items

How often do things going on at home make you tense and irritable on the job?

How often do the demands of your family interfere with your work on the job?

When you are at work, how often do you think about things going on at home?

7

Harassment and Discrimination

Kathleen M. Rospenda
Judith A. Richman

In recent years, there has been exponential growth in research on specific types of workplace harassment and discrimination—particularly sexual harassment and racial discrimination. However, there is a dearth of literature on the *overall* experience of workplace harassment and discrimination, that is, whether and how these experiences overlap, what general theories apply to this broad class of workplace stressors, and whether experiences of different kinds of harassment and discrimination lead to similar outcomes. In fact, anecdotal accounts of harassment and discrimination tend to indicate that different types of harassment and discrimination frequently occur together (e.g., "gendered racism," Essed, 1991), suggesting that distinctions between types may be artificial. Thus, the purpose of this chapter is to synthesize the literatures on various types of harassment and discrimination to provide an overall picture of the meaning and implications of these types of experiences in the workplace. We draw heavily from the sexual harassment literature, however, because theory development and overall quantity of research predominate in this area. We believe that much of what has been learned in the area of sexual harassment research can be applied to the study of other forms of harassment and discrimination.

We first articulate the distinction between harassment and discrimination and define these separate but related constructs. Then we discuss the prevalence of different types of harassment and discrimination at work and delineate key measurement issues. Next we present major theoretical models that have been applied to the study of harassment and discrimination. We then describe the antecedents, outcomes, and moderators associated with harassment and discrimination. Throughout the chapter, we highlight major empirical studies that have looked at these phenomena in work settings. We conclude with a discussion of fruitful future research directions and implications.

Definition of Workplace
Harassment and Discrimination

In the United States, when harassment is mentioned in the context of work, most people assume the reference is to sexual harassment. However, sexual harassment is only one form of workplace harassment actionable under U.S. civil rights laws (Platt, 1994). In the United States, such laws protect against employment discrimination based on race, ethnicity, color, national origin, sex, religion, age, and disability. Thus, the intent of these laws is to protect historically less powerful groups. The essence of harassment and discrimination as stressors involves perceiving differential treatment in the workplace based on some biological, physical, or social characteristic leading to the creation of an unwelcoming or hostile environment that can negatively affect targets' job satisfaction, mental and physical health, and ability to do the job.

Although we recognize that alternate "equal opportunity" forms exist that are not based on legally protected characteristics, the focus of this chapter is on those forms of harassment and discrimination that are covered under U.S. law. We should note, however, that legally proscribed forms of harassment not only tend to co-occur (as noted earlier) but also may occur alongside more generalized harassment (e.g., bullying) and even violence on the job. For example, Barling, Rogers, and Kelloway (2001) found that sexual harassment and workplace violence were highly correlated and predicted negative outcomes for victims in a similar way in a sample of in-home health and mental health care workers. Rospenda (2002) also found a moderate correlation between sexual harassment and generalized workplace harassment in a university-employed sample. We are unaware of research that has studied relationships between other illegal forms of harassment and generalized harassment or violence, but readers should keep in mind that many different types of mistreatment may co-occur in workplaces conducive to such behaviors. (See Chapter 8 in this volume, by Schat and Kelloway, for a discussion of more generalized forms of harassment that have often been conceptualized as workplace violence.)

We draw our definition of harassment from guidelines proposed by the U.S. Equal Employment Opportunity Commission (EEOC; 1993). Although the guidelines were ultimately withdrawn because of political pressures, they are still useful for purposes of definition. Under the guidelines,

> Harassment is verbal or physical conduct that denigrates or shows hostility or aversion toward an individual because of his/her race, color, religion, gender, national origin, age, or disability, or that of his/her relatives, friends, or associates, and that (i) has the purpose or effect of creating an intimidating, hostile, or offensive work environment; (ii) has the purpose or effect of unreasonably interfering with an individual's work performance; or (iii) otherwise adversely affects an individual's employment opportunities. (pp. 51268–51269)

Although these guidelines refer separately to the characteristics of race, color, and national origin, for the purposes of this chapter, we refer more generally to the construct of race as encompassing these forms of harassment and discrimination, which is consistent with most existing research. Also, sexual orientation is not mentioned by the guidelines, as it does not currently represent a protected characteristic under U.S. law. However, there has been movement toward including sexual orientation under civil rights laws (Kovach, 1995), and some U.S. states already have legal protections in place prohibiting discrimination on the basis of sexual orientation (Huang & Kleiner, 2000). Thus, we include this form of harassment and discrimination in our discussion.

Schneider, Hitlan, and Radhakrishnan (2000) noted that most research has not made a distinction between racial-ethnic harassment and discrimination. This comment is true of psychological research on other forms of harassment and discrimination as well. How does harassment differ from discrimination? Legal scholars have conceptualized *harassment* as more micro behaviors that cause harm to an individual in the workplace and *discrimination* as the more global context in which the harm occurs (Ehrenreich, 1999). For example, the net effect of sexual harassment experiences would be sex discrimination when the harassment serves to create a hostile environment or affect the terms or conditions of the job. Similarly, in their study of ethnic harassment, Schneider and colleagues (2000) viewed harassment as experiences that may contribute to a hostile environment, whereas ethnic discrimination was defined as "unequal job treatment or lack of positive opportunities because of one's race-ethnicity" (p. 3). In terms of harassment and discrimination in the workplace, then, we use the term *harassment* to refer to negative behaviors that are directed toward individuals because of their ascribed characteristics (e.g., sex, race, age, religion, disability, sexual orientation) and *discrimination* to refer to unequal treatment or opportunities at the job or occupational level because of one's ascribed characteristics rather than one's qualifications or job performance (e.g., Gutek, Cohen, & Tsui, 1996).

Our approach to the discussion of harassment and discrimination is similar to that taken in the sexual harassment literature. That is, drawing from Fitzgerald and colleagues' (Fitzgerald, Gelfand, & Drasgow, 1995; Fitzgerald, Swan, & Magley, 1997) work in the area of sexual harassment, we further distinguish between legal, behavioral, and psychological definitions of harassment and discrimination. A legal definition would be based on criteria for judging a particular set of experiences as constituting harassment or discrimination, as determined by law. A behavioral definition of harassment or discrimination references the measurement strategy employed, that is, whether subjects report experiencing behaviors that might be considered harassing or discriminatory. A psychological definition of harassment and discrimination refers to the impact of these experiences on victims (Fitzgerald, Swan, et al., 1997). Thus, researchers may call what they have measured harassment or discrimination, but targets and/or legal scholars may not agree. Alternatively, targets may label their experiences as harassing or discriminatory, but their specific experiences may not be incorporated in measures of these constructs and/or may not meet legal criteria for harassment or discrimination. Definitional issues remain a bone of contention. Our perspective here recognizes that the concepts of harassment and discrimination are aligned with legal constructs as well as corresponding behavioral constructs. Although we discuss these issues briefly, our focus is on harassment and discrimination as perceptual or psychological experiences and how these experiences affect targets.

We qualify our discussion by noting that harassing workplace experiences are likely a universal phenomenon. The interpretation of these experiences, however, is dependent on the cultural context in which they occur. That is, specific behaviors may or may not be interpreted as harassing, depending on the cultural "lens" through which they are viewed. For example, Mazur (2002) suggests that hostile environment types of sexual harassment are generally considered less problematic in Spain and France as a result of less prohibitive views on sexuality in those cultures. Likewise, laws and legislation related to discrimination differ across countries reflecting cultural differences in how harassment and discrimination are defined. Nevertheless, cross-cultural research supports the generalizability of conceptual models of sexual harassment (Gelfand, Fitzgerald, & Drasgow, 1995; Wasti, Bergman, Glomb, & Drasgow, 2000) and indicates that targets of sexual harassment exhibit similar negative psychological outcomes across cultures (Shupe, Cortina, Ramos, Fitzgerald, & Salisbury, 2002; Wasti et al., 2000). Although this research was limited to sexual harassment, it suggests that broad concepts of harassment and discrimination are to at least some extent universal, even if their specific manifestations differ by culture (Barak, 1997). Thus, portions of this review that deal with broader conceptual issues (e.g., models of harassment and discrimination) rather than more specific culture-bound issues such as prevalence, will likely be the most generalizable to non-U.S. contexts. (For more on international issues related to workplace stress, see Chapter 20, by Lin and Spector, in this volume.)

Prevalence of Harassment and Discrimination

Research on harassment and discrimination has generally proceeded with a narrow focus on specific types of experiences or, more frequently in non-occupational research, has utilized a broad single-item measure to assess whether an individual has ever experienced harassment or discrimination. Therefore, formulating an accurate assessment of the prevalence of these experiences is difficult. A national study conducted by Kessler, Mickelson, and Williams (1999) probably provides the best estimate of the prevalence of discrimination in the general population. Kessler et al. base their estimates on data collected for the Midlife Development in the United States (MIDUS) survey, a national telephone and mail survey of over 3,000 adults in the continental United States aged 25 to 74. Kessler et al. took the unique approach of combining overall assessments of perceived lifetime discrimination in a variety of domains (including work) as well as measuring more specific day-to-day experiences. They found that job-related discrimination events were more frequently cited than all other types of discrimination (e.g., hassled by police, denied a bank loan, prevented from renting/buying a home, denied/received inferior service): 6% of respondents reported being fired from a job, 13% reported not being given a promotion, and 16% reported not being hired for a job for discriminatory reasons at some time in their lives. Although the researchers did not find significant differences in perceived job discrimination for men versus women, whites were generally less likely to report these types of experiences compared with blacks and other ethnic minorities.

Kessler et al. (1999) also assessed nine specific day-to-day events (e.g., "people act as if you are inferior," "you are called names or insulted"). Although the researchers labeled these experiences as discriminatory, they would fit under our definition of harassment. Although they did not refer specifically to job contexts in measuring these events, Kessler et al. found that about 61% of their sample reported that they generally experience one or more of these behaviors on a day-to-day basis. Overall, whites reported a lower likelihood of these experiences (56%) compared with blacks (91%) and other minorities (81%).

Kessler et al. (1999) found that the four most frequent reasons attributed to these experiences by those who reported experiencing harassment or discrimination were race/ethnicity (37%), gender (33%), appearance (28%), and age (24%). Experiences were attributed to religion (7%), disability (4%), and sexual orientation (4%) far less often. These percentages do not sum to 100, as over 30% of those who reported harassment or discrimination attributed it to more than one reason. This suggests that experiences of harassment and discrimination may not clearly map to specific categories, or, alternatively, that different types of harassment and discrimination tend to occur together. Again, although Kessler et al. did not specifically assess harassment in the workplace, their data still provide compelling evidence that harassment is a widespread social phenomenon.

Unlike Kessler et al. (1999), Pavalko, Mossakowski, and Hamilton (2003) focused on work discrimination in a survey of 1,778 employed black and white women from the National Longitudinal Survey of Mature Women. Pavalko et al. found that about 16% of women respondents reported experiencing work discrimination between 1977 and 1982, and 12% reported experiencing work discrimination between 1984 and 1989. Although Pavalko et al.'s sample was less representative (women ranged in age from 47 to 62), the findings regarding overall work discrimination are similar to those reported in Kessler et al. (1999). Overall, 2% of the sample attributed discrimination experiences to race, 6% to age, 3% to gender, 3% to other, and 2% to multiple reasons. Black women were more likely than white women to attribute work discrimination to race, whereas white women were more likely to attribute it to age or gender. Not unexpectedly for this older sample, age was the most salient discriminatory factor, whereas Kessler et al. had found that race and gender were much more salient. This illustrates the importance of considering sample demographics when interpreting findings related to discrimination.

It is important to note that Kessler et al. (1999) and Pavalko et al.'s (2003) estimates may be understating the prevalence of these phenomena. Sexual harassment research has shown that when individuals are asked specifically whether they have experienced sexual harassment, prevalence estimates are lower than when they are asked whether or not they have experienced specific behaviors that fall under the domain of sexual harassment (Brooks & Perot, 1991; Fitzgerald et al., 1988). Pavalko and her colleagues (2003) acknowledge that this phenomenon is likely true of discrimination research in general.

The following sections detail prevalence rates for specific types of harassment and discrimination, which, as Pavalko et al. (2003) suspected, are generally higher than for overall estimates of discrimination and harassment. As others have noted in reference to research on sexual harassment, it is often difficult to compare prevalence estimates because of differing survey methodology and instrumentation (e.g., Arvey & Cavanaugh, 1995; Gruber, 1997). In our review of the literature, we found that the same caveat applies to research on other forms of harassment and discrimination.

Sexual Harassment and Sex Discrimination

Sexual harassment is the most frequently studied form of workplace harassment or discrimination. A widely accepted definition of sexual harassment is that it represents a "latent behavioral construct composed of three dimensions": gender harassment (i.e., insulting or degrading gender-related behaviors or remarks that convey hostility), unwanted sexual attention (i.e., pressure for sexual involvement of some sort that is *not* associated with actual or implied job outcomes), and sexual coercion (i.e., pressure for sexual involvement that *is* associated with actual or implied job outcomes) (Fitzgerald, Hulin, & Drasgow, 1994, p. 57). Gender harassment and unwanted sexual attention reflect the legal construct of "hostile environment" harassment, whereas sexual coercion reflects the legal construct of "quid pro quo" harassment.

A conservative estimate would be that about 50% of women will experience sexual harassment in the workplace at some time in their lives (Gutek, 1985; Koss et al., 1994; Loy & Stewart, 1984; see Rospenda, 1998, for a review; U.S. Merit Systems Protection Board [USMSPB], 1981, 1988, 1995), a finding that has been replicated outside of the United States (Barak,

Pitterman, & Yitzhaki, 1995; Canadian Human Rights Commission [CHRC], 1983; Crocker & Kalemba, 1999; Wise & Stanley, 1987). Gruber's (1997) review of the literature, however, indicated that sexual harassment is generally less prevalent for European women (particularly in Scandinavia, where women enjoy a higher level of social equality) than for American women. In terms of specific categories of sexual harassment, prevalence is higher for hostile environment–type experiences compared with quid pro quo–type experiences, although those who experience quid pro quo harassment generally also experience hostile environment sexual harassment (e.g., Gruber, 1997).

Only recently has it become more common to include men in studies of sexual harassment because it has traditionally been conceptualized as a "women's issue." For men, prevalence of sexual harassment has been found to be about 15% (USMSPB, 1981, 1988, 1995). Men have generally been found to report experiences of sexual harassment at much lower rates than women, although estimates have varied widely with prevalence at 40% or higher in some studies (e.g., Gutek, 1985; Morrow, McElroy, & Phillips, 1994), particularly those that have worded instruments so as to apply to men as well as women (e.g., Richman et al., 1999) or specifically to men (e.g., Waldo, Berdahl, & Fitzgerald, 1998). In fact, Richman et al.'s (1999) study of university employees indicated no gender differences in the prevalence of sexual harassment. However, what *was* salient was an interaction between gender and occupational status. Although higher-status women (i.e., faculty) had higher rates of sexual harassment than did men, lower-status men (i.e., clerical and service workers) had higher rates than did women in these occupational groups.

Other than Kessler et al.'s (1999) finding that 33% of a national sample reported ever being discriminated against because of their gender (48% of women and 11 % of men), few studies have looked at the prevalence of the broader category of sex or gender discrimination. In a longitudinal study of over 1,000 master of business administration graduates, Murrell, Olson, and Frieze (1995) found that 52% of 431 women respondents in 1984 indicated having experienced discrimination in their work at some time in their lives. Of these, approximately 4% mentioned sexual harassment experiences, and 82% (or 39% of all women respondents) mentioned that it was some other form of gender discrimination. In 1991, 83% of those experiencing discrimination (or about 28% of all women respondents) attributed it to gender-related reasons. Murrell et al. did not report data for men in their study.

Klonoff and Landrine (1995) used the Schedule of Sexist Events, a 20-item measure of sex discrimination in a variety of areas including work, in their study of 631 women (47% college students, the rest recruited from the community). About 60% of this sample indicated having had one or more experiences of work discrimination at some point in their lives because of their gender, whereas 37% of the sample had such an experience in the past year. Yoder and McDonald (1998) used the sexist discrimination in the workplace subscale of the Schedule of Sexist Events to measure discrimination in a national sample of 44 women firefighters. They found that 93% of the women reported one or more experiences with sexist workplace discrimination at work. Finally, in a 1987 telephone survey of 51 black and 50 white women in California, which conflated harassment and discrimination, Krieger (1990) found that up to 36% of the white women and 38% of the black women reported experiencing discrimination, being "prevented from doing something" or being "hassled or made to feel inferior because you're a woman" (Krieger, 1990, p. 1274) at some time when getting a job or when at work (this difference in prevalence between white and black women was not significant).

Although most studies utilized convenience samples and failed to consider whether gender discrimination might be perceived by men (see Kessler et al., 1999, for an exception), these results indicate that somewhere between 33% and 60% of women will experience gender discrimination at some point in their lives. Prevalence is likely higher for women in nontraditional occupations (e.g., firefighting; Yoder & Aniakudo, 1996). It is likely that Klonoff and Landrine's (1995) prevalence estimate was higher than most other studies because they asked multiple, specific questions about discriminatory experiences rather than rely on a single, more general question about discrimination. This supports the general view that prevalence estimates of harassment and discrimination are lower when respondents are forced to label their experiences as such. Similarly, although sexual harassment is considered to be a form of sex discrimination, Murrell et al. (1995) note that 36% of women who reported experiencing sexual harassment by 1991 did not label these experiences as discrimination. This highlights the importance of measuring both individual experiences and overall perceptions of harassment and discrimination at work.

Racial Harassment and Discrimination

Studies of racial or ethnic harassment and discrimination have typically revealed high prevalence rates, particularly for blacks. As described above, Kessler et al. (1999) found that about 37% of a national sample reported experiencing discrimination attributable to race/ethnicity, including 21% of non-Hispanic whites, 90% of non-Hispanic blacks, and 77% of "other" race/ethnicity. Like the majority of research on racial discrimination and harassment, however, Kessler et al.'s measures were not limited to workplace harassment and discrimination.

In a major study that did focus on workplace experiences, the U.S. Department of Defense (DOD) conducted a survey on equal opportunity and racial/ethnic issues in active duty personnel (Scarville, Button, Edwards, Lancaster, & Elig, 1999). Over 76,000 enlisted men and women in all branches of the military were surveyed resulting in a 53% response rate. The survey assessed 57 behaviors that might be considered racial/ethnic harassment, insensitivity, or discrimination. Results indicated that 62% of white respondents experienced one or more race-related offensive encounters (e.g., racist stories/jokes, offensive remarks) with other DOD personnel in the past 24 months, compared with between 69% and 78% of racial/ethnic minority group members. Four percent of whites reported experiencing discriminatory behaviors that had an impact on their career or assignment because of their race, compared with between 10% and 18% of racial/ethnic minorities. Similarly, only 4% of whites, compared with between 8% and 19% of racial/ethnic minorities, reported experiencing unfair evaluations at work due to their race. As would be expected, whites were generally found to experience the fewest racially harassing or discriminatory behaviors compared with racial/ethnic minority group members.

Research focusing on racial harassment and discrimination in civilian work settings has generally found slightly lower prevalence of harassment experiences but higher prevalence of discriminatory experiences, compared with the findings of Scarville et al. (1999), when separate estimates were reported. For example, Landrine and Klonoff (1996) found that about 54% of a sample of 153 black students, faculty, and staff of a large university reported being treated differently by an employer or boss because of their race in the past year, and 69% reported differential treatment by an employer or boss in their entire lives. Schneider et al. (2000) developed a measure specifically to assess experiences of ethnic harassment and found that 40% of a sample of Anglo and Hispanic school district employees reported one or more such experiences at work in the past 24 months (prevalence did not differ by employee ethnicity, Schneider et al. proposed, because Anglos were underrepresented in their work contexts). Finally, Krieger (1990) found that 4% of white women and up to 53% of black women in their community sample reported being discriminated against, prevented from doing something, hassled, or made to feel inferior at work, a difference that was highly significant. Although research in this area utilized widely differing samples, methodology, and measurement strategies, we conservatively estimate that about 40% of racial/ethnic minorities (and likely an even higher percentage of blacks) will experience racial harassment or discrimination at work some time in their lives.

Harassment and Discrimination
Related to Age, Disability, and Religion

There is very little empirical data on prevalence of workplace discrimination due to age, and we were unable to locate any research on age-related harassment. In a sample of over 1,600 managers (94% male, 88% were 40 years old or older) in the United Kingdom, McGoldrick and Arrowsmith (2001) found that up to 44% had experienced some form of discrimination at work because of being older. Interestingly, up to 30% had also reported some form of discrimination because of being younger, a possibility that is not often considered in age discrimination research. Although conducted nearly 30 years ago, Kasschau (1977) reported that age-related discrimination at work was reported at similar rates to racial harassment in a community sample of over 1,000 individuals aged 45 to 74: 13% of whites, 16% of Mexican Americans, and 23% of blacks reported being discriminated against because of their age in an employment situation at some time in their lives.

In terms of disability, anecdotal evidence suggests that discrimination and harassment of disabled individuals in the workplace is common (O'Keeffe, 1993). Balser (2000) describes a 1994 Louis Harris study that found 30% of a sample of adults reported experiencing job-related discrimination due to a disability. We were unable to locate any research on prevalence of harassment and discrimination due to religion.

Harassment and Discrimination Due to Sexual Orientation

Although research on the prevalence of workplace harassment and discrimination due to sexual orientation is also scarce, Croteau's (1996) thorough review of the literature indicated that between 25% and 66% of lesbian, gay, and bisexual workers reported experiencing discrimination on the job at some point in their lives. Croteau notes that sampling and methodological problems preclude "true" estimates of discrimination (p. 198). These rates, however, are consistent with prevalence estimates of workplace discrimination reported by other minority groups.

In sum, prevalence estimates indicate that workplace harassment and discrimination are widespread phenomena. Prevalence estimates are quite variable, however, depending on methodological factors such as sampling strategy, structure of questions, and reference period employed. Although studies often confounded harassment and discrimination, the general trend seems to suggest that workplace harassment experiences may be more common than work-related discrimination. Although most studies focus on experiences of minority groups, some research has demonstrated that majority group members also perceive harassment and discrimination (e.g., men perceive gender harassment, younger workers perceive age discrimination, whites perceive racial discrimination), a finding that has not received much attention in the research.

Measurement Issues

There are several measurement issues specific to harassment and discrimination as job-related stressors. First is the issue of construct definition, as we discussed in the introduction. As legal scholars and social science researchers have pointed out, harassment and discrimination are not the same thing yet are often confounded in research and theory (e.g., Ehrenreich, 1999; Schneider et al., 2000). Researchers in the area of racial harassment and discrimination have generally used the term "racial discrimination" to describe their measures. These measures often include items assessing experiences like being called racist names or being told racist jokes (e.g., Landrine & Klonoff, 1996; Sanchez & Brock, 1996), which more closely fit a definition of harassment. Although harassment and discrimination clearly have similar outcomes and are related constructs, they are not equivalent, and researchers should take care not to treat them as if they were.

A related issue is that researchers, particularly in the area of racial discrimination, have tended to confound personal experiences of harassment and discrimination (e.g., not hired because you are Black) with items that measure perceptions of how minorities are generally treated (e.g., "Blacks are treated badly at work"—Mays, Coleman, & Jackson, 1996, p. 329; "some of the policies and practices of this organization are racist/sexist"—Ensher, Grant-Vallone, & Donaldson, 2001, p. 61), or with items that measure responses to discrimination or harassment (e.g., "forced to take drastic steps . . . such as filing a grievance . . . to deal with some racist thing that was done to you"—Landrine & Klonoff, 1996, p. 165). Again, it is likely that personal experiences with harassment or discrimination are related to general feelings about how minorities are treated, and the severity of personally experienced harassment or discrimination is likely related to how people cope with it. Including these types of items in measures of harassment and discrimination, however, may distort obtained prevalence rates of these experiences as well as bias relationships with outcomes. Further, such studies may actually be tapping organizational climate, a factor that has been shown to be related to harassment and discrimination but that is conceptually distinct (e.g., Fitzgerald et al., 1994).

A third issue is whether researchers should measure specific harassing or discriminatory events versus a more global measure requiring respondents to specifically label their experiences as harassment or discrimination. In the sexual harassment arena, Fitzgerald and colleagues purposefully developed the Sexual Experiences Questionnaire (SEQ, the major instrument used to measure sexual harassment) to separate behavioral indicators of sexual harassment from the actual labeling of the experiences as sexual harassment, given that some individuals who report experiencing sexually harassing behaviors do not label these experiences as harassment (Fitzgerald et al., 1995; Fitzgerald et al., 1988). It has been demonstrated that measures requiring respondents to label their experiences as harassment or discrimination lead to lower prevalence estimates than questions about specific events (Brown, 2001) and that multi-item measures of specific events are more psychometrically sound (e.g., see Fitzgerald et al., 1988; Kessler et al., 1999; Pavalko et al., 2003).

Another issue involves the optimal time period for measurement: should harassment and discrimination be measured with reference to lifetime prevalence, or should the reference period be more time-limited? In the sexual harassment literature, the most widely used measures of sexual harassment (e.g., the SEQ and the USMSPB measures) have employed a 24-month reference period. However, Arvey and Cavanaugh (1995) argue that longer reference periods can lead to inaccurate recall, potentially biasing estimates of the prevalence of harassment. They recommended that researchers use reference periods of no longer than 12 months. Because research has found that chronic harassment can lead to more severe negative outcomes (e.g., Rospenda, Richman, Wislar, & Flaherty, 2000), it may be useful to gauge more recent experiences along with lifetime history of harassment and discrimination, as individuals with a history of exposure to such experiences may be especially vulnerable to negative outcomes (e.g., Kessler et al., 1999).

Because of the legal ramifications of workplace harassment and discrimination, there has been particular interest in measurement of these constructs, arguably more so than most other types of work stress. For example, accurately determining the prevalence of sexual harassment was a key pursuit in the early research. However, comparison of prevalence rates between studies was often impossible because of the differing measurement strategies used. To address this situation, Fitzgerald and her colleagues have pursued an extensive research program into the development and validation of the SEQ (see Fitzgerald, Drasgow, Hulin, Gelfand, & Magley, 1997; Fitzgerald et al., 1988; Schneider, Swan, & Fitzgerald, 1997), which makes it the measure of choice for many sexual harassment researchers. Although Fitzgerald, Swan, et al. (1997) caution against use of the SEQ to represent the legal construct of sexual harassment, this measure has helped to address the problem of comparability of measures (for further discussion of measurement issues related to sexual harassment, see Gutek & Done, 2001).

Researchers of other forms of harassment and discrimination have attempted to follow suit. For example, Schneider et al. (2000) constructed a measure similar in design to the SEQ to measure experiences of ethnic harassment. Similarly, Landrine and Klonoff (1996) have reported on the Schedule of Racist Events, which purports to measure racial discrimination in work and life contexts. However, no single measure of racial harassment/discrimination has achieved widespread usage. Researchers outside of the sexual harassment field still tend to develop their own instruments to measure harassment and discrimination, leading to the same problems with comparability of results as seen in the sexual harassment literature.

Major Theoretical Models of Harassment and Discrimination

Research on various types of workplace harassment and discrimination has generally reflected a stress orientation (e.g., Fitzgerald et al., 1994; Holzbauer & Berven, 1996; Landrine & Klonoff, 1996; Landrine, Klonoff, Gibbs, Manning, & Lund, 1995; McCann & Giles, 2002; Meyer, 1995; Richman, Flaherty, & Rospenda, 1996; Sanchez & Brock, 1996), though not always explicitly. Detailed models have also been tested, mainly to explain either antecedents or consequences of particular types of workplace harassment and discrimination. This is particularly true in the research on sexual harassment (e.g., Tangri, Burt, & Johnson, 1982) and racial harassment/discrimination (e.g., Guitierres, Saenz, & Green, 1994; James, 1994; Sanchez & Brock, 1996). To date, these areas have been afforded the most research attention, most likely because sexual and racial harassment and discrimination, more than other forms of harassment and discrimination, represent politically "hot topics." In this section, we describe the major models of harassment and discrimination that we feel might be usefully applied to the study of all forms of these experiences.

Probably the best known, most comprehensive, and most widely supported theoretical model in this area was developed by Fitzgerald and colleagues (Fitzgerald et al., 1994) to explain the antecedents and consequences of sexual harassment. Researchers have also successfully used this model to guide the study of ethnic (Schneider et al., 2000) and sexual orientation–related (Waldo, 1999) harassment. Drawing from an occupational stress paradigm, sexual harassment is conceptualized as one of a variety of other psychosocial work stressors, all of which can be associated with negative outcomes for individuals (Fitzgerald et al., 1994). This model posits that organizational and job context factors are primary antecedents of sexual harassment. More specifically, Fitzgerald et al. propose that a higher prevalence of sexual harassment will be found in situations characterized by a male-dominated job-gender context (e.g., high male-to-female ratio, historically male occupation) and harassment-tolerant organizational climate. The model also proposes that the effects of harassment are moderated by personal vulnerability and response or coping styles of targets. Particularly, those with certain demographic characteristics (e.g., younger, unmarried) and cognitive proclivities (e.g., sensitivity to harassment) and those who actively respond to harassment (e.g., filing a complaint, reporting) will be more likely to experience negative effects. Finally, the model posits that sexual harassment can affect targets in three domains: the job, mental health, and physical health (see Gutek & Koss, 1993, for a review). Although other occupational stressors are not directly incorporated in this model, Fitzgerald et al. (1994) assert that their measurement is crucial in determining a base level of stress in the workplace against which the effects of harassment can be compared. This model has been extensively tested in a wide variety of settings, and its main hypothesized relationships have generally been supported (e.g., Fitzgerald, Drasgow, et al., 1997; Glomb, Munson, Hulin, Bergman, & Drasgow, 1999; Glomb et al., 1997).

Other researchers have elaborated why workplace harassment represents a unique job stressor. Richman et al. (1996) note that models of workplace stress have historically focused on certain aspects of work, such as lack of control and overwork, and neglected workplace interpersonal relationships, a sentiment that other researchers have also expressed (Beehr, 1995;

Glowinkowski & Cooper, 1986; Spector, Dwyer, & Jex, 1988). Richman et al. argue that sexual harassment is a manifestation of interpersonally based alienation and lack of control at work, making it more distressing than typically studied job stressors linked to the structure of the job (Richman et al., 1996; Rospenda et al., 2000).

Although not specific to workplace settings, the work of Dion and colleagues has also demonstrated the utility of conceptualizing a variety of forms of discrimination from within a stress framework (e.g., Dion, Dion, & Pak, 1992; Dion & Earn, 1975). Dion and colleagues have found evidence that various forms of discrimination, for example racial (Dion et al., 1992), gender (Dion, 1975), and sexual orientation (Birt & Dion, 1987), are associated with a variety of negative mental health outcomes, even after statistically controlling for other life stressors (Dion et al., 1992; Pak, Dion, & Dion, 1991). In the racial harassment and discrimination literature, researchers have applied social identity theory to explain this phenomenon. Social identity theory (Tajfel & Turner, 1985) proposes that people conceptualize their own and others' identities on the basis of membership in social categories. As noted by James (1994), "race is a membership category that typically has strong identity influences for minority individuals" (p. 128) and is often tied to esteem. James (1994) notes that individuals are highly motivated to maintain esteem, or a positive sense of self-worth. Because racial harassment and discrimination experiences are inextricably tied to group membership, they can represent a significant threat to esteem and thus to the mental health of minority group members (James, 1994; James, Lovato, & Khoo, 1994). Sanchez and Brock (1996) note that such individuals are not immune to the effects of other more typically studied job stressors (e.g., role conflict and ambiguity); hence, racial harassment and discrimination represent an additional source of stress for minority group members. Researchers have also applied social identity theory to explore why groups who are underrepresented in certain occupations may feel increased pressure to perform (e.g., to increase acceptance by the majority group and maintain esteem) when faced with discrimination (Parker & Griffin, 2002).

Although most stress-based models of harassment and discrimination focus on negative outcomes associated with these experiences, other models have focused on explaining their antecedents. The most common are social interactionist, or "person-by-situation" models. These types of models are primarily seen in the sexual harassment literature and propose that workplace norms that tacitly endorse harassment facilitate harassment tendencies among men who are predisposed to harass (e.g., have hostile attitudes toward women, associate sex with power, endorse stereotypical sex role beliefs) (Pryor & Fitzgerald, 2003). Pryor and his colleagues have found support for these models (e.g., Pryor, LaVite, & Stoller, 1993) and argue that neither organizational nor personal characteristics of perpetrators are sufficient to explain the occurrence of sexually harassing behavior. Thus, it is important to consider the context of such experiences when they occur.

Similarly, Dekker and Barling (1998) surveyed a sample of male faculty and staff at a Canadian university and found that higher perceived organizational tolerance, sexualized work environment, and false beliefs about sexual harassment (e.g., women bring it on themselves) contributed to men's self-reported perpetration of sexually harassing behaviors. Additionally, perceptions of organizational tolerance were most strongly linked to perpetration of harassing behaviors when men had higher levels of false sexual harassment beliefs, adversarial sexual beliefs, and lower ability to see things from another's perspective, thus supporting a person-by-situation model.

Because this type of model focuses on the characteristics unique to each situation, it probably provides the most useful and generalizable framework for examining the antecedents of various types of workplace harassment and discrimination (for further information on models that have been applied to the study of sexual harassment, see Gutek & Done, 2001; O'Hare & O'Donohue, 1998; Tangri et al., 1982). These ideas have been theoretically discussed in the context of other forms of harassment and discrimination. For example, Duncan (2001) noted that ageism can be seen as a result of socialization processes that instill fear and anxiety about getting older. Structural factors in organizations, such as compulsory retirement, also serve to reinforce the idea that old age is a time of nonproductivity (Duncan, 2001, p. 27). However, we were unable to locate empirical research that applied person-by-situation models to study other forms of harassment and discrimination.

Finally, power differential models view harassment/discrimination as the effect of one individual unfairly or unequally exerting some form of held power (e.g., organizational power related to position, societal power, personal power) over another in the workplace. The most comprehensive of this class of models was developed by Cleveland and Kerst (1993), who incorporate different sources of perpetrator power as antecedents of sexual harassment. They assert that, in addition to power associated with position in the organizational hierarchy, individuals gain power from personal (e.g., through influence tactics and intelligence) and societal (e.g., social status) sources, a view that is consistent with French and Raven's (1959) well-known taxonomy of power sources. Cleveland and Kerst cite evidence that women are disadvantaged compared with men in terms of each of these sources of power. Cleveland and Kerst see women's disadvantaged societal and organizational statuses as contributing to work conditions that encourage sexual harassment. However, they also suggest that societal and organizational sources of power interact with the personal power of the harasser and the victim in explaining harassment, which is reminiscent of person-by-situation models. Finally, their model describes a process whereby organizational responses to sexual harassment provide feedback to either confirm or refute the power of the harasser as well as to reinforce or alter work conditions. Individual responses to harassment also serve to reinforce or alter the power of the victim. Cleveland and Kerst note that although power seems to be a robust explanation for sexual harassment, current research has not adequately tested its influence. They argue that research is needed to assess how specific types of power are related to sexual harassment as well as which sources of power are used by perpetrators at different organizational levels relative to victims. In qualitative research drawing on and elaborating Cleveland and Kerst's model, Rospenda, Richman, and Nawyn (1998) demonstrated that complex and varied sources of power come into play when explaining contrapower harassment (i.e., harassment in which the perpetrator is of lower organizational status than the target). Moreover, they suggest the utility of simultaneously considering the influence of gender, race, and class on power dynamics at organizational, sociocultural, and interpersonal or individual levels.

Antecedents of Harassment and Discrimination

Perpetrator Characteristics

Most of the research on perpetrator characteristics is limited to the area of sexual harassment and has been done by Pryor and his colleagues. As noted above, Pryor et al. (1993) found that men with certain proclivities to harass were more likely to do so when their organization was tolerant of harassment. More recently, Begany and Milburn (2002) found evidence that authoritarian personality coupled with hostile attitudes toward women and acceptance of rape myths were important in predicting likelihood to harass.

Target Characteristics

In terms of target characteristics that may be risk factors for sexual harassment, Pryor and Fitzgerald (2003) cite research evidence of history of childhood sexual abuse (Rosen & Martin, 1998) and egalitarian rather than traditional gender role orientation (Dall'Ara & Maass, 1999). Critics have argued that sexual harassment may be a function of individuals overreacting to normal workplace interactions, what some have termed the "whiner" hypothesis (e.g., Bowes-Sperry & Tata, 1999). Although research has shown those scoring higher on measures of neuroticism and narcissism have more sexual harassment experiences, the negative effects of harassment could not be explained entirely by personality vulnerability (Wislar, Richman, Fendrich, & Flaherty, 2002). Other research has also negated disposition as a major factor in explaining the relationships between sexual and racial harassment and outcomes (Glomb et al., 1999; Munson, Hulin, & Drasgow, 2000; Schneider et al., 2000).

Certain demographic characteristics of targets have also been linked to increased risk for harassment and discrimination. In terms of sexual harassment, race has not been consistently linked to increased risk for harassment (cf. Fain & Anderton, 1987; Wyatt & Riederle, 1995). However, marital status (single), age (younger), and lower education level have predicted sexual harassment for women (Coles, 1986; Fain & Anderton, 1987; Gutek & Dunwoody, 1987; LaFontaine & Trudeau, 1986; USMSPB, 1988). Being younger and single has also been linked to increased likelihood of perceiving discrimination for a variety of other reasons (e.g., Kessler et al., 1999). Sociological research indicates that these characteristics help determine status and personal power attributed to an individual in social interactions (Berger, Cohen, & Zelditch, 1972). This would lend support to models of harassment that speculate that those with lower power are more likely to experience harassment because lack of power makes it harder for targets to counter or resist these behaviors. Harned, Ormerod, Palmieri, Collinsworth, and Reed (2002) recently found some support for this contention in that lower organizational and sociocultural power were linked to higher levels of sexual harassment for military women.

There has been an increasing call for research on how demographic characteristics may interact to influence likelihood of harassment and discrimination. Some theorists have proposed a "double jeopardy" hypothesis (e.g., Beale, 1970) suggesting that membership in multiple minority groups may serve to increase risk for discrimination. Research that has examined the impact of multiple-group membership has mostly focused on the interplay of race and gender. These studies have shown that sexual harassment is often intertwined with racism such that black women's experiences of sexual harassment often include elements of racial stereotyping (Mecca & Rubin, 1999; Yoder & Aniakudo, 1996). Yoder and Aniakudo (1996) interviewed black women firefighters and found that they were unwilling to make distinctions about whether unfair treatment occurred because of their race or their gender, "noting instead that these facets of their lives were intertwined" (p. 266). In empirical research, Cortina, Fitzgerald, and Drasgow (2002) found that experiences of racial harassment were the strongest predictor of severe sexual harassment for a sample of over 400 employed Latinas, providing further evidence that different types of harassing experiences tend to co-occur in the workplace. It is likely that these relationships are not limited to sexual and racial harassment. Theorists have noted that "multiple jeopardy" may be an issue in aging (Pasupathi & Lockenhoff, 2002). For example, elderly adults who also belong to another stigmatized group may be at increased risk for discrimination (Pasupathi & Lockenhoff, 2002, p. 235). However, we could find no empirical research on this topic or on other forms of multiple jeopardy as related to harassment and discrimination.

Organizational Factors

In the area of sexual harassment, the most commonly studied antecedent of sexual harassment is organizational tolerance (e.g., Fitzgerald, Drasgow, et al., 1997; Harned et al., 2002; Richman, Rospenda, Flaherty, & Freels,

2003), which is the extent to which an organization tacitly endorses or fails to address sexual harassment (e.g., weak policy, lack of policy dissemination and/or enforcement) (Pryor & Fitzgerald, 2003). Empirical research has strongly supported the link between organizational tolerance and higher levels of sexual harassment in a variety of samples (Fitzgerald, Drasgow, et al., 1997; Glomb et al., 1999; Hulin, Fitzgerald, & Drasgow, 1996; LaFontaine & Trudeau, 1986; Richman et al., 2003; Timmerman & Bajema, 2000). Similarly, research on gay, lesbian, and bisexual workers indicates that those who perceived their organization's climate be unsupportive of nonheterosexual employees and whose organizations did not have policies supporting gay and lesbian employees (e.g., nondiscrimination policies) were more likely to experience sexual orientation–related harassment and discrimination (Ragins & Cornwell, 2001; Waldo, 1999).

Other known antecedents of sexual harassment include job-gender context (Fitzgerald et al., 1994; Pryor & Fitzgerald, 2003) and "sex ratio" of the job (Gutek & Morasch, 1982). Sexual harassment is more likely to occur in work contexts where men outnumber women or where women are performing "men's work" (Fitzgerald, Drasgow, et al., 1997; Fitzgerald et al., 1994; Glomb et al., 1999; Gruber, 1997). Gruber (1997) notes that organizational tolerance and job-gender context have been found to be antecedents of sexual harassment in North America as well as Europe. Although research supports job-gender context as an antecedent of sexual harassment, much of this research has been cross-sectional. Thus, it is possible that jobs high in harassment drive women out, such that sexual harassment is the antecedent of skewed sex ratios on the job. For example, in Antilla's (2002) exposé of the retail brokerage industry on Wall Street, she describes a "locker room environment" (p. 61) where unseemly harassing behavior was rampant and ignored. Although 50% of the brokers were women in the 1980s, only 1% were women in the 1990s when the job became much more lucrative (p. 101). She describes an environment in which the CEO set the tone of harassment and management took steps to ensure women were pushed out of the now more lucrative jobs (Antilla, 2002). Researchers have tended to ignore this potential reverse causality.

Like the finding that job-gender context is a risk factor for sexual harassment (e.g., Fitzgerald et al., 1994), researchers in other areas have found that other forms of imbalance in workplace demographics can contribute to increased likelihood of harassment and discrimination. For example, Hughes and Dodge (1997) found that black women working in jobs in which blacks were underrepresented experienced more "interpersonal prejudice" (i.e., racial harassment) and "institutional discrimination" (i.e., racial discrimination). Anglos have also been found to experience higher than expected levels of racial/ethnic harassment in settings where they represent a numerical minority (e.g., Schneider et al., 2000). Likewise, gay and lesbian employees in work groups that were mainly heterosexual were more likely to report sexual orientation–based work discrimination (Ragins & Cornwell, 2001).

Researchers have speculated that discrepancy in group proportions results in increased salience of group membership, a tendency for majority group members to exaggerate group differences in order to maintain group boundaries, and a tendency to perceive minority group members in stereotypical ways (e.g., Kanter, 1977), which can increase the likelihood of harassment and discrimination.

Outcomes

In 1996, Holzbauer and Berven hypothesized that the effects of various forms of workplace harassment and discrimination would be similar. Research has overwhelmingly proven them correct as well as supported Fitzgerald et al.'s (1994) model specifying the job, mental health, and physical health as the three main outcome domains of harassment.

Job Outcomes

One of the most consistent findings in workplace harassment and discrimination research is the relationship of harassing or discriminatory experiences to job satisfaction. Hughes and Dodge (1997) found that racial harassment and discrimination (measured as separate scales) were better predictors of job dissatisfaction than either psychosocial or structural job stressors in a sample of 79 black women employed full-time. Similarly, Sanchez and Brock (1996) found that perceived racial discrimination and harassment at work was associated with decreased job satisfaction and organizational commitment and increased work tension for a community sample of 139 Hispanic men and women, above and beyond the effects of role conflict and ambiguity. Research in the military has indicated that the most bothersome experiences of racial/ethnic harassment or discrimination led to decreased trust in coworkers and supervisors, thoughts about leaving the service, decreased productivity, and, less frequently, lost time from work (Scarville et al., 1999).

Age discrimination and sexual orientation–based harassment are also associated with negative job outcomes. Perceived age discrimination has been linked to decreased job satisfaction in older employees in several different industries (Hassell & Perrewé, 1993; Orpen, 1995), as well as decreased organizational commitment and job involvement (Orpen, 1995). Interestingly, consistent with McGoldrick and Arrowsmith's (2001) findings, Hassell and Perrewé (1993) found that younger workers also perceived age discrimination. In terms of sexual orientation, Waldo (1999) found that sexual orientation–based harassment was associated with decreased job satisfaction, and Ragins and Cornwell (2001) found that sexual orientation–based discrimination was associated with negative work attitudes.

In the sexual harassment literature, several major studies have revealed a variety of negative job outcomes for targets. Gutek (1985), in the most comprehensive study of its type, conducted a random telephone survey of sexual harassment in a community sample. Working with over 5,000 working residential numbers in Los Angeles County, Gutek obtained an admirable 77% compliance rate among eligible respondents for a final sample of 827 women and 405 men employed outside the home at least 20 hours per week. This was the first, and to date the only, study to gather data on the sexual harassment experiences of employed women *and* men in a large, representative (i.e., nonmilitary, nongovernment) sample. Gutek measured eight forms of potentially sexually harassing behavior at work, including complimentary and insulting sexual comments, looks and gestures, sexual and nonsexual touching, pressure for dates, and pressure for sexual relations. She found that women who experienced sexual touching or sexual remarks on the job had decreased job satisfaction, but men's experiences of sexual behavior at work were unrelated to job satisfaction. Notably, Gutek found that even "nonproblematic" sexual behavior at work was associated with decreased job satisfaction for women (p. 114). Gutek describes more severe consequences of sexually harassing experiences for women, including being fired or forced to quit. It should be noted that Gutek focused only on work experiences with those of the opposite sex, so her findings do not represent the totality of sexually harassing behaviors at work. Researchers have found that same-sex sexual harassment can represent a substantial portion of men's sexual harassment experiences and may actually result in more severe job and personal outcomes than opposite-sex harassment for men (DuBois, Knapp, Faley, & Kustis, 1998; Waldo et al., 1998).

In possibly the most widely cited and well-known set of studies, the United States Merit Systems Protection Board (USMSPB) conducted repeated surveys of large cross sections of federal employees. The USMSPB surveyed approximately 20,000 employees in 1980 and about 13,000 in 1987 and 1994, obtaining responses from over 8,000 employees in each survey year (USMSPB, 1981, 1988, 1995). The USMSPB focused on only six types of potentially sexually harassing behaviors: uninvited sexual remarks, letters or phone calls, touching, suggestive looks, pressure for dates, and pressure for sexual favors. Extrapolating from the results of the 1994 survey, the USMSPB estimated that sexual harassment may have caused nearly 20,000 federal employees to quit or change jobs in the 2 years prior to the 1994 survey. The USMSPB found that about 8% of survey respondents reported using sick leave as a result of being sexually harassed. The most common effect of sexual harassment was decreased productivity reported by 21% of respondents in 1994 (USMSPB, 1995).

Fitzgerald, Drasgow, et al. (1997) carried out the first major empirical test of Fitzgerald et al.'s (1994) comprehensive model of the antecedents and consequences of sexual harassment in a sample of 357 women employed by a utility company, oversampling those who worked in nontraditional jobs. In support of the model, Fitzgerald, Drasgow, et al. (1997) found that sexual harassment as measured by the SEQ was related to work withdrawal (i.e., avoidance of work tasks, absenteeism, tardiness) through its effects on job satisfaction and to job withdrawal (e.g., turnover intentions) through its effects on health conditions and health satisfaction. Glomb et al. (1999) tested the Fitzgerald et al. (1994) model with longitudinal data from a sample of nearly 300 women university employees and found that sexual harassment at one time point was associated with decreased job satisfaction and increased job withdrawal (through its effects on job satisfaction) 2 years later, demonstrating the persistence of negative effects of harassment over time. Although the general model has been tested mainly in samples of women, recent research in the military has shown that the basic relationships hold for men (Fitzgerald, Drasgow, & Magley, 1999) and across racial groups (Bergman & Drasgow, 2003). Glomb et al. (1997) and Richman-Hirsch and Glomb (2002) further extended the Fitzgerald et al. (1994) model by examining "ambient" sexual harassment (i.e., general level of harassment within a work group), demonstrating that even if women and men are not direct victims of sexual harassment, they can still experience negative job and psychological effects.

Along with their work in the area of racial/ethnic harassment and discrimination, the U.S. Department of Defense (DOD) has a major ongoing research program on sexual harassment of active duty military personnel. Lancaster (1999) presents a history of this program, focusing on surveys conducted in 1988 and 1995. About 38,000 active duty personnel were surveyed in 1988 and about 49,000 in 1995. Response rates exceeded 50% for each survey (see Hay & Elig, 1999, for more details). Data from the 1995 survey indicate that even moderate levels of sexual harassment negatively affect work satisfaction, satisfaction with coworkers, satisfaction with supervisors, commitment to the military, and productivity, especially for women (Magley, Waldo, Drasgow, & Fitzgerald, 1999).

Although much of the work on outcomes of sexual harassment has been carried out by Fitzgerald and her colleagues, independent research has supported negative associations between sexual harassment and aspects of job satisfaction (e.g., Morrow et al., 1994; Murry, Sivasubramaniam, & Jacques, 2001), organizational commitment (e.g., Morrow et al., 1994; Murry et al., 2001), work withdrawal, and turnover intentions (e.g., Murry et al., 2001). Research on discrimination has found similar effects in that women managers who report experiencing discrimination on the job exhibit decreased job satisfaction and organizational commitment (Murrell et al., 1995). Other research on nonfaculty university employees indicates that perceived sexism and gender discrimination are associated with decreased job satisfaction, particularly for women and those in female-dominated jobs (Bond, Punnett, Pyle, Cazeca, & Cooperman, 2004).

Mental Health Outcomes

Probably the most robust finding in the harassment and discrimination literature is that these experiences are linked with negative mental health outcomes such as depression, anxiety, and distress. Although Kessler et al. (1999) did not focus on workplace discrimination, it was the form of discrimination most frequently reported by respondents in their study. Kessler et al. found that both lifetime and daily experiences of discrimination and harassment were related to increased distress and major depression, a finding that did not vary when reason for discrimination was taken into account. Research in the military indicates that experiences of racial/ethnic harassment are associated with feelings of stress, anxiety, fear, and depression in active duty personnel (Scarville et al., 1999).

Pavalko et al.'s (2003) longitudinal research on the effects of work discrimination in a national sample of older women indicated that women who reported work discrimination of any kind between 1984 and 1989 had higher levels of psychological distress in 1989, controlling for prior health, gender and job attitudes, and work characteristics. These results help rule out critics' contentions that physical or emotional health problems can cause increased likelihood of perceiving discrimination rather than representing effects of discrimination.

In their study of ethnic harassment, Schneider et al. (2000) found that verbal harassment was linked to decreased life satisfaction in a sample of school district employees. Interestingly, Schneider et al. found a complex relationship between experiences of verbal harassment and workplace exclusion due to ethnicity in school district employee and graduate student samples such that those with high levels of exclusion but low levels of verbal harassment had the most negative effects on posttraumatic stress disorder (PTSD) symptoms and life satisfaction. Plots of the interactions indicated that those with high levels of verbal harassment had consistently poor outcomes across all levels of exclusion. This suggests that high levels of any type of harassing experiences outweigh any positive effects that may be associated with having lower levels of other harassing experiences.

Other forms of harassment and discrimination have also been linked to negative psychological outcomes. Hassell and Perrewé (1993) found that perceptions of age discrimination were linked with decreases in both self-esteem and feelings of personal control. Holzbauer and Berven (1996) provide a summary of anecdotal evidence of the devastating psychological consequences of disability harassment, including workplace harassment, and describe parallels with the literature on the consequences of sexual harassment. Likewise, Waldo (1999) found that sexual orientation–based harassment was significantly associated with psychological distress in a sample of gay, lesbian, or bisexual men and women.

In the sexual harassment literature, there is a vast amount of empirical evidence supporting relationships between sexual harassment and various negative mental health outcomes including overall well-being (e.g., Fitzgerald, Drasgow, et al., 1997; Fitzgerald, Drasgow, et al., 1999; Glomb et al., 1999; Glomb et al., 1997; Goldenhar, Swanson, Hurrell, Ruder, & Deddens, 1998; Magley et al., 1999; Munson et al., 2000; Piotrkowski, 1998) as well as more specific outcomes such as anxiety, hostility, depression (Richman et al., 1999), and PTSD (Dansky & Kilpatrick, 1997; Wolfe et al., 1998). Although their study was not limited to discrimination in the workplace, Klonoff, Landrine, and Campbell (2000) found that women who experienced higher levels of sexist discrimination also exhibited increased psychiatric symptoms (e.g., somatization, depression, anxiety) compared with men whereas women with few discrimination experiences had levels of symptomatology similar to men. They argue that sexist discrimination may be a root cause of commonly reported gender differences in psychiatric symptoms (p. 93).

Some research indicates that, although women and men experience similar psychological consequences of sexual harassment, women tend to be more negatively affected by these experiences because they experience a greater frequency of harassment compared with men (Barling et al., 1996; Magley et al., 1999). Other studies have shown that the most severe psychological outcomes of workplace harassment and discrimination occur when these experiences continue over time (e.g., Pryor, 1995; Rospenda et al., 2000). Unfortunately, research evidence has shown that, when it occurs, harassment tends to be chronic (Glomb et al., 1999; Rospenda et al., 2000). Anecdotal evidence has linked chronic sexual harassment, in particular, with suicidal thoughts and tendencies among targets (e.g., Antilla, 2002).

Physical Health

Harassment and discrimination have also been linked to physical health problems for targets. This line of research has primarily focused on the effects of racial harassment and discrimination on blood pressure. Results generally have supported a relationship between racial harassment and discrimination and blood pressure, though not always in the predicted direction. In a community study of black and white women, Krieger (1990) found that although racial discrimination was not associated with high blood pressure, gender discrimination was associated with *lower* blood pressure for black women. Krieger postulated that either the women in her study were repressing their anger and hostility about discrimination, or, alternatively, hypertension may somehow be affecting perceptions of stress (p. 1278). By contrast, James et al. (1994) found that higher levels of perceived organizational prejudice and discrimination were related to increased blood pressure for employed racial minorities. These effects were mediated by level of collective esteem, suggesting that discrimination affects blood pressure through its negative effects on feelings of self-worth, in support of social identity theory.

Research on other health-related outcomes of harassment and discrimination has also produced complex results. Schneider et al.'s (2000) study of ethnic harassment indicated that graduate students who had low levels of verbal harassment but high levels of exclusion due to ethnicity had the worst self-rated health. As noted above, this may indicate that low levels of harassment in one area will not protect individuals against negative effects if they are experiencing high levels of other types of harassment. Research in other civilian and military samples supports a relationship between experiences of workplace racial/ethnic harassment and discrimination and self-reported physical health problems (James, 1994; Scarville et al., 1999).

Anecdotal evidence also suggests that sexual harassment and sex discrimination are linked to health problems. For example, Antilla (2002) related an account of a woman in the brokerage industry who was diagnosed with chronic fatigue syndrome brought on by stress resulting from persistent gender-based harassment and discrimination (p. 191) limiting her ability to work. In their review of the literature, Gutek and Koss (1993) cited many qualitative studies and anecdotal accounts of the physical effects associated with sexual harassment. Most frequently, women reported experiencing "gastrointestinal disturbances, jaw tightness and teeth grinding, nervousness, binge-eating, headaches, inability to sleep, tiredness, nausea, loss of appetite, weight loss, and crying spells" (Gutek & Koss, 1993, p. 13). Goldenhar et al. (1998) found that sexual harassment and discrimination were the only job stressors associated with symptoms of nausea and headaches in a sample of female construction workers. It is notable that many of these symptoms are considered somatic manifestations of psychological distress by the medical profession. It is also notable that tests of the Fitzgerald et al. (1994) model generally have found that sexual harassment and harassment based on sexual orientation exert effects on self-reported physical health indirectly through their effects on psychological distress (Fitzgerald, Drasgow, et al., 1997; Fitzgerald et al., 1994; Glomb et al., 1999; Waldo, 1999). However, in one study, sexual harassment was also directly linked with physiological indicators of stress. Schneider, Tomaka, Palacios-Esquivel, & Goldsmith (2001) found that women who experienced sexist remarks from a male coworker in an experimental study displayed cardiac and vascular physiological reactions consistent with typical responses seen in stressful or threatening situations. Finally, sexual harassment but not other job stressors were associated with increased odds of self-reported serious illness, injury, or assault in a sample of university employees (Rospenda, Richman, Ehmke, & Zlatoper, 2004), suggesting that harassment may affect health in a multitude of ways.

Other Outcomes

Recently, interest in other potential outcomes of harassing experiences has been piqued. Although prior research had focused on the impact of harassment and discrimination on mental and physical health, it had neglected to examine effects on health-related behaviors. In the first large-scale study to address the linkage between harassment and behavioral outcomes, Richman et al. (1999) surveyed over 2,000 university employees and found that sexual harassment was linked to higher levels of drinking frequency and escapist drinking, increased odds of drinking to intoxication for women, and increased odds of heavy episodic drinking (consuming six or more drinks containing alcohol in a single day) and drinking to intoxication for men. In a report incorporating the second wave of data collection in this university sample, Rospenda et al. (2000) found that individuals who reported having sexual harassment experiences at two points in time, 1 year apart, also reported increased variability in drinking behavior compared with those who never experienced harassment. More specifically, chronically harassed individuals reported significantly greater amounts of alcohol consumed in a single day in the past 30 days, controlling for prior levels of drinking. In a study of disordered eating behaviors, Harned and Fitzgerald (2002) found that workplace sexual harassment was significantly linked to eating disorder symptoms (e.g., binge eating, vomiting) through its effects on psychological distress in two samples of women.

The results of these studies indicate the potential for the effects of harassment to lead to behaviors that can further affect the health of targets. However, not much is known about the extent to which targets of harassment and discrimination seek help from professional sources. Following the general stress literature, which links higher levels of life and work stress to increased use of health and mental health services (Manning, Jackson, & Fusilier, 1996; Miranda, Perez-Stable, Munoz, Hargreaves, & Henke, 1991; Sherbourne, 1988), Rospenda (2002) found that both men and women university employees who experienced sexual harassment were more likely to report use of at least one type of health or mental health service because of workplace problems compared with those who did not experience harassment, controlling for other job stressors and prior use of services.

Moderators and Mediators

Even though Fitzgerald et al.'s (1994) model proposed a variety of variables that may moderate the relationship between sexual harassment and outcomes, few harassment researchers have chosen to focus on potential moderators. This is true of research on other forms of harassment and discrimination as well. The limited research in this area, however, indicates a wide variety of potential moderators and mediators of harassment/discrimination-outcome relationships.

Target Characteristics

There has been little research empirically testing moderating effects of target characteristics. The research that has been done suggests that demographic characteristics of targets may moderate the extent to which targets experience negative outcomes of harassment and discrimination. For example, Kessler et al. (1999) found that discrimination was more strongly related to negative mental health outcomes for women, blacks, and low socioeconomic status respondents. Similarly, findings from the DOD equal opportunity survey indicated that racial/ethnic minorities were more likely to report negative job, psychological, and health outcomes associated with experiences of racial harassment and discrimination (Scarville et al., 1999).

There is also evidence that personality characteristics may influence the extent to which targets will experience negative outcomes. Dion et al. (1992) found that Chinese community members lower in the personality character- istic hardiness (as measured by locus of control) showed stronger negative psychological effects of racial discrimination than those high in hardiness. However, this study was not specific to work-related racial discrimination and was limited to one ethnic group. As noted earlier, sexual harassment research focusing on neuroticism, narcissism, and negative affectivity has generally not found these personality or dispositional traits to play a major role in explaining the effects of harassment on outcomes (e.g., Glomb et al., 1999; Wislar et al., 2002). Further research on personality variables that have not yet been studied could prove fruitful.

Research also suggests that cultural issues may affect outcomes associated with harassment. Shupe et al. (2002) found that cultural affiliation moder- ated relationships between sexual harassment and job outcomes in a sample of non-Hispanic white and Hispanic women working at a food-processing company. Shupe et al. argued that affiliation with mainstream U.S. culture was protective for Hispanic women because traditional Hispanic culture sanctions women for sexual behavior or even discussion of sexual matters. Thus, sexual harassment may affect traditional Hispanic women more strongly.

Coping Style

Fitzgerald et al.'s (1994) comprehensive model predicts that actively coping with sexual harassment (e.g., reporting, confronting, or filing a complaint against the perpetrator) will lead to more negative outcomes for targets as such actions can result in secondary stressors such as retaliation. Research has generally supported this prediction. For example, actively cop- ing with sexual harassment resulted in increased negative drinking outcomes for university-employed targets when the harassment continued (Richman, Rospenda, Flaherty, & Freels, 2001). Similarly, Stockdale (1998) analyzed the 1987 USMSPB data and found that men and women who responded to sexual harassment with "confrontative" (i.e., assertive) coping styles had worse work-related consequences than those who exhibited more passive coping. This was particularly true for men, contrary to expectations. Bergman, Langhout, Palmieri, Cortina, & Fitzgerald (2002) also found that assertive coping was often associated with retaliation, decreased job satis- faction, and increased psychological distress for men and women in the mil- itary. In an experimental study, Schneider et al. (2001) found that women who confronted a harassing coworker exhibited greater cardiovascular reactions than women who did not confront their coworker, providing physiological evidence that this type of coping response is often stressful.

By contrast, research on racial discrimination in a community sample of women demonstrated that black women who responded to unfair treatment by keeping quiet and accepting it were over four times more likely to report having hypertension than those who responded by talking to someone or taking action (Krieger, 1990). It is likely that keeping quiet did not stop the discrimination for the women in Krieger's sample. If this is the case, the results may be consistent with Richman et al. (2001) in that continued negative experiences may result in negative outcomes regardless of target's choice of coping mode. Studies should consider measuring effectiveness of coping to further explore this possibility.

Social Support

Research suggests that support is most likely to moderate the effects of stressors when support is matched to the stressor (e.g., Cohen & Wills, 1985). Thus, for workplace harassment or discrimination, support within the workplace should be a more effective buffer against negative outcomes than general levels of social support or social support from sources outside the workplace. Consistent with this hypothesis, Richman et al.'s (2001) research on university employees indicated that although overall social support had no moderating effects on negative drinking outcomes, coworker support did ameliorate the effects of sexual harassment in some cases. The results were complex, however, and a clear protective effect of coworker support was not apparent. Richman et al. note that in some cases coworker support may be occurring within drinking contexts. The impact of support within the workplace on other outcomes may be more interpretable. For example, Murry et al. (2001) found that sexual harassment was more strongly related to negative job outcomes when there was low social exchange with or low levels of support from supervisors. It is likely that supervisor support is a more critical moderator of harassment-outcome relationships because supervisors have more power to effectively end the harassment compared with coworkers.

Other Moderators and Mediators

In a study of police officers in the United Kingdom, Parker and Griffin (2002) found that gender harassment on the job was linked to psychological distress through its effects on overperformance demands for women but not for men. Overperformance demands refer to the pressure to exceed usual levels of performance in order to prove oneself within the workplace (p. 196). Parker and Griffin note that minority group members, in this case women, may be particularly likely to face overperformance demands at work because they are often judged more harshly than majority group members. They qualify their findings by noting that they may not be generalizable to other occupations and that further research is needed to clarify the circumstances under which discrimination and harassment can lead to other types of less productive responses such as decreased performance or job withdrawal.

Barling et al. (1996) proposed that sexual harassment exerts its effects on outcomes through work-related negative mood. Barling et al. tested this model in two studies. The first study drew from samples of Canadian hotel employees, office workers, and nurses and found support for the model: frequency of sexual harassment was associated with turnover intentions, psychosomatic health complaints, and dissatisfaction with supervisors and coworkers mainly through its effects on negative work-related mood. In a second study of women undergraduates, Barling et al. found similar results in that frequency of sexual harassment was associated with psychosomatic health complaints, decreased self-esteem, and lower grades through its effects on negative mood. Similarly, research in a sample of university employees has found that the effects of sexual harassment on drinking outcomes for both men and women were partially mediated by psychological distress (Richman, Shinsako, Rospenda, Flaherty, & Freels, 2002). This suggests that target's appraisal of harassment and discrimination experiences plays an important role in determining the severity of outcomes, consistent with stress theory (e.g., Lazarus & Folkman, 1984).

Future Research Directions

Given the amount of interest in harassment and discrimination due to race and gender, the relative lack of empirical research on harassment and discrimination due to age, disability, religion, and sexual orientation is striking. Expanding on Kasschau's (1977) comments regarding the extent to which some individuals may avoid age discrimination by looking and acting younger, we suggest that the dearth of research in these areas is due at least in part to the fact that religion, sexual orientation, and even many disabilities are generally less visible. Thus, it is more difficult to identify membership in these protected groups compared with the relative ease of identifying people by their gender and race. As a result, harassment and discrimination based on characteristics other than race and gender may be suffering from an "out of sight, out of mind" phenomenon.

However, by no means should other forms of harassment and discrimination be considered less important. Our literature review indicates that members of "less obvious" minority groups still perceive significant amounts of harassment and discrimination and suggests that the effects of these forms of harassment and discrimination are no less harmful. In fact, there are striking similarities and overlaps in antecedents and outcomes of various forms of harassment and discrimination suggesting that much of the existing theory in this area can be applied to the study of multiple forms of harassment and discrimination.

Although research on neglected forms of harassment and discrimination is needed, research on racial and gender discrimination in particular has demonstrated that it is often impossible, and undesirable, to study specific types of harassment and discrimination in isolation. Gender, race, and other ascribed characteristics work together to fashion individual identity (e.g., Reid & Comas-Diaz, 1990). Given evidence for interaction effects between gender and occupational status in prevalence of harassment, future research should also pay greater attention to the salience of low social class status. Thus, we recommend that researchers consider expanding their focus to include alternate forms of harassment and discrimination as well as consider multiple potential indicators of social status and power to fill these gaps in the research.

Although the need for large-scale, nationally representative research in this area is clear (as accurate prevalence rates cannot be obtained when those who experience the highest levels of harassment and discrimination may be the most likely to leave their jobs) (Sbraga & O'Donohue, 2000), there is also a need for more detailed studies of specific occupations. Research in the area of sexual harassment in particular has suggested that the risk of harassment in certain occupations, particularly law (e.g., Cortina, Lonsway, et al., 2002), medicine (e.g., Richman, Flaherty, Rospenda, & Christensen, 1992), and the military (e.g., Fitzgerald, Magley, Drasgow, & Waldo, 1999; Lancaster, 1999; Scarville et al., 1999), may be especially high. Sbraga and O'Donohue (2000) note that little is known about certain occupations because they have not been studied. For example, few researchers have looked at sexual harassment in blue-collar workers. Research is needed to more completely delineate risk factors specific to these and other occupations, which could then lead to tailored interventions to address harassment and discrimination.

Bowes-Sperry and Tata (1999) note the lack of research evaluating the impact of sexual harassment training. This observation was also more recently made by Pryor and Fitzgerald (2003) indicating that little progress is being made in this area. Pryor and Fitzgerald summarized the few research studies that have been done, which indicate some evidence of success in terms of participants' ratings of usefulness. A few experimental studies showed that training programs can affect people's perceptions of sexual harassment and possibly result in short-term reductions in harassing behavior among men with proclivities to harass. However, additional research is needed in this area.

Given that a social interactionist perspective is useful for describing a wide variety of workplace harassment and discrimination situations and that different forms of harassment and discrimination can co-occur, it is recommended that researchers continue to explore both the process and the form of harassment and discrimination experiences. This is best accomplished through longitudinal studies of the course of harassment and discrimination over time. Also, the use of statistical models with the capacity to model interactions between key variables is essential in order to better test, and consequently refine, theoretical models of mistreatment.

Finally, although existing longitudinal research demonstrates that the effects of harassment can persist over time (e.g., Glomb et al., 1999; Rospenda, 2002; Rospenda et al., 2000), little is known about how harassment experiences themselves evolve over time. Future research is needed to better understand the course of harassment and discrimination as well as how different forms of harassment and discrimination may be interrelated.

Implications

A review of the literature leaves no doubt that harassment and discrimination represent particularly serious forms of workplace stressors. Some researchers have attempted to explain why. Dion et al. (1992) see discrimination as a stressor that is particularly threatening to individuals because it is often unpredictable and uncontrollable. Consistent with this theory, Dion et al. (1992) have found evidence that those with higher levels of locus of control may be less negatively affected by discrimination. This has implications for organizations in that if employees can be made to feel more in control (i.e., more assured that the organization will not tolerate harassment or discrimination and will take complaints seriously), this may help protect the mental health of targeted employees. Because there is overwhelming evidence that organizational tolerance of harassment and discrimination predicts the prevalence of these experiences, it is clear that implementation and enforcement of antidiscrimination policies is crucial to reducing harassment and discrimination. Organizations with strong, highly visible, consistently enforced antidiscrimination policies will protect their employees in two ways. First, such policies will serve to decrease the incidence of harassment and discrimination. Second, such policies will serve to decrease the likelihood that targets' complaints of harassment or discrimination will be ignored, thereby also decreasing the likelihood of severe mental health or physical health consequences for these employees. Because perpetrators' attitudes and beliefs have also been shown to contribute to harassment (e.g., Dekker & Barling, 1998; Duncan, 2001; Pryor et al., 1993), another option for organizations is to implement training targeted to changing attitudes and promoting empathy for victims (Dekker & Barling, 1998). By taking preventive measures such as these, organizations will not only protect their employees from harassment and discrimination but will help protect the organization from costly lawsuits and workers' compensation claims resulting from harassment and discrimination.

Given that different forms of harassment and discrimination tend to co-occur, it would also make sense for organizations to formulate more global policies on diversity and nondiscrimination to make it clear that no forms of harassment and discrimination are tolerated. We suggest that these policies should cover *all* forms of harassment and discrimination, regardless of whether they are prohibited by law. Expanding on a statement made by Bond et al. (2004, p. 41) regarding why men may be negatively affected by sexism directed at their female colleagues, we suggest that *all* employees may be negatively affected when certain members of the workforce are devalued through harassment and discrimination. Bell, Quick, and Cycyota (2002) note that top management commitment, zero tolerance policies, notification to applicants and new hires that the workplace is harassment-free, regular organizational surveys to assess problems, and training programs to counter harassment (p. 162) are important tools for the prevention of harassment. Organizations that wish to ensure all employees are treated with respect would benefit from this advice.

Conclusion

This chapter reveals harassment and discrimination to be common organizational phenomena. We distinguish harassment from discrimination in that harassment refers to poor interpersonal treatment at work directed toward an individual because of his or her ascribed characteristics, and discrimination refers to differential treatment in terms of job opportunities or outcomes as a result of an individual's ascribed characteristics. We reviewed several theoretical models proposed by sexual harassment researchers that might be applied to the more general study of harassment and discrimination including models based on (a) occupational stress theory (explicitly), (b) social identity theory, (c) social interactionism, and (d) power differentials between perpetrators and targets. We argue that social interactionist models (i.e., person-by-situation models) may be most useful for the larger study of workplace harassment and discrimination. A recurring theme found in the literature was that different types of harassment and discrimination often occur together. Also, various forms of harassment and discrimination tend to share common antecedents, most notably in terms of skewed ratios of minority to majority groups on the job and an organizational climate that tolerates harassment and discrimination. Experiences of various forms of harassment and discrimination have similar negative effects on targets in terms of job, mental health, and physical health outcomes as well as health-related behaviors. Research on the moderators and mediators of the relationships between harassment (particularly harassment that is not based on sex) and discrimination and outcome variables has been scarce and has produced mixed findings. More research is needed on potential moderators of harassment and discrimination. Although the evidence suggests that various forms of harassment and discrimination have similar antecedents and outcomes, more research is also needed on understudied types of these experiences (e.g., age, disability, religion) in order to determine whether these results are generalizable. Finally, broader longitudinal research examining multiple types of harassment and discrimination experiences is needed to clarify exactly how (or whether) they co-occur and develop over time in people's work lives. Enforced organizational polices that prohibit harassment and discrimination are essential to the creation of a climate that does not tolerate harassment and discrimination.

References

Antilla, S. (2002). *Tales from the boom-boom room: Women vs. Wall Street.* Princeton, NJ: Bloomberg Press.

Arvey, R. D., & Cavanaugh, M. A. (1995). Using surveys to assess the prevalence of sexual harassment: Some methodological problems. *Journal of Social Issues, 51,* 39–52.

Balser, D. B. (2000). Perceptions of on-the-job discrimination and employees with disabilities. *Employee Responsibilities and Rights Journal, 12,* 179–197.

Barak, A. (1997). Cross-cultural perspectives on sexual harassment. In W. O'Donohue (Ed.), *Sexual harassment: Theory, research, and treatment* (pp. 263–300). Boston: Allyn & Bacon.

Barak, A., Pitterman, Y., & Yitzhaki, R. (1995). An empirical test of the role of power differential in originating sexual harassment. *Basic and Applied Social Psychology, 17,* 497–517.

Barling, J., Dekker, I., Loughlin, C. A., Kelloway, E. K., Fullagar, C., & Johnson, D. (1996). Prediction and replication of the organizational and personal consequences of workplace sexual harassment. *Journal of Managerial Psychology, 11*(5), 4–25.

Barling, J., Rogers, A. G., & Kelloway, E. K. (2001). Behind closed doors: In-home workers' experience of sexual harassment and workplace violence. *Journal of Occupational Health Psychology, 6*(3), 255–269.

Beale, F. M. (1970). Double jeopardy: To be Black and female. *New Generations, 5,* 40–42.

Beehr, T. A. (1995). *Psychological stress in the workplace.* London: Rutledge.

Begany, J. J., & Milburn, M. A. (2002). Psychological predictors of sexual harassment: Authoritarianism, hostile sexism, and rape myths. *Psychology of Men and Masculinity, 3,* 119–126.

Bell, M. P., Quick, J. C., & Cycyota, C. S. (2002). Assessment and prevention of sexual harassment of employees: An applied guide to creating healthy organizations. *International Journal of Selection and Assessment, 10*(1/2), 160–167.

Berger, J., Cohen, B. P., & Zelditch, M., Jr. (1972). Status characteristics and social interaction. *American Sociological Review, 37,* 241–255.

Bergman, M. E., & Drasgow, F. (2003). Race as a moderator in a model of sexual harassment: An empirical test. *Journal of Occupational Health Psychology, 8*(2), 131–145.

Bergman, M. E., Langhout, R. D., Palmieri, P. A., Cortina, L. M., & Fitzgerald, L. F. (2002). The (un)reasonableness of reporting: Antecedents and consequences of reporting sexual harassment. *Journal of Applied Psychology, 87,* 230–242.

Birt, C. M., & Dion, K. L. (1987). Relative deprivation theory and responses to discrimination in a gay male and lesbian sample. *British Journal of Social Psychology, 26*, 139–145.

Bond, M. A., Punnett, L., Pyle, J. L., Cazeca, D., & Cooperman, M. (2004). Gendered work conditions, health, and work outcomes. *Journal of Occupational Health Psychology, 9*, 28–45.

Bowes-Sperry, L., & Tata, J. (1999). A multiperspective framework of sexual harassment: Reviewing two decades of research. In G. N. Powell (Ed.), *Handbook of gender and work* (pp. 263–280). Thousand Oaks, CA: Sage.

Brooks, L., & Perot, A. R. (1991). Reporting sexual harassment: Exploring a predictive model. *Psychology of Women Quarterly, 15*, 31–47.

Brown, T. N. (2001). Measuring self-perceived racial and ethnic discrimination in social surveys. *Sociological Spectrum, 21*, 377–392.

Canadian Human Rights Commission (CHRC). (1983). *Unwanted sexual attention and sexual harassment: Results of a survey of Canadians.* Ottawa: CHRC/ Research and Special Studies Branch.

Cleveland, J. N., & Kerst, M. E. (1993). Sexual harassment and perceptions of power: An underarticulated relationship. *Journal of Vocational Behavior, 42*, 49–67.

Cohen, S., & Wills, T. A. (1985). Stress, social support, and the buffering hypothesis. *Psychological Bulletin, 98*(2), 310–357.

Coles, F. S. (1986). Forced to quit: Sexual harassment complaints and agency response. *Sex Roles, 14*(1/2), 81–95.

Cortina, L. M., Fitzgerald, L. F., & Drasgow, F. (2002). Contextualizing Latina experiences of sexual harassment: Preliminary tests of a structural model. *Basic and Applied Social Psychology, 24*(4), 295–311.

Cortina, L. M., Lonsway, K. A., Magley, V. J., Freeman, L. V., Collinsworth, L. L., Hunter, M., & Fitzgerald, L. F. (2002). What's gender got to do with it? Incivility in the federal courts. *Law & Social Inquiry, 27*, 235–270.

Crocker, D., & Kalemba, V. (1999). The incidence and impact of women's experiences of sexual harassment in Canadian workplaces. *Canadian Review of Sociology and Anthropology, 36*(4), 541–558.

Croteau, J. M. (1996). Research on the work experiences of lesbian, gay, and bisexual people: An integrative review of methodology and findings. *Journal of Vocational Behavior, 48*, 195–209.

Dall'Ara, E., & Maass, A. (1999). Studying sexual harassment in the laboratory: Are egalitarian women at higher risk? *Sex Roles, 41*, 681–704.

Dansky, B. S., & Kilpatrick, D. G. (1997). Effects of sexual harassment. In W. O'Donohue (Ed.), *Sexual harassment: Theory, research, and treatment* (pp. 152–174). Boston: Allyn & Bacon.

Dekker, I., & Barling, J. (1998). Personal and organizational predictors of workplace sexual harassment of women by men. *Journal of Occupational Health Psychology, 3*(1), 7–18.

Dion, K. L. (1975). Women's reactions to discrimination from members of the same or the opposite sex. *Journal of Research in Personality, 9*, 294–306.

Dion, K. L., Dion, K. K., & Pak, A. W. P. (1992). Personality-based hardiness as a buffer for discrimination-related stress in members of Toronto's Chinese community. *Canadian Journal of Behavioural Science, 24*(4), 517–536.

Dion, K. L., & Earn, B. M. (1975). The phenomenology of being a target of prejudice. *Journal of Personality and Social Psychology, 32*, 944–950.

DuBois, C. L. Z., Knapp, D., Faley, R. H., & Kustis, G. (1998). An empirical examination of same- and other-gender sexual harassment in the workplace. *Sex Roles, 39*(9/10), 731–749.

Duncan, C. (2001). Ageism, early exit, and the rationality of age-based discrimination. In I. Glover & M. Branine (Eds.), *Ageism in work and employment* (pp. 25–46). Aldershot, UK: Ashgate.

Ehrenreich, R. (1999). Dignity and discrimination: Toward a pluralistic understanding of workplace discrimination. *Georgetown Law Journal, 88*(1), 1–64.

Ensher, E. A., Grant-Vallone, E. J., & Donaldson, S. I. (2001). Effects of perceived discrimination on job satisfaction, organizational commitment, organizational citizenship behavior, and grievances. *Human Resource Development Quarterly, 12*(1), 53–72.

Equal Employment Opportunity Commission (EEOC). (1993). Notice of proposed rule making: Guidelines on harassment based on race, color, religion, gender, national origin, age, or disability. *Federal Register, 58*, 51266–51269.

Essed, P. (1991). *Understanding everyday racism: An interdisciplinary theory.* Newbury Park, CA: Sage.

Fain, T. C., & Anderton, D. L. (1987). Sexual harassment: Organizational context and diffuse status. *Sex Roles, 15*(5/6), 291–311.

Fitzgerald, L. F., Drasgow, F., Hulin, C. L., Gelfand, M. J., & Magley, V. J. (1997). Antecedents and consequences of sexual harassment in organizations: A test of an integrated model. *Journal of Applied Psychology, 82*, 578–589.

Fitzgerald, L. F., Drasgow, F., & Magley, V. J. (1999). Sexual harassment in the armed forces: A test of an integrated model. *Military Psychology, 11*(3), 329–343.

Fitzgerald, L. F., Gelfand, M. J., & Drasgow, F. (1995). Measuring sexual harassment: Theoretical and psychometric advances. *Basic and Applied Social Psychology, 17*(4), 425–445.

Fitzgerald, L. F., Hulin, C. L., & Drasgow, F. (1994). The antecedents and consequences of sexual harassment in organizations: An integrated model. In G. P. Keita & J. J. Hurrell, Jr. (Eds.), *Job stress in a changing workforce* (pp. 55–73). Washington, DC: American Psychological Association.

Fitzgerald, L. F., Magley, V. J., Drasgow, F., & Waldo, C. R. (1999). Measuring sexual harassment in the military: The Sexual Experiences Questionnaire (SEQ-DOD). *Military Psychology, 11*, 243–263.

Fitzgerald, L. F., Shullman, S. L., Bailey, N., Richards, M., Swecker, J., Gold, Y., Ormerod, A. J., & Weitzman, L. (1988). The incidence and dimensions of sexual harassment in academia and the workplace. *Journal of Vocational Behavior, 32*, 152–175.

Fitzgerald, L. F., Swan, S., & Magley, V. J. (1997). But was it really sexual harassment? Legal, behavioral, and psychological definitions of the workplace victimization of women. In W. O'Donohue (Ed.), *Sexual harassment: Theory, research, and treatment* (pp. 5–28). Boston: Allyn & Bacon.

French, J. R. P., Jr., & Raven, B. H. (1959). The bases of social power. In D. Cartwright (Ed.), *Studies in social power* (pp. 150–167). Ann Arbor: University of Michigan.

Gelfand, M. J., Fitzgerald, L. F., & Drasgow, F. (1995). The structure of sexual harassment: A confirmatory analysis across cultures and settings. *Journal of Vocational Behavior, 47*, 164–177.

Glomb, T. M., Munson, L. J., Hulin, C. L., Bergman, M. E., & Drasgow, F. (1999). Structural equation models of sexual harassment: Longitudinal explorations and cross-sectional generalizations. *Journal of Applied Psychology, 84,* 14–28.

Glomb, T. M., Richman, W. L., Hulin, C. L., Drasgow, F., Schneider, K. T., & Fitzgerald, L. F. (1997). Ambient sexual harassment: An integrated model of antecedents and consequences. *Organizational Behavior and Human Decision Processes, 71*(3), 309–328.

Glowinkowski, S. P., & Cooper, C. L. (1986). Managers and professionals in business/industrial settings: The research evidence. *Journal of Occupational Behavior and Management, 8*(2), 177–193.

Goldenhar, L. M., Swanson, N. G., Hurrell, J. J., Jr., Ruder, A., & Deddens, J. (1998). Stressors and adverse outcomes for female construction workers. *Journal of Occupational Health Psychology, 3,* 19–32.

Gruber, J. E. (1997). An epidemiology of sexual harassment: Evidence from North America and Europe. In W. O'Donohue (Ed.), *Sexual harassment: Theory, research, and treatment* (pp. 84–98). Boston: Allyn & Bacon.

Guitierres, S. E., Saenz, D. S., & Green, B. L. (1994). Job stress and health outcomes among White and Hispanic employees: A test of the person-environment fit model. In J. J. Hurrell, Jr. (Ed.), *Job stress in a changing workforce* (pp. 107–125). Washington, DC: American Psychological Association.

Gutek, B. A. (1985). *Sex and the workplace.* San Francisco: Jossey-Bass.

Gutek, B. A., Cohen, A. G., & Tsui, A. (1996). Reactions to perceived sex discrimination. *Human Relations, 49*(6), 791–813.

Gutek, B. A., & Done, R. S. (2001). Sexual harassment. In R. K. Unger (Ed.), *Handbook of the psychology of women and gender* (pp. 367–387). New York: Wiley.

Gutek, B. A., & Dunwoody, V. (1987). Understanding sex in the workplace. In A. H. Stromberg, L. Larwood, & B. A. Gutek (Eds.), *Women and work: An annual review* (Vol. 2, pp. 249–269). Newbury Park, CA: Sage.

Gutek, B. A., & Koss, M. P. (1993). Changed women and changed organizations: Consequences of and coping with sexual harassment. *Journal of Vocational Behavior, 42,* 1–21.

Gutek, B. A., & Morasch, B. (1982). Sex-ratios, sex-role spillover, and sexual harassment at work. *Journal of Social Issues, 38,* 55–74.

Harned, M. S., & Fitzgerald, L. F. (2002). Understanding a link between sexual harassment and eating disorder symptoms: A mediational analysis. *Journal of Consulting and Clinical Psychology, 70*(5), 1170–1181.

Harned, M. S., Ormerod, A. J., Palmieri, P. A., Collinsworth, L. L., & Reed, M. (2002). Sexual assault and other types of sexual harassment by workplace personnel: A comparison of antecedents and consequences. *Journal of Occupational Health Psychology, 7*(2), 174–188.

Hassell, B. L., & Perrewé, P. L. (1993). An examination of the relationship between older workers' perceptions of age discrimination and employee psychological states. *Journal of Managerial Issues, 5,* 109–120.

Hay, M. S., & Elig, T. W. (1999). The 1995 Department of Defense sexual harassment survey: Overview and methodology. *Military Psychology, 11*(3), 233–242.

Holzbauer, J. J., & Berven, N. L. (1996). Disability harassment: A new term for a long-standing problem. *Journal of Counseling and Development, 74*(May/June), 478–483.

Huang, C. I., & Kleiner, B. H. (2000). New developments concerning the discrimination and harassment of gays in the workplace. *Equal Opportunities International, 19*(6–7), 66–69.

Hughes, D., & Dodge, M. A. (1997). African American women in the workplace: Relationships between job conditions, racial bias at work, and perceived job quality. *American Journal of Community Psychology, 25*(5), 581–599.

Hulin, C. L., Fitzgerald, L. F., & Drasgow, F. (1996). Organizational influences on sexual harassment. In M. S. Stockdale (Ed.), *Sexual harassment in the workplace: Perspectives, frontiers, and response strategies* (pp. 127–151). Thousand Oaks, CA: Sage.

James, K. (1994). Social identity, work stress, and minority workers' health. In G. P. Keita & J. J. Hurrell, Jr. (Eds.), *Job stress in a changing workforce* (pp. 127–145). Washington, DC: American Psychological Association.

James, K., Lovato, C., & Khoo, G. (1994). Social identity correlates of minority workers' health. *Academy of Management Journal, 37*(2), 383–396.

Kanter, R. M. (1977). *Men and women of the corporation.* New York: Basic Books.

Kasschau, P. L. (1977). Age and race discrimination reported by middle-aged and older persons. *Social Forces, 55*(3), 728–742.

Kessler, R. C., Mickelson, K. D., & Williams, D. R. (1999). The prevalence, distribution, and mental health correlates of perceived discrimination in the United States. *Journal of Health and Social Behavior, 40,* 208–230.

Klonoff, E. A., & Landrine, H. (1995). The Schedule of Sexist Events: A measure of lifetime and recent sexist discrimination in women's lives. *Psychology of Women Quarterly, 19,* 439–472.

Klonoff, E. A., Landrine, H., & Campbell, R. (2000). Sexist discrimination may account for well-known gender differences in psychiatric symptoms. *Psychology of Women Quarterly, 24,* 93–99.

Koss, M. P., Goodman, L. A., Browne, A., Fitzgerald, L. F., Keita, G. P., & Russo, N. F. (1994). *No safe haven: Male violence against women at home, at work, and in the community.* Washington, DC: American Psychological Association.

Kovach, K. A. (1995). ENDA promises to ban employment discrimination for gays. Employment Non-Discrimination Act. *Personnel Journal, 74,* 48–49.

Krieger, N. (1990). Racial and gender discrimination: Risk factors for high blood pressure? *Social Science and Medicine, 30*(12), 1273–1281.

LaFontaine, E., & Trudeau, L. (1986). The frequency, sources, and correlates of sexual harassment among women in traditional male occupations. *Sex Roles, 15,* 433–442.

Lancaster, A. R. (1999). Department of Defense sexual harassment research: Historical perspectives and new initiatives. *Military Psychology, 11,* 219–231.

Landrine, H., & Klonoff, E. A. (1996). The Schedule of Racist Events: A measure of racial discrimination and a study of its negative physical and mental health consequences. *Journal of Black Psychology, 22,* 144–168.

Landrine, H., Klonoff, E. A., Gibbs, J., Manning, V., & Lund, M. (1995). Physical and psychiatric correlates of gender discrimination: An application of the Schedule of Sexist Events. *Psychology of Women Quarterly, 19,* 473–492.

Lazarus, R. S., & Folkman, S. (1984). *Stress, appraisal, and coping.* New York: Springer.

Loy, P. H., & Stewart, L. P. (1984). The extent and effects of the sexual harassment of working women. *Sociological Focus, 17,* 31–43.

Magley, V. J., Waldo, C. R., Drasgow, F., & Fitzgerald, L. F. (1999). The impact of sexual harassment on military personnel: Is it the same for men and women? *Military Psychology, 11*(3), 283–302.

Manning, M. R., Jackson, C. N., & Fusilier, M. R. (1996). Occupational stress and health care use. *Journal of Occupational Health Psychology, 1,* 100–109.

Mays, V. M., Coleman, L. M., & Jackson, J. S. (1996). Perceived race-based discrimination, employment status, and job stress in a national sample of Black women: Implications and health outcomes. *Journal of Occupational Health Psychology, 1,* 319–329.

Mazur, A. G. (2002). *Theorizing feminist policy.* Oxford, UK: Oxford University Press.

McCann, R., & Giles, H. (2002). Ageism in the workplace: A communication perspective. In T. D. Nelson (Ed.), *Ageism: Stereotyping and prejudice against older persons* (pp. 163–199). Cambridge: MIT Press.

McGoldrick, A. E., & Arrowsmith, J. (2001). Discrimination by age: The organizational response. In I. Glover & M. Branine (Eds.), *Ageism in work and employment* (pp. 75–95). Aldershot, UK: Ashgate.

Mecca, S. J., & Rubin, L. J. (1999). Definitional research on African American students and sexual harassment. *Psychology of Women Quarterly, 23,* 813–817.

Meyer, I. H. (1995). Minority stress and mental health in gay men. *Journal of Health and Social Behavior, 36,* 38–56.

Miranda, J., Perez-Stable, E. J., Munoz, R. F., Hargreaves, W., & Henke, C. J. (1991). Somatization, psychiatric disorder, and stress in utilization of ambulatory medical services. *Health Psychology, 10,* 46–51.

Morrow, P. C., McElroy, J. C., & Phillips, C. M. (1994). Sexual harassment behaviors and work-related perceptions and attitudes. *Journal of Vocational Behavior, 45,* 295–309.

Munson, L. J., Hulin, C. L., & Drasgow, F. (2000). Longitudinal analysis of dispositional influences and sexual harassment: Effects on job and psychological outcomes. *Personnel Psychology, 53,* 21–46.

Murrell, A. J., Olson, J. E., & Frieze, I. H. (1995). Sexual harassment and gender discrimination: A longitudinal study of women managers. *Journal of Social Issues, 51,* 139–149.

Murry, W. D., Sivasubramaniam, N., & Jacques, P. H. (2001). Supervisory support, social exchange relationships, and sexual harassment consequences: A test of competing models. *Leadership Quarterly, 12*(1), 1–29.

O'Hare, E. A., & O'Donohue, W. (1998). Sexual harassment: Identifying risk factors. *Archives of Sexual Behavior, 27,* 561–580.

O'Keeffe, J. (1993). Disability, discrimination and the Americans With Disabilities Act. *Consulting Psychology Journal, 45,* 3–9.

Orpen, C. (1995). The effects of perceived age discrimination on employee job satisfaction, organizational commitment and job involvement. *Psychology: A Quarterly Journal of Human Behavior, 32*(3/4), 55–56.

Pak, A. W.-P., Dion, K. L., & Dion, K. K. (1991). Social-psychological correlates of experienced discrimination: Test of the double jeopardy hypothesis. *International Journal of Intercultural Relations, 15,* 243–254.

Parker, S. K., & Griffin, M. A. (2002). What is so bad about a little name-calling? Negative consequences of gender harassment for overperformance demands and distress. *Journal of Occupational Health Psychology, 7*(3), 195–210.

Pasupathi, M., & Lockenhoff, C. E. (2002). Ageist behavior. In T. D. Nelson (Ed.), *Ageism: Stereotyping and prejudice against older persons* (pp. 201–246). Cambridge: MIT Press.

Pavalko, E. K., Mossakowski, K. N., & Hamilton, V. J. (2003). Does perceived discrimination affect health? Longitudinal relationships between work discrimination and women's physical and emotional health. *Journal of Health and Social Behavior, 43,* 18–33.

Piotrkowski, C. S. (1998). Gender harassment, job satisfaction, and distress among employed white and minority women. *Journal of Occupational Health Psychology, 3*(1), 33–43.

Platt, H. A. (1994, March). Nonsexual harassment claims hit HR's desk. *HR Magazine, 39,* 29–30, 32–34.

Pryor, J. B. (1995). The psychosocial impact of sexual harassment on women in the U.S. military. *Basic and Applied Social Psychology, 17,* 581–603.

Pryor, J. B., & Fitzgerald, L. F. (2003). Sexual harassment research in the United States. In S. Einarsen, H. Hoel, D. Zapf, & C. L. Cooper (Eds.), *Bullying and emotional abuse in the workplace: International perspectives in research and practice* (pp. 79–100). London: Taylor & Francis.

Pryor, J. B., LaVite, C. M., & Stoller, L. M. (1993). A social psychological analysis of sexual harassment: The person/situation interaction. *Journal of Vocational Behavior, 42,* 68–83.

Ragins, B. R., & Cornwell, J. M. (2001). Pink triangles: Antecedents and consequences of perceived workplace discrimination against gay and lesbian employees. *Journal of Applied Psychology, 86,* 1244–1261.

Reid, P. T., & Comas-Diaz, L. (1990). Gender and ethnicity: Perspectives on dual status. *Sex Roles, 22,* 397–408.

Richman, J. A., Flaherty, J. A., & Rospenda, K. M. (1996). Perceived workplace harassment experiences and problem drinking among physicians: Broadening the stress/alienation paradigm. *Addiction, 91*(3), 391–403.

Richman, J. A., Flaherty, J. A., Rospenda, K. M., & Christensen, M. L. (1992). Mental health consequences and correlates of reported medical student abuse. *Journal of the American Medical Association, 267*(5), 692–694.

Richman, J. A., Rospenda, K. M., Flaherty, J. A., & Freels, S. (2001). Workplace harassment, active coping, and alcohol-related outcomes. *Journal of Substance Abuse Treatment, 13*(3), 347–366.

Richman, J. A., Rospenda, K. M., Flaherty, J. A., & Freels, S. (2003, June). *Organizational tolerance for workplace harassment, prevalence, and distress and drinking over time.* Paper presented at the annual meeting of the Research Society on Alcoholism, Ft. Lauderdale, FL.

Richman, J. A., Rospenda, K. M., Nawyn, S. J., Flaherty, J. A., Fendrich, M., Drum, M. L., & Johnson, T. P. (1999). Sexual harassment and generalized workplace abuse among university employees: Prevalence and mental health correlates. *American Journal of Public Health, 89*(3), 358–363.

Richman, J. A., Shinsako, S. A., Rospenda, K. M., Flaherty, J. A., & Freels, S. (2002). Workplace harassment/abuse and alcohol-related outcomes: The mediating role of psychological distress. *Journal of Studies on Alcohol, 63,* 412–419.

Richman-Hirsch, W. L., & Glomb, T. M. (2002). Are men affected by the sexual harassment of women? Effects of ambient sexual harassment on men. In J. M. Brett & F. Drasgow (Eds.), *The psychology of work: Theoretically based empirical research.* Mahwah, NJ: Lawrence Erlbaum.

Rosen, L. N., & Martin, L. (1998). Childhood maltreatment history as a risk factor for sexual harassment among U.S. Army soldiers. *Violence and Victims, 13*(3), 269–286.

Rospenda, K. M. (1998). *Sexual and non-sexual harassment as interpersonal conflict stressors in the workplace: Effects on job, mental health, and physical health outcomes.* Unpublished doctoral dissertation, DePaul University, Chicago.

Rospenda, K. M. (2002). Workplace harassment, services utilization, and drinking outcomes. *Journal of Occupational Health Psychology, 7*(2), 141–155.

Rospenda, K. M., Richman, J. A., Ehmke, J. L. Z., & Zlatoper, K. W. (2004, April). *Is workplace harassment hazardous to your health?* Poster session presented at the annual meeting of the Society for Industrial and Organizational Psychology, Chicago.

Rospenda, K. M., Richman, J. A., & Nawyn, S. J. (1998). Doing power: The confluence of gender, race, and class in contrapower sexual harassment. *Gender & Society, 12,* 40–60.

Rospenda, K. M., Richman, J. A., Wislar, J. S., & Flaherty, J. A. (2000). Chronicity of sexual harassment and generalized work-place abuse: Effects on drinking outcomes. *Addiction, 95*(12), 1805–1820.

Sanchez, J. I., & Brock, P. (1996). Outcomes of perceived discrimination among Hispanic employees: Is diversity management a luxury or a necessity? *Academy of Management Journal, 39*(3), 704–719.

Sbraga, T. P., & O'Donohue, W. (2000). Sexual harassment. *Annual Review of Sex Research, 11,* 258–285.

Scarville, J., Button, S. B., Edwards, J. E., Lancaster, A. R., & Elig, T. W. (1999). *Armed Forces equal opportunity survey* (ADA-366037). Arlington, VA: Defense Manpower Data Center.

Schneider, K. T., Hitlan, R. T., & Radhakrishnan, P. (2000). An examination of the nature and correlates of ethnic harassment experiences in multiple contexts. *Journal of Applied Psychology, 85,* 3–12.

Schneider, K. T., Swan, S., & Fitzgerald, L. F. (1997). Job-related and psychological effects of sexual harassment in the workplace: Empirical evidence from two organizations. *Journal of Applied Psychology, 82*(3), 401–415.

Schneider, K. T., Tomaka, J., Palacios-Esquivel, R., & Goldsmith, S. D. (2001). Women's cognitive, affective, and physiological reactions to a male co-worker's sexist behavior. *Journal of Applied Social Psychology, 31,* 1995–2018.

Sherbourne, C. D. (1988). The role of social support and life stress events in use of mental health services. *Social Science and Medicine, 27,* 1393–1400.

Shupe, E. I., Cortina, L. M., Ramos, A., Fitzgerald, L. F., & Salisbury, J. (2002). The incidence and outcomes of sexual harassment among Hispanic and non-Hispanic White women: A comparison across levels of cultural affiliation. *Psychology of Women Quarterly, 26,* 298–308.

Spector, P. E., Dwyer, D. J., & Jex, S. M. (1988). Relation of job stressors to affective, health, and performance outcomes: A comparison of multiple data sources. *Journal of Applied Psychology, 73,* 11–19.

Stockdale, M. S. (1998). The direct and moderating influences of sexual-harassment pervasiveness, coping strategies, and gender on work-related outcomes. *Psychology of Women Quarterly, 22,* 521–535.

Tajfel, H., & Turner, J. C. (1985). The social identity theory of intergroup behavior. In S. Worchel & W. G. Austin (Eds.), *Psychology of intergroup relations* (2nd ed., pp. 7–24). Chicago: Nelson-Hall.

Tangri, S. S., Burt, M. R., & Johnson, L. B. (1982). Sexual harassment at work: Three explanatory models. *Journal of Social Issues, 38,* 33–54.

Timmerman, G., & Bajema, C. (2000). The impact of organizational culture on perceptions and experiences of sexual harassment. *Journal of Vocational Behavior, 57,* 188–205.

U.S. Merit Systems Protection Board (USMSPB). (1981). *Sexual harassment of federal workers: Is it a problem?* Washington, DC: Author.

U.S. Merit Systems Protection Board (USMSPB). (1988). *Sexual harassment in the federal government: An update.* Washington, DC: Author.

U.S. Merit Systems Protection Board (USMSPB). (1995). *Sexual harassment in the federal workplace: Trends, progress, continuing challenges.* Washington, DC: Author.

Waldo, C. R. (1999). Working in a majority context: A structural model of hetero-sexism as minority stress in the workplace. *Journal of Counseling Psychology, 46,* 218–232.

Waldo, C. R., Berdahl, J. L., & Fitzgerald, L. F. (1998). Are men sexually harassed? If so, by whom? *Law and Human Behavior, 22,* 59–79.

Wasti, S. A., Bergman, M. E., Glomb, T. M., & Drasgow, F. (2000). Test of the cross-cultural generalizability of a model of sexual harassment. *Journal of Applied Psychology, 85,* 766–778.

Wise, S., & Stanley, L. (1987). *Georgie Porgie: Sexual harassment in everyday life.* London: Pandora.

Wislar, J. S., Richman, J. A., Fendrich, M., & Flaherty, J. A. (2002). Sexual harass-ment, generalized workplace abuse and drinking outcomes: The role of person-ality vulnerability. *Journal of Drug Issues, 32,* 1071–1088.

Wolfe, J., Sharkansky, E. J., Read, J. P., Dawson, R., Martin, J. A., & Ouimette, P. C. (1998). Sexual harassment and assault as predictors of PTSD symptomology among U.S. female Persian Gulf War military personnel. *Journal of Interpersonal Violence, 13,* 40–57.

Wyatt, G. E., & Riederle, M. (1995). The prevalence and context of sexual harass-ment among African American and White American women. *Journal of Interpersonal Violence, 10,* 309–321.

Yoder, J. D., & Aniakudo, P. (1996). When pranks become harassment: The case of African-American women firefighters. *Sex Roles, 35*(5/6), 253–270.

Yoder, J. D., & McDonald, T. W. (1998). Measuring sexist discrimination in the workplace: Support for the validity of the Schedule of Sexist Events. *Psychology of Women Quarterly, 22,* 487–491.

8

Workplace Aggression

Aaron C. H. Schat

E. Kevin Kelloway

Work is, by its very nature, about violence—to the spirit as well as to the body. It is about ulcers as well as accidents, about shouting matches as well as fistfights, about nervous breakdowns as well as kicking the dog around. It is, above all (or beneath all), about daily humiliations. To survive the day is triumph enough for the walking wounded among the great many of us.

Studs Terkel, *Working* (1974, p. xi)

Workplace aggression is a serious occupational health problem that has garnered a great deal of media attention. Paradoxically, the attention has contributed to both increased social awareness of the problem and to inaccurate understanding of it. The media tend to report only on serious acts of workplace violence, facilitating increased awareness but sacrificing accurate understanding because they create the perception that such acts are prototypical. In fact, they represent a rare form of workplace aggression. Nevertheless, the seriousness of workplace aggression—in its various manifestations—is becoming more widely acknowledged, and the growing empirical literature is beginning to augment the limitations of the popular perceptions of the topic with more valid knowledge of aggression, its causes, consequences, and the means by which it can be addressed.

—

Authors' Note: Preparation of this chapter was supported by a Social Sciences and Humanities Research Council of Canada (SSHRC) doctoral fellowship and Ontario Graduate Scholarship to the first author and grants from both the SSHRC and the Nova Scotia Health Research Foundation to the second author. Correspondence concerning this article should be addressed to Aaron C. H. Schat, Michael G. DeGroote School of Business, McMaster University, 1280 Main Street West, Hamilton, Ontario, Canada, L8S 4M4. Electronic mail may be sent to schata@mcmaster.ca

Conceptualizing and Defining Workplace Aggression

One of the major limitations of the research on workplace aggression is that the terminology, definitions, and operationalizations of it vary greatly. In some cases, the terms *workplace aggression* and *workplace violence* have been used interchangeably. In others, they have been used to refer to different classes of behavior, with aggression typically reflecting nonphysical and violence reflecting physical behaviors. In addition, numerous other terms have been used to describe similar or related constructs, although the literatures have remained largely independent from one another. These other constructs include workplace harassment (e.g., Richman et al., 1999; Rospenda, 2002), emotional (e.g., Keashly, 1998, 2001), verbal (Cox, 1991), and psychological (e.g., Sheehan, Sheehan, White, Leibowitz, & Baldwin, 1990) abuse, victimization (e.g., Aquino, 2000; Aquino, Grover, Bradfield, & Allen, 1999), interpersonal organizational deviance (e.g., Bennett & Robinson, 2000), bullying (e.g., Einarsen, 1999; Hoel, Rayner, & Cooper, 1999), and mobbing (e.g., Leymann, 1996). There is a need to clarify the definitions of these constructs and more clearly delineate their relationships.

In this section, we seek to define the construct of workplace aggression and discuss how it relates to and is distinct from a number of conceptually related constructs. We have chosen to use the term *workplace aggression,* rather than *workplace violence* or the other terms discussed above, because it links research on workplace aggression with the broader body of research on human aggression (e.g., Anderson & Bushman, 2002; Berkowitz, 1993) and provides a general construct to which other antisocial behavior constructs can be related. Using the term *workplace aggression* and defining it broadly should help contribute to the integration of a body of research that has, to date, been fragmented.

Several researchers have proposed definitions of workplace aggression. For example, Neuman and Baron (1998) define it as "efforts by individuals to harm others with whom they work, or have worked, or the organizations in which they are presently, or were previously, employed" (p. 395). The drawback to this definition is that it limits workplace aggression to behaviors of current or former employees. This focus on intraorganizational sources of aggression is too narrow because it fails to consider aggression perpetrated by members of the public (e.g., customers, patients, or clients) who come into contact with individuals who are working and who commit an act of aggression during the course of an interaction with an employee (Peek-Asa, Runyan, & Zwerling, 2001). Second, its breadth results in the inclusion of behaviors that are specifically directed at organizations, some of which may be more appropriately considered acts of organizational deviance (e.g., Bennett & Robinson, 2000) than aggression. That being said, the distinction between acts directed at individuals versus organizations is not always clear as some acts (e.g., property damage, disclosing confidential company information) can be explicitly directed at an organization but enacted with the intention of harming an individual or individuals within the organization.

A second definition is offered by O'Leary-Kelly, Griffin, and Glew (1996), who focus on organization-motivated aggression that they define as "attempted injurious or destructive behavior initiated by either an organizational insider or outsider that is instigated by some factor in the organizational context" (p. 229). This definition includes aggression perpetrated by employees and members of the public, but its exclusive focus on organizational causes of aggression limits its utility as a general definition of workplace aggression.

Extending the existing definitions, we define workplace aggression as behavior by an individual or individuals within or outside an organization that is intended to physically or psychologically harm a worker or workers and occurs in a work-related context. There are several elements of this definition that make it an appropriate general definition of the construct. First, the target of the behavior is an individual within the organization, not the organization as a whole, which helps to distinguish aggression from organizational deviance (e.g., theft, sabotage). Second, the perpetrator of the aggressive behavior can be a member of either the organization or the public. Third, it focuses on behavior that is intended to do harm to an individual worker or groups of workers. This focus helps to distinguish aggression from behavior that results in unintentional harm (e.g., workplace accidents) and avoids excluding aggressive behavior that was intended to do harm but did not result in actual harm. Finally, considering behavior that occurs in a "work-related context" includes aggression that occurs during standard working hours at the primary workplace itself and also aggression that occurs when work-related duties are being carried out offsite or at a function that is related to work but is not part of a workday, per se.

In addition to the effects of direct exposure to workplace aggression, previous research has highlighted the role of vicariously experienced events. First, witnessing the death or injury of others has been consistently associated with the development of posttraumatic stress disorder (PTSD) symptoms (e.g., Meichenbaum, 1994; Vaitkus & Martin, 1991), and the traumatic nature of handling dead or wounded bodies has been identified in studies of combat stress (e.g., Sutker, Uddo, Brailey, Vasterling, & Errera, 1994; see also Lamerson & Kelloway, 1996). Research focusing on more common examples of workplace aggression (e.g., Rogers & Kelloway, 1997) has also noted that those who experience aggression vicariously (i.e., those who witness or hear about aggressive acts directed toward similar others) also experience adverse effects.

Relationship of Workplace Aggression to Other Constructs

Although the terms workplace aggression and violence have been used interchangeably, it is appropriate to make a distinction between them that is similar to the distinction that has been made in the general human aggression literature (e.g., Anderson & Bushman, 2002) and to a limited extent, the workplace aggression literature (e.g., Neuman & Baron, 1998). Specifically, *workplace aggression* is the more general term that comprises a variety of interpersonally harmful behaviors, whereas *workplace violence* is a specific type of workplace aggression consisting of behaviors that are physical in nature and that may cause physical harm. Accordingly, all violent behaviors are, by definition, aggressive whereas not all aggressive behaviors are violent. Some support for this distinction comes from Schat and Kelloway (2003) who provide factor analytic evidence that physically and nonphysically aggressive behaviors are empirically distinguishable.

There is also a need to consider how workplace aggression is related to workplace bullying and the similar constructs of workplace abuse, mistreatment, victimization, and mobbing. Although there are slight variations in the definitions of these terms, Keashly (2001) suggests that they generally refer to "interactions between organizational members that are characterized by repeated hostile verbal and nonverbal, often nonphysical behaviors directed at a person(s) such that the target's sense of him/herself as a competent worker and person is negatively affected" (p. 234). In general, the behaviors that compose these constructs would fall within our definition of workplace aggression; however, the definitions differ in three respects. First, bullying and these other constructs are often more narrowly defined to include only negative behavior that occurs frequently (e.g., weekly) and persists over a prolonged period of time (e.g., 6 months; see Hoel et al., 1999, for a review), which would exclude one-time or infrequent acts from the domain of bullying. Our definition is somewhat broader in that it does not specifically reference the frequency or duration of aggressive behavior. Second, the other definitions limit the source of the negative behaviors to organizational members, whereas our definition includes extraorganizational sources of aggression (e.g., members of the public) as well. Finally, they also include an explicit reference to outcomes, whereas we focus our definition on aggressive behavior, recognizing that personal and situational variables may influence whether and the extent to which negative outcomes will occur.

Workplace incivility (Andersson & Pearson, 1999) is another construct that is conceptually related to workplace aggression. It is defined as "low-intensity deviant behavior with ambiguous intent to harm the target, in violation of workplace norms for mutual respect. Uncivil behaviors are characteristically rude and discourteous, displaying a lack of regard for others" (p. 457). According to this definition, there is a degree of overlap between the constructs of workplace aggression and incivility. Uncivil behavior that is enacted with no intent to harm would not be considered aggressive, whereas that which is intended to harm would be considered a low-intensity form of workplace aggression. Andersson and Pearson (1999) suggest that incivility can be a precursor to more serious forms of aggression, which suggests that if aggressive behavior is classified along a continuum of severity or intensity, incivility would represent the low end of this continuum.

Recently, a number of researchers have included sexual harassment behaviors in their definitions and operationalizations of workplace violence and aggression (e.g., Barling, Rogers, & Kelloway, 2001; Richman et al., 1999; Rospenda, 2002). Therefore, consideration of the relationship between workplace aggression and sexual harassment is warranted. Based on our definition, workplace sexual harassment—which consists of gender harassment, unwanted sexual attention, and sexual coercion (Gelfand, Fitzgerald, & Drasgow, 1995)—is a unique form of workplace aggression that is characterized by sexualized or sex-related behavior. Recent factor analytic evidence suggests that sexual harassment is empirically distinct from, but related to, generalized work harassment (Fendrich, Woodward, & Richman, 2002).

Forms and Prevalence of Workplace Aggression

The most severe form of workplace aggression is a physical act of violence that results in death. Reports suggest that workplace homicide is the second leading cause of work-related death (Bureau of Labor Statistics, 1995). Based on media reports, the prototypical case of workplace aggression—and homicide in particular—involves a disgruntled former employee returning to his workplace and shooting his boss and coworkers (Smith, 1999). Despite the seriousness of such acts, in reality, they are quite rare and represent only a small proportion of work-related homicides. Most work-related homicides (80%) occur during armed robberies or other crimes perpetrated by nonemployees (Sygnatur & Toscano, 2000) who do not know the target of their aggression and whose motives are more likely to be instrumental than vengeful.

Physical assault represents another serious form of workplace violence and one that occurs more frequently than homicide. Published estimates of the frequency of physical assaults vary widely, with surveys suggesting that anywhere from 5% (U.S. Postal Service Commission [USPSC], 2000) to 30% (Pizzino, 1993, as cited in Pizzino, 2002) of the workforce experiencing such acts. The frequencies reported tend to vary as a function of the types of behavior that are asked about, the time frame covered by the survey, and the nature of the occupations included in the sample. Although physical assaults rarely have fatal results, they can cause physical injury and have adverse psychological consequences as well. Therefore, even the conservative exposure estimates belie the seriousness of this form of aggression.

In addition to physical aggression, there are a variety of other behaviors that are nonphysical but still aggressive in nature. Examples include yelling, swearing, insults, sarcasm, and spreading rumors (e.g., Keashly, 1998; Neuman & Baron, 1997). It should be pointed out that behaviors such as these have also been considered in the literature on workplace bullying (e.g., Hoel et al., 1999), which involves aggressive behavior at work that occurs frequently and takes place over a sustained period of time.

Nonphysical workplace aggression tends to receive very little public or media attention even though it represents the most common form of aggression (Greenberg & Barling, 1999; USPSC, 2000). For example, the survey by the USPSC (2000) found that 33% of the U.S. workforce reported experiencing verbal abuse at work. In a 1993 survey of public employees conducted in Canada by the Canadian Union of Public Employees (Pizzino, 1993, as cited in Pizzino, 2002), as many as 69% of respondents reported experiencing verbal aggression at work. There is also research evidence, which will be described later, suggesting that these forms of aggression have serious consequences for both individuals and organizations (e.g., Keashly, 1998; Schat & Kelloway, 2000) and may escalate into more serious acts of aggression (Glomb, 2002). Considered in light of their frequent occurrence, serious consequences, and potential to escalate, nonphysical acts of workplace aggression constitute an important dimension of the construct of workplace aggression and represent a serious occupational health concern.

Prevalence and Severity of Aggression From Different Sources

The frequency estimates that we have presented are averages based on the available survey data, which tend to vary as a function of the source of the aggression. Although not all surveys have source-specific data, those that do reveal a somewhat inconsistent pattern of results. The USPSC (2000) found that 2.3% of their national workforce sample reported physical assault from organizational outsiders (members of the public) and 3% from coworkers; 2.4% reported sexual harassment from outsiders and 14% from coworkers; and 7.7% reported verbal abuse from outsiders and 25% from coworkers. Summarizing the results of a survey of Canadian public sector employees by the Public Service Alliance of Canada, Pizzino (2002) states that 35% of the employees reported experiencing some form of aggression during the previous year, with verbal abuse accounting for 72% of the aggression reported. Of the aggression reported, clients accounted for 38% and supervisors accounted for 22%. Unfortunately, a more detailed breakdown of aggression type by aggression source is not provided, nor is it clear how the remaining 40% of the aggression reported by the survey respondents is divided across nonsupervisory coworkers, members of the public who are not clients, or others.

Source-specific frequency data can also be gleaned from LeBlanc and Kelloway's (2002) study, although percentages were not reported in the source article. Their results, based on me-an ratings on a 5-point scale measuring the frequency of exposure to various acts of aggression (ranging from 0 [0 times] to 4 [4 or more times]), indicate that nonphysical acts of aggression from members of the public ($M = 1.34$, $SD = 1.44$) occur more frequently than such acts by coworkers ($M = .73$, $SD = 1.09$). Between 45% and 55% of respondents reported experiencing nonphysical aggression from members of the public, and between 25% and 35% of the sample reported experiencing nonphysical aggression from coworkers (actual frequencies vary with the form of aggression). Violent acts by members of the public ($M = .41$, $SD = .82$) also occur more frequently than violence by coworkers ($M = .02$, $SD = .10$). Between 15% and 25% of respondents reported experiencing physical violence from members of the public, whereas fewer than 5% of respondents reported experiencing physical violence from coworkers.

On balance, the data suggest that workers are more likely to experience aggression from members of the public than from coworkers, although there are inconsistencies. Despite the apparently lower frequency of coworker aggression, however, the available evidence suggests that its psychological consequences are more severe than those of public aggression. In LeBlanc and Kelloway's (2002) study, public aggression predicted both perceived likelihood and fear of future violence but was not associated with emotional health, somatic health, or affective commitment. Coworker aggression, on the other hand, did not predict perceived likelihood or fear of aggression but was directly associated with reduced health and commitment and increased turnover intentions. The reason for this pattern of results requires further research to determine but we can suggest several potential explanations. One possibility is that aggression from members of the public (e.g., clients, patients, etc.) is perceived by workers in some occupations as being "part of the job" and therefore less likely to have adverse effects. A second possibility is that public aggression is less distressing because the target is unlikely to have contact with the specific aggressor again. On the other hand, aggression from coworkers is less likely to be perceived as intrinsic to a job and more likely to involve ongoing contact with the aggressor, making it more likely to cause distress and in turn affect workers' health, job attitudes, and behavior.

Another potential source of aggression at work that merits attention is one's partner or significant other. This type of aggression—in which domestic abuse spills over into the workplace—has been recognized as a distinct category in some existing typologies of workplace aggression (e.g., Peek-Asa et al., 2001) and the subject of a number of articles in the popular literature. However, empirical research on the topic is scarce (LeBlanc & Barling, in press).

Domestic abuse can spill over into the workplace in two major ways. First, the effects of domestic abuse can spill over when its target's work-related behavior and performance can be adversely affected. Second, the abusive behavior can itself spill over when an aggressive act is committed at the workplace either directly (as when the perpetrator physically enters the workplace) or indirectly (via phone calls, electronic mail, etc.). The 1999 General Social Survey on Victimization conducted by Statistics Canada indicates that 32.9% of women and 10.1% of men sampled reported missing paid employment and unpaid work due to partner-initiated victimization

(Johnson & Bunge, 2001). In addition, research by Riger, Ahrens, and Blickenstaff (2000) and Swanberg and Logan (2002, as cited in LeBlanc & Barling, in press) suggests that women who experience domestic abuse experience psychological distress and other problems that in turn lead to high levels of work-related tardiness and absenteeism, reduced job performance, and job loss due to quitting or being fired. These data demonstrate the potentially serious negative spillover effects of domestic abuse in the workplace and suggest the need for additional research in this area.

Theoretical Issues Related to Workplace Aggression

Workplace Aggression and the Stress Process Model

The most widely used theoretical approach to understanding the effects of experiencing workplace aggression is the process model of work stress that, in its simplified form, involves (a) an aversive environmental stimulus, (b) an individual's perception of and immediate psychological response(s) to the stimulus, and (c) various consequences of same (e.g., Kahn & Byosiere, 1990) that may relate to the individual's health (e.g., psychological and somatic) and work-related (e.g., job attitudes and behavior) functioning. These elements of the work stress process model have also been referred to as stressor, stress, and strain, respectively (e.g., Pratt & Barling, 1988). The model posits that an individual's perception of and immediate psychological response to a stressor mediates the effect of the stressor on subsequent functioning. A graphical depiction of the application of this model to workplace aggression is presented in Figure 8.1. As shown, aggressive behavior experienced by an individual represents the stressor, the individual's immediate psychological reaction (e.g., perceived vulnerability, fear, anxiety) represents stress, and the medium- and long-term consequences represent strain. Other variables and linkages that are included in Figure 8.1, including predictors, mediators, moderators, and consequences of workplace aggression, will be discussed later in the chapter.

There are a number of reasons why this model is appropriate for the study of workplace aggression and its consequences. First, it has been widely used in the broader work stress literature and thus sets the study of workplace aggression in this context. Second, it distinguishes between the aggressive event, an individual's immediate reaction to that event, and its subsequent effects. Third, it is general enough to be readily adapted to different research contexts. Finally, a variety of organizational, situational, and individual difference variables can be incorporated as moderators and mediators into this model.

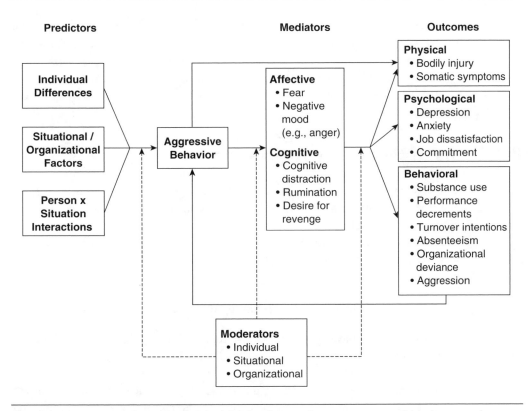

Figure 8.1   Comprehensive Model of the Predictors, Consequences, and Moderators of Workplace Aggression

Workplace Aggression as an Acute Versus Chronic Stressor

As Pratt and Barling (1988) point out, stressors can vary along a number of dimensions including time of onset, intensity, duration, and frequency of occurrence. Researchers have used these dimensions to distinguish between various stressors. Two common categories are acute and chronic stressors. Acute stressors begin at a specific time, have high intensity, short duration, and low frequency. Chronic stressors have no specific onset, range in intensity and duration, and occur frequently.

This distinction can be usefully applied to workplace aggression, although the classification is not straightforward and requires consideration of context. In general, an act of violence (e.g., physical assault) would be classified as an acute stressor because it has a specific beginning and end, is highly intense, and occurs rarely (although there may be occupations such as police work in which violent acts could be classified as chronic stressors). Nonphysical acts of aggression are more difficult to classify, particularly because their intensity and frequency of occurrence can vary so widely. Some behaviors that are highly intense and rarely occur would probably be most appropriately classified as acute (e.g., being yelled at, ridiculed), whereas others that have low intensity and occur more frequently would be most appropriately classified as chronic stressors (e.g., being ignored). Because the pattern of exposure to aggression varies across occupations (e.g., LeBlanc & Kelloway, 2002; USPSC, 2000), the classification of various forms of aggressive behavior as acute versus chronic stressors may be occupation-specific.

Predictors of Workplace Aggression

Investigation of the predictors of workplace aggression has recently received increased research attention. This research has focused on individual difference, situational and organizational predictors, and, to a lesser extent, the interaction between individual differences and situational factors. Each of these categories is discussed below.

Individual Difference Predictors of Workplace Aggression

Researchers have investigated whether individual difference variables—including demographic characteristics, dispositional traits, behavioral tendencies, and past experiences—significantly predict aggression. In general, demographic characteristics (e.g., gender, age, education) are not good predictors of aggressive behavior, although the research evidence shows that a number of dispositional and experience variables are.

Dispositional variables including trait anger, attitudes toward revenge, and attribution style have been found to account for a large proportion of variance in workplace aggression (Douglas & Martinko, 2001). Specifically, those with higher levels of trait anger, positive attitudes toward revenge, and hostile attribution style report behaving more aggressively at work than those with lower levels of these dispositional variables. Studies have also shown that individuals with the type A behavior pattern (Baron, Neuman, & Geddes, 1999) and neurotic tendencies (Jockin, Arvey, & McGue, 2001) are more likely to behave aggressively than type B and nonneurotic individuals, respectively. Drinking behavior—including the percentage of days one reports consuming alcohol (McFarlin, Fals-Stewart, Major, & Justice, 2001) and the quantity of alcohol consumption (Jockin et al., 2001)—is also positively associated with aggression. Greenberg and Barling (1999) measured aggressive behavior directed at coworkers, supervisors, and subordinates and found that quantity of alcohol consumption only predicted aggression directed at coworkers.

Previous experiences with aggression are also associated with self-reports of workplace aggression. Greenberg and Barling (1999) found that a history of behaving aggressively—operationalized as how often participants hit their parents, siblings, or others during and after high school—predicted coworker-directed aggression. Similarly, Douglas and Martinko (2001) found that exposure to aggressive cultures (e.g., growing up in neighborhoods where aggression occurred) is also associated with self-reports of aggressive behavior.

Frustration has also been shown to be associated with hostile and aggressive behavior (e.g., Fox & Spector, 1999). Although frustration is an internal state and thus most appropriately considered an individual difference characteristic, its experience is likely induced to some extent by situational factors that may be present in organizations. It is to considering these factors that we now turn our attention.

Situational and Organizational Predictors of Workplace Aggression

A number of situational and organizational factors have been suggested as potential predictors of workplace aggression. Among these is the concept of organizational climate (or the related concept of organizational culture). According to Naylor, Pritchard, and Ilgen's (1980) classic formulation, organizational climate involves organizational members' shared perceptions of the contingencies between behaviors that occur in the work environment and their consequences. With respect to aggression, characteristics of the organizational environment can lead to perceptions that aggressive behavior is discouraged or encouraged, which in turn may reduce or increase the likelihood of its occurrence. The construct of organizational tolerance—which is based on Naylor et al.'s conceptualization of climate—has been examined in the sexual harassment literature, and the available empirical data demonstrate that a tolerant organizational climate is a significant antecedent of sexual harassment (e.g., Fitzgerald, Drasgow, Hulin, Gelfand, & Magley, 1997). Only one study has examined the effects of organizational tolerance of aggression (Glomb, 2001, as cited in Glomb, Steel, and Arvey, 2002) and found that it did not predict reports of perpetrated aggression. However, more research is needed to examine the effects of the various potential manifestations of (in)tolerance including the presence and enforcement of a policy that addresses workplace aggression, work group norms, and attitudes of other organizational members (e.g., coworkers, supervisors) toward aggressive behavior at work.

Related to the notion that organizational climate may influence aggression is O'Leary-Kelly et al.'s (1996) concept of organization-motivated aggression, which involves situational factors within the organization that cause aggressive behavior to occur. Among the variables they propose as likely antecedents of aggression are modeling, aversive treatment, perceived rewards for behaving aggressively, and physical conditions of the environment (e.g., crowding, noise). Drawing on the O'Leary-Kelly et al. (1996) framework, a study by Robinson and O'Leary-Kelly (1998) demonstrated that the modeling of antisocial behavior by work group members is associated with the levels of antisocial behavior reported by individual work group members. These results were extended by Glomb and Liao (2003) who found that the overall mean level of aggression in a work group and an individual's reports of having been a target of aggression predicted employee self-reports of perpetrated aggression after controlling for a number of demographic and individual difference variables. Together, these studies demonstrate the reciprocal effects of workplace aggression in which experiencing aggression predicts perpetrated aggression and vice versa.

Changes in the workplace and the experience of injustice have also been posited as antecedents of aggression. A study by Skarlicki and Folger (1997) provides some support for this position. These authors found that perceptions of distributive, procedural, and interactional injustice accounted for a large proportion of variance in organizational retaliatory behavior. Although this construct does not reflect aggression per se, it is a conceptually related construct. Extending these results to aggression, Baron and Neuman (1996) found significant correlations between several workplace changes (e.g., budget and pay cuts, management changes) and reports of workplace aggression. In addition, Greenberg and Barling (1999) demonstrated that perceived procedural injustice and organizational use of surveillance and monitoring technology predict aggression directed toward supervisors but not toward coworkers or subordinates.

A recent study by Dietz, Robinson, Folger, Baron, and Schulz (2003) found evidence that community violence spills over into organizations. In their longitudinal study, they investigated the frequency of workplace aggression in 250 plants of a large organization and examined its association with the violent crime rates in the communities in which the plants reside. The results showed that violence in the community surrounding a plant predicted workplace aggression levels within the plant suggesting a spillover effect.

Individual Difference by Situation Interactions

Folger and Skarlicki (1998) proposed a "popcorn model" of workplace aggression, a model based primarily on the notion that characteristics of a person interact with situational characteristics—particularly perceived injustice—to cause workplace aggression. They suggest, for example, that people high in negative affectivity or neuroticism would be more sensitive to justice violations that would in turn lead to negative behavioral responses. Support for this comes from a study by Skarlicki, Folger, and Tesluk (1999) who found that the individual difference variables of negative affect and agreeableness interacted with perceived organizational injustice to predict retaliation behavior.

A study by Greenberg and Barling (1999) extended the Skarlicki et al. findings to the domain of workplace aggression specifically. In a sample of nonfaculty men working in a university setting, they observed several notable person-by-situation interaction effects (which they defined as effects that accounted for 2.5% of criterion variance, regardless of statistical significance). First, those with higher reported alcohol use who perceived procedural injustice were more likely to behave aggressively toward coworkers and subordinates. Second, those with a history of aggression who felt insecure about their jobs or who perceived procedural injustice were more likely to behave aggressively toward subordinates. Finally, those who consumed more alcohol and who experienced job insecurity were also more likely to be aggressive toward subordinates.

The results summarized here suggest that the investigation of person-by-situation interactions can inform our understanding of the antecedents of aggression. This research is important because it moves beyond the simplistic notion that individual characteristics rather than situational factors are the primary causes of aggression and away from the simplistic solutions that such a notion perpetuates (e.g., screening out "violent" individuals represents the primary means of prevention of workplace aggression). Clearly, more research is needed to understand how individual difference and situational factors interact to predict aggression. Longitudinal research is particularly important in this area to empirically test the causal assumptions that underlie this research.

_____ Outcomes of Exposure to Workplace Aggression

The consequences of aggression can be immediate or occur after the passage of time and can be generally categorized as psychological, physical, and behavioral. The type of consequence and the extent to which it becomes manifest is influenced by the type, severity, and frequency of the aggressive behavior as well as the presence of situational and individual difference variables that moderate the effects of aggression.

Before we discuss the potential consequences of workplace aggression, it should be understood that unless otherwise noted, the findings discussed are based on cross-sectional, self-report survey data. Thus, the causal assertions, although theoretically based, need to be substantiated by longitudinal research. In addition, the possibility of monomethod bias inflating the observed correlations exists. Competing with this, however, is the likelihood that the presence of range restriction in the aggression measures (the distributions of which are usually positively skewed) attenuates observed correlations with other variables.

Immediate Outcomes of Exposure to Workplace Aggression

The most salient outcomes of physical acts of aggression (i.e., violence) could include bodily injury or death. Besides these, however, the process model of work stress posits that an individual's perception of and immediate psychological response to a stressor mediates the effect of the stressor on subsequent functioning. Barling (1996) suggested three variables that would mediate the effects of workplace aggression on individual and organizational outcome variables: fear, negative mood, and cognitive difficulties. Of these, fear has received the most research attention.

Role of fear and expectations of future workplace aggression. Fear of future workplace aggression constitutes a combined affective and cognitive reaction to experiencing an act of workplace aggression in which an individual perceives an increased vulnerability to experiencing other aggressive acts in the future. Although the extent to which this variable reflects both affective and cognitive elements has not been extensively examined, it is likely that it consists of a negative mood state (i.e., being afraid) and negative thoughts (i.e., ruminations about the past and potential future acts of aggression). LeBlanc and Kelloway (2002) included measures of both fear and perceived likelihood of future aggression in their study, apparently in recognition of these affective and cognitive elements. The two variables were highly correlated ($r = .70$), and in their model, perceived likelihood was the immediate outcome of aggression, which in turn predicted fear of future aggression.

A number of studies have demonstrated that fear or threat appraisal is the immediate consequence of workplace aggression (e.g., Duffy & McGoldrick, 1990; LeBlanc & Kelloway, 2002; Sinclair, Martin, & Croll, 2002) and mediates its effects on outcomes such as psychological and somatic health, work attitudes (e.g., affective commitment), and withdrawal behaviors and intentions (e.g., job neglect, turnover intentions; Rogers & Kelloway, 1997; Schat & Kelloway, 2000). In their study of bank employees, Rogers and Kelloway found that fear fully mediated the effects of aggression on psychological and somatic health as well as affective commitment. In their study of health care workers and group home staff, Schat and Kelloway replicated Rogers and Kelloway's results and found that the mediating effect of fear also extended to counterproductive (i.e., neglect) behaviors such as tardiness. LeBlanc and Kelloway collected both coworker and public aggression data from a variety of occupations and found that only public aggression predicted fear and perceived likelihood of future aggression, whereas the effects of coworker aggression on health and work-related outcomes were direct and not mediated by fear. Barling et al. (2001) also found that fear of future exposure mediated the relationships between aggression and personal outcomes in their study of home care workers. Future research needs to replicate their results to determine whether the differential relationships are due to specifying the source of aggression, the wide variety of occupations in the sample, or some other factor. Despite some inconsistency, however, the research evidence suggests that fear represents one of the mechanisms by which aggression adversely influences people's health- and work-related functioning.

Affective responses to workplace aggression. Negative affect has also been posited as an immediate consequence of experiencing workplace aggression, which mediates its effects on health, behavior, and other outcomes (Barling, 1996). It can be manifested in various forms ranging from low-intensity affect such as depressed mood to high intensity affect such as anger and desire for revenge. The way in which affect is manifested is likely influenced by individual differences, situational factors, characteristics of the aggression experienced, and their interaction, and would also predict subsequent reactions. For example, the sequelae of depressed mood would likely include psychological and somatic health symptoms, decrements in job attitudes, and withdrawal behaviors, and more intense affective reactions such as anger would more likely lead to a desire for retribution and revenge (Bies & Tripp, 1998) and retaliatory behaviors such as reciprocated aggression (Glomb, 2002) or other explicit acts of deviance.

Medium- and Long-Term Consequences of Workplace Aggression

Psychological and somatic consequences. In addition to fear and negative mood, symptoms of anxiety and depression have been found to be associated with workplace aggression (LeBlanc & Kelloway, 2002; Northwestern National Life Insurance Company, 1993; Rogers & Kelloway, 1997; Schat & Kelloway, 2000). Work-related psychological consequences of aggression have also been observed and include negative work-related affect (Schat & Kelloway, 2003), job dissatisfaction (e.g., Budd, Arvey, & Lawless, 1996), and reduced affective commitment (Barling et al., 2001; Rogers & Kelloway, 1997). Research also shows that in some cases these psychological variables, particularly fear and emotional health, mediate the effects of aggression on physical and behavioral outcomes (e.g., LeBlanc & Kelloway, 2002; Rogers & Kelloway, 1997; Schat & Kelloway, 2000).

The distress that may result from workplace aggression can physiologically manifest in the form of somatic disturbances and illness. Symptoms include headaches, sleep difficulties, respiratory infections, and gastrointestinal problems (Rogers & Kelloway, 1997; Schat & Kelloway, 2000). Research on other work-related stressors has shown that they may result in other physical symptoms, such as muscoskeletal disorders, increased blood pressure, and cardiac problems as well, and it remains for future research to examine whether they are also predicted by exposure to workplace aggression.

Behavioral consequences. Whereas the psychological and physical outcomes most clearly demonstrate the negative effects of aggression on individuals, the behavioral outcomes demonstrate its negative effects on both individuals and organizations. The behavioral and behavioral intention variables that have been found to be associated with aggression and that may directly or indirectly affect organizations include withdrawal behaviors such as turnover intentions (Budd et al., 1996; Rogers & Kelloway, 1997), reduced productivity and performance (Barling et al., 2003; Budd et al., 1996), alcohol use (McFarlin et al., 2001; Richman et al., 1999; Rospenda, Richman, Wislar, Nawyn, & Flaherty, 2000), and counterproductive behaviors including job neglect (e.g., taking extended breaks, not sharing information; Schat & Kelloway, 2000), aggression (Glomb & Liao, 2003), and revenge and retaliation (Aquino, Tripp, & Bies, 2001; Bies & Tripp, 1998). Several of these studies provide preliminary evidence of reciprocal aggression—the notion that exposure to aggression causes those exposed to, in turn, behave more aggressively. Preliminary linkages related to this are incorporated into Figure 8.1, although further research is needed to more clearly establish the causality, mediational processes, and boundary conditions of the relationships among these phenomena.

Moderators of the Relationships Between Workplace Aggression and Its Consequences

We noted earlier that the use of the process model of work stress to study aggression provides a framework for testing for moderating effects. Moderators are variables that influence the main effects posited by the model, such as the relationship between workplace aggression and its mediator, the mediator and the outcome variables, or between workplace aggression and its distal outcomes (i.e., the direct effects of aggression, without the mediator). Although a number of different moderating (or interactive) effects are possible, from a work stress perspective, the most interesting and relevant effects are those that prevent or reduce the negative consequences of aggression. Accordingly, investigation of potential moderating variables represents a step toward identifying empirically supported means of workplace aggression prevention and intervention and is, therefore, an essential direction for research in this area. To date, however, few studies have investigated moderators of the relationship between workplace aggression and its sequelae. Of those that have, the evidence is promising but, as with the investigation of moderators of other work stress consequences (see Beehr, 1995, for a review), somewhat inconsistent.

Previous Exposure as Personal Vulnerability

In addition to the objective occurrence of an aggressive action, previous exposure to traumatic events may heighten individual reactions (Corneil, 1993; Mitchell & Bray, 1990). For example, in her studies of Israeli Army personnel, Solomon (1993, 1994) reports that the effects of repeated exposure to traumatic events are cumulative. These findings suggest that personal history with aggression may increase personal vulnerability such that those who have been previously targeted are more likely to experience adverse effects when exposed to aggressive acts in the workplace. Another implication that warrants investigation is whether a person who has been previously victimized is more likely than one who has not been previously victimized to experience anger and intentions to retaliate when the target of an aggressive act. In general, more research is needed to examine the extent to which, and conditions under which, previous experience of aggression—whether at work or in other contexts (see Lamerson & Kelloway, 1996)—exacerbates the effects of subsequent exposure to workplace aggression.

Perceived Control

One potential moderating variable that has been examined in the workplace aggression literature—albeit to a limited extent—is perceived control. In a study based on a sample of health care workers and a sample of group home staff, Schat and Kelloway (2000) examined whether three dimensions of perceived control—understanding, prediction, and influence (Sutton & Kahn, 1987)—interacted with workplace aggression to predict fear and interacted with fear to predict emotional well-being, somatic health, and neglect. None of the interaction effects examined were significant, although structural equation modeling revealed substantial direct effects of perceived control on fear and emotional well-being, suggesting the benefits of perceived control. Significantly, Schat and Kelloway only tested whether perceived control interacted with aggression to predict fear and interacted with fear to predict the outcome variables; they did not test whether perceived control interacted with workplace aggression to directly predict the outcome variables.

Social Support and Training

Social support has also been examined as a potential moderator of the effects of workplace aggression. In one study, Leather, Lawrence, Beale, Cox, and Dickson (1998) examined the moderating effects of both intraorganizational (e.g., personnel department) and extraorganizational (e.g., friends, family) sources of support on the relationships between exposure to workplace aggression and well-being, job satisfaction, and organizational commitment in a sample of pub licensees. No interactions involving extraorganizational support were significant, but a number of significant intraorganizational support interactions did emerge. In general, the pattern of interactions reveal that when intraorganizational support is present, people who are exposed to aggression do not experience decrements in well-being, satisfaction, or commitment. These results suggest that support plays a protective or stress-buffering role.

Schat and Kelloway (2003) extended Leather et al.'s (1998) results by testing the moderating effects of two forms of social support identified by House (1981)—instrumental and informational support—in a sample of health care workers. Instrumental support, which consists of behaviors that directly help a person in need (House, 1981), was found to moderate the relationships between aggression and three outcomes—emotional health, somatic health, and work-related affect (but not fear or job neglect). Informational support, which involves providing people with information they can use to cope with difficulties (House, 1981), was a significant moderator of the relationship between aggression and emotional health (and not the other criteria). In general, the patterns of the moderation effects were similar to those of Leather et al., in which support acts as a buffer against the negative consequences of aggression.

In their study, Schat and Kelloway (2003) conceptualized training as a form of informational support. Training programs aimed at helping workers prevent, confront, or otherwise constructively deal with aggressive behavior at work represent a promising means of intervention, although the effectiveness of such programs has yet to be rigorously examined. In addition to Schat and Kelloway (2003), an earlier study also provides preliminary evidence of the efficacy of training, in which health care workers who reported having received training related to workplace aggression exhibited higher levels of three dimensions of perceived control—understanding of the causes of the aggression, perceived ability to predict the nature and timing of aggressive behavior, and perceived ability to take action when confronted with aggression—than those who did not receive training (Schat & Kelloway, 2000). However, because training was not explicitly examined as a moderator in this study, its reported effects may be additive and therefore may exist independent of exposure to aggressive behavior. Taken together with the findings that control was associated with reduced fear and increased psychological and somatic health, these results suggest that training may provide information and techniques that help to mitigate the consequences of workplace aggression.

Measurement Issues Related to Workplace Aggression

Good measurement begins with a clear definition of the target construct. The definition presented earlier should provide the foundation for the development of a comprehensive and valid measure of workplace aggression. Although a number of different measures have been used in the extant literature, the operational definitions of aggression vary from study to study, and no measure has established itself as the standard measure of the construct. A measure that taps the broad range of aggressive behavior and has demonstrated validity does not yet exist. This represents a significant need in this area of research (Greenberg & Barling, 1999).

Measuring Workplace Aggression

Some of the existing measures of workplace aggression and related constructs include the Violence and Aggression at Work Scale (Barling et al., 2001; LeBlanc & Kelloway, 2002; Rogers & Kelloway, 1997; Schat & Kelloway, 2000, 2003), the Perceived Victimization Scales (Aquino, 2000; Aquino & Byron, 2002), the Work Harassment Scale (Björkqvist, Österman, &

Lagerspetz, 1994), the Interpersonal Deviance subscale of Bennett and Robinson's (2000) Workplace Deviance Scale, and the Scale of Aggressive Behavior used by Baron et al. (1999). Each of these measures consists of items tapping various forms of work-related aggressive behavior, although they vary with respect to how comprehensively they tap the domain and to the evidence that exists demonstrating their psychometric quality. For example, the Kelloway and colleagues' measure appears to be the most widely used, taps a broad range of physically aggressive behaviors and vicarious exposure to aggression, has shown known-groups validity (i.e., employees of bank branches with a known history of robbery had higher mean scores than employees of branches who had no history of robbery; Rogers & Kelloway, 1997), factorial validity (i.e., confirmatory factor analysis revealed that physical violence, nonphysical aggression, and vicarious exposure formed distinct yet correlated factors; Schat & Kelloway, 2003), and good internal consistency, and in several studies has correlated as hypothesized with a variety of outcome variables providing further validity evidence. A limitation of this measure, however, is that its coverage of nonphysical forms of aggression is limited to only a few items. Interestingly, several of the other measures referred to above tend to lack in their coverage of physical aggression but have a number of items tapping nonphysical aggression. It would seem that the next logical step in this area would be to synthesize the items from the existing measures into a single comprehensive measure of workplace aggression and to provide further assessment of the psychometric properties of this broader scale.

Measuring the context of workplace aggression. In addition to the need to measure the full range of aggressive behavior, there is a need for studies of aggression to more clearly identify—and measure—the context in which aggression occurs. One contextual element that is important to consider is the source of aggression, or more precisely, the nature of the relationship between the aggressor and target. There are a number of reasons for this need. First, the frequency of reported aggression appears to be related to source, with aggression from members of the public occurring more often than aggression from other employees (e.g., Greenberg & Barling, 1999). Second, the relational dynamics (e.g., perceived power, control) between the perpetrator and target of aggression are likely to influence the target's perceptions of the aggression and its consequences. For example, the dynamics of an encounter with an angry customer likely differ from the dynamics of an encounter with one's supervisor, which may influence the perceived stressfulness of the situation and, in turn, its effects on cognitive and health-related functioning. A recent study by LeBlanc and Kelloway (2002) provides preliminary evidence of such differences. They measured both public-initiated and coworker-initiated aggression and found that they were differentially associated with personal and organizational outcome variables. Coworker-initiated aggression directly predicted health (emotional and somatic) and affective commitment but not fear or turnover intentions, whereas public-initiated aggression predicted perceived likelihood and fear of future violence as well as turnover intentions but not health or affective commitment.

Other contextual elements that warrant examination involve the factors that immediately precipitate an aggressive act. Although the intent (or perceived intent) to harm is often included in definitions of aggression, this intent may have different causes. For example, someone may behave aggressively in response to aversive behavior by others. In such cases, the aggressive behavior is a hostile response to provocation and could be considered a form of reactive aggression (Buss, 1961), retaliation, or revenge (e.g., Bies & Tripp, 1998). This type of aggression is laden with affect and likely to be overt in its manifestation. In other cases, the aggressive behavior may be more premeditated and enacted for the purpose of manipulating a person or situation and achieving a certain desired outcome for the perpetrator. This type of behavior can be considered a form of instrumental aggression (Buss, 1961), is typically less affect-laden, and is more likely to be indirect, covert, and nonviolent in nature. This type of behavior is also more likely to be repeated, and therefore its effects are likely to accumulate over the time of exposure. It corresponds to most definitions of workplace bullying, a form of workplace aggression that research has shown to have particularly devastating effects (see Hoel et al., 1999, for a review). Despite the contributions of bullying research in this area, more work is needed to determine how to measure elements of context related to aggression, which in turn should facilitate a better understanding of contextual influences on the causes and effects of instrumental and hostile forms of aggressive work-related behavior. One possible means of measuring context is to use situation-specific measures of workplace aggression, as we discuss in the following section.

Measuring specific incidents versus aggregating across incidents. Most of the existing research on workplace aggression uses an aggregate approach to measurement in which survey respondents are asked to report the number of times they have engaged in or experienced various aggressive behaviors over a fixed period of time, typically 6 months or a year. These reports are then correlated with various predictor or outcome variables to investigate the association between the frequency of reported aggression and these variables. This approach is helpful in understanding the general pattern of relationships between aggressive work-related behavior and its proposed causes and consequences. However, because it aggregates individual instances of aggression over a period of time, specific characteristics of the situation are typically overlooked and the interplay between individual differences and organizational characteristics *within a specific incident of aggression* cannot be addressed.

To complement the existing aggregation-based research on workplace aggression, Glomb (2002) conducted two studies that focused on specific incidents of workplace aggression. The first study involved a series of structured interviews aimed at gathering in-depth information about work-related interactions involving anger and aggressive behavior. The second study used a measure in which participants identified a particularly salient episode of aggression they experienced (as either a perpetrator or target) and answered a number of specific questions about that episode (e.g., characteristics of the other person involved, the outcomes experienced as a result of the encounter). Several findings are notable: First, the pattern of frequency with which various forms of aggression occur seems to be consistent between aggregate and specific incident assessment of aggression, with nonphysical behaviors (e.g., yelling, insults) occurring more frequently than physically violent (e.g., physical assault) behaviors. Second, this approach to data collection revealed that less severe forms of aggressive behavior may be precursors of more severe aggressive behaviors. Third, this approach may also shed light on the reciprocal relationship between experienced and enacted aggression. Fourth, the detrimental effects of aggression were observed to be limited to job outcomes and not personal outcomes, a finding that is inconsistent with research based on aggregate assessments of aggression (e.g., Rogers & Kelloway, 1997) and which calls for further research to examine this inconsistency.

Overall, a research approach involving the investigation of specific incidents of aggression appears to be promising as a means of testing the generalizability of, and extending, the research using aggregate measures. In addition to the use of structured interviews and retrospective measures of specific incidents used by Glomb (2002), researchers should also consider using experience sampling methods (e.g., daily diaries) to investigate specific incidents of workplace aggression.

Potential Research Directions

In addition to the need for improved measurement of workplace aggression and other research directions that we have already discussed throughout this chapter, there are a number of other important directions for future research in this area. These include, but are not limited to, (a) research that examines whether the nature, predictors, and consequences of workplace aggression vary as a function of the source of aggression, (b) research that seeks to understand how workplace aggression and its consequences unfold over time, and (c) research that tests the efficacy of prevention and intervention efforts. Each of these research directions will be discussed below.

Much of the emerging research on workplace aggression has not distinguished between the various potential sources of aggression making it impossible to assess whether the types, predictors, and consequences of aggressive behavior are affected by the source of the behavior. A recent study by LeBlanc and Kelloway (2002) shows the potential importance of this distinction by demonstrating a different pattern of outcomes associated with coworker and public-initiated aggression.

There are a number of potential directions for research in this area. First, research is needed that more specifically measures intraorganizational sources of aggression (i.e., distinguishing between supervisors, peers, and subordinates) because the nature of these organizational relationships is likely to influence both the type and impact of the aggression that occurs. For example, a supervisor behaving aggressively toward a subordinate is likely to use more direct and overt forms of aggressive behavior than would a subordinate who is behaving aggressively toward a supervisor. The type of behavior may in turn influence the impact it has on the target. Second, research is needed to investigate whether there are different predictors of aggression from different sources. For example, do supervisors behave aggressively for instrumental reasons (e.g., as an influence tactic) whereas subordinates or coworkers behave aggressively in reaction to frustrating circumstances? Does the variance accounted for by individual difference and situational factors vary as a function of the source of aggression? These examples are merely illustrative of the types of issues that merit investigation.

There is a need for longitudinal research in many domains of psychological inquiry, and this need exists in the workplace aggression literature as well. The available studies are almost exclusively based on cross-sectional data, and the causal relationships that have been suggested must be substantiated with longitudinal or other appropriate methodologies.

Numerous researchers have espoused the importance of efforts aimed at preventing workplace aggression and addressing its potentially harmful effects. The following section highlights some of the work that has been done in this area and identifies several avenues for future research.

Implications for Practice, Policy, and Intervention

The negative consequences of workplace aggression for both individuals and organizations suggest the need for intervention efforts. These efforts should be primary—aimed at preventing aggressive behavior from occurring, and secondary—aimed at reducing the negative consequence of aggression that does occur. There are a number of general and specific suggestions for intervention that derive from the existing literature on workplace aggression. Some general suggestions include the following: First, interventions need to be sensitive to the source of aggression, targeting aggression that occurs from sources inside (e.g., coworkers, supervisors, subordinates) and outside (e.g., customers, clients, patients) organizations. The effectiveness of interventions is likely to be predicated on the congruence between the source of aggression that is of concern and the degree to which the intervention addresses this source. Second, the research suggests that different factors predict aggression directed at different targets. For example, workplace factors predict supervisor-directed aggression, and individual differences predict coworker aggression (Greenberg & Barling, 1999). Although there is limited research evidence for these differences, the available evidence suggests the need to consider the target when developing strategies to control aggression.

Job Design

LeBlanc and Kelloway (2002) developed the Risk for Violence Scale, a measure consisting of a number of job characteristics they posited as risk factors for workplace aggression from members of the public. Analyses revealed that 22 characteristics were associated with reports of aggression from members of the public, including exercising physical control over others, having contact with individuals taking medication, working alone, and disciplining others. Although some of these characteristics are essential elements of certain jobs and therefore difficult to modify, others are amenable to modification. For example, it would be possible for organizations to develop policies and practices that preclude the possibility of people working alone. Although this may result in increased labor costs, it could also reduce the risk of aggression, the outcomes of which can be harmful to individuals and costly to organizations.

Interventions to Increase Social Support

The buffering effects of intraorganizational social support on the outcomes of workplace aggression (Leather et al., 1998; Schat & Kelloway, 2003) suggest the potential benefits of interventions aimed at increasing the levels of social support for those who are exposed to workplace aggression. Modeling of socially supportive behavior is one means by which it might be increased. Indirect evidence of this possibility comes from Glomb and Liao (2003) who found that aggressive behavior by work group members is associated with self-reports of engaging in aggressive behavior. These results suggest the importance of modeling of negative behavior that occurs in work groups (O'Leary-Kelly et al., 1996) and could also be extended to positive behavior such as social support. If employees observe their supervisors or other coworkers exhibiting supportive behaviors to colleagues who experience aggression (e.g., covering their shifts, talking with them), they may be more likely to engage in such behaviors. It should be noted that the data on which this suggestion is based are limited and that more research is needed to assess the efficacy of such an intervention.

Crisis Response

In cases of serious acts of workplace violence, it is imperative that organizations have a crisis response program in place. Such incidents can lead to symptoms of anxiety, depression, anger, difficulties concentrating, and sleep disturbances (Robinson & Mitchell, 1993). One approach to crisis response has been referred to as critical incident stress debriefing (CISD). Although the characteristics of CISDs may vary, they generally involve the provision of help and assistance (by psychologists or other trained personnel) immediately following a traumatic event in order to prevent the development of serious or lasting negative consequences. CISDs would consist of elements such as ensuring confidentiality, providing individuals with the opportunity to talk about their perspective on, thoughts about, and emotional reactions to the incident, assessing psychological and physical symptoms, and providing information about stress responses and coping strategies (e.g., Mitchell & Bray, 1990).

In a study of the effectiveness of CISDs, Leonard and Alison (1999) compared the coping strategies and levels of anger of two groups of police officers that had experienced a traumatic event. One group of officers received CISD and the other did not. The results suggested that the CISD group exhibited more adaptive coping strategies and lower levels of anger than those in the non-CISD group. The lack of random assignment to conditions cast some doubt on the validity of these findings, although they do provide preliminary evidence of the efficacy of CISD following exposure to traumatic work-related events.

Despite these promising results, the research literature also provides a basis on which to question the effectiveness of CISD. First, in their review of 67 studies, Arendt and Elklit (2001) concluded that debriefing does not mitigate the effects of traumatic stress. Second, based on their meta-analytic review, van Emmerik, Kamphuis, Hulsbosch, and Emmelkamp (2002) found that single-session debriefing was less effective than other forms of intervention and less effective than no intervention in reducing the effects of traumatic stress. Finally, there is a growing list of studies suggesting that individuals receiving CISD interventions may experience exacerbated traumatic reactions and more adverse outcomes (Bisson, Jenkins, Alexander, & Bannister, 1997; Carlier, Lamberts, Van Uchelin, & Gersons, 1998; Kenardy, 2001; Mayou, Ehlers, & Hobbs, 2000; Small, Lumley, Donohue, Potter, & Waldenstroem, 2001). As Barling et al. (2003) note, these findings violate the widely accepted maxim that psychological interventions should in the first instance do no harm. The inconsistent findings as to the effectiveness of CISDs suggest the need for more research in this area to identify whether there are elements of CISDs that are helpful and should be retained and others that are harmful and should be excluded from such programs.

Training

Training programs can provide individuals with skills they can use to manage and respond to aggressive behavior, which should help to reduce the likelihood of aggression and its negative consequences. The basic aggression research suggests that some individuals behave aggressively because of a lack of social skills such as emotional sensitivity (Baron & Richardson, 1994). In situations in which deficiencies in social skills are the source of work-related aggressive behavior, training programs aimed at social skill development may be effective (Neuman & Baron, 1997).

Training that is more specifically directed at providing employees with information about how to anticipate and constructively respond to workplace aggression also represents a promising means of intervention (Schat & Kelloway, 2000). This training would likely include providing employees with information about the nature of aggressive behavior, ways of identifying risk factors, and means of defusing and responding to aggressive or potentially aggressive individuals. However, systematic assessment of the characteristics and effectiveness of training programs targeting workplace aggression has not been carried out and represents a significant research need in this area.

Epilogue

In this chapter, we have sought to summarize the research that has been done on workplace aggression, drawing primarily from the literature in industrial-organizational psychology, organizational behavior, and management. We began by addressing conceptual and definitional issues related to workplace aggression and discussed how it is similar to and distinct from various other forms of aversive work-related behaviors. We then presented statistics about the prevalence of various forms of aggression and discussed a number of measurement issues related to workplace aggression. We also described how the stress process model has been applied to workplace aggression and summarized research on its antecedents, consequences, and moderators. Finally, we identified a number of directions for future research and implications of the existing research for workplace aggression prevention and intervention. In conclusion, we note that the volume of research that has emerged on the topic of workplace aggression over the last 5 to 10 years has substantially contributed to our understanding of this construct, and we hope that addressing workplace aggression—through prevention and intervention—becomes a prominent feature of the research agenda in the years ahead.

References

Anderson, C. A., & Bushman, B. J. (2002). Human aggression. *Annual Review of Psychology, 53,* 27–51.

Andersson, L. M., & Pearson, C. M. (1999). Tit-for-tat? The spiraling effect of incivility in the workplace. *Academy of Management Review, 24,* 452–471.

Aquino, K. (2000). Structural and individual determinants of workplace victimization: The effects of hierarchical status and conflict management style. *Journal of Management, 26,* 171–193.

Aquino, K., & Byron, K. (2002). Dominant interpersonal behavior and perceived victimization in groups: Evidence for a curvilinear relationship. *Journal of Management, 28,* 69–87.

Aquino, K., Grover, S. L., Bradfield, M., & Allen, D. G. (1999). The effects of negative affectivity, hierarchical status, and self-determination on workplace victimization. *Academy of Management Journal, 42,* 260–272.

Aquino, K., Tripp, T. M., & Bies, R. J. (2001). How employees respond to personal offense: The effects of blame attribution, victim status, and offender status on revenge and reconciliation in the workplace. *Journal of Applied Psychology, 86,* 52–59.

Arendt, M., & Elklit, A. (2001). Effectiveness of psychological debriefing. *Acta Psychiatry Scandanavia, 104,* 423–437.

Barling, J. (1996). The prediction, experience, and consequences of workplace violence. In G. R. VandenBos & E. Q. Bulatao (Eds.), *Violence on the job: Identifying risks and developing solutions* (pp. 29–49). Washington, DC: American Psychological Association.

Barling, J., Hurrell, J. J., Braverman, M., Collins, J., Gelles, M. G., Scrivner, E., et al. (2003). *Terrorized workers: Employee well-being following 9/11.* Manuscript submitted for publication.

Barling, J., Rogers, A. G., & Kelloway, E. K. (2001). Behind closed doors: In-home workers' experience of sexual harassment and workplace violence. *Journal of Occupational Health Psychology, 6,* 255–269.

Baron, R. A., & Neuman, J. H. (1996). Workplace violence and workplace aggression: Evidence on their relative frequency and potential causes. *Aggressive Behavior, 22,* 161–173.

Baron, R. A., Neuman, J. H., & Geddes, D. (1999). Social and personal determinants of workplace aggression: Evidence for the impact of perceived injustice and the type A behaviour pattern. *Aggressive Behavior, 25,* 281–296.

Baron, R. A., & Richardson, D. R. (1994). *Human aggression* (2nd ed.). New York: Plenum.

Beehr, T. A. (1995). *Psychological stress in the workplace.* London: Routledge.

Bennett, R. J., & Robinson, S. L. (2000). Development of a measure of workplace deviance. *Journal of Applied Psychology, 85,* 349–360.

Berkowitz, L. (1993). *Aggression: Its causes, consequences, and control.* Philadelphia: Temple University Press.

Bies, R. J., & Tripp, T. M. (1998). Revenge in organizations: The good, the bad, and the ugly. In R. W. Griffin, A. O'Leary-Kelly, & J. M. Collins (Eds.), *Dysfunctional behavior in organizations: Non-violent dysfunctional behavior* (pp. 49–67). Stanford, CT: JAI.

Bisson, J. I., Jenkins, P. L., Alexander, J., & Bannister, C. (1997). Randomized controlled trial of psychological debriefing for victims of acute burn trauma. *British Journal of Psychiatry, 171,* 78–81.

Budd, J. W., Arvey, R. D., & Lawless, P. (1996). Correlates and consequences of workplace violence. *Journal of Occupational Health Psychology, 1,* 197–210.

Bureau of Labor Statistics. (1995, August 3). *News. National census of fatal occupational injuries, 1994* [News release]. Washington, DC: Author.

Buss, A. H. (1961). *The psychology of aggression.* New York: Wiley.

Carlier, I. V. E., Lamberts, R. D., Van Uchelin, A. J., & Gersons, B. P. R. (1998). Disaster-related posttraumatic stress in police officers: A field study of the impact of debriefing. *Stress Medicine, 14,* 143–148.

Corneil, D. W. (1993). *Prevalence of post traumatic stress disorders in a metropolitan fire department.* Unpublished doctoral dissertation, Johns Hopkins University, Baltimore.

Cox, H. (1991). Verbal abuse nationwide, part 2: Impact and modifications. *Nursing Management, 22,* 66–69.

Dietz, J., Robinson, S. L., Folger, R., Baron, R. A., & Schulz, M. (2003). The impact of community violence and an organization's procedural justice climate on workplace aggression. *Academy of Management Journal, 46,* 317–326.

Douglas, S. C., & Martinko, M. J. (2001). Exploring the role of individual differences in the prediction of workplace aggression. *Journal of Applied Psychology, 86,* 547–559.

Duffy, C. A., & McGoldrick, A. E. (1990). Stress and the bus driver in the U.K. transport industry. *Work & Stress, 4,* 17–27.

Einarsen, S. (1999). The nature and causes of bullying at work. *International Journal of Manpower, 20,* 16–27.

Fendrich, M., Woodward, P., & Richman, J. A. (2002). The structure of harassment and abuse in the workplace: A factorial comparison of two measures. *Violence and Victims, 17,* 491–505.

Fitzgerald, L. F., Drasgow, F., Hulin, C. L., Gelfand, M. J., & Magley, V. J. (1997). Antecedents and consequences of sexual harassment in organizations: A test of an integrated model. *Journal of Applied Psychology, 82,* 578–589.

Folger, R., & Skarlicki, D. P. (1998). A popcorn metaphor for employee aggression. In R. W. Griffin, A. O'Leary-Kelly, & J. M. Collins (Eds.), *Dysfunctional behavior in organizations: Violent and deviant behavior* (pp. 43–81). Stanford, CT: JAI.

Fox, S., & Spector, P. E. (1999). A model of work frustration-aggression. *Journal of Organizational Behavior, 20,* 915–931.

Gelfand, M. J., Fitzgerald, L. F., & Drasgow, F. (1995). The structure of sexual harassment: A confirmatory analysis across cultures and settings. *Journal of Vocational Behavior, 47,* 164–177.

Glomb, T. M. (2002). Workplace anger and aggression: Informing conceptual models with data from specific encounters. *Journal of Occupational Health Psychology, 7,* 20–36.

Glomb, T. M., & Liao, H. (2003). Interpersonal aggression in work groups: Social influence, reciprocal, and individual effect. *Academy of Management Journal, 46,* 486–496.

Glomb, T. M., Steel, P. D. G., & Arvey, R. D. (2002). Office sneers, snipes, and stab wounds: Antecedents, consequences, and implications of workplace violence and aggression. In R. G. Lord, R. Klimoski, & R. Kanfer (Eds.), *Emotions at work* (pp. 227–259). San Francisco: Jossey-Bass.

Greenberg, L, & Barling, J. (1999). Predicting employee aggression against co-workers, subordinates and supervisors: The roles of person behaviors and perceived workplace factors. *Journal of Organizational Behavior, 20,* 897–913.

Hoel, H., Rayner, C., & Cooper, C. L. (1999). Workplace bullying. In C. L. Cooper & I. T. Robertson (Eds.), *International review of industrial and organizational psychology* (Vol. 14, pp. 195–230). Chichester, UK: Wiley.

House, J. S. (1981). *Work stress and social support.* Reading, MA: Addison-Wesley.

Jockin, V., Arvey, R. D., & McGue, M. (2001). Perceived victimization moderates self-reports of workplace aggression and conflict. *Journal of Applied Psychology, 86,* 1262–1269.

Johnson, H., & Bunge, V. P. (2001). Prevalence and consequences of spousal assault in Canada. *Canadian Journal of Criminology, 43,* 27–45.

Kahn, R. L., & Byosiere, P. (1990). Stress in organizations. In M. D. Dunnette & L. M. Hough (Eds.), *Handbook of industrial and organizational psychology* (2nd ed., Vol. 3, pp. 571–650). Palo Alto, CA: Consulting Psychologists Press.

Keashly, L. (1998). Emotional abuse in the workplace: Conceptual and empirical issues. *Journal of Emotional Abuse, 1,* 85–115.

Keashly, L. (2001). Interpersonal and systemic aspects of emotional abuse at work: The target's perspective. *Violence and Victims, 16,* 233–268.

Kenardy, J. (2001). Posttraumatic stress prevention: How do we move forward? *Advances in Mind-Body Medicine, 17,* 183–186.

Lamerson, C. D., & Kelloway, E. K. (1996). Towards a model of peacekeeping stress. *Canadian Psychology, 37,* 195–204.

Leather, P., Lawrence, C., Beale, D., Cox, T., & Dickson, R. (1998). Exposure to occupational violence and the buffering effects of intra-organizational support. *Work & Stress, 12,* 161–178.

LeBlanc, M. M., & Barling, J. (in press). Understanding the many faces of workplace violence. In S. Fox & P. E. Spector (Eds.), *Counterproductive workplace behavior: An integration of both actor and recipient perspectives on causes and consequences.* Washington, DC: American Psychological Association.

LeBlanc, M. M., & Kelloway, E. K. (2002). Predictors and outcomes of workplace violence and aggression. *Journal of Applied Psychology, 87,* 444–453.

Leonard, R., & Alison, L. (1999). Critical incident stress debriefing and its effects on coping strategies and anger in a sample of Australian police officers involved in shooting incidents. *Work & Stress, 13,* 144–161.

Leymann, H. (1996). The content and development of mobbing at work. *European Journal of Work and Organizational Psychology, 5,* 165–184.

Mayou, R. A., Ehlers, A., & Hobbs, M. (2000). Psychological debriefing for road accident victims: Three-year follow up of randomized control trial. *British Journal of Psychiatry, 176,* 589–593.

McFarlin, S. K., Fals-Stewart, W., Major, D. A., & Justice, E. M. (2001). Alcohol use and workplace aggression: An examination of perpetration and victimization. *Journal of Substance Abuse, 13,* 303–321.

Meichenbaum, D. (1994). *A clinical handbook/practical therapist manual for assessing and treating adults with post-traumatic stress disorder (PTSD).* Waterloo, Ontario: Institute Press.

Mitchell, J., & Bray, G. (1990). *Emergency services stress.* Englewood Cliffs, NJ: Prentice Hall.

Naylor, J. C., Pritchard, R. D., & Ilgen, D. R. (1980). *A theory of behavior in organizations.* New York: Academic Press.

Neuman, J. H., & Baron, R. A. (1997). Aggression in the workplace. In R. A. Giacalone & J. Greenberg (Eds.), *Antisocial behavior in organizations* (pp. 37–67). Thousand Oaks, CA: Sage.

Neuman, J. H., & Baron, R. A. (1998). Workplace violence and workplace aggression: Evidence concerning specific forms, potential causes, and preferred targets. *Journal of Management, 24,* 391–419.

Northwestern National Life Insurance Company. (1993). *Fear and violence in the workplace: A survey documenting the experience of American workers.* Minneapolis, MN: Author.

O'Leary-Kelly, A. M., Griffin, R. W., & Glew, D. J. (1996). Organization-motivated aggression: A research framework. *Academy of Management Review, 21*, 225–253.

Peek-Asa, C., Runyan, C. W., & Zwerling, C. (2001). The role of surveillance and evaluation research in the reduction of violence against workers. *American Journal of Preventive Medicine, 20*, 141–148.

Pizzino, A. (2002). Dealing with violence in the workplace: The experience of Canadian unions. In M. Gill, B. Fisher, & V. Bowie (Eds.), *Violence at work: Causes, patterns, and prevention* (pp. 165–179). Cullompton, UK: Willan.

Pratt, L. I., & Barling, J. (1988). Differentiating between daily events, acute and chronic stressors: A framework and its implications. In J. J. Hurrell, Jr., L. R. Murphy, S. L. Sauter, & C. L. Cooper (Eds.), *Occupational stress: Issues and developments in research*. New York: Taylor & Francis.

Richman, J. A., Rospenda, K. M., Nawyn, S. J., Flaherty, J. A., Fendrich, M., Drum, M. L., & Johnson, T. P. (1999). Sexual harassment and generalized workplace abuse among university employees: Prevalence and mental health correlates. *American Journal of Public Health, 89*, 358–363.

Riger, S., Ahrens, C., & Blickenstaff, A. (2000). Measuring interference with employment and education reported by women with abusive partners: Preliminary data. *Violence and Victims, 15*, 161–172.

Robinson, R. C., & Mitchell, J. T. (1993). Evaluation of psychological debriefings. *Journal of Traumatic Stress, 6*, 367–382.

Robinson, S. L., & O'Leary-Kelly, A. M. (1998). Monkey see, monkey do: The influence of work groups on the antisocial behavior of employees. *Academy of Management Journal, 41*, 658–672.

Rogers, K., & Kelloway, E. K. (1997). Violence at work: Personal and organizational outcomes. *Journal of Occupational Health Psychology, 2*, 63–71.

Rospenda, K. M. (2002). Workplace harassment, services utilization, and drinking outcomes. *Journal of Occupational Health Psychology, 7*, 141–155.

Rospenda, K. M., Richman, J. A., Wislar, J. S., Nawyn, S. J., & Flaherty, J. A. (2000). Chronicity of workplace harassment and abuse: Effects on drinking outcomes. *Addiction, 95*, 1805–1820.

Schat, A. C. H., & Kelloway, E. K. (2000). The effects of perceived control on the outcomes of workplace aggression and violence. *Journal of Occupational Health Psychology, 4*, 386–402.

Schat, A. C. H., & Kelloway, E. K. (2003). Reducing the adverse consequences of workplace aggression and violence: The buffering effects of organizational support. *Journal of Occupational Health Psychology, 8*, 110–122.

Sheehan, K. H., Sheehan, D. V., White, K., Leibowitz, A., & Baldwin, D. C. (1990). A pilot study of medical student "abuse": Student perceptions of mistreatment and misconduct in medical school. *Journal of the American Medical Association, 263*, 533–537.

Sinclair, R. R., Martin, J. E., & Croll, L. W. (2002). A threat-appraisal perspective on employees' fears about antisocial workplace behavior. *Journal of Occupational Health Psychology, 7*, 37–56.

Skarlicki, D. P., & Folger, R. (1997). Retaliation in the workplace: The roles of distributive, procedural, and interactional justice. *Journal of Applied Psychology, 82*, 434–443.

Skarlicki, D. P., Folger, R., & Tesluk, P. (1999). Personality as a moderator in the relationship between fairness and retaliation. *Academy of Management Journal, 42,* 100–108.

Small, R., Lumley, J., Donohue, L., Potter, A., & Waldenstroem, U. (2001). Randomized controlled trial of midwife led debriefing to reduce maternal depression after operative childbirth. *British Medical Journal, 321,* 1043–1047.

Smith, G. (1999, June). Violence at work. *Benefits Canada, 23,* 22–27.

Solomon, Z. (1993). *Combat stress reactions: The enduring toll of war.* New York: Plenum.

Solomon, Z. (1994). *Coping with the Gulf War.* New York: Plenum.

Sutker, P. B., Uddo, M., Brailey, K., Vasterling, J. J., & Errera, P. (1994). Psychopathology in war-zone deployed and nondeployed: Operation Desert Storm troops assigned graves registration duties. *Journal of Abnormal Psychology, 103,* 383–390.

Sutton, R. I., & Kahn, R. L. (1987). Prediction, understanding, and control as antidotes to organizational stress. In J. W. Lorsch (Ed.), *Handbook of organizational behavior* (pp. 272–285). Englewood Cliffs, NJ: Prentice Hall.

Sygnatur, E. F., & Toscano, G. A. (2000, Spring). Work-related homicides: The facts. *Compensation and Working Conditions,* 3–8.

Terkel, S. (1974). *Working: People talk about what they do all day and how they feel about what they do.* New York: Pantheon.

U.S. Postal Service Commission on a Safe and Secure Workplace. (2000). *Report of the United States Postal Service Commission on a Safe and Secure Workplace.* New York: National Center on Addiction and Substance Abuse at Columbia University.

Vaitkus, M. A., & Martin, J. A. (1991). *Combat exposure and post-traumatic stress symptomatology among U.S. soldiers deployed to the Gulf War.* U.S. Army Medical Research Unit-Europe.

Van Emmerik, A. A. P., Kamphuis, J. H., Hulsbosch, A. M., & Emmelkamp, P. M. G. (2002). Single session debriefing after psychological trauma: A meta-analysis. *The Lancet, 340,* 768–771.

9

Physical Work Environment

Janetta Mitchell McCoy
Gary W. Evans

T his chapter focuses on the attributes and properties of the physical environment of work that produce stress. Many occupational stress studies overlook the physical components of the work environment in favor of discussing health and behavior in its psychosocial context (Cooper & Cartwright, 1997; Sparks & Cooper, 1999). Yet, the physical environment is constant and ubiquitous. All people experience it, and that experience is rarely neutral (Evans & McCoy, 1998). As such, changes in the physical environment provide a potentially powerful intervention tool for enhancing organized work.

In today's sophisticated, technological society, the physical setting of the office is important because it is the place that most people go to do their work. Increasingly, the work done in an office environment is intellectual: thinking, communicating, reading, and writing. The physical office work environment is typically one of an organization's most costly budget items—second only to the cost of its human capital. Thus, organizational performance is optimized when the physical environment supports the needs and requirements of the personnel, providing a place where individuals can think and groups can effectively communicate. Performance (and organizational success) is compromised when the physical environment interferes with actions taken toward achievement (Becker & Steele, 1995). One result of that interference is stress. The purpose of this chapter is to demonstrate how stress is linked to the physical work environment of the office. Our focus is on the office because it is the largest and most rapidly

Authors' Note: In addition to the editors for their comments and direction, we thank Frank Becker, Eric Sundstrom, and Jean Wineman for critical feedback on earlier drafts of this chapter.

changing work environment. The future of work is, to a large extent, the future of the office.

This chapter is organized in three parts. First, we define stress outcomes related to physical characteristics of work. The major focus of this chapter (part two) is the critical research linking specific features of the physical environment to stress in the office. Finally, we conclude with suggestions and recommendations for future studies calling for further theoretical development that incorporates a more ecological perspective.

Stress and the Physical Environment

Stress occurs when environmental demands tax or exceed the adaptive capabilities of the organism resulting in psychological or physiological changes. Our focus in this chapter is on physical characteristics of office settings associated with stress effects. We include five stress outcomes in this chapter. In a subsequent section, we discuss other potential markers of stress, such as job satisfaction, that warrant further investigation.

Physiological markers of stress, which can occur without subjective awareness of environmental demands, include elevated cardiovascular activity (e.g., blood pressure), heightened physiological arousal (e.g., skin conductance), and shifts in both the sympathetic adrenal medullary system (SAM) (e.g., epinephrine, norepinephrine) and the hypothalamic-pituitary adrenocortical axis (HPA) (e.g., cortisol). There is increasing evidence that chronic elevations of the SAM and HPA result in disease (Cohen, Kessler, & Gordon, 1995; McEwen, 1998). With the exception of noise, physical aspects of work settings have not been studied for stress-related diseases.

The most ubiquitous index of psychological stress in the work environment is self-reports of negative affect, typically including assessments of stress, fatigue, tension, workload pressure, and various forms of anxiety (Cohen et al., 1995). Some studies use well-validated, reliable stress assessment instruments. Most, unfortunately, do not. Another common index of psychological stress is task performance. Many individuals can overcome the negative impacts of stressors on task performance as long as the stressor is not severe, the duration of performance is not prolonged, or the task does not require maximum cognitive capacity. To put it differently, stressors in the work environment can interfere with very complex cognitive tasks and are more likely to adversely affect performance if the stressor is prolonged or of high intensity. Task complexity primarily refers to the number and predictability of signals that need to be attended to, the level of comprehension and understanding required, and the capacity of working memory required (Cohen, Evans, Stokols, & Krantz, 1986; Evans, 2001).

These facts about stress and task performance also illustrate an important and challenging aspect of studying occupational stress and human behavior. Investigations of environmental demands in isolation frequently do not provide the full picture of human stress impacts. One must also take into consideration other variables that can moderate the linkages between stressors and human responses. In the case of task performance, the nature of the individual's job is critical in understanding whether the environment will make a difference in performance (Cohen et al., 1986; Evans & Cohen, 1987).

In addition to self-reports of negative affect and task performance, physical stressors in the workplace influence two other qualities of human behavior. Stressors that are uncontrollable, as many suboptimal physical qualities typically are, lead to motivational deficits related to learned help-lessness. Human beings and other organisms, after repeated failed attempts to cope with a stressor, will learn that the outcomes of their behaviors are independent of their efforts to correct the situation. Among the manifestations of learned helplessness is diminished motivation in task persistence (Cohen, 1980; Glass & Singer, 1972; Peterson, Maier, & Seligman, 1993).

Social relationships are also affected by stressor exposure in the workplace. The elevated negative affect associated with work stress can adversely affect cooperative behaviors such as social support, altruistic behaviors, and teamwork. Workplace stressors also increase hostility, frustration, and aggressive tendencies. Greater conflict and fewer positive social interactions follow stress.

Summarizing, workplace stressors can negatively affect human biological and psychological processes. Biological markers of stress include SAM- and HPA-related processes as well as disease morbidity. In this chapter, we focus on the former, given the paucity of data on the latter in the office context. Psychological markers include self-reports of stress, tension, workload pressure, and anxiety. Task performance under certain conditions (high-complexity tasks, high-intensity or long-duration stressor exposure) is negatively affected by work stressors. Motivation to persist on tasks and positive, cooperative social interaction are both at risk in suboptimal working conditions.

Linking the Physical Work Environment to Stress in the Office

Stress effects of the physical work environment on its occupants may be highly detrimental to the individual as well as the organization. Whereas the physical environment can be objectively measured, the relationship of an occupant's stress to the physical space is not always so clear-cut. If the physical components of the work environment are supportive of activities necessary for accomplishing work and supporting the social relationships inherent in an organization, the attributes and properties of that environment may go unnoticed. On the other hand, when the physical components of the work environment interfere with occupant performance and social necessities, that interference is likely to result in stress.

Risk Factors of the
Physical Office Environment

Elements of the physical office environment can elevate stress. Risk factors in the physical office environment include spatial organization, architectonic details, ambient conditions, and resources, as well the view or visual access from the workspace. As environmental stressors, the physical features and properties of the office can influence physiological processes, produce negative affect, limit motivation and performance, and impede social interaction. We will review how each of these physical properties of the work environment can affect health and behavior. We also note where relevant data exist on moderators of the physical characteristics. Theoretically, physical work characteristics can also function as coping resources that help workers better handle work demands. For example, views of natural scenes appear to attenuate high workload demands.

Spatial Organization

Spatial organization determines the level of enclosure, adjacencies, density, and territoriality in an office. The organization of space encompasses the size, shape, allocation, and division of space, including furniture configuration and circulation routes.

In a 5-year program of research examining 80 different organizations, the Buffalo Organization for Social and Technical Innovation (BOSTI) (Brill, Margulis, & Konar, 1984) documented the longitudinal impacts of changes in the spatial organization of offices for more than 6,000 office workers. Workers in open-plan cubicles wanted more enclosure in order to have more control over interruptions, visual exposure, and other distractions that interfered with their work. The layout or arrangement of office space was related to interference in social interactions. Although greater enclosure assured more privacy, it did not interfere with communication. With increased job complexity and responsibility, need for individual focus and concentration has also increased. Provision for privacy and control promotes individual effectiveness. People with less perceived control over social interaction at work are more likely to experience symptoms of stress, such as depression and anxiety (Griffin, Fuhrer, Stansfeld, & Marmot, 2002).

The International Workplace Studies Program (IWSP) has conducted extensive case studies of numerous large corporate organizations to understand how the physical work environment supports workplace initiatives that encourage high performance, such as teamwork, telecommuting, and cross-functional collaboration (Becker & Steele, 1995). Spatial provisions for effective teamwork should include individual work areas for concentration and reflection as well as space for collaboration and informal communication.

Workplace qualities with the strongest effects on well-functioning team performance include ability to do distraction-free solo work, support for impromptu interactions, support for meetings and undistracted group work, and location near or within easy access of coworkers (Brill, Weidemann, & BOSTI Associates, 2001).

Wineman and Serrato's (1999) review of best practices for workplace design supports Allen's (1977) proposition that communication is an important underpinning of performance and that spatial organization of team workspace can enhance communication. Simply put, workers will talk with others who are in close proximity. Such social interaction encourages sharing of ideas and better coordination of activities. Proximity of workstations and informal gathering places fostering informal interaction are also important ingredients supporting collaboration (Sundstrom, Demuse, & Futrell, 1990).

Spatial organization may imply various office types with differing levels of enclosure. Duffy (1997) defines four relevant categories of office types: hive, cell, den, and club. Each category suggests unique patterns of work based on task, interaction, and autonomy as well as distinctive levels of enclosure. These categories are useful metaphors for understanding how the level of enclosure fits the needs and expectations of the occupant and in turn indicate potential for stress. Level of enclosure implies a division of space and level of privacy between one person and another. The level of enclosure can determine the level of distraction, crowding, status, efficiency, and territoriality experienced by the worker.

Duffy's *hive* category indicates that space required may be satisfied by open, ganged cubicles easily defined by simple space standards. Little interaction and little autonomy are expected. The *cell* category suggests enclosed offices or individual workstations with high partitions in order to conduct high-level cognitive work. Individual concentration is paramount with little interaction; high autonomy is expected. The *den* is an open group space, appropriate for people working together with a balance of different or interdependent skills. The den provides a context for high interaction with little autonomy for both meeting spaces and individual workspaces. The *club* is also a group space and suggests high-level work carried out by individuals who need to work both collaboratively and individually; work processes may be constantly evolving and require a diverse, complex, adaptable range of settings based on a wide variety of tasks for high interaction and high autonomy.

Although open-plan offices imply facilitated interaction and communication, not all employees want or need such interaction. Likewise, some communication needs to be confidential; the inability to control the level and quality of interaction and communication may result in negative affect and interfere with tasks requiring concentration (Wineman, 1982; Hatch, 1984; Sundstrom, Herbert, & Brown, 1982). Managers react more negatively to open office plan configurations, on average, than clerical workers, and numerous studies suggest that open offices make it more difficult to regulate social interaction (Sundstrom, 1986).

For many years, designers and office furniture manufacturers have touted the efficiency and cost effectiveness of the hive or cubicle in an open office, but evidence suggests that such offices offer little protection against distraction (Brill et al., 2001). With the proliferation of the open-plan office (Brill et al., 2001; Becker & Steele, 1995) has come a stream of inquiries regarding the impact of noise, visual distraction, and the lack of privacy when walls and doors are absent. For many people who work in a nonenclosed office, the sound of others talking or walking by or the noise produced by keyboards, telephone, and copy machines significantly interferes with intellectual work (Jukes, 2000; Loewen & Suedfeld, 1992; Sundstrom, Herbert, et al., 1982; Sundstrom, Town, Brown, Forman, & McGee, 1982). Without adequate enclosure to minimize distraction, workers express feelings of discontent and fatigue (Sundstrom, 1986; Wineman, 1982).

It is not unusual for studies to report some measure of unhappiness or dissatisfaction with open-plan offices. Oldham and Brass (1979) found that occupants of open-plan offices felt their jobs were less significant. Oldham and Rotchford (1983) found that those in such offices reported their tasks to be less important and were significantly more likely to leave their desks for breaks and lunch. In a longitudinal study, employees perceived that stress increased following relocation from private offices to open offices and that stress did not abate even after an adjustment period (Brennan, Chugh, & Kline, 2002).

An individual private office, or Duffy's cell, suggests the most privacy and least distraction, allowing doors to be closed for confidential conversations or to eliminate visual and auditory distractions from office activity and equipment. Similarly, adjacencies are important in an office layout to minimize distractions and maximize efficiency. Locating team members near meeting areas and essential equipment can encourage efficient use of time. Locating a noisy task group next to another noisy department may isolate noise distractions from those groups who require quiet and concentration. (More discussion of noise follows under ambient conditions.) Further, distractions of seeing others' activities or perceiving one's own activities constantly under observation may limit concentration and thus compromise job performance (O'Neil, 1994; Lipman-Blumen & Leavitt, 1999; Sundstrom et al., 1982). Those who work in adjacent areas are likely to develop some level of interpersonal relationship, which can be important in the development of essential social interactions (Becker & Steele, 1995; McCoy, 2002).

Density and crowding may affect stress experienced by office occupants. Crowding reduces employees' behavioral options: A space that is too small for the number of people present may result in unwanted or forced interaction (Baum & Paulus, 1987). Density is the number of people in a given area. In the office work environment, this has performance implications as the level of stress increases. Many laboratory and residential studies show that crowding interferes with complex task performance and motivation (Baum & Paulus, 1987). There is also evidence that the ability to regulate social interaction that often accompanies crowding diminishes task motivation (Evans, 2001). High-density, crowded spaces tend to result in less liking of both people and places as well as withdrawal and less helping behavior (Baum & Paulus, 1987; Evans, 2001). Oldham & Fried (1987), for example, noted that clerical workers were more withdrawn as a function of more crowded offices. Stokols, Smith, and Proctor (1975) found that workers had greater feelings of crowding and behavior constraint when partitions were added to a high-density setting.

Another perspective on crowded workplaces applied behavior-setting theory (Wicker, 1987). Hypothesizing that when too many or too few staff members were used to operate a behavior setting, in this case branch banks, Oxley and Barerra (1984) discovered that employees of small branches reported a greater sense that they are needed and that their jobs and hard work are important when either too many or too few worked in the branch; these feelings were significantly related to greater job satisfaction, greater identification with the bank, and less tardiness.

Fried (1990) reported that employees in high-density, open-plan offices were more likely to report more fatigue than those with more enclosure and less density. Hedge (1984) found that in a survey of 1,200 employees, 40% of those in an open plan reported frequent headaches whereas only 20% of employees in enclosed offices reported frequent headaches. In either of these cases, however, it is difficult to draw meaningful conclusions without knowing many other, more specific details about the space, the organization, and the workload. Nonetheless, it is unlikely that tired or ill employees are high performers or that their social interaction is optimal.

Spatial organization can have profound effects on wayfinding or navigation within office buildings. Wayfinding has implications for stress in visitors because of being lost or frustrated in finding their destinations. Building occupants also suffer when others have wayfinding difficulties. Staff time is taken up helping people become oriented; and when visitors finally reach their destination, they may be irritable and frustrated (Evans & Garling, 1991; Kaplan & Kaplan, 1982). Problems in wayfinding within interior spaces are strongly influenced by the overall plan of space. Spaces that are simpler and resemble regular geometric shapes are easier to understand and navigate (Weisman, 1982). Distinctive interior markers that provide differentiations (Evans, 1980), distinctive landmarks placed as major decision points (Evans & McCoy, 1998), and views of the external environment (Garling, Book, & Lindberg, 1986) all enhance wayfinding in buildings. Good informational systems such as signs and directories can aide in building navigation but are not as effective as the above factors.

In summary, research indicates that spatial organization of an office can provide functional opportunities for workers to do their work effectively and efficiently without undue distraction or threat. Work environments that provide workers with the opportunity to think and concentrate on their work, controlling the number and level of distractions, may minimize the experience of stress.

Architectonic Details

Architectonic details are the fixed or stationary aesthetics of the workplace. They include ornaments or materials intended to embellish the environment but do not necessarily involve structural organization. These elements of the physical environment are often overlooked, but as Becker and Steele's (1995) case studies suggest, decorative styles, surface treatments, signage, color, and artwork may encourage team identity and purpose. Interpretation of architectonic details relies heavily on *how* they are used rather than the specific item of use. Architectonic details may be risk factors for stress in the office environment (see Table 9.1).

Table 9.1   Links of Architectonic Details to Stress Effects in the Office Environment Identified in Research

Stress Effects	Potential Risk Factors of Architectonic Details
Affective Appraisal	Style and color preferences Participatory selection Status markers Stimulation/deprivation
Motivation	Stimulation/deprivation Personalization
Task Performance	Sharing of ideas Dominance/persuasion
Physiological Symptoms	Arousal
Social Interaction	Participatory selection Territorial markers

Architectonic details may imbue meaning and have symbolic significance (Rapoport, 1990; Mazumdar, 1992) reflecting values and norms of the people and the organization (Brill et al., 1984). Such details may be a form of nonverbal communication from the organization reflecting management's value of the employees. Personal articles displayed by employees on desks and walls often reflect their personal identity. Such displays of personalization, deliberate decoration, or modification of the office by its occupants reflect their identities and mark their boundaries or territories (Sommer, 1974; Sundstrom, 1986; Heidmets, 1994; Wells, 2000). McCoy (2000) found that members of highly creative teams tend to personalize with objects reflective of their professional successes, whereas members of less creative teams tend to display artifacts reflective of their personal lives.

Wineman and Serrato's (1999) review of best practices in corporate facilities design and McCoy's (2000) study of government teams suggest that display of artifacts or products of work is an opportunity to share ideas or work in progress with other group members and with individuals in the larger organization.

Wells and Thelen's (2002) survey of office personalization in 20 small businesses found that people want to personalize their workspace and that personalization is significantly associated with employee well-being.

Artwork, materials, and finishes may be highly relevant to those who participate in their selection or those trained in their use, thus enhancing job satisfaction. However, if such artifacts or details provided by management are deemed irrelevant, meaningless, extraneous, or frivolous, they may result in negative affect (McCoy, 2002; Rapoport, 1990). For instance, prominently displayed portraits of all male, white historical leaders in a conference room was distracting and irritating to many female minority staff and resulted in negative affect (McCoy, 2000).

Mazumdar's (1992) ethnographic study of organizational work life describes the intensity of the deprivation felt by those whose work environment eliminated status indicators such as a corner office. With this loss, members experienced the humiliation of loss of status or prestige, resulting in increased levels of stress. Team members who felt deprived exhibited a range of responses: to distance oneself from other members, to groan and complain to reduce anxiety, to plead with those in authority to avoid or divert the deprivation, to fight for what they wanted, to quit the organization, or even to file a lawsuit for reinstatement or for damages.

In summary, architectonic details as the overall aesthetic of the office are important and can be risk factors for stress. Architectonic details influence perceived stress by reflecting the individual, team, and organizational identity, values, and norms—encouraging performance and achievement. As markers of status and territory, architectonic details may encourage job satisfaction, motivation, and social interaction. Deprived of appropriate, meaningful architectonic details, worker motivation and performance may be diminished.

Ambient Conditions

Ambient conditions are the most researched physical stressors in office settings. Ambient conditions include illumination, heating, ventilation, and sound. Thermal conditions, air quality, noise, and lighting have both objective and subjective indicators, and their extremes have been demonstrated to influence task performance, negative affect, physiological symptoms, and social interaction. Whereas there are published "ideal" temperature ranges and lighting levels (for specific tasks), there is some controversy about the value of such a narrow range of environmental specification constituting a single comfortable temperature or level of light. Perhaps more important is that people prefer variable temperatures and lighting levels that they can control (Gerlach, 1974; Kuller & Laike, 1998; Veitch & McColl, 1995; Veitch & Newsham, 1998).

Direct or objective measures of the ambient properties of the work environment may indicate or predict performance and affective appraisal. They also indicate a clear connection between the physical environment and the psychosocial issues relevant to work performance. Klitzman and Stellman (1989) found that adverse environmental conditions, especially poor air quality, noise, ergonomic conditions, and lack of privacy affected perceived worker satisfaction. Extremes of ambient conditions may influence health and well-being and may compromise the ability of the occupant to think and to interact with others.

Illumination. The system and quality of lighting in the workplace can influence the health and well-being of building occupants. Glare causes eyestrain and headaches; glare can also contribute to accidents due to the inability to see distraction and potential dangers (Veitch, 2001). This has age implications: As we age our eyes change and we need more illumination. Occupants with some control over their workspace lighting (and other building systems) report fewer building-related illnesses (Sterling, Sterling, Hartel, & McIntyre, 1983).

Rea, Oulette, and Kennedy (1985) noted that participants tend to modify their posture to maintain visual performance under lighting conditions that would otherwise reduce task visibility. Such awkward or slouching postures may lead to musculoskeletal or other health problems. Sauter, Gottlieb, Jones, Dodson, and Rohrer (1983) found that computer-based workers who feel socially isolated may react more negatively to lighting and ergonomic conditions. Workers with similar ambient conditions who were not socially isolated did not indicate the significant associations between physical conditions and negative mood.

Claims that lighting quality or quantity can create or change moods are not well supported, but studies of light levels do tend to suggest that increased light elevates physiological arousal, suggesting greater alertness for shift workers (Campbell & Dawson, 1990). When offices are darker, employees are more likely to leave when they have a choice, such as during lunchtime or breaks (Oldham & Fried, 1987). There is also evidence that exposure to daylight, particularly in the winter season, helps regulate circadian rhythm and prevents mild depression in some people (Veitch, 2001).

Air quality. Indoor air quality (IAQ) has been the focus of considerable research (Dorgan & Dorgan, 2000) relating IAQ to health and well-being, task performance, and job satisfaction. When IAQ is not satisfactory, both employee and other building occupants' health can be affected. Factors that determine indoor air quality include temperature, humidity, room air motion, and contaminants. Sick building syndrome (SBS) is used to describe a range of symptoms (such as eye, nose, and throat irritation, dryness of mucous membranes and skin, nosebleeds, skin rash, mental fatigue, headache, cough, hoarseness, wheezing, nausea, and dizziness) that appear when employees are at work and disappear when they are away from work (Burge, Hedge, Wilson, Bass, & Robertson, 1987). SBS is related to increased absenteeism as well as job performance (Jones et al., 1995).

Ambient pollutants can also affect worker stress by interfering with task performance (National Research Council, 1991) and by influencing emotional affect and interpersonal behaviors. Polluted air leads to negative emotions (Evans, 1994; Rotton & Cohen, 2000), reduces interpersonal attraction and elevates hostility, and under certain conditions can even increase aggressive behaviors (Evans, 1994; Rotton & Cohen, 2000). Measured contaminants compromising the air quality of the office environment include fungi, carbon dioxide, formaldehyde, carbon monoxide, and total volatile organic compounds (e.g., alpha-pinene, d-limonene, acetone, pentanal, hexanal, heptanal, nonanal, and acetic acid). Sources of these contaminants include many common materials such as carpet, construction materials such as plywood, office equipment such as copiers and printers, and the building air-conditioning system.

Hedge, Sterling, and Sterling (1986) found that office workers in naturally ventilated buildings suffered fewer SBS symptoms in comparison to workers in air-conditioned buildings. However, this pattern of results was not uniform across various departments within the same sample of buildings. Persons with higher job satisfaction appeared less reactive to SBS.

From the results of a questionnaire on environmental conditions given to 4,479 workers from 27 air-conditioned office buildings, Hedge, Erikson, and Rubin (1996) found significant associations between symptoms of sick buildings and computer use, level of job stress, and amount of job dissatisfaction. Workers reporting high job stress also reported more symptoms of SBS. Similarly, workers reporting low job satisfaction reported more symptoms of SBS. Although there were no objective measures of worker productivity, workers were asked to indicate how much their work had been disrupted by each of the environmental conditions and their SBS symptoms. Results show that inappropriate thermal conditions (too warm or too cold), inadequate ventilation, distracting noise, and glaring lighting were the most disruptive to work. Many of the symptoms reported are not specific to poor IAQ and could be a consequence of poor lighting and other stressful work conditions.

Thermal conditions. The effect of temperature on building occupants depends on the type of work being done, the amount of clothing worn, and the length of time spent in a high or low temperature. The effect of temperature on work is inconclusive (Gifford, 1997). However, there are some general patterns. Productivity drops when temperatures rise to a very hot range (McCormick, 1976). Productivity drops in the performance of work that requires fine movement and sensitive touch when the temperatures fall into a cold range (Fox, 1967; Enander, 1987). Cool offices may improve performance of some cognitive tasks and reduce fatigue, but in general, the more complex the task, the more performance will worsen with extremes of hot or cold.

Thermal conditions have been shown to affect behavior in complex ways, depending on other factors. People report they feel more crowded when temperatures are higher (Ruback & Pandey, 1992). Anderson (1989) proposed that negative feelings mediate the relationship between heat and aggression. Negative affect increases aggressive behavior; but as temperatures become uncomfortably hot, aggression dissipates. This may be because extremely high heat is debilitating.

Noise. Noise is one of the most common annoyances in offices (Becker, 1981; Sundstrom, 1986). Exposure to unwanted sounds in the work environment has been linked with a variety of stress effects, including elevated cardiovascular and neuroendocrine activity, fatigue, inability to concentrate, and reduced motivation. The influence of noise exposure on performance has been found to be contingent on a number of factors, including the nature of the noise and the type of task involved. The effects of unpredictable noise are more severe than those of predictable noise; noise effects on performance increase with task complexity (Broadbent, 1971; Evans & Hygge, in press).

In a questionnaire distributed to 143 office workers, Leather, Beale, and Sullivan (2003) found no main effect for high noise levels (of air-conditioning, telephones, office machines, people talking, and street noise) with stress. They did, however, find a moderator effect between noise exposure and job stress, with higher noise exacerbating negative effects of job strain, organizational commitment, and well-being. This again suggests that although the physical characteristics of an environment might not be stressful in themselves, they nevertheless influence the negative impact of some simultaneously occurring psychosocial stress.

Noise-related stress is often associated with other psychosocial conditions. Lercher, Hortnagl, and Kofler (1993) found that annoyance with noise at work had a small positive association with diastolic blood pressure. This relationship was significantly amplified among workers high in job dissatisfaction and low in social support on the job. Performance on tasks with few information-processing demands does not seem influenced by noise (Broadbent, 1971; Evans & Hygge, in press; Smith & Jones, 1992). Sundstrom, Town, Rice, Osborn, and Brill (1994) demonstrated that relative to workers who experienced no change or reductions in noise, those who experienced more office noise after relocating reported greater disturbance from noise, were less satisfied with their new work environment, and had the lowest levels of overall job satisfaction, although self- and supervisor-rated job performance did not change. The apparent absence of noise-related productivity deficiency parallels results from many lab and field studies.

A number of experimental and field studies have demonstrated that exposure to uncontrollable noise leads to motivation deficiencies (Cohen & Spacapan, 1984; Evans & Stecker, in press). One aftereffect index, task persistence, was used in a series of experiments by Glass and Singer (1972). They found that when individuals were exposed to uncontrollable noise, they were less likely to persist on challenging puzzles following noise exposure. Numerous laboratory and field studies have replicated the Glass and Singer results (Cohen, 1980; Evans, 2001). Although loud, unexpected noise is not common in office environments, when short-term exposure to loud noise is accompanied by demanding tasks, habituation may be blocked but performance can be maintained, at least under many circumstances (e.g., short-term tasks that do not demand large amounts of attention or memory), by additional cognitive effort.

Problems with relatively low levels of noise have increasingly become a source of stress with the use of open-office or systems furniture (Brill et al., 2001; Sundstrom, 1986). Low-intensity noise may be capable of producing performance deficits as well, particularly when information-processing demands are high. Irrelevant speech, in comparison with nonspeech-related stimuli at normal conversational volume, disrupts memory when load is high (Jones & Morris, 1992). These findings are interesting as well because they support the notion that quality of sound, not just intensity, may be important.

Loewen and Suedfeld (1992) found that representative, open-office noise of low intensity interfered with complex but not simple task performance. In a simulated open-office experiment, Evans and Johnson (1999) found that typical low-intensity office noise had no adverse effect on simple tasks, but stress hormones were elevated and task motivation was reduced following a 3-hour exposure period. Although there was physiological, motivational, and observational evidence of elevated stress for low-intensity noise exposure, workers' self-reports and a simple index of productivity were unaffected by low-intensity noise.

Evans and Johnson's findings of elevated neuroendocrine stress hormones when working under noise matches some occupational noise studies conducted in blue-collar settings where higher noise levels can occur than those found in typical office environments. In general, the industrial noise literature reveals a mixed pattern of findings linking noise to elevated blood pressure and other disease endpoints such as coronary heart disease (Berglund & Lindvall, 1995; Medical Research Council, 1997). Evidence suggests that noise is most likely to elevate blood pressure in work settings when it is unpredictable and uncontrollable, when workers must maintain high cognitive or physical performance, and when the duration of exposure is extended over long periods of time (Evans, 2001). Noise also suppresses altruism (Cohen & Spacapan, 1984). Both laboratory and field studies have converged on the adverse social impacts of noise. Because noise interferes with social interaction and communications, it is reasonable to suspect (although no data exist to our knowledge) that noise would interfere with the development and maintenance of socially supportive relationships.

To summarize, the effects of ambient conditions on stress experienced in the office work environment are significant. Stress may result from thermal discomfort, noise, and poor air quality. The ability of the individual worker to control environmental stressors also plays an important role in determining the level of stress experienced from ambient conditions in the office environment.

Resources

Physical features of the work environment include resources—accessibility to and functional characteristics of equipment and services that support occupants' work. Resources include equipment such as computers, copiers, and phones. Resources also include access to facilities management services, physical fitness areas, parking facilities, and food service. Amabile's interviews of office workers revealed that of the nine qualities that encouraged creativity, 52% of respondents stated that it was very important to have "access to the necessary resources, including facilities, equipment, information, funds, and people" (1988, p. 146; see also Amabile, 1993). Likewise, the office may be conceptualized as a tool, not just as a place to house tools (Brill et al., 1984). In this instance, the office (the building, its furniture and equipment) is just one part of a larger information-handling system, the goal of which is "to add value to information in a managed process" (p. 28).

The ability to perform work-related tasks is often directly related to availability and functional qualities of equipment. Feature resources such as fitness areas and food service, although not essential to the task at hand, may be relevant to job stress and thus employee retention. Ergonomic features of furniture and equipment contribute quantitatively to task performance and a sense of well-being as well as to job satisfaction and interpersonal relations within the office. Inadequate and inaccessible resources may compromise performance by evoking role conflict and role ambiguity. Resources may be a source of stress if they are not appropriate for the task at hand, if they require skills beyond that of the user, or if they show potential for injury or undue fatigue for the worker (see Table 9.2). With the increased use of the VDT has come rising levels of employee fatigue, muscular tension, musculoskeletal complaints, stress symptoms, and eyestrain (Kleeman, 1989; Stellman, Klitzman, Gordon, & Snow, 1987).

The use of VDTs, and poorly designed furniture in general, has been linked to problems such as eyestrain and neck, shoulder, and back pain, fatigue, repetitive strain injuries, and reductions in job satisfaction as well as stress (Goodrich, 1982; Kleeman, 1989; Stellman et al., 1987; Sundstrom, 1987; Wineman, 1986). Often such injuries and stress will be minimized through ergonomic support and training regarding the use of ergonomic equipment (Chung & Choi, 1997).

VDT users in general report the highest levels of office (environmental) satisfaction and the highest levels of visual and musculoskeletal symptoms but the lowest levels of job satisfaction. Kleeman (1989) argues that although there are studies that show that VDT users are more prone to stress symptoms and to stress-related health problems than are non-VDT users, their studies also show that clerical VDT workers are not generally subject to greater job stress than traditional clerical workers, although they were less satisfied with their jobs. Kleeman concludes that there may be an interactive effect between VDT use and other elements of the physical work environment

Table 9.2   Links from Resources to Stress Effects in the Office Environment
Identified in Research

Stress Effects	Potential Risk Factors of Resources
Affective Appraisal	Ergonomic features Control over pace Participatory ergonomic plan
Motivation	Safety Control over pace Participatory ergonomic plan
Task Performance	Accessibility Availability Fit to task Feature resources Ergonomic qualities Control over pace
Physiological Symptoms	Ergonomic features Participatory ergonomic plan Workload demand
Social Interaction	Safety Control over pace Participatory ergonomic plan Workload demand

(e.g., lighting, noise control, workstation furniture) that in certain combinations leads to greater stress.

Carlopio and Gardner (1992) surveyed 370 employees within four departments of a large bank and found that employees with PCs were more satisfied with their jobs and felt less crowded than nonusers. However, they were not more satisfied with the health and safety aspects of the physical work environments. Carlopio and Gardner also found an interaction between job type and ergonomic furniture. Clerical employees do not seem to differ in terms of environmental satisfaction based on whether they have ergonomic furniture. However, professionals and managers were more likely to be satisfied with the workplace than those without ergonomic furniture.

Resources can also affect social relationships. For example, many studies have found that the introduction of computer technology, particularly in clerical jobs, reduced social support and also led to feelings of reduced job control (Evans, Johansson, & Carrere, 1994). These results are similar to the findings in the initial Tavistock coal-mining studies that indicate that in the design of new work systems, equal weight should be given to social and technical factors (Mumford, 1994).

The National Institute for Occupational Safety and Health (NIOSH; 1997) outlines five psychosocial factors that are related to back and upper extremity disorders: job satisfaction, workload, monotonous work, job control, and social support. Ferreira and Saldiva (2002) found an association between poor psychosocial environments and musculoskeletal disorder (MSD) in subjects involved in computer-telephone interactive tasks. Self-reports of boredom and monotonous work are associated with neck symptoms and neck and shoulder pain (Ryan & Brampton, 1988; Linton, 1999). The studies of Lindstrom, Leino, Seitsamo, and Torstila (1997) and Villaneuva, Sotoyama, Jonai, Takeuchi, and Saito (1996) suggest that computer use factors such as monitor height have an effect on neck and upper limb muscle strain, particularly when workload is intense. Similarly, Lundberg and colleagues have shown in a series of studies that the adverse impacts of poor biomechanics of musculoskeletal disorders are exacerbated by job stress (Lundberg et al., 1994

Arnetz and Wiholm's (1997) longitudinal study of 116 advanced telecommunications design employees found that the higher the pressure of the workload, or mental stress level, the higher the psychosomatic stress symptoms: mental fatigue, headache, restlessness, irritation, moodiness, and difficulty concentrating. Arnetz and Wiholm focused on workers' interaction with video display units (VDUs) including physical illnesses and musculoskeletal disorders.

Smith's (1985) study of machine-paced work in which technology dictates the pace, showed that workers end up taking insufficient breaks. Henning, Sauter, and Kreig (1992) also suggest that a lack of synchrony between the internal physiologic rhythms of a worker and the rhythms set by a computer in data input tasks leads to significant stress. Providing workers more control over the pace of their work can reduce stress. High task repetition and short cycle times of tasks that force high repetitive strains are major ergonomic risk factors for the development of MSDs.

In an ergonomic intervention study with 340 workers in a chemical plant, Maciel (1998) found that a participatory ergonomics program was effective in diminishing repetitive strain injuries (RSIs) due to workstation and physical environment. Forming work teams to meet regularly to discuss needed ergonomic improvements of their work environments, the organization was able to identify and implement needed workplace changes and reduce work-related stress and pain complaints. Results from quarterly questionnaires showed positive results. Job satisfaction and performance rose while injury and complaints diminished.

In summary, resources that work well and support the worker, allowing the work to be done efficiently and effectively, are highly valued in the office environment. However, resources are linked to the level of stress experienced by workers in the office environment to the extent that they are inaccessible and unavailable and when inappropriate to the task to be performed. Ergonomic features and participatory ergonomic plans may prevent or alleviate some level of stress. Alternatively, resources that require the worker to keep up with a demanding pace of work rather than allow the worker to set the pace are stressful.

Views From the Workspace

Views are the observable features within or visible from the work area, including what can be seen in adjacent workspaces and what can be seen from windows. Views may be natural (i.e., rivers, plants, sky) or built (corridors, other buildings, a parking lot), and views may be intimate (into a small garden) or panoramic (from a tall office building across the landscape). Views are evaluated based on scale and content. Although there is little evidence that views directly affect worker stress (Table 9.3), some outdoor views may have restorative value, thus counteracting stressful work (Heerwagen, 1990; Kaplan, Talbot, & Kaplan, 1988). Views from a hospital room have salutary properties, shortening recovery time for surgery and reducing pain medications (Ulrich, 1984, 1993). Physiological stress is also attenuated by contact with nature (Hartig, Evans, Jamner, Davis, & Garling, 2003), and some evidence shows nearby, accessible nature moderates aggressive behavior (Kuo, 2002). There is also some evidence that contact with nature buffers the negative impact of stressful life events on children's mental health (Wells & Evans, 2003).

Table 9.3   Links From Resources to Stress Effects in the Office Environment Identified in Research

Stress Effects	Potential Risk Factors of Views
Job Satisfaction	Preference for views of nature Amount of sunlight penetration
Affective Appraisal	Symbol of status Access to daylight Positive affect
Motivation	
Task Performance	
Physiological Symptoms	Restorative qualities Nature content
Social Interaction	Positive affect

Kaplan et al. (1988) report responses from a survey of three groups of office workers indicating employees whose outdoor views included only built components (such as roads or buildings) experienced higher levels of job stress than others. In contrast, workers who could see at least some natural elements (such as trees and grass) reflected higher job satisfaction levels than did either those with views of built elements outdoors or those with no outdoor views from their desks at all. These findings complement findings on view preferences.

There is limited evidence of adverse effects of "windowlessness" (Collins, 1975), though this could be due to the quality of light from windows rather than lack of view. Satisfaction with and performance in windowless rooms appear to depend on the function of the space, its size, and the duration of time spent there. However, as described previously, the preference for windows is notable. In the Netherlands, legislation mandates that no person be assigned a workspace further than 16 feet from a window (Duffy, 1997).

Leather, Pygras, Beale, and Lawrence (1998) explored the potential interaction between windows in the workplace and job stress. They found that sunlight penetration had a direct positive effect on job satisfaction, intention to quit, and general well-being. Access to a view of nature, on the other hand, buffered the negative impact of job stress on intention to quit and had similar, though marginal, effects on general well-being.

Conclusions and Recommendations

Noise, poor air quality, and open office design have the most obvious stress effects on office workers. For noise, the data are multimethodological, revealing self-reports of negative affect, physiological stress, decrements in complex task performance, and diminished motivation. For air quality and open office design, the results are largely restricted to self-reports of negative affect. For open-plan office settings, negative interpersonal relationships in relation to difficulties in social regulation have been uncovered as well. There is also good evidence that window views of nature can alleviate the adverse effects of other sources of stress (e.g., high workload demands) in the workplace.

In this final section of the chapter, we present some arguments about why there may be undetected stress effects from the physical settings wherein people work. We also lay out a research agenda for further work on the physical environment and occupational stress.

The holy grail of negative environmental impacts at work is productivity. Thus, for many analysts, unless a variable diminishes productivity, little or no concern is raised. This is a mistake for several reasons. First, individuals can maintain productivity under stress unless the task is very complex or the stressor exposure level quite intense. Mobilization of coping resources to maintain performance under stress comes at the price of elevated physiological stress. This has been shown repeatedly in laboratory and field studies of noise, for example (Evans, 2001). Second, a narrow focus on productivity ignores high organizational costs that appear related to worker well-being (Becker & Steele, 1995). Workers who are dissatisfied, even when productive, are harder to retain. Third, an employee's own interest in personal growth and skill development may be depressed by a suboptimal working environment. Fourth, the critical need for effective teamwork in many jobs will likely continue to grow in importance, and interpersonal relationships can be adversely affected by working in a poor physical setting. Both negative affect (e.g., tension, irritability) as well as social withdrawal in response to social interaction regulation difficulties can lead to interpersonal difficulties. Noise, crowding, inadequate climatic conditions (e.g. temperature), and poorly designed open office plans all interfere with interpersonal relationships essential to teams.

Another reason that stress affects of the physical environment have gone undetected is the tendency to study environmental stressors in isolation from psychosocial qualities of the organizational environment. The nature of work tasks, the level of decision latitude, degree of cooperation, and workload demands are all likely moderators of the impacts of physical working conditions on stress (Evans et al., 1994). For example, as indicated earlier, the physiological stress outcomes of exposure to noise are significantly accentuated by demanding tasks. Shift work also elevates the negative impacts of noise on physiological stress (Cesana et al., 1982; Ottmann, Rutenfranz, Neidhart, & Boucsein, 1987). Noise also interacts with job satisfaction to influence physiological stress. Dissatisfied workers functioning under noise have higher blood pressure than relatively satisfied workers doing their job under noisy conditions (Matthews, Cottingham, Talbott, Kuller, & Siegel, 1987). Workers with higher job satisfaction also appear less reactive to SBS (Hedge et al., 1986). This interaction is likely due to status-related issues and variable needs for confidential communication. Several studies have also shown exacerbated musculoskeletal problems in response to poor ergonomic conditions among those with higher job strain (Evans et al., 1994).

The critical role of personal control or decision latitude at work has been investigated with respect to stress and health outcomes (Karasek & Theorell, 1990; Sauter, Hurrell, & Cooper, 1989). Many poor physical working conditions potentially contribute to lower personal control at work. The importance of the uncontrollability of physical conditions has been demonstrated most clearly in laboratory and field experiments with noise. Exposure to uncontrollable as compared with controllable noise has profound implications for motivation and possibly physiological stress responses (Evans & Stecker, in press). Less task persistence, negative affect, and, under some chronic noisy conditions, depressive symptomatology follow exposure to uncontrollable noise.

Stress effects of the physical environment of work may also go undetected because of the typical approach of researchers to examine environmental stressors in isolation. Although there are excellent scientific reasons to examine one environmental variable's relationship to an outcome while holding other variables constant, the experimental rigor achieved may lead to underestimation of stress effects of the physical environment. Environmental stressors often covary. Poor lighting often accompanies inadequate climatic regulation and noisy or poorly designed workstations. The experience of one isolated stressor alone may be quite different compared with experience of the same stressor embedded in a multiplicity of other environmental stressors. The confluence of many small, rather modest suboptimal conditions may have cumulative effects. The combination of many small hassles from the physical environment may aggregate into stress impacts that are not appreciated when each physical stressor is studied singly.

Temporal issues have been largely ignored in occupational stress research. At least two aspects of time are potentially salient in thinking about stress and the physical environment at work. One is the duration of exposure. Task performance and physiological stress under laboratory conditions in relation to noise and crowding are both duration sensitive. Longer exposure causes different, more negative impacts than shorter exposure (Evans, 2001). This occurs for many different psychosocial stressors as well, unless at extreme intensity, the chronicity of stressor exposure may be more critical than intensity (Lepore, 1995). Yet most studies of the physical environment and stress at work either ignore exposure duration or restrict their analysis to short-term, acute exposures.

A second temporal issue in investigating physical stressors at work is the delay in impacts. Following, but not during exposure to several environmental stressors—unless the exposure duration is prolonged—few or modest impacts on task performance are typically noted. However, immediately following exposure, negative task motivation effects are noted (Cohen, 1980; Glass & Singer, 1972). For example, Evans and Johnson (2000) found no impacts of typical open-office noise on simple clerical tasks. However, immediately following a 3-hour working session in noise versus quiet, experienced clerical workers were less persistent on a challenging task. Another cost of coping successfully with an environmental stressor, as indicated by concurrent productivity, may be diminished motivation. Evans and Johnson also found elevated physiological stress in these same clerical workers.

Aftereffects of exposure to poor working conditions can also be manifested cross-situationally. Negative interpersonal relationships among family members are sensitive to both working (Repetti, 1993) and commuting conditions (Wener, Evans, Phillips, & Nadler, 2003). High job strain as well as more demanding commuting experiences spill over into the home environment, interfering with harmonious family relationships.

The role of physical characteristics of work as stressors may often be rather subtle. Few dramatic, direct impacts on stress are to be expected, particularly in office settings in economically developed countries where the intensity of physical stressors is typically low or moderate. However, this does not mean the physical environment of work plays no role or only a minor one in occupational stress. Research strategies that take better account of the ecology of the work setting are more likely to demonstrate heretofore largely undiscovered impacts of physical working conditions on worker health and well-being. Interactive relationships with psychosocial variables, particularly job strain (i.e., demands and control) and task demands are two key variables that have largely been ignored in occupational stress and the physical environment. Temporal aspects of exposure duration and time-lagged impacts of working conditions warrant further consideration. Finally, the natural covariation of working conditions suggests an alternative research strategy in which the experience of multiple accumulated suboptimal physical and psychosocial working conditions is modeled. A more ecological theoretical framework implies a different set of research strategies for investigating occupational stress and the physical environment.

References

Allen, T. (1977). *Managing the flow of technology.* Cambridge: MIT Press.

Amabile, T. (1988). A model of creativity and innovation in organizations. *Research in Organizational Behavior, 10,* 23–167.

Amabile, T. (1993). Motivational synergy: Toward new conceptualizations of intrinsic and extrinsic motivation in the workplace. *Human Resource Management Review, 3,* 185–201.

Anderson, C. (1989). Temperature and aggression: Effects on quarterly, yearly, and city rates of violent and nonviolent crime. *Journal of Personality and Social Psychology, 52,* 1161–1173.

Arnetz, B., & Wiholm C. (1997). Technological stress: Psychophysiological symptoms in modern offices. *Journal of Psychosomatic Research, 43*(1), 35–42.

Baum, A., & Paulus, P. (1987). Crowding. In D. Stokols & I. Altman (Eds.), *Handbook of environmental psychology* (pp. 534–570). New York: Wiley.

Becker, F. (1981). *Workspace: Creating environments in organizations.* New York: Praeger.

Becker, F., & Steele, F. (1995). *Workplace by design.* San Francisco: Jossey-Bass.

Berglund, B., & Lindvall, T. (1995). Community noise: WHO noise criterion document. *Archives of the Center for Sensory Research, 2,* 1–195.

Brennan, A., Chugh, J., & Kline, T. (2002). Traditional versus open office design: A longitudinal field study. *Environment and Behavior, 344,* 279–299.

Brill, M., Margulis, S., & Konar, E. (1984). *Using office design to increase productivity* (Vols. 1, 2). Buffalo, NY: Workplace Design and Productivity.

Brill, M., Weidemann, S., & BOSTI Associates. (2001). *Disproving widespread myths about workplace design.* Jasper, IN: Kimball International.

Broadbent, D. E. (1971). *Decision and stress.* New York: Cambridge University Press.

Burge, S., Hedge, A., Wilson, S., Bass, J., & Robertson, A. (1987). Sick building syndrome: A study of 4,373 office workers. *Annals of Occupational Hygiene, 31,* 493–504.

Campbell, S., & Dawson, D. (1990). Enhancement of nighttime alertness and performance with bright ambient light. *Physiology & Behavior, 48,* 317–320.

Carlopio, J., & Gardner, D. (1992). Direct and interactive effects of the physical work environment on attitudes. *Environment and Behavior, 24,* 579–601.

Cesana, G., Ferrario, M., Curti, R., Aznettini, R., Greico, A., Sega, R., et al. (1982). Work stress and urinary catecholamine excretion in shift workers exposed to noise: Epinephrine and norepinephrine. *La Medicina Del Lavaro, 73,* 99–109.

Chung, M. K., & Choi, K. (1997, December). Ergonomic analysis of musculoskeletal discomforts among conversational VDT operators. *Computers & Industrial Engineering, 33,* 521–524.

Cohen, S. (1980). Aftereffects of stress on human performance and social behavior: A review of research and theory. *Psychological Bulletin, 88,* 82–108.

Cohen, S., Evans, G., Stokols, D., & Krantz, D. (1986). *Behavior, health, and environmental stress*. New York: Plenum Press.

Cohen, S., Kessler, R. C., & Gordon, L. (1995). Strategies for measuring stress in studies of psychiatric and physical disorders. In S. Cohen, R. C. Kessler, & L. Gordon (Eds.), *Measuring stress* (pp. 3–28). New York: Oxford University Press.

Cohen, S., & Spacapan, S. (1984). The social psychology of noise. In D. M. Jones & A. J. Chapman (Eds.), *Noise and society* (pp. 221–245). New York: Wiley.

Collins, B. (1975). *Windows and people: A literature survey* (NBS Building Science Series 70). Washington, DC: U.S. Government Printing Office.

Cooper, C., & Cartwright, S. (1997). An intervention strategy for workplace stress. *Journal of Psychosomatic Research, 43,* 7–16.

Dorgan, C. E., & Dorgan, C. B. (2000). Assessment of link between productivity and indoor air quality. In D. Clements-Croome (Ed.), *Creating the productive workplace*. London: E&FN Spon.

Duffy, F. (1997). *The new office*. London: Conran Octopus.

Enander, A. (1987). Effects of moderate cold on performance of psychomotor and cognitive tasks. *Ergonomics, 30,* 1431–1445.

Evans, G. W. (1980). Environmental cognition. *Psychological Bulletin, 88,* 259–287.

Evans, G. W. (1994). The psychological costs of chronic exposure to ambient air pollution. In R. L. Isaacson & K. F. Jensen (Eds.), *The vulnerable brain and environmental risks: Vol. 3. Toxins in air and water* (pp. 167–182). New York: Plenum.

Evans, G. W. (2001). Environmental stress and health. In A. Baum, T. Revenson, & J. Singer (Eds.), *Handbook of health psychology* (pp. 365–385). Mahwah, NJ: Lawrence Erlbaum.

Evans, G. W., & Cohen, S. (1987). *Environmental stress*. In D. Stokols & I. Altman (Eds.), *Handbook of environmental psychology* (Vol. 1, pp. 571–610). New York: Wiley.

Evans, G. W., & Garling, T. (1991). Environment, cognition and action: The need for integration. In T. Garling & G. W. Evans (Eds.), *Environment, cognition, and action* (pp. 3–17). New York: Oxford University Press.

Evans, G. W., & Hygge, S. (in press). Noise and performance in children and adults. In L. Luxon & D. Prasher (Eds.), *Noise and its effects*. London: Whurr.

Evans, G. W., Johansson, G., & Carrere, S. (1994). Psychosocial factors and the physical environment: Inter-relations in the workplace. In C. Cooper & I. Robertson (Eds.), *International review of industrial and organizational psychology* (Vol. 9). New York: Wiley.

Evans, G. W., & Johnson, D. (2000). Stress and open-office noise. *Journal of Applied Psychology, 85,* 779–783.

Evans, G. W., Lepore, S., & Schroeder, A. (1996). The role of architecture in human responses to crowding. *Journal of Personality and Social Psychology, 70,* 41–46.

Evans, G. W., & McCoy, J. (1998). When buildings don't work: The role of architecture in human health. *Journal of Environmental Psychology, 18,* 85–94.

Evans, G. W., & Stecker, R. (in press). Motivational consequences of environmental stress. *Journal of Environmental Psychology*.

Ferreira, M., & Saldiva, P. (2002). Computer-telephone interactive tasks: Predictors of musculoskeletal disorders according to work analysis and worker's perception. *Applied Ergonomics, 33,* 147–153.

Fox, W. (1967). Human performance in the cold. *Human Factors, 9,* 203–220.

Fried, Y. (1990). Workspace characteristics, behavioral interferences, and screening ability as joint predictors of employee reactions: An examination of the intensification approach. *Journal of Organizational Behavior, 11,* 267–280.

Garling, T., Book, A., & Lindberg, E. (1986). Spatial orientation and wayfinding in the designed environment: A conceptual analysis and some suggestions for post occupancy evaluation. *Journal of Architectural and Planning Research, 3,* 55–64.

Gerlach, K. (1974). Environmental design to counter occupational boredom. *Journal of Architectural Research, 3,* 15–19.

Gifford, R. (1997). *Environmental psychology: Principles and practice* (2nd ed.). Boston: Allyn & Bacon.

Glass, D., & Singer, J. (1972). *Urban stress: Experience on noise and social stressors.* New York: Academic Press.

Goodrich, R. (1982). Seven office evaluations: A review. *Environment and Behavior, 14,* 353–378.

Griffin, J. M., Fuhrer, R., Stansfeld, S. A., & Marmot, M. (2002). The importance of low control at work and home on depression and anxiety: Do these effects vary by gender and social class? *Social Science & Medicine, 54*(5), 783–798.

Hartig, T., Evans, G. W., Jamner, L. D., Davis, D., & Garling, T. (2003). Tracking restoration in natural and urban field settings. *Journal of Environmental Psychology, 23,* 109–124.

Hatch, C. (1984). *The scope of social architecture.* Toronto: Van Nostrand Reinhold.

Hedge, A. (1984). Suggestive evidence for a relationship between office design and self-reports of ill-health among office workers in the United Kingdom. *Journal of Architectural Planning and Research, 1,* 163–174.

Hedge, A., Erikson, W., & Rubin, G. (1996). Predicting sick building syndrome at the individual and aggregate levels. *Environment International, 22,* 3–19.

Hedge, A., Sterling, E., & Sterling T. (1986). Evaluating office environments: The case for macroergonomic approach. In O. Brown & H. Hendrix (Eds.), *Human factors in organizational design and management* (pp. 419–424). Amsterdam: Elsevier.

Heerwagen, J. H. (1990). The psychological aspects of windows and window design. *Coming of age.* Proceedings of EDRA/21. 269–280. Champaign-Urbana, IL.

Heidmets, M. (1994). The phenomenon of personalization of the environment: A theoretical analysis. *Journal of Russian and East European Psychology, 32,* 41–85.

Henning, R., Sauter, S., & Kreig, E. (1992). Work rhythm and physiological rhythms in repetitive computer work: Effects of synchronization on well-being. *International Journal of Human-Computer Interaction, 4,* 233–243.

Jones, D., & Morris, N. (1992). Irrelevant speech and cognition. In D. J. Jones & A. Smith (Eds.), *Handbook of human performance* (Vol. 1, pp. 29–53). London: Academic.

Jones, P., Vaughan, N., Grajewski, T., Jenkins, H., O'Sullivan, P., Hillier, W., et al. (1995). *New guidelines for the design of healthy office environments.* Summary report to the SERC/DTI, GR/H38645, p. 7. London: University College Cardiff and University College London.

Jukes, J. (2000). Optimizing the working environment. In D. Clements-Croome (Ed.), *Creating the productive workplace.* London: E&FN Spon.

Kaplan, R., & Kaplan, S. (1982). *Cognition and environment.* New York: Praeger.

Kaplan, S., Talbot, J., & Kaplan, R. (1988). *Coping with daily hassles: The impact of nearby nature on the work environment.* (Project Report, Urban Forestry Unit Cooperative Agreement 23-85-08) U.S. Forest Service, North Central Experiment Station, St. Paul, MN.

Karasek, R., & Theorell, T. (1990). *Healthy work.* New York: Basic Books.

Kleeman, W. (1989). The politics of office design. *Environment and Behavior, 20*(5), 537–549.

Klitzman, S., & Stellman, J. (1989). The impact of the physical environment on the psychological well-being of office workers. *Social Science and Medicine, 29*(6), 733–742.

Kuller, R., & Laike, T. (1998). The impact of flicker from fluorescent lighting on well-being, performance and physiological arousal. *Ergonomics, 41,* 433–447.

Kuo, F. E. (2002). Bridging the gap: How scientists can make a difference. In R. Bechtel & A. Churchman (Eds.), *Handbook of environmental psychology* (pp. 335–346). New York: Wiley.

Leather, P., Beale, D., & Sullivan, L. (2003). Noise, psychosocial stress and their interaction in the workplace. *Journal of Environmental Psychology, 23,* 213–222.

Leather, P., Pygras, M., Beale, D., & Lawrence, C. (1998). Windows in the workplace: Sunlight, view, and occupational stress. *Environment and Behavior, 30*(6), 739–762.

Lepore, S. (1995). Measurement of chronic stressors. In S. Cohen, R. Kessler, & L. Gordon (Eds.), *Measuring stress* (pp. 102–121). New York: Oxford University Press.

Lercher, P., Hortnagl, J., & Kofler, W. (1993). Work noise annoyance and blood pressure: Combined effects with stressful working conditions. *International Archives of Occupational and Environmental Health, 65,* 23–28.

Lindstrom, K., Leino, T., Seitsamo, J., & Torstila, I. (1997). A longitudinal study of work characteristics and health complaints among insurance employees in VDT work. *International Journal of Human-Computer Interaction, 9*(4), 343–368.

Linton, S. (1999). Risk factors for neck and back pain in a working population in Sweden. *Work Stress, 4,* 41–49.

Lipman-Blumen, J., & Leavitt, H. (1999). *Hot groups: Seeding them, feeding them, and using them to ignite your organization.* New York: Oxford University Press.

Loewen, L, & Suedfeld, P. (1992). Cognitive and arousal effects of masking office noise. *Environment and Behavior, 24,* 381–395.

Lundberg, U., Kadefors, R., Melin, B., Palmerud, G., Hassmen, P., Engstrom, M., et al. (1994). Psychophysiological stress and EMG activity of the trapezius muscle. *International Journal of Behavioral Medicine, 1,* 354–370.

Maciel, R. (1998). Participatory ergonomics and organizational change. *International Journal of Industrial Ergonomics, 22,* 319–325.

Matthews, K., Cottington, E., Talbott, E., Kuller, L., & Siegel, J. (1987). Stressful work conditions and diastolic blood pressure among blue-collar factory workers. *American Journal of Epidemiology, 126,* 280–291.

Mazumdar, S. (1992). "Sir, please do not take away my cubicle": The phenomenon of environmental deprivation. *Environment and Behavior, 24,* 691–722.

McCormick, E. (1976). *Human factors in engineering and design.* New York: McGraw-Hill.

McCoy, J. (2000). The creative work environment: The relationship of the physical environment and creative teamwork at a state agency—A case study. (Doctoral dissertation, University of Wisconsin–Milwaukee, 2000). *Dissertation Abstracts International, 61, 03A*.

McCoy, J. (2002). Work environments: The changing workplace. In R. Bechtel & A. Churchman (Eds.), *Handbook of environmental psychology*. New York: Wiley.

McEwen, B. (1998). Protective and damaging effects of stress mediators. *New England Journal of Medicine, 338*(3), 171–179.

Medical Research Council. (1997). The nonauditory effects of noise (IEH Report R 10.) Leicester, UK: Institute for Environment and Health.

Mumford, E. (1994). New treatments or old remedies: Is business process reengineering really socio-technical design? *Journal of Strategic Information Systems, 3*(4), 313–326.

National Institute for Occupational Safety and Health (NIOSH). (1997). *Musculoskeletal disorders and workplace factors*. Washington, DC: U.S. Department of Health and Human Services.

National Research Council. (1991). *Environmental epidemiology*. Washington, DC: National Academy Press.

Oldham, G., & Brass, D. (1979). Employee reactions to an open office: A natural occurring, quasi-experiment. *Administrative Science Quarterly, 24*, 267–284.

Oldham, G., & Fried, Y. (1987). Employee reactions to workspace characteristics. *Journal of Applied Psychology, 72*, 75–80.

Oldham, G., & Rotchford, N. (1983). Relationships between office characteristics and employee reaction: A study of the physical environment. *Administrative Science Quarterly, 28*, 542–556.

O'Neill, J. (1994). Work space adjustability, storage and enclosure as predictors of employee reactions and performance. *Environment and Behavior, 26*, 504–526.

Ottmann, W., Rutenfranz, J., Neidhart, B., & Boucsein, W. (1987). Combined effects of shift work and noise on catecholamine excretion and electrodermal activity. In A. Oginski, J. Pokorski, & J. Rutenfranz (Eds.), Contemporary advances in shift work research. *Proceedings of the Eighth International Symposium on Night and Shift Work, Krakow, Poland*, 65–75.

Oxley, D., & Barrera, M., Jr. (1984). Undermanning theory and the workplace: Implications of setting size for job satisfaction and social support. *Environment and Behavior, 16*, 211–234.

Peterson, C., Maier, S., & Seligman, M. E. P. (1993). *Learned helplessness*. New York: Oxford University Press.

Rapoport, A. (1990). *The meaning of the built environment: A nonverbal communication approach*. Tucson: University of Arizona Press.

Rea, M., Oulette, M., & Kennedy, M. (1985). Lighting and task parameters affecting posture, performance, and subjective ratings. *Journal of the Illuminating Engineering Society, 13*, 231–238.

Repetti, R. (1993). The effect of workload and the social environment at work on health. In L. Goldberger & S. Breznitz (Eds.), *Handbook of stress* (2nd ed.). New York: Free Press.

Rotton, J., & Cohen, E. G. (2000). Violence is a curvilinear function of temperature in Dallas: A replication. *Journal of Personality and Social Psychology, 78*, 1074–1081.

Ruback, R., & Pandey, J. (1992). Very hot and really crowded: Quasi-experimental investigations of Indian "empos." *Environment and Behavior, 24*, 5257–5554.

Ryan, G., & Brampton, M. (1988). Comparison of data process operators with and without upper limb symptoms. *Community Health Studies, 12*(1), 63–68.

Sauter, S., Gottlieb, M., Jones, K., Dodson, V., & Rohrer, K. (1983). Job and health implications of VDT use: Initial results of the Wisconsin-NIOSH study. *Communications of the AGM, 26,* 284–294.

Sauter, S., Hurrell, J. J., & Cooper, C. L. (Eds.). (1989). *Job control and worker health.* New York: Wiley.

Smith, A., & Jones, D. (Eds.). (1992). Noise and performance. *Handbook of human performance* (Vol. 1, pp. 1–28). London: Academic.

Smith, M. (1985). Machine-paced work and stress. In D. L. Cooper & M. J. Smith (Eds.), *Job stress and blue collar work* (pp. 51–64). New York: Wiley.

Sommer, R. (1974). *Tight spaces: Hard architecture and how to humanize it.* Englewood Cliffs, NJ: Prentice Hall.

Sparks, K., & Cooper, C. (1999). Occupational differences in the work-strain relationship towards the use of situational specific modes. *Journal of Occupational and Organizational Psychology, 72,* 219–229.

Stellman, J., Klitzman, S., Gordon, G., & Snow, B. (1987). Work environment and the well-being of clerical and VDT workers. *Journal of Occupational Behaviour, 8,* 95–114.

Sterling, E., Sterling, T., Hartel, D., & McIntyre, E. (1983). *Health and comfort in modern office buildings: Results of a work environment survey.* Vancouver, BC: TDS Limited.

Stokols, D., Smith, T., & Proctor, J. (1975). Partitioning and perceived crowding in a public space. *American Behavioral Scientist, 18,* 792–814.

Sundstrom, E. (1986). *Work places: The psychology of the physical environment in offices and factories.* New York: Cambridge University Press.

Sundstrom, E. (1987). Work environments: Offices and factories. In D. Stokols & I. Altman (Eds.), *Handbook of environmental psychology* (pp. 733–782). New York: Wiley.

Sundstrom, E., Demuse, K., & Futrell, D. (1990). Work teams: Applications and effectiveness. *American Psychologist, 45*(2), 120–133.

Sundstrom, E., Herbert, R., & Brown, D. (1982). Privacy and communication in an open-plan office: A case study. *Environment and Behavior, 14,* 379–392.

Sundstrom, E., Town, J., Brown, D., Forman, A., & McGee, C. (1982). Physical enclosure, type of job and privacy in the office. *Environment and Behavior, 14,* 543–559.

Sundstrom, E., Town, J., Rice, R., Osborn, D., & Brill, M. (1994). Office noise, satisfaction, and performance. *Environment and Behavior, 26,* 195–222.

Ulrich, R. (1984). View from the window may influence recovery from surgery. *Science, 224,* 420–421.

Ulrich, R. (1993). Biophilia, biophobia, and natural landscapes. In S. Kellert & E. Wilson (Eds.), *The biophilia hypothesis.* Washington, DC: Island Press.

Veitch, J. (2001). Lighting quality contributions from biopsychological processes. *Journal of the Illuminating Engineering Society, 30*(3), 3–16.

Veitch, J., & McColl, S. (1995). On the modulation of fluorescent light: Flicker rate and spectral distribution effects on visual performance and visual comfort. *Light Research and Technology, 27,* 243–256.

Veitch, J., & Newsham, G. (1998). Determinants of light quality: State of the science. *Journal of the Illuminating Engineering Society, 27*(1), 92–106.

Villaneuva, M., Sotoyama, M., Jonai, H., Takeuchi, Y., & Saito, S. (1996). Adjustments of posture and viewing parameters of the eye to changes in the screen height of the visual display terminal. *Ergonomics, 39,* 933–945.

Weisman, G. (1982). Evaluating architectural legibility. *Environment and Behavior, 13,* 189–204.

Wells, M. (2000). Office clutter or meaningful personal displays: The role of office personalization in employee and organizational well-being. *Journal of Environmental Psychology, 20,* 239–255.

Wells, M., & Thelen, L. (2002). What does your workspace say about you? The influence of personality, status, and workspace on personalization. *Environment and Behavior, 34*(3), 300–321.

Wells, N. M., & Evans, G. W. (2003). Nearby nature: A buffer of life stress among rural children. *Environment and Behavior, 35,* 311–330.

Wener, R. E., Evans, G. W., Phillips, D., & Nadler, N. (2003). Running for the 7:45: The effects of public transit improvements on commuter stress. *Transportation, 30,* 203–220.

Wicker, A. (1987). Behavior settings reconsidered: Temporal stages, resources, internal dynamics, contest. In D. Stokols & I. Altman (Eds.), *Handbook of environmental psychology* (Vol. 1, pp. 613–654). New York: Wiley.

Wineman, J. (1982). The office environment as a source of stress. In G. W. Evans (Ed.), *Environmental stress* (pp. 256–285). New York: Cambridge University Press.

Wineman, J. (1986). Current issues and future directions. In J. Wineman (Ed.), *Behavioral issues in office design.* New York: Van Nostrand Reinhold.

Wineman, J., & Serrato, M. (1999). Facility design for high-performance teams. In E. Sundstrom & Associates (Eds.), *Supporting work team effectiveness: Best management practices for fostering high performance.* San Francisco: Jossey-Bass.

10 Workplace Safety

Leanne Barlow
Roderick D. Iverson

Workplace Safety

There is a plethora of evidence to conclude that occupational stress affects employees' health and well-being (Semmer, 2003). Although there are multiple models of stress (e.g., Karasek & Theorell, 1990; Siegrist, 2001), a common characteristic is the negative psychological and physiological impact on employees. One such impact is workplace safety. Workplace safety is important from a human and economic perspective. In Canada, for example, just over three workers die every working day from an occupational injury, one employee out of 38 is injured seriously enough to miss at least one day of work, and one time-loss injury occurs every 19 seconds worked (Human Resources Development Canada [HRDC], 2000).

In the United States, an estimated 6,529 fatal and approximately 13 million nonfatal occupational injuries occurred in 1992 (Leigh, Markowitz, Fahs, Shin, & Landrigan, 1997); and in Australia, compensated injuries resulted in an average of 2 months lost work in 1998–1999 (National Occupational Health and Safety Commission [NOHSC], 2000). Leigh, Macaskill, Kuosma, and Mandryk (1999) have estimated that worldwide there are over 100 million injuries annually. In terms of the economic impact, in Australia the cost of each workplace injury is estimated to be around $7,000 (NOHSC, 2000). Marshall (1996) estimated the cost of each workplace injury and fatality in Canada to be $6,000 and $492,000, respectively, with a total annual cost of $9.3 billion (HRDC, 2000). In the United States, the total cost of workplace injuries has been estimated to be $145 billion annually (Leigh et al., 1997).

In order to understand the impact of stress on workplace safety, a clearer understanding of these terms is required. Workplace safety is most commonly discussed in terms of the physical well-being of employees. Common examples of workplace safety are the wearing of protective equipment, the following of safety procedures, and the reporting of accidents through proper channels (Parker, Axtell, & Turner, 2001). Doverspike and Blumental (2001) found that workplace safety is primarily measured using three major factors: physical safety, working conditions, and the responsibility for the physical safety of others. An employee's emotional well-being or psychological safety is a component of workplace safety not often treated as a separate factor but present within the three measurement factors. Psychological safety includes the ability to handle role conflicts, manage diverse roles, and handle duties of multiple positions (Doverspike & Blumental, 2001). Barling and Frone (2004), in reviewing the workplace safety literature, observe that there is not a clear distinction between physical and psychological health-related injuries. This makes the reporting of safety results difficult to interpret and the development of safety intervention strategies problematic.

Hurrell, Nelson, and Simmons (1998) note that although there are different conceptions of occupational stress, it generally falls into three categories. First, job *stressors* are defined as "work-related environmental conditions (or exposure) that affect the health and well-being of the worker" (Hurrell et al., 1998, p. 368). Second, *strains* reflect the psychological and physiological reactions to these conditions or exposure; and third, *health status* is the long-term consequences of job stressors. For example, occupational stress causes some employees to focus narrowly on specific aspects of their environment; workers may focus more on productivity outputs than on taking the required safety steps, which can compromise their safety (Probst & Brubaker, 2001). The perceived occupational stress may vary among individuals and cause different reactions (e.g., ill health and decreased well-being) in those exposed to the particular stressors; reactions vary from physiological (elevated blood pressure), psychological (tenseness), to behavioral (alcohol use, or use of protective equipment) (Israel, Baker, Goldenhar, Heaney, & Schurman, 1996). In addition, research indicates that job stress can lead to anxiety, depression, job dissatisfaction, chemical dependencies, and alcohol abuse (Sauter, Murphy, & Hurrell, 1990).

There are numerous conceptual models of stress. For example, the seminal models comprise incompatible person-environment (P-E) fit (French, Caplan, & Harrison, 1982), job demands-control (Karasek, 1979), transactional or cognitive appraisal (Lazarus, 1966), state-trait process (Spielberger, Jacobs, Russell, & Crane, 1983), and preventive stress management (Quick & Quick, 1984). Spielberger, Vagg, & Wasala (2003) note that although these models have different emphases, they should be considered as complementary in their conceptualization of stress and form the foundation of current models. We provide a brief summary of some of the current stress models.

Spielberger et al. (2003), applying a P-E fit framework, define specific job-related stressors to include employee duties and responsibilities, job condition and requirements, and support from the organization, supervisor, and coworker. The severity of the stressor and the characteristics of the employee then determine the psychological or physical outcomes, resulting in adverse behavioral consequences such as turnover, absenteeism, and health problems.

Nelson and Simmons (2003) have developed a "holistic" model that incorporates a variety of stressors that are broken down into categories encompassing role demands, interpersonal demands, physical demands, workplace policies, and job conditions. These categories are argued to affect stress in either a positive or a negative manner depending on individual differences. This results in a variety of outcomes that affect one's health, performance, and/or family and work relationships.

A model by Heaney (2003) uses the physical, social, and organizational conditions, or stressors, as the starting point, which leads to a variety of short- and long-term outcomes. The individual's resources and the social or organizational resources that are available affect these stressors. Similarities are found in the model of Israel et al. (1996) who discuss stressors caused from psychosocial-environmental conditions that are moderated by social, psychological, biophysical, behavioral, and genetic variables leading to a variety of short- and long-term physiological, psychological, or behavioral outcomes.

In their model, Quillian-Wolever and Wolever (2003) consider the internal and external environmental impacts on the stressor and outline three courses of action: avoid the stressor, change the stressor, or change the response to the stressor. The three courses of action are achieved by breaking the strategies down into physical, emotional, cognitive, and solution-focused approaches.

Recognizing the importance of understanding stress in the workplace, this chapter will examine the causes and predictors of workplace safety, identify measurement issues, and discuss the outcomes and implications in relation to practice, policy, and intervention. In Figure 10.1, we show an integrated model to understand the relationship between occupational stress and safety.

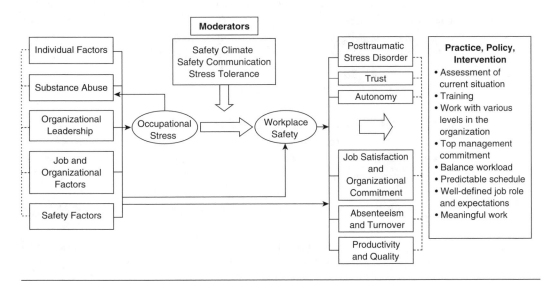

Figure 10.1   A Model of Workplace Safety

Causes and Predictors

Research has focused on individual factors, substance abuse, job and organizational factors, and safety factors as all being determinants of workplace safety. The causal links found between stress and workplace safety will be examined in greater detail throughout this section of the chapter.

Individual Factors

Many studies have examined the role of individual characteristics of demographics and personality that may cause an individual to have a predisposition to stress and a proneness to accidents (e.g., Iverson & Erwin, 1997; Kamp & Krause, 1997; Lawton & Parker, 1998).

Studies on occupational stress have found gender to be associated with different reactions to workplace injuries and illnesses. Women tend to report higher psychological stress, and men report more physical illness as a result of occupational stress (Ilgen, 1990; Spielberger et al., 2003). Men have also been found to have more injuries in the workplace than women have (Frone, 1998). This finding is consistent with that of Doverspike and Blumental (2001), who found that psychological safety is a major factor of work associated with jobs held more by women than men. Research regarding workplace injures has tended to focus on riskier jobs that are predominately held by men. However, Doverspike and Blumental specifically examined the differences between genders in the workplace when dealing with stress. Men primarily working in more physically demanding jobs account for the higher reporting of physical injuries related to occupational stress (Frone, 1998). Women, on the other hand, are often in a work environment in which the physical demands are significantly less, but the psychological stress is higher. Therefore, women report higher incidence of psychological injuries related to occupational stress. Iverson and Erwin (1997), however, observed women to be more vulnerable to occupational injury than men when undertaking similar work in a manufacturing plant. The authors proposed that work-family conflicts might account for the results.

Individual characteristics such as positive and negative affectivity (Iverson & Erwin, 1997), agreeableness, conscientiousness, intellect (Cellar, Nelson, Yorke, & Bauer, 2001), trustfulness, naïveté, self-sufficiency, recklessness, anxiety/depression, and risk-taking (Lawton & Parker, 1998) have been examined in relation to workplace injury potential. Previous studies suggest that personality traits may explain accidents and injuries in the workplace. Kamp and Krause (1997) found that some characteristics of neurosis and social maladjustment were significantly related to accident rates. Iverson and Erwin (1997) reported positive affectivity (individuals are generally positive and enthusiastic in nature) and negative affectivity (individuals display negative emotions and experiences) to be strong predictors of injuries in the following year.

Other personal factors that have been associated with an employee's accident rate include cognitive factors (including perception of stress), skills, attitudes, values, beliefs, emotional state, occupation, and biodata (e.g., age, education, tenure) (e.g., Barling, Kelloway, & Iverson, 2003b; Hansen, 1989; Kamp & Krause, 1997). Of course, skills and temporary emotional states can be influenced through workplace interventions such as training, but attitudes and beliefs are more difficult to modify. Job tenure has an impact on workplace safety through environmental factors such as workload, boredom, and physical hazards. In a study of adolescent workers conducted by Frone (1998), a positive relationship was found between tenure and work injuries. This relationship is explained by recognition that job tenure represents greater job-related experience and increased job assignments that entail greater skill and risk potential. Job tenure, therefore, with its additional responsibilities, may cause increased stress, negatively affecting an employee's safety performance.

However, Lawton and Parker (1998) point out that past research found it impossible to produce a stable profile of an accident-prone individual. The relationship between personality and accidents is not straightforward, and the evidence is mixed.

Substance Abuse

The use of tobacco, alcohol, and drugs to cope with occupational stress is common (Bass, 1990); but, as displayed in Figure 10.1, substance abuse is a major cause of stress. The effect of alcohol use on work-related injuries is met with great uncertainty, according to Stallones and Kraus (1993). Research on the topic has been quite unsystematic in the testing of substance levels in individuals involved in accidents, and the majority of studies are based on self-reports. As a result, the magnitude of the problem is unknown. The number of injuries related to substance abuse may, in fact, be significantly higher than believed because innocent bystanders may have been injured from the actions of someone under the influence (Stallones & Kraus, 1993).

Webb et al. (1994) found after reviewing previous studies on alcohol and occupational injuries that it was not possible to conclude that alcohol has a causal role in workplace injuries. The authors suggest that it is the social and psychological condition or symptom of excessive alcohol consumption that increases the risk of accidental injuries. Frone (1998) reported that adolescent workers' substance abuse was associated with workplace injuries. The study reported that results were inconclusive for older individuals, perhaps because adults felt there would be negative implications to reporting substance abuse while at work, such as job loss. However, the adolescent group studied was forthcoming with their substance use information (see Frone, 2004, for a more complete discussion).

Organizational Leadership

The quality and level of leadership is a major predictor of workplace safety. Leadership makes a significant difference in the prevention and occurrence of stress in the workplace (Bass, 1990), which influences the number of workplace injuries and illnesses. Current research has identified three distinct leadership approaches (Hofmann & Morgeson, 2004).

The first leadership approach is behavioral, which involves active monitoring and administering of rewards for performing the appropriate workplace behavior. A majority of the research on leadership and safety uses a behavioral perspective. Studies have found that a supportive managerial relationship is important in reducing the number of workplace accidents (Hofmann & Morgeson, 1999).

The second leadership approach is situational, which occurs through the leader's behavior influencing the subordinates. In research conducted on groups with a leader and groups without a leader, the groups with a leader were more likely to deal better with stress than those without a leader. The presence of a leader in a stressful situation tends to speed up the decision making, which at times does not provide the best solutions; but providing structure to the employees can be very powerful and beneficial (Bass, 1990). Situational leadership through the promotion of safe work practices by the supervisors/managers is effective in reducing workplace accidents and assists employees in coping with stress, which reduces the number of workplace accidents.

The third leadership approach uses power and influence through aspects of social exchange. Social exchange occurs when one party acts in a way that benefits another, with the implicit obligation for reciprocity (Hofmann & Morgeson, 1999). Perceived organizational support (POS) is one type of social exchange that involves increasing the willingness to make suggestions to improve the organization. Based on this definition by Hofmann and Morgeson (1999), POS should increase the level of safety communication and safety concerns.

Other forms of influential leadership are leader-member exchange, transformational leadership or transactional leadership. Leader-member exchange (LMX) fosters an open, constructive communication that therefore creates openness to raising safety concerns (Hofmann & Morgeson, 1999). LMX has been found to be significantly related to safety communication, safety commitment, and accidents. Studies have found that the higher the quality of interaction among employees and supervisors, the greater the emphasis on safety, which positively influences the safety climate and safety performance (e.g., Hofmann & Morgeson, 1999; Hofmann, Morgeson, & Gerras, 2003).

Transformational leadership can also be linked to workplace safety because it influences employee attitudes and other work outcomes such as trust in management, organizational commitment, satisfaction with leadership, and work performance (Barling, Loughlin, & Kelloway, 2002). This style of leadership focuses on development and encourages people to commit themselves to more challenging tasks by adding an increased awareness of larger issues and shifts the goals away from personal safety toward achievement (Bass, 1990). A transformational leader considers safety as a moral obligation (Zohar, 1980, 2003a), and, as a result, it is associated with decreased occupational injuries. Transactional leadership, in contrast, focuses on organizing tasks and getting people to perform more reliably and efficiently and is therefore more effective with highly routinized work (Zohar, 2003a). A transactional leader provides structure and consideration to a given situation (Bass, 1990).

Although the leadership approach will depend on organizational factors or human resource practices, what is important to recognize is that a leadership style can affect employees' level of stress, which in turn affects workplace safety.

Job and Organizational Factors

The work-related environmental conditions in which staff is immersed will affect employees' level of occupation stress and their health and well-being (Hurrell et al., 1998). Many job and organizational factors have been found to affect workplace safety (Hofmann & Morgeson, 1999; Iverson & Erwin, 1997). Employee behavior can be determined by aspects of the work environment (Kamp & Krause, 1997), and it plays a key role in causation of individual accidents and injuries. Every organization will have a multitude of factors or aspects to each of its jobs that differentiates them from those of another organization; however, commonalities exist in workplace factors that affect occupational safety.

Research indicates that organizations that have health and safety committees are associated with lower numbers of workplace injuries through their positive impact on the safety climate (Turner & Parker, 2004). The organizational climate is influenced by the commitment to improving working conditions (stress is a component of employees' working conditions) (Zohar, 1980) and procedures regarding workplace safety. A lack of procedures, organizational pressure to perform the job, poor communication, and a poor social climate will all have a negative impact on the overall safety performance of employees and their stress level (Hofmann & Stetzer, 1996). An effective health and safety committee will increase the level of safety communication among supervisors and workers, develop procedures for situations that involve risk, and create a positive emphasis on the safety climate by demonstrating a concerted organizational effort to create a healthier, safer work environment for employees. The emphasis on improving the production design and outputs through consideration of the safety aspect creates an orderly plant with a controlled work environment, and improving the level of communication among managers and workers not only improves the social and psychological climate but also the safety climate at work (Zohar, 1980).

The person-environment fit of an employee is another aspect that can have a significant impact on the employee's stress level. A poor or incompatible person-environment fit will produce a psychological strain or stress, which results in greater illness and/or accidents at work (Spielberger et al., 2003). A poor fit may also result from an incompatible job fit. The job fit is determined by ensuring the worker is able to meet the requirements of that particular job. Problems arise when a worker is hired to perform a job for which the employee is lacking the appropriate knowledge and skills. Any problems associated with fit issues will increase an employee's stress level, leading to increased propensity for occupational accidents (Spielberger et al., 2003). There is current research interest in the role of human resource bundles in addressing these problems.

The impact of stress on workplace safety is of growing concern and importance to human resource (HR) practitioners. The relationships between innovative workplace practices and health and safety are complex, to say the least. In a study conducted by Askenazy (2001), a variety of HR practices, such as autonomous work teams, job rotation, and total quality management (TQM), were examined in relation to health and safety in the workplace. A comparison of Japanese and U.S. automotive plants found that Japan's rate of occupational injuries was seven times lower with "lean production" methods, but it was later learned that Japan had a large number of undeclared injury cases. Examination of companies in the United States found that organizations that had implemented these innovative work practices experienced a dramatic increase in occupational injuries and illness (Askenazy, 2001). Nevertheless, several concerns can be raised in terms of the methodology that used multiple establishment surveys, as well as the nature of the HR practices.

Current research is now focused on high-performance work systems (HPWS) and their association with occupational stress and injuries. HPWS are based on employee involvement and empowerment that increases the quality of work life for employees and therefore should assist in decreasing stress in the workplace and reducing the number of workplace accidents. According to Way (2002), a HPWS is a "set of distinct but interrelated HRM practices that together select, develop, retain, and motivate a workforce" (p. 765). Zacharatos, Barling, and Iverson (in press) found HPWS (i.e., comprising employment security, selective hiring, training, teams, reduced status distinctions, information sharing, contingent compensation, transformational leadership, job quality, and measurement) to decrease occupational injuries at the individual and organizational level (based on a sample of HR and safety inspectors across 138 organizations). Another variation on the HPWS framework was the study by Barling, Kelloway, and Iverson (2003b). These researchers observed that high-quality work (comprising extensive training, variety, and autonomy) reduced injuries.

Recent research by Kaminski (2001) employing a variety of individual HR practices such as performance-based pay, contingent employees, training, and teamwork found that the training hours and work teams were associated with decreased injuries. In another study, Vredenburgh (2002) reported that hiring practices predict occupational injuries. Although it is beyond the scope of this chapter to discuss all HR practices, we direct readers to the article by Zacharatos et al. (in press) who, in proposing HPWS, discuss employment security, selective hiring, training, teams, reduced status distinctions, information sharing, contingent compensation, transformational leadership, job quality, and measurement. As we previously noted, the relationship between innovative practices or HPWS and injuries is complicated. Although some researchers characterize the HPWS as a commitment-based approach (Barling & Hutchinson, 2000), others characterize it from a labor process perspective. That is, work is actually intensified by some of these practices or systems. Shirom, Westman, and Melamed (1999), studying a sample of blue-collar employees, observed that those employees on a performance-contingent pay system experienced higher levels of depression and somatic complaints in comparison with their counterparts only paid for the time worked.

In summary, HR practices can influence the safety climate in the organization (Neal & Griffin, 2004) and engage employees, leading to lower stress and fewer occupational injuries. Conversely, there is also evidence that some of these practices, such as contingent pay, may increase stress leading to decreased safety.

Safety Factors

The literature identifies numerous safety factors. Safety climate refers to the perceptions of policies, procedures, and practices relating to safety (Zohar, 1980, 2003b; Neal & Griffin, 2004). Zohar (1980) described organizational climate as having a "psychological utility serving as a frame of reference for guiding appropriate and adaptive task behaviors" (p. 96). Safety climate reflects the overall impression of the importance the organization places on safety. It is generally agreed that safety climate is the predominate antecedent to safety behavior. As stress has a negative influence on this, safety climate needs to be managed effectively for workplace safety.

Two components of safety behavior are participation and compliance. Barling and Hutchinson (2000) characterize these two approaches as commitment and control in maximizing occupational safety. A commitment-based approach improves the perceived safety climate by increasing the trust in management and loyalty to the organization. Employees perceive that management is acting in their best interests by allowing them greater participation in decision making, increased training, and so on. The control-based approach, in contrast, is outcome-focused and emphasizes that rewards or punishment be used to increase efficiency. Overall, a commitment-based approach would be more effective to health and safety than a control orientation (Barling & Hutchinson, 2000). Zohar (1980), studying a sample of factories, observed that a major factor to a successful safety program was management commitment to the safety program. Factories experiencing low accident rates all had top management that supported safety programs and advocated safety in production design and outputs, overall plant operation, environmental conditions, and use of protective safety equipment.

The different attitudes and perceptions held by managers and supervisors about safety in an organization will create different safety behaviors in employees, which affects safety performance (Hofmann & Stetzer, 1996) and occupational stress. Safety knowledge and motivation are factors that are important in predicting safety compliance (Probst, 2004).

The effects of stress within these causal factors leading to workplace injuries are not always clear—more often studies reflect the direct link of cause and effect (injury). Our model (see Figure 10.1) attempts to reflect this by demonstrating the direct and indirect effects via occupational stress.

Known Moderators

In an effort to understand the relationship between stress and workplace safety, researchers have identified many potential moderators (see Figure 10.1). One that is particularly pertinent is safety climate. It is the most well-known and commonly investigated moderator relating to workplace safety (Hofmann, et al., 2003). Safety climate, as stated previously, relates to the employees' overall impression of safety in the organization based on policies and procedures (Zohar, 1980, 2000) that are relevant to employees' safety (Varonen & Mattila, 2000). Hofmann et al. (2003) have demonstrated the moderating effects of safety climate on the relationship between LMX and subordinate safety citizenship behavior. Specifically, the researchers observed that high-quality LMX relationships promoted expanded safety citizenship role definition when there was a positive safety climate, which is no surprise because the style of leadership makes a significant difference in employees' occupational stress level.

Safety climate has also been found to act as a mediator. Research has found that the safety climate played an intervening role between employees' behavior and their safety performance (Griffin & Neal, 2000). In another study, Barling et al. (2002) reported that the perceived safety climate mediated the relationship between safety-specific transformational leadership and occupational safety. Transformational leadership went beyond ergonomic and regulatory approaches in promoting a positive safety climate leading to safety-related events and decreased occupational injuries. Management's commitment to safety-related issues was far-reaching and strengthened the safety climate.

Although there is sparse empirical evidence, another potential moderator is safety communication. The quality of safety communication that occurs among managers and employees will influence the safety climate (Zohar, 1980). The more concern expressed by managers for employees and the more open the leader-member exchange, the greater the promotion of safety as a priority in the organization. Inconsistencies among departments are often found in an organization due to the priority the manager assigns to safety communication (Zohar, 2000). A concerted effort by management in communicating the priority of workplace safety results in a lower accident rate. This is critical for understanding the importance of leadership in mitigating the occurrence of stress (Bass, 1990).

At the individual level, another possible moderator is stress tolerance, the ability of an individual to contend with stress of a situational and temporary nature. Everyone experiences stress in the workplace, but some individuals are more likely to react in a way that leads to mistakes and errors, as previously mentioned (Probst & Brubaker, 2001). Individuals with a low stress tolerance have been shown to become more flustered and have a reduction in the quality and breadth of their attention and focus (Forcier, Walters, Brasher, & Jones, 2001). Therefore, an individual with low stress tolerance is at increased risk of being involved in a workplace accident causing injury.

Measurement and Design Issues

There are a number of measurement and design issues surrounding the relationship between stress and workplace safety. One such issue is the use of objective injury data collected from company records versus subject self-report data collected from individuals. In the past, doubt has been cast over the accuracy of self-report data and associated problems such as common method variance. Grunberg, Moore, and Greenberg (1996) have questioned the rationale of discounting self-reports by inquiring into what incentives would make employees intentionally falsify injury reports. In fact, Barling et al. (2003b) have noted that it is entirely possible for management to underestimate the real extent of injuries. In any event, employing multiple measures (e.g., self-report, medical records, organizational records, workers' compensation data) would make measurement of workplace safety more robust (Eisenberg & MacDonald, 1988). Another measurement issue pertains to the frequency and the severity of injuries. Frequency relates to the number of times an event occurs, and severity relates to amount of lost time from that event. This has implications for understanding the influence of levels of occupational stress. Other measurement issues include micro-accidents, in which employees experience injuries but require no time off from work (Zohar, 2000), and near misses (Zacharatos et al., in press). Finally, level of analysis (i.e., individual, group, and organization) continues to be a salient issue through the use of measures such as safety climate, arguably a group rather than an individual phenomenon (Hofmann et al., 2003; Zohar, 2003a, 2003b).

There are two main design issues. The first is the preponderance of research based on cross-sectional rather than longitudinal designs (Iverson & Erwin,

1997; Parker et al., 2001; Probst & Brubaker, 2001). This obviously has causation implications. Another issue is the types of samples studied—the majority of research is on male blue-collar employees engaged in manufacturing, mining, or outdoor work, although more current studies include samples such as hospital, service, and multiple-occupation employees (Barling, Kelloway, & Iverson, 2003a, Vredenburgh, 2002).

Measurement and design issues are important for disentangling the stress-safety relationship. If we cannot accurately operationalize and test the relationship, it limits our ability to generalize and specifically test and develop interventions to increase workplace safety.

Outcomes

As shown in Figure 10.1, occupational stress and the implications on workplace safety are significant as demonstrated so far, and the effects have far-reaching ramifications. Stress in the workplace was found to cause a 20% decrease in interest in the quality of work from a sample of high-skilled employees (Argyris, 1960). When workers are disengaged, they are more likely to be injured. In Argyris's particular study, conflict in the workplace increased as the level of stress increased, and there was a rise in employee unfriendliness. Workers were found to have had an elevated desire to unionize as a result of the negative work environment. Not surprisingly, the absentee and turnover rates also increased, but this study did not indicate if the absence rate was a result of injuries suffered in the workplace. Conversely, we do know that the higher the level of job satisfaction, the more safely employees work (Barling et al., 2003b).

The literature identifies several consequences of occupational injuries. Asmundson, Norton, Allerdings, Norton, and Larsen (1998) have observed that a substantial portion of employees suffering workplace injuries experience symptoms consistent with posttraumatic stress disorder (PTSD). These persistent psychological symptoms can include re-experiencing the injury (e.g., nightmares), hyperarousal (e.g., sleep difficulties), and the avoidance of feelings or activities related to the injury.

A lingering problem that employees suffer is trying to make sense of their environments and assessing their propensity for future harm following an accident. The two theories of normal accidents (Perrow, 1984, 1994) and high-reliability organizations (Roberts, 1990; Weick, Sutcliffe, & Obstfeld, 1999) help us understand the perceived accident risk of employees. In an environment of complex technological systems, following an accident employees may blame management (defensive attribution error) due to management's inability to comprehend the complexities of the systems involved. This results in negative attitudes such as distrust of management (Barling et al., 2003a; Clarke, 1999). Clarke (1999), for example, reported that train drivers attributed to managers and supervisors less knowledge and care regarding occupational safety than they actually had. In addition, employees have also linked accidents to perceived lack of control. Following an injury, employees may experience lowered controllability appraisals of their jobs and the environment, and these beliefs are enduring. Further, Reason, Parker and Lawton (1998) argued that this perception by employees may be accurate due to management tightening their use of procedures and rules following the accident.

In addition to trust and autonomy, workplace injuries would be expected to lower other attitudes, such as job satisfaction and organizational commitment, and increase withdrawal behavior, such as absenteeism and turnover (Barling et al., 2003a). As these attitudes and behaviors may be viewed as "voicing" disenchantment with the organization, other possible outcomes include lower productivity and quality of work.

Implications for Practice, Policy, and Intervention

Organizational and HR practices can influence an employee's stress level, which will have implications for not only accidents in the workplace but job satisfaction, absenteeism, turnover, productivity, and quality output. In fact, HR practices have more impact on safety than on production (Kaminski, 2001). The greatest challenge, though, is to make health and safety a more strategic core consideration in the way work is conducted (Brotherton, 2003).

Levi, Sauter, and Shimomitsu (1999) suggest that employers analyze the work situation as they have an obligation to the employee to detect stressors and remedy the situation. An ideal workplace will be structured to have safety systems that workers engage in at all times; and through the use of workplace interventions, employees' emotional states will be positively influenced (Kamp & Krause, 1997).

A variety of HR practices can lead to decreased stress and assist in creating a safer positive work environment. Training, for example, can help an individual to cope with job stressors. Focusing on the recruitment phase can also be a key to ensuring the employee has the appropriate fit with the job and skills required. During the recruitment phase, measuring the employee for the specific traits that are required for the job will enable the appropriate placement of the candidate and guide the accompanying training decisions (Kamp & Krause, 1997).

A majority of attempts to prevent stress have been directed at the individual so far. Preventative measures need to examine the working conditions and investigate primary, secondary, and tertiary interventions (Israel et al., 1996; Semmer, 2003). The goal of a primary intervention is to reduce the risk factor or alter the nature of the job stressor before employees experience stress-related symptoms. This is a very proactive approach and often targets physical-environmental and psychosocial conditions. Secondary interventions prevent existing short-term stress symptoms from becoming chronic by altering aspects of the environment that are responsible. An example of a secondary intervention would be changing the way people respond to the stressors. This form of intervention could also alter the physical or psychosocial environment. Finally, a tertiary intervention would take the form of a program designed to treat employees that have been dealing with long-term negative effects associated with work.

Prevention strategies must take into account causal mechanisms and factors that perpetuate the psychological disorders (Sauter et al., 1990). An assessment of the job stressors and organizational needs is a critical component of an intervention. The intervention must be tailored to the organization with the prevention interventions aimed at various levels in the organization (individual, work group, department, and top management) (Israel et al., 1996; Sauter et al., 1990).

Specific job design interventions aimed at improving the working conditions should focus on the workload, work pace, schedule, role stressors, career security factors, interpersonal relations, and job content, as each of these factors can increase employee health risks (Sauter et al., 1990). Balancing out the workload and increasing an employee's control in relation to the pace of work and decisions will decrease the health risks associated with these. Creating a predictable schedule that is compatible with outside work demands will also decrease the health risks associated with a rotating work schedule. Providing employees with a well-defined job role with clear expectations and reducing the ambiguity of long-term job opportunities with the company will have a positive impact on reducing health risks. Finally, providing employees with meaningful work that allows them to utilize their skills will decrease the impact of job stressors.

Organizations need an awareness and appreciation of psychological disorders as workplace problems and an understanding of work risk factors, including recognition of their signs and symptoms, to reduce stressful work conditions and provide treatment to employees (Sauter et al., 1990). Early detection and preventative strategies for job stressors will have a positive impact on the reduction of workplace injuries. Work environment changes need to focus on ergonomic changes, job content, and work organization (Semmer, 2003). Based on several case studies, Israel et al. (1996) observed modifying factors such as social support and control over decisions to provide competencies for dealing with short- and long-term responses to stress. Control over decisions came in many forms, from greater job autonomy to employee participation in health and safety committees. Also keys to successful interventions were training the trainers to be more effective recognizing and treating stress-related disorders in the workplace and enlisting support of top management to sustain an organizationwide change in workplace safety policies and attitudes. A summary of these implications appears in Figure 10.1.

Future Research

Disentangling the complex relationship between stress and workplace safety is a difficult but not impossible task. Nevertheless, current research has a number of limitations that restrict our ability to employ the various approaches outlined in the chapter. There are several avenues for future research. A most important issue is the low base rates for occupational injuries, which impedes our ability to find significant causes. Researchers need to focus on measures such as frequency and severity as well as microaccidents and near misses. In addition, there is a definite need for better research designs (e.g., longitudinal design, time-frame, and multilevel) to establish causation. Improved measures (i.e., multiple items rather than single items) and greater standardization (e.g., high quality of work or high-performance work systems) (Barling et al., 2003b; Zacharatos et al., in press) would also contribute to the generalizability of findings. The opportunity to use available archival data sets (e.g., specification and monomethod issues) needs to be weighed against understanding the process by which injuries occur (Godard, 2001). To date there are few moderator variables in the literature (e.g., safety climate). This limits our ability to understand the buffering effects on injuries and suggests that other moderators (e.g., job satisfaction) require exploration. Finally, we know very little about the consequences of injuries (e.g., psychological contract violations) and the success of intervention strategies. To contribute to the health and well-being of employees, researchers need to be aware of these types of issues in future research.

In conclusion, organizations that are concerned about their bottom line (e.g., profits and productivity) need to be also worried about the safety of their employees (Ilgen, 1990). Workplace safety programs need to address not only physical safety but psychological safety. There are numerous challenges organizations face, such as the time frame in which to implement programs, resources, commitment from top management and unions, integration of health-related programs into the organizationwide operations, and the legislation and policies mandated (Israel et al., 1996).

Epilogue

Thus, it can be seen that the occupational stress associated with workplace safety is twofold: it serves as a multifaceted predictor. In this chapter, we found support for individual, substance abuse, organizational leadership, job and organizational, and safety factors. In addition, stress also serves as a consequence. The organizational and personal consequences of getting hurt comprise posttraumatic stress disorder, trust, autonomy, job satisfaction, organizational commitment, absenteeism, turnover, productivity, and quality. However, occupational stress is amenable to interventions (Sauter et al., 1990), and workplace safety is a human and economic imperative that provides a "win-win" for employees, organizations, and society.

References

Argyris, C. (1960). Organizational effectiveness under stress. *Harvard Business Review, 38,* 137–146.

Askenazy, P. (2001). Innovative workplace practices and occupational injuries and illnesses in the United States. *Economic and Industrial Democracy, 22,* 485–516.

Asmundson, G. J., Norton, G. R., Allerdings, M. D., Norton, P. J., & Larsen, D. K. (1998). Posttraumatic stress disorder and work-related injury. *Journal of Anxiety Disorders, 12,* 57–69.

Barling, J., & Frone, M. R. (2004). Occupational injuries: Prevalence, costs, and setting the stage. In J. Barling & M. R. Frone (Eds.), *Psychology of workplace safety.* Washington, DC: American Psychological Association.

Barling, J., & Hutchinson, I. (2000). Commitment vs. control-based safety practices, safety reputation, and perceived safety climate. *Canadian Journal of Administrative Sciences, 17,* 76–84.

Barling, J., Kelloway, K. E., & Iverson, R. D. (2003a). Accidental outcomes: Attitudinal consequences of workplace injuries. *Journal of Occupational Health Psychology, 8*(1), 74–85.

Barling, J., Kelloway, K. E., & Iverson, R. D. (2003b). High-quality work, job satisfaction, and occupational injuries. *Journal of Applied Psychology, 88,* 276–283.

Barling, J., Loughlin, C., & Kelloway, K. E. (2002). Development and test of a model linking safety-specific transformational leadership and occupational safety. *Journal of Applied Psychology, 87,* 488–496.

Bass, B. M. (1990). *Bass & Stodgill's handbook of leadership theory, research, and managerial applications* (3rd ed.). New York: Free Press.

Brotherton, C. (2003). The role of external policies in shaping organizational health and safety. In D. A. Hofmann & L. E. Tetrick (Eds.), *Health and safety in organizations: A multilevel perspective* (pp. 372–396). San Francisco: Jossey-Bass.

Cellar, D. F., Nelson, Z. C., Yorke, C. M., & Bauer, C. (2001). The five-factor model and safety in the workplace: Investigating the relationships between personality and accident involvement. *Journal of Prevention and Intervention in the Community, 22,* 43–52.

Clarke, S. (1999). Perceptions of organizational safety: Implications for the development of safety culture. *Journal of Organizational Behavior, 20,* 185–198.

Doverspike, D., & Blumental, A. (2001). Gender issues in the measurement of physical and psychological safety. *Journal of Prevention and Intervention in the Community, 22,* 21–34.

Eisenberg, W. M., & MacDonald, H. (1988). Evaluating workplace injury and illness records: Testing a procedure. *Monthly Labor Review, 111,* 58–60.

Forcier, B. H., Walters, A. E., Brasher, E. E., & Jones, J. W. (2001). Creating a safer working environment through psychological assessment: A review of a measure of safety consciousness. *Journal of Prevention and Intervention in the Community, 22,* 53–65.

French, J. R. P., Jr., Caplan, R. D., & Harrison, R. V. (1982). *The mechanisms of job stress and strain.* London: Wiley.

Frone, M. R. (1998). Predictors of work injuries among employed adolescents. *Journal of Applied Psychology, 83,* 565–576.

Frone, M. R. (2004). Alcohol, drugs, and workplace safety outcomes: A view from a general model of employee substance use and productivity. In J. Barling & M. R. Frone (Eds.), *Psychology of workplace safety*. Washington, DC: American Psychological Association.

Godard, J. (2001). New dawn or bad moon rising? Using large scale government administered workplace surveys and the future of Canadian IR research. *Relations Industrielles/Industrial Relations, 56,* 3–33.

Griffin, M. A., & Neal, A. (2000). Perceptions of safety at work: A framework for linking safety climate to safety performance, knowledge, and motivation. *Journal of Occupational Health Psychology, 5,* 347–358.

Grunberg, L., Moore, S., & Greenberg, E. (1996). The relationship of employee ownership and participation to workplace safety. *Economic and Industrial Democracy, 17,* 221–241.

Hansen, C. P. (1989). A causal model of the relationship among accidents, biodata, personality, and cognitive factors. *Journal of Applied Psychology, 74,* 81–90.

Heaney, C. A. (2003). Worksite health interventions: Targets for change and strategies for attaining them. In J. C. Quick & L. E. Tetrick (Eds.), *Handbook of occupational health psychology* (pp. 305–324). Washington, DC: American Psychological Association.

Hofmann, D. A., & Morgeson, F. P. (1999). Safety-related behavior as a social exchange: The role of perceived organizational support and leader-member exchange. *Journal of Applied Psychology, 84,* 286–296.

Hofmann, D. A., & Morgeson, F. P. (2004). The role of leadership in safety. In J. Barling & M. R. Frone (Eds.), *Psychology of workplace safety*. Washington, DC: American Psychological Association.

Hofmann, D. A., Morgeson, F. P., & Gerras, S. J. (2003). Climate as a moderator of the relationship between leader-member exchange and content specific citizenship: Safety climate as an exemplar. *Journal of Applied Psychology, 88,* 170–178.

Hofmann, D. A., & Stetzer, A. (1996). A cross-level investigation of factors influencing unsafe behaviors and accidents. *Personnel Psychology, 49,* 307–339.

Human Resources Development Canada. (2000). *Work safely for a healthy future: Statistical analysis occupational injuries and fatalities Canada*. Ottawa, ON: Author.

Hurrell, J. J., Nelson, D. L., & Simmons, B. L. (1998). Measuring job stressors and strains: Where we have been, where we are, and where we need to go. *Journal of Occupational Health Psychology, 3,* 368–389.

Ilgen, D. R. (1990). Health issues at work. *American Psychologist, 45,* 273–283.

Israel, B. A., Baker, E. A., Goldenhar, L. M., Heaney, C. A., & Schurman, S. J. (1996). Occupational stress, safety, and health: Conceptual framework and principles for effective prevention interventions. *Journal of Occupational Health Psychology, 4,* 261–286.

Iverson, R. D., & Erwin, P. J. (1997). Predicting occupational injury: The role of affectivity. *Journal of Occupational and Organizational Psychology, 70,* 113–128.

Kaminski, M. (2001). Unintended consequences: Organizational practices and their impact on workplace safety and productivity. *Journal of Occupational Health Psychology, 6,* 127–138.

Kamp, J., & Krause, T. R. (1997). Selecting safe employees: A behavioral science perspective. *Professional Safety, 42*(4), 24–28.

Karasek, R. A. (1979). Job demands, job decision latitude, and mental strain: Implications for job redesign. *Administrative Science Quarterly, 24,* 285–307.

Karasek, R. A., & Theorell, T. (1990). *Healthy work: Stress, productivity and the reconstruction of working life.* New York: Basic Books.

Lawton, R., & Parker, D. (1998). Individual differences in accident liability: A review and integrative approach. *Human Factors, 40, 655–671.*

Lazarus, R. S. (1966). *Psychological stress and the coping process.* New York: McGraw-Hill.

Leigh, J. P., Macaskill, P., Kuosma, E., & Mandryk, J. (1999). Global burden of disease and injury due to occupational factors. *Epidemiology, 10,* 626–631.

Leigh, J. P., Markowitz, S. B., Fahs, M., Shin, C., & Landrigan, P. J. (1997). Occupational injury and illness in the U.S.: Estimates of costs, morbidity and mortality. *Archives of Internal Medicine, 157,* 1557–1568.

Levi, L., Sauter, S. L., & Shimomitsu, T. (1999). Work-related stress—It's time to act. *Journal of Occupational Health Psychology, 4,* 394–396.

Marshall, K. (1996, Summer). A job to die for. *Perspectives on Labour and Income,* 26–31.

National Occupational Health and Safety Commission. (2000). *Compendium of workers' compensation statistics, Australia, 1998–1999.* Canberra, NSW: Author.

Neal, A., & Griffin, M. A. (2004). Safety climate and safety at work. In J. Barling & M. R. Frone (Eds.), *Psychology of workplace safety.* Washington, DC: American Psychological Association.

Nelson, D. L., & Simmons, B. L. (2003). Health psychology and work stress: A more positive approach. In J. C. Quick & L. E. Tetrick (Eds.), *Handbook of occupational health psychology* (pp. 97–119). Washington, DC: American Psychological Association.

Parker, S. K., Axtell, C. M., & Turner, N. (2001). Designing a safer workplace: Importance of job autonomy, communication quality, and supportive supervisors. *Journal of Occupational Health Psychology, 6,* 211–228.

Perrow, C. (1984). *Normal accidents: Living with high-risk technologies.* New York: Basic Books.

Perrow, C. (1994). Accidents in high-risk systems. *Technological Studies, 1,* 1–20.

Probst, T. M. (2004). Job insecurity: Exploring a new threat to employee safety. In J. Barling & M. R. Frone (Eds.), *Psychology of workplace safety.* Washington, DC: American Psychological Association.

Probst, T. M., & Brubaker, T. L. (2001). The effects of job insecurity on employee safety outcomes: Cross-sectional and longitudinal explorations. *Journal of Occupational Health Psychology, 6,* 139–159.

Quick, J. C., & Quick, J. D. (1984). *Organizational stress and preventative management.* New York: McGraw-Hill.

Quillian-Wolever, R. E., & Wolever, M. E. (2003). Stress management at work. In J. C. Quick & L. E. Tetrick (Eds.), *Handbook of occupational health psychology* (pp. 355–376). Washington, DC: American Psychological Association.

Reason, J., Parker, D., & Lawton, R. (1998). Organizational controls and safety: The varieties of rule-related behavior. *Journal of Occupational and Organizational Psychology, 71,* 289–304.

Roberts, K. H. (1990). Some characteristics of one type of high reliability organizations. *Organization Science, 2,* 160–176.

Sauter, S. L., Murphy, L. R., & Hurrell, J. J. (1990). Prevention of work-related psychological disorders. *American Psychologist, 45,* 1146–1158.

Semmer, N. K. (2003). Job stress interventions and organization of work. In J. C. Quick & L. E. Tetrick (Eds.), *Handbook of occupational health psychology* (pp. 325–354). Washington, DC: American Psychological Association.

Shirom, A., Westman, M., & Melamed, S. (1999). The effects of pay systems on blue-collar employees' emotional distress: The mediating effects of objective and subjective work monotony. *Human Relations, 52,* 1077–1097.

Siegrist, J. (2001). A theory of occupational stress. In J. Dunham (Ed.), *Stress in the workplace* (pp. 52–66). London: Whurr.

Spielberger, C. D., Jacobs, G., Russell, S., & Crane, R. S. (Eds.). (1983). *Assessment of anger: The State-Trait Anger Scale* (Vol. 2). Hillsdale, NJ: Lawrence Erlbaum.

Spielberger, C. D., Vagg, P. R., & Wasala, C. F. (2003). Occupational stress: Job pressures and lack of support. In J. C. Quick & L. E. Tetrick (Eds.), *Handbook of occupational health psychology* (pp. 185–200). Washington, DC: American Psychological Association.

Stallones, L., & Kraus, J. F. (1993). The occurrence and epidemiologic features of alcohol-related occupational injuries. *Addiction, 88,* 945–951.

Turner, N., & Parker, S. K. (2004). The effect of teamwork on safety processes and outcomes. In J. Barling & M. R. Frone (Eds.), *Psychology of workplace safety.* Washington, DC: American Psychological Association.

Varonen, U., & Mattila, M. (2000). The safety climate and its relationship to safety practices, safety of the work environment and occupational accidents in eight wood-processing companies. *Accident Analysis and Prevention, 32,* 761–769.

Vredenburgh, A. G. (2002). Organizational safety: Which management practices are most effective in reducing employee injury rates? *Journal of Safety Research, 33,* 259–276.

Way, S. A. (2002). High performance work systems and intermediate indicators of firm performance within the U.S. small business sector. *Journal of Management, 28*(6), 765–785.

Webb, G. R., Redman, S., Hennrikus, D. J., Kelman, R. G., Gibberd, R. W., & Sanson-Fisher, R. W. (1994). The relationships between high-risk and problem drinking and the occurrence of work injuries and related absences. *Journal of Studies on Alcohol, 55,* 436–446.

Weick, K. E., Sutcliffe, K. M., & Obstfeld, D. (1999). Organizing for high reliability: Processes of collective mindfulness. *Research in Organizational Behavior, 21,* 81–123.

Zacharatos, A., Barling, J., & Iverson, R. D. (in press). High-performance work systems and occupational safety. *Journal of Applied Psychology.*

Zohar, D. (1980). Safety climate in industrial organizations: Theoretical and applied implications. *Journal of Applied Psychology, 65,* 96–102.

Zohar, D. (2000). A group-level model of safety climate: Testing the effect of group climate on microaccidents in manufacturing jobs. *Journal of Applied Psychology, 85,* 587–596.

Zohar, D. (2003a). The influence of leadership and climate on occupational health and safety. In D. A. Hofmann & L. E. Tetrick (Eds.), *Health and safety in organizations: A multilevel perspective* (pp. 201–229). San Francisco: Jossey-Bass.

Zohar, D. (2003b). Safety climate: Conceptual and measurement issues. In J. C. Quick & L. E. Tetrick (Eds.), *Handbook of occupational health psychology* (pp. 123–142). Washington, DC: American Psychological Association.

11 Economic Stressors

Tahira M. Probst

To do nothing may be to be nothing for many Americans.

Judge and Hulin (1993, p. 413)

In an era of record unemployment, massive layoffs, and a sluggish economy, many of today's workers face the economic stressors of unemployment, underemployment, and job insecurity. Although each of these three stressors is conceptually distinct, they do have similar antecedents and consequences associated with them. As the quote by Judge and Hulin above suggests, a person's job is one of the most important mechanisms through which he or she gains a sense of identity. Whether that job is threatened (as with job insecurity), compromised financially with respect to status (as with underemployment), or lost (as with unemployment), theory and empirical research overwhelmingly suggest that the resulting consequences are significant, negative, and widespread.

The purpose of this chapter is to define and discuss the prevalence of these economic stressors in the workplace; review major theoretical models and empirical studies associated with job insecurity, underemployment, and unemployment; delineate the individual, organizational, and societal outcomes that may result from these work stressors; suggest future research needs; and discuss implications for practice, policy, and intervention.

Defining Economic Stress

The concept of economic stress gained prominence in the 1980s and was the focus of a series of theoretical and empirical articles and books by sociologist Patricia Voydanoff (Voydanoff, 1984, 1987, 1990; Voydanoff & Majka,

Exhibit 11.1   Components of Economic Stress Described by Voydanoff (1990)

| | *Source of Stress* | |
	Employment	Income
Objective Stressors	<u>Employment Instability</u> • Duration of periods of unemployment • Number of periods of unemployment • Extent of underemployment • Downward mobility • Forced early retirement	<u>Economic Deprivation</u> • Inability to meet current financial needs • Loss of income and financial resources
Subjective Stressors	<u>Employment Uncertainty</u> • Concern about possible layoff • Assessment of onset of, duration of, and recovery from layoff • Concern about reduction in income	<u>Economic Strain</u> • Perceived financial adequacy • Financial concerns and worries • Adjustment to change in financial status

1988). According to Voydanoff (1990), economic stress refers to aspects of economic life that are potential stressors for employees and their families and consists of both objective and subjective components reflecting the employment and income dimensions of the worker-earner role. Objective indicators of economic stress include employment instability (e.g., the frequency and length of unemployment versus employment) and economic deprivation (e.g., low income or income loss), whereas employment uncertainty (e.g., one's assessment of the probability of unemployment) and economic strain (e.g., the evaluation of one's current financial status) are considered to be subjective indicators of economic stress (Kinnunen & Pulkkinen, 1998). See Exhibit 11.1 for a complete summary of the dimensions and sources of economic stress as outlined by Voydanoff (1990).

Although there are many directions a chapter on economic stressors could take, the focus of this chapter will be on the three specific aspects of economic stress that have been most heavily researched by industrial/organizational and occupational health psychologists: unemployment, underemployment, and job insecurity. Not coincidentally, these areas will be tackled in order ranging from most to least objective in nature. It is relatively easy to ascertain when someone is unemployed; there is less agreement on what it means to be underemployed; and there are even fewer objective standards by which one can identify someone as holding an insecure job. Yet, all of these conditions can be sources of economic stress and can have significant implications for those affected individuals. Below we begin with an overview of the definition and prevalence of these three stressors.

Definition and Prevalence of Unemployment, Underemployment, and Job Insecurity

Unemployment. Unemployment is an objectively measured stressor that involves a loss or lack of employment and a loss of income. According to the U.S. federal government, "persons are classified as unemployed if they do not have a job, have actively looked for work in the prior 4 weeks, and are currently available for work" (Bureau of Labor Statistics [BLS], 2001). At the time of writing (June 2003), the current federal unemployment rate in the United States stood at a 9-year high of 6.4%, accounting for 9.4 million workers. Of those, 2 million had been unemployed for over 6 months. At the same time, the labor force participation rate was at a 10-year low of 66.2%.

It is important to note that the preceding unemployment and labor statistics do not take into account the so-called 1.4 million "marginally attached" workers or the .5 million "discouraged" workers. Marginal workers are unemployed individuals who want to work but did not actively seek work during the 4 weeks preceding the federal government survey, whereas discouraged workers are defined as those who were not currently looking for work due to a belief that there was no work available for them. Thus, these individuals did not meet the strict government definition of unemployed yet would be considered unemployed by most organizational researchers.

Underemployment. Although politicians, the press, and the public largely focus on the national unemployment rate as the primary indicator of the health of the economy, many researchers would argue that an additional indicator, underemployment, might provide a more comprehensive and accurate picture of the economic well-being of American families (Feldman, 1996; Zvonkovic, 1988).

Whereas unemployment is federally defined and tracked, there is less agreement regarding what constitutes underemployment or how many people can be categorized as such. Underemployment has been defined as a discrepancy between "satisfactory employment" (Kaufman, 1982) and current employment wherein the current employment is seen as inferior or of lower quality (Feldman, 1996). Thus, underemployment is always defined relative to some standard; however, that standard can be assessed either objectively (via a comparison of income and position status relative to a comparable cohort) or subjectively (via one's own assessment of income and position relative to what it has been in the past and/or should be).

In a review of the underemployment literature, Feldman (1996) proposed five criteria to determine the extent of an individual's underemployment. The first criterion assesses whether and to what extent an employee possesses more formal education than the position requires. The second criterion evaluates whether the employee is more highly skilled and has more work experience than is required for the job. These two dimensions constitute what is commonly referred to as being "overqualified" for a job. The third criterion assesses whether the person is involuntarily (rather than voluntarily) employed outside his or her area of formal training. The fourth component of underemployment considers if the employee is involuntarily employed on a part-time, intermittent, temporary, or otherwise contingent basis. Finally, the fifth aspect of underemployment focuses on the employee's earnings. If the employee's wages are 20% less than had been earned previously or 20% less than a comparable cohort, then the person is said to be underemployed.

As might be expected given the many definitions of underemployment, it is difficult to achieve a consensus regarding the prevalence of the phenomenon. However, although there is no government-sanctioned definition of underemployment, the Economic Policy Institute (EPS; 2003), a nonprofit, nonpartisan think tank, defines underemployment as including the unemployed, discouraged workers, involuntary part-timers (part-time workers who would prefer full-time work), and other individuals who want to work but face one or more barriers such as lack of transportation or child care. Using this definition, the Economic Policy Institute estimated that underemployment rose to 10.3% in June of 2003, the highest rate in the United States since 1994 when the Institute began to track these levels.

Similarly, although the federal government does not define underemployment, it does track workforce "underutilization," which is defined as including the total number of unemployed workers plus all marginally attached workers and those individuals who are involuntarily employed part-time for economic reasons. Using this definition, the Bureau of Labor Statistics (2003) estimated that underutilization of the workforce rose to 10.6% in June of 2003, the highest rate in the United States since 1995 when the bureau began to track this measure.

According to Feldman (1996), the above figures may be misleading because they do not take into account the definitions of underemployment used by most organizational researchers. He estimated that a figure of 25% underemployment of today's workforce might be more accurate and used the following statistics to support this higher number:

• About 25% of the workforce is employed in a part-time or temporary position. Of those, one third of the part-time workers and two thirds of the temporary workers would prefer permanent full-time positions (Ansberry, 1993; Feldman & Doerpinghaus, 1992; Morrow, 1993).

• Laid-off workers, when they do find reemployment, often obtain jobs that pay less and are of significantly lower quality than their previous jobs. Without job retraining, dislocated workers have typically been found to earn only 75% of what they might have earned had the layoff not occurred (Washington State Board for Community and Technical Colleges, 2000). For example, in their study of laid-off steelworkers, Leana and Feldman (1992) reported that "only 66% of the re-employed were working full-time, 85% were making 40% or less money than in their former jobs, and 70% reported receiving significantly fewer fringe benefits than in their previous jobs" (Feldman, 1996, p. 386). Blue-collar workers are not the only group affected by this trend. Rose (2003) reports that laid-off white-collar professionals are increasingly working part-time and in blue-collar jobs to make ends meet.

- Finally, many individuals who are entering the workforce for the first time (i.e., recent high school and college graduates) are accepting positions for which they are overqualified. Estimates of underemployment among this group range from 12% to 36% in the United States (Feldman, 1996).

Clearly, regardless of one's preference of definition or metric for assessing the prevalence of this phenomenon, too many of today's employees can be considered to be underemployed. In addition, this number is not expected to fall in the foreseeable future (EPS, 2003).

Job insecurity. The last economic stressor that we will consider is job insecurity. Although it may be an overstatement to say there are perhaps as many definitions of job insecurity as there are studies on the topic, there is nonetheless no agreed-on definition for this seemingly simple construct. Many studies fail to define the construct entirely or simply ask participants to indicate "the likelihood of losing their job in the next year," or if they "expect a change in their employment for the worse" (Probst, 2003a).

Greenhalgh and Rosenblatt (1984) were among the first researchers to provide a rigorous definition of the job insecurity construct as well as explicate some important organizational outcomes of the phenomenon. They defined job insecurity as "a perceived powerlessness to maintain desired continuity in a threatened job situation" (p. 438). Based on this definition, Ashford, Lee, and Bobko (1989) developed a measure of job insecurity that incorporated (a) the range of work situation features that could be in jeopardy, (b) the valence of each such feature, (c) the subjective probability of losing each feature, and (d) the number of sources of threat. Thus, job insecurity = [(σ importance of job feature × likelihood of losing job feature) + (σ importance of job loss × likelihood of job loss)] × perceived powerlessness to resist threat.

However, Probst (2003a) argued there are several potential drawbacks to defining and measuring job insecurity as such. First, research has found that employees do not always make a conceptual distinction between perceptions of "loss of job features" and "loss of employment" (Roskies & Louis-Guerin, 1990). Second, when conceptualizing job security, it is important to clearly distinguish *dimensions* of the construct itself from those variables that might *moderate* the relationships between the construct and outcome variables of interest. For example, job importance has been shown to moderate the effects of job insecurity on employee outcomes (Probst, 2000).

Based on the preceding arguments, Probst (2003a) developed an alternative theoretically grounded and empirically tested definition and measurement of job security that defined job security as "the perceived stability and continuance of one's job as one knows it" (p. 452). In contrast to other definitions of job security (e.g., Ashford et al., 1989; Greenhalgh & Rosenblatt, 1984), this definition does not attach or include any attitudinal or affective reactions to perceived job insecurity. Job insecurity is not predicted to occur only when individuals perceive that the future of their jobs is unstable *and* negatively react to it. Rather, it is proposed that job insecurity exists when the future of the individual's job is perceived to be unstable or at risk. Restricting the definition and measurement of job security to *perceptions* of job security allows researchers then to explore the moderators of the relationship between the individual's perception of job insecurity and his or her evaluative and affective responses to that perception.

Research shows that job insecurity is on the rise in today's workforce. Commercial rivalries around the globe, government deregulation of industry, and the ever-increasing pace of organizational technology change have led organizations worldwide to take extreme measures in order to remain competitive. Organizational restructuring in the form of corporate downsizing, mergers and acquisitions, plant closings, and workforce reorganizations affect millions of workers each year. According to the Society for Human Resource Management (2001), 43% of U.S. organizations conducted employee layoffs in 2000 and 2001 (prior to the events of September 11), with corporate reductions averaging 10 to 13% of the workforce. As a result, a large proportion of today's workforce is concerned about job loss. Whereas only 11% of workers reported being fearful of involuntary job loss during the recession years of the early 1990s, a survey conducted during the boom years of the late 1990s found that 37% of workers were fearful of being laid off in the near future (Belton, 1999). One can only presume that with the recent recession, these numbers have increased.

Summary. Unemployment, underemployment, and job insecurity are at historically high levels in today's workforce. Over 6% of the workforce is unemployed, approximately 25% are underemployed, and over one third worry about losing their jobs in the near future. Given the prevalence of these economic stressors, it is important to examine their causes and outcomes. Thus, the next section of the chapter presents an integration of the major theoretical models of the antecedents and consequences of unemployment, underemployment, and job insecurity.

An Integrated Model of the Causes and Consequences of Economic Stress

Despite the fact that unemployment, underemployment, and job insecurity are conceptually distinct phenomena and have been largely researched independently of each other, not surprisingly they do share similar antecedents and consequences. Because of this similarity in the causes and effects of these

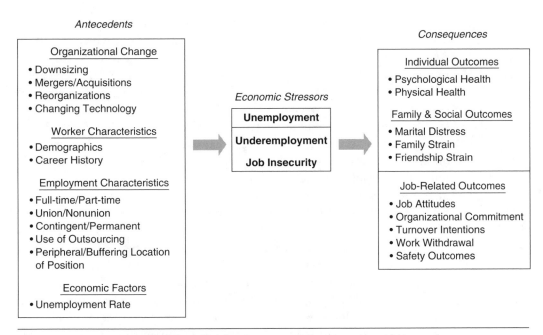

Figure 11.1   An Integrated Model of the Causes and Consequences of Unemployment,
                    Underemployment, and Job Insecurity.

economic stressors, it may be beneficial for the field of occupational health
to view these stressors in an integrated manner. Thus, the model presented
in Figure 11.1 and described below is an integration of three major theoretical models of unemployment (Warr, 1987), underemployment (Feldman,
1996), and job insecurity (Probst, 2002a).

Antecedents of Economic Stress

The predictors of economic stress at work can be summarized in four
categories: organizational change characteristics, worker characteristics,
employment characteristics, and economic factors. Organizational change
characteristics refer to downsizing, mergers and acquisitions, reorganizations,
and changing technology. Worker characteristics that predict economic stress
are primarily demographic in nature but also include the career history of
the worker. Employment characteristics pertain to the contractual relationship that the employee has with the organization (e.g., full-time/part-time,
contingent vs. permanent worker). Finally, economic indicators such as the
federal unemployment rate are expected to predict employee unemployment,
underemployment, and job insecurity. Empirical evidence for each of these
antecedents will be described below.

Organizational change characteristics. Formal announcement of layoffs, an
upcoming merger or acquisition, organizational restructuring, and/or downsizing are all potential organizational change characteristics that may increase

employee job insecurity and lead to job loss or underemployment (Ashford et al., 1989; Probst, 2003a, 2002b; Roskies & Louis-Guerin, 1990). Annually, approximately 500,000 U.S. employees can expect to lose their jobs as a result of these transitions (Simons, 1998). Fortune 500 companies alone reduced their total workforce from an aggregate 14.1 million employees to 11.6 million between 1983 and 1993. Recent years have seen record layoffs posted with 2 million jobs lost in 2001 and 1.4 million in 2002.

In addition to actual job loss, organizational change characteristics have also been shown to predict fears of job loss. Marks and Mirvis (1985) found fears of job loss and layoffs to be the most common consequence of a merger among both lower-level employees and senior executives. Turnley and Feldman (1999) found that workplace restructuring resulted in severe perceived psychological contract violations. Employees felt their expectations regarding job security, compensation, and opportunities for advancement were not realized. Similarly, Olson and Tetrick (1988) found that workplace reorganizations had a negative impact on satisfaction with job security.

An additional antecedent of economic stress may be related to changing organizational technology. A change in the technological systems of an organization can have a profound effect on the security of those positions experiencing the technology change. According to Hulin and Roznowski (1985), as the level of technological complexity required in an organization changes, so do the worker requirements, which can, in turn, affect the security of those individuals who cannot adapt to the change or whose skills are no longer required (i.e., obsolescence). Thus, technological change can increase job insecurity and eventually lead to job loss for those workers whose skills and/or positions are obsolete.

Finally, organizational change characteristics have also been found to predict underemployment. As organizational technology becomes more advanced and as organizations become leaner and meaner, "increasing numbers of highly-skilled workers are forced to take pay cuts and/or lower level jobs just to keep their employment" (Feldman, 1996, p. 391). If laid off, these workers often must accept pay cuts or demotions in order to find reemployment, thus reducing their rate of wage recovery.

Worker characteristics. Worker characteristics refers to a variety of individual differences variables that increase an individual's susceptibility to being laid off, perceiving that his or her job is insecure, or being underemployed. These variables include the employee gender and race, absenteeism rates, grievance filing, organizational tenure, career history, and education level.

Government data provided by the Bureau of Labor Statistics (2003) show that the rate of unemployment is traditionally higher among racial minorities than among whites. Among African Americans, the rate of unemployment has typically been double that of whites (e.g., 12% versus 5.6% unemployment in June 2003). Hispanics also face consistently higher levels of unemployment (7.4%) than do whites. Although the actual rates of unemployment for women are not higher than for men, research indicates that women tend to suffer from greater downward mobility than do men (Feldman, 1996; Newman, 1988). Not surprisingly, racial minorities and women have also been shown to experience higher levels of underemployment (Leana & Feldman, 1992; Newman, 1988) than their white counterparts and tend to remain unemployed for longer periods of time than do whites.

Employee absenteeism has also been theorized to be a predictor of economic stress (Probst, 2002a). Workers who are frequently absent are less likely to be secure in their position and are more likely to face involuntary turnover than workers who do not absent themselves as often. In support of this, Probst (2002a) found a negative relationship between absenteeism rates and job security among government workers, such that higher rates of absenteeism were related to less job security.

Research has also shown that workers who file grievances are less likely to be promoted, receive lower performance evaluations following the grievance activity, and have higher voluntary and involuntary turnover rates (Carnevale, Olson, & O'Connor, 1992; Lewin, 1987). In addition, Probst (2002a) found a significant negative relationship between government employee rates of grievance filing and their job security perceptions. Thus, although employees may be utilizing a company-endorsed grievance system, doing so may come at a price to the employee's job security, upward job mobility, and employment.

The frequent implementation of "last hired, first fired" lends credence to the suggestion that job longevity or organizational seniority may provoke feelings of security (Luthans & Sommer, 1999). In addition, Feldman (1996) suggests that older workers are less likely to be laid off than their younger counterparts due to seniority protections. However, he also cautions that, if laid off, older workers typically face more difficultly in finding reemployment. Thus, age may be negatively correlated with job insecurity and unemployment but positively correlated with underemployment.

An employee's career history is also expected to be related to his or her vulnerability to economic stress. Research (Kjos, 1988; Leana, Feldman, & Tan, 1998) suggests that employees who have been laid off in the past, have been laid off for longer periods of time, or are career plateaued are more likely to face underemployment. Feldman (1996) suggests this may be due to a marketplace stigma associated with having been laid off.

Finally, individuals with more education typically tend to hold positions of greater power within organizations. Thus, individuals with more education might perceive their job to be more secure than would individuals with little education (Roskies & Louis-Guerin, 1990). In addition, research indicates that workers with more education tend to experience fewer layoffs and less underemployment than their less educated counterparts (Feldman, 1996; Leana & Feldman, 1992; Newman, 1988). Thus, education appears to provide some protection against the economic stressors of job insecurity, underemployment, and unemployment.

Employment characteristics. *Employment characteristics* refers to the contractual relationship that an employee has with his or her organization. This includes whether the worker is employed on a temporary or contingent basis versus a permanent one; whether the worker is employed part-time versus full-time; and whether the job falls under union jurisdiction. Nonbinding, temporary, or part-time contracts are expected to result in lower job security, greater underemployment, and a higher likelihood of resulting in unemployment because these characteristics implicitly suggest a briefer tenure with the organization than a binding, permanent, full-time contract would suggest. In addition, these types of contractual arrangements also tend to pay less and offer fewer employee benefits, such as retirement and health benefits, than permanent or full-time arrangements. On the other hand, union affiliation might be expected to result in higher perceptions of job security and less underemployment and unemployment than no union affiliation. Because union employees have some formal recourse when they perceive their jobs to be threatened and are mandated by law (Worker Adjustment and Retraining Notification Act, 1989) to participate in any organizational mass layoff plans, one might expect that, all other things being equal, they would be less immediately susceptible to the economic stressors of unemployment, underemployment, and job insecurity. However, as noted above, lower levels of education, such as is associated with blue-collar, nonprofessional positions, would be associated with more economic stress.

The increasing reliance on outsourcing is another organizational trend that has implications for employee job insecurity, underemployment, and unemployment. Outsourcing is the delegation of major noncore organizational functions to specialized and efficient service providers (Elmuti, 2003). Between 1996 and 2001, U.S. businesses tripled their use of outsourcing and spent more than $300 billion for outsourced services (Elmuti, 2003). According to a recent study conducted by Bardhan and Kroll (2003), as many as 14 million white-collar service jobs in the United States are currently at risk of being outsourced to employees and organizations located outside the United States.

The implications of outsourcing were forecast nearly two decades ago by Hulin and Roznowski (1985) as they argued that the *proximity* of one's job in relation to the organizational technology can often be more important than the job itself in determining the security or vulnerability of that position. Positions can be classified into two different categories: (a) those that are core or essential (D'Aveni, 1989) to transforming organizational input into organizational output; and (b) those that are located in the buffering or peripheral systems of an organization (Hulin & Roznowski, 1985). According to Hulin and Roznowski (1985), all components other than the core technology systems exist solely to support the core activities. Thus, these buffering or peripheral positions are more likely to be seen as unnecessary or easily replaced than those found in the core organizational systems. And it is exactly these buffering functions that are increasingly being outsourced by organizations.

Similarly, Feldman (1996) predicted that levels of underemployment are likely to be higher in the buffering or peripheral systems of an organization. Specifically, he predicted that underemployment would be greater among managers, staff workers, and marketing and R&D employees. Line workers and nonmanagers (i.e., those individuals most directly involved in the transformation of organizational input into organizational output) are expected to be less vulnerable to unemployment and underemployment. Empirical support for this proposition is evidenced by the large numbers of organizations that downsize by cutting layers of middle management, organizational bureaucracy, and other nonessential positions (D'Aveni, 1989).

Economic factors. Economic factors are the last set of antecedents of economic stress. Clearly, when the state of the economy is poor, rates of unemployment increase. During the recessions of the mid-1970s, early 1980s, early 1990s, and our current recession, unemployment rates in the United States rose from lows of 4% to record highs of 9%, 10.8%, 7.6%, and 6.3% respectively (BLS, 2003). As the state of the economy worsens, the likelihood of underemployment also increases due to low levels of job creation and a scarcity of high-wage jobs (Fasenfest & Perrucci, 1994; Feldman, 1996; Zvonkovic, 1988). Finally, as the economy worsens and news of mass layoffs looms large in the public eye, employee perceptions of job insecurity are also likely to rise.

Consequences of Unemployment, Underemployment, and Job Insecurity

According to Warr's (1987) vitamin model of work and unemployment, individuals require nine environmental "vitamins" in order to maintain their psychological health: opportunity for control, opportunity for skill use, externally generated goals, variety, environmental clarity, availability of money, physical security, opportunity for interpersonal contact, and valued social position. Many of these vitamins are threatened or compromised under conditions of unemployment, underemployment, and job insecurity. For example, unemployed individuals have lost control over their employment status; their skills are no longer being utilized. The external structure and opportunities for social interaction that work provided are gone, and a loss of income and valued social position accompany job loss. Underemployed individuals are similarly "malnourished" or "deficient" with respect to their work-related vitamin needs. As noted earlier, the skills of underemployed individuals are frequently underutilized; income is often reduced substantially; and one's social position can be compromised as a result of underemployment. Finally, a loss of control over one's employment security, low environmental clarity, and an anticipation of a loss of income accompany employee job insecurity. Based on Warr's (1987) model, one would expect that the consequences of economic stress would be extensive and overwhelmingly negative as a result of these vitamin needs being compromised.

Indeed, research has found that individuals faced with unemployment, underemployment, or job insecurity experience strikingly similar outcomes that fall into one of three primary categories: individual outcomes, family and social outcomes, and job-related outcomes. The first two categories contain outcomes that have been witnessed among the unemployed, the underemployed, and the job insecure. The last category, however, contains outcomes that are relevant to only the underemployed and individuals faced with job insecurity but are not applicable to the unemployed due to their lack of employment relationship with an organization.

Individual outcomes. Numerous empirical studies have documented the negative impact that unemployment, underemployment, and job insecurity can have on the psychological and physical health of the affected individual. Unemployment has been found to be one of the top 10 traumatic life experiences (Spera, Buhrfeind, & Pennebaker, 1994). In a review of unemployment research conducted between the years 1994 and 1998, Hanisch (1999) reported that virtually every study documents negative psychological and physical outcomes for the affected individual. Psychologically, the studies reviewed in Hanisch (1999) indicate that the unemployed exhibit increases in hostility, depression, anxiety, psychiatric illness, worry, strain, stress, suicide attempts, alcohol abuse, violent behavior, anger, fear, paranoia, loneliness, pessimism, despair, and social isolation. In addition, individuals affected by unemployment exhibit decreases in self-esteem, positive affect, life satisfaction, perceptions of competence, feelings of mastery, aspiration level, and social identity (Hanisch, 1999).

There are multiple negative physical health effects as well to being unemployed. Unemployed individuals suffer from more headaches, stomachaches, sleep problems, lack of energy, and death from stroke, heart, and kidney disease than individuals who are employed. In addition, unemployment is associated with an increase in disability, hypertension, ulcers, vision problems, cholesterol levels, and other doctor-diagnosed illnesses (Hanisch, 1999).

Although the research on the psychological and physical health effects of underemployment is not as extensive, it does suggest that underemployment takes its toll on affected employees. Psychologically, empirical research has found underemployment to be associated with increases in depression, suicide, and learned helplessness and decreases in self-esteem and general affect (Dooley, Prause, & Ham-Rowbottom, 2000; Stack, 1982). Physically, underemployment has been reported to be associated with fatigue, backache, and muscular pains (Benavides, Benach, Diez-Roux, & Roman, 2000) as well as a host of other physical health factors (Friedland, 2000). In addition, analyses appear to suggest that the causal effect of underemployment on health is stronger than the effect of health on employment status (Friedland, 2000).

With respect to job insecurity, research from as early as the 1970s suggests that this economic stressor can have a detrimental effect on employee health outcomes. Cobb (1974) found that the stress of possible job termination was associated with significant increases in norepinephrine excretion, serum creatinine, serum uric acid, and serum cholesterol. Research since then has supported the finding that employees with low job security report a greater incidence of physical health conditions (Cottington, Matthews, Talbot, & Kuller, 1986; Dooley, Rook, & Catalano, 1987; Kuhnert, Sims, & Lahey, 1989; Probst, 2000, 2002a, 2003b; Roskies & Louis-Guerin, 1990) when compared with employees with secure jobs. More recently, in a four-wave longitudinal study of employees facing an organizational restructuring, Pollard (2001) found that job insecurity and role ambiguity significantly predicted higher blood pressure and cholesterol levels.

Job insecurity has also been associated with higher levels of general psychological distress (Dekker & Schaufeli, 1995; Probst, 2000, 2002a, 2003b) and with increased medical consultations for psychological distress (Catalano, Rook, & Dooley, 1986). Roskies and Louis-Guerin (1990) reported that job insecurity among managers was related to an increase in anxiety, depression, and general distress. Finally, Kuhnert et al. (1989) found that job insecurity was related to overall increases in somatization, depression, anxiety, and hostility.

To summarize, research on job insecurity, underemployment, and unemployment all seems to indicate that these economic stressors have negative implications for the psychological and physical health and well-being of affected workers.

Family and social outcomes. In addition to affecting the workers themselves, the phenomena of unemployment, underemployment, and job insecurity have grave implications for the families of affected employees and greater society. Research on unemployment has documented increases in spousal abuse, marital stress and dissolution, wife battering, and spousal depression and psychiatric disorders (Hanisch, 1999). At the same time, decreases in spousal well-being and spousal contact with friends have also been reported (Hanisch, 1999). In addition, there is a growing body of research that suggests the children of unemployed workers are also negatively affected. Increases in family conflict, child abuse, family violence, and aggression and hostility toward children have been documented, as well as decreases in family cohesion and the physical and mental well-being of children. Finally, research indicates that children of unemployed individuals act out more frequently, exhibit greater cognitive difficulties, and achieve lower levels of academic performance than children of employed individuals (Harland, Reijneveld, Brugman, Verloove-Vanhorick, & Verhulst, 2002) and are at increased risk of accidents (Stroem, 2002).

Similar findings have been documented for the families of underemployed individuals (Feldman, 1996). Zvonkovic (1988) found that underemployed husbands and their wives were less satisfied with their finances and marital relationship than a matched sample of fully employed couples. In addition, children of the underemployed face the challenges associated with parental job relocations (Newman, 1988), fewer material possessions compared with their peers (Leventman, 1981), and frequent premature entry into the workforce to make family ends meet (Newman, 1988). Finally, as has been reported in studies of unemployment, the underemployed also face social isolation as a result of their reduced financial situation and their inability to afford former leisure activities or to reciprocate social niceties (Leana & Feldman, 1992; Newman, 1988).

The implications of job insecurity on family and other social relationships have not been as well researched. However, what evidence there is suggests a trend similar to that described above for the economic stressors of unemployment and underemployment. Work and family research clearly suggests that these two spheres of life do not operate independently of each other. Therefore, it is not surprising that research has found that the economic worries of one member of a couple cross over to predict the job security of the other partner (Mauno & Kinnunen, 2002). Westman, Etzion, and Danon (2001), in their study of job insecurity and the crossover of burnout among married couples found that job insecurity was related to burnout and that the burnout experienced by one member of the couple influenced the burnout reported by the other member. More important, couples who were experiencing job insecurity exhibited higher levels of both given and received social undermining toward one another, behaviors that display negative affect and negative evaluation. Similar findings were reported by Burke and Greenglass (1999), who found that organizational restructuring predicted work-family conflict.

Children of parents who are experiencing job insecurity are also not immune from its negative effects. Barling, Dupré, and Hepburn (1998) found that children's perceptions of work, work beliefs, and work attitudes are influenced by their parents' job insecurity. Further, undergraduate student grades were negatively associated with children's perceptions of their parent's job insecurity (Barling & Mendelson, 1997). In an exploration of those findings, Barling, Zacharatos, and Hepburn (1998) report that this relationship is mediated by children's cognitive difficulties. This series of relationships is particularly alarming, as it suggests a potential negative cyclical relationship whereby parental job insecurity is related to lower academic performance and potentially fewer and/or lower-quality employment opportunities for their children.

Job-related outcomes. Extensive research has been conducted on the job-related outcomes associated with underemployment and job insecurity. A recent meta-analysis by Sverke, Hellgren, and Näswall (2002) summarizing the effects of job insecurity reported that insecure employees experience decreased job satisfaction (e.g., Ashford et al., 1989; Davy, Kinicki, & Scheck, 1991; Grunberg, Moore, & Greenberg, 1998), are less involved in their jobs (Kuhnert & Palmer, 1991), are less committed to the organization and more likely to quit their jobs (Ashford et al., 1989; Davy et al., 1991), place less trust in management (e.g., Ashford et al., 1989), and have lower levels of performance than workers with more job security (e.g., Abramis, 1994). Other studies not reviewed in the meta-analysis report significantly higher levels of job-related stress (Tombaugh & White, 1990), more work withdrawal behaviors such as absenteeism, tardiness, and work task avoidance (Probst, 1998), and lower levels of creativity (Probst & Tierney, 2003) among less secure workers.

Finally, recent research also suggests that worker safety can be compromised as a result of job insecurity. Landisberger, Cahill, and Schnall (1999) reported detrimental effects on employee health and injury rates in a variety of industries that were implementing lean production cultures. Probst and Brubaker (2001) found that employees who perceive their jobs to be insecure report lower levels of safety knowledge and reduced motivation to comply with safety policies. In turn, these variables were related to a decrease in safety compliance and an increase in job-related accidents and injuries. In a laboratory experiment, Probst (2002b) found that individuals threatened with layoffs displayed higher productivity than individuals who were not threatened with layoffs but also violated more safety policies and produced lower-quality products than their secure counterparts.

Research on the effects of underemployment has found a similar myriad of negative job-related outcomes (Feldman, 1996). Underemployed individuals have more negative career attitudes than their fully employed counterparts (Feldman, Doerpinghaus, & Turnley, 1994), reporting more career disillusionment and frustration (Borgen, Amundson, & Harder, 1988) and heavier reliance on non-performance-based behaviors to get ahead at work (Feldman & Weitz, 1991). Similar to the consequences of job insecurity, underemployment has also been shown to be related to higher levels of employee turnover (Burris, 1983; Borgen & Amundson, 1984; Feldman et al., 1994), lower levels of job satisfaction (Bolino & Feldman, 2000; Feldman & Turnley, 1995), and lower levels of self-reported employee performance (Bolino & Feldman, 2000).

Moderators of the Effects of Economic Stress

Despite the overwhelming evidence indicating that economic stress has enormous negative implications for individuals, organizations, and society, research also suggests that certain variables moderate the effects of economic stress by serving to either mitigate or exacerbate its consequences. Moderators of the effects of economic stress can be classified as individual differences moderators and organizational level moderators.

Individual differences moderators. Several characteristics that vary individually have been shown to moderate the effects of economic stress. Probst and Lawler (2003) found that cultural values influence the extent to which employees reacted negatively to perceived job insecurity, such that individuals with a collectivist cultural orientation (Triandis, 1995) were more likely to report lowered job satisfaction, more job stress, and more turnover intentions as a function of job insecurity than their individualistic counterparts. In a study of job insecurity in China, Probst and Yi (2003) examined the Chinese concept of *guanxi* (interpersonal connections) in relation to outcomes of job insecurity and found that employees with high levels of *guanxi* were more adversely affected by the perception of job insecurity—experiencing more negative work and job security satisfaction, greater turnover intentions, and more job stress—than employees with lower levels of *guanxi*. Together, these results suggest that culture can play an important role in predicting employee reactions to economic stress. They also suggest that multinational organizations need to take culture into account when implementing organizational changes in collectivist societies.

Self-efficacy for adapting to organizational change has also been found to moderate the effects of job insecurity on employee outcomes (Probst, 2001). Based on the theory of self-efficacy (Bandura, 1982), Probst (2001) predicted that self-efficacy would serve to buffer the stress of working in an organization undergoing a major transition, but only when the employee's outcome expectancy was positive. Results indicated that high self-efficacy was associated with more positive attitudinal and behavioral job-related outcomes. However, the positive effects of self-efficacy were attenuated when outcome expectancies (i.e., perceptions of job security) were low. Thus, to attenuate the effects of economic stress associated with organizational change, her results suggest that organizations should increase communication during times of organizational transition to improve the accuracy of job security perceptions and to increase the extent to which employees feel capable of handling pending organizational changes.

Similar research also suggests that workplace control (i.e., the ability to protect oneself from negative events at work) may be an important moderator of the stress associated with job insecurity. Based on data from 187 black South African gold miners, Barling and Kelloway (1996) concluded that perceived workplace control moderated the relationship between job insecurity and somatic symptoms and blood pressure. Job insecurity was positively associated with somatic symptoms and blood pressure when perceived workplace control was low but unrelated to these outcomes when perceived workplace control was high. Thus, similar to the self-efficacy findings noted above, individuals who perceive that they are able to protect themselves from negative events at work may be less vulnerable to the effects of economic stressors.

Another variable that has been theorized to buffer the effects of job insecurity on employee outcomes is emotional intelligence. Jordan, Ashkanasy, and Hartel (2002) argue that because emotional intelligence regulates the way in which individuals manage emotions, it will moderate the effects of job insecurity on emotional reactions and behaviors. Specifically, they predict that low emotional intelligence employees will be more likely to experience negative emotional reactions to job insecurity and utilize more negative coping strategies than high emotional intelligence employees. Although they do make predictions regarding underemployment and unemployment, by extension, one would predict similar relationships for low emotional intelligence individuals experiencing underemployment or unemployment.

A final individual differences variable, job involvement, has also been shown to moderate the effects of job insecurity on employee outcomes. In a study of 283 public sector employees experiencing workplace reorganization, Probst (2000) found that employees who were highly invested in their jobs were more adversely affected by job insecurity than less-invested employees. Specifically, highly involved employees reported more negative job attitudes, more health problems, and a higher level of psychological distress than their less-involved counterparts when they perceived their jobs to be threatened. These results and those of other similar research (e.g., Wiesenfeld, Brockner, Petzall, Wolf, & Bailey, 2001) imply that individuals who consider their jobs to be quite important, and whose jobs may be significant to their self-identity or financial security, are more at risk for negative outcomes as a result of job insecurity than individuals who are relatively indifferent to their jobs. Again, by extension, one would expect that similar findings would be found in the contexts of underemployment and unemployment as well.

Although there are organizational implications to the individual differences research discussed above, there are limitations to modifying individual differences variables. For example, organizations cannot change employee cultural values or levels of job involvement in an effort to ward off the negative effects of economic stress. However, research has shown that there are a number of organizational interventions that can be utilized to moderate the effects of economic stress, and these will be discussed below.

Organizational level moderators. One of the major sources of stress during times of organizational change is the uncertainty associated with such change. Whether an organization is restructuring, merging with another organization, or downsizing, research has shown that employees face great job insecurity during those periods. Recently, there have been a series of studies (Appelbaum & Donia, 2001; Probst, 2003c; Schweiger & DeNisi, 1991) conducted to assess the effectiveness of one organizational intervention—increased organizational communication—designed to reduce the consequences of such uncertainty.

Buono and Bowditch (1989) first noted that during times of organizational transition, the rumor mill often plays a greater role in employee perceptions than reality does, and it is this reliance on the rumor mill, and the absence of factual information, that can exacerbate employee anxiety. In a first attempt to assess whether enhanced organizational communication could dampen the dysfunctional effects of an organizational merger, Schweiger and DeNisi (1991) examined the effectiveness of a "realistic merger preview" in reducing employee uncertainty. Analogous to a realistic job preview, a realistic merger preview provides detailed information regarding the timeline of the merger, how the merger will affect employees, and other pertinent information. In a rare longitudinal field experiment in this context, Schweiger and DeNisi (1991) were able to provide realistic merger previews to employees in one plant while having a control plant where the merger was managed in a more traditional format. Although both plants experienced initial negative effects as a result of the announced upcoming merger, the plant that was offered a realistic merger preview rebounded more quickly from the negative effects, whereas employees in the control plant continued to report negative job attitudes, a lack of trust toward the company, and lower levels of self-reported performance 4 months following the merger announcement. Thus, as the authors noted, "a realistic merger preview seems to function at least as an inoculation that makes employees resistant to the negative effects of mergers and acquisitions, and its effects may go beyond that" (p. 129).

Similarly, based on data from nine case studies, Appelbaum and Donia (2001) developed a model for providing a "realistic downsizing preview" to counter the negative effects associated with surviving an organizational downsizing, known as survivor syndrome. Based on their analysis, they concluded that it is critical to continuously inform employees when downsizing is being considered in order to ward off the negative effects and to ensure that employees understand and are able to adapt to their new psychological contract with the organization.

Finally, a study conducted by Probst (2003c) found that organizational communication was critical in attenuating the negative effects of job insecurity on employee safety and health outcomes and job attitudes. In this multiorganization field study, she found that when job security was high, there were no differences in outcomes between employees who perceived low versus high levels of organizational communication. However, when employees felt their jobs were insecure, employees who perceived organizational communication was lacking reported twice as many accidents, over three times as many near accidents, lower job satisfaction, and more physical ailments than employees who were satisfied with the level of communication within the organization.

The preceding three studies suggest that organizational communication can play a pivotal role in attenuating the negative effects of job insecurity, downsizings, and mergers on employee physical and psychological outcomes. The attractiveness of this intervention is enhanced when one considers that providing increased communication within an organization is a relatively low-cost endeavor. For example, e-mail is free and bulletin board postings are inexpensive. Thus, organizations should strongly consider providing employees with brief daily or weekly updates regarding future organizational changes or events to help avoid the negative effects of economic stress on employees.

A slightly more involved organizational intervention found to reduce the negative effects of job insecurity is to increase employee participative decision making. Over the past two decades, there has been an increase in the popularity of employee participative decision-making initiatives within organizations (Liden & Tewksbury, 1995; Weber, 1990). Ironically, this increase in participative decision making comes as a direct result of organizational trends during the past two decades involving a flattening of their hierarchies and a reduction in their reliance on middle managers. Thus, some of the same organizational events that engender employee job insecurity simultaneously result in employees being more frequently asked to participate in and contribute to important organizational decision making.

Whereas job insecurity is associated with a lack of control perceived by employees, participative decision making has been found to be effective within organizations precisely because it allows employees to have a substantial voice in job-related decisions. Therefore, Probst (2003d) argued that organizations that provide their employees with participative decision-making opportunities offer their employees the chance to regain control over important aspects of their jobs that is otherwise lost under conditions of job insecurity. Data on the job satisfaction and turnover intentions of 807 employees in six different companies appeared to confirm this hypothesis (Probst, 2003d). Employees with greater participative decision-making opportunities reported fewer negative job-related consequences as a function of job insecurity compared with employees with fewer participative decision-making opportunities.

A final organizational intervention that shows promise in attenuating some of the worst effects of job insecurity involves the organizational safety climate under which employees work. As noted above, research is beginning to suggest that job insecurity has a detrimental effect on employee safety attitudes, behaviors, and outcomes (Grunberg et al., 1998; Probst, 2002b; Probst & Brubaker, 2001). However, recent research indicates that the effects of job insecurity on safety may be moderated by the extent to which the organization is seen as valuing and emphasizing safety. In a study of light manufacturing employees, Probst (2004) found that when employees perceived a weak organizational safety climate, job insecurity was related to lower levels of safety knowledge, less employee safety compliance, a greater number of employee accidents, more near miss incidents, a greater likelihood of workplace injury, and a greater incidence of repetitive motion injuries. However, when employees perceived that the organizational safety climate was strong, the slope of the relationships between job insecurity and these safety outcomes was consistently attenuated. These results suggest that particularly during times of organizational transition and employee economic stress, it is wise for organizations to consistently send a strong message regarding the importance of safety to their employees. In today's weakened economy with its record layoffs, organizations should consider the messages being conveyed to workers who may be seeking such cues as to the optimal means of retaining their jobs.

Unresolved Questions and Future Research Needs

Despite the large body of research that has been conducted on the antecedents, consequences, and moderators of economic stressors, there remain a large number of unresolved questions that beg empirical inquiry. In addition, there are a number of measurement issues that plague the field and impede the successful integration of the research that has been conducted to date.

Measurement Issues

The key measurement issues in the area of economic stress concern the definition of, dimensionality of, and measures used to identify individuals suffering from economic stress. As noted earlier, a continuing problem in the field of job insecurity research has been the lack of a comprehensive definition and measurement of job security, with many studies failing to define the construct and/or using one- or two-item indicators to measure job security. In addition, there is no consensus regarding the dimensionality of job insecurity (Sverke et al., 2002). Is job insecurity a global perception about the future of one's job or does it break down into a variety of different facets (e.g., security regarding organizational status, employment security, career opportunities)? Without an agreed-on definition of what constitutes job insecurity and a consistently used measure, it is difficult for the field to integrate the knowledge that has already been gained.

Research into the causes and consequences of underemployment is similarly hampered by definitional problems. Although underemployment implies a relative deprivation of sorts, there is no consensus regarding what is the appropriate comparison for determining which individuals are relatively deprived. For example, is the appropriate comparison one's previous work history and pay, or should the comparison be to a cohort matched by age, gender, years of experience, and so forth? In addition to questions surrounding the appropriate comparison group, an equally important unresolved question concerns the level of relative deprivation. For example, some researchers define underemployment as 33% less pay than earned in a previous job (Elder, 1974), whereas others have used a 20% income loss as the standard (Zvonkovich, 1988). Still other researchers and government entities define underemployment based on involuntary part-time work. A final question concerns the measurement of underemployment and whether underemployment is more appropriately classified as a discrete or continuous variable. Is a measurement of different levels of underemployment meaningful, or is a categorization of "fully employed" versus "underemployed" equally informative?

There are competing definitions of unemployment as well. Whereas the federal government only considers individuals to be unemployed if they do not have a job, have actively looked for work in the prior 4 weeks, and are currently available for work, unemployment researchers take a much broader and more inclusive definition that frequently overlaps with the government's definition of underemployed individuals.

The lack of consistent definitions and measures for economic stressors poses several challenges for researchers. First, it is difficult to accurately assess the prevalence of the phenomena without agreed-on definitions. Second, it is difficult and sometimes unwise to compare the results of research on the same topic that have used different definitions or classification systems. Finally, interventions aimed at particular groups of employees or individuals are difficult to implement if there is no consensus regarding who is most appropriately targeted.

Future Research Needs

In addition to the pressing measurement issues outlined above, there are many other avenues of research that await attention by investigators in the field of economic stressors. First, although the review was by no means comprehensive, it is apparent from the discussion of research on moderators of economic stress that much of the moderator research has focused on individual differences variables rather than organizational interventions. Unfortunately, this type of research, although identifying employees and individuals more likely to be adversely affected by economic stress, does not provide organizations with practical interventions to ameliorate the negative effects of economic stress.

The overwhelming number of cross-sectional studies on the effects of economic stress highlights another pressing need for future research. For the field to progress, greater efforts should be made to conduct longitudinal research that incorporates time as an independent variable of interest. When longitudinal research is conducted, the data collection intervals are often based on experimental convenience rather than on empirically or theoretically derived temporal intervals thought to underlie the processes under investigation (Kelly & McGrath, 1988). Some causal processes take longer to unfold than others. Therefore, it is important to specify in our theories of organizational change and economic stress, and confirm empirically, the temporal intervals required for these inferred causal processes to unfold.

In addition to specifying the temporal intervals, it is equally important to determine the temporal shape (Kelly & McGrath, 1988) of theorized causal processes. For example, does job insecurity have a cumulative negative effect on individuals that gradually worsens with time? Do mergers and acquisitions result in an all-at-once persistent change in job attitudes, or do these attitude changes decay over time? Are the effects of unemployment immediately seen, or do they gradually worsen or improve over time? The conflicting findings of researchers in the field of economic stress may be more a function of when measurements were obtained and the temporal shape of the process being examined than a causal effect that truly exists.

A related avenue of future research concerns a better examination of the process by which economic stress results in negative consequences for affected individuals. Although the research reviewed in this chapter shows time and again a multitude of negative outcomes, very little research investigates mediators of the process (i.e., why these negative outcomes occur as a function of economic stress). A notable exception to this trend is the recent research conducted by Price, Choi, and Vinokur (2002) that examined the chain of events that lead from job loss to depression, impaired functioning, and poor health. In their longitudinal research conducted over a 2-year period, they found that financial strain and loss of personal control were critical mediators of the relationship between job loss and the above outcomes. Additional research such as this is needed to clarify the mechanisms by which job loss, underemployment, and job insecurity lead to adverse outcomes.

Finally, there is a need for multilevel research to be conducted on the antecedents and consequences of economic stressors. Research on the topic of economic stress is currently being conducted at many different levels (i.e., economic level, community level, workgroup level, and individual employee level). However, these different streams of research are largely being conducted independent of each other (e.g., economic researchers focusing primarily on more macro level data collection and psychological researchers collecting primarily micro level data). However, with the advent of sophisticated data analytic techniques, such as hierarchical linear modeling (HLM), each of these units of analysis can be fruitfully explored in an integrated examination of the contribution of macro and micro level variables on the processes of interest.

Implications for Practice, Policy, and Intervention

Although theory and research on economic stress (the model presented in Figure 11.1 being no exception) typically consider job insecurity, underemployment, and unemployment to be separate independent stressors, they should be considered as linked nonrecursive phenomena (Burchell, 1992). Individuals in insecure jobs are more likely to become unemployed. Unemployed individuals are more likely to regain employment at a lower level than had been enjoyed prior to the layoff, thus becoming underemployed (Kjos, 1988; Leana et al., 1998). Underemployed individuals are theorized to have higher levels of absenteeism and lower job performance and to engage in fewer organizational citizenship behaviors (Feldman, 1996). As noted earlier, these variables have been found to be related to lower job security. Thus, job insecurity, underemployment, and unemployment are closely and likely causally related in a nonrecursive fashion, resulting in affected workers falling into a downward spiral of decreasing job mobility. Accordingly, any response to today's increasing levels of economic stress should be developed and implemented in a systematic integrated fashion.

The onus of responding to today's economic stress falls on three different entities, each of which bears responsibility for minimizing the likelihood of, and consequences from, job insecurity, underemployment, and unemployment: (a) individual employees; (b) employing organizations; and (c) federal, state, and local governments.

Implications for Individuals: Choosing the Right Job in the First Place

The Bureau of Labor Statistics estimates that 5.9 million college graduates (17%) work in jobs that do not require a bachelor's degree (Fleetwood & Shelley, 2000). Not surprisingly, an equal percentage (or one in six college graduates) earn less than the median for all high school graduates (Dohm & Wyatt, 2002). Fleetwood and Shelley (2000) theorize that the relatively large number of college graduates holding non-college-level jobs may be due to (a) a genuine preference for non-college-level work; (b) an unwillingness to relocate to obtain a college-level job; or (c) an inability to find a college-level position due to poor academic preparation or marginal academic skills. Regardless of the reason, as Feldman (1996) notes, "At a minimum, this suggests that students do not receive (or do not utilize) adequate career planning services. . . . It may also suggest that there are more students who are attending 4-year liberal arts colleges than can benefit from them" (p. 404).

These data imply that individuals need to bear a large portion of the responsibility for ensuring that they do not become underemployed by seeking out career counseling early, having discussions with high school guidance counselors, and choosing the appropriate level of education needed to obtain a job in their chosen career field. Despite the lure of having "the college experience," vocational institutes or technical training schools may provide a quicker path to a skilled position than a 4-year college education for a certain segment of the workforce-bound population (Feldman, 1996).

For the majority of the workforce-bound population, however, the data are clear that higher education does have its benefits in terms of future career options, better promotion opportunities, and higher earnings. Although not requiring a college degree, many jobs nonetheless may still be classified as "college preferred" (Dohm & Wyatt, 2002). And data show that a college degree results in an average "earnings premium" of 61% over a high school diploma (Crosby, 2000). In addition, more-educated workers appear to be less vulnerable to layoffs and underemployment than their less-educated counterparts (Feldman, 1996).

In summary, the primary implication of research on economic stress for individuals is to allocate sufficient time and energy to career planning. Choose a career based on thorough research into the knowledge, skills, and abilities

(KSAs) required for the occupation, an analysis of one's own skills and abilities, an investigation into the occupational outlook for that career, and an understanding of the necessary level of education to enter that occupation.

Organizational Responsibilities: Is Downsizing Really the Answer?

Although individuals bear a certain degree of responsibility for ensuring their economic well-being, employing organizations shoulder an equivalent, if not greater, obligation for preventing economic stress among their employees. Given that organizational change characteristics, such as downsizing, mergers and acquisitions, and other forms of restructuring, play a major role in determining whether an employee will suffer from job insecurity, underemployment, or unemployment, it is worthwhile to examine some of the reasons that organizations undertake these drastic measures and whether they pay off.

Advocates of downsizing cite lower overhead, less bureaucracy, and increases in productivity and profits as a few of the anticipated benefits (Cascio, 1993). However, research shows that these benefits frequently do not materialize. According to Cascio (1993), less than one third of restructuring firms reported profit increases; stock prices of downsizing companies did not improve over a 3-year period compared with those of stable employers; and the average improvement in return on assets (ROA) for corporate downsizers was a negligible 0.3%, 2 years after downsizing (Morris, Cascio, & Young, 1999).

Despite the fact that the anticipated benefits of downsizing do not often materialize, more than 85% of Fortune 1,000 companies downsized between 1987 and 1991, and more than 50% downsized in 1990 alone (Cascio, 1993). At the same time, more than 50% of downsizers reported that they began the downsizing with no outplacement programs or similar policies to minimize the negative effects of the restructuring on their employees (Cascio, 1993). These numbers indicate that there are many steps organizations could be taking to minimize economic stress among their employees.

What can organizations do? According to Morris et al. (1999), organizations must first determine if downsizing is truly needed, why it is being considered, what the expected benefits will be, and if the research shows that they are likely to transpire. Second, if an organization must downsize, downsize assets, not employees. Not only is this better for the employees; research indicates it is better for the organization. Whereas the ROA of so-called "employment downsizers" declined in the year following the layoffs, the ROA for "asset downsizers" actually increased by nearly 2% (Morris et al., 1999). Third, despite the fact that staffing requirements will naturally fluctuate over the course of the business cycle, repeated downsizing and upsizing of the workforce can be costlier than maintaining a stable workforce after taking into account the costs associated with unemployment assistance, rehiring, severance packages, retraining, and other forms of outplacement assistance

(Morris et al., 1999). In addition to these tangible costs, the costs associated with layoff survivor syndrome (Brockner, 1985)—the myriad consequences seen among employees not laid off—can be severe. Layoff survivors are more risk averse, stressed, anxious, and distrustful of management; experience more role ambiguity and role conflict; and report lower self-confidence, morale, and job satisfaction than employees in stable companies.

Finally, if an organization makes the decision to downsize, it should downsize in as humane a manner as possible to minimize the effects of resulting economic stress for employees. The 1989 Worker Adjustment and Retraining Notification (WARN) Act requires employers to provide employees with 60 days advance notice of covered plant closings and mass layoffs. In addition to providing adequate advance notice, organizations should be prepared to provide outplacement assistance to affected workers. Finally, they should ensure that the lines of communication remain open with their employees. As noted in the review of research on the effects of organizational communication, an enhanced effort at maintaining communication with employees can result in an attenuation of some of the negative effects of the restructuring.

Governmental Policies and Programs

The last major entities that are part of any concerted effort to prevent and combat the negative effects of economic stress are the federal, state, and local governments. As part of their social safety net, federal and state governments provide unemployment wages to laid-off employees. Over 96% of all wage and salaried civilian jobs are covered by unemployment insurance or unemployment compensation. Typically, 26 weeks of unemployment benefits are offered; however, under poor economic conditions, the federal government has granted additional weeks. For example, in May of 2003, President Bush signed legislation to grant an additional 13 weeks of benefits largely due to the poor economy. In addition, employees in certain states, such as Oregon and Washington, that were hardest hit by the economic downturn were offered an additional 26 weeks beyond that.

In addition to financially supporting unemployed workers, government agencies also provide retraining for laid-off workers in order to facilitate their entry into a different occupation with more long-term growth opportunities. The 1998 Workforce Investment Act, a federal job training reform law, provides block grants to states that target employment and training for dislocated workers, disadvantaged adults, and disadvantaged youth. The majority of the dislocated worker funds go to local areas, which are responsible for providing reemployment services through one-stop centers and employment and training providers.

Compared with the vast government resources aimed at alleviating the economic stress of the unemployed, there are relatively few government programs designed to mitigate the stress associated with underemployment or job insecurity. Under the Department of Commerce, the Economic Development

Agency provides grants to nonprofit and local governments for projects that alleviate unemployment and underemployment in economically distressed areas. Since 1965, this agency has invested $16 billion across its programs (averaging approximately $400 million per year). However, this figure pales in comparison with the amount spent each year—$2.2 billion in 2002 alone—on the unemployed for unemployment insurance. Thus, government appears to spend more money on short-term fixes than on long-term prevention.

Epilogue

Unemployment, underemployment, and job insecurity are at historically high levels in today's workforce. Over 6% of the workforce is unemployed, approximately 25% are underemployed, and over one third worry about losing their jobs in the near future. This chapter developed an integrated model of the causes and consequences of such economic stress and reviewed major theoretical and empirical research that suggests the consequences of these economic stressors can be severe and affect not only employees, but also their families, society, and employing organizations. Finally, future directions for research were suggested, as were implications for individual, organizational, and governmental practice, policy, and intervention.

References

Abramis, D. J. (1994). Relationship of job stressors to job performance: Linear or an inverted-U? *Psychological Reports, 75,* 547–558.

Ansberry, C. (1993, March 11). Workers are forced to take more jobs with fewer benefits. *Wall Street Journal,* pp. A1, A9.

Appelbaum, S. H., & Donia, M. (2001). The realistic downsizing preview: A multiple case study, part 1: The methodology and results of data collection. *Career Development International, 6,* 128–148.

Ashford, S., Lee, C., & Bobko, P. (1989). Content, causes, and consequences of job insecurity: A theory-based measure and substantive test. *Academy of Management Journal, 32,* 803–829.

Bandura, A. (1982). Self-efficacy mechanism in human agency. *American Psychologist, 37,* 122–147.

Bardhan, A. D., & Kroll, C. A. (2003). *The new wave of outsourcing.* University of California, Berkeley, Fisher Center for Real Estate and Urban Economics.

Barling, J., Dupré, K. E., & Hepburn, C. G. (1998). Effects of parents' job insecurity on children's work beliefs and attitudes. *Journal of Applied Psychology, 83,* 112–118.

Barling, J., & Kelloway, E. K. (1996). Job insecurity and health: The moderating role of workplace control. *Stress Medicine, 12,* 253–259.

Barling, J., & Mendelson, M. B. (1997). Parents' job insecurity affects children's grade performance through the indirect effects of beliefs in an unjust world and negative mood. *Journal of Occupational Health Psychology, 4,* 347–355.

Barling, J., Zacharatos, A., & Hepburn, C. G. (1998). Parents' job insecurity affects children's academic performance through cognitive difficulties. *Journal of Applied Psychology, 84,* 437–444.

Belton, B. (1999, February 17). Fed chief: Tech advances raise job insecurity. *USA Today,* p. B2.

Benavides, F. G., Benach, J., Diez-Roux, A. V., & Roman, C. (2000). How do types of employment relate to health indicators? Findings from the Second European Survey on working conditions. *Journal of Epidemiology and Community Health, 54,* 494–501.

Bolino, M. C., & Feldman, D. C. (2000). The antecedents and consequences of underemployment among expatriates. *Journal of Organizational Behavior, 21,* 889–911.

Borgen, W., & Amundson, N. (1984). *The experience of unemployment: Implications for counseling the unemployed.* Scarborough, Ontario: Nelson Canada.

Borgen, W., Amundson, N., & Harder, H. G. (1988). The experience of underemployment. *Journal of Employment Counseling, 25,* 149–159.

Brockner, J. (1985). Layoffs, self-esteem, and survivor guilt: Motivational, affective, and attitudinal consequences. *Organizational Behavior and Human Decision Processes, 36,* 229–244.

Buono, A. F., & Bowditch, J. L. (1989). *The human side of mergers and acquisitions: Managing collisions between people, cultures, and organizations.* San Francisco: Jossey Bass.

Burchell, B. (1992). Towards a social psychology of the labour market: Or why we need to understand the labour market before we can understand unemployment. *Journal of Occupational and Organizational Psychology, 65,* 345–354.

Bureau of Labor Statistics (BLS). (2001). *Labor force statistics from the Current Population Survey.* Retrieved July 7, 2003, from www.bls.gov/cps/cps_faq.htm

Bureau of Labor Statistics (BLS). (2003). *Alternative measures of labor underutilization.* Retrieved July 7, 2003, from www.stats.bls.gov/news.release/empsit.t12.htm

Burke, R. J., & Greenglass, E. R. (1999). Work-family conflict, spouse support, and nursing staff well-being during organizational restructuring. *Journal of Occupational Health Psychology, 4,* 327–336.

Burris, B. H. (1983). The human effects of underemployment. *Social Problems, 31,* 96–110.

Carnevale, P. J., Olson, J. B., & O'Connor, K. M. (1992, June). *Reciprocity and informality in a laboratory grievance system.* Paper presented at the International Association of Conflict Management, Minneapolis, MN.

Cascio, W. F. (1993). Downsizing: What do we know? What have we learned? *Academy of Management Executive, 7,* 95–104.

Catalano, R., Rook, K., & Dooley, D. (1986). Labor markets and help-seeking: A test of the employment security hypothesis. *Journal of Health and Social Behavior, 27,* 277–287.

Cobb, S. (1974). Physiologic changes in men whose jobs were abolished. *Journal of Psychosomatic Research, 18,* 245–258.

Cottington, E. M., Matthews, K. A., Talbot, E., & Kuller, L. H. (1986). Occupational stress, suppressed anger, and hypertension. *Psychosomatic Medicine, 48,* 249–260.

Crosby, O. (2000, Winter). Degrees to dollars: Earnings of college graduates in 1998. *Occupational Outlook Quarterly,* 31–38.

D'Aveni, R. A. (1989). The aftermath of organizational decline: A longitudinal study of the strategic and managerial characteristics of declining firms. *Academy of Management Journal, 32,* 577–605.

Davy, J., Kinicki, A., & Scheck, C. (1991). Developing and testing a model of survivor responses to layoffs. *Journal of Vocational Behavior, 38,* 302–317.

Dekker, S. W., & Schaufeli, W. B. (1995). The effects of job insecurity on psychological health and withdrawal: A longitudinal study. *Australian Psychologist, 30,* 57–63.

Dohm, A., & Wyatt, I. (2002, Fall). College at work: Outlook and earnings for college graduates, 2000–10. *Occupational Outlook Quarterly,* 3–15.

Dooley, D., Prause, J., & Ham-Rowbottom, K. A. (2000). Underemployment and depression: Longitudinal relationships. *Journal of Health & Social Behavior, 41,* 421–436.

Dooley, D., Rook, K., & Catalano, R. (1987). Job and non-job stressors and their moderators. *Journal of Occupational Psychology, 60,* 115–132.

Economic Policy Institute. (2003). Economic snapshots. Retrieved July 7, 2003, from www.epinet.org/content.cfm/webfeatures_snapshots_archive_04232003

Elder, G. (1974). *Children of the Great Depression: Social change in life experiences.* Chicago: University of Chicago Press.

Elmuti, D. (2003). The perceived impact of outsourcing on organizational performance. *Mid-American Journal of Business, 18*(2), 33–41.

Fasenfest, D., & Perrucci, R. (1994). Changes in occupation and income, 1979–1989: An analysis of the impact of place and race. *International Journal of Contemporary Sociology, 31,* 203–233.

Feldman, D. C. (1996). The nature, antecedents, and consequences of underemployment. *Journal of Management, 22,* 385–407.

Feldman, D. C., & Doerpinghaus, H. I. (1992). Patterns of part-time employment. *Journal of Vocational Behavior, 41,* 282–294.

Feldman, D. C., Doerpinghaus, H. I., & Turnley, W. H. (1994). Managing temporary workers: A permanent HRM challenge. *Organizational Dynamics, 23,* 1–15.

Feldman, D. C., & Turnley, W. H. (1995). Underemployment among recent college graduates. *Journal of Organizational Behavior, 16,* 691–706.

Feldman, D. C., & Weitz, B. A. (1991). From the invisible hand to the gladhand: Understanding the nature of a careerist orientation to work. *Human Resource Management, 30,* 237–257.

Fleetwood, C., & Shelley, K. (2000, Fall). The outlook for college graduates, 1998–2008: A balancing act. *Occupational Outlook Quarterly,* 3–9.

Friedland, D. S. (2000). Underemployment: Consequences for the health and well-being of workers (Doctoral dissertation, University of Michigan, 2000). *Dissertation Abstracts International, 61,* 1119.

Greenhalgh, L., & Rosenblatt, Z. (1984). Job insecurity: Towards conceptual clarity. *Academy of Management Review, 9,* 438–448.

Grunberg, L., Moore, S., & Greenberg, E. S. (1998). Work stress and problem alcohol behavior: A test of the spillover model. *Journal of Organizational Behavior, 19,* 487–502.

Hanisch, K. (1999). Job loss and unemployment research from 1994 to 1998: A review and recommendations for research and intervention. *Journal of Vocational Behavior, 55,* 188–220.

Harland, P., Reijneveld, S. A., Brugman, E., Verloove-Vanhorick, S. P., & Verhulst, F. C. (2002). Family factors and life events as risk factors for behavioral and emotional problems in children. *European Child & Adolescent Psychiatry, 11,* 176–184.

Hulin, C. L., & Roznowski, M. (1985). Organizational technologies: Effects on organizations' characteristics and individuals' responses. *Research in Organizational Behavior, 7,* 39–85.

Jordan, P. J., Ashkanasy, N. M., & Hartel, C. E. J. (2002). Emotional intelligence as a moderator of emotional and behavioral reactions to job insecurity. *Academy of Management Review, 27,* 361–372.

Judge, T. A., & Hulin, C. L. (1993). Job satisfaction as a reflection of disposition: A multiple source causal analysis. *Organizational Behavior and Human Decision Processes, 56,* 388–421.

Kaufman, H. (1982). *Professionals in search of work.* New York: Wiley.

Kelly, J. R., & McGrath, J. E. (1988). *On time and method.* Newbury Park, CA: Sage.

Kinnunen, U., & Pulkkinen, L. (1998). Linking economic stress to marital quality among Finnish marital couples. *Journal of Family Issues, 19,* 705–724.

Kjos, D. (1988). Job search activity patterns of successful and unsuccessful job seekers. *Journal of Employment Counseling, 5,* 4–6.

Kuhnert, K., & Palmer, D. R. (1991). Job security, health and the intrinsic and extrinsic characteristics of work. *Group and Organization Studies, 16,* 178–192.

Kuhnert, K., Sims, R., & Lahey, M. (1989). The relationship between job security and employees' health. *Group and Organization Studies, 14,* 399–410.

Landisberger, P. A., Cahill, J., & Schnall, P. (1999). The impact of lean production and related new systems of work organization on worker health. *Journal of Occupational Health Psychology, 4,* 108–130.

Leana, C. R., & Feldman, D. C. (1992). *Coping with job loss: How individuals, organizations, and communities respond to layoffs.* New York: Lexington Books.

Leana, C. R., Feldman, D. C., & Tan, G. Y. (1998). Research predictors of coping behavior after a layoff. *Journal of Organizational Behavior, 19,* 85–97.

Leventman, P. (1981). *Professionals out of work.* New York: Free Press.

Lewin, D. (1987). Dispute resolution in the non-union firm: A theoretical and empirical analysis. *Journal of Conflict Resolution, 31,* 465–502.

Liden, R. C., & Tewksbury, T. W. (1995). Empowerment and work teams. In G. R. Ferris, S. D. Rosen, & O. T. Barnum (Eds.), *Handbook of human resource management* (pp. 386–403). Cambridge, MA: Blackwell.

Luthans, B., & Sommer, S. M. (1999). The impact of downsizing on workplace attitudes: Differing reactions of managers and staff in a health care organization. *Group and Organization Management, 24,* 46–70.

Marks, M. L., & Mirvis, P. H. (1985). Merger syndrome: Stress and uncertainty. *Mergers and Acquisitions, 20,* 50–55.

Mauno, S., & Kinnunen, U. (2002). Perceived job insecurity among dual-earner couples: Do its antecedents vary according to gender, economic sector and the measure used? *Journal of Occupational and Organizational Psychology, 75,* 295–314.

Morris, J. R., Cascio, W. F., & Young, C. E. (1999). Downsizing after all these years: Questions and answers about who did it, how many did it, and who benefited from it. *Organizational Dynamics, 27,* 78–87.

Morrow, L. (1993, March 29). The temping of America. *Time,* 40–47.

Newman, K. S. (1988). *Falling from grace.* New York: Free Press.

Olson, D. A., & Tetrick, L. E. (1988). Organizational restructuring: The impact on role perceptions, work relationships, and satisfaction. *Group and Organization Studies, 13,* 374–388.

Pollard, T. M. (2001). Changes in mental well-being, blood pressure and total cholesterol levels during workplace reorganization: The impact of uncertainty. *Work & Stress, 15,* 14–28.

Price, R. H., Choi, J. N., & Vinokur, A. D. (2002). Links in the chain of adversity following job loss: How financial strain and loss of personal control lead to depression, impaired functioning, and poor health. *Journal of Occupational Health Psychology, 7,* 302–312.

Probst, T. M. (1998). *Antecedents and consequences of job insecurity: Development and test of an integrated model.* Unpublished doctoral dissertation, University of Illinois at Urbana-Champaign.

Probst, T. M. (2000). Wedded to the job: Moderating effects of job involvement on the consequences of job insecurity. *Journal of Occupational Health Psychology, 5,* 63–73.

Probst, T. M. (2001, May). *Self-efficacy for adapting to organizational transitions: It helps, but only when the prospects are bright.* Paper presented at the meeting of the Western Psychological Association, Maui, HI.

Probst, T. M. (2002a). The impact of job insecurity on employee work attitudes, job adaptation, and organizational withdrawal behaviors. In J. M. Brett & F. Drasgow (Eds.), *The psychology of work: Theoretically based empirical research* (pp. 141–168). Hillsdale, NJ: Lawrence Erlbaum.

Probst, T. M. (2002b). Layoffs and tradeoffs: Production, quality, and safety demands under the threat of job loss. *Journal of Occupational Health Psychology, 7,* 211–220.

Probst, T. M. (2003a). Development and validation of the Job Security Index and the Job Security Satisfaction Scale: A classical test theory and IRT approach. *Journal of Occupational and Organizational Psychology, 76,* 451–467.

Probst, T. M. (2003b). Exploring employee outcomes of organizational restructuring: A Solomon four-group study. *Group & Organization Management, 28,* 416–439.

Probst, T. M. (2003c). *Organizational communication: A method to stemming job insecurity's madness?* Unpublished manuscript, Washington State University, Vancouver.

Probst, T. M. (2003d, March). *Participative decision making: A simple solution to job insecurity's consequences?* Paper presented at the 3rd biennial APA/NIOSH Conference on Work, Stress, and Health, Toronto, Canada.

Probst, T. M. (2004). Safety and insecurity: Exploring the moderating effect of organizational safety climate. *Journal of Occupational Health Psychology, 9,* 3–10.

Probst, T. M., & Brubaker, T. L. (2001). The effects of job insecurity on employee safety outcomes: Cross-sectional and longitudinal explorations. *Journal of Occupational Health Psychology, 6,* 139–159.

Probst, T. M., & Lawler, J. (2003). *Cultural values as moderators of the outcomes of job insecurity: The role of individualism and collectivism.* Unpublished manuscript, Washington State University, Vancouver.

Probst, T. M., & Tierney, B. (2003). *Productivity and creativity: The ups and downs of employee job insecurity.* Unpublished manuscript, Washington State University, Vancouver.

Probst, T. M., & Yi, X. (2003). *Guanxi in Chinese organizations: A help or hindrance in insecure times?* Manuscript submitted for publication.

Rose, B. (2003, April 4). Underemployment has onetime professionals working part-time, blue-collar jobs. *Knight Ridder Tribune Business News*, p. 1.

Roskies, E., & Louis-Guerin, C. (1990). Job insecurity in managers: Antecedents and consequences. *Journal of Organizational Behavior, 11*, 345–359.

Schweiger, D. M., & DeNisi, A. S. (1991). Communication with employees following a merger: A longitudinal field experiment. *Academy of Management Journal, 34*, 110–135.

Simons, J. (1998, November 18). Despite low unemployment, layoffs soar—Corporate mergers and overseas turmoil are cited as causes. *Wall Street Journal*, p. A2.

Society for Human Resource Management. (2001). *Layoffs and job security survey*. Alexandria, VA: Author.

Spera, S. P., Buhrfeind, E. D., & Pennebaker, J. W. (1994). Expressive writing and coping with job loss. *Academy of Management Journal, 37*, 722–733.

Stack, S. (1982). Suicide in Detroit 1975: Changes and continuities. *Suicide and Life-Threatening Behavior, 12*, 67–83.

Stroem, S. (2002). Keep out of the reach of children: Parental unemployment and children's accident risks in Sweden 1991–1993. *International Journal of Social Welfare, 11*, 40–52.

Sverke, M., Hellgren, J., & Näswall, K. (2002). No security: A meta-analysis and review of job insecurity and its consequences. *Journal of Occupational Health Psychology, 7*, 242–264.

Tombaugh, J. R., & White, L. P. (1990). Downsizing: An empirical assessment of survivors' perceptions in a postlayoff environment. *Organization Development Journal, 8*, 32–43.

Triandis, H. C. (1995). *Individualism and collectivism*. Boulder, CO: Westview.

Turnley, W. H., & Feldman, D. C. (1999). The impact of psychological contract violation on exit, voice, loyalty, and neglect. *Human Relations, 52*, 895–922.

Voydanoff, P. (1984). Economic distress and families: Policy issues. *Journal of Family Issues, 5*, 273–288.

Voydanoff, P. (1987). *Work and family life*. Newbury Park, CA: Sage.

Voydanoff, P. (1990). Economic distress and family relations: A review of the eighties. *Journal of Marriage and the Family, 52*, 1099–1115.

Voydanoff, P., & Majka, L. C. (1988). *Families and economic distress: Coping strategies and social policy*. Newbury Park, CA: Sage.

Warr, P. B. (1987). *Work, unemployment, and mental health*. Oxford, UK: Clarendon Press.

Washington State Board for Community and Technical Colleges. (2000). *Worker retraining: Sixth accountability report for the Worker Retraining Program*. Retrieved July 4, 2003, from www.perkins.ctc.edu/data/rsrchrpts/WFEd AccountReportYr6.doc

Weber, J. (1990, December 10). Farewell, fast track. *BusinessWeek*, 192–200.

Westman, M., Etzion, D., & Danon, E. (2001). Job insecurity and crossover of burnout in married couples. *Journal of Organizational Behavior, 22*, 467–481.

Wiesenfeld, B. M., Brockner, J., Petzall, B., Wolf, R., & Bailey, J. (2001). Stress and coping among layoff survivors: A self-affirmation analysis. *Anxiety, Stress and Coping: An International Journal, 14*, 15–34.

Worker Adjustment and Retraining Notification Act, 29 U.S.C. § 2101 (1989).

Zvonkovic, A. M. (1988). Underemployment: Individual and marital adjustment to income loss. *Lifestyles, 9*, 161–178.

12

Technology

Michael D. Coovert

Lori Foster Thompson

J. Philip Craiger

The Definition and Prevalence of Computer-Supported Work

Technology is nearly ubiquitous in the workplace. Broadly defined as advancements in software, hardware, and associated services, "computer support" has transformed the world of work, and this trend shows no sign of abating (Coovert & Thompson, 2001; Wilson, 1991). According to recent surveys, many innovations in changing the workplace with computers have occurred during the last decade alone, primarily within white-collar occupations (Andries, Smulders, & Dhondt, 2002).

Jobs and employees are affected by both new innovations and increasing access to more familiar technologies. For example, dramatic work transformations will likely result from late breaking advances in wearable computers that extend human capabilities by allowing people to do things like see what is behind them while facing forward (Negroponte & Gershenfeld, 1995). Meanwhile, work is also changing because more familiar technologies (cell phones, laptops, wireless connections, etc.) have become smaller, faster, cheaper, and generally more available than ever before, providing access even to small businesses and small-budget operations.

The impact of new innovations and increasing access to "old" ones has been felt throughout the work world. In fact, it is hard to imagine a profession that remains untouched by the effects of technology. Consider the dental hygienist whose job now consists of operating new machines that perform tasks he once completed manually. Imagine the accountant who now spends most of her time on complex cases because these days prospective clients with basic needs tend to "do" their own taxes at home via their personal computers. Think about the person whose office work has shifted from typewriters and memos to personal computers, laptops, PDAs, cell phones, e-mail, intelligent agent assistants, and beyond.

Clearly, these changes have produced both intended and unintended effects. A large-scale survey by Andries et al. (2002) over a 5-year period demonstrated that the use of a computer results in more qualified work, and indeed few people would dispute the assertion that recent advancements in technology have afforded personal and professional efficiencies previously unimaginable. At the same time, many would agree that the consequences of technology have not been uniformly positive. Sometimes technology results in more than a well-connected, productive, efficient worker. Sometimes it results in stress.

Technology can create stress both directly through workers' contact with computer support and indirectly via workplace changes that have been driven by computer support. This is a subtle but important distinction. With regard to technology's direct effects, the mere exposure to innovations such as computer monitoring software can be stressful and so can events such as computer viruses and unintentionally deleted files. Moreover, repetitive use of technological tools (e.g., keyboard, mouse) can produce musculoskeletal stress and strain as can prolonged exposure to poorly positioned monitors (Straker & Mekhora, 2000).

It is also necessary to consider the effects of technology from a more global or macro perspective. In this regard, technology can have indirect effects that are sometimes viewed as by-products of increasing degrees of technological sophistication. These by-products include increased work pace, noise, and mental workload, for example. They also involve the rapidly changing nature of jobs that are continually reconfigured as the technological tools for completing them evolve. Additionally, the need to work on a computer anchored to an office increases exposure to everyday office stressors (office noise, light). Although none of these stressors is the direct result of human-computer interaction, all are clearly implicated in the relationship between technology and workplace stress. This chapter reviews technology's indirect consequences as well as its direct effects on work stress. Our aim is to focus on some of the most common computer-related stress issues, which cut across many jobs and professions.

Major Theoretical Models

There are a few basic approaches that can be used to understand the impact of technology on workers. The following pages highlight two such models. One comes from the field of ergonomics (human factors), and the other involves the perspective of socio-technical systems theory. An overview of each is now provided.

Ergonomics

The field of ergonomics is concerned with finding an appropriate match between the capabilities of an individual and the products that must be interacted with. This area can target the use of workplace tools such as a keyboard, workstation, or chair; or it can emphasize nonwork activities such as the operation of a car or VCR. In the workplace, the focus is on the interaction of the human with technology with the goal of human-centered design. In order to achieve this goal, ergonomics incorporates the work of three relevant subdisciplines: anatomy, physiology, and psychology (Blakemore & Jennett, 2001).

A good physical fit between a person and a device is achieved, in part, through a thorough understanding of human anatomy. Biomechanics is the study of the operation of muscles and extremities, and anthropometrics provides data on the dimensions of the human body in various postures. Human physiology is concerned with establishing standards for work rate, workload, and energy requirements, and environmental physiology focuses on the physical working conditions (e.g., temperature, noise, lighting). Finally, psychology's focus is on understanding the human as an information processor. This includes sensation, perception, memory demands/requirements, and decision making.

In short, the ergonomic approach to minimizing technology-driven stress is based on the pursuit of truly human-centered work environments. Such environments are believed to occur when there is a clear understanding of (a) the human in terms of anatomy, physiology, and psychology; (b) the environment in terms of physiology and the task; and (c) the necessary functioning of the device or job from an ergonomic standpoint. This perspective extends beyond physical jobs and includes concerns regarding cognitive ergonomics, which involves understanding the cognitive demands of work and fitting the job or technology to employees' mental representations of work.

Socio-technical Systems

Work in the area of socio-technical systems also provides a framework for understanding the relationships between technology and stress. The idea that work consists of interactions between two separate systems, a technical system and a social system, was developed by Eric Trist and the Tavistock Institute (Trist, 1950, 1981). While working with the National Coal Board in England, Trist recognized the need to understand the two separate systems. By that time, the technological revolution in mining had moved work to the "long-wall method," which broke jobs down into one-man/one-task roles. This was in sharp contrast to the historical "short-wall method," in which small groups of workers took responsibility for the entire work process. Working to understand the differences between high-producing/high-morale mines and low-producing/low-morale mines, Trist found that successful mines had relatively autonomous teams with interchanging roles and activities and very little supervision (characteristics of the traditional short-wall method of mining). Even with the higher level of mechanization produced by the technological revolution, effective work groups found ways to recover group cohesion, self-regulation, and participation in decision making.

In 1950, Trist recognized that

> work organizations exist to do work—which involves people using technological artifacts (whether hard or soft) to carry out sets of tasks related to specific overall purposes. Accordingly, a conceptual reframing was proposed in which work organizations were envisaged as socio-technical systems rather than simply as social systems. (1981., p. 10)

Thus, Trist (1981) maintained that the social and technical systems (i.e., the people and equipment) were the substantive factors of note. "Economic performance and job satisfaction were outcomes, the level of which depended on the goodness of fit between the substantive factors" (p. 10).

Principles of socio-technical systems include the following (Trist, 1981): First, the unit of analysis is the work system rather than the single jobs into which the unit is decomposed. Second, the central unit is the work group as opposed to the individual worker. Third, the system is regulated by the work group instead of external individuals such as supervisors. Fourth, individuals develop multiple skills and can take on multiple roles. Fifth, the individual is complementary to the technology (machine) rather than an extension of it. Sixth, this structure is variety-increasing for both the individual and the organization in contrast to the variety-decreasing mode of a traditional bureaucracy.

Research Linking Technology to Work Stress: Major Empirical Studies

Technology as a stressor manifests itself both psychologically and physiologically, and not all individuals are affected the same way. Psychologically, anxiety can be caused by technology and so can role overload, role conflict, and a host of negative attitudes. Physiological symptoms include pain, heart and blood pressure problems, and musculoskeletal disorders.

Many studies spanning several different research areas have looked at the psychologically and physiologically stressful outcomes to which technology directly and indirectly exposes workers. In this section of the chapter, we review the research linking technology and its by-products to physiological stresses and strains. In addition, we consider the psychological consequences of a work world characterized by increasing exposure to technology.

Those who study workplace stressors typically report their findings in one of two ways, either under the rubric of the disorder (e.g., work-related musculoskeletal disorders, pain) or by the source of the stressor (e.g., noise, electronic performance monitoring). Below we follow a similar format beginning with findings reported by disorder followed by some findings reported by stressor or stressor source. Additional detailed discussion of these factors can be found in Coovert and Thompson (2003).

Technology-Driven Stress and Its Antecedents

Physical pains and strains. Using a computer full-time can result in physical and mental strain, which can be followed by physical pains and strains. Indeed, technology-driven work stress has been blamed for a number of noteworthy health problems. Over 50 million Americans have high blood pressure, and in nearly all the cases, the cause is unknown. Stress may be a factor. With regard to cardiac health and well-being, Karasek and Theorell (1990) maintain that up to 23% of heart disease could be prevented (saving 150,000 lives per year) if the level of job strain was reduced in high-strain occupations.

The potential effects of stress-inducing technology are not limited to heart disease and blood pressure problems. The literature has demonstrated a clearly established causal link between stress and work-related musculoskeletal disorders of the upper extremities (Pransky, Robertson, & Moon, 2002). Moreover, work-related musculoskeletal disorders are quite prevalent in the workforce. According to the Occupational Safety and Health Administration (OSHA; 2003), there are over 600,000 injuries and illnesses yearly, and work-related musculoskeletal disorders account for 34% of all lost days reported to the Bureau of Labor Statistics. These claims cost more than $20 billion per year and consume one of every three dollars paid out by workers' compensation.

Noteworthy disagreements exist concerning the specifics of some of the physiological manifestations of technology-driven stress. For instance, debates about how to define repetitive stress injuries persist (Szabo & King, 2000). Szabo and King (2000) contend that repetitive stress disorders have been defined by society and politics. Indeed, medical doctors examining workers claiming to have repetitive stress disorders often fail to concur with the patient's self-diagnosis.

There is also disagreement about the specifics of pain, prompting ongoing research to clarify this issue. Most hypotheses about muscle pain agree that it results from muscle cell activation. Following activation, damage can occur as a result of calcium accumulation, hypoxia, or the effects of energy deficits. Unfortunately, there has not been a causal relationship established between activation and pain as measured by traditional tools such as electromyography. Knardahl (2002) maintains that the sustained low-level motor activation associated with computer work is not enough to cause pain in the traditional model. His hypothesis is that in work typified by computer usage, muscle pain originates from the blood vessel-nociceptor (pain-specific nerves) interactions of the connective tissue of a muscle. Roe and Knardahl

(2002), however, measured blood fluxes during tracking tasks of computer operators and found that blood fluxed during the tracking task and then there was a pooling of blood (hyperemia) when the task ended. This pooling, they hypothesized, is what leads to pain.

Over the past several years many researchers have specifically examined technological factors related to neck and shoulder pain. For example, research has demonstrated an unambiguous relationship between poor typing skills and the long hours secretarial and clerical staffs spend putting extreme pressure on the neck flexion. Given the extent to which computers pervade office work today, Evans and Patterson (2000) examined the degree to which poor typing skills might be associated with upper extremity pain experienced by those in professional and managerial positions. Conducting an epidemiological field study, Evans and Patterson (2000) focused on such positions in seven different companies and measured typing skills, hours of computer use, tension, and workstation setup (was the workstation ergonomically correct?). Their results indicated that tension scores were the most predictive of neck and shoulder pain for those in managerial and other professional jobs with high computer use.

A 6-year epidemiological field study was conducted by Aaras, Horgen, Bjorset, Ro, and Walsoe (2001) examining the relationship between workplace lighting, ergonomic work stations, and optometric corrections (giving the worker an optometric examination and glasses if needed) and the outcome variables of musculoskeletal pain and visual and psychosocial stress. The focus of their research was solely on video display unit operators. Aaras et al. (2001) divided participants into three groups, and at the beginning of the study gave one group optimal lighting, ergonomically correct workstations (supported the forearm on the table top), and optometric corrections if needed. Two years later the second group had the same intervention, and 4 years later the third group received the changes. All groups reported significant reductions in shoulder and back pain as well as visual discomfort. No significant differences were found, however, for reduction in psychosocial stress.

The role of psychological stress in contributing to work-related musculoskeletal disorders in the shoulder region has been investigated by McLean and Urquhart (2002). These researchers manipulated work pace and distractions in the environment as psychological stressors. Physiological activity in key muscles that are used to support the shoulder during typing tasks was monitored. Their findings indicated that the muscles are differentially susceptible to the two sources of stress, but neither source alone is capable of significantly increasing muscle activity (which would lead to pain) as reflected by the amplitude of a myoelectric signal.

Seppala (2001) conducted a broad-based study of computer-supported office workers in which several professional groups (lawyers, architects, engineers, etc.) were surveyed about the impact of psychosocial and organizational factors on musculoskeletal discomfort and psychological stress. Their findings support the premise that both psychosocial factors and organizational factors are determinants of perceptions of stress and musculoskeletal disorders. Vision problems were also found to be related. Women tended to report the symptoms of stress and musculoskeletal discomfort more often than men. Looking more closely at the findings, many of the by-products of technological sophistication were related to stress, including workload and haste, management and work atmosphere, work demands, and defects in the workplace. It is interesting to note that the same predictors were related to both the psychological and musculoskeletal discomforts.

Technology-Driven Stressors and Their Outcomes

Mouse input devices. A contributing factor to many musculoskeletal symptoms is improper use of a device or the use of a device that is poorly designed and thereby places too much strain on a portion of the musculoskeletal system. As an input device, the mouse is ubiquitous, but its constant use can lead to work-induced problems. In a large-scale survey of nearly 1,300 computer users, Hagberg, Tornqvist, and Toomingas (2002) found a relationship between computer mouse position or task work and an average productivity decrease of 14% for men and women who reported musculoskeletal symptoms attributed to the mouse.

Research by Cook, Burgess-Limerick, and Chang (2000) also examined the relationship between mouse usage and physiological stress levels. Their results demonstrated a relationship between arm abduction (which is specific to mouse use) and musculoskeletal symptoms of the neck and upper extremity.

Psychological stress may exacerbate the mouse's negative effects on musculoskeletal symptoms. A study conducted by Wahlstrom, Hagberg, Johnson, Svensson, and Rempel (2002) investigated the role of stress in computer mouse work. These authors manipulated stress via time pressure and negative verbal provocation and measured physiological reactions and mood states. In the stress conditions, heart rate, blood pressure, and muscle activity specific to the mouse-use muscles were all significantly higher than in the control conditions.

Office noise and lighting. Despite advances in wireless technology and mobile computing, many workers are still tethered to their office computers. They spend increasing amounts of time in the office, which extends their exposure to undesirable elements such as office noise. A couple of recent studies have examined the effect of office noise on stress levels and performance. Evans and Johnson (2000) ran a study in which office workers were randomly assigned to either a quiet control or a low-noise condition (meant to simulate the noise in a typical open-office environment). Participants in the open-office noise condition produced less than workers in the quiet control condition. They also made fewer adjustments to their workstations. This is important because postural invariance is one of the risk factors for the development of musculoskeletal disorders. The groups, however, did not differ in self-reported levels of perceived stress.

The impact of noise and light has also been examined by Takahashi et al. (2001). Their design was a 2 luminance (high, low) × 2 noise (high 70 dB, low) factorial design, and video display unit workers were randomly assigned to one of the four experimental conditions. Dependent measures included several physiological measures as well as subjective reports of fatigue. In the two noisy conditions, participants reported significantly higher levels of stress and fatigue. In the two high luminance conditions, a visual reaction test and critical flicker fusion frequency were affected the most. In summary, their results demonstrate that high luminance coupled with noise will lead to greater levels of stress/fatigue and will negatively affect mental activities.

Isolation. Depending on how it is used, technology may isolate workers and increase stress or expand a worker's social network and produce the opposite effect. Consider the case of a teleworker, for example. The literature indicates that social needs are partly satisfied by interactions with others in the workplace (Timpka & Sjoberg, 1998; Viller & Sommerville, 2000). By removing employees from the workplace, telework arrangements can limit people's exposure to coworkers, which could reduce social support (Coovert & Thompson, 2003).

This is significant because research has shown that social support can help shield workers from the negative effects of job strain. Using survey research methodology, Sargent and Terry (2000) investigated the role of social support and its relationship to various work outcomes within a job strain model perspective. Results highlighted the importance of having a good overall social support network, beginning with the supervisor at work and extending through nonwork support networks. Specifically, Sargent and Terry's (2000) results demonstrated that having high levels of supervisory support can eliminate the negative effects of high job strain on job satisfaction and feelings of depersonalization. In addition, high levels of nonwork and coworker support reduced the negative effects of job strain on work performance. Research by Searle, Bright, and Bochner (2001) failed to demonstrate a relationship between social support and stress; however, it did highlight the effects of social support on arousal, satisfaction, and perceived performance. Yeuk-Mui's (2001) investigation of call center employees revealed that reliable coworkers and supportive management contribute to job satisfaction and stress reduction. Other studies have also indicated that a lack of social support from managers and peers predicts a range of musculoskeletal problems (Halford & Cohen, 2003).

Thus, technological solutions such as telecommuting opportunities may increase stress by reducing the social support stemming from interactions with coworkers. On the other hand, technology could actually be used to combat isolation and enhance social support in telework and other environments. It is known that older individuals use the Internet (e-mail) as a form of social support, and this leads to lower levels of life stress for these people (Wright, 2000). It is also widely known that not all time spent on work computers is actually work-related. In fact, according to some researchers (Lavoie & Pychyl, 2001), nearly half of all individuals report using the Web for some form of cyberslacking and procrastination. Taken together, these trends suggest that technology may have the potential to reduce feelings of isolation and stress experienced by workers. The caveat is that people must feel comfortable using their work computers to socialize. This comfort level and its potentially beneficial effects may become increasingly unlikely in the days to come due to the trend toward electronic performance monitoring that can pressure workers to stay on task and discourage them from socializing (Amick & Smith, 1992).

Electronic performance monitoring. Electronic performance monitoring is a stressor that has received much attention in recent years. The term *electronic performance monitoring* has been used to refer to a wide range of technologies that may in fact prompt a rather heterogeneous set of stressors (Ambrose, Alder, & Noel, 1998). Indeed, definitional problems have been known to cause difficulties in interpreting the impact of electronic monitoring on stress (Lund, 1992). Semantic confusion has also been implicated in the widespread disagreement over the benefits and costs of electronic performance monitoring (Ambrose et al., 1998).

To clear up this confusion, Ambrose et al. (1998) classified electronic performance monitoring into several categories. We have modified Ambrose et al.'s (1998) framework to accommodate distinctions made by Lund (1992) and Westin (1992) and to incorporate some of the newer practices (e.g., reviewing employee e-mail and Web browsing activities) not included in previous taxonomies. As shown in Figure 12.1, our framework consists of two broad categories: performance monitoring and behavior monitoring.

As its name implies, performance monitoring is narrow in focus and concentrates exclusively on data pertaining to *task performance*. Performance monitoring can involve quantitative data (e.g., keystrokes, claims per hour, etc.), which is generally captured by computer hardware and peripherals and is continuous in nature (Lund, 1992). It can also include qualitative monitoring (e.g., listening in on a telephone call to assess a customer service representative's courtesy or determine whether a call center operator mentioned a sales or promotion campaign). Qualitative monitoring is typically discrete in nature and performed by a supervisor (Lund, 1992). In general, electronic performance monitoring is important from the employer's perspective because it can provide accurate insights into the actual productivity of the workers on certain jobs. For example, employers can see real-time data reflecting the amount of typing employees are currently doing, examine that data across any time period of the day, and compare it with standards of performance.

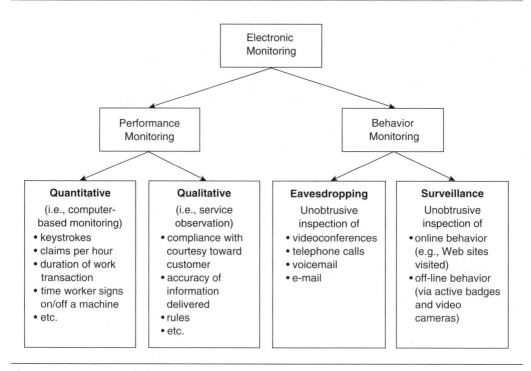

Figure 12.1   Forms of Electronic Monitoring

The second category, work behavior monitoring, refers to a broader practice that captures both task and nontask behaviors. Work behavior monitoring can involve eavesdropping or surveillance. Eavesdropping exposes employers to a range of employees' work and nonwork voicemail, e-mail, and telephone calls (not just work calls as in the preceding example). Some employers have estimated that a sizable percentage of the e-mail received at work is not task-related (Guernsey, 2000). Consequently, those who review this type of information are privy to a great deal of personal information.

In addition to eavesdropping, work behavior monitoring involves surveillance. Surveillance includes monitoring online behaviors (e.g., software that records Web sites visited) and/or offline behaviors (e.g., video cameras in break rooms and active badges that track the number and duration of bathroom breaks). It allows employers to assess the task-relatedness of employees' on-the-clock behaviors and the appropriateness of their use of the company's time and resources. It may even track off-the-clock behaviors when workers log on to company intranets from home.

Although there is some overlap between the two categories, electronic performance monitoring and behavior monitoring generate some very different concerns. The debate surrounding behavior monitoring involves the issues of privacy and invasiveness; conversely, concerns regarding performance monitoring often entail workload, pace, and related issues (Ambrose et al., 1998). Although behavior monitoring has received a great deal of media attention, very little empirical work has examined its effects on work stress.

Performance monitoring, however, has been studied a bit more extensively and is reviewed next.

There is a substantial amount of empirical evidence showing that computer performance monitoring can create stress and related health problems for employees (Alder & Tompkins, 1997; Ambrose et al., 1998). For example, Alder and Tompkins (1997) have described investigations supported by a study conducted by the University of Wisconsin and the Communication Workers of America that compared monitored workers with their nonmonitored counterparts. According to these authors, 81% of monitored workers reported depression compared with 69% of those not monitored. Additionally, 72% reported feeling extreme anxiety, whereas only 57% of nonmonitored workers expressed this problem. Last, workers whose employers monitored their keystroke entries were twice as likely to complain of sore wrists as were those whose employers did not track keystroke data.

A 1992 study by Smith, Carayon, Sanders, Lim, and LeGrande also supported the contention that electronic performance monitoring induces stress. After surveying 745 employees spanning seven different companies, the researchers concluded that compared with unmonitored employees, workers whose performance was electronically monitored perceived their working conditions as more stressful and reported higher levels of psychological tension, depression, job boredom, anxiety, anger, health complaints, and fatigue.

One important area of performance monitoring research involves customer services representatives working in call centers. There is presently a great deal of interest in the stress experienced by this sizable population of workers (Ferreira & Saldiva, 2002; Halford & Cohen, 2003; Yeuk-Mui, 2001). This is a special profession to be examined because "repetitive movements and prolonged static sitting postures occur in complex situations where communication skills, cordiality, responsibility, and efficiency are expected from operators under the effect of time pressure, ambitious goals and direct monitoring of performance" (Ferreira & Saldiva, 2002, p. 147). A wide variety of quantitative and qualitative performance data are collected, including the number of incoming and outgoing calls, the duration for which employees are logged on to the telephone system, and a breakdown of the time spent on each call. These systems often allow management to monitor real-time displays of the work status of all call service representatives (Yeuk-Mui, 2001). Managers may also selectively listen in on the conversations to ensure employees are complying with rules and procedures, sales or promotion campaigns, and courtesy requirements (Westin, 1992).

To investigate this population, Halford and Cohen (2003) conducted a survey of 67 employees who were currently working in call centers or had recently ceased working in this type of environment. All participants were drawn from a banking call center that dealt with incoming calls concerning consumer debt collection. For this study, respondents were interviewed individually and asked a variety of questions pertaining to their health, workplace conditions, ergonomic and health/safety factors, psychosocial factors, and computer use factors. Results indicated that monitoring of performance was significantly associated with musculoskeletal problems, and the authors concluded that electronic performance monitoring, in concert with heavy workload, created a pressurized environment in which operator stress played a noteworthy role in the development of musculoskeletal problems.

Findings such as these raise questions about the mechanisms through which computer performance monitoring adversely affects the stress and musculoskeletal health of employees such as those working in call centers. Some have asserted that the collection of electronic performance data can have direct psychological effects as well as indirect effects stemming from job design changes (Smith, Carayon, Sanders, Lim, & LeGrande, 1992). By prompting job design changes, electronic performance monitoring may indirectly affect psychosocial work factors that can trigger stress-related disorders.

Monotonous work, social support, and intensified workload are three psychosocial factors that have been identified by the National Institute for Occupational Safety and Health (NIOSH) as having relationships with back and upper extremity disorders (Halford & Cohen, 2003). With regard to monotony, Amick and Smith (1992) have argued that deskilling (work rationalization and standardization) is one of the most serious job stress aspects of electronic performance monitoring. Although boredom, repetition, and monotony did not significantly predict musculoskeletal problems in Halford and Cohen's (2003) research, the authors noted that the electronically monitored call center workers surveyed in their study reported very strong feelings of boredom, repetition, monotony, and dissatisfaction.

Electronically monitored employees may also experience stress due to a lack of social support. Workers who are constantly monitored often fear that off-task behaviors such as chatting with coworkers will result in reprimands. As a result, electronic performance monitoring systems can limit interactions among coworkers and lead to social isolation resulting in depression, loneliness, and stress (Amick & Smith, 1992).

Workload is one of the most clearly implicated culprits contributing to the monitoring-stress linkage. Many call centers, for example, calculate the average work time (i.e., the number of seconds it takes an operator to process a customer call, on average) and then set unrealistic or excessively difficult performance standards that violate workers' right to health (Ambrose et al., 1998; DiTecco, Cwitco, Arsenault, & André, 1992). In this manner, electronic performance monitoring may increase the workload, work pace, or time pressure experienced by employees. This constant pressure from electronic performance feedback can be more stressful than the intermittent deadlines that characterize jobs that are not electronically monitored (Amick & Smith, 1992).

Fear of job loss and associated feelings of stress are especially likely to occur among employees who have difficulty meeting performance standards (Schleifer & Shell, 1992). Thus, demanding performance standards paired with electronic performance monitoring is a recipe for stress. This notion is consistent with laboratory research indicating that people performing difficult jobs are especially prone to the negative effects of electronic performance monitoring. Social facilitation is one popular theory used to explain this finding. The social facilitation effect refers to the fact that the presence of others boosts performance of easy tasks and hinders performance of difficult tasks. In a similar vein, laboratory research has shown that the presence of monitoring enhances the mood of people working on easy tasks, whereas it dampens moods and increases stress levels of those working on difficult tasks (Davidson & Henderson, 2000).

Clearly, meeting the challenging performance standards set by management and tracked by electronic performance-monitoring systems creates a pressure to increase productivity from a quantitative standpoint. This pressure is often at odds with the quality requirements enforced by the organization. The result is role conflict, which is one of the classic stressors in the occupational health literature (DiTecco et al., 1992). Consider the example of a call center worker. The computer tracks the average amount of time it takes an operator to complete calls, and operators are pressured to keep this time to a minimum in order to process as many calls as possible. Unrealistic call time objectives conflict with the worker's desire to provide quality customer service, and they also conflict with management's demands for quality (e.g., courtesy, fully satisfying customers' business needs, etc.). "The operator who knows she/he is continuously monitored can experience conflict in meeting the needs of the system over the needs of the customer" (Amick & Smith, 1992, p. 12). The end result is psychological and physical stress.

Research by DiTecco et al. (1992) supports this assertion. These authors surveyed a cross-sectional random sample of more than 700 telephone operators and found that conflicting demands contributed to the stress experienced by respondents. A total of 70% of the sample indicated that difficulty serving a customer well while still keeping call time down largely contributed to the stress they felt at work (DiTecco et al., 1992).

In sum, computer monitoring is a powerful tool, and the decision to use it should not be taken lightly. Employers have a right to be able to evaluate employees' performance on the job, and for some jobs, such as teleworkers, employers may have few options other than some form of electronic performance monitoring. One downside of performance monitoring, however, is that it may create stress and resistance on the part of workers who feel their privacy has been invaded and the systems are not fair. In the end, psychological barriers against monitoring, supervision, and the organization may result unless interventions are implemented to minimize the negative consequences of computer monitoring.

Risk Factors, Moderators, and Interventions: Countering Technology-Induced Stress

Understanding the types of interventions that may reduce techo-stress requires a clear grasp of the risk factors and variables that moderate the technology-stress connection. Various risk factors can increase the likelihood that technology will result in stress just as known moderators can reduce the potential for negative technology-related fallout. Many of these moderators are within an organization's control making them excellent candidates for programs to decrease the stressful impact of technology in the workplace. The following pages describe variables that exacerbate or curtail technology's negative effect on work stress. Research-based ideas for countering the stressful effects of technology are also described and evaluated.

Personality and Demographic Moderators

For starters, individual differences (personality, demographic variables) play a role in employees' reactions to technology. Although these variables themselves are not easily changed via organizational interventions, their identification is critical. Knowing who is at risk for technology-induced stress can inform training design leading to programs tailored to high-risk populations.

Studies seeking to identify high-risk populations have shown that certain types of people have more trouble coping with changes in technology than others. Technology evolves continually. For instance, new versions of familiar software applications seem to be emerging with increasing frequency. Installing new software requires people to learn the nuances of an unfamiliar user interface while mastering the new functionality of the application (i.e., learning what the system can do or can no longer do). The need to adapt to a technological change such as this can be viewed as anything from a challenge to a hassle to a threat, and a number of researchers have tried to identify the variables that predict adverse reactions to technological evolutions.

To examine this issue, Shigemi, Mino, and Tsuda (2000) developed a scale to measure workers' mental health and job stress. Factor analysis yielded six factors: anxiety and depression, severe depression, lack of interpersonal network/social support, poor social activity, insomnia, and lack of a positive attitude. After verifying that this factor structure was stable across multiple administrations of the instrument, Shigemi et al. (2000) examined the predictive properties of the six variables. The major finding was that the anxiety and depression factor had a significant and stable relationship with the stress-related perceptions of experiencing too much responsibility at work and an inability to keep up with new technology.

Other researchers have examined whether well-known personality variables such as locus of control help minimize the stress produced by changing technology. People with an internal locus-of-control orientation tend to believe they possess control over their fate. Conversely, those with an external orientation believe that chance, luck, or other uncontrollable outside factors regulate their rewards. Coovert and Goldstein (1980) found that compared with people with internal locus-of-control orientations, "externals" were less satisfied with computer technology and less accepting of the changes prompted by technology. Meanwhile, Aiello and Svec (1993) found that externals feel significantly more anxious as a result of computer monitoring than do internals.

The literature also indicates that particular demographic subgroups are prone to technology's negative impact. For example, Mikkelsen, Ogaard, Lindoe, and Olsen (2002) looked at the degree to which different types of people experience computer anxiety. A survey was administered as part of a large Norwegian research effort, and several hundred individuals responded to questions on their backgrounds and jobs. Structural equation modeling was employed to assess a model of computer anxiety. Results revealed that gender, age, education, decision authority, and training were predictive of computer anxiety. Managers tended to have less anxiety than did nonmanagers. The authors state that to minimize computer anxiety in an organization, user involvement (i.e., participation, control) and active practical-use training should accompany the introduction of new technology. Groups that should receive special attention include women, less educated, and older employees.

Training can be an effective solution for high-risk populations. Researchers such as Beckers and Schmidt (2001) have advocated the use of training as an intervention to help individuals reduce computer anxiety and stress. After developing and administering a scale to measure six different factors of computer anxiety, Beckers and Schmidt (2001) found that the two most predictive dimensions were computer self-efficacy and computer literacy. Both of these factors were strongly related to physical arousal and affect. Thus, developing a training program to enhance computer self-efficacy and literacy could lead to decreased computer anxiety. A similar study by Venkatesh (2000) looked at ease of use in three different organizations and arrived at similar conclusions. In 1980, Coovert and Goldstein made a complementary argument addressing the role of computer attitudes during both training and selection.

Ergonomics

Ergonomics focuses on fitting technology to the worker in part because people operating in uncomfortable environments are prone to strain and stress. Realistically, many of today's office workers spend large portions of their days holed up in cubicles facing glowing computer monitors, operating keyboards and mouse devices (often in a repetitive fashion) to accomplish their duties (Coovert & Thompson, 2003). Failing to attend to ergonomic concerns within these and other work environments puts employees at risk for stress.

Several ergonomic strategies have evolved for stress reduction and the (hoped for) elimination of work-related pain. These strategies range from work equipment/workstation design changes to workforce education and training programs on the causes and treatment of stress and pain. To date, there appears to be no silver bullet for eradicating problems in this area. Indeed, many studies report inconsistent and inconclusive findings (e.g., Smith & Bayehi, 2000).

Technological interventions. A potential solution to the harmful effects of repetitive mouse use involves a redesigned mouse that does not force the arm into unnatural positions, thereby relieving the strain on the neck and upper extremity of the user's body. One design is the Anir/Renaissance mouse (Aaras, Dainoff, Ro, & Thoresen, 2002), which allows a more neutral position of the wrist compared with a traditional mouse. (The mouse stands upright and is gripped almost like a joy stick.) Several studies extending over 3 years report a significant reduction in pain for neck, shoulders, forearm, wrist, and hand when this type of mouse is used.

A rather innovative method for adjusting technology to human requirements involves the real-time monitoring of stress levels. One application of this approach has occurred in the domain of virtual reality. Virtual reality training systems have become more and more common over the past decade. These are especially useful for teaching employees to perform jobs in which training in the real environment is threatening, hazardous, or simply too expensive to do on a routine basis. A problem associated with virtual reality training systems, however, is that the trainee can become quite ill (similar to simulator sickness or seasickness). This is a type of technology-induced workplace stress that should be avoided at all costs because when it is present the training will not be nearly as effective as it could be, and the trainees will not want to participate (for reasons that are all too obvious to anyone who has gotten sick in such a training environment!). Recent work (Stoermer, Mager, Roessler, Mueller-Spahn, & Bullinger, 2000) has taken a stride toward addressing this problem by monitoring several aspects of the trainee: mental workload, stress, and behavioral and physiological parameters in real time. Analysis also occurs in real time, and when appropriate, feedback to the trainee and changes in the virtual environment are made "on the fly" to keep the trainees' monitored parameters within a desired range. This intervention is implemented to minimize user discomfort and stress, enhance cognitive functioning, and maximize the procedural skills the trainee needs for the task at hand, thus enhancing the training experience.

Personnel interventions. Personnel interventions involve things like ergonomic awareness programs, on-the-job exercise programs, and ergonomic training. As noted by Coovert and Thompson (2003), one straightforward approach that can be easily implemented by most organizations is a training program designed to promote ergonomic awareness. Such programs teach employees the correct way to perform tasks as well as how to properly use the equipment and tools associated with their work to prevent forces that stress workers' joints.

But what is the best method for teaching employees to use these techniques? Some suggest that active learning may be key. Active learning has been a buzzword in education and training for quite some time, and its effectiveness for training people to reduce musculoskeletal problems was investigated by Bohr (2000). Bohr conducted a field experiment in which workers of a reservation center were randomly assigned to one of three conditions: control, traditional education (e.g., lecture), or participatory education (active learning). The focus of the training was on a program to decrease the incidence of musculoskeletal injuries associated with computer use. Baseline data were gathered, and additional data were collected 3, 6, and 12 months after the intervention. Bohr (2000) noted that those who received education (either traditional or participatory) reported less pain, discomfort, and stress than did those in the control group. Those in the participatory education program additionally reported a significantly better perception of their overall health than both the controls and those in the traditional training group.

Taking Steps to Minimize Role Stressors

As noted earlier, technology (e.g., software used to monitor employee performance) may create stress by prompting role conflict. Research by Joshi and Rai (2000) supports the contention that role conflict and role ambiguity may shape reactions to technology. Similar conclusions were drawn by Postle (2002), who studied European care managers working with older individuals. Postle (2002) asserts that the nature of the care manager's job has changed significantly since the introduction of legislation forcing these managers to spend more time on paperwork and computer work and less time building and maintaining the relationships clients need. The nature of the work is increasingly reductionistic, and this splitting of time between computer work and clients has led to greater levels of role ambiguity and conflict for the care managers. The rising levels of role conflict and role ambiguity have led to increased stress and turnover, causing staffing problems. Some have argued the current U.S. nursing shortage has been caused by the same mechanism: increased levels of role conflict, role overload, and stress, coupled with decreased job satisfaction and heightened turnover. Significantly, these studies indicate that the negative fallout of technology may be minimized when interventions are designed to reduce conflict and ambiguity. The design of such interventions may benefit from a socio-technical systems viewpoint.

Taking a Systems View

As discussed earlier, the socio-technical systems framework is a philosophy about how work and organizational systems should be designed. Keeping the social system of work on an even keel with the technical system is critical and requires careful attention to the manner in which technology is incorporated into workers' jobs, and it also encourages opportunities for worker input. In this regard, the literature suggests that interventions as straightforward as quality circles (groups of employees who meet regularly to discuss and propose solutions to problems) can significantly reduce the stress associated with telework (Konradt, Schmook, Wilm, & Hertel, 2000). In general, attending to systems principles while designing jobs and introducing technological innovations should minimize negative reactions to technology.

Dvash and Mannheim (2001) examined the human and job design characteristics that moderate stress in an automated manufacturing technology (AMT) environment. In particular, they examined reactions to technological coupling and their relationship to job control characteristics and workers' psychological well-being. Coupling is a design characteristic of many manufacturing systems. The manufacturing processes can vary from being very tightly coupled to more fluid or lightly (semi-) coupled. The job characteristics examined by Dvash and Mannheim (2001) were timing and method control, monitoring, problem-solving demand, and production responsibility. The psychological variables were satisfaction and "mental health." Data from over 200 AMT operators indicated that technological coupling was negatively related to timing and method control and to both psychological variables. The variables positively related to worker satisfaction were problem solving, production responsibility, timing, and method control. The positive consequence of problem solving, responsibility, and the like is perhaps unsurprising when viewed in light of the systems perspective that technology works best when it is variety-increasing and regulated by its users.

Studies such as Dvash and Mannheim's (2001) provide information about the interactions between the social and technical aspects of organizations and can be used to guide interventions designed to create a better harmony between the two systems. Interestingly, a variable called "desirability of control" was found to moderate Dvash and Mannheim's (2001) psychological well-being findings, suggesting that operators' responses to technological coupling were influenced by their desire for control. Overall, this emphasizes that individual worker differences may shape the degree to which interventions reduce the effects of technology on stress.

With regard to electronic performance monitoring, stress can be minimized by attending to the way the data gathered through performance-tracking tools are used. Indeed, Yeuk-Mui (2001) has suggested that the effects of electronic performance monitoring on stress depend on how the performance data generated by information technology are used. Similarly, Alder and Tompkins (1997) maintain that when organizations "use data obtained through electronic means in a concertive manner by emphasizing two-way communication and supportive feedback, they are likely to reap positive results" (p. 259).

A large survey conducted by Holman, Chissick, and Totterdell (2002) supports these points and emphasizes the socio-technical systems view that technology works best when it complements rather than dictates workers' jobs. Holman et al.'s (2002) survey was designed to explore the linkages between electronic performance monitoring, well-being, and control, and it was based on the authors' assertion that monitoring has three components. The first is related to performance (such as providing feedback or setting criterion levels of performance). The second is a beneficial feedback purpose used to provide developmental information to the worker and not employed for punitive purposes. The third is the perceived intensity of the monitoring. Several hundred call center employees whose performance was constantly monitored responded to the questionnaire. Results revealed that the first two components (performance-related and beneficial purposes) were positively related to well-being whereas perceived intensity was negatively related. It is important to point out that supervisory support and job control moderated the relationship between intensity and well-being. Thus, as discussed next, job control can help buffer workers from technology-induced stress.

Control and Participation

The issue of control comes up often (e.g., locus of control) when considering the technology-stress linkage. According to Schleifer (1992), long-term benefits of electronic performance monitoring can be realized if organizations use these data to increase workers' sense of competence and control rather than use the information to control workers. There has been a long-standing interest in the psychological literature concerning the effects of control on a myriad of affective, cognitive, and physiological variables (Parker & Price, 1994). Technological tools (and procedures for using them) provide people with varying levels of real or perceived process control (Douthitt & Aiello, 2001), and low levels of perceived control are associated with high levels of physical symptoms, emotional distress, and role stress (Spector, 1986). For example, Ekman, Andersson, Hagberg, and Hjelm (2000) demonstrated a relationship between loss of control (in terms of work planning) and musculoskeletal health/well-being among computer users, especially those who are female.

Researchers have suggested that stress can be alleviated by allowing workers to participate in or otherwise control decisions surrounding an electronic performance monitoring system (Alder & Tompkins, 1997; Amick & Smith, 1992). Strategies designed to enhance perceptions of control have been implemented in the domain of computer monitoring with varying levels of success. One technique focuses on communicating the presence of monitoring to workers whose performance was being "watched." This way, employees can better control which behaviors are captured electronically. A common method for doing this involves including little windows or icons on employees' screens to report when monitoring is in progress. After integrating the findings from several literatures and conducting two additional studies, Zweig and Webster (2002) concluded that such strategies, which manipulate the characteristics of monitoring systems, do not alleviate the invasion of privacy perceived by many employees. Simply keeping workers informed about the status of computer monitoring may therefore be less than optimal for enhancing perceptions of control and reducing the stress resulting from electronic performance monitoring.

Fortunately, other interventions have realized greater success. Techniques designed to promote employee participation, for instance, have been shown to be quite effective both within and outside the computer-monitoring domain. The empowerment, participatory decision making, and employee voice literatures all emphasize the importance of allowing workers the chance to provide input. This practice not only increases employees' sense of procedural justice but also boosts their perceptions of control (Douthitt & Aiello, 2001; McFarlin & Sweeney, 1996; Menon, 1999; Parker & Price, 1994; Spector, 1986) and can therefore decrease technology-induced stress. An example is provided by the work of Douthitt and Aiello (2001) that showed that an intervention to enhance perceptions of input (e.g., asking people how they feel their performance should be evaluated for bonus purposes and allowing them to choose the color of their computer screen) reversed some of the negative effects of computer monitoring.

Carayon and Karsh (2000) investigated the role of participation in the acceptance of a new imaging technology introduced in two organizations. Each organization replaced existing computer technology with the new imaging system. In one organization, the old technology was merely replaced and workers were instructed to use the new system. In the other organization, workers participated in the implementation of the new imaging system. Using questionnaires and structured and semistructured interviews, Carayon and Karsh (2000) found that workers who participated in the implementation rated the imaging systems more favorably and also reported higher levels of job satisfaction than did those in the nonparticipation organization. Reductions in stress, it is hoped, followed suit.

A longitudinal study by Korunka and Vitouch (1999) resulted in similar findings. They followed the implementation of a new technology in 10 companies over a 2-year period measuring variables at five different points in time. Data were structured such that there was an implementation sample and a control sample. Personal variables were assessed as well as situational factors (job design, implementation content, and implementation context). These factors were used to predict employees' strain response via structural equation modeling. Findings confirmed that negative consequences from the implementation of the technology are to be expected if employees are not given the chance to participate in the implementation process.

According to the work of Shadur, Kienzle, and Rodwell (1999), participation and involvement are most likely when employees feel committed to the organization and view the climate as supportive, thereby suggesting that the mitigating effects of participation and control on stress may be best viewed through a larger nomological net that also takes affective and organizational variables into account.

Conclusion

In sum, many factors can mitigate the unintended, stressful consequences of technological innovation. Identifying and attending to moderators such as human-centered technology design, role stressors, socio-technical fit, employee input, perceived control, personality, training, and demographics can aim interventions in fruitful directions and help minimize the stressful fallout of technology in the workplace.

Notably, some of the problems discussed in this chapter will probably diminish as technology advances. Advances in voice recognition software, for example, may reduce the need for keyboard and mouse devices, thereby minimizing the stress created by these tools. Moreover, although this chapter has focused on technology's negative side effects, it is important to acknowledge that some aspects of technology can promote health and well-being. Indeed, as we move toward the future, technology itself can be part of the solution to work stress problems. Coovert and Thompson (2003) describe the concept of cooperative buildings that are dynamic, user-friendly, technically rich structures and that include a number of fascinating features such as adaptive electronic assistance, smart rooms, and support for informal interactions among on- and off-site workers. Cooperative buildings may help future workers overcome technology-induced problems such as stress stemming from isolation and musculoskeletal strain.

As new technologies such as cooperative buildings emerge, much more research will be needed. Indeed, the intersection between technology and work stress already provides very fertile ground for research. We therefore conclude by highlighting four example areas in need of empirical attention.

First, although this chapter has separately addressed a number of computer-related stressors (e.g., keyboard/mouse issues, electronic monitoring), it is important to acknowledge that these stressors do not occur in isolation. Each profession is exposed to a unique combination of stressors. For example, systems administrators (i.e., individuals responsible for making sure an organization's computing services work) not only encounter the stress stemming from equipment upgrades and malfunctions, they are also subject to anxiety resulting from "internal customers" (e.g., agitated computer users who themselves struggle to deal with upgrades, viruses, breakdowns, and the like). In the end, stressors such as work overload, role ambiguity, role conflict, and little autonomy characterize the systems administrator position and lead to exhaustion among these professionals (Moore, 2000).

Clearly, profession-specific combinations of stressors create a need for studies examining special populations as well as studies investigating the manner in which various component stressors interact. Studies testing theoretically rich, multivariate models of the relationships among technology-related stressors (including both the physical ergonomic factors and the psychosocial work factors), workers, and organizations are needed (Carayon, Smith, & Haims, 1999; Coovert & Thompson, 2001). Work stress stems not only from the technology used by the worker but also the job tasks performed, the physical and social environment of the workplace, and the structure of the organization. Consequently, future research should account for these factors to facilitate a better understanding of the effects of technology, job task, work environment, and organization structure on employee stress (Lund, 1992).

Second, there has recently been much popular media attention to electronic work behavior monitoring (e.g., watchdog technologies that report Internet usage and eavesdropping tools that give employers access to workers' e-mail), with less input from the scientific community on the topic. Although there are distinct similarities between electronic behavior monitoring and computer performance monitoring, important differences exist. As noted earlier and suggested in Figure 12.1, traditional forms of computer performance monitoring track task performance, whereas surveillance and eavesdropping tools police a broad range of work and nonwork behaviors. This distinction may cause workers to respond to the two types of technology differently, creating unanticipated stress reactions among those exposed to watchdog technologies. For example, we know very little about the effects that unintended and potentially improper "pop-up" Web sites may have on the stress levels of monitored employees who are using the Internet for work. Similarly, research should look at the manner in which e-mail monitoring affects stress levels, particularly when employees inadvertently encounter inappropriate e-mail. In short, research on the effects of behavior monitoring tools is sorely needed.

Third, all signs indicate that employers and workers will increasingly rely on intelligent software agents in the days to come (Coovert & Thompson, 2001). These tools can work autonomously and adaptively to provide the types of assistance another person could otherwise offer. Future research should investigate the kinds of stress involved in interacting with nonhuman teammates and identify ways for mitigating these stressors.

Fourth and finally, advances in wireless technology have facilitated trends toward mobile, "nomadic" computing that allows employees to journey with their equipment and work on the go. This trend sparks a host of questions involving the effects of nomadic work styles on multitasking tendencies, divided attention, workload, and stress. Empirical investigations are needed to inform the practice of mobile computing, which has outpaced research in this area by leaps and bounds.

References

Aaras, A., Dainoff, M., Ro, O., & Thoresen, M. (2002). Can a more neutral position of the forearm when operating a computer mouse reduce the pain level for VDU operators? *International Journal of Industrial Ergonomics, 30,* 307–324.

Aaras, A., Horgen, G., Bjorset, H. H., Ro, O., & Walsoe, H. (2001). Musculoskeletal, visual, and psychosocial stress in VDU operators before and after multidisciplinary ergonomic interventions: A 6-year prospective study—Part 2. *Applied Ergonomics, 32,* 559–571.

Aiello, J. R., & Svec, C. M. (1993). Computer monitoring of work performance: Extending the social facilitation framework to electronic presence. *Journal of Applied Social Psychology, 23,* 537–548.

Alder, G. S., & Tompkins, P. K. (1997). Electronic performance monitoring: An organizational justice and concertive control perspective. *Management Communication Quarterly, 10, 259–288.*

Ambrose, M. L., Alder, G. S., & Noel, T. W. (1998). Electronic performance monitoring: A consideration of rights. In M. Schminke (Ed.), *Managerial ethics: Moral management of people and process* (pp. 61–79). Mahwah, NJ: Lawrence Erlbaum.

Amick, B. C., III, & Smith, M. J. (1992). Stress, computer-based work monitoring and measurement systems: A conceptual overview. *Applied Ergonomics, 23,* 6–16.

Andries, F., Smulders, P. G. W., & Dhondt, S. (2002). The use of computers among workers in the European Union and its impact on the quality of work. *Behaviour & Information Technology, 21,* 441–447.

Beckers, J. J., & Schmidt, H. G. (2001). The structure of computer anxiety: A six factor model. *Computers in Human Behavior, 17,* 35–49.

Blakemore, C., & Jennett, S. (Eds.). (2001). *The Oxford companion to the body.* Oxford, UK: Oxford University Press.

Bohr, P. C. (2000). Efficacy of office ergonomic education. *Journal of Occupational Rehabilitation, 10,* 243–255.

Carayon, P., & Karsh, B. T. (2000). Socio-technical issues in the implementation of imaging technology. *Behavior & Information Technology, 19,* 247–262.

Carayon, P., Smith, M. J., & Haims, M. C. (1999). Work organization, job stress, and work-related musculoskeletal disorders. *Human Factors, 41,* 644–663.

Cook, C., Burgess-Limerick, R., & Chang, S. W. (2000). The prevalence of neck and upper extremity musculoskeletal symptoms in computer mouse users. *International Journal of Industrial Ergonomics, 26,* 347–356.

Coovert, M. D., & Goldstein, M. A. (1980). Locus of control as a predictor of users' attitude toward computers. *Psychological Reports, 47,* 1167–1173.

Coovert, M. D., & Thompson, L. F. (2001). *Computer supported cooperative work: Issues and implications for workers, organizations, and human resource management.* Thousand Oaks, CA: Sage.

Coovert, M. D., & Thompson, L. F. (2003). Technology and workplace health. In J. C. Quick & L. E. Tetrick (Eds.), *Handbook of occupational health psychology* (pp. 221–241). Washington, DC: American Psychological Association.

Davidson, R., & Henderson, R. (2000). Electronic performance monitoring: A laboratory investigation of the influence of monitoring and difficulty on task performance, mood state, and self-reported stress levels. *Journal of Applied Social Psychology, 30,* 906–920.

DiTecco, D., Cwitco, G., Arsenault, A., & André, M. (1992). Operator stress and monitoring practices. *Applied Ergonomics, 23,* 29–34.

Douthitt, E. A., & Aiello, J. R. (2001). The role of participation and control in the effects of computer monitoring on fairness perceptions, task satisfaction, and performance. *Journal of Applied Psychology, 86,* 867–874.

Dvash, A., & Mannheim, B. (2001). Technological coupling, job characteristics and operators' well being as moderated by desirability of control. *Behaviour & Information Technology, 20,* 225–236.

Ekman, A., Andersson, A., Hagberg, M., & Hjelm, E. W. (2000). Gender differences in musculoskeletal health of computer and mouse users in the Swedish workforce. *Occupational Medicine (Oxford), 50,* 608–613.

Evans, G. W., & Johnson, D. (2000). Stress and open office noise. *Journal of Applied Psychology, 85,* 779–783.

Evans, O., & Patterson, K. (2000). Predictors of neck and shoulder pain in non-secretarial computer users. *International Journal of Industrial Ergonomics, 26,* 357–365.

Ferreira, M., Jr., & Saldiva, P. H. N. (2002). Computer-telephone interactive tasks: Predictors of musculoskeletal disorders according to work analysis and workers' perception. *Applied Ergonomics, 33,* 147–153.

Guernsey, L. (2000, April 5). Monitoring of office e-mail is increasing. *New York Times,* p. C1.

Hagberg, M., Tornqvist, E. W., & Toomingas, A. (2002). Self-reported reduced productivity due to musculoskeletal symptoms: Associations with workplace and individual factors among white-collar computer users. *Journal of Occupational Rehabilitation, 12,* 151–162.

Halford, V., & Cohen, H. H. (2003). Technology use and psychosocial factors in the self-reporting of musculoskeletal disorder symptoms in call center workers. *Journal of Safety Research, 34,* 167–173.

Holman, D., Chissick, C., & Totterdell, P. (2002). The effects of performance monitoring on emotional labor and well-being in call centers. *Motivation and Emotion, 26,* 57–81.

Joshi, K., & Rai, A. (2000). Impact of the quality of information products on information systems users' job satisfaction: An empirical investigation. *Information Systems Journal, 10,* 232–345.

Karasek, R. A., & Theorell, T. (1990). *Healthy work.* New York: Basic Books.

Knardahl, S. (2002). Psychophysiological mechanisms of pain in computer work: The blood vessel-nociceptor interaction hypothesis. *Work & Stress, 16,* 179–189.

Konradt, U., Schmook, R., Wilm, A., & Hertel, G. (2000). Health circles for teleworkers: Selective results on stress, strain, and coping styles. *Health Education Research, 15,* 327–338.

Korunka, C., & Vitouch, O. (1999). Effects of the implementation of information technology on employees' strain and job satisfaction: A context-dependent approach. *Work & Stress, 13,* 341–363.

Lavoie, J. A., & Pychyl, T. A. (2001). Cyberslacking and the procrastination super-highway: A web-based survey of online procrastination, attitudes, and emotion. *Social Science Computer Review, 19,* 431–444.

Lund, J. (1992). Electronic performance monitoring: A review of research issues. *Applied Ergonomics, 23,* 54–58.

McFarlin, D. B., & Sweeney, P. D. (1996). Does having a say matter only if you get your way? Instrumental and value-expressive effects of employee voice. *Basic and Applied Social Psychology, 18,* 289–303.

McLean, L., & Urquhart, N. (2002). The influence of psychological stressors on myoelectrical signal activity in the shoulder region during a data entry task. *Work & Stress, 16,* 138–153.

Menon, S. T. (1999). Psychological empowerment: Definition, measurement, and validation. *Canadian Journal of Behavioural Science, 31,* 161–164.

Mikkelsen, A., Ogaard, T., Lindoe, P. H., & Olsen, O. E. (2002). Job characteristics and computer anxiety in the production industry. *Computers in Human Behavior, 18,* 223–239.

Moore, J. E. (2000). One road to turnover: An examination of work exhaustion in technology professionals. *MIS Quarterly, 24,* 141–168.

Negroponte, N., & Gershenfeld, N. (1995). Wearable computing. *Wired, 3*(12), 256.

Occupational Safety and Health Administration. (2003). *Work-related musculo-skeletal disorders.* Retrieved September 19, 2003, from www.osha.gov/pls/oshaweb/owadisp.show_document

Parker, L. E., & Price, R. H. (1994). Empowered managers and empowered workers: The effects of managerial support and managerial perceived control on workers' sense of control over decision making. *Human Relations, 47,* 911–928.

Postle, K. (2002). Working tension between the ideal and the reality: Ambiguities and tensions in care managers' work. *British Journal of Social Work, 32,* 335–351.

Pransky, G., Robertson, M. M., & Moon, S. D. (2002). Stress and work-related upper extremity disorders: Implications for prevention and management. *American Journal of Industrial Medicine, 41,* 443–455.

Roe, C., & Knardahl, S. (2002). Muscle activity and blood flux during standardized data terminal work. *International Journal of Industrial Ergonomics, 30,* 251–264.

Sargent, L. D., & Terry, D. J. (2000). The moderating role of social support in Karasek's job strain model. *Work & Stress, 14,* 245–261.

Schleifer, L. M. (1992). Electronic performance monitoring (EPM). *Applied Ergonomics, 23,* 4–5.

Schleifer, L. M., & Shell, R. L. (1992). A review and reappraisal of electronic performance monitoring, performance standards and stress allowances. *Applied Ergonomics, 23,* 49–53.

Searle, B., Bright, J. E., & Bochner, S. (2001). Helping people to sort it out: The role of social support in the job strain model. *Work & Stress, 15,* 328–346.

Seppala, P. (2001). Experience of stress, musculoskeletal discomfort, and eyestrain in computer based office work: A study in municipal workplaces. *International Journal of Human-Computer Interaction, 13,* 279–304.

Shadur, M. A., Kienzle, R., & Rodwell, J. J. (1999). The relationship between organizational climate and employee perceptions of involvement: The importance of support. *Group & Organizational Management, 24,* 479–503.

Shigemi, J., Mino, Y., & Tsuda, T. (2000). Stability of factor structure and correlation with perceived job stress in a general health questionnaire: A three-wave survey over one year in Japanese workers. *Journal of Occupational Health, 42,* 284–291.

Smith, M. J., & Bayehi, A. D. (2000). Do ergonomic improvements increase computer workers' productivity? An intervention study in a call center. *Ergonomics, 46,* 3–18.

Smith, M. J., Carayon, P., Sanders, K. J., Lim, S. Y., & LeGrande, D. (1992). Employee stress and health complaints in jobs with and without electronic performance monitoring. *Applied Ergonomics, 23,* 17–27.

Spector, P. E. (1986). Perceived control by employees: A meta-analysis of studies concerning autonomy and participation at work. *Human Relations, 39,* 1005–1016.

Stoermer, R., Mager, R., Roessler, A., Mueller-Spahn, F., & Bullinger, A. H. (2000). Monitoring human-virtual reality interaction: A time series analysis approach. *Cyberpsychology & Behavior, 3,* 401–406.

Straker, L., & Mekhora, K. (2000). An evaluation of visual display unit placement by electromyography, posture, discomfort and preference. *International Journal of Industrial Ergonomics, 26,* 389–398.

Szabo, R. M., & King, K. J. (2000). Repetitive stress injury: Diagnosis or self-fulfilling prophecy? *Journal of Bone and Joint Surgery, 82a,* 1314–1344.

Takahashi, K., Sasaki, H., Saito, T., Hosokawa, T., Kurasaki, M., & Saito, K. (2001). Combined effects of working environmental conditions in VDT work. *Ergonomics, 44,* 562–570.

Timpka, T., & Sjoberg, C. (1998). Development of systems for support of collaboration in health care: The design arenas. *Artificial Intelligence in Medicine, 12,* 125–136.

Trist, E. L. (1950). *The relations of social and technical systems in coal-mining.* Paper presented to the meeting of the British Psychological Society, Industrial Section.

Trist, E. L. (1981). The evolution of socio-technical systems. In A. H. Van de Ven and W. F. Joyce (Eds.), *Perspectives on organization design and behavior.* New York: Wiley.

Venkatesh, V. (2000). Determinants of perceived ease of use: Integrating control, intrinsic motivation, and emotion into the technology acceptance model. *Information Systems Research, 11,* 342–365.

Viller, S., & Sommerville, I. (2000). Ethnographically informed analysis for software engineers. *International Journal of Human Computer Studies, 53,* 169–196.

Wahlstrom, J., Hagberg, M., Johnson, P. W., Svensson, J., & Rempel, D. (2002). Influence of time pressure and verbal provocation on physiological and psychological reactions during work with a computer mouse. *European Journal of Applied Physiology, 87,* 257–263.

Westin, A. F. (1992). Two key factors that belong in a macroergonomic analysis of electronic monitoring: Employee perceptions of fairness and the climate of organizational trust or distrust. *Applied Ergonomics, 23,* 35–42.

Wilson, P. (1991). *Computer supported cooperative work.* Oxford, UK: Intellect.

Wright, K. (2000). Computer-mediated social support, older adults, and coping. *Journal of Communication, 50,* 100–118.

Yeuk-Mui, M. T. (2001). Information technology in frontline service work organization. *Journal of Sociology, 37,* 177–206.

Zweig, D., & Webster, J. (2002). Where is the line between benign and invasive? An examination of psychological barriers to the acceptance of awareness monitoring systems. *Journal of Organizational Behavior, 23,* 605–633.

13 Industrial Relations

Lori Francis

E. Kevin Kelloway

The practice of industrial relations is characterized by conflict and change and, as a result, is inherently stressful (Bluen & Barling, 1988; Fried, 1993). Involvement in strikes (Barling & Milligan, 1987), collective bargaining (Bluen & Jubiler-Lurie, 1990), and participation in union activities (Kelloway & Barling, 1994) have all been associated with stress. Despite consistent empirical evidence, the practice of industrial relations has not been incorporated in the larger organizational stress literature (Bluen & Barling, 1987, 1988) and is often overlooked in reviews of stressors in the workplace (e.g., Kahn & Byosiere, 1992). In this chapter, we consider the ways in which industrial relations practice is a source of workplace stress. We note that our chapter builds on and extends Bluen and Barling's (1987, 1988) seminal work on the psychological stressors associated with industrial relations by incorporating and emphasizing research that has appeared since the publication of their review. In particular, we identify specific stressors associated with industrial relations, evaluate theoretical models of industrial relations stress, review the major empirical research in this area, and highlight areas of particular importance for future research and application in industrial relations practice.

Prevalence of Industrial Relations Events

Before we begin a detailed discussion of stressors associated with industrial relations, we provide some context for that discussion by considering the

Authors' Note: This work was supported by grants from the Nova Scotia Health Research Foundation to both authors. The authors thank C. Gail Hepburn for comments on an earlier version of this chapter.

prevalence of industrial relations events in today's workforce. An examination of recent statistics generated from census data reveals that a substantial portion of the workforce is unionized. In 2002, 13.2% of the U.S. workforce belonged to a labor union, with union membership rising to over 20% in New York, Alaska, Hawaii, and Michigan (U.S. Department of Labor [USDL], n.d.). Of unionized employees in the United States, 46% work in government organizations and 54% in private industry (USDL, n.d.). Almost half of the union members in the United States work in traditionally white-collar roles. Unionization rates are even higher in other countries. Data from the 2002 labor force survey reveals that union density among employees in the United Kingdom is 29% (National Statistics Online, n.d.). As of 2002, 30.3% of the Canadian workforce was unionized (Akyeampong, 2003). When considering only the public sector, 72.5% of Canadian public servants are unionized (Akyeampong, 2003).

Statistics are also available for the incidence of labor strikes. During 2001, there were 379 strikes lasting more than 10 days in Canada. These incidences resulted in 223,800 individuals off the job and 2,231,100 missed work days (International Labour Office [ILO], n.d.). During the same year, there were 675 such strikes in Australia, contributing to 225,700 employees off the job and 393,100 days not worked (ILO, n.d.). Available strike statistics for the United States include only those incidents involving more than 1,000 employees, and as such the number of reported strikes is lower. During 2001, 29 strikes in the United States met this criterion. However, those 29 disputes resulted in 99,100 workers off the job and 1,151,300 days not worked.

As we demonstrated in the paragraphs above, industrial relations and industrial relations events directly affect a substantial portion of the workforce. As such, it is important to consider the stressors to which these individuals are exposed during their industrial relations involvement and the resulting potential for the experience of stress and strain. Beyond those employees directly involved in unions, we also point out that exposure to industrial relations–related stressors is not confined to those who belong to a union. Nonunionized individuals are affected by unions in a number of ways. For instance, those who occupy management positions in a unionized organization may actively engage industrial relations practice via collective bargaining with the union. Similarly, nonunionized employees who work in a unionized environment may be exposed to the conflict that arises in labor-management relations. For instance, they may experience a strike at their workplace or be party to a grievance. Family members of active union members may feel stress resulting from their relatives' involvement in the union such as when they endure financial strain if a family member goes on strike or when they have to balance the family member's additional work-load because of a union role. Finally, members of the general public are party to industrial relations events in the form of labor disputes. Individuals may be placed in a position in which they are negatively affected by lost services during a strike (e.g., Day, Stinson, & Catano, 2002) or lockout, or they may have to make a decision about whether or not to cross a picket line (Kelloway, Francis, & Catano, & Dupre, 2004).

Given the far-reaching nature of industrial relations events, it becomes apparent that stressors associated with industrial relations affect a large number of people in a multitude of ways. As exposure to stressors is associated with a number of negative health issues, further attention must be given to the existence of stressors in the industrial relations setting. To set the stage for a consideration of the nature and impact of stressors in industrial relations activities, we will first examine the existing theoretical work on this issue.

Theoretical Models of Industrial Relations Stress

Despite the fact that stressful activities play a large role in industrial relations, no single overarching, theoretical framework of the relationship between industrial relations and stress has emerged. The most comprehensive theoretical discussion of industrial relations stressors to date was provided by Bluen and Barling (1988). Additionally, recent research on exposure to workplace injustice as a stressor (e.g., Cropanzano, Goldman, & Benson, Chapter 4 in the current volume; Elovainio, Kivimaki, & Helkama, 2001; Elovainio, Kivimaki, & Vahtera, 2002; Kivimaki, Elovainio, Vahtera, & Ferrie, 2003; Tepper, 2001) has theoretical implications for the study of stress in industrial relations. In this section, we review Bluen and Barling's theoretical discussion of industrial relations stress and discuss the implications that organizational justice research has for the study of the stress associated with industrial relations.

Bluen and Barling (1988): Conflict and Change as Industrial Relations Stressors

In seeking to explicate the relationship between stress and industrial relations, Bluen and Barling (1988) noted that conflict and change are two central and interrelated dynamics of industrial relations. Both conflict and change have been identified as sources of stress (Dohrenwend & Dohrenwend, 1974; Kahn & Byosiere, 1992; Kahn, Wolfe, Quinn, Snoek, & Rosenthal, 1964). Bluen and Barling (1988) argued that as the two primary dynamics underlying industrial relations are stressful, the potential for stress among those involved in the practice of industrial relations is high. The nature of conflict and change as they relate to stress associated with industrial relations is considered below.

Researchers have long noted that conflict is inherent in industrial relations (Bluen & Barling, 1988; Fox, 1973). In describing the conflict-based context in which industrial relations activities are conducted, Bluen and Barling (1989) drew on a distinction made earlier by Fox. Fox (1973) discussed industrial relations from two different perspectives, unitary and pluralist, and noted the role of conflict within these two frames of reference. According to the tenets of the unitary approach, there is a single source of loyalty and authority within an organization. An organization functioning under unitary ideology works toward organizational goals presumably determined by company management. The consonance implied by the unitary perspective essentially negates the existence of conflict. Applied to a labor relations environment, the unitary approach implies that management and workers share priorities that are conducive to the attainment of such organizational goals without any conflict of interest. Such a perspective indeed dominates the discussion of the "new" human resources (Kelloway, Barling, & Harvey, 1998).

Given the tangible existence of conflict in industrial relations events, the conflict-free unitary perspective does not represent the reality of industrial relations practice. However, Fox (1973) pointed out that some maintain the notion of unitary organizations as this view tends to reflect the interests of management in that it suggests that all stakeholders are focussed on advancing organizational goals. Bluen and Barling (1988) warn that adherence to a unitary ideology negates the existence of fundamental conflicts in the workplace. As a result, the existence and impact of industrial relations stressors may be ignored or underestimated.

Fox (1973) argued that the pluralist perspective provides a more accurate depiction of organizations in general and industrial relations in particular, as it recognizes the existence of multiple groups within an organization. The various groups have different leaders and objectives. In the case of industrial relations, the management and the union are the two major groups. Management seeks to maximize profits and reduce costs, whereas labor groups are concerned with issues such as wages, job security, and working conditions (Bluen, 1994). The acknowledgement of different groups within an organization by the pluralist perspective recognizes that conflict is a naturally occurring component in industrial relations practice. In fact, Fox (1973) noted that the existence of conflict indicates that all involved parties are being heard.

The experience of conflict is generally recognized as a prevalent work-related stressor (Kahn & Byosiere, 1992; Kahn et al., 1964; Sauter, Murphy, & Hurrell, 1991). As such, the acknowledgement of conflict in labor-management interactions provides solid theoretical support for the proposal that industrial relations can be stressful. Conflict is a common theme in both industrial relations incidents such as grievances, collective bargaining, and labor disputes and in industrial relations roles themselves.

Bluen and Barling (1988) also identified change as a stress-provoking dynamic in the practice of industrial relations. They pointed out that conflict and change are interrelated, as change can both result from and cause conflict. Change is a frequently noted stressor (Dohrenwend & Dohrenwend, 1974; Kahn & Byosiere, 1992). Dohrenwend and Dohrenwend (1974) argue that major life events requiring adaptation on the part of the individual are stressors and that exposure to these stressors can ultimately contribute to strain-related symptoms, including illness. Such work-related events as a change in financial state, a change in work responsibilities, and a change in working hours or conditions have been noted among the life events that are stress provoking (Holmes & Rahe, 1967; Rahe, 1989). An examination of the context of labor-management relations reveals that change is an unavoidable and potentially stressful reality in industrial relations practice.

There are both external and internal forces for change that influence labor-management relations. External forces such as changing government regulations, economic fluctuations, and technological development place pressure on industrial relations systems to adapt to these environmental realities. As such, industrial relations practitioners must respond to and incorporate those external forces in their industrial relations activities. Internal factors for change include new contracts and changes among the players in a particular industrial relations unit. For instance, union members have to adapt to new provisions in collective agreements and to the appearance of new individuals in the union and in management. Finally, industrial relations events in and of themselves can create changes in the day-to-day lives of those affected by the event. For example, striking workers and their families may have to change their spending patterns and get by on substantially reduced income during a labor dispute. Similarly, management employees may be called upon to assume additional and new duties to replace striking workers during a dispute. Again, changes in work hours or conditions are noted as stressful life events. Research supports the proposition that changes in working patterns due to an industrial relations dispute are stressors. Lusa, Hakkanen, Luukkonen, and Viikari-Juntera (2002) reported that nonunionized employees in fire stations experienced stress as a result of filling in for striking firefighters, with one particular stressor being different and smaller shifts.

Injustice as an Industrial Relations Stressor

Recent research demonstrates that exposure to injustice is associated with increased reports of stress and strain (e.g., Cropanzano et al., current volume; Elovainio et al., 2001, 2002; Francis, Kelloway, Barling, & Keeley, 2003; Kivimaki et al., 2003; Tepper, 2001; Zohar, 1995). One can argue that many industrial relations events hinge on issues of fairness. For instance, unionized employees file grievances in response to a perceived violation of the collective agreement. In her model of unionization, Brett (1980) identified dissatisfaction as the "trigger" of unionization drives, and Kelloway, Francis, Catano, and Teed (2004) point out that dissatisfaction may be a reaction to injustice. Similarly, Barling, Fullagar, & Kelloway (1992) point to the role of unions in ensuring fair processes as a central motive for unionization. Before further discussion of the possible links between injustice and industrial relations stress, we must first introduce some important terms from the organizational justice literature.

Research in organizational justice is concerned with employees' perceptions of fairness in organizations. The justice literature has considered three types of fairness judgments that employees may make about their workplaces. Individuals can assess the fairness of outcomes (distributive justice), the fairness of processes (procedural justice), and the fairness of the interpersonal treatment they receive (interactional justice). Organizational justice has been repeatedly associated with positive workplace attitudes and behavior, whereas injustice has been found to result in undesirable reactions (Cohen-Charash & Spector, 2001; Cropanzano & Greenberg, 1997).

It is apparent that employees recognize unfair treatment on the part of their employers as a stressor. A number of recent investigations reveal that perceptions of distributive, procedural, and interactional injustice are associated with increased reports of stress and strain. Francis et al. (2003) found that those who perceived a high degree of distributive, procedural, or interactional injustice in their work setting also reported increased emotional strain. In addition, perceptions of injustice explained variance in stress reactions not accounted for by low job control or job insecurity. Similarly, Tepper (2001) found that perceptions of procedural and distributive injustice were associated with increased emotional strain symptoms including depression, emotional exhaustion, and anxiety. Elovainio and his colleagues (Elovainio et al., 2001, 2002; Kivimaki et al., 2003) report a consistent relationship between perceptions of procedural and interactional injustice and increased experience of emotional strain, increased illness-related work absences, and decreased self-reported health status.

Although no studies to date have directly examined the role of perceived injustice in stress stemming from industrial relations practice, researchers agree that issues of fairness are pertinent to industrial relations activities and practice (e.g., Barling et al., 1992; Brett, 1980). For instance, perceived fairness of interpersonal treatment during negotiation may affect the progress of collective bargaining. Similarly, perceptions of a distributively fair rate of pay could determine the salary demands that union representatives make during collective bargaining and ultimately affect the outcome of the bargaining process. Finally, perceptions of procedural injustice in the application of the collective agreement may influence a person's decision to file a grievance. To the extent that industrial relations activities are affected by perceptions of injustice, theoretical work from the justice literature, particularly that relating injustice to health outcomes, may be useful in the development of a comprehensive framework for the future study of industrial relations stress.

Industrial Relations and Stress: Terminology and Definitions

Before we articulate the stressors associated with industrial relations, it is necessary to explicitly introduce terminology that will be used in the discussion that follows. The organizational stress literature distinguishes among the concepts stressor, stress, and strain. The present work will use the stressor, stress, strain framework as described by Pratt and Barling (1988). *Stress* refers to any state experienced by an individual characterized by arousal and displeasure (Kristensen, 1996). A *stressor* then is any environmental factor experienced by individuals that increases the likelihood that they will feel stress (Kristensen, 1996). *Strain* represents the category of adverse responses to stress (Kahn & Byosiere, 1992).

Stressors in Industrial Relations

Work stressors take a number of forms. They can originate in the physical environment, in the contents of a job, or in the social aspects of one's role at work (Sauter et al., 1991). The practice of industrial relations appears to expose individuals to two broad categories of stressors: those that are *common* to a number of work settings and those that are *unique* to industrial relations. For instance, a person who assumes a union role may experience the common work stressor role overload (Kahn et al., 1964) if their union job is demanding of their time. Stressors unique to the industrial relations setting would include such occurrences as grievance filing and aspects of collective bargaining.

The types of stressors prevalent in the practice of industrial relations may vary considerably. Some industrial relations stressors are episodic, others enduring, and still others transient. Pratt and Barling (1988) distinguished between acute, chronic, catastrophic, and daily stressors, and we suggest that this is a useful framework in characterizing industrial relations stressors. According to Pratt and Barling's (1988) model, stressors are differentiated along several dimensions, including frequency of occurrence, intensity, duration, and predictability of onset. A *chronic* stressor has no specific onset, may be of short or long duration, repeats frequently, and may be of either low or high intensity. In the context of industrial relations, chronic stress is conceivably represented by the industrial relations climate (Dastmalchian, Blyton, & Adamson, 1989), that is, the extent to which the relations between management and labor are characterized by cooperation, conflict, trust, or suspicion. *Acute* stressors have a specific time onset, are typically of short duration, are of high intensity, and have a low frequency. Filing a grievance or participation in a strike or other industrial action would be acute stressors in the practice of industrial relations. *Daily* stressors have specific onset, are of short duration, are of low intensity, and are typically infrequent. Misunderstandings or misinterpretations of the collective agreement are examples of daily stressors in an industrial relations environment. Finally, *catastrophic* stressors have a specific onset, occur infrequently, have a high intensity, and may be of either long or short duration. The main distinction between acute and catastrophic stressors is in the intensity of the stressor. Catastrophic stressors typically involve a direct threat to life, loss of life, and/or major property damage. Strikes that erupt into picket line violence (e.g., Francis & Kelloway, 2004) may be examples of catastrophic stressors in an industrial relations context.

Stress in Industrial Relations

We suggest that the stress an individual may feel following exposure to industrial relations stressors is the same as that experienced following work-related stressors in general. As such, we use the popular transactional theory of stress suggested by Lazarus and his colleagues (e.g., Lazarus, DeLongis, Folkman, & Gruen, 1985; Lazarus & Folkman, 1984) to guide the current discussion. According to this model of stress, the environment may contain stressors, but they are in fact only perceived as stressful if an appraisal of the situation indicates that the environmental demands outweigh the capabilities of the individual. Thus perceptions of stress are associated with an internal state of arousal and displeasure (Kristensen, 1996). If a situation is perceived as stressful, the individual may experience strain.

Strain in Industrial Relations

The strain that may result following exposure to industrial relations stressors is similar to the experience of strain in general. Strain can manifest in a number of ways, including physical illness (Kristensen, 1996; Mohren, Swaen, Borm, Bast, & Galama, 2001) and psychological symptoms (e.g., Billings & Moos, 1982; Tepper, 2001; Zohar, 1995). Individual and organizationally relevant behavior may also be affected by stress. Individuals experiencing a state of stress may display such actions as increased alcohol consumption (Frone, 1999; Jones & Boye, 1992) and increased absence from work (Manning & Osland, 1989). In the sections that follow, we extend our consideration of stressors, stress, and strain in industrial relations.

Stressors Associated With Industrial Relations

As we have alluded to in previous sections, the practice of industrial relations includes many activities that are inherently stressful for the individuals involved. Some of these stressors arise from situations unique to industrial relations, and others reflect the types of stressors that are common to the work setting in general. Many of the stressors prevalent in industrial relations practice stem from the often conflictual and sometimes antagonistic relations between labor and management. Representatives of management are concerned with the productivity and profitability of organizations, whereas labor representatives are primarily interested in the welfare of the workers (Bluen, 1994). Lawlor and Mohrman (1987) noted that even in situations in which union and management appear to concur, such agreement is often the result of competitive threats or resource depletion rather than a fundamental acceptance of the other side's view. In this section, we illustrate the stressful nature of industrial relations practice by highlighting some of the stressors associated with a number of industrial relations events. In particular, we will discuss the ways in which grievances, bargaining, and labor disputes such as strikes and lockouts can contribute to perceptions of stress among those involved in these activities.

A grievance is an allegation, typically made by an employee through the union, that one party, typically the employer, has violated a provision of the collective agreement (i.e., the contract). Most often, the collective agreement will detail a grievance-handling procedure that attempts to ensure a fair hearing and resolution of such complaints (Barling et al., 1992). The grievance process is an event exclusive to industrial relations and to that extent presents unique stressors for the individuals involved. Almost all aspects of grievance filing are stressful for the involved parties. Employees who file a grievance perceive that they have been treated unfairly in some way by their employer. These employees may also worry about the outcome of the grievance and the extent to which the procedure will resolve the perceived injustice. Moreover, a grievance may bring members into conflict with other members (e.g., invoking a seniority right to "bump" another union member and assume his or her position). At the same time, the steward and the union members involved in the grievance may face criticism from company management or fellow employees who disagree with their action or be called upon to defend the grievance in a hearing, which may be a source of stress for some individuals.

Beyond the stressors introduced by the unique nature of the grievance process, being involved in a grievance can also increase a person's exposure to other common work-related stressors. For example, handling a grievance likely increases the workload of the union steward, contributing to the experience of *role overload,* a well-documented stressor that occurs when the demands of one's role exceed the amount of time one has to meet those demands (Kahn et al., 1964). Union grievance officers or stewards may also experience considerable conflict. Although they are elected to represent members, union officials are also responsible for the accurate implementation of union policies. In that case, officials often have to explain to members that a grievance is not the same as a complaint or a simple feeling of injustice and thus may feel torn between a responsibility to the membership and a responsibility to properly implement procedures.

Collective bargaining is a form of joint labor-management decision making. During the collective bargaining process, teams representing both the union and management come together to negotiate a contract that will govern the conditions of employment between unionized employees and management. This represents a unique situation in which both labor and management have much to gain or lose depending on the outcome of the bargaining process. The inherent conflict of interest between labor and management contributes to an antagonistic approach to bargaining that can be stress inducing (Bluen & Barling, 1988). In fact, previous research has demonstrated a link between participation in collective bargaining and such indicators of strain as elevated blood pressure, increased anxiety levels, and decreased psychological well-being (Bluen & Jubiler-Lurie, 1990). The stressors inherent in the collective bargaining process are numerous and diverse. For instance, the bargaining can be a tense process during which negotiators encounter considerable conflict and uncertainty (Bluen & Jubiler-Lurie, 1990). In fact, negotiators often become the targets for criticism from the opposing team or feel vulnerable to the opponents' threats of job action. Moreover, negotiators may feel immense pressure to reach a settlement that will please the body they represent, be it the union or the company. This pressure may weigh heavily on individual negotiators and contribute to perceptions of stress.

Involvement in collective bargaining can also increase a person's exposure to a number of well-documented work-related stressors. A number of role characteristics, including role conflict and role overload, have been identified as stressors (Kahn et al., 1964). These role characteristics are likely to appear in the context of collective bargaining. One type of role conflict evident in the bargaining process is *person-role conflict* (Bluen & Barling, 1988). Person-role conflict occurs when one's role responsibilities require one to support a position that he or she does not personally hold. When negotiating, representatives of the union and management must adhere to the mandates they have been given by the people they represent. This may mean that individuals are arguing against their own opinions and beliefs to represent a mandated viewpoint and could experience stress as a result.

Interrole conflict exists when employees face incompatible demands from two or more roles. The experience of interrole conflict has been associated with increased incidents of strain (Kahn et al., 1964). Individuals involved in the collective bargaining process may experience several types of interrole conflict. For instance, bargaining and other union-related activities can involve lengthy time commitments, and accordingly those active in the union may feel conflict between their responsibilities to their employer and to their union. Alternatively, the large time commitment involved in industrial relations roles, including being a member of a negotiation team, can contribute to the experience of union-family conflict as industrial relations commitments hinder one's ability to meet family commitments.

Intrarole conflict can occur whenever individuals in a single role face incompatible demands from two or more sources (Kahn et al., 1964). It is certainly reasonable to expect that those involved in collective bargaining would experience intrarole conflict and thus be vulnerable to the associated negative health-related outcomes. For instance, members of the negotiation team may feel conflicting expectations from the union executive and the rank-and-file members. For example, members may expect union representatives on the negotiation team to adopt a militant and aggressive style toward management—postures unlikely to lead to an effective bargaining effort and thus not supported by the union executive.

Individuals involved in collective bargaining may be vulnerable to role overload (Kahn et al., 1964). The bargaining process can be a lengthy engagement during which members of both teams dedicate long hours to bargaining sessions and team meetings. This level of involvement can contribute to stressors such as falling behind in one's regular work assignment. Additionally, the bargaining process often occurs in a limited time frame due to such constraints as contract expiry dates and legal strike deadlines. Those involved in negotiations may be overwhelmed by the amount of work they have to accomplish in a short time.

Another stressful characteristic of industrial relations practice is the potential for a breakdown of labor-management relations (Bluen & Barling, 1988; Bluen, 1994). When labor-management negotiations fail, a strike or a lockout may occur. During a strike, the union executive makes a decision, with endorsement of the majority of union members, to walk off the job. In terms of lockouts, the company management makes a decision to prevent employees from working. Although some argue that strikes bring about beneficial outcomes for workers, such as improved communication between parties (e.g., Shirom, 1982), we assert that striking and locked-out employees face a number of stressors. While off the job, striking and locked-out workers may experience financial stress as they do not receive regular pay and are forced to get by on often meager strike pay (Bluen, 1994). Additionally, workers on a picket line sometimes feel intense job insecurity as they may perceive a risk of losing their jobs to replacement workers or plant closure. Picketing employees may also be involved in incidents of aggression as replacement workers, management employees, and members of the public attempt to cross the picket line or voice their views against the strike.

Those involved in a strike or lockout may also experience some of the role-related stressors described above. For example, a person who does not agree in principle with striking but is participating in a strike to support the union or earn strike pay may experience person-role conflict. If members of a striker's family do not support the strike, the individual may feel interrole conflict between family and union roles. Representatives of company management may also feel interrole conflict during a strike or lockout. To the extent that they view picketing workers as colleagues, nonunionized employees may feel torn between their commitment to their coworkers and their loyalty to the company.

From the discussion thus far it is clear that there are a number of stressors associated with the practice of industrial relations. At this point, it is relevant to consider the factors that increase one's exposure to such stressors. We suggest that those who are highly active in labor-management relations and assume official industrial relations roles are the most at risk for exposure to the stressors associated with industrial relations. There are empirical data supporting this suggestion. First, union members report higher levels of role conflict than do comparable nonmembers (Odewahn & Petty, 1980; Shirom & Kirmeyer, 1988). Within the union membership, active union members (Kelloway & Barling, 1994) and union leaders (e.g., Kelloway & Barling, 1994; Nicholson, 1976) report higher exposure to stressors than do nonactive union members.

Based on Nicholson's (1979) definition of union democracy, Kelloway and Barling (1993) defined behavioral union participation as a unidimensional and cumulative construct. Thus, although the majority of union members do not participate actively in union activities, a minority attend meetings, a handful serve on union committees and hold union office, and only three to four members will be actively involved in collective bargaining. Empirical data confirm the expectation that level of behavioral participation in the union is predictive of increased exposure to industrial relations stressors such as conflict between union and family roles and, in turn, increased reports of stress stemming from industrial relations (Kelloway & Barling, 1994; Kelloway, Catano, & Carroll, 2000). In addition, Kelloway and Barling (1994) found that union involvement was associated with decreased job satisfaction and increased role conflict and role ambiguity compared with inactive union members.

Participation in strike action is also associated with increased exposure to stressors and ultimately with increased reports of stress (Barling & Milligan, 1987). Although strikes are comparatively rare (Bluen, 1994), when a strike does occur, participation is often mandatory in that all members are expected to participate whether or not they support the action. Participants in such action may experience considerable conflict as they adopt a role (i.e., striker) that may be inconsistent with their professional identity or self-image. Indeed, some recent data (Catano & Kelloway, 2004) suggest that worry about the effects of a strike as well as the perceived legitimacy of strike action are important predictors of strike voting and strike behavior.

Apart from behavioral involvement, there is some evidence that attitudinal variables such as union commitment (Kelloway, Catano, & Southwell, 1992), psychological involvement in the union (the parallel to job involvement, Kelloway et al., 2000), and perceptions of union instrumentality (Kelloway & Barling, 1993) are predictors of exposure to industrial relations stressors and, in turn, the experience of stress and strain. Kelloway et al. (2000) reported that one's degree of *psychological involvement* with the union is predictive of union participation and propensity to strike. The construct of psychological union involvement reflects individuals' identification with their union and the importance they place on union-related activities. Kelloway et al. (2000) reported that psychological involvement with the union was positively related to the number of hours per week a person was involved in union-related activities and other behavioral indications of participation, including holding a union office, voting in union elections, and talking with other members about problems such as grievances. Additionally, psychological involvement directly predicted willingness to engage in strike action and the length of time a person was willing to stay on strike. Of particular interest in the current chapter, Kelloway et al. (2000) also examined the predictive relationship between union involvement and stress. They found that those who were more highly involved in union activities reported higher levels of stress stemming from industrial relations. As such, a high degree of psychological involvement with the union is a valuable predictor of exposure to industrial relations stressors and the resulting potential for stress.

Perceptions of *union instrumentality* have also been associated with participation in the union (Barling et al., 1992; Kelloway & Barling, 1993) and by extension with exposure to industrial relations stressors. Union members are more likely support and take part in union activities such as voting, filing grievances, and serving in a union role if they perceive that the union is effective (see Barling et al., 1992). As such, those who feel that the union is instrumental in achieving valued goals are more likely to be involved in industrial relations–related activities and roles, accordingly putting themselves at risk of exposure to the associated stressors and the experience of stress and strain. For example, individuals who see the action as instrumental are more willing to (a) vote for initial strike action, (b) support the strike by picketing, and (c) vote to continue the strike (Catano & Kelloway, 2004).

Union commitment is an important predictor of participation in industrial relations activities (Barling et al., 1992; Kelloway & Barling, 1993). Gordon, Philpot, Burt, Thompson, and Spiller (1980) defined a four-dimensional construct of union commitment that included union loyalty, willingness to work for the union, responsibility to the union, and belief in unionism. Subsequent research has focused on loyalty, responsibility, and willingness (Kelloway et al., 1992). Gordon et al. (1980) found that union commitment is positively related to union participation, including such actions as holding an elected union position and attending union meetings. Given that individuals who have a high degree of commitment to the union more actively participate in industrial relations activities, it is possible that they are at increased risk for exposure to stressors and the experience of stress and strain. Certainly, Kelloway et al. (2000) found that a high degree of perceived responsibility to the union was predictive of increased stress in a sample of union stewards. However, other components of union commitment, namely willingness to work for the union and union loyalty, were not associated with increased reports of stress. In fact, union loyalty was negatively related to stress stemming from industrial relations practice. Potential reasons for these findings are considered in the following section on moderators of industrial relations stress.

Moderators of Industrial Relations Stress

Given the potential negative consequences associated with exposure to industrial relations stressors, such as emotional exhaustion and somatic complaints, it is important to consider factors that moderate or buffer the experience of stress in the presence of these stressors (Bluen & Barling, 1988). Three potential moderators that are particularly relevant to the study of stress and industrial relations are union commitment (Kelloway et al., 2000), union instrumentality, and perceived support (Bluen & Barling, 1988; Bluen & Jubiler-Lurie, 1990).

As noted earlier, union commitment is an important predictor of union participation (Barling et al., 1992; Gordon et al., 1980; Kelloway & Barling, 1993). Given that being committed to the union increases the likelihood of participation in union activities, one might assume that it uniformly increases the likelihood that a person will be exposed to industrial relations stressors. However, Kelloway et al. (2000) found that one facet of union commitment, namely union loyalty, was negatively associated with self-reported stress associated with industrial relations involvement. That is, those stewards who were highly loyal to the union felt less industrial relations–related stress than did those who were less loyal. Although Kelloway et al. (2000) did not directly test for moderation, this pattern of results implies that feeling a high degree of loyalty may provide a buffer to industrial relations stressors. Given that union loyalty is viewed as the most valuable aspect of commitment in the prediction of union participation (Fullagar & Barling, 1989), future studies should more fully examine the predictive and moderating roles of union commitment, in general, and union loyalty in particular.

We also listed perceptions of *union instrumentality* as an important predictor of union participation (Barling et al., 1992; Kelloway & Barling, 1993) and by extension exposure to industrial relations stressors. However, some existing data suggest that perceptions of instrumentality may also play a moderating role in the relationship between industrial relations stressors and strain. Shirom and Kirmeyer (1988) reported that union instrumentality moderated the relationship between stress and strain in a sample of union members. Those members who thought their union was effective experienced less perceived stress and strain than did those who felt their union was ineffective. Based on this evidence, union officials must recognize the stress that is encountered by their members and make efforts to increase the effectiveness of industrial relations endeavours.

Social support has also been identified as an important moderator of the relationship between exposure to stressors and reports of stress and strain, both in general (e.g., Cohen & Willis, 1985; House, 1981) and with respect to industrial relations–related stress in particular (Bluen & Edelstein, 1993; Bluen & Jubiler-Lurie, 1990; Fried & Tiegs, 1993). Perceived support from various sources, including family members, union officials, and the union itself (Shore, Tetrick, Sinclair, & Newton, 1994), can protect individuals from the negative impact of industrial relations stressors. Bluen and Jubiler-Lurie (1990) found that industrial relations negotiators from both management and labor who had high levels of family support experienced less psychological distress than did those with low levels of support. Fried and

Tiegs (1993) reported that union stewards are an important source of support for rank-and-file union members. They found that strain was highest among those employees who experienced role stressors and perceived little social support from their union steward. Similarly, Bluen and Edelstein (1993) determined that the union itself is a valuable source of support for workers during stressful situations (see also Shore et al., 1994). After experiencing a mining disaster, miners who perceived their union as supportive of their emotional responses reported less psychological distress than did witnesses who did not perceive their union as supportive.

Outcomes of Industrial Relations Stress

The stress literature has documented a number of severe outcomes of work-related stress. Symptoms of strain have been classified into four main categories: physical, psychological, behavioral, and organizational. Physiological outcomes of stress include cancer, gastrointestinal illness, and cardiovascular disease (Kristensen, 1996; Quick, Quick, Nelson, & Hurrell, 1997) as well as increased incidence of the common cold (Mohren et al., 2001). Psychological manifestations of stress include anxiety (e.g., Billings & Moos, 1982), depression (e.g., Tepper 2001; Zohar, 1995), job dissatisfaction (Ulleberg & Rundmo, 1997), and cognitive failure (Kivimaki & Lusa, 1994). Common behavioral strain symptoms are increased alcohol (Cooper, Frone, Russell, & Mudar, 1995; Frone, 1999; Frone, Cooper, & Russell, 1994; Jones & Boye, 1992), nicotine (Cooper et al., 1995; Parrott, 1995), and psychotherapeutic drug (Cooper et al., 1995) consumption. Organizational strain-related outcomes include decreased job performance (Blau, 1981; Stewart & Barling, 1996) and increased absenteeism and turnover (Greiner, Krause, Ragland, & Fisher, 1998; Manning & Osland, 1989).

A number of studies have considered the strain resulting from exposure to industrial relations stressors and have determined that it is similar to the symptoms of strain described above. Increased blood pressure, a precursor of heart disease (Cooper & Marshall, 1976), is one physical outcome associated with involvement in industrial relations practice (Bluen & Jubiler-Lurie, 1990). However, much of the research to date on strain resulting from industrial relations activities has focussed on psychological manifestations of strain. Psychological indices of strain stemming from industrial relations involvement include increased reports of anxiety and decreased psychological well-being (Bluen & Jubiler-Lurie, 1990), emotional exhaustion (Nandram & Klandermans, 1993), and decreased job satisfaction (Kelloway, Barling, & Shah, 1993). Other studies have considered the psychological strain resulting from participation in a strike. Disruptive organizational events like strikes and lockouts have been associated with short- and long-term stress responses such as withdrawal, exhaustion, psychological distress, decreased perceptions of health, and decreased general functioning (MacBride, Lancee, & Freeman, 1981;

Milburn, Schuler, & Watman, 1983). Barling and Milligan (1987) demonstrated that strain resulting from strike participation does not necessarily dissipate with the end of the dispute. They found that symptoms such as psychological distress and psychosomatic complaints persisted up to 6 months following the dispute. To further consider the relationship between industrial relations stressors and strain, a number of the studies that have examined this link are reviewed in the following section.

Empirical Investigations of Industrial Relations Stress

Thus far we have made the argument that stressors are prevalent in several aspects of industrial relations practice, including participation in industrial relations–related activities and in fulfilling particular union and managerial industrial relations roles. Bluen and Barling (1988) structured their review of the industrial relations stress literature in terms of stress and strain associated with labor-management relations in general and stress associated with industrial relations roles. Following a similar structure, we will present some of the major empirical investigations pertaining to industrial relations stress.

Stress and the Labor-Management Relationship

Several studies have considered the stress resulting from participation in conflict-ridden labor-management relationships. The studies we will review here include Bluen and Jubiler-Lurie's (1990) study of the stress and strain associated with collective bargaining and two studies of the strain experienced by striking workers (Barling & Milligan, 1987; MacBride et al., 1981).

Bluen and Jubiler-Lurie (1990) investigated the stress associated with labor-management negotiations. They hypothesized that involvement in the process of collective bargaining would result in perceptions of stress and the experience of strain. Students role-playing in collective bargaining assumed the roles of labor and management in a simulated hostile bargaining session. Compared with a control group of students engaged in a similar participative project that was not related to industrial relations, the industrial relations group displayed greater increases in anxiety as well as more negative changes in blood pressure. Thus, even in a simulated setting, the practice of collective bargaining is stress inducing. Bluen and Jubiler-Lurie (1990) extended the study described above by investigating the stress experienced by labor and management representatives involved in actual negotiations. Again they found that bargaining gave rise to strain.

Another stressful characteristic of industrial relations practice occurs when labor-management relations break down (Bluen & Barling, 1988; Bluen, 1994). When labor and management are unable to resolve their differences, there is a possibility of a disruptive situation such as a strike or a lockout. MacBride et al. (1981) investigated the psychosocial impact of a labor dispute among a group of air traffic controllers. During the dispute, controllers exhibited increased psychological distress, decreased perceptions of health, decreased general functioning, and increased anxiety compared with the follow-up assessments after the dispute ended. MacBride et al. (1981) concluded that the labor dispute did not provide an outlet for job frustrations but rather aggravated tension and resulted in strain among the air traffic controllers.

Barling and Milligan (1987) also considered the psychological consequences of a labor dispute. They assessed the strain experienced by community college faculty during a 22-day strike and again 2 and 6 months after the labor unrest. During the strike action, there was a significant correlation between industrial relations events and strain. Specifically, negatively perceived industrial relations events were associated with decreased marital functioning, psychological distress, and psychosomatic complaints. In addition, Barling and Milligan (1987) found that the effect of negatively perceived industrial relations events on psychological well-being continued to manifest both 2 and 6 months after the end of the strike. This study demonstrates that industrial relations activities can result in the persistent experience of strain for those involved. However, Barling and Milligan (1987) noted that this particular strike ended with back-to-work legislation rather than the two parties reaching an agreement. Future research should examine the impact that the type of resolution has on strain, as it may contribute to increased vulnerability and prolonged negative effects on psychological well-being.

Stress in Industrial Relations Roles

Bluen and Barling (1988) suggested that union activity can be stressful for individuals involved in a number of union roles, including the union leaders, the stewards, and the rank-and-file members. In this section, we will review some of the empirical studies that have examined the stress associated with particular industrial relations roles.

Kelloway and Barling (1994) distinguished between passive union members, active union members, and union leaders. Passive members did not participate in union activities, active members participated by attending union meetings, and union leaders held elected office in the union. Their sample comprised a union of faculty members and a union of university support staff. Kelloway and Barling (1994) reported an ordering of stress outcomes such that leaders and active union members reported more negatively perceived industrial relations events, positively perceived industrial relations events, role ambiguity, role conflict, and job dissatisfaction than did passive union members. It is possible, of course, that members become active in the union as a means of dealing with stress or dissatisfaction (Barling et al., 1992), suggesting that stress causes activism rather than the other way around. However, Kelloway and Barling (1994) replicated their study with 6-month longitudinal data. The longitudinal component of this study supported a model in which activity in the union measured at time one predicted positively perceived industrial relations events, job dissatisfaction, and role ambiguity 6 months later. Results for negatively perceived industrial relations stress approached but did not attain statistical significance.

Consistent with these data, researchers have focused on the union steward as a central role in industrial relations (Barling et al., 1992). The union steward is exposed to a variety of stressors while engaged in industrial relations activities. Union stewards have many duties, including representing members, representing the union, handling grievances, and negotiating (Nicholson, 1976). Martin and Berthiaume (1993) investigated a number of factors that affect the stress experienced by union stewards, including role expectations, motivations for holding office, grievance-handling strategies, and their commitment to the employer and the union. They concluded that the steward's role is generally ambiguous. Role ambiguity is a well-documented stressor characterized by an unclear understanding of what a particular role entails (Kahn et al., 1964). Higher role ambiguity was reported for those stewards who choose to remain stewards in order to serve the union, those who attempt to maintain a working relationship between the union and management in grievance handling, and those who are highly committed to the union. Given that these attributes are desirable in union stewards, attempts should be made to decrease the role ambiguity, and thus the stress, encountered by union stewards (Martin & Berthiaume, 1993). If stewards are able to function in a less ambiguous role, it is likely that they will not only experience less stress but also better serve the union.

The steward's role expectations also affected the experience of role ambiguity (Martin & Berthiaume, 1993). Stewards who indicated that they represented the interests of both the union and its members experienced more role ambiguity. This finding may result from the pressure to balance responsibilities to the union and the employees, especially when they are in disagreement. Likewise, stewards who believed the steward's role was to represent management experienced increased role ambiguity. This finding is intuitive, as the steward's prescribed role generally does not include representing management.

Interestingly, Martin and Berthiaume (1993) found that the steward's motivation for maintaining office influenced both role ambiguity and role conflict. Stewards who took union office for personal reasons such as achieving power and prestige were likely to experience both increased role conflict and role ambiguity. It appears that an individual seeking office for personal reasons is not as highly invested in the union and therefore does not serve the union as well, resulting in ambiguity and conflict.

Kelloway et al. (2000) also considered the experience of industrial relations–related stress among union stewards. They found that psychological involvement with the union was a unique predictor of union participation, strike-related militancy, and industrial relations–related stress. In particular, those stewards who placed a high degree of importance on their union activity and more strongly believed that their union activity was a central life interest reported higher incidence of union participation, greater propensity to strike, a willingness to stay on strike for a longer period of time, and of particular importance for the current discussion, more conflict between their union and family roles and greater union-related stress.

The work of both Martin and Berthiaume (1993) and Kelloway et al. (2000) suggest that it is not simply holding a steward's position that determines the extent and nature of the stress experienced by an individual steward. Rather, individual attitudes relating to the steward's union involvement, reasons for participating, and expectations about the position are important contributors to the amount of role-related stress one reports. These findings further support our earlier argument that union-related attitudes are an important class of predictors in the study of industrial relations stressors and stress.

In addition to stewards, rank-and-file union members are also exposed to stressors in their roles. Nandram and Klandermans (1993) investigated the stress experienced by union members. They found that active members of unions experienced role overload and role conflict, both of which were significantly correlated with emotional exhaustion. Half of the active union members sampled indicated that they had experienced emotional exhaustion as a result of their union activities. In addition, combined role stressors affected emotional exhaustion more so than the individual role stressors alone. Thus, the more frequently a unionized individual encounters different role stressors, the higher the level of emotional exhaustion.

Shirom and Kirmeyer (1988) investigated the effects of union membership versus nonmembership on stress and strain. They found that, relative to nonmembers, unionized workers report higher levels of role ambiguity and role conflict. These authors suggest that union members are likely to experience higher role conflict because of their conflicting loyalty to their employer and the union. However, the increased reports of exposure to role stressors did not predict the incidence of somatic strain symptoms.

Very little research has directly investigated the impact of industrial relations stress on managers (Bluen & Barling, 1988). Bluen and Barling surmise that the diverging concerns of unions and management can place managers in a stressful position. Work supervisors are particularly open to stress because they are the liaison between management and labor working face-to-face with unionized employees as they handle labor complaints such as grievances. In this capacity, much responsibility falls on the supervisor to ensure healthy labor-management relations (Bluen & Barling, 1988).

Kelloway et al. (1993) investigated the influence of industrial relations stress among a group of industrial relations practitioners who primarily represented management. As daily hassles are predictive of stress in general (Lu, 1991), Kelloway et al. (1993) sought to determine if daily industrial relations–related hassles cause strain. In particular, they examined the impact of industrial relations hassles on strain via their impact on mood. They suggested that positively perceived industrial relations events contribute to positive mood, which in turn directly predicts job satisfaction. Alternatively, they hypothesized that negatively perceived industrial relations events contribute to negative affect, which in turn contributes to decreased job satisfaction.

Kelloway et al. (1993) asked industrial relations practitioners to complete measures of industrial relations stress, mood, and job satisfaction on a daily basis for a period of 20 days. They found that mood mediated the relationship between stressful industrial relations events and job satisfaction. Negative industrial relations stress was fully mediated by mood, but positive industrial relations stress had both direct and mediated impact on job satisfaction. Kelloway et al. (1993) extended their study to consider the time frame over which positively and negatively perceived industrial relations events predict job satisfaction. They found that positively perceived industrial relations events affected job satisfaction only on the day that the event occurred. However, negatively perceived industrial relations events had a lagged effect and affected industrial relations stress in the days following the experience of the event. Thus, daily industrial relations activities can be stressful, with negatively perceived industrial relations events having a more enduring effect than positive industrial relations events.

Measurement Issues

As mentioned earlier, the study of industrial relations stress has not been well integrated into the stress literature. It comes as no surprise, then, that the measurement of industrial relations stress has been at best poorly addressed. Typically, studies of the stress associated with industrial relations have taken one of two approaches; use/adaptation of the Industrial Relations Events Scale (Bluen & Barling, 1987) or adaptation of other preexisting stress scales to an industrial relations context.

The Industrial Relations Events Scale (Bluen & Barling, 1987) is a 44-item instrument patterned on measures of life events. Participants are asked to rate whether or not they have experienced an event and whether the effect of the event was positive or negative. Three scores—occurrence, positive industrial relations events, and negative industrial relations events—are obtained and can both offer insight about the number of industrial relations stressors to which an individual is exposed and provide information on the impact, be it positive or negative, of that stressor. The scale includes such incidents as experiencing an inconsistency between industrial relations policy and practice, joining a union, being involved in negotiations, and experiencing a strike or lockout. Respondents are asked to indicate the extent to which they view such events as favorable or unfavorable. Events that are perceived as unfavorable may have negative implications for a person's health and well-being, as they may result in the increased experience of strain.

Bluen and Barling (1987) provide detailed evidence for the test-retest reliability and the convergent, discriminant, and known-groups validity of the scale. Generally, the psychometric properties of the scale are satisfactory. Although originally developed in South Africa, the scale has also been used in North America (e.g., Kelloway & Barling, 1994; Kelloway et al., 2000). Kelloway et al. (1993) used a 25-item short form of the Industrial Relations Events Scale.

Investigators have also used previously established stress-related scales in either their original or adapted forms to study stress in industrial relations. Perhaps the scales most frequently used in this manner are the role conflict and role ambiguity measures originally developed by Rizzo, House, and Lirtzman (1970). However, Kelloway et al. (2000) also adapted the Kopelman, Greenhaus, and Connolly (1983) Work-Family Conflict Scale to measure union-family conflict. Although scales adapted in this way demonstrate acceptable internal consistency, the effects of such adaptation on scale validity are unknown, and, as such, more attention must be directed toward issues of measurement in the study of industrial relations stress.

Examination of the literature suggests that measurement issues have been neglected in the study of industrial relations stress. The paucity of validated, existing measures limits the strength of the conclusions researchers can make about the nature and extent of industrial relations stress. As such, there is considerable potential for scale development. Researchers should endeavor to develop and test measures that are specific to the industrial relations context.

Toward a Future Research Agenda

The research described in the current chapter indicates that industrial relations can be stressful. Evidence of the stressors associated with industrial relations is especially pertinent when one considers that a large portion of the work force is engaged in industrial relations activities. In addition, many nonunionized employees may be engaged in industrial relations practice on behalf of management.

Stress in industrial relations has been generally overlooked by organizational psychologists (Bluen & Barling, 1988; Fried, 1993). This neglect may be a function of a larger trend in organizational psychology to overlook industrial relations issues in general (Barling, 1988). A 1993 special issue of the *Journal of Organizational Behavior* was dedicated to industrial relations stress. In concluding that issue, Tetrick & Fried (1993) noted that ignoring industrial relations stress was a considerable oversight and that many avenues for future research remain to be addressed. However, very little research on industrial relations stress has been added to the literature since that time, and many issues remain unexplored.

Tetrick and Fried (1993) suggested that industrial relations stress should be examined within the context of the total work environment. Issues such as the relationship between industrial relations stress and the nature of the industrial relations climate should be studied. It is not known if an affable labor-management relationship attenuates the stress associated with industrial relations or if a hostile industrial relations climate exacerbates stress. In addition, the effect of both various managerial policies and procedures and the industrial relations history of an organization on the stress associated with labor relations stress is unknown.

The impact of industrial relations stress is not confined to those directly involved in labor-management relations. Members of various third parties can be exposed to stressors stemming from industrial relations incidents. For instance, it appears that labor disputes can be a direct source of stress for multiple parties. Strikes and lockouts are a source of considerable stress for stakeholders who are denied valuable services during a dispute. Greenglass, Fiksenbaum, Goldstein, and Desiato (2002) found that students whose academic year was truncated by a lengthy faculty strike experienced both anger and anxiety as a result of the dispute. On a similar note, Day et al. (2002) found that university students experienced impaired psychological well-being as a result of anticipating a strike by their professors. In other instances, individuals have to make difficult decisions regarding whether or not to cross a picket line to obtain services. Although crossing may result in criticism from striking workers, not crossing may mean going without necessary services.

Members of third parties may also be vicariously exposed to industrial relations stress. For example, family members may be affected by the stress and strain experienced by their relatives who are involved in activities such as bargaining or a labor dispute. Even though industrial relations stress is not confined to those involved in industrial relations, very little research has considered its impact on various third-party stakeholders. Future research should consider the manner in which industrial relations–related stressors directly and vicariously affect members of third parties.

To date, much of the research on industrial relations stress has emphasized the stressors experienced by those in unionized roles. Less research has considered the experience of industrial relations practitioners representing management. Similarly, the existing literature had emphasized labor relations as they occur in unionized settings. However, interactions between management and employees also occur outside unionized settings. To achieve a more complete understanding of the stressors associated with industrial relations, researchers must recognize and explore the experience of individuals who are not unionized.

We noted earlier that strain, including industrial relations–related strain, can be described in four major categories; physiological, psychological, behavioral, and organizational. To date, much of the existing research on industrial relations–related strain has focused on such psychological outcomes as anxiety (Bluen & Jubiler-Lurie, 1990), emotional exhaustion (Nandram & Klandermans, 1993), and psychological distress (MacBride et al., 1981; Milburn et al., 1983), with few studies considering the physiological, behavioral, and organizational outcomes. We encourage researchers to expand the domain of strain-related outcomes that they include in studies of industrial relations stress. The inclusion of a broader spectrum of strain symptoms will improve our understanding of the impact of industrial relations stressors on the individual, the union, and the organization.

Implications for Practice

Throughout this chapter, we have illustrated the ways in which various aspects of industrial relations are potentially stressful. Such a demonstration carries a number of important implications for those actively engaged in industrial relations. As a starting point, unions, management, and individuals involved in the practice of industrial relations must acknowledge the fact that industrial relations activities expose people to a number of stressors that may result in stress and strain. Once the stressful nature of industrial relations has been recognized, steps can be taken to reduce the stressors prevalent in industrial relations and help individuals better manage unavoidable stressors.

In keeping with the tenets of preventative stress management (Quick et al., 1997), we suggest that efforts to avoid, offset, or mitigate the stress associated with industrial relations must exist at both the organizational and individual levels of industrial relations practice. In other words, we propose that a major implication of recognizing the role of stress in industrial relations is that both organizations and individuals must take responsibility for addressing the problem. Organizational stress management initiatives would involve actions on the part of the union or the company as a whole. For instance, unions might ensure that their representatives receive adequate stress management training before they assume elected union roles. Alternatively, individual efforts reflect the steps that practitioners of industrial relations can take themselves to help manage relevant stressors such as leading a balanced lifestyle that includes a healthy diet and fitness plan.

Organizational and individual attempts to manage stress can occur at different times in the stress process. Primary stress prevention efforts involve the reduction or removal of the actual stressors (Hepburn, Loughlin, & Barling, 1997). For example, in the case of industrial relations–related stress, unions may be able to reduce the amount of role ambiguity reported by stewards (Martin & Berthiaume, 1993) by providing elected officials with clear job descriptions that remove some of the uncertainty in their roles. Clear ground rules for making decisions on potential grievances also help stewards deal with a potential source of role conflict. Similarly, stewards themselves may reduce their susceptibility to industrial relations stressors in a number of ways. For instance, they might avoid role overload by delegating some of their tasks to an assistant.

Secondary interventions focus on minimizing the negative impact of the response once a person has recognized the onset of a feeling of stress (Hepburn et al., 1997). Secondary initiatives at the organizational level in the industrial relations context might involve efforts such as providing free massage therapy services for members of negotiating teams who are feeling pressured to secure a contract. Similarly, individuals on the negotiating team might address their perceptions of stress by taking breaks to exercise and relax.

Finally, tertiary intervention strategies are used after the fact to help those individuals who have not been able to effectively manage or cope with stress and are now experiencing symptoms of strain (Hepburn et al., 1997). An industrial relations example of an organizationally driven tertiary initiative would be a case in which the union executive sponsored stress counseling for striking workers who were reporting strain associated with a lengthy labor dispute. To take this example to an individual level, striking workers who can recognize symptoms of strain and know to seek out treatment are engaging in effective tertiary intervention efforts.

Epilogue

The theory and research presented in the current chapter indicate that industrial relations can be stressful. Industrial relations–related stressors have been associated with such negative outcomes as job dissatisfaction (Kelloway et al., 1993), emotional exhaustion (Nandram & Klandermans, 1993), and psychological distress (Barling & Milligan, 1987; Bluen & Jubiler-Lurie, 1990; MacBride et al., 1981). Given that negative reactions to stress can have deleterious effects for the individual, the union, and the employer, it is important to gain an understanding of the stressors, individual reactions, moderating factors, and consequences of stress associated with industrial relations. However, research in this important area has declined. If a full understanding of the relationship between stress and the practice of industrial relations is to be obtained, research interest in this area must be regenerated.

References

Akyeampong, E. B. (2003). Fact sheet on unionization. *Perspectives on labor and income, 47*(7), 2–25. Ottawa, ON: Statistics Canada.

Barling, J. (1988). Industrial relations: A "blind spot" in the teaching, research, and practice of industrial/organizational psychology. *Canadian Psychology, 29,* 103–108.

Barling, J., Fullagar, C., & Kelloway, E. K. (1992). *The union and its members: A psychological approach.* Oxford, UK: Oxford University Press.

Barling, J., & Milligan, J. (1987). Some psychological consequences of striking: A six month, longitudinal study. *Journal of Occupational Behavior, 8,* 127–138.

Billings, A. G., & Moos, R. H. (1982). Stressful life events and symptoms: A longitudinal model. *Health Psychology, 1,* 99–117.

Blau, G. (1981). Organizational investigation of job stress, social support, service length and job strain. *Organizational Behavior and Human Performance, 27,* 279–302.

Bluen, S. D. (1994). The psychology of strikes. In C. L. Cooper & I. T. Robertson (Eds.), *International review of industrial and organizational psychology* (Vol. 9, pp. 113–135). London: Wiley.

Bluen, S. D., & Barling, J. (1987). Stress and the industrial relations process: Development of the Industrial Relations Event Scale. *South African Journal of Psychology, 17,* 150–159.

Bluen, S. D., & Barling, J. (1988). Psychological stressors associated with industrial relations. In C. L. Cooper & R. Payne (Eds.), *Causes, coping and consequences of stress at work.* London: Wiley.

Bluen, S. D., & Edelstein, I. (1993). Trade union support following an underground explosion. *Journal of Organizational Behavior, 14,* 473–480.

Bluen, S. D., & Jubiler-Lurie, V. G. (1990). Some consequences of labor-management negotiations: Laboratory and field studies. *Journal of Organizational Behavior, 11,* 105–118.

Brett, J. M. (1980). Why employees want unions. *Organizational Dynamics, 8,* 47–59.

Catano, V. M., & Kelloway, E. K. (2004). *Predictors of strike voting and strike behavior.* Unpublished manuscript.

Cohen, S., & Willis, T. A. (1985). Stress, social support, and the buffering hypothesis. *Psychological Bulletin, 98,* 310–357.

Cohen-Charash, Y., & Spector, P. E. (2001). The role of justice in organizations: A meta-analysis. *Organizational Behavior and Human Decision Processes, 86,* 278–321.

Cooper, C. L., & Marshall, J. (1976). Occupational sources of stress: A review of the literature relating to coronary heart disease and mental health. *Journal of Occupational Psychology, 49,* 11–28.

Cooper, M. L., Frone, M. R., Russell, M., & Mudar, P. (1995). Drinking to regulate positive and negative emotions: A motivational model of alcohol use. *Journal of Personality and Social Psychology, 69,* 990–1005.

Cropanzano, R., & Greenberg, J. (1997). Progress in organizational justice: Tunneling through the maze. In C. L. Cooper & I. T. Robertson (Eds.), *International review of industrial and organizational psychology* (Vol. 12, pp. 317–372). London: Wiley.

Dastmalchian, A., Blyton, P., & Adamson, R. (1989). Industrial relations climate: Testing a construct. *Journal of Occupational Psychology, 62,* 21–32.

Day, A. L., Stinson, V., & Catano, V. M. (2002, April). *Strike threats: Predictors of strain outcomes in affected third parties.* Paper presented at the meeting of the Society for Industrial and Organizational Psychology, Toronto, ON.

Dohrenwend, B. S., & Dohrenwend, B. P. (Eds.). (1974). *Stressful life events.* New York: Wiley.

Elovainio, M., Kivimaki, M., & Helkama, K. (2001). Organizational justice evaluations, job control, and occupational strain. *Journal of Applied Psychology, 86,* 418–424.

Elovainio, M., Kivimaki, M., & Vahtera, J. (2002). Organizational justice: Evidence of a new psychosocial predictor of health. *American Journal of Public Health, 92,* 105–108.

Fox, A. (1973). Industrial relations: A social critique of pluralist ideology. In J. Child (Ed.), *Man and organization.* London: Allen and Unwin.

Francis, L., Cameron, J. E., & Kelloway, E. K. (2004). *Picket line violence*. Unpublished manuscript.

Francis, L., Kelloway, E. K., Barling, J., & Keeley, C. (2003, March). *The impact of organizational injustice on the experience of stress*. Paper presented at the Work, Stress and Health Conference, Toronto, ON.

Fried, Y. (1993). Integrating domains of work stress and industrial relations: Introduction and overview. *Journal of Organizational Behavior, 14,* 397–399.

Fried, Y., & Tiegs, R. B. (1993). The main effect model versus the buffering model of shop steward social support: A study of rank-and-file auto workers in the U.S.A. *Journal of Organizational Behavior, 14,* 481–493.

Frone, M. R. (1999). Work stress and alcohol use. *Alcohol Research & Health, 23,* 284–291.

Frone, M. R., Cooper, M. L., & Russell, M. (1994). Stressful life events, gender, and substance use: An application of tobit regression. *Psychology of Addictive Behaviors, 8,* 59–69.

Fullagar, C., & Barling, J. (1989). A longitudinal test of a model of the antecedents and consequences of union loyalty. *Journal of Applied Psychology, 74,* 213–227.

Gordon, M. E., Philpot, J. W., Burt, R. E., Thompson, C. A., & Spiller, W. E. (1980). Commitment to the union: Development of a measure and examination of its correlates. *Journal of Applied Psychology, 65,* 474–499.

Greenglass, E. R., Fiksenbaum, L., Goldstein, L., & Desiato, C. (2002). Stressful effects of a university faculty strike on students: Implications for coping. *Interchange, 33,* 261–279.

Greiner, B. A., Krause, N., Ragland, D. R., & Fisher, J. M. (1998). Objective stress factors, accidents, and absenteeism in transit operators: A theoretical framework and empirical evidence. *Journal of Occupational Health Psychology, 3,* 130–146.

Hepburn, C. G., Loughlin, C. A., & Barling, J. (1997). Coping with chronic work stress. In B. H. Gottleib (Ed.), *Coping with chronic work stress*. New York: Plenum.

Holmes, T. H., & Rahe, R. H. (1967). The Social Readjustment Rating Scale. *Journal of Psychosomatic Research, 11,* 213–218.

House, J. S. (1981). *Work stress and social support*. Reading, MA: Addison-Wesley.

International Labour Office. (n.d.). Yearbook of labor statistics. In Statistics Canada (2003). *Strikes and lockouts, workers involved and workdays not worked*. Retrieved July 25, 2003, from www.statcan.ca/english/Pgdb/labor30a.htm

Jones, J. W., & Boye, M. W. (1992). Job stress and employee counterproductivity. In J. C. Quick, L. R. Murphy, & J. J. Hurrell (Eds.), *Stress and well-being at work*. Washington DC: American Psychological Association.

Kahn, R. L., & Byosiere, P. (1992). Stress in organizations. In M. D. Dunnette & L. M. Hough (Eds.), *Handbook of industrial and organizational psychology* (Vol. 3). Palo Alto, CA: Consulting Psychologists Press.

Kahn, R. L., Wolfe, D. M., Quinn, R. P., Snoek, J. D., & Rosenthal, R. A. (1964). *Organizational stress: Studies in role conflict and ambiguity*. New York: Wiley.

Kelloway, E. K., & Barling, J. (1993). Members' participation in local union activities: Measurement, prediction and replication. *Journal of Applied Psychology, 78,* 262–279.

Kelloway, E. K., & Barling, J. (1994). Industrial relations stress and union activism: Costs and benefits of participation. *Proceedings of the 46th annual meeting of the Industrial Relations Research Association,* Boston, MA, 442–451.

Kelloway, E. K., Barling, J., & Harvey, S. (1998). Changing employment relations: What can unions do? *Canadian Psychology, 39,* 124–132.

Kelloway, E. K., Barling, J., & Shah, A. (1993). Industrial relations stress and job satisfaction: Concurrent effects and mediation. *Journal of Organizational Behavior, 14,* 447–457.

Kelloway, E. K., Catano, V. M., & Carroll, A. (2000). Psychological involvement in the union. *Canadian Journal of Behavioral Science, 32,* 163–167.

Kelloway, E. K., Catano, V. M., & Southwell, R. R. (1992). The construct validity of union commitment: Development and dimensionality of a shorter scale. *Journal of Occupational and Organizational Psychology, 65,* 197–211.

Kelloway, E. K., Francis, L. D., Catano, V. M., & Dupre, K. E. (2004). *Third party support for strike action.* Manuscript submitted for publication.

Kelloway, E. K., Francis, L. D., Catano, V. M., & Teed, M. (2004). *Predicting protest: Solidarity, injustice and instrumentality as predictors.* Manuscript submitted for publication.

Kivimaki, M., Elovainio, M., Vahtera, J., & Ferrie, J. E. (2003). Organisational justice and health of employees: Prospective cohort study. *Occupational and Environmental Medicine, 60,* 27–34.

Kivimaki, M., & Lusa, S. (1994). Stress and cognitive performance of fire fighters during smoke diving. *Stress Medicine, 10,* 63–68.

Kopelman, R. E., Greenhaus, J. H., & Connolly, T. F. (1983). A model of work, family, and interrole conflict: A construct validation study. *Organizational Behavior and Human Performance, 32,* 198–215.

Kristensen, T. S. (1996). Job stress and cardiovascular disease: A theoretical critical review. *Journal of Occupational Health Psychology, 3,* 246–260.

Lawlor, E. E., & Mohrman, S. A. (1987). Union and the new management. *The Academy of Management Review, 1,* 293–300.

Lazarus, R. S., Delongis, A., Folkman, S., & Gruen, R. (1985). Stress and adaptational outcomes: The problem of confounded measures. *American Psychologist, 40,* 770–779.

Lazarus, R. S., & Folkman, S. (1984). *Stress, appraisal, and coping.* New York: Springer.

Lu, L. (1991). Daily hassles and mental health: A longitudinal study. *British Journal of Psychology, 82,* 125–133.

Lusa, S., Hakkanen, M., Luukkonen, R., & Viikari-Juntura, E. (2002). Perceived physical work capacity, stress, sleep disturbance and occupational accidents among firefighters working during a strike. *Work & Stress, 16,* 264–274.

MacBride, A., Lancee, W., & Freeman, S. J. J. (1981). The psychosocial impact of a labor dispute. *Journal of Occupational Psychology, 54,* 125–133.

Manning, M. R., & Osland, J. S. (1989). The relationship between absenteeism and stress. *Work & Stress, 3,* 223–235.

Martin, J. E., & Berthiaume, R. D. (1993). Stress and the union steward's role. *Journal of Organizational Behavior, 14,* 433–466.

Milburn, T. W., Schuler, R. S., & Watman, K. H. (1983). Organizational crisis: Part 2. Strategies and responses. *Human Relations, 36,* 1161–1180.

Mohren, D. C. L., Swaen, G. M. H., Borm, P. J. A., Bast, A., & Galama, J. M. D. (2001). Psychological job demands as a risk factor for common cold in a Dutch working population. *Journal of Psychosomatic Research, 50,* 21–27.

Nandram, S. S., & Klandermans, B. (1993). Stress experienced by active members of trade unions. *Journal of Organizational Behavior, 14*, 415–431.

National Statistics Online. (n.d.). *Union membership: Broadly flat in 2002 compared with 2001.* Retrieved July 28, 2003, from www.statistics.gov.uk/CCI/nugget .asp?ID=4&Pos=1&ColRank=2&Rank=896

Nicholson, N. (1976). The role of the shop steward: An empirical case study. *Industrial Relations Journal, 7*, 15–26.

Nicholson, N. (1979). Industrial relations climate: A case study approach. *Personnel Review, 8*, 20–25.

Odewahn, C. A., & Petty, M. M. (1980). A comparison of levels of job satisfaction, role stress, and personal competence between union members and nonmembers. *Academy of Management Journal, 23*, 150–155.

Parrott, A. C. (1995). Stress modulation over the day in cigarette smokers. *Addiction, 90*, 233–244.

Pratt, L. I., & Barling, J. (1988). Differentiating between daily events, acute and chronic stressors: A framework and its implications. In J. J. Hurrell, Jr., L. R. Murphy, S. L. Sauter, & C. L. Cooper (Eds.), *Occupational stress: Issues and development in research* (pp. 41–53). London: Taylor & Francis.

Quick, J. C., Quick, J. D., Nelson, D. L., & Hurrell, J. J., Jr. (1997). *Preventive stress management in organizations.* Washington, DC: American Psychological Association.

Rahe, R. H. (1989). Stressful life events. In T. W. Miller (Ed.), *International Universities Press stress and health series* (Monograph 4, pp. 5–11). Madison, CT: International Universities Press.

Rizzo, J. R., House, R. J., & Lirtzman, S. I. (1970). Role conflict and ambiguity in complex organizations. *Administrative Science Quarterly, 15*(2), 150–163.

Sauter, S. L., Murphy, L. R., & Hurrell, J. J., Jr. (1991). Prevention of work-related psychological disorders: A national strategy proposed by the National Institute for Occupational Safety and Health (NIOSH). *American Psychologist, 45*, 1146–1158.

Shirom, A. (1982). Strike characteristics as determinants of strike settlements: A chief negotiator's viewpoint. *Journal of Applied Psychology, 67*, 45–52.

Shirom, A., & Kirmeyer, S. (1988). The effects of unions on blue-collar role stresses and somatic strains. *Journal of Organizational Behavior, 9*, 29–42.

Shore, L. M., Tetrick, L. E., Sinclair, R. R., & Newton, L. A. (1994). Validation of a measure of perceived union support. *Journal of Applied Psychology, 79*, 971–977.

Stewart, W., & Barling, J. (1996). Daily work stress, mood and interpersonal job performance: A mediational model. *Work & Stress, 10*, 336–351.

Tepper, B. J. (2001). Health consequences of organizational injustice: Tests of main and interactive effects. *Organizational Behavior and Human Decision Processes, 86*, 197–215.

Tetrick, L. E., & Fried, Y. (1993). Industrial relations: Stress induction or stress reduction? *Journal of Organizational Behavior, 14*, 511–514.

Ulleberg, P., & Rundmo, T. (1997). Job stress, social support, job satisfaction and absenteeism among offshore oil personnel. *Work & Stress, 11*, 215–228.

U.S. Department of Labor, Bureau of Labor Statistics. (n.d.). *Trends in union membership.* Retrieved July 23, 2003, from www.aflcio.org/aboutunions/ joinunions/whyjoin/

Zohar, D. (1995). The justice perspective of job stress. *Journal of Organizational Behavior, 16*, 487–495.

14 Organizational Politics

Ken Harris

K. Michele Kacmar

Like stress, politics is ubiquitous in organizations. Perhaps because of its omnipresence, agreement on a definition of politics is difficult to reach. There have been numerous definitions of organizational politics presented in the literature including an entire article devoted to defining the construct (Drory & Romm, 1990). Although a number of different aspects of the definition were discussed by Drory and Romm, they failed to offer their own definition. In a recent review piece, Kacmar and Baron (1999) drew on the work of Drory and Romm as well as other conceptualizations to arrive at the following definition: "Organizational politics involves actions by individuals which are directed toward the goal of furthering their own self-interests without regard for the well-being of others or their organization" (p. 4). We will use this as the working definition for this chapter.

In addition to both being ever-present in organizations, stress and politics share a number of other common characteristics. For example, politics, like stress, is subjective and rests in the eye of the beholder. Exposure to a particular person, event, or environment often results in different levels of perceptions of political activity and experienced stress. Events perceived as political or stressful also produce different behavioral reactions in individuals. Some may try to flee the political or stressful situation by permanently (i.e., turning over) or temporarily (i.e., increased absenteeism or mentally checking out) exiting, whereas others may be invigorated by the situation and use the resulting adrenal rush that comes from being exposed to political behavior or a stressor to motivate themselves to rise to the challenge or use the situation to their advantage.

Because individuals' recognition of and reaction to political behavior varies greatly, the large majority of empirical investigations have examined perceptions of organizational politics rather than political behavior.

Theoretical support for this approach can be found in Lewin's work (1936) as well as the finding that perceptions of organizational politics relate to political behaviors (Valle & Perrewé, 2000). Thus, in this chapter, when we refer to politics, we are actually referring to an individual's perceptions of politics in the work environment.

Prevalence of Politics in the Workplace

Certain characteristics, such as people, policies, and history, are present in most if not every company. Some researchers have suggested that politics and stress should be placed in the same category (Ferris, Adams, Kolodinsky, Hochwarter, & Ammeter, 2003; Kacmar & Baron, 1999). As suggested by Ferris, Russ, and Fandt (1989), politics (i.e., self-interested behaviors) thrives in situations in which there is uncertainty or ambiguity. Thus, when discussing the prevalence of exposure to organizational politics, most employees face situations that are not 100% clear, certain, and/or dictated by company rules or policies. When conditions in an organization are perceived as being uncertain or ambiguous, individuals are able to "make their own rules" and act in ways that will benefit themselves (i.e., engage in political behaviors). Because of the uncertainty and inconsistency surrounding political behavior, one predictable outcome is stress.

Major Theoretical Models of Politics

In 1981, Porter, Allen, and Angle wrote a conceptual paper in the *Research in Organizational Behavior* series on organizational politics. They noted the paucity of work in the area and stated that the few papers published were primarily macro (subunit) as opposed to micro (individual) in nature. One potential reason for the overall lack of work in the area, especially at the micro level, was the absence of a commonly accepted theoretical framework.

Ferris et al. (1989) changed this when they proposed an extensive model of organizational politics perceptions (see Figure 14.1). Their model hypothesized antecedents, outcomes, and moderators of the relationships between politics and outcomes. They divided antecedents into three categories: organizational influences, job/work environment influences, and personal influences.

As depicted in Figure 14.1, the hypothesized organizational influences included an organization's level of centralization, level of formalization, the hierarchical level, and the span of control for each of the organizational individuals. The hypothesized job/work environment influences included job autonomy, skill variety, feedback, advancement opportunities, and interactions with others (either coworkers or supervisors). Finally, the hypothesized personal influences included age, sex, Machiavellianism, and self-monitoring. The predicted outcomes from perceptions of organizational politics were job involvement, job satisfaction, organizational withdrawal in the forms of

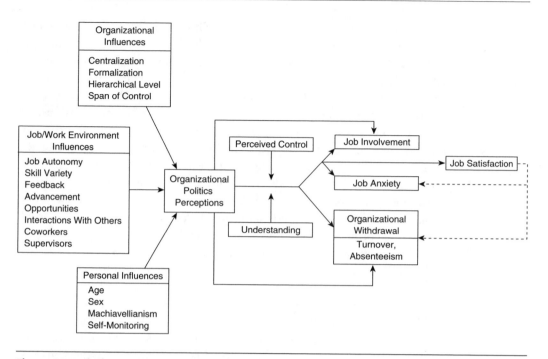

Figure 14.1   The Ferris, Russ, and Fandt (1989) Model

increased turnover and increased absenteeism, and most important to the present chapter, job anxiety. In the original model, Ferris et al. (1989) predicted only two moderators, perceived understanding and control. These moderators were predicted based on their ability to decrease feelings of ambiguity and uncertainty, which were thought to decrease the negative relationships between politics and outcomes, including stress.

In the years following the introduction of the conceptual model of organizational politics perceptions, most links in the model were empirically tested and supported (e.g., Cropanzano, Howes, Grandey, & Toth, 1997; Ferris, Frink, Galang, et al., 1996; Ferris & Kacmar, 1992; Kacmar, Bozeman, Carlson, & Anthony, 1999; Parker, Dipboye, & Jackson, 1995; Valle & Perrewé, 2000). In addition to investigating the links hypothesized in the Ferris et al. (1989) model, numerous researchers extended the original model by examining different predictors (organizational size, accountability, person-organization fit, participation/involvement, positive affectivity, and negative affectivity), moderators (demographic influences, tolerance for ambiguity, generalized self-efficacy, and task self-efficacy), and outcomes (organizational commitment, justice reactions, trust, organizational cynicism, job performance, organizational citizenship behaviors, and political behaviors) of organizational politics (e.g., Cropanzano et al., 1997; Kacmar et al., 1999; Maslyn & Fedor, 1998; Randall, Cropanzano, Bormann, & Birjulin, 1999; Vigoda, 2000; Zhou & Ferris, 1995).

One such extension was conducted by Zhou and Ferris (1995), in which the researchers examined satisfaction with different aspects of the job including the job itself, coworkers, supervision, pay, and promotion opportunities. The findings from this study showed that politics was negatively related to satisfaction with each of the dimensions of job satisfaction. Another extension was the Cropanzano et al. (1997) study, in which the relationships between politics and outcomes such as organizational support and organizational citizenship behaviors were examined. Still another extension of the Ferris et al. (1989) model occurred in the Kacmar et al. (1999) study. The researchers extended the model by examining different predictors (career development and cooperation) and new outcomes including performance and organizational satisfaction, and all of these links were empirically supported.

With the considerable amount of work performed on organizational politics, recent review articles (Ferris et al., 2003; Kacmar & Baron, 1999) provided updates, syntheses, and directions for future research. Both of these articles summarized the empirical work performed on politics, with the Ferris et al. (2003) article providing an updated model (see Figure 14.2) based on the findings since the initial Ferris et al. (1989) model was proposed. With specific reference to stress, this new model included not only the link between perceptions of organizational politics and job anxiety but also a link between politics and tension.

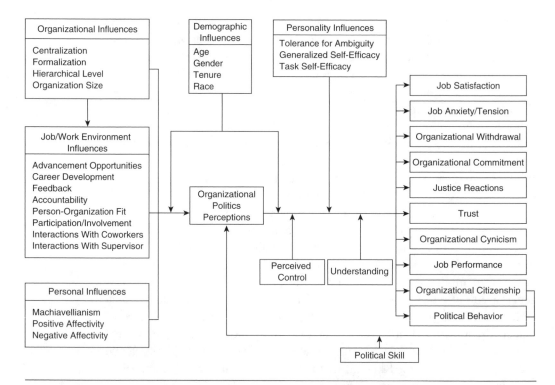

Figure 14.2   The Ferris, Adams, Kolodinsky, Hochwarter, and Ammeter (2003) Model

Predictors of Politics

Two early studies attempted to identify personal characteristics of organizational politicians—essentially, those traits of individuals who engage in politics (Allen, Madison, Porter, Renwick, & Mayes, 1979; Vrendenburgh & Maurer, 1984). As was previously mentioned, feelings of uncertainty and a lack of control are central to both perceptions of organizational politics (Ferris et al., 1989; Jex & Beehr, 1991) and are central to its being viewed as a stressor (e.g., Edwards, 1992; Parker & DeCotiis, 1983). Thus, causes and predictors of organizational politics are often those aspects of the organization, job/work, or individual that increase uncertainty and feelings of being out of control.

As can be seen in Figure 14.1, Ferris et al. (1989) identified a number of causes/predictors, and the large majority of these have been supported in various research efforts (Ferris et al., 2003; Kacmar & Baron, 1999). Since Ferris et al's. (1989) proposed model, the hypothesized predictors and a number of others have been empirically investigated. A full listing of the predictors of organizational politics is provided in Table 14.1, and we will begin by discussing organizational influences.

Organizational influence predictors. Vrendenburgh and Maurer (1984) were among the first researchers to explicitly suggest organizational predictors of politics. Their list of organizational predictors, which is highly similar to predictors of stress, included a lack of resources, segmentation of information, organizational opportunity structure, goal and task interdependence, ambiguous goals and roles, and organizational climate and history. Ambiguity was the only organizational predictor investigated, with Madison, Allen, Porter, Renwick, and Mayes (1980) finding that one quarter of subjects felt that higher levels of ambiguity led to increased politics.

Ferris et al. (1989) added to Vrendenburgh and Maurer's (1984) list by proposing centralization, formalization, hierarchical level, and span of control as organizational predictors. All of these variables have been examined, and the results have been mostly as hypothesized. For centralization, Fedor, Ferris, Harrell-Cook, and Russ (1998); Ferris, Frink, Galang, et al. (1996); and Kacmar et al. (1999) found positive relationships whereas Parker et al. (1995) established a negative one. The discrepancy between these findings is most likely due to the fact that Parker et al. created their own measure of politics rather than using an established scale. All three of the studies examining formalization found a negative relationship with politics (Fedor et al., 1998; Ferris, Frink, Galang, et al., 1996; Ferris & Kacmar, 1992). The results for hierarchical level have been mixed. More specifically, DuBrin (1988) found a negative relationship, Parker et al. (1995) recorded a nonsignificant relationship, and three studies (Drory, 1993; Ferris, Frink, Galang, et al., 1996; Ferris & Kacmar, 1992) found a positive relationship. Not only are these findings inconsistent with one another, but they also contradict earlier work that suggested that although those at higher levels

Table 14.1   Summary of Predictors of Organizational Politics

Characteristic	Study	Finding
Organizational Influences		
Ambiguity	Madison et al., 1980	Positive
Centralization	Fedor et al., 1998	Positive
	Ferris, Frink, Galang, et al., 1996	Positive
	Kacmar et al., 1999	Positive
	Parker et al., 1995	Negative
Formalization	Fedor et al., 1998	Negative
	Ferris, Frink, Galang, et al., 1996	Negative
	Ferris & Kacmar, 1992	Negative
Hierarchical Level	Drory, 1993	Positive
	DuBrin, 1988	Negative
	Ferris, Frink, Galang, et al., 1996	Positive
	Ferris & Kacmar, 1992	Positive
	Parker et al., 1995	Not Significant
Size of the Organization	Fedor et al., 1998	Negative
Span of Control	Anderson, 1994	Not Significant
	Ferris & Kacmar, 1992	Not Significant
Unionization	Fedor et al., 1998	Not Significant
Job/Work Context Influences		
Accountability	Ferris et al., 1997	Positive
Advancement Opportunities	Ferris, Frink, Galang, et al., 1996	Negative
	Ferris & Kacmar, 1992	Negative
	Kacmar et al., 1999	Negative
Autonomy	Anderson, 1994	Negative
	Ferris & Kacmar, 1992	Negative
	Zanzi et al., 1991	Not Significant
Career Development	Kacmar et al., 1999	Negative
	Parker et al., 1995	Negative
Cooperation	Kacmar et al., 1999	Negative
	Parker et al., 1995	Negative
Feedback	Ferris & Kacmar, 1992	Negative
	Kacmar et al., 1999	Negative
	Parker et al., 1995	Negative
Interactions With Coworkers	Kacmar et al., 1999	Negative
	Parker et al., 1995	Negative
Interactions With Supervisor	Ferris & Kacmar, 1992	Negative
	Kacmar et al., 1999	Negative
Relationship With Supervisor	Ferris & Kacmar, 1992	Negative
	Kacmar et al., 1999	Negative
Skill Variety	Ferris & Kacmar, 1992	Negative

Characteristic	Study	Finding
Personal Influences		
Age	Anderson, 1994	Not Significant
	Ferris, Frink, Bhawuk, et al., 1996	Not Significant
	Ferris, Frink, Galang, et al., 1996	Not Significant
	Ferris & Kacmar, 1992 (2 studies)	Negative/Positive
	Parker et al., 1995	Not Significant
Education	Anderson, 1994	Not Significant
	Parker et al., 1995	Positive
Gender	Drory, 1993	Not Significant
	Fedor et al., 1998	Not Significant
	Ferris, Frink, Bhawuk, et al., 1996	Negative
	Ferris, Frink, Galang, et al., 1996	Negative
	Ferris & Kacmar, 1992	Not Significant
	Parker et al., 1995	Not Significant
Locus of Control	Biberman, 1985	Not Significant
	Kirchmeyer, 1990	Positive for males, Not Significant for females
Machiavellianism	Biberman, 1985	Positive
Need for Power	Kirchmeyer, 1990	Not Significant for males, Positive for females
Negative Affectivity	Valle et al., 2002	Positive
Race	Ferris, Frink, Bhawuk, et al., 1996	Positive
	Parker et al., 1995	Not Significant
Self-Esteem	Biberman, 1985	Not Significant
Self-Monitoring	Ferris & Kacmar, 1992	Not Significant
	Kirchmeyer, 1990	Positive
Tenure	Anderson, 1994	Not Significant
	DuBrin, 1988	Negative
	Ferris, Frink, Bhawuk, et al., 1996	Positive
	Ferris, Frink, Galang, et al., 1996	Positive
	Ferris & Kacmar, 1992	Negative
	Fedor et al., 1998	Negative

engaged in more politics, those at lower levels perceived more politics (e.g., Gandz & Murray, 1980). The divergence in findings is most likely due to the type of samples used. Respondents from nonmanagement samples watched the political activities being enacted around them but were unable to participate in the process, leading to higher perceptions of politics than respondents from management samples who actively engaged in politics rather than simply watching from the sidelines. Finally, all of the studies (Anderson,

1994; Ferris & Kacmar, 1992, two studies) found nonsignificant relationships between span of control and politics.

Two other organizational influences that have been empirically investigated include the size of the organization and unionization. The Fedor et al. (1998) study investigated organization size and found a negative relationship with politics and that unionization was not related to organizational politics.

Job/work context predictors. Ferris et al. (1989) also hypothesized advancement opportunities, job autonomy, feedback, interactions with coworkers and supervisors, and skill variety as job/work context predictors of organizational politics. Ferris, Frink, Galang, et al. (1996), Ferris and Kacmar (1992, both studies), and Kacmar et al. (1999) found negative relationships between advancement opportunities and politics. Concerning the relationship with autonomy, Anderson (1994) and Ferris and Kacmar (1992) reported negative correlations, and Zanzi, Arthur, and Shamir (1991) found a nonsignificant relationship. The difference is most likely due to how autonomy was measured in the Zanzi et al. study. Specifically, these authors asked respondents how much autonomy had guided their career choices, not how much autonomy they experienced in their job. Feedback has been consistently shown to have a negative relationship with politics (Ferris & Kacmar, 1992; Kacmar et al., 1999; Parker et al., 1995) as have both interactions with coworkers (Kacmar et al., 1999; Parker et al., 1995) and interactions with supervisors (Ferris & Kacmar, 1992; Kacmar et al., 1999). Skill variety has been examined only by Ferris and Kacmar (1992), and a negative relationship was found.

Accountability, career development, and cooperation are three other job/work context predictors of politics that have been investigated. Ferris et al. (1997) reported a positive correlation between accountability and politics. For career development and cooperation, both predictors were tested in two studies (Kacmar et al., 1999; Parker et al., 1995), and the results showed negative relationships with politics.

Personal influence predictors. Allen et al. (1979) asked respondents to list personal characteristics and adjectives describing individuals who engaged in political behaviors. Adjectives that were on more than 10% of respondents' lists were articulate, sensitive, socially adept, competent, popular, extroverted, self-confident, aggressive, ambitious, devious, "organization man," highly intelligent, and logical. Vrendenburgh and Maurer (1984) added the personal characteristics of expedient, venturesome, shrewd, authoritarian, cynical, and locus of control. Of these variables, only locus of control has been empirically validated by Kirchmeyer (1990), who found a positive relationship for males but a nonsignificant relationship for females, and Biberman (1985), who found a nonsignificant overall relationship. These results are not surprising as individuals who are high in locus of control may or may not be more likely to perceive politics.

Ferris et al. (1989) hypothesized age, gender, Machiavellianism, and self-monitoring as additional individual predictors of politics. Each of these four variables has been empirically investigated with varying results. Of the six studies examining age and politics, one reported a negative correlation (Ferris & Kacmar, 1992, Study 1), one reported a positive correlation (Ferris & Kacmar, 1992, Study 2), and four found nonsignificant relationships (Anderson, 1994; Ferris, Frink, Bhawuk, Zhou, & Gilmore, 1996; Ferris, Frink, Galang, et al., 1996; Parker et al., 1995). The results from these six studies show that older workers exhibit no differences in perceiving politics, with the single negative (Ferris & Kacmar, 1992, Study 1) and positive correlations (Ferris & Kacmar, 1992, Study 2) likely being functions of unique samples. The results for gender are similar, as two studies reported negative correlations (Ferris, Frink, Bhawuk, et al., 1996; Ferris, Frink, Galang, et al., 1996), and four found nonsignificant relationships (Drory, 1993; Fedor et al., 1998; Ferris & Kacmar, 1992, Study 1; Parker et al., 1995). Machiavellianism was only investigated in one study (Biberman, 1985), which reported a positive relationship with politics. Finally, for self-monitoring, Kirchmeyer (1990) found a positive relationship with politics, but Ferris and Kacmar (1992, Study 2) found a nonsignificant relationship. These discrepant findings are somewhat surprising, as individuals who are high in self-monitoring are more aware of their environments and therefore more likely to perceive higher levels of politics than their low-self-monitoring counterparts. Thus, future research on the relationship between self-monitoring and politics is warranted.

A number of other personal characteristics have been investigated as predictors of politics. For studies of individuals' education levels, one study (Parker et al., 1995) found a positive relationship, whereas the second study (Anderson, 1994) found a nonsignificant relationship. Kirchmeyer (1990) investigated an individual's need for power and found a positive correlation for males but a nonsignificant correlation for females. Two studies examined the relationship between race and politics, and one found that minorities viewed their environments as higher in politics (Ferris, Frink, Bhawuk, et al., 1996) whereas the other found a nonignificant relationship (Parker et al., 1995). Self-esteem was investigated in one study, but the relationship reported was not significant (Biberman, 1985). Tenure has been investigated in six studies, with two reporting positive relationships (Ferris, Frink, Bhawuk, et al., 1996; Ferris, Frink, Galang, et al., 1996), Anderson (1994) reporting a nonsignificant relationship, and three studies reporting negative correlations (DuBrin, 1988; Ferris & Kacmar, 1992; Fedor et al., 1998). Finally, Valle, Witt, and Hochwarter (2002) investigated individuals' levels of negative affectivity as personal predictors of politics. Their results found that individuals who are higher in negative affectivity were more likely to perceive organizational politics.

Moderators of the Politics-Stress Relationship

In general, findings have shown that organizational politics has negative consequences for both the individual and the organization (e.g., higher job anxiety, lower organizational citizenship behaviors, lower levels of satisfaction with multiple different aspects of the job, increased intentions to leave the organization, and lower perceptions of organizational support) (Ferris et al., 2003; Kacmar & Baron, 1999). However, it appears that some of these negative relationships are moderated by several different variables. Although the moderating effects on a variety of politics-outcome relationships have been investigated, we focus here primarily on just those that relate to the politics-stress relationship.

Vrendenburgh and Maurer (1984) predicted that an individual's sensitivity to organizational politics will moderate the manner and degree in which predictors result in either political behavior or the perceptions of political behavior. The authors' reasoning behind this argument was that individuals with higher sensitivities will be better at acquiring information needed to determine how to act in various political situations. Ferris et al. (1989) expanded on the work by Vrendenburgh and Maurer (1984) when they introduced understanding and perceived control as moderators of the relationships between politics and outcomes. Their hypothesized relationships were based on Tetrick and LaRocco's (1987) work in the area of stress. Specifically, they posited that if individuals recognize the existence of politics in their organization but have minimal understanding or perceive little control over the processes, then politics will be perceived as a threat and will result in negative outcomes such as high levels of experienced stress. On the other hand, if individuals have high levels of understanding or perceived control, they will be more likely to think of politics as an opportunity to increase the benefits received and will result in more favorable or less negative outcomes (i.e., less perceived stress).

The first test of understanding as a moderator was conducted by Ferris, Frink, Gilmore, and Kacmar (1994). In this study, the researchers used organizational tenure as a proxy for understanding and found the interactive effect between politics and understanding lessened job anxiety. Ferris, Frink, Bhawuk, et al. (1996) and Ferris, Frink, Galang, et al. (1996) investigated understanding measured with Tetrick and LaRocco's (1987) understanding measure. The results of these studies found support for understanding as a moderator between politics and job anxiety.

Concerning studies of control as moderator, Ferris et al. (1993) examined this prediction in two separate studies. The first study operationalized control as supervisor status and found support for the moderation between politics and job anxiety. The second study measured control perceptions using an instrument developed to measure the degree to which individuals believed they could influence 16 aspects of their jobs and found support for the moderation between politics and outcomes.

More recent studies have examined other variables as moderators of politics-outcomes relationships. Three that are particularly relevant to the present chapter are level of commitment, self-efficacy, and teamwork perceptions. The first was conducted by Hochwarter, Perrewé, Ferris, and Guercio (1999), who investigated the level of affective commitment as moderator between politics and tension and found support for this contention. The second involved self-efficacy as a moderator of different politics-outcomes relationships (Bozeman, Perrewé, Hochwarter, & Brymer, 2001). The findings showed that individuals who were high in self-efficacy experienced fewer negative outcomes from perceptions of politics. The third and final study of specific interest involved teamwork perceptions as a moderator of the politics–job satisfaction relationship (Valle & Witt, 2001). Results showed that under high levels of perceived teamwork importance, the negative impacts of politics were minimized. On the other hand, when there were low levels of teamwork importance, the negative impact of politics on job satisfaction was the highest.

Measurement of Politics

Attempts to measure the impact of political activities in the workplace date back to 1978 when DuBrin published a book titled *Winning Office Politics*. In this book, he introduced a 100-item politics test that required respondents to indicate whether the items were true or false about themselves. The responses were scored using a pre-established answer key with one point being awarded for responses that matched the key. Resulting scores ranged from 100 to 0. Individuals scoring 90 or more were informed that they were power-hungry individuals with an uncontrollable tendency to act politically, whereas those scoring less than 35 were dubbed innocent lambs who believed that working hard was all that was needed to reap organizational rewards. Biberman (1985) used 50 items from this scale to test hypotheses about one's propensity to engage in political activities at work, and DuBrin (1988) published a shorter version of the scale, but no future researchers made use of the scale.

Another way in which politics has been measured in past research is via vignettes. Drory and Romm (1990) developed 15 critical incident vignettes to measure what they viewed as the key components of organizational politics. Similarly, Kirchmeyer (1990) used 20 vignettes to measure political behavior. Her vignettes were based on the seminal research performed by Gandz and Murray (1980), who asked respondents to describe how they got their way in their organizations.

In 1991, Kacmar and Ferris developed the Perceptions of Organizational Politics Scale (POPS). This scale consisted of the following three dimensions that reflected the variety of ways in which politics could be enacted in organizations: "general political behavior" (e.g., people in this organization attempt to build themselves up by tearing others down), "going along to get ahead" (e.g., agreeing with powerful others is the best alternative in this organization), and "policies and procedures" (e.g., when it comes to pay raise and promotion decisions, policies are irrelevant). This scale, or versions of it, has been used widely in the politics research arena (Cropanzano et al., 1997; Fedor et al., 1998; Ferris et al., 1993; Ferris, Frink, Bhawuk, et al., 1996;

Ferris, Frink, Galang, et al., 1996; Ferris et al., 1994; Ferris & Kacmar, 1992; Gilmore, Ferris, Dulebohn, & Harrell-Cook, 1996; Hochwarter, Witt, & Kacmar, 2000; Nye & Witt, 1993; Randall et al., 1999; Valle & Perrewé, 2000; Witt, 1998; Witt, Andrews, & Kacmar, 2000).

In 1997, Kacmar and Carlson conducted a series of studies designed to further validate the POPS. Applying structural equation modeling to a combined sample of over 2,500, they located a few of the original items that did not perform well and replaced them with others. The revised POPS had the same three dimensions but was composed of 15 rather than 12 items. As with the original POPS, the 15 items can be used as a unidimensional measure, or any of the subscales can be used to measure a more specific type of politics.

Outcomes of Politics

Now that we have discussed predictors and moderators of relationships with politics, we will turn our focus to the outcomes of organizational politics. Table 14.2 provides a summary of the outcomes frequently examined. Given that the focus of this book is on stress, we begin by reviewing the work performed on this outcome.

Table 14.2   Summary of Outcomes of Organizational Politics

Outcome	Study	Finding
Absenteeism	Gilmore et al., 1996	Not Significant
Actual Turnover	Witt, 1999	Positive
Innovation and Creativity	Anderson, 1994	Negative
	Parker et al., 1995	Negative
Intent to turnover	Anderson, 1994	Positive
	Cropanzano et al., 1997, both studies	Positive
	Hochwarter et al., 1999	Positive
	Kacmar et al., 1999	Positive
	Maslyn & Fedor, 1998	Positive
	Randall et al., 1999	Positive
Job Anxiety/Stress/Tension	Anderson, 1994	Positive
	Cropanzano et al., 1997	Positive
	Ferris et al., 1993	Negative
	Ferris et al., 1994	Positive
	Ferris, Frink, Bhawuk, et al., 1996	Positive
	Ferris, Frink, Galang, et al., 1996	Positive
	Hochwarter et al., 1999	Positive
	Kacmar et al., 1999	Positive
	Vigoda, 2002	Positive
Job Involvement	Biberman, 1985	Not Significant
	Cropanzano et al., 1997, both studies	Negative
	Ferris & Kacmar, 1992	Positive
Job Satisfaction	Anderson, 1994	Negative
	Biberman, 1985	Not Significant

Outcome	Study	Finding
	Cropanzano et al., 1997, both studies	Negative
	Ferris, Frink, Bhawuk, et al., 1996	Negative
	Ferris, Frink, Galang, et al., 1996	Negative
	Ferris & Kacmar, 1992, both studies	Negative
	Harrell-Cook et al., 1999	Negative
	Kacmar et al., 1999	Negative
	Nye & Witt, 1993	Negative
	Parker et al., 1995	Negative
	Randall et al., 1999	Negative
	Valle & Perrewé, 2000	Negative
	Valle & Witt, 2001	Negative
	Witt et al., 2000	Negative
Organizational Citizenship Behavior	Cropanzano et al., 1997, both studies	Not Significant
	Randall et al., 1999	Negative
Organizational Commitment	Cropanzano et al., 1997, Study 1	Positive
	Cropanzano et al., 1997, Study 2	Negative
	Drory, 1993, continuance	Not Significant
	Nye & Witt, 1993	Negative
	Randall et al., 1999, affective	Negative
	Randall et al., 1999, continuance	Not Significant
	Wilson, 1995, affective	Negative
Organizational Productivity	Anderson, 1994	Negative
Organizational Satisfaction	Kacmar et al., 1999	Negative
Organizational Support	Cropanzano et al., 1997, both studies	Negative
	Nye & Witt, 1993	Negative
	Randall et al., 1999	Negative
Perceptions of Equal Opportunity Employment Opportunities	Nye & Witt, 1993	Negative
	Parker et al., 1995	Negative
Performance		
Self-Appraisal	Kacmar et al., 1999	Negative
Supervisor Rating	Hochwarter et al., 2000	Not Significant
	Witt, 1998	Negative
Political Behaviors	Valle & Perrewé, 2000	Positive
Reward Accuracy	Anderson, 1994	Negative
Satisfaction (other than job)		
Coworkers	Drory, 1993	Negative
Pay	Zhou & Ferris, 1995	Negative
Promotion Opportunities	Zhou & Ferris, 1995	Negative
Supervision	Anderson, 1994	Negative
With Service	Zhou & Ferris, 1995	Negative
With Operation	Drory, 1993	Negative
	Ferris, Frink, Galang, et al., 1996	Negative
	Zhou & Ferris, 1995	Negative
	Vigoda, 2000	Negative
	Vigoda, 2000	Negative

To date, a total of nine studies have examined the politics-stress relationship. The majority of these studies—eight of nine—reported a positive relationship (Anderson, 1994; Cropanzano et al., 1997; Ferris et al., 1994; Ferris, Frink, Bhawuk, et al., 1996; Ferris, Frink, Galang, et al., 1996; Hochwarter et al., 1999; Kacmar et al., 1999; Vigoda, 2002). This relationship held for a variety of measures of stress, including job tension, somatic tension, general fatigue, and burnout, providing even more evidence that the relationship between these two variables is indeed positive (Cropanzano et al., 1997).

Numerous scholars have predicted that job satisfaction (e.g., Ferris et al., 1989; Vrendenburgh & Maurer, 1984) would be directly affected by organizational politics, and this outcome has received the highest number of empirical investigations (Ferris et al., 2003; Kacmar & Baron, 1999). Although Biberman (1985) found a nonsignificant relationship between politics and job satisfaction, every other study reported a negative correlation (Anderson, 1994; Cropanzano et al., 1997, both studies; Ferris, Frink, Bhawuk, et al., 1996; Ferris, Frink, Galang, et al., 1996; Ferris & Kacmar, 1992, both studies; Harrell-Cook, Ferris, & Dulebohn, 1999; Kacmar et al., 1999; Nye & Witt, 1993; Parker et al., 1995; Randall et al., 1999; Valle & Perrewé, 2000; Valle & Witt, 2001; Witt, Andrews, & Kacmar, 2000).

The relationship between organizational politics and organizational commitment also has received considerable attention, but the results have been more equivocal than those for job satisfaction. Cropanzano et al. (1997) published an article that included two studies, one of which found a positive relationship between politics and organizational commitment and the other a negative relationship. Nye and Witt (1993) and Wilson (1995) reported negative relationships similar to the negative correlation between politics and affective commitment found by Randall et al. (1999). However, Drory (1993) recorded a nonsignificant relationship between politics and continuance commitment, and Randall et al. (1999) reported a nonsignificant correlation between politics and continuance commitment.

The findings between politics and job involvement have been mixed, with results showing a positive relationship (Ferris & Kacmar, 1992), a negative relationship (Cropanzano et al., 1997, both studies), and a nonsignificant relationship (Biberman, 1985). More consistent results have been reported for organizational withdrawal. For turnover intentions, all five studies (Anderson, 1994; Cropanzano et al., 1997; Ferris, Frink, Bhawuk, et al., 1996; Ferris, Frink, Galang, et al., 1996; Hochwarter et al., 1999; Kacmar et al., 1999; Maslyn & Fedor, 1998; Randall et al., 1999) reported positive relationships with politics. For actual turnover, Witt (1999) has been the only researcher to investigate this outcome, and he found a positive relationship with politics. For absenteeism, only the Gilmore et al. (1996) study investigated this relationship, and the researchers found a nonsignificant correlation.

Limited and inconsistent results have been reported for organizational citizenship behaviors (OCBs). One study found a nonsignificant relationship with politics (Cropanzano et al., 1997), whereas Randall et al. (1999) found a negative relationship between politics and OCBs. Theory and conceptual work on politics (Ferris et al., 1989; Kacmar & Baron, 1999) would predict that organizations that are high on politics would have lower levels of OCBs, but as yet there is not enough research to definitely say this is an established relationship. Another outcome variable, organizational support, has received considerable research, and the results have all reported strong, negative relationships (Cropanzano et al., 1997, both studies; Nye & Witt, 1993; Randall et al., 1999).

Some other outcome variables that have been found to have negative relationships with politics include satisfaction with pay (Zhou & Ferris, 1995), satisfaction with supervision (Drory, 1993; Ferris, Frink, Galang, et al., 1996; Zhou & Ferris, 1995), satisfaction with coworkers (Drory, 1993; Zhou & Ferris, 1995), satisfaction with promotion and advancement opportunities (Anderson, 1994; Zhou & Ferris, 1995), organizational satisfaction (Kacmar et al., 1999), innovation and creativity (Anderson, 1994; Parker et al., 1995), reward accuracy (Anderson, 1994), perceptions of equal opportunity employment opportunities (Nye & Witt, 1993; Parker et al., 1995), and organizational productivity (Anderson, 1994). Additionally, three studies have examined the relationships between politics and performance ratings. Kacmar et al. (1999) examined the relationship between politics and self-appraisals of performance and recorded a negative relationship. Two other studies (Hochwarter et al., 2000; Witt, 1998) investigated supervisor ratings of performance, with Hochwarter et al. finding a nonsignificant relationship with supervisor-rated performance and Witt finding a negative relationship. Finally, Valle and Perrewé (2000) found that perceptions of politics positively relate to actual political behaviors.

Major Empirical Studies of Politics

As has been discussed in the previous sections, the large majority of organizational politics studies have been micro in nature and focused on the individual as the unit of analysis. However, before we begin a discussion of the major empirical studies of organizational politics at the individual level, we wanted to mention a few research efforts using different units of analysis.

Two organizational level studies were conducted by Riley (1983) and Zahra (1987). Riley conducted 20 interviews at two different organizations to determine the symbols used to create political images, and she found that there were three main structuring mechanisms: signification, legitimation, and dominance. Zahra collected data from 55 different firms and found politics to be related to different stages of the strategic process and negatively related with overall company performance. Two other studies (Galang & Ferris, 1997; Prasad & Rubenstein, 1994) investigated politics at the departmental level, and both of these studies found that politics played an important role in different departments. Finally, a number of other studies investigated organizational politics at the procedure or policy levels, all of which indicated that a lack of coherent organizational polices led to increased politics in the work environment (e.g., Gandz & Murray, 1980; Kacmar & Carlson, 1997; Madison et al., 1980).

Now we will discuss a number of the major empirical studies on organizational politics at the individual level as these are the studies that have established politics as a work stressor. The beginning of these studies can be traced back to the development of the testable model by Ferris et al. (1989), and the large majority of empirical investigations have been conducted by Ferris and colleagues (e.g., Fedor et al., 1998; Ferris, Frink, Bhawuk, et al., 1996; Ferris, Frink, Galang, et al., 1996; Ferris & Kacmar, 1992; Gilmore et al., 1996; Zhou & Ferris, 1995).

In chronological order, one of the earliest empirical studies was conducted by Ferris and Kacmar (1992), which investigated predictors and outcomes from politics. Shortly thereafter, Drory (1993) examined the relationships between politics and job attitudes, and Nye and Witt (1993) investigated the dimensions and a few outcomes from politics. Anderson's (1994) study worked at creating a measure and investigated a number of predictors and outcomes from politics. Four major empirical studies (Ferris, Frink, Bhawuk, et al., 1996; Ferris, Frink, Galang, et al., 1996; Gilmore et al., 1996; Zhou & Ferris, 1995) then focused considerable attention on outcomes, with Zhou and Ferris investigating different types of satisfaction and Gilmore et al. primarily focusing on the relationship between politics and absenteeism.

Cropanzano et al. (1997) examined politics and organizational support and both of these constructs' relationships with behaviors, attitudes, and stress. The authors extended Ferris et al.'s (1989) original model as they found that politics was not significantly related to OCBs and was negatively related to organizational support. Fedor et al. (1998) investigated organizational and individual predictors of politics and found that formalization, size of the organization, and tenure were negatively related to politics, centralization was positively related to politics, and unionization and gender were not significantly related. Randall et al. (1999) focused on outcomes from politics including job attitudes, performance, and OCBs. The findings from this study indicated that politics was positively related to turnover intentions, not significantly related to continuance commitment, and negatively related to job satisfaction, organizational citizenship behaviors, affective commitment, and organizational support. Kacmar et al. (1999) replicated and extended Ferris et al.'s (1989) model by examining different predictors and outcomes. In their study, the authors' extensions found that cooperation was a negative predictor of politics, and organizational satisfaction and self-appraisal of performance are outcomes that are negatively related to politics. Finally, one of the most recent major empirical investigations of politics was conducted by Valle and Perrewé (2000), in which the researchers found that perceptions of politics were positively related to both turnover intentions and political behaviors.

Future Research Needs

As has been evidenced by the previous sections as well as recent reviews of research on politics (Ferris et al., 2003; Kacmar & Baron, 1999), a considerable amount of work has been performed on the topic. However, there are still a number of areas that are in need of future investigation, and we bring particular attention to three of these.

First, there is a need to investigate the long-term impacts of organizational politics on individuals. Surprisingly, few (if any) research designs have been longitudinal, thus leaving unanswered a number of questions related to the impact of politics over time. For example, the research findings have suggested that, in general, organizational politics has a negative impact on desired organizational outcomes (i.e., job satisfaction, organizational support, job anxiety, and turnover intentions), but this might change over time. More specifically, employees who perceive political environments might experience short-term adverse consequences, but in the long term, these individuals may become used to and almost accustomed to the politics. As a result of this "becoming accustomed," the negative consequences from politics (Ferris et al., 2003; Kacmar & Baron, 1999) might be minimized or level off after a certain point. On the other hand, individuals may be able to adequately deal or cope with organizational politics in the short term, but long-term exposure to this kind of perceived stressor can result in damage to one's body (e.g., ulcers, acid reflux).

A second area for future research is to continue to investigate and gain additional insight into the antecedents, moderators, and consequences related to organizational politics. In particular, outcomes such as aggressive behaviors (Kacmar & Baron, 1999), relationships with different forms of organizational justice (Cohen-Charash & Spector, 2001; Colquitt, Conlon, Wesson, Porter, & Ng, 2001), levels of trust, and different aspects of performance including helping behaviors, group performance, and performance ratings by different individuals (i.e., self-ratings, supervisors, coworkers, and subordinates) are important areas to focus on in the future. Additionally, some research efforts (Ferris et al., 2003; Kacmar et al., 1999) have shown that politics serves as a mediator for various relationships. Continuing research in this area is important as relationships between predictors or antecedents with outcomes, including stress, may in fact be spurious as their relationships are a function of their relations with organizational politics.

A third area for future research is to investigate organizational politics in a cross-cultural context. Although a good deal is known about politics in the United States (where the majority of organizational politics research has been performed) and can be naturally extended to other Western cultures, little is known about politics in Eastern cultures. This is important to investigate as U.S. theories do not always apply cross-culturally (Hofstede, 1980; Kagitcibasi & Berry, 1989), and some of the cultural dimensions may have a considerable impact on perceptions of politics as well as correlates with politics. It is possible that individuals in individualistic cultures may pay more attention to self-interested actions than individuals in collectivistic cultures. Another consideration relates to the dimension of power distance (Hofstede, 1980). Individuals in cultures that are high on power distance may be accustomed to actions that would be considered political behaviors by U.S. standards (a country low in power distance); therefore these behaviors may be perceived differently.

Implications for Practice, Policy, and Intervention

As research has repeatedly shown, politics is more likely to occur in ambiguous and uncertain work environments. If managers wish to curtail political activity in their organizations, they need to create unambiguous work environments. There are a variety of ways to accomplish this. One of the most effective is to behave consistently. Rewarding one employee for a specific behavior but not others results in perceptions of politics. Thus, managers should strive to develop polices that are fair, communicate these policies to their employees, and then consistently enforce them.

Another way in which managers can reduce perceptions of politics is through goal-setting activities. Meeting individually with employees to set goals specific to them can help reinforce the effort-to-performance and performance-to-reward links needed to motivate individuals to perform their jobs effectively. However, for goal setting to be helpful in reducing perceptions of politics in the workplace, the goals must be compatible with the work environment. That is, achievement of a goal at the expense of others in the organization must be viewed as failing to achieve one's goals. Focusing attention not only on achieving the goal but on how the goal can and should be achieved should result in a more collegial organizational environment and one lacking in both politics and stress.

Epilogue

As this chapter has shown, politics and stress share a variety of characteristics. For instance, both are in the eye of the beholder; that is, what one person views as a political action or a stressor, another may not. Another similarity is that it is virtually impossible to rid the organization of either politics or stress. A final similarity is in how individuals react to political or stressful situations. Although some may embrace the situation and prosper from it, others may run and hide. Thus, organizational decision makers need to be aware of the potential causes and consequences of politics and stress so that they can take steps to minimize the negative effects both can have on an organization's bottom line.

References

Allen, R. W., Madison, D. L., Porter, L. W., Renwick, P. A., & Mayes, B. T. (1979). Organizational politics: Tactics and characteristics of its actors. *California Management Review, 22,* 77–83.

Anderson, T. P. (1994). Creating measures of dysfunctional office and organizational politics: The DOOP and short for DOOP scales. *Psychology, 31,* 24–34.

Biberman, G. (1985). Personality and characteristic work attitudes of persons with high, moderate, and low political tendencies. *Psychological Reports, 57,* 1303–1310.

Bozeman, D. P., Perrewé, P. L., Hochwarter, W. A., & Brymer, R. A. (2001). Organizational politics, perceived control, and work outcomes: Boundary conditions on the effects of politics. *Journal of Applied Social Psychology, 31,* 486–503.

Cohen-Charash, Y., & Spector, P. E. (2001). The role of justice in organizations: A meta-analysis. *Organizational Behavior and Human Decision Processes, 86,* 278–321.

Colquitt, J. A., Conlon, D. E., Wesson, M. J., Porter, C., & Ng, K. Y. (2001). Justice at the millennium: A meta-analytic review of 25 years of organizational justice research. *Journal of Applied Psychology, 86,* 425–445.

Cropanzano, R., Howes, J. C., Grandey, A. A., & Toth, P. (1997). The relationship of organizational politics and support to work behaviors, attitudes, and stress. *Journal of Organizational Behavior, 18,* 159–180.

Drory, A. (1993). Perceived political climate and job attitudes. *Organization Studies, 14,* 59–71.

Drory, A., & Romm, T. (1990). The definition of organizational politics: A review. *Human Relations, 43,* 1133–1154.

DuBrin, A. J. (1988). Career maturity, organizational rank, and political behavioral tendencies: A correlational analysis of organizational politics and career experiences. *Psychological Reports, 63,* 531–537.

Edwards, J. R. (1992). A cybernetic theory of stress, coping, and well-being in organizations. *Academy of Management Review, 17,* 238–274.

Fedor, D., Ferris, G. R., Harrell-Cook, G., & Russ, G. S. (1998). The dimensions of politics perceptions and their organizational and individual predictors. *Journal of Applied Social Psychology, 28,* 1760–1797.

Ferris, G. R., Adams, G., Kolodinsky, R., Hochwarter, W., & Ammeter, A. (2003). Perceptions of organizational politics: Theory and research directions. In F. Dansereau & F. Yammarino (Eds.), *Multi-level issues in the organizational sciences.* Oxford, UK: JAI.

Ferris, G. R., Brand, J. F., Brand, S., Rowland, K. M., Gilmore, D. C., King, T. R., et al. (1993). Politics and control in organizations. In E. J. Lawler, B. J. O'Brien, & K. Heimer (Eds.), *Advances in group processes* (Vol. 10, pp. 83–111). Greenwich, CT: JAI.

Ferris, G. R., Dulebohn, J. H., Frink, D. D., George-Falvy, J., Mitchell, T. R., & Matthews, L. M. (1997). Job and organizational characteristics, accountability, and employee influence. *Journal of Managerial Issues, 9,* 162–175.

Ferris, G. R., Frink, D. D., Bhawuk, D. P. S., Zhou, J., & Gilmore, D. C. (1996). Reactions of diversity groups to politics in the workplace. *Journal of Management, 22,* 23–44.

Ferris, G. R., Frink, D. D., Galang, M. C., Zhou, J., Kacmar, K. M., & Howard, J. L. (1996). Perceptions of organizational politics: Prediction, stress-related implications, and outcomes. *Human Relations, 49,* 233–266.

Ferris, G. R., Frink, D. D., Gilmore, D. C., & Kacmar, K. M. (1994). Understanding as an antidote for the dysfunctional consequences of organizational politics as a stressor. *Journal of Applied Social Psychology, 24,* 1204–1220.

Ferris, G. R., & Kacmar, K. M. (1992). Perceptions of organizational politics. *Journal of Management, 18,* 93–116.

Ferris, G. R., Russ, G. S., & Fandt, P. M. (1989). Politics in organizations. In R. A. Giacalone & P. Rosenfeld (Eds.), *Impression management in the organization* (pp. 143–170). Hillsdale, NJ: Lawrence Erlbaum.

Galang, M. C., & Ferris, G. R. (1997). Human resource department power and influence through symbolic action. *Human Relations, 50,* 1403–1426.

Gandz, J., & Murray, V. V. (1980). The experience of workplace politics. *Academy of Management Journal, 23,* 237–251.

Gilmore, D. C., Ferris, G. R., Dulebohn, J. H., & Harrell-Cook, G. (1996). Organizational politics and employee attendance. *Group and Organizational Management, 21,* 481–494.

Harrell-Cook, G., Ferris, G. R., & Dulebohn, J. H. (1999). Political behaviors as moderators of the perceptions of organizational politics-work outcomes relationships. *Journal of Organizational Behavior, 20,* 1093–1106.

Hochwarter, W. A., Perrewé, P. L., Ferris, G. R., & Guercio, R. (1999). Commitment as an antidote to the tension and turnover consequences of organizational politics. *Journal of Vocational Behavior, 55,* 277–297.

Hochwarter, W. A., Witt, L. A., & Kacmar, K. M. (2000). The moderating effects of perceptions of organizational politics on the conscientiousness–sales performance relationship. *Journal of Applied Psychology, 85,* 472–478.

Hofstede, G. (1980, Summer). Motivation, leadership, and organization: Do American theories apply abroad? *Organizational Dynamics,* 42–63.

Jex, S. M., & Beehr, T. A. (1991). Emerging theoretical and methodological issues in the study of work-related stress. In G. R. Ferris & K. M. Rowland (Eds.), *Research in personnel and human resources management* (Vol. 9, pp. 311–365). Greenwich, CT: JAI.

Kacmar, K. M., & Baron, R. A. (1999). Organizational politics: The state of the field, links to related processes, and an agenda for future research. In G. R. Ferris (Ed.), *Research in personnel and human resources management* (Vol. 17, pp. 1–39). Stamford, CT: JAI.

Kacmar, K. M., Bozeman, D. P., Carlson, D. S., & Anthony, W. P. (1999). An examination of the perceptions of organizational politics model: Replication and extension. *Human Relations, 52,* 383–416.

Kacmar, K. M., & Carlson, D. S. (1997). Further validation of the Perceptions of Politics Scale (POPS): A multi-sample approach. *Journal of Management, 23*(5), 627–658.

Kacmar, K. M., & Ferris, G. R. (1991). Perceptions of Organizational Politics Scale (POPS): Development and construct validation. *Educational and Psychological Measurement, 51,* 193–205.

Kagitcibasi, C., & Berry, J. W. (1989). Cross-cultural psychology: Current research and trends. *Annual Review of Psychology, 40,* 493–531.

Kirchmeyer, C. (1990). A profile of managers active in office politics. *Basic and Applied Social Psychology, 11,* 339–356.

Lewin, K. (1936). *Principles of topological psychology.* New York: McGraw-Hill.

Madison, D. L., Allen, R. W., Porter, L. W., Renwick, P. A., & Mayes, B. T. (1980). Organizational politics: An exploration of managers' perceptions. *Human Relations, 33,* 79–100.

Maslyn, J., & Fedor, D. B. (1998). Perceptions of politics: Does measuring different foci matter? *Journal of Applied Psychology, 84,* 645–653.

Nye, L. G., & Witt, L. A. (1993). Dimensionality and construct validity of the Perceptions of Organizational Politics Scale (POPS). *Educational and Psychological Measurement, 53,* 821–829.

Parker, C. P., Dipboye, R. L., & Jackson, S. L. (1995). Perceptions of organizational politics: An investigation of antecedents and consequences. *Journal of Management, 21,* 891–912.

Parker, D. F., & DeCotiis, T. A. (1983). Organizational determinants of job stress. *Organizational Behavior and Human Performance, 32,* 160–177.

Porter, L. W., Allen, R. W., & Angle, H. L. (1981). The politics of upward influence in organizations. In L. L. Cummings & B. M. Staw (Eds.), *Research in organizational behavior* (Vol. 3, pp. 109–149). Greenwich, CT: JAI.

Prasad, L., & Rubenstein, A. H. (1994). Power and organizational politics during new product development: A conceptual framework. *Journal of Scientific & Industrial Research, 53,* 397–407.

Randall, M. L., Cropanzano, R., Bormann, C. A., & Birjulin, A. (1999). Organizational politics and organizational support as predictors of work attitudes, job performance, and organizational citizenship behavior. *Journal of Organizational Behavior, 20,* 159–174.

Riley, P. (1983). A structuralist account of political culture. *Administrative Science Quarterly, 28,* 414–437.

Tetrick, L. E., & LaRocco, J. M. (1987). Understanding, prediction, and control as moderators of the relationship between perceived stress, satisfaction, and psychological well-being. *Journal of Applied Psychology, 72,* 538–543.

Valle, M., & Perrewé, P. L. (2000). Do politics perceptions relate to political behaviors? Tests of an implicit assumption and expanded model. *Human Relations, 53,* 359–386.

Valle, M., & Witt, L. A. (2001). The moderating effect of teamwork perceptions on the organizational politics–job satisfaction relationship. *Journal of Social Psychology, 141,* 379–388.

Valle, M., Witt, L. A., & Hochwarter, W. (2002). Dispositions and organizational politics perceptions: The influence of positive and negative affectivity. *Journal of Managerial Research, 2,* 121–128.

Vigoda, E. (2000). Internal politics in public administration systems: An empirical examination of its relationship with job congruence, organizational citizenship behavior, and in-role performance. *Public Personnel Management, 29,* 185–210.

Vigoda, E. (2002). Stress-related aftermaths to workplace politics: The relationships among politics, job distress, and aggressive behavior in organizations. *Journal of Organizational Behavior, 23,* 571–591.

Vrendenburgh, D. J., & Maurer, J. G. (1984). A process framework of organizational politics. *Human Relations, 37,* 47–66.

Wilson, P. A. (1995). The effects of politics and power on the organizational commitment of federal executives. *Journal of Management, 21,* 101–118.

Witt, L. A. (1998). Enhancing organizational goal congruence: A solution to organizational politics. *Journal of Applied Psychology, 83,* 666–674.

Witt, L. A. (1999, August). *I am outta here: Organizational politics vs. personality predicting turnover.* Paper presented at the 59th Annual National Meeting of the Academy of Management, Chicago.

Witt, L. A., Andrews, M. C., & Kacmar, K. M. (2000). The role of participation in decision-making in the organizational politics-job satisfaction relationship. *Human Relations, 53,* 341–358.

Zahra, S. A. (1987). Organizational politics and the strategic process. *Journal of Business Ethics, 6,* 579–587.

Zanzi, A., Arthur, M., & Shamir, B. (1991). The relationship between career concerns and political tactics in organizations. *Journal of Organizational Behavior, 12,* 219–233.

Zhou, J., & Ferris, G. R. (1995). The dimensions and consequences of organizational politics perceptions: A confirmatory analysis. *Journal of Applied Social Psychology, 25,* 1747–1764.

15

Terrorism

Michelle Inness
Julian Barling

I n Oklahoma City in 1995, right-wing extremists Timothy McVeigh and Terry Nichols killed 168 people and injured hundreds more in a bombing of the Alfred P. Murrah Federal Building. Dr. Barnett Slepian, a physician performing legal abortions, was shot and killed in 1998 in Buffalo, New York, by James Kopp, an antiabortion militant. Revolutionary Armed Forces of Colombia (FARC) guerrillas kidnapped two brothers, French businessmen in Colombia, releasing one shortly after the abduction with a hefty ransom demand for the other. In what has been called the largest terrorist attack in history, suicide bombers commandeered four American passenger airplanes on September 11, 2001, and flew them into the Twin Towers of the World Trade Center in New York and the Pentagon in Washington D.C., killing an estimated 3,000 people and injuring another 250.

These are but a few examples of recent acts of terrorism. A common feature among them is that each act has been waged in or against a workplace or against individuals as a result of their occupation. Workplaces may be particularly attractive targets for terrorists for several reasons: (a) large numbers of people congregate in them, (b) they are present at predictable times during the day, providing a "social address" where an individual or group can easily be found (Barling, 1990), (c) attacks on workplaces will gain significant public attention (Scotti, 1986), and (d) workplaces may be perfect targets from an ideological perspective, as particular workplaces may be selected because they represent an ideology that runs counter to that of the terrorists (Drake, 1998). Given that these features of workplaces are unlikely to change, it is also possible to predict that acts of terrorism against workplaces will continue in the future.

This chapter examines terrorism in its relationship to the workplace. We will provide a definition of terrorism, discuss some reasons why specific workplaces may be targeted by terrorists, and describe the impact of being a target of terrorism on individual well-being and behavior and potential outcomes to the organization. In doing so, we provide an overview of the psychological literature on terrorism in the workplace and explore a rich new area for research.

Defining Terrorism

Terrorism has been defined in the literature in a number of ways. In an effort to devise a consensual working definition of terrorism, Schmid and Jongman (1988) analyzed 109 definitions of terrorism and extracted their core and shared components. Common to the majority of these definitions are the notions that terrorism (a) involves intentional violence or aggression, (b) is motivated by an agenda that is inherently political, (c) is conducted for the purpose of creating fear among a populace, and (d) uses this fear to achieve a desired goal, which may be fear itself, to elicit desired behavior or to "send a message" (Schmid & Jongman, 1988).

Several distinctions can be made about the nature of terrorism. First, terrorism can be distinguished from other forms of organizational violence by its underlying intention (Van Fleet & Van Fleet, 1998). Whereas other forms of organizational violence are based on instrumental motives such as obtaining a resource or reactive motives such as retaliation (Little, Jones, Henrich, & Hawley, 2003), acts of terrorism are invariably based on the motivation to evoke fear. For this reason, the individuals and organizations targeted by terrorists are not necessarily the terrorist groups' primary enemy but may include apolitical and innocent civilians. Nevertheless, it is typically the primary enemy from whom a response is ultimately desired (Drake, 1998).

Second, it is important to recognize that despite the common characteristics that define acts of terrorism, there is a great deal of variation in the targets of terrorism, the nature of terrorist organizations, and the strategies used to evoke terror (Van Fleet & Van Fleet, 1998). For instance, workplaces that have been targets of terrorism have included government buildings, embassies, various businesses, office buildings, trains and subways, shopping centers and markets, aircraft and airports, banks, hotels, and universities. People who work in certain industries have also been more vulnerable, such as members of government, diplomats, businesspeople, peacekeepers, and police officers. In addition, terrorists or terrorist networks can differ in size, motivation, tactics, resources, culture, organizational structure, and method. The victims of terrorism can include organizations, groups, or individuals (Van Fleet & Van Fleet, 1998) and, as in the attacks of 9/11, physical structures.

Third, from the perspective of the victims of terrorism, attacks may seem to be random and have often been described as "indiscriminate," a term suggestive of the perception that little thought or planning contributed to the terrorists' selection of a target. Terrorist attacks, however, are typically anything but random. There are a number of factors that may contribute to terrorists' choice of target, but central among them is the terrorists' particular ideology. The terrorists consider organizations or people who represent ideologies that are inconsistent with their own to be legitimate targets, and the terrorists may justify the violence directed at these targets by holding them responsible for an undesirable state of affairs in the world (Drake, 1998).

Theoretical Development on the Impact of Terrorism

With few exceptions (e.g., Barling et al., 2003), theoretical development on the topic of terrorism has been relatively sparse. A number of explanations for this paucity of research can be hypothesized. First, terrorism has only recently emerged in the Western world's public consciousness as a prominent social problem. Second, terrorist attacks can be characterized as an acute work stressor, and acute stressors have been relatively neglected in the work stress literature (Pratt & Barling, 1988; van der Ploeg, Kleber, & van der Velden, 2000), perhaps because of the difficulty of predicting their onset. Nevertheless, acute stressors can often be more psychologically devastating and their effects more enduring than chronic stressors, which speaks to the importance of understanding their effects (Beehr, Jex, Stacy, & Murray, 2000). Third, existing models of work stress such as the demand-control model (Karasek, 1979), the vitamin model (Warr, 1994), and the effort-reward imbalance model (Siegrist & Peter, 1994) address the experience of work stress within the context of one's work role (Jackson & Schuler, 1985). However, little is known about how stressors that originate outside of the organization and outside of one's typical work experience affect one's job (Ryan, West, & Carr, 2003; Byron & Peterson, 2002). Perhaps as a result of these factors, research on terrorism has been limited to post hoc investigations, and there have been very few theoretical advances on the relationship between the experience of terrorism and subsequent strain.

Because theory should provide explanations for the relationships among variables and drive research (Sutton & Staw, 1995), it is appropriate to conceptualize terrorism at work in a way that enables an understanding and predictions about its link with personal and organizational well-being. One model of the underpinnings of the relationship between workplace terrorism and subsequent well-being has been described by Barling et al. (2003). These authors suggest that the individual's subjective appraisal of the event is a critical predictor of the experience of terrorism and the extent of resulting strain and explains why individuals respond to the same events with different levels of adaptation. This appraisal is made along five main dimensions, each with implications for well-being.

The first dimension is perceived control, which refers to the extent to which individuals believe they have agency over stressful events at work. Generally, the greater one's perceived control in a stressful situation, the better one's subsequent well-being (Terry & Jimmieson, 1999). Extending these findings somewhat, it has also been suggested that incidents such as natural disasters involving a complete lack of control may result in less strain than incidents in which individuals' perception of personal control has been actively weakened by another person or group (Baum, Fleming, & Davidson, 1983). The second dimension in Barling et al.'s (2003) framework is the individual's causal attributions for the event. People who experience negative or unexpected events tend to search for an explanation for these events (Heider, 1958; Kelley, 1973). When an individual attributes the causes of negative events to external sources, sense of personal power may be undermined and well-being may suffer. Third, stressful events that are caused by another person's intentional attempt to harm the victim, as opposed to accidents or natural disasters, may be more detrimental to well-being (Barling et al., 2003). Fourth, different types of disasters are associated with different "low points," the point in time at which the individual no longer feels that the reoccurrence of the disaster is likely (Baum & Fleming, 1993). Individuals' distress will persist until the low point is reached so that the longer it takes to reach the low point, the more persistent the distress. As long as individuals believe that the terrorist act might occur or recur, the low point will not be reached. Finally, events that create uncertainty about one's future are more likely to be detrimental to well-being (Barling et al., 2003).

According to this model, terrorist attacks constitute a stressor that is highly likely to threaten well-being. Specifically, in a terrorist attack, people are likely to feel that their personal control has been limited or eliminated. Individuals may also tend to make an external attribution for the attack, perceiving that they were unable to exert agency over their own fate, with detrimental consequences to well-being. The intentional nature of the attacks may cause victims additional distress (e.g., North & Pfefferbaum, 2002; Smith & North, 1993; Rubonis & Bickman, 1991). The time taken to reach the low point after a terrorist attack may be prolonged, particularly if there are ongoing government warnings of the likelihood of recurrence (Barling et al., 2003; Baum, 1991). Finally, terrorist attacks can create an enormous amount of uncertainty about the future. Following an attack, people may live in fear of future attacks or face uncertainty regarding the future of their job, their organization, and their lives. Although the experiences of workplace violence and terrorism experienced at work often differ in terms of magnitude, the literature on workplace violence provides additional evidence for hypothesizing effects of terrorism on well-being. Specifically, the literature on workplace violence suggests that the fear of future aggression has been identified as a major consequence of experiencing or witnessing aggression or violence and is a central predictor of subsequent well-being (Barling, Rogers, & Kelloway, 2001; Budd, Arvey, & Lawless, 1996; Schat & Kelloway, 2000).

When Terrorism Exerts Its Greatest Impact

Existing research on terrorism has contributed much to identifying situational and individual difference factors contributing to the duration and severity of distress following a terrorist attack (e.g., Desivilya, Gal, & Ayalon, 1996; Rubonis & Bickman, 1991). With respect to situational factors, people who were directly victimized in the terrorist attack on 9/11 or who were in close proximity to the attack were more likely to experience extreme stress reactions than people whose involvement was more peripheral (Piotrkowski & Brannen, 2002; Schlenger et al., 2002). Similarly, people who personally witnessed the attacks were more likely to suffer psychological impairment than people whose exposure was limited to media reports of these events. In addition, people who have lost relatively more in a terrorist attack are more likely to suffer higher levels of distress following a terrorist attack (Silver, Holman, McIntosh, Poulin, & Gil-Rivas, 2002).

The extent of the disaster caused by the event is another important determinant of individuals' stress reactions. Specifically, the likelihood of adverse effects of a disaster will be greater when it results in a more extreme rate of injury, loss of human life or threat to human life, or more extensive damage to property and/or when it creates persistent and dramatic problems for the community (Norris, Friedman, & Watson, 2002). For example, in a review of 52 studies on the psychological outcomes following disasters, Rubonis and Bickman (1991) found that the rate of human casualties in a disaster is related to subsequent psychopathology among members of the victimized population.

Research has also identified a number of individual difference factors that may moderate a highly stressful experience such as terrorism and subsequent psychological outcomes. Characteristics such as negative affectivity (Houkes, Janssen, de Jonge, & Bakker, 2003) and, conversely, positive emotions such as gratitude, interest, and love (Frederickson, Tugade, Waugh, & Larkin, 2003) and empathy (Regehr, Goldberg, & Hughes, 2002) are related to strain after a traumatic event, possibly through the impact of affect on resilience (Frederickson et al., 2003). Demographic characteristics (e.g., gender, minority group status) may also make subsequent strain more likely. Having a preexisting disorder such as depression or anxiety may make an individual more vulnerable to the effects of terrorism on well-being (Silver et al., 2002). Finally, people tend to be motivated to see the world as a fairly predictable and safe place. A traumatic event such as a terrorist attack can seriously challenge this worldview (McFarlane & de Girolamo, 1996). To the extent that people feel that their perception of the world as safe, predictable, and within their control is lost, individuals may feel distress and become more vulnerable to psychopathology (Piotrkowski & Brannen, 2002).

The multivariate risk/resilience model (Freedy, Kilpatrick, & Resnick, 1993) was developed to explain individual reactions to disasters, but it can also be applied to other acute stressors as well (Byron & Peterson, 2002). This model incorporates individual difference and situational factors before, during, and after the experience of an acute disaster that moderate an individual's reaction to the disaster. These stressors include personality characteristics (such as the individual's dispositional optimism) and situational factors (such as the extent to which the individual receives social support on an ongoing basis, targeted social support, or social support received in direct response to the disaster and the individual's exposure to the disaster) (Byron & Peterson, 2002). In an empirical study, Byron and Peterson (2002) examined the effects of these factors on individual psychological strain and job dissatisfaction following the terrorist attacks of September 11. They found that both targeted social support and degree of exposure to the disaster were associated with subsequent psychological well-being and strain, respectively, and that dispositional optimism and coworker support predicted job satisfaction.

The Effect of Terrorism on Well-Being

In this section we examine the effect of experiencing a disaster on personal well-being and work-related well-being. We then examine various factors that may moderate the effect of terrorism on well-being, and we look at the potential impact of terrorism on the organization as a whole. We hypothesize important effects largely on the basis of literature examining the effects of other (nonterrorism) acute stressors on well-being. At the outset, it is important to recognize that at present there is little to no empirical research specifically looking at the effects of terrorism at work on personal and organizational well-being. We present these topics as a way of initiating the process of conceptualization of potential outcomes and motivating future research. In doing so, we hope to provide some direction for future research on the impact of terrorism on the workplace. The topics covered herein are not meant to be exhaustive but are intended to provide an overview of some of the main psychological outcomes found to result from acute stress.

Effects on Personal Well-Being

By far, the bulk of empirical research examining the outcomes of terrorism has focused on the effects of terrorism on the well-being of people in the general population (e.g., North & Pfefferbaum, 2002; Silver et al., 2002). In the literature on terrorism, as in many literatures, well-being has largely been conceptualized in terms of the presence or absence of illness or distress (for discussion, see Inness & Barling, 2003). The most commonly examined indicators of well-being following stress include general psychological distress that may include symptoms of depression, anxiety and fear, emotional upset, loss of concentration, and sleep disturbance, as well as posttraumatic stress disorder (PTSD; North & Pfefferbaum, 2002; Hanson, Kilpatrick, Falsetti, & Resnick, 1995).

Of the research that has examined well-being following a terrorist attack, most studies have focused on the incidence of psychological distress in the *general population* in the months following a terrorist attack (e.g., Schlenger et al., 2002) and over time (e.g., Galea et al., 2002). With few exceptions (Byron & Peterson, 2002), empirical investigations focusing on *employees* or *organizations* that have experienced terrorism in their workplace are rare. The findings of studies on distress in the general population, however, may be informative for predicting the effect on well-being that employees may experience if their organization has been the target of terrorism. It is likely, however, that rates of distress in the general population will be conservative when compared with rates of distress within an organization that was directly targeted.

Nevertheless, an awareness of the effects of terrorism in general on well-being can provide an important basis for understanding workplace-based terrorism.

Posttraumatic stress disorder. A number of studies have suggested that people who are victimized by terrorist attacks may develop clinically significant symptoms severe enough for a diagnosis of PTSD (North & Pfefferbaum, 2002). Research suggests that acts of intentional malfeasance such as terrorist attacks are more likely than are accidents to result in PTSD. Data suggest that within 1 week of the attacks of September 11, 44% of a random sample reported being bothered "extremely" or "quite a bit" by the attacks, and approximately one in five people reported experiencing at least one symptom of PTSD (Schuster et al., 2002). A separate study by Piotrkowski and Brannen (2002) conducted 25 weeks after the attacks of 9/11 with a sample of people with relatively low levels of exposure to the attacks suggested that people reported an average of over four symptoms of PTSD, and 28% of the sample reported seven or more symptoms. A separate study with a sample of people living outside of New York City found that approximately 17% of the sample reported posttraumatic stress symptoms 2 months after the attacks and 5.8% had symptoms as long as 6 months after the attacks (Silver et al., 2002). Similar to research on subclinical psychological symptoms, research on PTSD suggests that the more centrally involved or proximal an individual is to an attack (Schlenger et al., 2002), the more extreme the events experienced (Shalev et al., 1998); and the shorter the length of time since the attack (Silver et al., 2002), the greater the likelihood of subsequent clinical diagnosis such as PTSD or major depression. This speaks to the heightened likelihood of negative psychological outcomes following an attack in which one's organization was directly targeted.

Vulnerability and helplessness. Empirical research suggests that in the aftermath of terrorism, one frequent response is a heightened feeling of personal vulnerability (Eidelson & Eidelson, 2003). Vulnerability reflects individuals' perception of being consistently in danger and having insufficient control over external threat to garner a sense of safety (Beck, Emery, & Greenberg,

1985). People with a relatively high perception of personal vulnerability tend to have concomitant levels of anxiety and may engage in catastrophic thinking, an exaggerated perception that their personal circumstances will substantially deteriorate at some point and that this fate is predestined and beyond personal control. Although moderate levels of anxiety may be functional when confronted with a severe acute stressor, very high levels can be a detriment to the individuals' overall quality of life.

A second outcome of the loss of perceived control that may follow the experience of terrorism in the workplace is a perception of helplessness, the belief that one's actions will fail to produce desired results, even with extensive effort and planning (Eidelson & Eidelson, 2003). Similar to perceived vulnerability, helplessness is often self-perpetuating, as the belief that one's actions are futile limits an individual's motivation to attempt new or challenging tasks.

Research on the duration of distress following a terrorist attack suggests that the negative impact of terrorism on an individual's fear of a future attack may linger. Many studies examining incidence rates of psychopathology and distress in a population proximal to a disaster site have shown elevated levels of distress that have persisted months after the attacks (Galea et al., 2002; Schlenger et al., 2002). A series of studies (Baum, Gatchel, & Schaeffer, 1983; Davidson, Baum, Fleming, & Gisriel, 1986) examined the psychological outcomes of residents who lived near Three Mile Island following the disaster in 1979. Psychological distress and a perceived loss of control were still apparent over 1 (Baum et al., 1983) and 2 (Davidson et al., 1986) years following the event for people who resided in the vicinity of the disaster.

Other research suggests that nearly 38% of a sample of 2,729 participants reported having fears of future attacks as long as 6 months after the September 11 terrorist attacks (Silver et al., 2002). Research examining subclinical psychological responses to the September 11 attacks suggests that even people who were not personally involved in the attacks suffered from recurring painful memories of the event (DeLisi et al., 2003; Schlenger et al., 2002), anxiety, fear of future terrorism and fear of harm to their family (Silver et al., 2002), and event-related strain (Byron & Peterson, 2002). For instance, in one study, fears of future terrorism were present in two thirds of the sample 2 months after the attack, and over one third of the sample still remained fearful after 6 months (Silver et al., 2002). In another study, having recurring memories of the attack was found to be the most common postattack outcome among New Yorkers (DeLisi et al., 2003). Other studies suggest that an increase in physical ailments can also be associated with a terrorist attack. For instance, a substantial increase in stress-related and respiratory illness emerged among members of the New York City Fire Department who worked among substantial dust and debris to provide emergency medical services following the attacks (Banauch et al., 2002).

Sense of loss. In the aftermath of a disaster, individuals can feel that they have suffered major losses, some tangible, others intangible. In a disaster, people can lose physical resources such as their belongings (Freedy, Saladin, Kilpatrick, Resnick, & Saunders, 1994), they may grieve the loss of friends and coworkers, and they can also feel that they have lost psychosocial resources including a lost routine, a lost sense of control over their outcomes, and a loss of optimism and goals for the future (Smith & Freedy, 2000). In a study of victims of hurricane Hugo, loss of resources accounted for more variance in individuals' postdisaster well-being than their coping strategies. Perhaps more relevant to the types of losses one is likely to incur in an incident of terrorism in the workplace is that of psychosocial losses. For instance, in the terrorist attacks on 9/11, many people lost their entire workplace and many of their coworkers. Research has shown that perceptions of losses such as these are often concomitant with suffering through an acute traumatic event and can have a significant impact on postdisaster functioning (Norris Friedman, Watson, Byrne, Diaz, Kaniasty, 2002; Smith & Freedy, 2000).

Somatic complaints. Research on work stress suggests that the experience of stress may lead to somatic health complaints. The bulk of research on the physiological effects of work stress has looked at chronic stressors (e.g., Fox, Dwyer, & Ganster, 1993). Acute stressors and traumas, however, may also lead to physical ailments such as headaches and sleep disruptions (Braverman, 1992). Following a traumatic event such as a terrorist attack, individuals may suffer physical ailments as a direct result of injuries incurred during the attack or as indirect effects of the psychological trauma of the event. Indeed, one explanation for the increased absenteeism immediately following the attack in New York on 9/11 is the possibility that individuals' physical health had suffered as a result (Byron & Peterson, 2002).

Effects on Well-Being That Are Directly Related to One's Work Role

Role ambiguity and performance. Role ambiguity reflects a level of uncertainty or lack of clarity regarding one's job or role (Breaugh & Colihan, 1994). Role ambiguity includes the uncertainty about one's responsibility, how to carry out that responsibility, how responsibilities are evaluated, and the consequences of not fulfilling one's role responsibilities (Eys & Carron, 2001). When an organization has been the target of terrorism, the work environment may be quite disorganized. If coworkers have been killed or injured, the resources required to perform one's job have been destroyed, or, as was the case in the attacks on September 11, the workplace itself has been destroyed, individuals may be unsure of how to go about performing their normal job-related tasks. Lacking clarity regarding one's job impairs people from accomplishing their job-related goals. When employees are unsure about what is expected of them, they may have difficulty plotting a course of action, and, as a result, their job performance may suffer (Beauchamp, Bray, Eys, & Carron, 2002).

Threats to self-efficacy. Self-efficacy reflects the belief that a person can organize and execute specific behaviors (Bandura, 1997). Efficacy beliefs are acquired through mastery experiences and a clear understanding of the behaviors and tasks that are required. In the face of a terrorist attack, the work environment may be quite chaotic and the precondition of understanding one's requisite behavior may be challenged. Perceived self-efficacy has also been found to affect job performance (Stajkovic & Luthans, 1998), and ultimately detriments in organizationwide performance may result. Bandura (1977, 1997) suggests that low efficacy beliefs can become a self-fulfilling prophesy as they discourage individuals from attempting or persisting at certain tasks. Unsuccessful performance merely serves to confirm negative beliefs about one's own ability and, therefore, further discourages the individuals from being motivated to persist on a task. Over time, this can lead to or perpetuate depression (Abramson, Seligman, & Teasdale, 1978). At the same time, however, self-efficacy beliefs could also have positive outcomes on work performance. High levels of preexisting self-efficacy have been found to buffer the negative effects of work stressors on well-being (Jex & Bliese, 1999). It remains to be seen whether these results extend to a stressor as extreme as workplace terrorism.

Absenteeism. Empirical studies on absenteeism distinguish between two main stress-related reasons for employee absences (Bakker, Demerouti, de Boer, & Schaufeli, 2003; Johns, 1997). One reason for absenteeism is employees' desire to withdraw from aversive circumstances at work. Employees who are absent for this reason tend to have relatively lower levels of job satisfaction and commitment and see absences as an escape from or protest against aversive characteristics of the work environment (Mathieu & Kohler, 1990; Sagie, 1998). Absenteeism may also be a way of recuperating from stress when individuals do not possess the resources required to deal with demands in the workplace. In this case, employees may not be dissatisfied with the work environment but instead use time away from work to recuperate from work-related stress caused by excessive job demands or from other personal difficulties such as psychological distress, physical ailments or injury, or other sources of diminished personal resources (Johns, 1997). The latter case may be more consistent with the increases in absenteeism following a terrorist attack.

Immediately following a terrorist attack, employee absenteeism may increase for a number of possible reasons. First, individuals may find it difficult to confront the workplace. For example, some people developed phobias that made it very difficult to confront the workplace following 9/11. Byron and Peterson's (2002) findings suggest that employees who experienced more strain following the 9/11 attacks were more likely to be absent from work in the weeks following the event. Second, employees who are physically injured may need to be absent from work in order to recuperate. Third, employees may become sick as a result of a compromised immunological system.

Fourth, employees' personal resources may be compromised, given the prevalence of various forms of psychological distress that tend to follow a terrorist attack. In the wake of a tragedy such as terrorism, employees may be proffering a great deal of social support to their colleagues. This may increase the likelihood that employees will experience emotional exhaustion or depression and require respite from the workplace (Bakker et al., 2003).

Although absenteeism has often been perceived as a negative organizational behavior following a terrorist attack, absenteeism may ultimately prevent turnover resulting from the accumulation of stress that can lead to chronic depression or disability (Bakker et al., 2003; Fredrickson et al., 2003). It may be preferable for employees to take time away from the workplace in order to recover as opposed to either remaining physically present and unable to concentrate on their work or leaving the organization, outcomes that have been found to be related to the experience of workplace violence (e.g., LeBlanc & Kelloway, 2002; Schat & Kelloway, 2000).

Prejudice and hostility. Following a terrorist attack, hatred for the attacker may generalize to hatred for other groups with characteristics similar to the attacker even if those groups do not support violence or have any obvious association with acts of violence. There are two theories that suggest that this may strain interpersonal relations within the organization between members of different demographic groups (Sauter, Murphy, & Hurrell, 1990).

Social categorization theory suggests that individuals assign people, including themselves, to social categories or groups (Tajfel, 1982) and generally tend to prefer members of their own social groups (Tajfel, 1978, 1982; Tajfel & Turner, 2001). How an individual defines the in-group (and thus the out-group) in a given instance is critical to determining against whom prejudice may be directed. One ramification of being targeted by terrorist action is that it may make in-group/out-group distinctions more salient, which may elicit prejudice, particularly if these distinctions are made on the basis of ethnicity. Following the attacks on 9/11, there were significant increases in documented cases of racism in the United States (Barling et al., 2003).

A second theory, terror management theory (Greenberg, Pyszczynski, & Solomon, 1986), concurs with these findings. Terror management theory suggests that the existence of culture serves two main functions: It provides the individual with a worldview through establishing a system of values, moral codes of conduct, and meanings that can be used to direct behavior, and it provides a gauge by which people develop their self-esteem as they evaluate their personal actions against these morals and codes (Greenberg et al., 1986). According to terror management theory, when individuals are confronted with their own mortality, biases against members of cultures other than their own may increase (Dechesne, Janssen, & van Knippenberg, 2000; Harmon-Jones, Greenberg, Solomon, & Simon, 1996) and can cause increases in negative reactions to people with different values or beliefs (Greenberg, Simon, Pyszczynski, Solomon, & Chatel, 1992). In the work context, this may make victims of politically motivated acts such as terrorism less open to working with people from different backgrounds or organizations that support a different system of morality. By extension, it may be hypothesized that racially linked selection and promotion decisions may follow—a serious problem in its own right—and this may in turn put the firm at considerable liability for legal action or human rights complaints. In addition, organizational initiative, such as affirmative action might be adversely affected.

Potential Moderators of the Relationship Between Terrorism and Distress

Based on work stress research in organizational contexts, we know that some characteristics of the job situation moderate the effects of work stress on well-being. These include leadership, organizational support, and job involvement; and these variables may also moderate the stress of experiencing terrorism on work outcomes. Each of these will be discussed.

Transformational leadership. The moderating effects of sound leadership on strain have been noted by researchers (Dionne, Yammarino, Atwater, & James, 2002); indeed, it is during times of crisis that leaders can exact their greatest influence (Sivanathan, Barling, Loughlin, & Kelloway, 2003). Leaders can quell chaos and ambiguity in an organization by creating a vision for the future of the organization and for employees, providing social support, communicating a sense of hope, and keeping employees up-to-date on new developments as events unfold.

Transformational leadership is a process by which leaders empower subordinates to be agents of organizational change (Yukl & Van Fleet, 1992). Transformational leadership consists of four main dimensions. First, idealized influence occurs when the leader does what is best for the greater good of the organization rather than his or her personal preferences. Second, inspirational motivation occurs when leaders provide followers with a sense of meaning associated with the tasks that they are asked to be engaged in and a sense of optimism and enthusiasm for the tasks that they are asked to perform. Third, transformational leaders tend to provide intellectual stimulation to their followers, helping and encouraging them to question existing ideas and epistemologies and to innovate and make intellectual contributions to their tasks. Finally, individualized consideration occurs through the individual support, mentoring, and coaching of each follower.

There is accumulating evidence to suggest that transformational leadership substantially influences employee performance (Barling, Weber, & Kelloway, 1996; Dvir, Eden, Avolio, & Shamir, 2002) via both self-efficacy and social support (Chen & Bliese, 2002; Rhoades & Eisenberger, 2002).

Leadership can exert an influence on efficacy perceptions by enhancing role clarity among followers (Chen & Bliese, 2002) affecting, in turn, job performance (Stajkovic & Luthans, 1998). Leadership also affects employee performance by creating a sense of personal identification with the leader and the work unit, thus motivating performance (Kark, Shamir, & Chen, 2003).

Perceived organizational support. Perceived organizational support refers to employees' subjective perception of the extent to which their work organization values their contributions and cares about their well-being (Eisenberger, Huntington, Hutchison, & Sowa, 1986; Rhoades & Eisenberger, 2002; Shore & Shore, 1995). Organizations and their representatives can provide a variety of supportive functions including emotional support involving caring and empathy, instrumental or tangible support, informational support or guidance in finding a solution to a problem, and appraisal support involving providing information relevant to self-evaluation (see Wills, 1985, for full discussion). Organizationally supportive practices such as supportive supervision affect the extent to which the individual has control over his or her job and life, which in turn has positive implications for reducing stress levels (Thomas & Ganster, 1995); and individuals with high perceived organizational support are less likely to seek out and accept jobs in alternative organizations (Eisenberger, Fasolo, & Davis-LaMastro, 1990). Research suggests that organizational support buffers the effect of stress on somatic tension, general fatigue, and burnout (Cropanzano, Howes, Grandey, & Toth, 1997) and produces relatively better psychological outcomes overall. It has been suggested that economic, counseling, and information support may all be of assistance to victims. Following the terrorist attacks of 9/11, some organizations provided tangible support (e.g., assistance with accommodation), with anecdotal reports suggesting that positive consequences ensued for the recipients (Barling et al., 2003).

Job involvement. Job involvement refers to the extent to which employees psychologically identify with their jobs (Probst, 2000) or consider the job central to their lives (Kanungo, 1982; Lodahl & Kejnar, 1965). Employees who have high levels of job involvement are more strongly affected by their work experiences. Although we are aware of no research that has examined job involvement as a moderator of the relationship between experiencing terrorism and subsequent strain, some research has suggested that people who are high in job involvement are more likely to experience health problems as an outcome of workplace stress (Frone, Russell, & Cooper, 1995) or negative behavioral and physical outcomes as a result of job insecurity (Probst, 2000). This research suggests that people who are relatively more involved in their jobs experience work events with greater intensity. In light of this evidence, employees with a high level of job involvement may respond more intensely to the experience of terrorism at work.

Terrorism and the Organization _____

The functioning of the organization may suffer in several ways as a result of a terrorist attack. Organizations may suffer direct and indirect financial costs as a result of terrorism. These costs may be incurred when organizations lose members through death, injury, or turnover, making it necessary for organizations to hire, socialize, and train new employees. Organizations may also need to assist workers with medical or psychological treatments. This may involve the use of in-house employee assistance programs or may involve making payments for these services to external treatment centers. These financial costs to the organization may lead to other organizational problems to the extent that attention is diverted from other workplace issues (Van Fleet & Van Fleet, 1998).

A second way that organizations may be affected by terrorism is via the reciprocal relationship between employee and organizational well-being (Tetrick, 2002). When employee well-being suffers, there is likely to be concomitant declines in organizational productivity (Jex & Bliese, 1999). Increases in employee absenteeism or turnover are also likely (Byron & Peterson, 2002; Van Fleet & Van Fleet, 1998) as people may be unable to concentrate on their work, may want to stay at home with family members, or may be fearful of returning to work and experiencing another attack. Others may be physically incapable of working as a result of injury (Van Fleet & Van Fleet, 1998). Organizational responses to a disaster such as terrorism may also have an important effect on individual well-being. Employees may expect their organizations to take responsibility for their well-being following a disaster. Following the 9/11 attacks, employees were more satisfied if their company exhibited compassion through means such as sending out empathetic companywide e-mails or organizing fundraisers or blood drives (Byron & Peterson, 2002; Dutton, Frost, Worline, Lilius, & Kanov, 2002).

Third, an individual does not have to be a member of an organization that has been targeted by terrorists to experience psychological distress following an attack. Some people work in occupations that force them to deal with the aftermath of a terrorist disaster. Such is the case for occupations such as investigators, emergency service personnel, and body handlers. One study examined outcomes of the Oklahoma City bombing on people whose job it was to handle the bodies of the deceased, and found they experienced subsequent increase in alcohol consumption and physical ailments (Tucker et al., 2002).

Other people may work in organizations that are similar to the one targeted for attack. People in these organizations may feel an increased level of vulnerability and fear of a future attack. For instance, people who work in commercial aviation may experience anxiety after a terrorist attack on another airline. Although this issue has not been addressed directly, research has suggested that following a terrorist attack, the general public tends to fear future attacks (Silver et al., 2002). It is therefore reasonable to expect this anxiety to exist in at least comparable levels among people who are in similar organizations or occupations to those targeted by terrorists.

Research Issues

Conducting research on the immediate psychological effects of a terrorist attack poses both practical and ethical challenges. First, given that terrorism is by its very nature unanticipated and the aftermath of terrorism can be so chaotic, it would be unlikely that data collection strategies would be in place immediately following an attack. The time needed to begin data collection may therefore preclude early assessments of psychological distress. Second, even if it is possible to quickly initiate data collection, considerations would need to be made regarding the ethics of collecting data with a sample of people who have recently been the target of terrorism. Ideally, researchers would wait until their sample population has dealt with the practical problems associated with the aftermath of the disaster to begin data collection (North & Pfefferbaum, 2002). Third, ethics also plays a role in conducting laboratory investigations. Given that the effects of experiencing terrorism can evoke a significant amount of stress, attempting to elicit this level of stress in the laboratory is likely to be precluded on ethical grounds (Barling, Bluen, & Fain, 1987). Finally, another consideration in research on terrorism is the heterogeneity of various types of terrorism, terrorists, the terrorists' reasons for attacking a given organization, and their methods. It is too early to hypothesize whether these variations may moderate the relationship between experiencing workplace terrorism as a stressor and subsequent strain on the part of the target. This may pose a potential limitation on the generalizability of research findings.

The nature of the challenges inherent in conducting research on terrorism reinforces the argument for regular surveillance of workplace stress and related disorders (Sauter et al., 1990). When we have regular collection of data on stress and related conditions, we optimize the chances of having good "pre" data from which to assess the effects of a terrorist attack or disaster. It might also suggest the need to adopt an opportunistic strategy whereby studies are prepared a priori and initiated should a terrorist attack occur.

Implications for Organizational Practice and Policy

The organization has a critical role to play in facilitating recovery of a devastated workforce. A variety of organizational responses may be required, and the best strategy for implementing these responses may require having the necessary infrastructure in place prior to a terrorist attack including a plan for a response to such an event.

Formal organizational responses to terrorism should include the use of employee assistance programs (EAPs). Although efficacy of EAPs following a terrorist attack has yet to be established, the assistance offered by these programs has been confirmed in studies on other stressors (for a detailed discussion, see Cooper, Dewe, & O'Driscoll, 2003). Following a terrorist attack, EAPs may provide employees with easily accessible counseling and support, identify symptoms that may indicate serious distress or psychopathology, and provide treatment or referrals for employees suffering trauma. Organizations, in conjunction with EAPs, also need to identify people who may be at higher risk for subsequent strain following a terrorist attack, such as people who sustained injury or who were close with people who suffered or died. Outreach services may be a vital conduit to access at-risk populations (Miller, 2002).

Developing an emergency response plan may also help employees retain or regain a sense of personal control before, during, and following a traumatic event such as a terrorist act. Training people to maximize their safety and help others in need may increase chances of escape from potentially violent situations (Van Fleet & Van Fleet, 1998). These formal responses to emergency situations can give employees reason to feel that their organization is supportive of their needs, and this perceived support may in turn encourage employees to demonstrate citizenship to the organization.

Should an act of terrorism occur, workplaces are responsible for providing on-scene mass casualty intervention. Immediate and short-term responses may include critical incident stress debriefing (CISD) that can be administered through workplace EAPs. CISD is a structured group meeting facilitated by a trained CISD team and involving only the personnel directly affected by the critical incident. The purpose of the debriefing is to mitigate acute stress resulting from traumatization and accelerate the normal recovery of ordinary people who are suffering through typical but painful reactions to an abnormal event. CISD is typically conducted 24 hours after the event by a trained CISD mental health professional. It is an early response intervention and not intended to substitute for psychotherapy or to act as a stand-alone intervention (Everly & Mitchell, 1995). Nevertheless, a recent meta-analysis suggests that CISD is an effective strategy for reducing acute stress in a wide variety of stressful events (Everly & Boyle, 1999).

On an ongoing basis, the workplace can act as a conduit of information for survivors of an attack. Lack of information can be potentially traumatic and can be harmful if rumors lead to panic. Communication networks within the organization and between the organization and the community can facilitate timely information.

Summary

The intent of this chapter was twofold. First, we provided an overview of the extant research on terrorism, particularly as it relates to stress and well-being.

Second, we hoped to extend the existing conceptualization of terrorism to include its potential effects on the workplace, particularly in light of the fact that terrorist attacks are often targeted at workplaces or at employees because they hold a particular occupational position. Overall, research on terrorism suggests that terrorism has been found to exert substantial effects on individual well-being as well as costs to the organization. We encourage future empirical examinations to delve more deeply into the effects of terrorism on what may be considered the crossroads of individual and organizational well-being: the individual's work experiences following a terrorist attack.

Workers and workplaces have been and likely will continue to be targets of terrorism. The threat of terrorism poses tremendous challenges to both employees and employers. How employers prepare for and respond to such events will have critical consequences for the health and well-being of both employees and organizations.

References

Abramson, L. Y., Seligman, M. E., & Teasdale, J. D. (1978). Learned helplessness in humans: Critique and reformulation. *Journal of Abnormal Psychology, 87*, 49–74.

Bakker, A. B., Demerouti, E., de Boer, E., & Schaufeli, W. B. (2003). Job demands and job resources as predictors of absence duration and frequency. *Journal of Vocational Behavior, 62*, 341–356.

Banauch, G., McLaughlin, M., Hirschhorn, R., Corrigan, M., Kelly, K., & Prezant, D. (2002). Injuries and illness among New York City Fire Department rescue workers after responding to the World Trade Center attacks. *JAMA: Journal of the American Medical Association, 288*, 1581–1584.

Bandura, A. (1977). Self-efficacy: Toward a unifying theory of behavioral change. *Psychological Review, 84*, 191–215.

Bandura, A. (1997). *Self-efficacy: The exercise of control.* New York: W. H. Freeman.

Barling, J. (1990). *Employment, stress and family functioning.* New York: Wiley.

Barling, J., Bluen, S. D., & Fain, R. (1987). Psychological functioning following an acute disaster. *Journal of Applied Psychology, 72*, 683–690.

Barling, J., Hurrell, J. J., Jr., Braverman, M., Collins, R. L., Gelles, M. G., Scrivner, E., & Keita, J. (2003). *Terrorized workers: Employee well-being following 9/11.* Unpublished manuscript.

Barling, J., Rogers, A. G., & Kelloway, E. K. (2001). Behind closed doors: In-home workers' experience of sexual harassment and workplace violence. *Journal of Occupational Health Psychology, 6*, 255–269.

Barling, J., Weber, T., & Kelloway, E. K. (1996). Effects of transformational leadership training on attitudinal and financial outcomes: A field experiment. *Journal of Applied Psychology, 81*, 827–832.

Baum, A. (1991). Toxins, technology, and natural disasters. In A. Monal & R. S. Lazarus (Eds.), *Stress and coping: An anthology* (3rd ed., pp. 97–139). New York: Columbia University Press.

Baum, A., & Fleming, I. (1993). Implications of psychological research on stress and technological accidents. *American Psychologist, 48,* 665–672.

Baum, A., Fleming, R., & Davidson, L. M. (1983). Natural disaster and technological catastrophe. *Environment and Behavior, 15,* 333–354.

Baum, A., Gatchel, R. J., & Schaeffer, M. A. (1983). Emotional, behavioral, and physiological effects of chronic stress at Three Mile Island. *Journal of Consulting and Clinical Psychology, 51,* 565–572.

Beauchamp, M. R., Bray, S. R., Eys, M. A., & Carron, A. V. (2002). Role ambiguity, role efficacy, and role performance: Multidimensional and mediational relationships within interdependent sport teams. *Group Dynamics, 6,* 229–242.

Beck, A. T., Emery, G., & Greenberg, R. L. (1985). *Anxiety disorders and phobias: A cognitive perspective.* New York: Basic Books.

Beehr, T. A., Jex, S. M., Stacy, B. A., & Murray, M. A. (2000). Work stressors and coworker support as predictors of individual strain and job performance. *Journal of Organizational Behavior, 21,* 391–405.

Braverman, M. (1992). Posttrauma crisis intervention in the workplace. In J. C. Quick & L. R. Murphy (Eds.), *Stress and well-being at work: Assessments and interventions for occupational mental health* (pp. 299–316). Washington, DC: American Psychological Association.

Breaugh, J. A., & Colihan, J. P. (1994). Measuring facets of job ambiguity: Construct validity evidence. *Journal of Applied Psychology, 79,* 191–202.

Budd, J. W., Arvey, R. D., & Lawless, P. (1996). Correlates and consequences of workplace violence. *Journal of Occupational Health Psychology, 1,* 197–210.

Byron, K., & Peterson, S. (2002). The impact of a large-scale traumatic event on individual and organizational outcomes: Exploring employee and company reactions to September 11, 2001. *Journal of Organizational Behavior, 23,* 895–910.

Chen, G., & Bliese, P. D. (2002). The role of different levels of leadership in predicting self- and collective efficacy: Evidence for discontinuity. *Journal of Applied Psychology, 87,* 549–556.

Cooper, C. L., Dewe, P., & O'Driscoll, M. (2003). Employee assistance programs. In J. C. Quick & L. E. Tetrick (Eds.), *Handbook of occupational health psychology* (pp. 289–304). Washington, DC: American Psychological Association.

Cropanzano, R., Howes, J. C., Grandey, A. A., & Toth, P. (1997). The relationship of organizational politics and support to work behaviors, attitudes, and stress. *Journal of Organizational Behavior, 18,* 159–180.

Davidson, L. M., Baum, A., Fleming, I., & Gisriel, M. M. (1986). Toxic exposure and chronic stress at Three Mile Island. In A. H. Lebovits & A. Baum (Eds.), *Advances in environmental psychology: Vol. 6. Exposure to hazardous substances: Psychological parameters* (pp. 35–46). Hillsdale, NJ: Lawrence Erlbaum.

Dechesne, M., Janssen, J., & van Knippenberg, A. (2000). Derogation and distancing as terror management strategies: The moderating role of need for closure and permeability of group boundaries. *Journal of Personality and Social Psychology, 79,* 923–932.

DeLisi, L. E., Maurizio, A., Yost, M., Papparozzi, C. F., Fulchino, C., Katz, C. L., et al. (2003). A survey of New Yorkers after the Sept. 11, 2001, terrorist attacks. *American Journal of Psychiatry, 160,* 780–783.

Desivilya, H. S., Gal, R., & Ayalon, O. (1996). Extent of victimization, traumatic stress symptoms, and adjustment of terrorist assault survivors: A long-term follow-up. *Journal of Traumatic Stress, 9,* 881–889.

Dionne, S. D., Yammarino, F. J., Atwater, L. E., & James, L. R. (2002). Neutralizing substitutes for leadership theory: Leadership effects and common-source bias. *Journal of Applied Psychology, 87,* 454–464.

Drake, C. J. M. (1998). The role of ideology in terrorists' target selection. *Terrorism and Political Violence, 10,* 53–85.

Dutton, J. E., Frost, P. J., Worline, M. C., Lilius, J. M., & Kanov, J. M. (2002). Leading in times of trauma. *Harvard Business Review, 80*(1), 54–61.

Dvir, T., Eden, D., Avolio, B. J., & Shamir, B. (2002). Impact of transformational leadership on follower development and performance: A field experiment. *Academy of Management Journal, 45,* 735–744.

Eidelson, R. J., & Eidelson, J. I. (2003). Five beliefs that propel groups toward conflict. *American Psychologist, 58,* 182–192.

Eisenberger, R., Fasolo, P., & Davis-LaMastro, V. (1990). Perceived organizational support and employee diligence, commitment, and innovation. *Journal of Applied Psychology, 75,* 51–59.

Eisenberger, R., Huntington, R., Hutchison, S., & Sowa, D. (1986). Perceived organizational support. *Journal of Applied Psychology, 71,* 500–507.

Everly, G. S., & Boyle, S. H. (1999). Critical incident stress debriefing (CISD): A meta-analysis. *International Journal of Emergency Mental Health, 1,* 165–168.

Everly, G. S., & Mitchell, J. T. (1995). Prevention of work-related posttraumatic stress: The critical incident stress debriefing process. In L. R. Murphy & J. J. Hurrell, Jr. (Eds.), *Job stress interventions* (pp. 173–183). Washington, DC: American Psychological Association.

Eys, M., & Carron, A. V. (2001). Role ambiguity, task cohesion, and task self-efficacy. *Small Group Research, 32,* 356–373.

Fox, M. L., Dwyer, D. J., & Ganster, D. C. (1993). Effects of stressful job demands and control on physiological and attitudinal outcomes in a hospital setting. *Academy of Management Journal, 36,* 289–318.

Fredrickson, B. L., Tugade, M. M., Waugh, C. E., & Larkin, G. R. (2003). What good are positive emotions in crisis? A prospective study of resilience and emotions following the terrorist attacks on the United States on September 11th, 2001. *Journal of Personality and Social Psychology, 84,* 365–376.

Freedy, J. R., Kilpatrick, D. G., & Resnick, H. S. (1993). Natural disasters and mental health: Theory, assessment, and intervention. *Journal of Social Behavior and Personality, 8,* 49–103.

Freedy, J. R., Saladin, M. E., Kilpatrick, D. G., Resnick, H. S., & Saunders, B. E. (1994). Understanding acute psychological distress following natural disaster. *Journal of Traumatic Stress, 7,* 257–273.

Frone, M. R., Russell, M., & Cooper, M. L. (1995). Job stressors, job involvement and employee health: A test of identity theory. *Journal of Occupational and Organizational Psychology, 68,* 1–11.

Galea, S., Ahern, J., Resnick, H., Kilpatrick, D., Bucuvalas, M., Gold, J., & Vlahov, D. (2002). Psychological sequelae of the September 11 terrorist attacks in New York City. *New England Journal of Medicine, 346,* 982–987.

Greenberg, J., Pyszczynski, T., & Solomon, S. (1986). The causes and consequences of a need for self-esteem: A terror management theory. In R. F. Baumeister (Ed.), *Public self and private self* (pp. 189–207). New York: Springer-Verlag.

Greenberg, J., Simon, L., Pyszczynski, T., Solomon, S., & Chatel, D. (1992). Terror management and tolerance: Does mortality salience always intensify negative reactions to others who threaten one's worldview? *Journal of Personality and Social Psychology, 63,* 212–220.

Hanson, R. F., Kilpatrick, D. G., Falsetti, S. A., & Resnick, H. S. (1995). Violent crime and mental health. In J. R. Freedy & S. E. Hobfoll (Eds.), *Traumatic stress: From theory to practice* (pp. 129–161). New York: Plenum Press.

Harmon-Jones, E., Greenberg, J., Solomon, S., & Simon, L. (1996). The effects of mortality salience on intergroup bias between minimal groups. *European Journal of Social Psychology, 26,* 677–681.

Heider, F. (1958). *The psychology of interpersonal relations.* Oxford, UK: Wiley.

Houkes, I., Janssen, P. P. M., de Jonge, J., & Bakker, A. B. (2003). Personality, work characteristics and employee well-being: A longitudinal analysis of additive and moderating effects. *Journal of Occupational Health Psychology, 8,* 20–38.

Inness, M., & Barling, J. (2003). Putting health back into occupational health psychology. In *The British Psychological Society, Occupational Psychology Conference 2003, Book of Proceedings.* London: British Psychological Society.

Jackson, S. E., & Schuler, R. S. (1985). A meta-analysis and conceptual critique of research on role ambiguity and role conflict in work settings. *Organizational Behavior and Human Decision Processes, 36,* 16–78.

Jex, S. M., & Bliese, P. D. (1999). Efficacy beliefs as a moderator of the impact of work-related stressors: A multilevel study. *Journal of Applied Psychology, 84,* 349–361.

Johns G. (1997). Contemporary research on absence from work: Correlates, causes and consequences. *International Review of Industrial and Organizational Psychology 12,* 115–173.

Kanungo, R. N. (1982). Measurement of job and work involvement. *Journal of Applied Psychology, 67,* 341–349.

Karasek, R. A. (1979). Job demands, job decision latitude, and mental strain: Implications for job redesign. *Administrative Science Quarterly, 24,* 285–307.

Kark, R., Shamir, B., & Chen, G. (2003). The two faces of transformational leadership: Empowerment and dependency. *Journal of Applied Psychology, 88,* 246–255.

Kelley, H. H. (1973). The processes of causal attribution. *American Psychologist, 28,* 107–128.

LeBlanc, M. M., & Kelloway, E. K. (2002). Predictors and outcomes of workplace violence and aggression. *Journal of Applied Psychology, 87,* 444–453.

Little, T. D., Jones, S. M., Henrich, C. C., & Hawley, P. H. (2003). Disentangling the "whys" from the "whats" of aggressive behaviour. *International Journal of Behavioral Development, 27,* 122–133.

Lodahl, T. M., & Kejnar, M. (1965). The definition and measurement of job involvement. *Journal of Applied Psychology, 49,* 24–33.

Mathieu, J. E., & Kohler, S. S. (1990). A test of the interactive effects of organizational commitment and job involvement on various types of absence. *Journal of Vocational Behavior, 36,* 33–44.

McFarlane, A. C., & de Girolamo, G. (1996). The nature of traumatic stressors and the epidemiology of posttraumatic reactions. In B. A. van der Kolk & A. C. McFarlane (Eds.), *Traumatic stress: The effects of overwhelming experience on mind, body, and society* (pp. 129–154). New York: Guilford Press.

Miller, L. (2002). Psychological interventions for terroristic trauma: Symptoms, syndromes, and treatment strategies. *Psychotherapy: Theory/research/practice/ training, 39,* 283–296.

Norris, F. H., Friedman, M. J., & Watson, P. J. (2002). 60,000 disaster victims speak: Part 2. Summary and implications of the disaster mental health research. *Psychiatry: Interpersonal and Biological Processes, 65,* 240–260.

Norris, F. H., Friedman, M. J., Watson, P. J., Byrne, C. M., Diaz, E., & Kaniasty, K. (2002). 60,000 disaster victims speak: Part 1. An empirical review of the empirical literature, 1981–2001. *Psychiatry: Interpersonal and Biological Processes, 65,* 207–239.

North, C. S., & Pfefferbaum, B. (2002). Research on the mental health effects of terrorism. *JAMA: Journal of the American Medical Association, 288,* 633–636.

Piotrkowski, C. S., & Brannen, S. J. (2002). Exposure, threat appraisal, and lost confidence as predictors of PTSD symptoms following September 11, 2001. *American Journal of Orthopsychiatry, 72,* 476–485.

Pratt, L., & Barling, J. (1988). Differentiating daily hassles, acute and chronic stressors: A framework and its implications. In J. R. Hurrell, L. R. Murphy, S. L. Sauter, & C. L. Cooper (Eds.), *Occupational stress: Issues and developments in research* (pp. 41–53). London: Taylor & Francis.

Probst, T. M. (2000). Wedded to the job: Moderating effects of job involvement on the consequences of job insecurity. *Journal of Occupational Health Psychology, 5,* 63–73.

Regehr, C., Goldberg, G., & Hughes, J. (2002). Exposure to human tragedy, empathy, and trauma in ambulance paramedics. *American Journal of Orthopsychiatry, 72,* 505–513.

Rhoades, L., & Eisenberger, R. (2002). Perceived organizational support: A review of the literature. *Journal of Applied Psychology, 87,* 698–714.

Rubonis, A. V., & Bickman, L. (1991). Psychological impairment in the wake of disaster: The disaster-psychopathology relationship. *Psychological Bulletin, 109,* 384–399.

Ryan, A. M., West, B. J., & Carr, J. Z. (2003). Effects of the terrorist attacks of 9/11/01 on employee attitudes. *Journal of Applied Psychology, 88,* 647–659.

Sagie, A. (1998). Employee absenteeism, organizational commitment, and job satisfaction: Another look. *Journal of Vocational Behavior, 52,* 156–171.

Sauter, S. L., Murphy, L. R., & Hurrell, J. J. (1990). Prevention of work-related psychological disorders: A national strategy proposed by the National Institute for Occupational Safety and Health (NIOSH). *American Psychologist, 45,* 1146–1158.

Schat, A. C., & Kelloway, E. K. (2000). Effects of perceived control on the outcomes of workplace aggression and violence. *Journal of Occupational Health Psychology, 5,* 386–402.

Schlenger, W. E., Caddell, J. M., Ebert, L., Jordan, B. K., Rourke, K. M., Wilson, D., et al. (2002). Psychological reactions to terrorist attacks: Findings from the National Study of Americans' Reactions to September 11. *JAMA: Journal of the American Medical Association, 288,* 581–588.

Schmid, A. P., & Jongman, A. J. (1988). *Political terrorism: A new guide to actors, authors, concepts, data bases, theories, and literature.* New Brunswick, NJ: Transaction Books.

Schuster, M. A., Stein, B. D., Jaycox, L. H., Collins, R. L., Marshall, G. N., Elliott, M. N., et al. (2002). A national survey of stress reactions after the September 11, 2001, terrorist attacks. *New England Journal of Medicine, 345,* 1507–1512.

Scotti, A. J. (1986). *Executive safety and international terrorism: A guide for travelers.* Englewood Cliffs, NJ: Prentice Hall.

Shalev, A. Y., Freedman, S., Peri, T., Brandes, D., Sahar, T., Orr, S. P., & Pitman, R. K. (1998). Prospective study of posttraumatic stress disorder and depression following trauma. *American Journal of Psychiatry, 155,* 630–637.

Shore, L. M., & Shore, T. H. (1995). Perceived organizational support and organizational justice. In R. Cropanzano & K. Kacmar (Eds.), *Organizational politics, justice, and support* (pp. 149–164). Westport, CT: Quorum.

Siegrist, J., & Peter, R. (1994). Job stressors and coping characteristics in work-related disease: Issues of validity. *Work & Stress. Special Issue: A Healthier Work Environment, 8,* 130–140.

Silver, R. C., Holman, E. A., McIntosh, D. N., Poulin, M., & Gil-Rivas, V. (2002). Nationwide longitudinal study of psychological responses to September 11. *JAMA: Journal of the American Medical Association, 288,* 1235–1244.

Sivanathan, N., Barling, J., Loughlin, C., & Kelloway, E. K. (2003). *Leading others to well-being: Transformational leadership and well-being.* Manuscript submitted for publication.

Smith, B. W., & Freedy, J. R. (2000). Psychosocial resource loss as a mediator of the effects of flood exposure on psychological distress and physical symptoms. *Journal of Traumatic Stress, 13,* 349–357.

Smith, M., & North, C. S. (1993). PTSD: Synthesis of research and clinical studies: The Australia bushfire disaster. In J. P. Wilson & B. Raphael (Eds.), *International handbook of traumatic stress syndromes.* New York: Plenum Press.

Stajkovic, A. D., & Luthans, F. (1998). Self-efficacy and work-related performance: A meta-analysis. *Psychological Bulletin, 124,* 240–261.

Sutton, R. I., & Staw, B. M. (1995). What theory is not. *Administrative Science Quarterly, 40,* 371–384.

Tajfel, H. (1978). *Differentiation between social groups: Studies in the social psychology of intergroup relations.* Oxford, UK: Academic.

Tajfel, H. (1982). Social psychology of intergroup relations. *Annual Review of Psychology, 33,* 1–39.

Tajfel, H., & Turner, J. (2001). An integrative theory of intergroup conflict. In M. A. Hogg & D. Abrams (Eds.), *Intergroup relations: Essential readings. Key readings in social psychology* (pp. 94–109). Philadelphia: Psychology Press.

Terry, D. J., & Jimmieson, N. L. (1999). Work control and employee well-being: A decade review. In C. L. Cooper & I. T. Robertson (Eds.), *International review of industrial and organizational psychology 1999* (Vol. 14, pp. 95–148). New York: Wiley.

Tetrick, L. (2002). Individual and organizational health. In P. L. Perrewé & D. C. Ganster (Eds.), *Research in occupational stress and well-being: Vol. 2. Historical and current perspectives on stress and health.* Greenwich, CT: JAI.

Thomas, L. T., & Ganster, D. C. (1995). Impact of family-supportive work variables on work-family conflict and strain: A control perspective. *Journal of Applied Psychology, 80,* 6–15.

Tucker, P., Pfefferbaum, B., Doughty, D. E., Jones, D. E., Jordan, F. B., & Nixon, S. J. (2002). Body handlers after terrorism in Oklahoma City: Predictors of posttraumatic stress and other symptoms. *American Journal of Orthopsychiatry, 72,* 469–475.

Van der Ploeg, E., Kleber, R. J., & van der Velden, P. G. (2000). Acute and chronic stress at work: Implications for psychological health. *Gedrag & Gezondheid: Tijdschrift voor Psychologie en Gezondheid, 28,* 172–185.

Van Fleet, E. W., & Van Fleet, D. D. (1998). Terrorism and the workplace: Concepts and recommendations. In R. W. Griffin & A. O'Leary-Kelly (Eds.), *Dysfunctional behavior in organizations: Violent and deviant behavior* (Monographs in organizational behavior and industrial relation, Vol. 23, Parts A & B, pp. 165–201). New York: Elsevier Science/JAI.

Warr, P. (1994). A conceptual framework for the study of work and mental health. *Work & Stress. Special Issue: A Healthier Work Environment, 8,* 84–97.

Wills, T. A. (1985). Supportive functions of interpersonal relationships. In S. Cohen & L. S. Syme (Eds.), *Social support and health* (pp. 61–82). San Diego, CA: Academic.

Yukl, G., & Van Fleet, D. D. (1992). Theory and research on leadership in organizations. In M. D. Dunnette & L. M. Hough (Eds.), *Handbook of industrial and organizational psychology* (2nd ed., Vol. 3, pp. 147–197). Palo Alto, CA: Consulting Psychologists Press.

PART II

Special Populations

16 Editors' Overview: Special Populations

Efforts to understand the experience of stress in the workplace have resulted in a proliferation of theoretical models (e.g., Karasek & Theorell, 1990; Siegrist, 1996; Sauter, Murphy, & Hurrell, 1990; Warr, 1987) that vary in their "breadth" (i.e., the number of organizational conditions considered) as well as the functional relationships specified between stressors and outcomes (e.g., the specification of moderated or curvilinear relationships). Underpinning each of these models is a more generic specification that distinguishes between stressors (i.e., the objective organizational condition), stress (i.e., the reaction to the stressor), and strain (i.e., the outcomes associated with prolonged exposure to the stressor; Pratt & Barling, 1988). Following from transactional views of stress (e.g., Lazarus & Folkman, 1984), researchers recognize that each of the linkages (i.e., stressor-stress, stress-strain) may be moderated by a host of individual factors.

The chapters in this section focus on "special populations," groups defined by demographic differences for whom the stress process is potentially different than it is for some referent group. Thus, the chapters focus on issues related to gender (Desmarais & Alksnis), cultural or national origin (Liu & Spector), older (Barnes-Farnell) and younger workers (Loughlin & Lang), and employment status (i.e., part-time and contingent work, Gallagher) and ask how these characteristics might affect the experience of workplace stress.

Within the context of a generic stress model, at least several potential effects are plausible. First, demographically defined groups may experience different stressors than do the referent group. For example, Gallagher notes that part-time and contingent workers are concerned about whether they get enough hours of employment or assignments within a pay period. Although economic insecurity may be endemic, this particular form of a work stressor is not generally shared with full-time employees.

Second, individuals may experience the same stressors but to a different degree based on demographic differences. Thus, it is clear that both women and men have family responsibilities. However, it is equally evident that women disproportionately assume primary responsibility for both child care and elder care (see, e.g., Gignac, Kelloway, & Gottlieb, 1996). As a result of this, one might expect to find reports of more work-family stress among women than men.

Third, it is possible that different groups may experience the same stressors but have different reactions to the same objective event. That is, work-related stressors may have particular relevance for individuals from particular groups. Whether as a result of socialization experiences, cultural norms, or developmental stages, there are numerous examples in which members of a population may be especially vulnerable to workplace stressors. For example, older workers may be especially vulnerable to issues of workload (Nygard, Huuhtanen, Tuomi, & Martikainen, 1997). In contrast, younger workers may be more vulnerable to stressors associated with interpersonal conflict in the workplace (Frone, 2000).

Finally, some stress outcomes may be of particular relevance for certain groups of workers. Thus, the impact of work characteristics on educational outcomes (e.g., skipping class, doing homework, grades; see Barling, Rogers, & Kelloway, 1995) has been examined for young workers but is rarely seen as a form of strain for other groups of workers.

In considering these issues, the authors of the respective chapters also identify numerous considerations for future research. Many of these are based on the recognition that science is a process of continually refining the independent variables (e.g., Campbell & Stanley, 1963). Researchers begin with the observation that the stress process might differ according to some demographic characteristic. As Desmarais and Alksnis point out with regard to gender, the demographic characteristic is often a marker for a host of social, cultural, and economic differences. As these refinements occur, it is important to return to the original observation and ask whether or not it is still appropriate to focus on the original demographic variable as the basis for empirical inquiry.

One issue that is apparent as we consider various populations is the use of frequently unspecified or poorly defined referent groups. Individuals in contingent and part-time work arrangements are distinguished from full-time employees. Younger workers and older workers are distinguished from the rest of the workforce. Loughlin and Lang identify the definition of "young" workers as problematic, obscuring substantial within-group differences. This point is equally true for referent groups; there are perhaps as many differences within any given group as there are between groups.

Despite these caveats, the study of special populations makes a valuable contribution to our understanding of workplace stress. Examining differences across age, gender, national/cultural origin, or employment status provides a means of testing the boundary conditions of our theories. Moreover, the quest to understand why stress processes or experiences may be different in a special population has the potential to inform our understanding of the stress process for all populations. In addressing these issues, the chapters presented in this section both challenge and inform our understanding of workplace stress.

References

Barling, J., Rogers, K., & Kelloway, E. K. (1995). Some effects of teenagers' part-time employment: It's the quantity and quality of work that makes the difference. *Journal of Organizational Behavior, 16,* 143–152.

Campbell, D. T., & Stanley, J. C. (1963). *Experimental and quasi-experimental designs for research.* Boston: Houghton Mifflin.

Frone, M. R. (2000). Interpersonal conflict at work and psychological outcomes: Testing a model among young workers. *Journal of Occupational Health Psychology, 5,* 246–255.

Gignac, M. A., Kelloway, E. K., & Gottlieb, B. (1996). The impact of caregiving on employment: A mediational model of work-family conflict. *Canadian Journal of Aging, 15,* 514–524.

Karasek, R. A., & Theorell, T. (1990). *Healthy work: Stress productivity and the reconstruction of working life.* New York: Basic Books.

Lazarus, R. S., & Folkman, S. (1984). *Stress, appraisal, and coping.* New York: Springer.

Nygard, C. H., Huuhtanen, P., Tuomi, K., & Martikainen, R. (1997). Perceived work changes between 1981 and 1992 among aging workers in Finland. *Scandinavian Journal of Work, Environment & Health, 23* (Suppl. 1), 12–19.

Pratt, L. I., & Barling, J. (1988). Differentiating between daily events, acute and chronic stressors: A framework and its implications. In J. J. Hurrell, L. R. Murphy, S. L. Sauter, & C. L. Cooper (Eds.), *Occupational stress: Issues and development in research* (pp. 41–53). London: Taylor & Francis.

Sauter, S. L., Murphy, L. R., & Hurrell, J. J. (1990). Prevention of work-related psychological disorders: A national strategy proposed by the National Institute for Occupational Safety and Health (NIOSH). *American Psychologist, 45,* 1146–1158.

Siegrist, J. (1996). Adverse health effects of high effort/low reward conditions. *Journal of Occupational Health Psychology, 1,* 27–41.

Warr, P. B. (1987). *Work employment and mental health.* Oxford, UK: Oxford University Press.

17

Young Workers

Catherine Loughlin

Katherine Lang

She thought she could handle the stress. . . . But then, one night after weeks of 18-hour days and constant travel, she staggered home at 7 A.M. Not to sleep. To shower. As she stood in the water, she started crying. . . . JP Morgan isn't the only firm driving its young employees insane. . . . All hire the brightest Ivy League grads and make them a deal: We will pay you $60,000 or more a year and give you glimpses of corporate luxury. . . . In exchange, you must work 70, 80, 100 hours a week through the best years of your life.

Laura Vanderkam, *USA Today*

Broken Dreams . . . Canada's most highly educated generation— a group of young adults who have, nevertheless, found that education doesn't necessarily guarantee the kind of rewards [their] parents' generation experienced.

Tess Kalinowski, *Toronto Star*

Young Workers' Stress

When most of us think of "young workers," we have images of high school students asking, "Do you want fries with that?" at the local fast-food restaurant. Many young workers do work in frontline services; however, around the globe they are employed in a wide range of occupations. Although it

Authors' Note: This study was supported by a grant from the Social Sciences and Humanities Research Council of Canada to Dr. Catherine Loughlin.

would be unusual to talk about "adult workers" without acknowledging different experiences based on industries, jobs, or levels within organizations, it is common to generalize about "young workers" as though they are a homogeneous group. Like adults, young workers will share some attributes with their age cohort; however, their experiences of work will also vary depending on the jobs, industries, and countries in which they work. Many young workers are exposed to stress and strain in these jobs, and we need to begin discussing the effects of this, not just on young workers' current health and productivity but on their development into healthy adults. Companies are increasingly aware that their own future viability may depend on this group of workers. Demographic trends predict a smaller supply of young workers and increasing retirements among baby boomers in the near future (Dohm, 2000). Unfortunately, there is limited understanding to inform choices. For example, what are the defining characteristics of young workers? How do their experiences of stress at work compare with those of their adult counterparts?

In this chapter, we will begin by framing our discussion about young workers' stress (e.g., what are the rates of exposure to paid employment and to work stress among youth?). Next, we will consider the major theoretical models of relevance to this topic. We will then discuss specific predictors (e.g., workload, interpersonal conflict), mediators (e.g., cognitive appraisal or coping), moderators (e.g., work quantity, personality), and outcomes (e.g., psychological and physical health) associated with young workers' stress. We will also address key measurement issues and outline future research needs. Finally, we will consider implications for practice, policy, and intervention. We will take a critical perspective and hope to move beyond some of the assumptions about young workers that do not stand up to empirical scrutiny.

Defining Young Workers and Work Stress

In keeping with the literature on work stress, we will refer to strains (e.g., anxiety) as outcomes resulting from stress (e.g., the response) associated with work-related stressors (e.g., workload). As has been discussed elsewhere, work stress is the response to a work-related situation that is perceived to be challenging or threatening to a person's well-being. Young workers are defined as individuals between the ages of 15 and 24 who are working for pay on a full-time, part-time, or casual basis. This includes workers who attend school (working evenings, weekends, and during the summer) as well as those who have entered the adult workforce (Loughlin & Barling, 1999).

Young workers can be subdivided further into two categories: those between 15 and 19 and those between 20 and 24. The younger group is more likely to have high school students and part-time workers in it, whereas the older group will be composed of more full-time workers and nonstudents.

These groups of workers may have different interests, aspirations, and needs in the workplace. It should also be noted that these categories are extending at both ends as youth enter the labor force at earlier ages and stay in school longer to gain access to higher-quality jobs, often not becoming independent from their parents until their early 30s (Livingstone, 1999). Unfortunately, education is not a panacea, and despite high levels of education, young workers are often seriously affected by recessions and find it difficult to find work even when the economy is on an upswing (Coy, Conlin, & Thornton, 2002).

In terms of a breakdown by gender and occupation, young men tend to participate in the labor force slightly more than young women, and almost half of both sexes work in sales and services. For young women, the next largest concentrations of work are in business, finance, and administrative occupations whereas for young men the next most popular areas of work are skilled trades, transport, and manufacturing (Ontario Association of Youth Employment Centres [OAYEC], 2001). It appears that the gendering of certain sectors and occupations happens early in young workers' labor force participation. This is interesting because there is evidence to suggest that relatively young workers' (mean age 26 years) experience of stress can vary based on sex (Babin & Boles, 1998). Further, if we take the adult literature into account, the possibility also exists that sex and race can interact to influence experiences of work stress (e.g., among women and black Americans, high-effort coping combined with high occupational status can actually increase stress and blood pressure ratings; Light et al., 1995). The potential for these types of interactions will need to be borne in mind throughout our discussion.

Because by definition stressors must be perceived as a problem before stress or strain can result, it is important to know what a good job looks like from a young person's perspective. In a longitudinal study of over 10,000 young people between 15 and adulthood, Bibby (2001) surveyed the work values of two generations, *millennials* (born since 1985) and *generation X* (born between 1965 and 1984). He listed the job characteristics that over half the respondents of high school age thought were critical in a "good" job (averaged across the sexes): 86% said the work must be interesting, 76% said it must give them a feeling of accomplishment, 68% said there must be chances for advancement, 66% said it should pay well, 63% said other people should be friendly and helpful, 59% would like it to add something to other people's lives, and 57% want job security. In terms of differences based on sex, the only characteristic in which there was more than a 10% difference in ratings was "adding something to other people's lives" (which females were much more likely to rate as an important aspect of a job). Another interesting finding from this research concerns the degree to which young people worry about their future employment before they finish school; 66% identify "what they will do for work when they finish school" as a core concern. In this sense, thinking about future employment in and of itself can be stressful for young people. Bibby (2001) also notes that by the time young people graduate from postsecondary education (and often confront the reality of student loans), the order of priorities in a job changes slightly (i.e., pay jumps in the rankings, with the ordering of the other characteristics staying basically the same). This supports calls from other researchers to adopt a life span perspective in our research (e.g., Griffiths, 1999) whereby the effects of employment are considered across age categories.

Prevalence of Paid Employment and Exposure to Work Stress Among Youth

Recent statistics show that 66.3% of Canadian youth participated in the workforce in 2002, a rate roughly equivalent to the overall labor force participation rate (66.9%; Statistics Canada, 2003). These numbers are surprisingly similar to those found in other countries. Young workers' participation rates in the United States in 2003 hovered around 67% during the peak summer months (U.S. Department of Labor, 2003), whereas the equivalent rates in Thailand and Australia were 68.2% and 59.6% respectively (National Statistical Office, 2003; Australian Bureau of Statistics, 2003). The current participation rate in the United Kingdom (47%) is slightly lower. It should also be noted that participation rates can vary widely depending on whether or not school is in session. This being said, recent increases in school enrollment during the summer months may mean that it will become easier to accurately measure young workers' participation in the workforce year-round.

Given these participation rates, calls for more research into the formative occupational experiences of young workers are not surprising (e.g., Frone, 2000; Loughlin & Barling, 2001). Adolescents are psychologically impressionable (e.g., Erikson, 1963; Krosnick & Alwin, 1989) and physically vulnerable (Zejda et al., 1993) during this stage of development. However, although most would agree that exposure to work stress could have serious implications for young workers' well-being as they progress into adulthood, we know of little empirical data measuring its societywide prevalence rates. In contrast, anecdotal or observational reports of young workers' stress are common. For example, references have been made to the high prevalence of stress among young workers in the service sector (e.g., Garson, 1988), the technology sector (Lessard & Baldwin, 2000), and military sectors (Dolan, Crouch, West, & Castro, 2001).

A recent Canadian survey of almost 37,000 people did attempt to gauge societywide prevalence rates of work stress across age categories (Statistics Canada, 2003). This survey asked individuals working for the past 12 months how stressful they perceived "most" days at work to be. Thirty-three percent of older workers (age 25–64) found their jobs to be "quite a bit" or "extremely stressful," whereas 21% of young workers (age 15–24) reported likewise. Given that work stress supposedly peaks in middle age, the extent to which higher perceptions of stress are distributed equally across the large grouping of older workers is unclear. Another interesting finding from this survey concerned the proportion of young female workers describing their workday as "a bit stressful" or "extremely stressful" (24%) as compared with young males (17%). Thus, in general, young workers perceive less stress at work than older workers; however, when broken down by gender, young women perceive more stress at work than young men.

Before leaving this section, one demographic factor other than sex that can significantly influence young people's experiences of work-related stress and strain should be mentioned. Education can be a defining factor for young people. Young workers without any postsecondary education face almost three times the unemployment rate of their counterparts with some postsecondary education. They also face lower incomes (OAYEC, 2001). Early unemployment has been linked to delays in young people forming their own unique work personalities (Ruiz-Quintanilla & Claes, 1994), in inhibiting proactive career planning (Claes & Ruiz-Quintanilla, 1998), and in lowering self-esteem (Goldsmith, Veum, & Darity, 1997). Young workers who are out of school and unemployed risk being marginalized and excluded from the mainstream job market (Canadian Council on Social Development [CCSD], 2002). Unemployment can lead to a vicious cycle whereby the stress and disappointment of failing to get a job can lead to lowered self-esteem, expectations, and minor psychiatric illnesses that may further impair the job search process, making unemployment even more likely (Furnham, 1985). Although this chapter focuses on stress related to employment, unemployment among young workers can be a serious work-related stressor in and of itself and has been dealt with elsewhere (e.g., Winefield, Winefield, Tiggemann, & Goldney, 1991).

Major Theoretical Models

In the adult literature, research on work and health typically focuses on how individuals experience their work and their engagement in this work rather than on the number of hours they work in a week. However, despite a large body of research over the past few decades focusing on work and health in adults (e.g., Cullen, 1999; Karasek & Theorell, 1990; Sauter, Murphy, & Hurrell, 1990; Warr, 1987), for the most part, we do not know how these findings generalize to young workers (Frone, 1999). With the exception of some sociologists (e.g., Lowe, 2000; Shanahan, Finch, Mortimer, & Ryu, 1991) and organizational psychologists (e.g., Loughlin, Frone, & Barling, 2002), research has primarily focused on the negative effects of unemployment or employment quantity on young workers' psychological and physical health (e.g., Marks & Fleming, 1999; Steinberg & Dornbusch, 1991; Winefield, Winefield, Tiggemann, & Goldney, 1991). In this section, we will briefly outline several models of work stress from the adult literature that link relationships between stressors, mediators/moderators, and the outcomes of work stress. We will then discuss how some of these elements generalize to young workers based on the research that has been done.

Finally, we will consider two models specifically developed for studying the psychology of work stress in young workers.

Job content concerns the job itself (i.e., intrinsic factors), and this is the focus of the first model from the adult literature, the job characteristics model. This model explains how job content can lead to three critical psychological states necessary for emotional health: (a) a feeling of personal responsibility for one's work, (b) experiencing one's work as meaningful, and (c) having knowledge of the results of one's performance (Hackman & Oldham, 1980). Five basic job elements are believed necessary for these three psychologically healthy states. First, skill variety is the degree to which one is involved in different activities related to one's work involving the use of various skills and abilities. Second, task identity is the degree to which a job involves the completion of a whole and recognizable piece of work (i.e., seeing a project through to completion). Third, task significance reflects the impact of one's work on others' lives or work, both inside and outside the organization. Fourth, feedback from the job is the amount of information one receives about the effectiveness of one's performance. Finally, autonomy is the degree to which one's job provides freedom in determining the scheduling of work/procedures necessary to carry out this work (Hackman & Oldham, 1980).

Autonomy is particularly important to most workers, and our next theoretical model of work stress, the demand-control model, emphasizes the importance of autonomy for health-related outcomes among adults (e.g., Karasek & Theorell, 1990). Lack of input into decision making in one's job has been found to result in emotional distress, lowered self-esteem, job dissatisfaction, increased tension, anxiety, depression, irritation, somatic complaints, and alienation (Nord, 1977; Sauter et al., 1990; Wall, Corbett, Martin, Clegg, & Jackson, 1990). Low job-decision latitude has even been associated with increased mortality among workers (Astrand, Hanson, & Isacson, 1989; Theorell, Perski, Orth-Gomer, Hamsten, & de Faire, 1991). In contrast, increasing worker control over their jobs has been found to improve work motivation, performance, job satisfaction, and mental health, as well as reducing employee turnover (Wall & Clegg, 1981; Wall et al., 1990). Typically, high demands at work are not considered problematic per se, unless accompanied by a lack of control (i.e., autonomy).

Our third major theoretical model from the adult literature was proposed by researchers at the National Institute for Occupational Safety and Health (NIOSH) in the United States and is perhaps the most comprehensive model of work stress for understanding how participation in the workforce can be linked to outcomes such as affective disturbances, negative behavioral and lifestyle patterns, and chemical dependencies (Sauter et al., 1990). This model aims to understand and thereby prevent psychological disorders in workers as well as improve workplace mental health services. These authors list six primary workplace stressors: (a) job content, (b) autonomy (concerning workload/pace), (c) work scheduling, (d) role stressors, (e) career security factors, and (f) interpersonal relationships at work. This model of work stress has been widely accepted and at least parts of the model have been tested across cultures (Yousef, 1999). One final point should be noted before leaving the NIOSH model; Sauter et al. (1990) identified workers in the service industry as being at increased risk for psychological disorders. Jobs in the service industry in North America tend to be insecure, pay poorly, and offer little career potential (e.g., Krahn, 1991). Because so many young workers do work in this industry, there is good reason to monitor stress in their work environments.

To our knowledge, no one has specifically tested these models on young workers. However, we have good reason to believe that at least four of the six NIOSH factors are important to young workers. Job content (e.g., skill use), opportunities for initiative and autonomy, role stressors, and opportunities for social interaction at work have all emerged as important in studies of young workers (e.g., Greenberger, Steinberg, & Ruggiero, 1982; O'Brien & Feather, 1990; Stern, Stone, Hopkins, & McMillion, 1990). Further, as early as 1982, Greenberger et al. (1982) proposed three dimensions along which adolescent jobs should be compared that sound quite similar to stressors identified by NIOSH: opportunities for learning (i.e., use of skills), exercising initiative or autonomy (e.g., participation in decision making), and social interactions. In contrast, the other two NIOSH factors have been considered less important to adolescents. For example, perhaps because students are not legally allowed to work after midnight or to be scheduled for work hours that conflict with school (e.g., Krahn, 1991), some consider work scheduling to be less of an issue for young people. Also, because most students do not intend to continue in the same jobs once having finished their education, it is argued that career security factors are less important to young workers (Greenberger & Steinberg, 1986). We will return to these issues shortly.

Three other models of work stress from the adult literature should be mentioned briefly because of their possible application to young workers. The person-environment fit model is based on the premise that it may be possible to match individuals to environments in such a way as to reduce overall stress (Caplan, Cobb, French, Harrison, & Pinneau, 1975). The second and third models emphasize the role of extrinsic factors in contributing to work stress. The effort-reward model suggests that the combination of high effort and low reward is pathogenic (Siegrist, 1996), and the lifestyle incongruity model emphasizes the extent to which income from one's job influences stress (i.e., it is the extent to which one's consumption habits outstrip one's job-based socioeconomic status that is stressful; Dressler, 1990). Research on young workers suggests that these models may also be relevant. Finch, Shannahan, Mortimer, and Ryu (1991) have noted that low pay, high turnover, and lack of opportunity for advancement are all problematic among young workers, and extrinsic aspects of work can affect their experiences of stress (Mortimer, Harley, & Staff, 2002). In fact, Shanahan et al. (1991) point out that when asked about their reasons for participating in the workplace, adolescents are straightforward in indicating that the most tangible product of their labor is the money, and few recognize or emphasize their interest in learning new skills, enhancing their abilities, or gaining experience in their field of choice. This is interesting, because youth are typically reliant on their parents for basic financial support, and therefore their jobs are economically less consequential than those of adults (Shanahan et al., 1991). This also seems to conflict with what youth themselves cite as most important in their jobs (e.g., Bibby, 2001). There is the potential for confusion here, and it is important to recognize that asking young workers about their initial reasons for taking a job (e.g., to make money) is not the same as asking them what is most important to them in the job they have (e.g., interesting work).

In terms of models specifically designed for young workers, two models are relevant: Frone's (2000) model of interpersonal work conflict suggests that young people have low tolerance for conflict in the workplace. Moreover, it recognizes that the interpersonal conflict with supervisors and coworkers may be differentially related to organizational and personal outcomes. Research has found that interpersonal conflict at work is negatively related to job satisfaction and positively related to depression among adults. Second, Lubbers, Loughlin, and Zweig (2004) have proposed a model of healthy work for young workers that not only takes into account mediators such as self-efficacy and negative affect but also predicts young workers' job-related performance in addition to their physical and psychological health (both these models will be discussed further in the major empirical studies section).

Predictors (i.e., Work Stressors) Specifically Related to Young Workers

In their comprehensive review of youth mental health, Mortimer et al. (2002) criticize the "near-exclusive focus on adolescent hours of employment" and the "scant empirical scrutiny" of work quality in the literature (pp. 190–191) and call on policymakers to begin attending to the quality of youth employment. In terms of employment quality, similar job characteristics to those listed in the adult literature are relevant (e.g., autonomy, social interactions, skill use). For example, the perception of being in control has proven to be a very important factor in the work experiences of adolescents, particularly because adolescence is widely recognized as a period of personal and social growth that can affect one's potential for future development (Finch et al., 1991). Social relationships are also important moderators of the relationship between work stressors and outcomes. Unfortunately, social relationships can be a particular stressor for young workers. In fact, Greenberger, Steinberg, Vaux, and McAuliffe (1980) reported early on that the workplace is not typically a source of close personal relationships for adolescents. They believe this is due to the amount of time teenagers work alone, under time pressure, as well as on irregular shifts. The quality of the work does seem to make a difference in this regard, and Mortimer and Shanahan (1991) later found that jobs better utilizing young workers' skills and eliciting high job involvement were related to the development of closer relationships on the job. Thus, these predictors can interact in their relationships with outcomes.

A survey of 25,000 workers in Canada (Williams, 2003) reported the prevalence of five sources of work stress across age categories (see Table 17.1). The results are interesting but must be interpreted with caution because the survey does not appear to have controlled for work status (i.e., the proportion of workers in each category working on a part-time vs. full-time basis). For example, 25% of young workers cited "too many demands/hours" as stressful whereas 36.5% of adults between the ages of 25 and 64 reported likewise. However, we do not know the extent to which "too many hours" was less stressful for young workers because they were working part-time. Interestingly, a greater proportion of young workers attributed work-related stress to "risk of accident/injury" (18%) than adult workers ages 25 to 64 (13%), and 17% of young workers identified "threat of layoff/job loss" as stressful compared with 14.5% of older workers. Given that part-time/ contract workers also tend to be exposed to more hazards on the job and have less secure positions than do full-time workers, these findings would also suggest that higher proportions of individuals may be working part-time in the younger group and that this may be influencing the findings. Other stressors would seem to be less confounded by work status. For example, whereas 13.25% of adult workers reported "having to learn computer skills" as stressful, only 8% of young workers said likewise. Although not a large difference, this seems reasonable because young workers are a product of the information age and cite technology as their biggest advantage (Wah, 1999).

Table 17.1   Sources of Work Stress Across Age Categories

Source of Workplace Stress

	Too many demands/ hours	*Risk of accident/ injury*	*Poor interpersonal relations*	*Threat of layoff/ job loss*	*Having to learn computer skills*
Total all ages	34	13	16	14	11
15–24 years	25	18	16	17	8 E
25–34 years	37	15	17	15	10
35–44 years	37	12	16	15	12
45–54 years	38	13	15	16	15
55–64 years	34	12	13	12	16

SOURCE: General Social Survey, 2000.

NOTE: Multiple responses permitted. Data with a coefficient of variation (CV) from 16.6% to 33.3% are identified by an (E) and should be interpreted with caution.

Concerning unique stressors for young workers that go beyond those found in the adult literature, Mortimer et al. (2002) emphasized the importance of "compatibility" between school and work and argued that this is perhaps the most significant predictor of mental health outcomes for young workers (e.g., depression while in high school and 4 years later). These researchers also found that early workplace stressors could be stress "sensitizing" 4 years after high school, diminishing young people's coping strategies and enhancing distress. Role conflict and time pressure can combine to produce a significant work stressor among those who are participants in both education and the workplace. Because school is supposed to be a young person's primary focus (Shanahan et al., 1991), when work interferes with school (or family), stress is a common experience (Babin & Boles, 1998). In a recent study, Loughlin, Frone, and Barling (2002) also found that those young workers who were most job-involved suffered the most negative effects from low-quality employment. Again, this may be because of pressure to make school their primary focus. It should be noted that this type of stressor could also occur anytime individuals attempt to combine high-demand roles such as student and worker and thus is not confined only to workers between the ages of 15 and 24.

Another stressor that is somewhat unique to this cohort is the notion of failed expectations (as illustrated in the quote at the beginning of the chapter). Many young workers enjoy the benefits of working in the non-standard workforce, which allows them the flexibility to juggle school and work. However, approximately 20% of youth in 1999 worked part-time because full-time jobs were not available (OAYEC, 2000). To the extent that they seek full-time work and cannot find it, this underemployment (not unlike unemployment as discussed earlier) will be a stressor for young workers trying to establish themselves in the adult labor market. When entering the workforce today, young workers are idealistic and optimistic compared with their older counterparts (those over age 35). For example, young workers in the United States are more likely than their older counterparts to believe that hard work will let them get ahead in the workplace (American Federation of Labor and Congress of Industrial Organizations [AFL-CIO], n.d.). Once in the workforce, however, young workers may begin to feel disillusioned as many of their hopes and dreams related to work are not realized (Coy et al., 2002). Young people find it necessary to adjust their values to reflect the opportunity for value fulfillment in the workforce. Young workers are seen to have "unrealistically high goals" when entering the workforce (Johnson, 2001, p. 316), which leads them to a revision of goals and values as they gain more experience in the labor market. Perhaps partially in response to this disappointment with work for need fulfillment, young workers have indicated that a key area of importance for them is more time for families and more help with child care (AFL-CIO, n.d.). Work for many has become a means to an end; meaning in life is derived from family and other social experiences outside of work, not from work itself

(Kersten, 2002). Young workers can be particularly hard hit by shifts in the economy (Coy et al., 2002). Much like older workers, young workers perceive that they are discriminated against based on their age (Renshaw, 2000). Youths are thought to be at a disadvantage when competing with older workers with more seniority and experience. The current economic climate is difficult for all workers, but young workers may bear the brunt of it as older workers are holding jobs that could be filled by young workers (Armour, 2002). Although this situation is predicted to ease in the near future due to labor shortages (and the demand for young workers to increase considerably), for now it can be a stressor for young people trying to find their places in the world of work. Further, to the extent that calls for the abolishment of mandatory retirement are successful, this competition for jobs could persist.

Another stressor among young workers relates to the physical environment, and young workers can face physical hazards even in jobs that might not seem dangerous (e.g., the food service industry; Castillo, 1999; Loughlin & Barling, 2001; Loughlin, Barling, & Kelloway, 2002). In fact, most injuries among young workers occur in the hospitality and retail sectors (CCSD, 2002). Needless to say, unsafe work can be a significant stressor in the workplace, particularly if young people lack the confidence to ask for changes. An intriguing example to consider in this regard is that of young people employed in the military (assuming, as in North America, they have enlisted by choice). Because until now there has been the perception that young people only work in the service sector of the economy and that young workers are protected from long hours of employment and/or hazardous work (Mortimer et al., 2002), this is an interesting example to consider. The United Nations Convention on the Rights of the Child allows children as young as 15 to enter combat; the United States has some 7,000 17-year-olds in its military forces and has been a leading opponent of the call for a "straight 18s protocol." Canada and Britain also recruit 17-year-olds (Schuler, 1999). Although this group may be a minority of young workers in North America, and we would not consider soldiers in countries with conscription to be "employees," it is interesting to note that large parts of our organizational literature in other areas (e.g., leadership) are built on military samples. Nonetheless, little organizational research looks at the experiences of young soldiers. This is a group worth looking at, given some of the stressors to which they are exposed and the serious consequences of work stress for their psychological and physical health now and in the future. In countries with the draft (e.g., Israel at the age of 18 years), the effects of these stressors are likely to be exacerbated to the extent that these individuals are not "serving" by choice.

Finally, and perhaps most important, it must be noted that stressors for young workers will vary widely depending on the particular job in question. For example, young workers in the service sector will have their own unique set of stressors (e.g., interpersonal stressors often take precedence). In some cases, these young workers may find themselves in a position not unlike previous generations in the manufacturing sector wherein a human assembly line has simply replaced a mechanical one (i.e., serving one customer or client after another in an endless stream of unrewarding or unfulfilling service-based interactions). The point here is not that service jobs are bad in and of themselves or that other sectors (e.g., technology) are not prone to stressful working conditions (e.g., Lessard & Baldwin, 2000); the point is to recognize that if we are to progress in this area, we must move beyond generalizations and acknowledge that young workers are exposed to a variety of experiences at work, and their experiences of stress and strain will vary accordingly. For example, young career soldiers identify their top stressors as not being able to use the skills they were trained for, doing tedious tasks, and a lack of communication from above (Dolan et al., 2001). Although some of these stressors overlap with those identified earlier in other young workers (e.g., skill utilization), some are also unique (e.g., communication from above). Young soldiers are also concerned about the failure of the military to live up to their expectations, which seems consistent with the experiences of much of their cohort. However, this study took this one step further and identified those whom young soldiers held responsible for their disappointment with their jobs. In this case, they perceived their leaders to be unable or unwilling to protect them from institutional sources of stress (Dolan et al., 2001). Perhaps what was most revealing in this study was that when leaders' perceptions of young people's primary stressors were measured, they did not match young soldiers' self-reports. These findings speak to the need to sample individuals directly for their perceptions of stressors in the workplace.

Mediators and Moderators of Stressor-Strain Relationships in Young Workers

In much of the discussion above, we have assumed direct links between stressors in the work environment and outcomes for young workers. However, there are also variables that will mediate and moderate these relationships. In the next few pages, we will discuss mediators and moderators of particular relevance to young workers.

Mediators. Developmental studies have found that adolescent coping behavior may be less developed than that of adults (Shanahan et al., 1991). Problem-focused coping is often an effective way of dealing with stressful situations (Yagil, 1998). However, problem-focused coping is likely to require a certain degree of self-confidence that young workers may not have when they first enter the workforce. In this regard, some authors argue that exposure to work can actually help young workers develop coping skills. Presuming outcomes are not perceived as negative (in which case stressors may have a sensitizing effect), the mastery of difficult tasks, even if experienced as stressful, is believed to enhance self-efficacy, inoculate against future reactivity to stressors, strengthen motivational structures, and increase the propensity to seek challenging environments in the future (Mortimer et al., 2002). These experiences, if successful, will become protective, effectively "steeling" the adolescent for future challenges. There is some additional support for this position. A study of Swiss young workers found that coping skills did develop over time and that there was a significant relationship between time in occupation and job control, social stressors, felt work appreciation, positive life attitudes, and job satisfaction (Kaelin et al., 2000). The mediating influences of both negative affect and self-efficacy have also been studied recently in predicting young workers' psychological and physical health as well as their job performance (Lubbers, Loughlin, & Zweig, in press). This study found that affect seemed to be the most important mediator in terms of predicting young workers' psychological and physical health based on their job experiences.

Moderators. Young workers' reactions to stressors in the workplace may be moderated by several personal or situational variables. Extensive research has been done in an attempt to identify and test the presence and effects of moderators in adult working populations; however, fewer studies have focused specifically on young workers. Moderators can also interact with each other, making it difficult to tease out causal relationships in some cases. For example, although potential job stressors such as time pressures or responsibilities for things outside one's control increase the likelihood of young workers exhibiting depressive symptoms (Shanahan et al., 1991), high levels of perceived person-job (P-J) fit are more likely to create higher levels of self-esteem in young workers. Moreover, depressive affect is moderated to some extent by the availability of social support networks during especially stressful times (Mortimer & Shanahan, 1994). These types of interactions can make theory building a challenge.

Personal variables. Even in similar occupations, exposure to work stress can vary based on demographic variables. For example, Mortimer et al. (2002) found that students from lower socioeconomic backgrounds and those who perform less well in school tend to move into jobs with more stressors in the environment. Personality factors such as the propensity for positive or negative affect may also enhance or reduce the impact of work stressors, although only negative affect (NA) has been found to significantly affect stressor-strain connections in adult samples (Hurrell, Nelson, & Simmons, 1998). Job involvement is another personal variable that may moderate stressor-strain relationships for young workers. Loughlin, Frone, and Barling (2002) found that job involvement moderated the relation between intrinsic work quality and psychological health among young workers (effects were most negative for those who were most involved in their jobs). Another set of moderators that generalizes from the adult literature is the tendency to use alcohol, cigarettes, and mood-altering substances as tools for coping with work stress. In young workers, this behavior is connected not only to the quality but also the quantity of hours worked (Shanahan et al., 1991). For example, adolescents working 10 or more hours per week have been found to be at an increased risk for frequent and/or heavy drinking (Kouvonen & Lintonen, 2002).

Situational variables. Perhaps the most important moderator of relationships between predictors and outcomes for young workers in school relates to the quantity of work in which young people engage, with more than 20 hours per week being most detrimental (e.g., Loughlin & Barling, 1998). Situational variables such as cultural expectations and the availability of social support may also moderate stressor-strain relationships among young workers. Support from parents and peers, support from supervisors, and the extent to which the work and school domains complement and mutually support each other have all been found to be important in this regard (Shanahan et al., 1991).

Interestingly, participation in the workforce by young people has also been found to fundamentally change family relationships, and in this case, work may also influence social support networks. Work may enable young people to become more emotionally and financially independent from their parents thereby changing the nature of the parent-child relationship. The influence of parents on working adolescents may diminish simply because employment cuts into the time that would otherwise be spent with parents. Furthermore, it is reasonable to believe that what the adolescent is doing at work, if it has implications for the adolescent's own psychological development, will also have consequences for relationships with parents and other family members. Of course, these moderators will also interact with individuals' own coping mechanisms in determining whether outcomes are positive, neutral, or negative.

Outcomes

As mentioned previously, researchers have consistently argued that the quality of the work environment is critical in determining successful job performance, physical health, safety, and psychological health among adults (Schaubroeck & Ganster, 1991; Kinicki, McKee, & Wade, 1996; Sauter & Hurrell, 1999; Sauter et al., 1990). In contrast, research on young workers in this regard has been notably lacking (Frone, 1999), and adolescent work has rarely been linked to mental health outcomes (Mortimer et al., 2002). What research has been done linking work to psychological and somatic health seems to suggest that the consequences of part-time work for adolescent development depend on the quantity and/or quality of the employment (e.g., Frone, 1999; Loughlin & Barling, 1999).

Although working can provide young people with opportunities to learn skills that may be useful in the future and can reward them with benefits such as pay and increased freedom, youth employment can also affect young people negatively. Many aspects of their work, such as long hours, role conflict, or time pressures, can be associated with psychological problems including depression. In their study of American high school students, Shanahan et al. (1991) found no significant differences in depressed mood between workers and nonworkers; however, they did find that particular working conditions seemed to influence depressive affect. For example, among ninth-grade students, self-direction was particularly important for boys in predicting depressed mood, whereas for girls, work-school conflict seemed the most important. It is also interesting to note that relationships between job skills and work hours differed between the sexes. Thus, we must be careful about generalizing across sexes. In summary, researchers who suggest negative associations between work and outcomes in adolescents are increasingly pointing to underemployment as the primary cause of problems (i.e., work of a low economic, physical, psychological, or social quality) as opposed to the quantity of hours worked. Economists have recognized the negative effects of poor-quality employment early in one's life for some time and talk about the economic "scarring" that is believed to occur when negative early labor market experiences affect subsequent employment outcomes (Betcherman & Morissette, 1994). Researchers are now recognizing the social and psychological equivalents (Lowe, 2000).

In contrast to the above, the most prevalent view voiced by parents and teenagers continues to be that paid work builds character, instills a positive work ethic, and is a positive experience for youth (Mortimer et al., 2002). In general, in comparison with their nonworking peers, moderate participation in the workforce may well lead adolescents to skill mastery more quickly. Research has found that when the number of hours worked is controlled for, students working during the school year can be more successful in various high school activities, and those having supervisory experience were most successful at activities requiring leadership or people skills (Mael, Morath, & McLellan, 1997). However, this relationship does not continue indefinitely, and higher quantities of participation in the workforce can take a toll. In addition, although there is little doubt that exposure to employment situations improves certain abilities in young people, it is important to recognize that mastery is likely the result of the quality, not the quantity, of work. Some argue that work experiences influence mastery in young people in a way that is different from their impact in adults (Finch et al., 1991). However, it must be kept in mind that control or mastery orientations are not fixed traits but are cumulative responses to a series of successes and failures throughout life. Work experiences likely influence employed adolescents' mastery orientation by affecting their propensity to view themselves as being in control, including, for example, having an internal locus of control, self-determination and confidence, and recognizing their level of competence. In their longitudinal study, Lubbers et al. (in press) found that perceived job self-efficacy fully mediated the relationship between interpersonal work conflict and the outcomes of job performance and health in young workers on full-time, short-term work assignments. Thus, stressors that diminish young workers' perceptions of their self-efficacy are likely to be the most troublesome for current and future well-being.

Major Empirical Studies of Stressor-Strain Relationships in Young Workers

Although not much empirical research has been conducted on this topic, a few recent empirical studies are instructive. Mortimer et al. (2002) gleaned important findings about the consequences of work quality (e.g., intrinsic and extrinsic factors, work intensity, and work-school compatibility) for youth mental health. This study addressed selection into employment and examined both short- and long-term mental health consequences. The authors found that although girls were more likely to work than boys during their high school years, factors such as socioeconomic status and nationality did not significantly predict either who worked and who did not during the 10th, 11th, or 12th grade or the level of compatibility between work and school. They also found that although the intrinsic qualities of work did not affect well-being or depressive affect, work-school compatibility and the perception that employment enhanced relationships with their friends led to positive mental health outcomes (Mortimer et al., 2002). Additionally, those adolescents who reported more stressors during the 10th and 11th grades were more likely to manifest depressive affect in the 12th grade (except in those students who felt that their work and school activities were especially compatible). Finally, early work stressors had a lasting effect on young adults' depressive affect up to 4 years after high school.

Frone's (2000) study pointed out the importance of interpersonal conflict at work in predicting young workers' psychological outcomes. This study found that interpersonal conflict with supervisors was negatively related to organizational commitment and job satisfaction and positively related to turnover intentions, whereas interpersonal conflict with coworkers was positively related to depression and somatic symptoms and negatively related to self-esteem among young workers.

Finally, the longitudinal study by Lubbers et al. (in press) of 195 young workers tested social cognitive and affective events theories in studying links between job experiences and health. Interpersonal conflict at the beginning of a work term was linked to job performance and health at the end of the work term via job self-efficacy and job-related affect. Furthermore, job-related affect mediated the relationship between intrinsic job characteristics at the beginning of a work term and job performance and health at the end. The findings offer insight into how job experiences translate into health and performance during a formative period in workers' lives. In keeping with Frone's (2000) study above, these findings also emphasize the need for more research into interpersonal work conflict as a predictor of young workers' outcomes.

Key Measurement Issues

Researchers in the field of occupational stress have faced a number of measurement challenges. For example, in the adult literature, a wide variety of instruments are used, data are often collected using inconsistent methodologies, and results are interpreted idiosyncratically (Williams & Cooper, 1998). The debate over self-report versus observational stress measures continues (as covered in much detail elsewhere in this book), and there are compelling arguments for triangulation strategies combining multiple stress measures. Finally, the effectiveness of established measurement tools has been questioned given changes in the nature of work and employment demographics. Instruments that work in one culture or organization may not generalize to another setting, and as Pousette and Hanse (2002) demonstrated, a "group-sensitive" model is most appropriate for measuring constructs in this area. All of these measurement challenges also apply to the study of young workers' stress. For example, given developmental differences, the extent to which various instruments developed for adult populations generalize to young workers is largely unknown.

In addition to the measurement challenges typically faced by occupational stress researchers in general, a few additional challenges face those studying stress in young workers. First, as pointed out by Castillo (1999), in her discussion of occupational health and safety in young workers, we cannot assume that youth are simply "little adults" (p. 180). Prior to full psychological and physical maturation, they may be uniquely susceptible to stressors in the workplace. Exposure to stressors during critical periods of development may also permanently alter the trajectory of normal development. For example, Zejda et al. (1993) found that among young farmers, chronic respiratory symptoms from environmental hazards were due both to more intense occupational exposure and to working during a critical period of lung development.

Another measurement challenge in studying young workers' stress is that we are discussing "work stress" during a stage of development that is already defined by some researchers as a social problem in and of itself (i.e., adolescence; Epstein, 1998). At times, this will make it difficult to separate normal developmental changes from those associated with negative or positive influences from the work environment in which young workers participate. For example, it is difficult to determine the extent to which separating from one's family social-support network is due to normal developmental changes versus depressive symptoms linked to stressors like lack of control in the work environment. Further, not all young people will be attracted to work at equal intensities in adolescence, and we must recognize that selection into employment while still in school may also affect measures of relationships between stressors and strain in this group of workers (Frone, 1999).

Interestingly, the most pressing issue concerning measurement in this area may simply be that the measures and models used for studying work and health in adults have rarely been applied to studying young workers. Only recently have organizational psychologists begun to adapt measures and models from the adult literature to the study of young workers (e.g., Frone, 2000; Lubbers et al., in press). Other researchers have pointed out that work-related injuries and illnesses in youth are typically ignored in the psychological field (Castillo, 1999), and the study of work stress is no exception.

Implications for Practice, Policy, and Intervention

Based on an understanding of the needs of young workers and what we have learned from the work stress literature, we can now consider four recommendations for reducing young workers' experiences of stress at work.

First, support young workers in learning opportunities at work, given the need for skill use and opportunities for learning discussed throughout earlier sections of this chapter. Assuming the work is of high quality, young workers can derive much benefit from contact with the world of work (Organization for Economic Cooperation and Development [OECD], 2002). They develop a network of potential employers, gain work experience, explore different career options, and are exposed to mentors. Organizations that are most successful in providing young workers with learning opportunities start early (Lancaster & Stillman, 2002). Partnerships are formed with high school students through mentoring, internship, and cooperative education programs. Recognizing the importance of early experiences in the workplace, some governments are now requiring that cooperative education, work experience, and school-work transition programs be provided to all interested students (Provincial Partnership Council, 2002). However, the quality of these experiences will be pivotal in determining their value (Lubbers et al., in press). Training within the organization should expose young workers to a range of employment experiences and people. According to an AFL-CIO survey (n.d.), 86% of young workers see putting more emphasis on education and skills training for employees as very important. Organizations providing early learning opportunities to young workers benefit as well from building the organization's talent pool and infusing the organization with the enthusiasm young workers can bring to the workplace.

Second, create a meaningful work experience. As outlined in the models earlier in this chapter, job content (e.g., task identity or significance) is important in contributing to psychologically healthy mental states. Young workers want to feel that they are engaged in work that has meaning (Lancaster & Stillman, 2002). Not only do they want to know what they are doing in the greater scheme of the organization, but they also want to know why they are doing it. Organizations should ensure that young workers are familiar with the organizational mission, strategy, and culture, and organizations should show young workers how their jobs contribute to the organization as a whole (Grensing-Pophal, 1999). Even if they are not working full-time, young workers should be integrated into the organization. As mentioned previously, young workers enter the workforce with enthusiasm but are soon overwhelmed by feelings of disillusionment and betrayal. Of course, young workers are also looking for a realistic portrayal of the work they will be doing in the organization, and it is important that managers do not promise what they cannot produce in terms of a meaningful work experience.

Third, provide opportunities for advancement. As mentioned earlier, autonomy and participation in decision making are critical to young workers, and many of them feel that jobs are not living up to their expectations. They often feel that they must look outside their current organization for promotion opportunities (Renshaw, 2000). It is predicted that young workers will be more loyal than their older counterparts, and it is suggested that young workers are not averse to staying with an organization for the course of their entire career if the situation is right for them (Lancaster & Stillman, 2002). This loyalty is not perceived to be matched by organizations (Coy et al., 2002). Young workers fall into entry-level jobs with little opportunity for advancement, often due to a perception that they must pay their dues before moving into better positions (Lieber, 1999). However, it makes sense for organizations to involve young workers more in decision making and to open opportunities for increased levels of responsibility in the organization. This will pay off from young workers' perspectives because they are better using their skills, but it will also likely pay off from the organizations' perspectives in terms of improved recruiting and retention opportunities (Lieber, 1999).

Finally, encourage and support work/school/life balance. Especially for young workers still in school, the workplace is one of many priorities. Companies should help young workers manage potentially conflicting demands if they are still in school. The older part of this cohort also may need help managing work-home conflict, especially if they have young children. In summary, flexibility may be the key to supporting balance for young workers in general. Flexibility for young workers could encompass work hours as well as work locations in some sectors (e.g., telecommuting). Lifestyle-focused benefits (e.g., time-off bonuses to manage other life priorities, or opportunities to travel and work in other locations) may also be effective means of attracting and retaining young workers (Laurie & Laurie, 1999).

Future Research Needs

Much like research in the adult literature (as discussed elsewhere in this book), there is a need to broaden the measures we use in measuring young workers' stress. There are some variables for which only self-reports are valid (e.g., only employees can tell us how much autonomy they perceive there to be in their work). Further, as illustrated in the example of young soldiers, other sources (e.g., leaders) may lack insight into the experiences of individuals being surveyed. However, there are also compelling reasons for utilizing multiple data sources in our research (e.g., observational or physiological measures). There is also a need for multidisciplinary approaches to the study of occupational stress in young workers (e.g., in which sociologists, psychologists, and other researchers look more closely at each other's work and begin to incorporate each other's findings into their models).

Concerning areas for future research that relate to young workers' stress in particular, some variables from the adult literature may have been dismissed prematurely in the case of young workers and need to be studied empirically. For example, it has been argued that work scheduling is less important to adolescents because students are not legally allowed to work after midnight or to be scheduled for work hours that conflict with school (e.g., Krahn, 1991). However, as discussed earlier, work-school conflict often emerges as a major stressor for young workers. Research must be done to reconcile conflicting findings. Career security is another factor overlapping with the NIOSH model of work stress that has been assumed unimportant for young workers (Greenberger & Steinberg, 1986). As temporary jobs become permanent in the new economy, this conclusion may no longer be valid. Future research will need to explore these types of relationships.

Another area ripe for research concerns moderators of relations between stressors and strain in young workers. Numerous moderators studied in research on adult work stress have not been considered for young workers. For example, whereas the impatience irritability (II) component of type A behavior patterns (TABP) in adults has been positively related to self-report measures of perceived stress, the achievement striving (AS) component has been linked to less perceived stress (Day & Jreige, 2002). At a most basic level this would suggest that young workers high in AS may be better equipped to handle stress in the workplace. It is unclear to what extent these findings can be generalized to adolescents (remember the personality sets of adolescents may not be fully developed when they enter the workplace), but it is worth investigating. Other potential moderators from the adult literature are enhanced organizational commitment or collective efficacy; they lessen the impact of workplace stressors by making employees feel that they and their work groups are better equipped to handle stressful situations (Zellars, Hochwarter, Perrewé, Miles, & Kiewitz, 2001; Siu, 2002). These variables have the potential to ease role conflict and buffer against some of the negative impact of work stress. Although the extent to which young, and often part-time or contract, workers have opportunities to develop these buffers is unknown, they may be worth considering.

Finally, the most pressing need in this area is simply to study the topic. We need to begin testing measures and models from the adult literature to determine the extent to which they generalize to young workers' experiences of stress and strain. Within industrial/organizational psychology, the lack of focus on links between young people's work quality and their health may be in part because many young people work on a part-time/contract basis and our literature tends to focus on full-time workers in large organizations. There has also been a tendency to treat young people's work as "transitional" and therefore not worthy of study (Loughlin & Barling, 2001). However, regardless of the reason for the neglect, we need to begin studying experiences of work, and work stress in particular, across the life span.

Epilogue

Policymakers are recognizing the workplace as a critical context for enhancing the health and quality of citizens' lives (Lowe, 2000). In a recent speech on "how to become the healthiest nation on Earth," the Canadian health commissioner was succinct: "Poor jobs equal poor health" (Romanow, 2003). For at least a decade now, researchers have been warning about the polarization of work into good and bad jobs in our service- and knowledge-based economies and the threat this poses to young workers (Krahn, 1991). Research has also found teenagers to be more influenced than adults by their work environments, possibly exaggerating any negative effects (Lorence & Mortimer, 1985). There is an urgent need to consider the effects of job quality on employees, including young workers, at different stages in their work lives (Griffiths, 1999).

There are good reasons for society to care about young workers' experiences of work stress. For example, characteristics of work that contribute to job strain also increase anger (directed at coworkers, supervisors, and customers) in young service sector workers (in models that controlled for dispositional negative affect and work status; Fitzgerald, Haythornthwaite, Suchday, & Ewart, 2002). Further, adults may have more input in this regard than they might think. A study in Germany found that attachment to adults not only predicted aggression and delinquency among young German apprentices but also the extent to which young people were optimistic about their occupational futures (Silverberg, Vazsonyi, Schlegel, & Schmidt, 1998).

It is time we acknowledge the role early work experiences can play in shaping young workers and begin to deliberately design workplaces accordingly. This is not an impossible task, and even in sectors such as food and beverage services that are notorious for low-quality work it can be done (e.g., Starbucks; Schlosser, 2001). Of course, before we can design workplaces that contribute to the health and productivity of young workers in the twenty-first century, we must understand how these relationships work. Researchers must begin to intervene accordingly based on these findings.

References

American Federation of Labor and Congress of Industrial Organizations (AFL-CIO). (n.d.). *High hopes, little trust*. Retrieved November 18, 2002, from www .aflcio.org/articles/high_hopes/index.htm

Armour, S. (2002, October 10). Young workers feel stuck as older ones don't retire. *USA Today* [Electronic version].

Astrand, N. E., Hanson, B. S., & Isacson, S. O. (1989). Job demands, job decision latitude, job support and social network factors as predictors of mortality in a Swedish pulp and paper company. *British Journal of Industrial Medicine, 46,* 334–340.

Australian Bureau of Statistics. (2003). Retrieved July 14, 2003, from abs.gov.au

Babin, B. J., & Boles, J. S. (1998). Employee behavior in a service environment: A model and test of potential differences between men and women. *Journal of Marketing, 62*(2), 77–91.

Betcherman, G., & Morissette, R. (1994). *Recent youth labour market experiences in Canada* (Business and Labour Market Analysis, 63). Ottawa, ON: Statistics Canada.

Bibby, R. W. (2001). *Canada's teens: Today, yesterday, and tomorrow.* Toronto, ON: Stoddart.

Canadian Council on Social Development (CCSD). (2002). *The progress of Canada's children.* Ottawa, ON.

Caplan, R. D., Cobb, S., French, J. R. P., Harrison, R. V., & Pinneau, S. R. (1975). *Job demands and worker health: Main effects and occupational differences.* Washington, DC: U.S. Government Printing Office.

Castillo, D. N. (1999). Occupational safety and health in young people. In J. Barling & K. Kelloway (Eds.), *Young workers: Varieties of experience* (pp. 159–200). Washington, DC: American Psychological Association.

Claes, R., & Ruiz-Quintanilla, S. A. (1998). Influences of early career experiences, occupational group, and national culture on proactive career behavior. *Journal of Vocational Behavior, 52,* 357–378.

Coy, P., Conlin, M., & Thornton, E. (2002, November 4). A lost generation? Young and mid-career job seekers are bearing the brunt of U.S. layoffs. *BusinessWeek* [Electronic version].

Cullen, M. R. (1999). Personal reflections on occupational health in the twentieth century: Spiraling to the future. *Annual Review of Public Health, 20,* 1–13.

Day, A. L., & Jreige, S. (2002). Examining type A behavior pattern to explain the relationship between job stressors and psychological outcomes. *Journal of Occupational Health Psychology, 7*(2), 109–120.

Dohm, A. (2000). Gauging the labor force effects of retiring baby-boomers. *Monthly Labor Review, 123*(7), 17–25.

Dolan, C. A., Crouch, C. L., West, P., & Castro, C. A. (2001). *Sources of stress and coping strategies among U.S. soldiers and their leaders.* Paper presented at the meeting of the European Health Psychology Conference, St. Andrews, Scotland.

Dressler, W. W. (1990). Lifestyle, stress, and blood pressure in a Southern Black community. *Psychosomatic Medicine, 52,* 182–198.

Epstein, J. S. (1998). Introduction: Generation X, youth culture, and identity. In J. S. Epstein (Ed.), *Youth culture: Identity in a postmodern world.* Oxford, UK: Blackwell.

Erikson, E. H. (1963). *Childhood and society.* New York: Norton.

Finch, M. D., Shanahan, M. J., Mortimer, J. T., & Ryu, S. (1991). Work experience and control orientation in adolescence. *American Sociological Review, 56,* 597–611.

Fitzgerald, S. T., Haythornthwaite, J. A., Suchday, S., & Ewart, C. K. (2002). Anger in young black and white workers: Effects of job control, dissatisfaction, and support. *Journal of Behavioral Medicine, 26*(4), 283–296.

Frone, M. R. (1999). Developmental consequences of youth employment. In J. Barling & E. K. Kelloway (Eds.), *Young workers: Varieties of experiences* (pp. 89–128). Washington, DC: American Psychological Association.

Frone, M. R. (2000). Interpersonal conflict at work and psychological outcomes: Testing a model among young workers. *Journal of Occupational Health Psychology, 5,* 246–255.

Furnham, A. (1985). Youth unemployment: A review of the literature. *Journal of Adolescence, 8,* 109–124.

Garson, B. (1988). *The electronic sweatshop: How computers are transforming the office of the future into the factory of the past.* New York: Penguin Books.

Goldsmith, A. H., Veum, J. R., & Darity, W. (1997). Unemployment, joblessness, psychological well-being and self-esteem: Theory and evidence. *Journal of Socio-economics, 26*(2), 133–158.

Greenberger, E., & Steinberg, L. D. (1986). *When teenagers work: The psychological and social costs of adolescent employment.* New York: Basic Books.

Greenberger, E., Steinberg, L. D., & Ruggiero, M. (1982). A job is a job . . . or is it? *Work and Occupations, 9,* 79–96.

Greenberger, E., Steinberg, L. D., Vaux, A., & McAuliffe, S. (1980). Adolescents who work: Effects of part-time employment on family and peer relations. *Journal of Youth and Adolescence, 9,* 189–202.

Grensing-Pophal, L. (1999, October). Teens at work: Handle with care. *HR Magazine,* 55–59.

Griffiths, A. (1999). Work design and management: The older worker. *Experimental Aging Research, 25,* 411–420.

Hackman, J. R., & Oldham, G. R. (1980). *Work redesign.* Reading, MA: Addison-Wesley.

Hurrell, J. J., Nelson, D. L., & Simmons, B. L. (1998). Measuring job stressors and strains: Where we have been, where we are, and where we need to go. *Journal of Occupational Health Psychology, 3*(4), 368–389.

Johnson, M. K. (2001). Change in job values during the transition to adulthood. *Work and Occupations, 28,* 315–345.

Kaelin, W., Semmer, N. K., Elfering, A., Techan, F., Dauwalder, J. P., Heunert, S., von Roten, F. C. (2000). Work characteristics and well-being of Swiss apprentices entering the labor market. *Swiss Journal of Psychology, 59*(4), 272–290.

Kalinowski, T. (2003, March 12). Broken dreams: Under-30s earn less than in 1980. *Toronto Star,* pp. A1, A8.

Karasek, R. A., & Theorell, T. (1990). *Healthy work: Stress, productivity and the reconstruction of working life.* New York: Basic Books.

Kersten, D. (2002, August 15). Twentysomethings adjust to life in a recession. *USA Today* [Electronic version].

Kinicki, A. J., McKee, F. M., & Wade, K. J. (1996). Annual review, 1991–1995: Occupational health. *Journal of Vocational Behavior, 49,* 190–220.

Kouvonen, A, & Lintonen, T. (2002). Adolescent part-time work and heavy drinking in Finland. *Addiction, 97*(3), 311–318.

Krahn, H. (1991). Youth employment. In R. Barnhorst & L. C. Johnson (Eds.), *The state of the child in Ontario* (pp. 139–159). Toronto, ON: Oxford University Press.

Krosnick, J. A., & Alwin, D. F. (1989). Aging and susceptibility to attitude change. *Journal of Personality and Social Psychology, 57,* 416–425.

Lancaster, L. C., & Stillman, D. (2002). *When generations collide*. New York: HarperCollins.

Laurie, N., & Laurie, M. (1999, December 13). What do young employees want? A life outside the office. *Canadian HR Reporter, 12*, G3.

Lessard, B., & Baldwin, S. (2000). *True tales of working the Web*. New York: McGraw-Hill.

Lieber, R. (1999). First jobs aren't child's play. *Fast Company, 25* [Electronic version].

Light, K. C., Brownley, K. A., Turner, J. R., Hinderliter, A. L., Girdler, S. S., Sherwood, A., & Anderson, N. B. (1995). Job status and high-effort coping influence work blood pressure in women and blacks. *Hypertension, 25*, 554–559.

Livingstone, D. W. (1999). *The education-jobs gap: Underemployment or economic democracy*. Toronto, ON: Garamond Press.

Lorence, J., & Mortimer, J. T. (1985). Job involvement through the life course: A panel study of three age groups. *American Sociological Review, 50*, 618–638.

Loughlin, C. A., & Barling, J. (1998). Teenagers' part-time employment and their work-related attitudes and aspirations. *Journal of Organizational Behavior, 19*(2), 197–207.

Loughlin, C. A., & Barling, J. (1999). The nature of youth employment quality. In J. Barling & K. Kelloway (Eds.), *Young workers: Varieties of experience* (pp. 17–36). Washington, DC: American Psychological Association.

Loughlin C. A., & Barling, J. (2001). Young workers' work values, attitudes, and behaviors. *Journal of Occupational and Organizational Psychology, 74*, 543–558.

Loughlin, C., Barling, J., & Kelloway, E. K. (2002). Development and test of a model linking safety-specific transformational leadership and occupational safety. *Journal of Applied Psychology, 87*(3), 488–496.

Loughlin, C., Frone, M., & Barling, J. (2002, April). *Work and well-being in young workers: Contrasting exposure and involvement*. Paper presented at the meeting of the SIOP Conference, Toronto, ON.

Lowe, G. S. (2000). *The quality of work: A people-centered agenda*. Don Mills, ON: Oxford University Press.

Lubbers, R., Loughlin, C., & Zweig, D. (2004). Common pathways to health and performance: Job self-efficacy and affect among young workers. *Journal of Vocational Behavior*.

Mael, F. A., Morath, R. A., & McLellan, J. A. (1997). Dimensions of adolescent employment. *Career Development Quarterly, 45*(4), 351–368.

Marks, G. N., & Fleming, N. (1999). Influences and consequences of well-being among Australian young people: 1980–1995. *Social Indicators Research, 46*, 301–323.

Mortimer, J. T., Harley, C., & Staff, J. (2002). The quality of work and youth mental health. *Work and Occupations, 29*(2), 166–197.

Mortimer, J. T., & Shanahan, M. J. (1991, June). *Adolescent work experience and relations with peers*. Paper presented at the meeting of the American Sociological Association, Cincinnati, OH.

Mortimer, J. T., & Shanahan, M. J. (1994). Adolescent work experience and family relationships. *Work and Occupations, 21*(4), 369–384.

National Statistical Office. (2003). *Thailand*. Retrieved July 14, 2003, from nso.go.th

Nord, W. R. (1977). Job satisfaction reconsidered. *American Psychologist, 32*, 1026–1035.

O'Brien, G. E., & Feather, N. T. (1990). The relative effects of unemployment and quality of employment on the affect, work values and personal control of adolescents. *Journal of Occupational Psychology, 63*, 151–165.

Ontario Association of Youth Employment Centres (OAYEC). (2000). *Window on youth employment.* Toronto, ON: Author.

Ontario Association of Youth Employment Centres (OAYEC). (2001). *Double cohort: Implications for work-bound youth.* Toronto, ON: Author.

Organization for Economic Cooperation and Development (OECD). (2002). *OECD employment outlook.* Paris: Author.

Pousette, A., & Hanse, J. J. (2002). Job characteristics as predictors of ill-health and sickness absenteeism in different occupational types: A multi-group structural equation modeling approach. *Work & Stress, 16*(3), 229–250.

Provincial Partnership Council. (2002). *Passport to prosperity.* Retrieved November 18, 2002, from www.edu.gov.on.ca/eng/general/elemsec/job/passport/passport.pdf

Renshaw, R. (2000, July 12). Young, willing and unable? *The Times* [Electronic version].

Romanow, R. (2003, May). *Connecting the dots: From health care and illness to wellbeing.* Paper presented at the meeting of the International Foundation's Public Service Award, Ottawa, ON.

Ruiz-Quintanilla, S. A., & Claes, R. (1994). *Determinants of underemployment during the early career* (Working Paper 94–06). Cornell University, Centre for Advanced Human Resource Studies, Ithaca, NY.

Sauter, S. L., & Hurrell, J. J. (1999). Occupational health psychology: Origins, content, and direction. *Professional Psychology: Research and Practice, 30*(2), 117–122.

Sauter, S. L., Murphy, L. R., & Hurrell, J. J. (1990). Prevention of work-related psychological disorders: A national strategy proposed by the National Institute for Occupational Safety and Health (NIOSH). *American Psychologist, 45*(10), 1146–1158.

Schaubroeck, J., & Ganster, D. C. (1991). Beyond the call of duty: A field study of extra-role behavior in voluntary organizations. *Human Relations, 44,* 569–582.

Schlosser, E. (2001). *Fast food nation: The dark side of the all-American meal.* Boston: Houghton Mifflin.

Schuler, C. (1999). *Childhood's end: Young soldiers try to go home.* ABC News. Retrieved Sept. 15, 2003, from www.abcnews.go.com/sections/world/dailynews/childsoldiers991020.html

Shanahan, M. J., Finch, M., Mortimer, J. T., & Ryu, S. (1991). Adolescent work experience and depressive affect. *Social Psychology Quarterly, 54*(4), 299–317.

Siegrist, J. (1996). Adverse health effects of high-effort/low-reward conditions. *Journal of Occupational Health Psychology, 1,* 27–41.

Silverberg, S. B., Vazsonyi, A. T., Schlegel, A. E., & Schmidt, S. (1998). Adolescent apprentices in Germany: Adult attachment, job expectations, and delinquency attitudes. *Journal of Adolescent Research, 13*(3), 254–271.

Siu, O. (2002). Occupational stressors and well-being among Chinese employees: The role of organizational commitment. *Applied Psychology: An International Review, 51*(4), 527–544.

Statistics Canada. (2003). *Canadian Community Health Survey. Mental Health and Well-Being.* Retrieved October 6, 2003, from www.statcan.ca/english/freepub/82–617XIE/index.htm

Steinberg, L. D., & Dornbusch, S. M. (1991). Negative correlates of part-time employment during adolescence: Replication and elaboration. *Developmental Psychology, 27,* 304–313.

Stern, D., Stone, J. R., Hopkins, C., & McMillion, M. (1990). Quality of student's work experience and orientation toward work. *Perspectives on Labour and Income, 4,* 15–21.

Theorell, T., Perski, A., Orth-Gomer, K., Hamsten, A., & de Faire, U. (1991). The effects of the strain of returning to work on the risk of cardiac death after a first myocardial infarction before the age of 45. *International Journal of Cardiology, 30,* 61–67.

U.S. Department of Labor, Bureau of Labor Statistics. (2003). Employment and unemployment among youth—Summer 2003. Retrieved October 6, 2003, from www.bls.gov/news.release/youth.nr0.htm

Vanderkam, L. (2003, August 21). White-collar sweatshops batter young workers. *USA. Today* [Electronic version].

Wah, L. (1999, April 8). The generation 2001 workforce. *Management Review, 88,* 8.

Wall, T. D., & Clegg, C. W. (1981). A longitudinal field study of group work redesign. *Journal of Occupational Behavior, 2,* 31–49.

Wall, T. D., Corbett, J. M., Martin, R., Clegg, C. W., & Jackson, P. R. (1990). Advanced manufacturing technology, work design, and performance: A change study. *Journal of Applied Psychology, 75*(6), 691–697.

Warr, P. (1987). *Work, unemployment and mental health.* Oxford, UK: Oxford University Press.

Williams, C. (2003). Sources of workplace stress. *Perspectives-on-labour and income* (Catalogue no. 75-001–XPE Autumn 2003), Statistics Canada, 15, 3, 23–30.

Williams, S., & Cooper, C. L. (1998). Measuring occupational stress: Development of the pressure management indicator. *Journal of Occupational Health Psychology, 3*(4), 306–321.

Winefield, A. H., Winefield, H. R., Tiggemann, M., & Goldney, R. D. (1991). A longitudinal study of the psychological effects of unemployment and unsatisfactory employment on young adults. *Journal of Applied Psychology, 76,* 424–431.

Yagil, D. (1998). If anything can go wrong it will: Occupational stress among inexperienced teachers. *International Journal of Stress of Management, 5*(3), 179–188.

Yousef, D. A. (1999). Antecedents and consequences of job stressors: A study in a Third World setting. *International Journal of Stress of Management, 6*(4), 265–282.

Zejda, J. E., Hurst, T. S., Rhodes, C. S., Barber, E. M., McDuffie, H. H., & Dosman, J. A. (1993). Respiratory health of swine producers: Focus on young workers. *Chest, 103*(3), 702–710.

Zellars, K. L., Hochwarter, W. A., Perrewé, P. L., Miles, A. K., & Kiewitz, C. (2001). Beyond self-efficacy: Interactive effects of role conflict and perceived collective efficacy. *Journal of Managerial Issues, 13*(4), 483–499.

18

Older Workers

Janet L. Barnes-Farrell

Older workers represent a large and growing presence in the workforce in many parts of the world. Fullerton and Toossi (2001) reported a 21% increase in the U.S. civilian labor force aged 55 and older between the years 1990 and 2000, and projections through the year 2010 indicate that growth in this sector will continue throughout the decade. As a percentage of the total civilian labor force, it is expected that "over 55" workers will constitute almost 17% of the labor force by the year 2010. Labor force participation rates tend to drop off beginning at about age 55, due primarily to early and "normal" retirements. However, labor force participation rates among members of this group have also shown a steady upward trend since 1990, with a projected labor force participation rate of 37% among those 55 and older by the year 2010 (up from 30% in 1990). Notably, among those aged 55 to 64, participation rates are expected to exceed 60% by the year 2010, and participation rates among those aged 65 to 74 are expected to exceed 22% by 2010.

These figures represent a variety of converging forces including increased life span, the coming of age of the baby boom generation, economic policies (e.g., increasing the standard retirement age that qualifies an individual for full social security benefits), and effective elimination of mandatory retirement policies from most civilian occupations in the United States. In other parts of the world, growth in this population sector is also evident, although labor force participation rates among members of the over-55 sector vary dramatically, in part because of differing employment opportunities and economic policies that provide incentives to withdraw from the labor market at a relatively early age. In fact, among nations in the European Union, there has been a concerted effort to develop policies that will help to increase the participation of older individuals in the labor pool in order to ease the economic and social burden of supporting individuals who leave the workforce early (Organization for Economic Cooperation and Development [OECD],

2002). In summary, the potential size of the older workforce has grown, and the economic need to take advantage of this resource by encouraging older adults to continue working and by providing them with opportunities to maintain healthy, satisfying, and productive work lives is important.

To do this, we need to understand special considerations for age that may be needed in the design of work and work environments. The problem of designing workplaces, work, and organizational practices that meet the needs of individuals from this segment of the workforce requires an understanding of the unique concerns of older workers as they relate to stress. Some of these concerns emanate from age-related changes that have the potential to increase the experienced physical, cognitive, and emotional demands that work places on older workers. For example, older workers are faced with the need to maintain performance levels in the face of changing physical, cognitive, and emotional reserves. They must do so at a time in their lives when for many workers chronic health concerns produce additional physical and emotional demands. In addition, older workers must cope with a variety of role-related transitions and social processes that are experienced as stressful, such as career plateaus, obsolescence, retirement decisions, and age discrimination.

Stress Models of Particular Relevance to Older Workers

Other chapters in this book deal in detail with the variety of stress models that have been proposed to account for the nature and impact of stress in the workplace. However, before moving to a consideration of the external stressors and other risk factors that are of particular significance for older workers, it is useful to point out the theoretical frameworks that have most often been invoked in the study of occupational stress for this segment of the workforce. In the context of understanding stress as it relates to older workers, most research is consistent with the notion of person-environment fit (P-E fit) as the basis for predicting whether work will be experienced as stressful. Within this framework, however, two particular classes of models are of significance.

First are those models that focus on workers' responses to features of work design such as physical and mental workload, shift work, and aspects of the physical work environment. What we know about changing physical capabilities and mental skills suggests that there should be age-related differences in reactions to physical stressors and that those responsible for workplace design must take note of these reactions in order to accommodate the needs of older workers and make it possible for them to maintain adequate performance levels without experiencing strain. For example, research that emphasizes the physical demands of work has tended to rely on models of stress that capture the typical characteristics of task design and work environments that may tax the capabilities of workers. Much of the work carried out by epidemiologists and human factors psychologists tends to emphasize this concern for identifying gaps between task and work environment physical/cognitive demands and the capabilities/limitations of workers. A mismatch between the two is seen as a primary source of the stress response. As such, a clear understanding of the physical and cognitive demands of work as well as the capabilities and limitations of human operators serves as a critical source of information for predicting stress responses and developing interventions to prevent or mitigate stress responses. In this stream of research, the focus is on the interaction between work demands and worker capabilities and the identification of interventions aimed at reducing the gap between the two via work and workplace redesign or training efforts.

Second are those models that focus on psychosocial stressors, such as Karasek's (1979) demand-control model, models that highlight worker perceptions and coping styles as an important step in the stress process (e.g., Lazarus & Folkman, 1984), and models that give explicit attention to organizational sources of stress in the form of role conflict, role ambiguity, and role overload (cf. Ivancevich & Matteson, 1980; Kahn & Byosiere, 1992). Such models, represented primarily in the work of organizational psychologists, are pertinent to the changing and unique role expectations of workers who are in the latter stages of their careers. These models also place emphasis on the important role of cognitive appraisal in determining whether a particular set of circumstances is likely to be experienced as stressful by workers. As such, they draw attention to the importance of a variety of individual difference variables (e.g., perceived self-efficacy) that are likely to influence appraisal of the situation by the worker, coping strategies for managing role stresses, and stress-related outcomes.

In the following sections, I will review a variety of stress-related concerns that have been identified with respect to aging and work. Because work concerned with work stress processes and outcomes among older workers is widely dispersed across a number of methodological and theoretical approaches, this discussion is not organized around a single theoretical approach. Instead, I will begin with a consideration of risk factors for work stress that are pertinent to older workers. This is followed by discussions of measurement issues particular to the study of occupational stress in this population, a summary of empirical findings regarding the experience and outcomes of occupational stress for this segment of the workforce, recommendations for future research, and implications for practice, policy, and organizational interventions.

Risk Factors for Experienced Stress and Strain Among Older Workers

Risk factors for experienced stress and strain among older workers generally fall into four categories: individual characteristics of workers that are known to be age-related; work and task design factors that may conflict with worker capabilities and characteristics; social, organizational, and cultural environment factors of particular relevance to older workers; and life stage issues.

Worker Characteristics

Large bodies of work concerned with the aging process have documented a variety of physical, cognitive, and emotional changes that accompany aging. Some of these changes have the potential to affect the ability of workers to meet the physical, cognitive, and socioemotional demands of work. Likewise, they may affect the physical and emotional toll that working under demanding conditions exacts from workers. To the extent that such changes create gaps between worker capabilities and work demands, they may be considered as risk factors for stress and strain among older workers. In this section, a number of conclusions that emerge from several published reviews of the changes that accompany adult aging are highlighted.

Several aspects of physical work capacity systematically decline with age. Aerobic capacity, muscular strength and endurance, and tolerance for thermal stress show decrements with increasing age (Shephard, 1999). Likewise, circadian functioning declines with decreased ability to adapt to shifts in waking/sleeping schedules (Smith, Folkard, & Fuller, 2003). Sensory changes that have the potential to affect work skills include decreased visual acuity and visual accommodation and reduced auditory sensitivity (Schwerha & McMullin, 2002). In addition, psychomotor abilities, including manual dexterity and finger dexterity, begin to decline once workers move into their 40s and beyond (cf. Avolio & Waldman, 1994). Nonetheless, the extent to which such decrements are likely to increase the risk of performance or safety problems depends substantially on the nature of physical job requirements.

Studies of cognitive abilities across the life span show a number of age-related changes that are relevant to an individual's ability to function effectively at work (cf. Schaie & Willis, 1993). At the broadest level, the speed of cognitive processing decreases with age, particularly as adults move into their 60s and beyond, with implications for capacity to carry out time-dependent problem-solving tasks or environmental monitoring tasks. This general slowing of response to information-processing demands is evidenced in increased response latencies to a wide variety of tasks and in difficulty with time-paced tasks. In addition, recall and working memory both decline with age. However, a fair representation of the research on cognition and aging would also point out that certain aspects of cognition are more affected by aging than others. In particular, fluid cognitive abilities (e.g., abstract reasoning and speeded responding) are more negatively affected by aging than crystallized abilities (e.g., social and verbal reasoning). Even fluid abilities seem to be responsive to educational interventions until quite late in life, and the rate of decline is attenuated by regular engagement in tasks that require these abilities (cf. Park, 1994; Willis & Schaie, 1986). Furthermore, some aspects of intellectual development continue to increase or at least plateau and remain stable well into the 70s. Notably, those aspects of cognitive functioning (sometimes known as cognitive pragmatics) that rely on expert knowledge (or wisdom) do not show declines with age.

Perhaps related to changes in cognitive functioning, the manner in which learners prefer to acquire new skills differs between younger and older learners, with older learners preferring more active, experiential learning approaches and preferring to learn at a somewhat slower pace (Mead & Fisk, 1998). Older learners also rely on somewhat different strategies during the learning process than younger workers (Delgoulet & Marquie, 2002).

Longitudinal research on personality traits indicates that most traits are quite stable throughout the life course. However, some changes in affect and orientation are notable. Patterns of change in affect and attitudes tend to reflect a general movement in the direction of depressed affect and a dampening of emotional responsiveness with age (Lawton, Kleban, Rajagopal, & Dean, 1992). This provides one possible explanation for the failure of older workers to react strongly to stressors in both work and life domains.

Normal aging is also accompanied by increased frequency and severity of health concerns. In addition to decreased cardiovascular, sensory-perceptual, and physiological functioning noted above, declines in the immune response, skeletal integrity, and vestibular functioning put older workers at increased risk of injury (e.g., slips and falls) and disease. Many older workers function with a variety of chronic health conditions, such as arthritis and chronic back pain, which also prompt them to carry out work duties while coping with some degree of pain or mobility impairment. All of these have implications for physical stamina and the ability to sustain physically and mentally demanding work. Furthermore, health concerns serve as stressors themselves, insofar as they threaten a worker's ability to maintain a steady income.

Other characteristics of older workers are not necessarily a natural product of the aging process but are either an outgrowth of workers' accumulated experiences as they negotiate a life of work or reflect situational variables that differentially affect the work experiences of older workers. For example, there is evidence of age-related shifts in the kinds of coping strategies that adults use to manage stressful experiences, as well as skill in using such strategies. It has been argued that older workers are more experienced at using cognitive strategies to regulate their emotions; this may allow them to respond more calmly to stressors (Hansson, Robson, & Limas, 2001). Osipow and Doty (1985) have also suggested that older workers learn to take advantage of coping resources so they are better able to manage similar amounts of stress than younger workers are; in addition, they are more likely to be in senior positions that provide them with access to sources of support that may not be readily available to younger workers. Of course, the observation of better-developed coping skills among older workers could also represent a self-selection phenomenon, with older workers who don't develop good coping skills succumbing to the physical and emotional demands of work and leaving the workforce early.

In a similar vein, Maurer (2001) posits that another work-related individual difference characteristic, self-efficacy for development, may be negatively related to age. Development self-efficacy is of increasing importance for many jobs because of its role in motivating workers to engage in development of new skills. Maurer's argument is based on the observation that development mastery experiences, vicarious experiences, and persuasion experiences that contribute to development self-efficacy beliefs are less likely to be offered to older workers. Mullan and Gorman (1972) also reported that older and more senior workers are more likely to have negative attitudes toward change because they see it as a loss of status. Taken together, these findings suggest characteristics that would disincline older workers to initiate participation in training for the development of new skills.

An important caveat to this overview of age-related changes and characteristics is one very consistent finding from life span studies: Adults evidence substantial heterogeneity in aging. This is a recurring theme of findings from the gerontological literature with respect to cognitive and physical abilities, health status, recuperative abilities, and most other characteristics relevant to work functioning. Although studies of age-related change report between-group differences on a number of variables relevant to functioning at work, they also report considerable within-group heterogeneity, which tends to increase with age. This may reflect the accumulation of diverse life experiences that accrue for older workers; it may reflect their responses to facilitating or debilitating environments. Nonetheless, it suggests that we should refrain from relying too heavily on information about population characteristics when considering the implications of age for a particular individual worker.

Work and Task Design

The discussion above regarding characteristics of older members of our workforce makes it clear that questions of work stress only make sense when we consider them in the context of particular work environments and task designs. A wide variety of work and task conditions have been identified as potential stressors for all workers, regardless of age. These have been discussed in other chapters. Furthermore, the changes that accompany aging do not imply that all jobs, tasks, and work environments will be more demanding for older workers than they are for younger workers. However, they do provide some guidance in thinking about the conditions under which older workers are most likely to encounter difficulties in maintaining performance levels, conditions under which coping mechanisms are most likely to be called into play, conditions under which older workers are most likely to report experienced stress, and conditions under which older workers are most likely to experience negative personal and work-related outcomes including performance decrements, injuries, negative work attitudes, and mental and physical health symptoms.

Because aging is accompanied by a variety of physical changes that imply reduced capacity in several domains, physical and cognitive task and workplace stressors may be of particular consequence for older workers. For example, jobs that require heavy lifting, work that that calls heavily on fluid aspects of intellectual functioning, tasks that involve external pacing and substantial time pressure, and tasks that involve environmental monitoring and divided attention all produce chronic demands that may be experienced as stressful to many workers, but they may be of particular significance to older workers. Likewise, noisy, hot, and cold work environments may be physically more taxing to older workers than they are to younger workers. In addition, work schedules that require night work and rotating shifts will be more demanding for older workers than they will be for younger workers because of the disruptions to circadian rhythm and sleep patterns that they produce.

More broadly, it has been argued that workload is a particular risk factor for older workers. This is based on the premise that older workers are working at higher capacity than younger workers, leaving them with fewer reserves for coping with additional stressors that may impinge on them from personal or work-related sources (Nygard, Huuhtanen, Tuomi, & Martikainen, 1997).

Other features of job design, such as the widespread incorporation of technology in the workplace, may produce both threats and opportunities for older workers. Technological innovations provide many opportunities to adjust task design to meet the needs of older workers: Adjustable illumination and font sizes on computer displays, keyboards with larger keys and less sensitive keypads, voice recognition software, and ergonomically designed workstations provide a few examples of the ways that technology can provide adaptive resources for older workers to accomplish tasks. The diffusion of technology throughout all levels of most organizations also signals a basic shift in the nature of work, with a general increase in emphasis on information and information handling as key components of work and decreased emphasis on physical and motor skills. On the other hand, new technologies often require skill sets that many older workers have not developed. The threat of obsolescence that this raises can serve as a stressor that is particularly salient to older workers.

More generally, shifts in the nature of work in the past two decades have increased the importance of adaptability and willingness to acquire and implement new skills (Yeatts, Folts, & Knapp, 1999). Although this creates an environment in which all workers must be willing to adapt to changes in task design and skill requirements on a regular basis, it creates special pressures for older and more senior workers whose successful performance is based on well-practiced skills and strategies that may no longer be sufficient and in some cases may be counterproductive. Coupled with disincentives that may be present in the work environment for older workers to engage in training and development, change as a feature of work has the potential to serve as an important stressor for older workers.

When job design is framed in terms of role requirements, special attention should be paid to stresses for older workers that may emanate from issues of role overload and role underload. Older workers are often in responsible positions, so they may be at increased risk for experiencing stress from responsibility for other people. As organizations move to flatter structures, this situation is exacerbated. On the other hand, when managers make work assignments based on stereotyped expectations about declining skills and motivation of older workers (Rosen & Jerdee, 1985), the outcome can be a gradual erosion of responsibilities for older workers. This produces a role underload situation that likewise has the potential to be stressful.

Finally, considerations of the impact of work design on older workers must recognize the long-term nature of their exposure to stressors, whether they are environmental stressors (e.g., exposure to high noise levels) or psychosocial stressors (e.g., time pressures, role overload, and so forth).

Social/Organizational/Cultural Environment

Distinct from work design, the social environment in which work takes place exerts on workers a variety of pressures that may be experienced as stressful or that may reduce a worker's ability to cope effectively with work demands. These include subtle (and not-so-subtle) hints about what older workers "can" and "should" do, changes in the availability of social networks to provide moral support, organizational cultures that value or devalue experience and "wisdom," and cultural expectations about the appropriateness and value of encouraging older workers to continue their participation in the workforce.

To begin with, negative impressions of the capabilities and behaviors of older workers conveyed by age stereotypes, coupled with workers' perceptions of waning work skills, interfere with development and maintenance of a positive self-image. Furthermore, real and perceived age discrimination create an environment in which older workers may feel threats to their job security and may experience anxiety about becoming re-employed should they lose their jobs.

Workplace norms and expectations about appropriate career trajectories (i.e., the sense that an individual is "on schedule" or "stalled" with respect to career advancement) produce another set of pressures for older workers. Likewise, occupational and organizational expectations about the appropriate timing of retirement can be a source of stress for individuals whose personal preferences are in conflict with those expectations (Settersten, 1998).

Social support provides an important buffer against stressful work conditions, particularly role overload and role conflict. However, as members of their cohort retire or move to other positions and organizations, many older workers find themselves with a reduced social network.

Organizational cultures and the values they convey also play a role in creating an environment that is less welcoming or more welcoming of older workers. For example, organizational cultures that value experience, loyalty, and diversity provide a very different set of circumstances for older workers than cultures that value youth, change, and creativity.

It should also be recognized that the international sociopolitical context in which work takes place has consequences for older workers. Cultural differences in the value placed on wisdom and respect given to older adults and differences in social and economic policies that encourage or discourage working until late in life produce pressures that may differ substantially for older workers in different parts of the world.

Life Stage Issues

Another class of stressors closely associated with advancing age is represented by career issues and decisions associated with career transitions. Coping with career plateaus and wrestling with decisions about if and when to retire from the workforce represent problems that cause considerable distress and distraction for many older workers. Even workers between the ages of 30 and 50 (so-called midcareer workers) must wrestle with the role transitions that accompany movement from the first half to the second half of one's working life. The shift in perspectives and shift in ways of functioning necessitated by this transition have been identified as sources of stress (Schabracq & Winnubst, 1998).

Furthermore, as noted above, economic and social pressures to continue working or discontinue working as one nears "typical" retirement age represent a source of stress of particular relevance to workers in their 60s and beyond. The extent and direction of such pressures may depend on one's gender, family situation, and cultural context.

Measurement Concerns

Several measurement and research design issues need to be recognized when age is the focus of attention in studies of stress and work. These include basic concerns with how we operationalize age constructs, research design and interpretation issues, and reporting biases that may influence the outcomes of survey research.

Measuring Age

Interpretation and application of what is known about the adult aging process to problems of occupational stress require careful attention to the operationalization of "older worker" that is used in studies concerned with age and aging. The underlying variable *age* represents a continuous variable.

Nonetheless, age is often treated as a categorical variable in discussions of the problems of older workers. Implicit in the term *older worker* is the idea that we can easily define a subset of members on that continuous variable that is conceptually distinct and internally homogeneous. However, classification as an older worker is a slippery topic. An examination of published literature on issues of aging and work reveals that the chronological boundary used to identify the target population of interest in this chapter—older workers— varies substantially, ranging from 40 to 75 (Stein & Rocco, 2001). This has the potential to result in considerable confusion in the interpretation of studies that draw conclusions based on comparisons of "older" and "younger" workers, without attending to the fact that different standards for inclusion in the older category may produce distinctly different conclusions.

So, what makes an individual an older worker? Is an older worker an individual who is legally protected from age discrimination? Is an older worker someone who is over 65? Over 55? Over 45? Does a person's mere existence for an extended period of time qualify him or her for membership in the "older worker" category? Or does "older" imply a state of mind that doesn't occur until an individual reports that he or she feels old?

The most readily recognized indicator of age is *chronological age*, which is generally reported as a demographic variable in studies of workplace functioning. Some studies of aging treat chronological age as a continuous variable, focusing on correlational data and other functions that map linear (or nonlinear) relationships between chronological age and a variety of worker characteristics and behaviors. However, many studies emphasize comparisons between fairly broad groupings of workers; members of each group are treated as interchangeable with respect to age. Although such groupings certainly differ with respect to the mean chronological age of their members, the boundaries that distinguish categories for purposes of comparison have the potential to affect the results of studies and conclusions that are drawn. Boundaries sometimes reflect statistical characteristics of the data, such as the distribution of age in the sample being observed (e.g., comparisons of workers in the upper and lower quartiles of the age distribution for a particular sample) or other characteristics, such as legal status (as discussed below).

It has been argued that *psychological indicators of age* (e.g., self- and other perceptions of how old an individual looks, feels, and acts) offer an alternative way of representing how the aging process is experienced that is distinct from the mere passing of time. Several researchers have reported work-related outcomes that are uniquely associated with psychological indicators of age (cf. Barak, 1987; Barnes-Farrell & Piotrowski, 1991; Cleveland, Shore, & Murphy, 1997). These outcomes include affective reactions to work such as organizational commitment and work-related stresses and strains.

Likewise, researchers who focus on impairments to functional abilities that accrue with the passage of time recognize that people differ with respect to the rate at which their functional capabilities change as they age. They have introduced the concept of *functional* age. From the standpoint of understanding the work capacities and limitations of older workers, they argue that functional age is a more relevant indicator than chronological age. The application of functional age to occupational functioning has been criticized by Salthouse (1986) and others as inappropriately assuming that the relationship between age and function is one of uniform decline. Although Salthouse concluded that there is a reasonable role for functional age in mapping rates of biological aging, he argued that workplace capabilities and performance are not well represented by the concept of functional age.

Finally, it is important to recognize that social policies and legal frameworks for treating older workers hinge on rather crude categorizations of workers that set the cutting point for "older" as low as 40 (the chronological age defining protection under the Older Americans Act) or as high as 65 to 67 (the age at which one qualifies for full social security benefits). Such definitions have less to do with the way individual workers or groups of workers in different age categories think, feel, or act and more to do with the way they are treated by social and legal systems.

Research Design Concerns

A particular concern in the design of studies that examine aging and stress in the workplace is the frequent confounding of age with cohort and period effects (Firebaugh, 1997). Much of the research on which our knowledge of aging and stress is based uses single cross-sectional studies. As such, it is not possible to disentangle age effects from cohort and period effects when age differences are observed. To do so, researchers must make use of either repeated cross-sectional studies or panel studies, depending on the change that is of primary interest. In fact, rotating (i.e., repeated) panel studies capture the strengths of both repeated cross-sectional data and panel data (Firebaugh, 1997).

Likewise, many studies that examine relationships between age and performance, stress, affect, or other purported outcomes of aging are plagued by a natural confounding of age with experience, seniority, and other variables that covary with age. This makes it difficult to distinguish the extent to which natural aging processes are the source of these outcomes or whether experience and seniority are the major causal agents.

Survey Measures: Response Biases

Interpretation of survey-based evidence regarding age-related differences in responses to work conditions must be tempered by awareness of age-related declines and cohort effects in reporting of affect (Griffiths, 1999). Such reporting biases can interfere with accurate interpretation of similarities and differences in the way older and younger workers experience the work environment. When differences are observed, it is important to triangulate the phenomenon using alternative indicators that are less influenced by such reporting biases.

Linear and Nonlinear Relationships

Typical approaches to studying worker age as it relates to workplace stress and other outcomes emphasize linear functions. Evidence regarding the nature of stressor-strain relationships and gerontological work on the nature of the aging process suggests the importance of being alert to nonlinear functions when we ask questions about the manner in which age and occupational stress are related. This also reinforces the importance of thinking carefully about how and why we operationally define the category "older worker."

Experience and Consequences of Occupational Stress for Older Workers

The discussions above identify a host of conditions under which work may create adaptive challenges or personal threats for older workers. But this begs the question: Do older workers experience work stress that affects their work behaviors and personal well-being? Empirical studies that directly examine the impact of stressful work conditions on older workers or the relative impact of such conditions on workers of different ages provide some insight into this question. In addition to reports of experienced work stress, studies of the effects of work on psychological health use dependent variables like job dissatisfaction, reduced motivation and aspiration levels, anxiety, and depression. Physical health outcomes include sleep quality, fatigue, muscuskeletal disorders, and other body pains. Behavioral outcomes of interest include performance decrements, accidents, and withdrawal behaviors such as absence and early retirement. In light of the multitude of ways that stress and strain have been operationalized in empirical work, I have not attempted a comprehensive review of empirical studies that include age as a variable or that target samples of older workers. The review is selective, with the goal of illustrating what is known about the extent to which work stress is experienced by older workers and the extent to which it exacts a toll in terms of performance, work attitudes and behaviors, and personal health and well-being.

Reports of the extent to which older workers are prone to such outcomes represent a mixed bag. Griffiths (1999) and others (cf. Lundberg et al., 1999) report that older workers more commonly report both stress and psychophysiological stress responses. Likewise, Griffiths reported that work design–related stressors predict sickness, absence, and early retirement among older workers.

Physical health complaints generally increase with age. However, the fact that health complaints are significantly increased among those who report working under stressful conditions has particular ramifications for older workers. For example, the rising prevalence of 24/7 operations has drawn increased attention to the impact of nonstandard work schedules on workers' lives. This is an area in which clear concern has been expressed regarding disproportionate risks for older workers. Older workers (notably those over the age of 50) suffer more adverse health consequences from shift work than younger workers, particularly with respect to decreased sleep length (Tepas, Duchon, & Gersten, 1993).

Notwithstanding the increased health concerns with which older workers must contend, most older workers (under the age of 74) report that health does not impair their ability to carry out work and housework (Sterns & Miklos, 1995), although the percentage who report impairments nearly doubles between the early 60s (12%) and the early 70s (22%). Although most older workers do not report that their physical health compromises their ability to carry out work and home activities, when physical health does suffer, older workers are more likely than younger workers to depart the workforce permanently.

One might expect accidents and injuries to be a natural consequence of mismatches between older workers' sensory and physical capacities and workplace demands. Actually, the frequency of accidents is lower among older workers. However, injuries and disabilities that result from accidents (particularly falls) are more severe among older workers, and recuperation periods are longer. Although absenteeism rates are generally low among older workers, disabilities resulting from such injuries produce absences that are extended in length; they also speed early exit from full-time labor force participation. Furthermore, health concerns have the unfortunate and ironic effect of both increasing the early exit of some workers whose health problems make it difficult or impossible to carry out their normal work activities on a regular basis (cf. Huuhtanen, 1994; Mutchler, Burr, Massagli, & Pienta, 1999) and delaying the exit of others who carry on working (sometimes at reduced capacity) in order to maintain critical health care benefits (Feldman, 2003).

Barnes-Farrell and Piotrowski (1991) observed a positive correlation between a psychosocial measure of age (feeling older than one's age) and the frequency/extent of stress-related outcomes including mental and physical fatigue, physical health symptoms, and maladaptive coping behaviors (e.g., alcohol consumption) in a large sample of manufacturing workers. A similar pattern of results was observed in a more recent survey project that examined the on-the-job and off-the-job stresses and strains of health care workers from several nations (Barnes-Farrell, Rumery, & Swody, 2002). Although levels of experienced stress and patterns of relationships differed somewhat from nation to nation, researchers reported significant relationships between a similar psychosocial measure of age and physical and mental fatigue, effort required to meet work demands, and perceptions of decreased work ability. However, they also pointed out that these findings were specific to workers' self-perceptions about their age. In examining the relationship between chronological age and work stress, these researchers reported that "one of the most uniform findings was the failure to observe significant positive relationships between chronological age and indicators of stress, strain, or declining performance" (p. 95). On the other hand, another recent study of nurses in Northern Ireland (Kircaldy & Martin, 2000) indicated that although all nurses in their sample reported fairly high levels of stress and strain from work and family sources, older nurses reported more stress and poorer psychological health than younger nurses.

Studies that focus on the introduction of new technologies have found that age and seniority are associated with anxiety about computer use and negative attitudes toward computerized technologies, which are seen as a threat to employment (Marquie, Thon, & Baracat, 1994). In laboratory examinations of older workers' responses to the demands of computer-based work, Czaja and Sharit (1993) reported only minimal age differences in performance, but age was associated with increased perceptions of demand and fatigue when the work was paced. In a second laboratory study that focused on stress-related reactions to computer-based work, older participants reported increased workload for mentally challenging computer tasks. However, they experienced less stress than younger subjects on an information retrieval task that involved a more socially interactive telephone component. The findings led the researchers to conclude that age effects for experienced stress on computer-based work depend on the nature of the task (Sharit et al., 1998).

Shifting the emphasis to psychosocial sources of stress, Osipow and Doty (1985) found that the nature of stress experiences reported by older workers is linked to the higher seniority and status typical of this group. They found that older workers reported experiencing more stress from responsibility for people and workload and less stress from physical stressors than younger workers. Furthermore, an extensive study of work and aging among Scandinavian workers in a wide variety of occupations conducted as part of the FinnAge program reported that declines in "work ability" (the ability to carry out work at full capacity) among workers 45 years and older were associated with stressors such as role conflict, fear of making mistakes, lack of influence, lack of professional development, and unsupportive supervisor attitudes (Ilmarinen et al., 1991).

Several studies have focused particularly on an outcome that is only available to older workers—retirement. Of course, retirement does not always represent a response to workplace distress. It is also a reaction to rewards and pressures external to the workplace. However, it has also been identified as an escape response for older workers responding to "push" forces from the workplace (Barnes-Farrell, 2003). Research on the relationship between retirement planning and indicators of experienced stress such as tension and fatigue has found that when jobs are increasingly experienced as stressful, older workers will begin planning to leave the workplace (Ekerdt & DeViney, 1993). Although Ekerdt and DeViney's study points out the relationship between stress and an important type of withdrawal behavior that is primarily available to older workers, it should be noted that the relationship they observed was between stress and retirement planning; they did *not* observe a relationship between worker age and proximity to retirement per se. Lin and Hsieh (2001) found that stressful work conditions associated with increased workload were related to increased intention to take early retirement. Similarly, Herzog, House, and Morgan (1991) found that workers in stressful or unrewarding jobs preferred to reduce their work commitments or retire completely. Likewise, it has been observed that workers who have plateaued with respect to their careers or their job duties are more likely to respond to pressures to exit the organization via acceptance of early retirement offers (Farr & Ringseis, 2002). It has also been observed that anxieties regarding re-employment among older workers involved in downsizing are common. Such anxieties are exacerbated by the belief that older worker stereotypes and age discrimination may impair their ability to become re-employed. Thus, many older workers simply give up and leave the workforce, particularly if they are eligible for early or on-time retirement benefits.

On the other hand, despite the variety of challenges that work demands pose for older workers, research that has assessed the relationship between age and work performance concludes that age and work performance are *not* systematically related. Several reviews of this literature have come to similar conclusions (McEvoy & Cascio, 1989; Rhodes, 1983; Waldman & Avolio, 1986). In fact, age-based differences in performance effectiveness are fairly rare. How can this be? One possible explanation is that older workers learn to work around those skill areas that have begun to decline, essentially redesigning their jobs and accomplishing tasks in ways that rely more heavily on those skills that increase with age (e.g., wisdom) or are unrelated to age and de-emphasizing those abilities and skills that decline with age (e.g., physical strength). Another explanation relies on the argument that older workers are willing to invest additional effort, effectively dipping into their reserves in order to maintain performance levels. In this case, we would expect experienced stress to be evidenced in the form of some of the other outcomes described above such as fatigue, affective outcomes, and health outcomes. Finally, it may be that self-selection processes and management task assignments operate to remove workers from jobs and tasks for which they are no longer well suited.

Furthermore, in contrast to work that reports increased stress and stress-related outcomes among older workers, a number of studies provide evidence that older workers are more resistant to stress and its consequences than we might expect. For example, the preponderance of evidence shows a positive correlation between age and work-related attitudes, although the sources of satisfaction that form the basis for those attitudes may differ across the life course (Sterns & Miklos, 1995). Several recent studies provide additional evidence that older workers are not systematically more likely to experience work stress and attendant negative outcomes. Remondet and Hansson (1991) reported that threats to personal control emanating from work demands, lack of growth opportunities, personal crises, and work conditions were generally associated with increased job and generalized stress as well as personal and job outcomes such as depression, injuries, absenteeism, decreased job satisfaction, and decreased job performance. However, a comparison of the older workers in their study (aged 54–72) with those classified as middle-aged (aged 30–53) indicated that older workers reported *less* stress, greater job satisfaction, and fewer concerns with control at work than their younger counterparts. Likewise, a recent study of managers found that age was positively related to job and mental well-being and older managers reported fewer sources of stress and higher internal locus of control than younger managers (Siu, Spector, Cooper, & Donald, 2001). In a similar vein, Swanson, Power, and Simpson (1996) described a study of male and female physicians in Scotland in which they found that older physicians reported less occupational stress and more job satisfaction (as measured by the Occupational Stress Inventory) than did younger physicians. A study of workers in a very different environment highlights the important role of perceived control among older workers. Perrewé and Anthony (1990) surveyed a sample of steel pipe workers and showed that when they perceived control over their work, older workers reported fewer demands and less health strain than younger workers.

What can we conclude from this? Clearly, the relationship between age and occupational stress is not a simple one, and broadbrush statements about the relative vulnerability of older workers to work stress cannot do justice to the complexity of this situation. Furthermore, methodological limitations of many of the studies that provide evidence regarding age and work stress make it difficult to identify the processes and conditions that are responsible for stress outcomes that were reported. The results provided by these studies do suggest that stress responses exact costs from older workers, but the nature of those costs is probably highly dependent on the nature of the job and the organizational context in which work takes place. Nonetheless, one consistent message did emerge from these studies that should be of particular interest to work organizations: Early exit from the organization (and often from active labor force participation) through retirement is an option that is psychologically and practically available to members of this segment of the workforce, and there is evidence that older workers faced with stressful work conditions of various kinds exercise this option. This should prompt organizations to pay much closer attention to the needs of older members of their workforce and how they can design work systems that are consistent with those needs. Failure to do so is likely to exact a very high cost in terms of valuable human resources that will be lost to the organization.

Future Research Needs

The bulk of empirical work that has directly examined work stress as it relates to our aging workforce has focused on potentially stressful gaps between occupational demands (especially physical and cognitive demands) and worker capabilities. Although much work remains to be done in this arena, a research agenda concerned with sources and implications of work stress for older workers must move beyond consideration of general risk factors to systematically acknowledge and explore mediating processes that are particularly relevant to older workers and contextual variables that are likely to buffer or exacerbate work stress for this population. I would like to suggest five areas that would particularly benefit from increased research attention. The first is primarily concerned with measurement issues relevant to the operationalization and study of age as it pertains to issues of work and stress. The second is concerned with independent and dependent variables that have not received sufficient research attention in this population. The remaining three are illustrative of the need for additional research on individual difference variables and context variables that are likely to be important in understanding the complex manner in which age figures into experiences of work stress and responses to work stress.

To begin with, as noted earlier, age is most often indexed with narrowly or broadly defined bands of chronological age. A number of authors have pointed out the potential value of using other indicators of age in the study of work attitudes and behaviors. However, with the exception of attempts to measure functional age, most research concerned with work stress continues to be limited to chronological indicators of age. In particular, a clearer understanding of how work stress contributes to psychological construals of age and how they in turn manifest in work attitudes and behaviors would help to clarify the relationships between worker age, work stress, and responses to stressful work.

Second, our understanding of the conditions under which older workers experience work as stressful would benefit from systematic attention to individual characteristics and the broader psychosocial context in which work takes place. For example, although the stresses of balancing work and family role demands are heavily studied for young parents, relatively little attention has been paid to the nature of the interface between work and nonwork domains of older workers. Likewise, the impact of gender on the manner in which role stresses of late career workers are experienced and the coping strategies that men and women use to manage those stresses form an understudied domain. In addition, theory-based cross-cultural studies should form the basis for understanding how cultural and socioeconomic forces that affect our expectations and treatment of older workers affect psychosocial sources of stress for this population.

More generally, systematic attention to role stresses unique to older workers (e.g., age discrimination, work-retirement role transitions) and inclusion of older workers in studies that have traditionally focused almost exclusively on early career workers (e.g., work-life balance) would provide organizations with clearer guidance on how best to assist older workers in managing such stresses in a constructive way.

If we look at the problem of work stress among workers from the perspective of seeking ways to effectively utilize this segment of our labor force, it is tempting (and common) to focus almost exclusively on the study of distress and interventions designed to mitigate distress, performance decrements, and negative personal outcomes among workers. However, another constructive direction for future research would be to focus on sources of eustress among older workers. Why do some individuals continue to work and thrive on (often very demanding) work well into their 70s and beyond? What characteristics of individuals, work environments, and tasks promote this situation? Are characteristics of the work environment that promote eustress different among older workers than they are among younger members of the workforce? There is much to be learned here.

In addition, the contrast between laboratory studies indicating declines in a variety of job-relevant abilities (e.g., cognitive abilities and psychomotor skills) and reviews of field evidence that conclude that job performance does *not* systematically decline with age begs for additional research aimed at understanding why this is so. This seeming paradox may be explained in part by the fact that the demands of many jobs are simply not sufficient to reveal diminished capacities. Undoubtedly, self-selection in work settings also provides a partial explanation for these findings. However, other explanations emphasize the role of compensatory mechanisms that allow older workers to utilize alternative skills and strategies to accomplish their work in an effective fashion. In particular, the role of experience and the form of expertise popularly known as wisdom deserve considerably more attention as vehicles for understanding how older workers adapt effectively to work demands.

Implications for Practice, Policy, and Intervention

A clear understanding of how older workers function and the kinds of work conditions that are experienced as stressful or that place older workers at high risk for adverse performance, health, and safety outcomes leads naturally to questions about areas in which we can reasonably introduce interventions that target known risk factors. Current knowledge about the stressful impacts of work and work environments on older workers suggests five likely targets for such intervention work.

Ergonomic Interventions

First, ergonomic interventions aimed at redesigning work conditions, work tasks, and work tools to conform to the changing physical and cognitive needs of older workers show great promise for maintaining worker functioning and performance. For example, taking advantage of adaptive technology, work sites can be designed to accommodate the declining visual adaptive capabilities of older workers. Tools that require less grip strength allow those who have reduced physical strength to maintain performance levels without increased stress on physical reserves. Such interventions are of particular significance for jobs that have large physical components. However, they are also highly relevant for the large proportion of jobs that require the use of technology to carry out important tasks. For example, opportunities to apply what is known about sensory, psychomotor, and cognitive changes during aging to the design of human-computer interfaces are immense. The technology to adapt workstations and other workplace tools to the needs of older workers already exists; what is needed is an appreciation of the kinds of features that would most benefit older workers' changing physical, sensory, and cognitive profiles.

Furthermore, reports from the European Union community suggest that there are two particular features of jobs that continue to create inappropriate levels of physical demand for (younger and) older workers. These include the requirement of maintaining tiring postures and carrying out repetitive motions over long periods of time (Ilmarinen, 2002). Task redesign and other ergonomic interventions that reduce the need for extended exposure to such task stressors should be a high priority for human factors psychologists who have the opportunity to intervene in this domain.

Finally, Schwerha and McMullin (2002) recently published an agenda for ergonomic research in aging that points out particular industries and aspects of work that can particularly benefit from ergonomic research and interventions aimed at the needs of older workers. They singled out human-computer interaction and ergonomic challenges in the health care workforce, retail and e-commerce, and transportation industries as noteworthy examples of occupations and industries that should receive high priority for the development of ergonomic interventions responsive to older workers.

Training Interventions

Training programs also have an important place in managing older workers' ability to respond to demanding work. For example, it has been demonstrated that training interventions can mitigate the declines in fluid abilities associated with increased age. Perhaps of more importance is recognition that active efforts should be made to provide training and development opportunities for older workers and to encourage participation in those efforts. This is important in order to avoid creeping skill obsolescence and minimize the gap between worker skills and changing job demands. Extra efforts may be necessary to increase development self-efficacy among older workers, in part to counteract lowered expectancies that emanate from an acceptance of older worker stereotypes that characterize older workers as less willing to develop new skills and less capable of doing so. Furthermore, in order to obtain maximum benefits from training programs that include older workers, instructional design should incorporate learning approaches that are consistent with the needs and orientations of older workers. For example, it has been demonstrated that older workers prefer experiential learning approaches to conceptual learning approaches and utilize different strategies during the learning process (cf. Mead & Fisk, 1998; Gist & Rosen, 1988). In addition, trainers should recognize that providing older workers with an opportunity to proceed at a slower pace is likely to have a payoff in terms of increased acquisition of skills, effectively eliminating age differences in learning performance in many cases. Development of training programs that are inadvertently designed to capitalize on the learning orientations of younger workers creates obstacles for older trainees and fails to capitalize on their abilities to acquire new skills.

Interventions Focused on Support and Control

A common theme of many studies of occupational stress is an emphasis on the role of personal control as a vehicle for managing challenging work conditions. A prime example is work based on Karasek's demand-control model, which argues that demanding jobs, which would otherwise produce distress, will be appraised as challenging when workers are provided with considerable decision latitude (i.e., control). Several approaches to providing increased control that might be particularly beneficial for older workers have been suggested, such as involving older workers in job redesign efforts, offering flexible work schedules and job sharing, and providing self-paced training modules for skill development. Likewise, social support has been identified in numerous studies as an important buffer between stressful work conditions and negative outcomes. Managers can help by encouraging the development of strong cross-generation social networks among coworkers and by engaging in supportive management practices that are sensitive to the needs of older workers.

Interventions Aimed at Stereotypes and Expectations

Educational efforts aimed at dispelling misunderstandings and overgeneralizations about the capabilities and characteristics of older workers can be important on two counts. On one hand, such efforts increase the likelihood that managers and others who influence the work assignments of older workers will recognize the value (for the organization as well as individual workers) of looking beyond stereotypic expectations and treating older workers as individuals. Likewise, the dynamics of teams can be more effective if coworkers are unfettered by inappropriate expectations about the capabilities and limitations of their more senior members. However, because older workers themselves frequently endorse stereotyped beliefs about aging, interventions aimed at dispelling age stereotypes also have the potential to affect older workers' aspirations, goals, and behaviors at work. They free workers to assess their own capabilities and aspirations without the burden of stereotypic expectations about what people their age can and cannot do.

Job Redesign Aimed at Optimizing Workloads

More generally, it should be recognized that role demands for older workers should be consistent with their capabilities. Although recent work in the field of occupational health has tended to emphasize problems of task overload and role overload, a case can be made for some groups of older workers that the primary issue to address is one of role underload, particularly qualitative underload. When managers begin shifting the more challenging assignments to younger workers and fail to include older workers in updating efforts, they unwittingly create a situation of role underload that contributes to the experienced boredom and stress of workers who are no longer challenged by their work. Interventions aimed at taking advantage of the increased experience that older workers often bring to the job and interventions designed to encourage older workers to develop and apply new skills can remedy this situation.

Epilogue

Older workers represent a substantial and growing segment of the workforce that employers cannot afford to ignore. Characteristics that differentiate this population from other members of the workforce put them at increased risk of stress and strain from some classes of task and work design stressors that are present in many jobs and at decreased risk of adverse consequences from others. Furthermore, older workers must contend with some kinds of psychosocial stressors (e.g., age discrimination, transition to retirement) that are unique to members of this group. However, the relationship between age and work stress is complex, as are worker responses to workplace stress. Although available knowledge about the interactions between older workers and workplace demands provides substantial guidance for ergonomic and work design interventions that can improve the work and personal lives of older workers, there are significant gaps in our knowledge of the interplay between age and occupational stress processes and outcomes that remain for researchers to address.

References

Avolio, B. J., & Waldman, D. (1994). Variations in cognitive, perceptual, and psychomotor abilities across the working life span: Examining the effects of race, sex, experience, education, and occupational type. *Psychology and Aging, 9,* 430–442.

Barak, B. (1987). Cognitive age: A new multidimensional approach to measuring age identity. *International Journal of Ageing and Human Development, 25*, 109–128.

Barnes-Farrell, J. (2003). Beyond health and wealth: Attitudinal and other influences on retirement decision making. In G. Adams & T. Beehr (Eds.), *Retirement: Reasons, processes, and results* (pp. 158–187). New York: Springer.

Barnes-Farrell, J., & Piotrowski, M. (1991). Discrepancies between chronological age and personal age as a reflection of unrelieved worker stress. *Work & Stress, 5*, 177–187.

Barnes-Farrell, J., Rumery, S., & Swody, C. (2002). How do concepts of age relate to work and off-the-job stresses and strains? A field study of health care workers in five nations. *Experimental Aging Research, 28*, 87–98.

Cleveland, J. N., Shore, L. M., & Murphy, K. R. (1997). Person- and context-oriented perceptual age measures: Additional evidence of distinctiveness and usefulness. *Journal of Organizational Behavior, 18*, 239–251.

Czaja, S. J., & Sharit, J. (1993). Age differences in the performance of computer-based work. *Psychology and Aging, 8*, 59–67.

Delgoulet, C., & Marquie, J. C. (2002). Age differences in learning maintenance skills: A field study. *Experimental Aging Research, 28*, 25–37.

Ekerdt, D., & DeViney, S. (1993). Evidence for a pre-retirement process among older male workers. *Journals of Gerontology, 48*, S35–S43.

Farr, J., & Ringseis, E. (2002). The older worker in organizational context: Beyond the individual. In C. Cooper & I. Robertson (Eds.), *International review of industrial and organizational psychology, 2002* (Vol. 17, pp. 31–75). New York: Wiley.

Feldman, D. (2003). Endgame: The design and implementation of early retirement incentive programs. In G. Adams & T. Beehr (Eds.), *Retirement: Reasons, processes, and results* (pp. 83–114). New York: Springer.

Firebaugh, G. (1997). *Analyzing repeated surveys.* Thousand Oaks, CA: Sage.

Fullerton, H. N., & Toossi, M. (2001). Labor force projections to 2010: Steady growth and changing composition. *Monthly Labor Review, 124*(11), 21–38.

Gist, M., & Rosen, A. (1988). The influence of training method and trainee age on the acquisition of computer skills. *Personnel Psychology, 41*, 255–265.

Griffiths, A. (1999). Work design and management—The older worker. *Experimental Aging Research, 25*, 411–420.

Hansson, R., Robson, S., & Limas, M. (2001). Stress and coping among older workers. *Work: Journal of Prevention, Assessment and Rehabilitation, 17*, 247–256.

Herzog, A., House, J., & Morgan, J. (1991). Relation of work and retirement to health and well-being in older age. *Psychology and Aging, 6*, 202–211.

Huuhtanen, P. (1994). Improving the working conditions of older people: An analysis of attitudes toward early retirement. In G. Keita & J. Hurrell (Eds.), *Job stress in a changing workforce: Investigating gender diversity and family issues* (pp. 197–206). Washington, DC: APA.

Ilmarinen, J. (2002). Physical requirements associated with the work of aging workers in the European Union. *Experimental Aging Research, 28*, 7–23.

Ilmarinen, J., Tuomi, K., Eskelinen, L., Nygard, C. H., Huuhtanen, P., & Klockars, M. (1991). Summary and recommendations of a project involving cross-sectional and follow-up studies on the aging worker in Finnish municipal occupations, 1981–1985. *Scandinavian Journal of Work, Environment & Health, 17* (Suppl. 1), 135–141.

Ivancevich, J., & Matteson, M. (1980). *Stress and work: A managerial perspective.* Glenview, IL: Scott Foresman.

Kahn, R., & Byosiere, P. (1992). Stress in organizations. In M. Dunnette & L. Hough (Eds.), *Handbook of industrial and organizational psychology* (2nd ed., Vol. 3, pp. 571–650). Palo Alto, CA: Consulting Psychologists Press.

Karasek, R. (1979). Job demands, job decision latitude, and mental strain: Implications for job redesign. *Administrative Quarterly, 24,* 285–307.

Kirkcaldy, B., & Martin, T. (2000). Job stress and satisfaction among nurses: Individual differences. *Stress Medicine, 16,* 77–89.

Lawton, M. P., Kleban, M., Rajagopal, D., & Dean, J. (1992). Dimensions of affective experience in three age groups. *Psychology and Aging, 7,* 171–184.

Lazarus, R., & Folkman, S. (1984). *Stress, appraisal and coping.* New York: Springer.

Lin, T. C., & Hsieh, A. T. (2001). Impact of job stress on early retirement intention. *International Journal of Stress Management, 8,* 243–247.

Lundberg, U., Dohns, I., Melin, B., Sandsjoe, L., Palmerud, G., Kadefors, R., Edstroem, M., & Parr, D. (1999). Psychophysiological stress responses, muscle tension, and neck and shoulder pain among supermarket cashiers. *Journal of Occupational Health Psychology, 4,* 245–255.

Marquie, J., Thon, B., & Baracat, B. (1994). Age influence on attitudes of office workers faced with new computerized technologies. *Applied Ergonomics, 25,* 130–142.

Maurer, T. (2001). Career-relevant learning and development, worker age, and beliefs about self-efficacy for development. *Journal of Management, 27,* 123–140.

McEvoy, G., & Cascio, W. (1989). Cumulative evidence of the relationship between employee age and job performance. *Journal of Applied Psychology, 74,* 11–17.

Mead, S., & Fisk, A. (1998). Measuring skill acquisition and retention with an ATM simulator: The need for age-specific training. *Human Factors, 40,* 516–523.

Mullan, C., & Gorman, L. (1972). Facilitating adaptation to change: A case study in retraining middle-aged and older workers at Aer Lingus. *Industrial Gerontology, 15,* 23–29.

Mutchler, J., Burr, M., Massagli, M., & Pienta, A. (1999). Work transitions and health in later life. *Journals of Gerontology (B): Psychological Sciences and Social Sciences, 54,* S252–S261.

Nygard, C. H., Huuhtanen, P., Tuomi, K., & Martikainen, R. (1997). Perceived work changes between 1981 and 1992 among aging workers in Finland. *Scandinavian Journal of Work, Environment & Health, 23*(Suppl. 1), 12–19.

Organization for Economic Cooperation and Development. (2002). Increasing employment: The role of later retirement. *OECD Economic Outlook 2002, 72,* 1–21.

Osipow, S., & Doty, R. (1985). Occupational stress, strain, and coping across the life span. *Journal of Vocational Behavior, 27,* 98–108.

Park, D. (1994). Aging, cognition and work. *Human Performance, 7,* 187–205.

Perrewé, P., & Anthony, W. (1990). Stress in a steel pipe mill: The impact of job demands, personal control, and employee age on somatic complaints. *Journal of Social Behavior and Personality, 5,* 77–90.

Remondet, J., & Hansson, R. (1991). Job-related threats to control among older employees. *Journal of Social Issues, 47,* 129–141.

Rhodes, S. (1983). Age-related differences in work attitudes and behavior: A review and conceptual analysis. *Psychological Bulletin, 93,* 328–367.

Rosen, B., & Jerdee, T. (1985). *Older employees: New roles for valued resources.* Homewood, IL: Dow Jones-Irwin.

Salthouse, T. (1986). Functional age: Examination of a concept. In J. Birren, P. Robinson, & J. Livingstone (Eds.), *Age, health and employment* (pp. 78–92). Englewood Cliffs, NJ: Prentice Hall.

Schabracq, M., & Winnubst, J. (1998). Senior employees. In M. Schabracq, J. Winnubst, & C. Cooper (Eds.), *Handbook of work and health psychology* (pp. 275–294). New York: Wiley.

Schaie, K. W., & Willis, S. L. (1993). Age difference patterns of psychometric intelligence in adulthood: Generalizability within and across ability domains. *Psychology and Aging, 8,* 44–55.

Schwerha, D., & McMullin, D. (2002). Prioritizing ergonomic research in aging for the 21st century American workforce. *Experimental Aging Research, 28,* 99–110.

Settersten, R. (1998). Time, age, and the transition to retirement: New evidence on life-course flexibility? *International Journal of Aging and Human Development, 47,* 177–203.

Sharit, J., Czaja, S., Nair, S., Hoag, D., Leonard, D., & Dilsen, E. (1998). Subjective experience of stress, workload, and bodily discomfort as a function of age and type of computer work. *Work & Stress, 12,* 125–144.

Shephard, R. (1999). Age and physical work capacity. *Experimental Aging Research, 25,* 331–343.

Siu, O., Spector, P., Cooper, C., & Donald, I. (2001). Age differences in coping and locus of control: A study of managerial stress in Hong Kong. *Psychology and Aging, 16,* 707–710.

Smith, C., Folkard, S., & Fuller, J. (2003). In J. C. Quick & L. Tetrick (Eds.), *Handbook of occupational health psychology* (pp. 163–183). Washington, DC: American Psychological Association.

Stein, D., & Rocco, T. (2001). *The older worker: Myths and realities.* ERIC Clearinghouse on Adult, Career, and Vocational Education [www.cete.org/acve/].

Sterns, H., & Miklos, S. (1995). The aging worker in a changing environment: Organizational and individual issues. *Journal of Vocational Behavior, 47,* 248–268.

Swanson, V., Power, K., & Simpson, R. (1996). A comparison of stress and job satisfaction in female and male GPs and consultants. *Stress Medicine, 12,* 17–26.

Tepas, D., Duchon, J., & Gersten, A. (1993). Shiftwork and the older worker. *Experimental Aging Research, 19,* 295–320.

Waldman, D., & Avolio, B. (1986). A meta-analysis of age differences in job performance. *Journal of Applied Psychology, 71,* 33–38.

Willis, S., & Schaie, K. W. (1986). Training the elderly on the ability factors of spatial orientation and inductive reasoning. *Psychology and Aging, 1,* 239–247.

Yeatts, D. E., Folts, W. E., & Knapp, J. (1999). Older worker's adaptation to a changing workplace: Employment issues for the 21st century. *Educational Gerontology, 25,* 331–347.

19

Gender Issues

Serge Desmarais
Christine Alksnis

Popular stereotypes convey fundamental differences in the way men and women feel, think, act, and relate to others. These gendered differences are assumed to exist in all social spheres, including work and family life. Yet the life circumstances of most women and men have changed dramatically over the past few decades, with evidence of greater similarity (Barnett & Hyde, 2001). We can attribute much of this shift to women's increasing entry into the paid workforce (Davidson & Burke, 2000; Reskin & Padavic, 1994; see also Fielden & Cooper, 2002). For instance, data from the United States show that women's participation in the labor force has gone from approximately 18% in the late 1800s to roughly 59% in 1996 (see Stroh & Reilly, 1999). A similar pattern has been observed in many other industrialized countries (International Labour Office, 1996; also see Powell, 1999b; Stroh & Reilly, 1999). Women's workforce participation in some European countries is even higher with 69% of women employed in Great Britain and over 70% in Denmark and Sweden (Fielden & Cooper, 2002). In North America, 78% of couples are dual-earner couples, and 75% of these dual-earner families have both partners working full-time (Bond, Galinsky, & Swanberg, 1998). Hence, the majority of women and men spend a substantial portion of the day in paid employment followed by some shared time with their partners and/or children.

In this chapter, we have the challenging task of summarizing and organizing the vast literature related to gender and work stress. Several authors before us have attempted to synthesize, expand, and provide some framework to research on gender, work, and stress (e.g., Barnett, Biener, & Baruch, 1987; Nelson & Burke, 2002b; Powell, 1999a, for reviews). The research reveals that work stress can have severe negative consequences for both men and women (Galinsky, Kim, & Bond, 2001; Guelzow, Bird, & Koball, 1991; Larson & Almeida, 1999; Paden & Buehler, 1995; Perry-Jenkins, Repetti, & Crouter, 2000). What is less clear is whether women experience unique forms of occupational stress—the evidence on this issue is not definitive (Westman, 2002). At this point, it seems appropriate to caution the reader that studies examining the connection between gender and work stress vary substantially in terms of methodology, sampling procedures, and measures (Westman, 2002); these differences may go a long way toward explaining the many contradictions in research findings. Furthermore, it seems safe to say that there are differences in the way women and men experience, express, and cope with work stress. Indeed, some have argued that the complexity of the interaction of gender with predictors of stress is such that trying to isolate the role of gender in stress may be nearly impossible (Nelson & Burke, 2002a). Our perception is more optimistic, and we hope that this chapter will help tease out how the norms and roles associated with gender influence this complex relationship.

One of our main contributions to the efforts of reviewers who have preceded us involves casting an even wider net in our integration of existing research by reviewing material from psychology, sociology, family studies, social work, and business. We review the most pertinent research and provide what we hope is a slightly different view of these issues by organizing the most relevant research into common themes informed by social psychological theories. Like Barnett and Hyde (2001), we believe that many of the theories on which social scientists commonly rely to explain the connection between gender and work no longer match our contemporary realities—at least in the context of most industrialized countries. We revisit this issue in our conclusion, wherein we consider whether the current approach to our studies of gender and work stress serves to reinforce normative expectations about gender differences.

We believe that gender can have several possible effects on work stress. First, women and men can experience different stressors or varying levels of the same stressors; we review the literature related to the gendered nature of work stressors in the section entitled "Review of Sources of Stress at Work." Second, women and men may have different reactions to stressors such that they experience different levels of strain; we review the literature that speaks to this issue in the section "Review of Effects of Work Stress." Third, the stressor-strain relations observed for women and men may be different. Gender-linked patterns may be attributable to the fact that gender acts as a moderator in these relationships (i.e., events that act as stressors for men do not do so for women or vice versa). Alternatively, these patterns may be attributable to the use of different coping strategies by men and women. We review the literature on stress-strain relationships in "Review of Strategies for Coping With Stress." Prior to reviewing the research, however, let us consider the theories that have guided our survey of the literature.

Theoretical Overview

A Brief Overview of Gender Socialization

According to social learning theory (Bandura, 1986), the acquisition of gender norms follows the same pattern as any other form of socialization or learned behaviors; it is a set of rules and expectations learned through observation rather than biologically determined or learned through conditioning (Bandura, 1986). Children are provided with countless opportunities to observe "appropriate" gender behaviors by watching people in their immediate environment (e.g., parents, family members, and friends). In addition, the exemplars of gender behaviors available in many media (e.g., television, movies) provide relevant illustration of how to be a man or a woman. Teachers, peers, and family also directly reinforce gender-based differential treatment and expectations. Even children's own expectations concerning career choices, which begin as early as elementary school (Stroh & Reilly, 1999), are rewarded when consistent with the traditional gendered expectations. It has been posited that early socialization may determine the jobs women and men consider socially acceptable (Cohen & Swim, 1995; Melamed, 1995, 1996; Witkowski & Leicht, 1995), their adoption of a traditional gendered arrangement of families (Haddock, Zimmerman, & Lyness, 2003), and the salary men and women feel entitled to earn (Desmarais & Curtis, 1999). By adulthood, acquired knowledge about the role of men and women can translate into role division along traditional lines, pressures to conform to traditional roles, and role conflict that exacerbate the pressures of work and family demands for members of both sexes. Reactions to role conflict tend to fall along gendered lines, with women more concerned about family stressors and men responding more to work-related pressures (Duxbury & Higgins, 1991).

The social learning approach has been critiqued for its essentialist view of gender development (see, e.g., Bem, 1981, 1985; Deaux & Lafrance, 1998). Although it is undeniable that children develop their gendered notions of self and society via the same observationally based mechanisms with which they learn other types of behaviors, children are not simply the passive recipients of gendered information. Instead, children show signs of active involvement in their gender norm acquisition, likely because of the powerful gender context that pervades society. The role of social structure in the acquisition of gender norms is highlighted by social role theory.

Social Role Theory

Gender has been conceptualized as a "diffuse" status characteristic. Specifically, in Western society, and perhaps in most nations, men and their roles are ascribed more respect, honor, and importance (Berger, Fisek, Norman, & Zelditch, 1977; Carli, 1991; Meeker & Wetzel-O'Neill, 1985;

Ridgeway & Diekema, 1992; Wagner & Berger, 1997). Eagly (1987, 1997) acknowledges this state of affairs in her social role theory and goes on to propose that the existing gendered division of labor within society is the root cause of sex differences in behavior. Specifically, people make inferences about the correspondence between the gender-linked actions performed by men and women and their inner dispositions (Eagly & Karau, 2002) such that gender acts as a marker for the social role that adults fill. By virtue of their exposure to the traditional social roles of women and men, people learn and eventually express the behavioral tendencies that they have observed and come to believe are desirable for each sex (Eagly, 1987). In effect, they have been provided with scripts for their behaviors that in turn influence their attitudes, behaviors, and expectations throughout their lives.

As mentioned earlier, the normative division of roles, in which men are expected to be in paid occupations and women are more likely to be in the homemaker role, is very relevant to the explanation of the gendered patterns of responses to work stress. This prescribed separation of roles is said to affect two types of gender-related beliefs: (a) the expectations that people have for the traits and behaviors shown by women and men, or *descriptive norms,* and (b) the beliefs that women and men have about their own abilities and the skills they could and/or should develop, or *injunctive norms* (see Cialdini & Trost, 1998). People come to perceive biological sex as the determinant of psychosocial gender characteristics; these perceptions are characterized by gender unidimensionality (Korabik, 1999), with men being attributed all the masculine "agentic" traits such as assertiveness, ambition, and achievement orientation and women being assigned "communal" qualities, defined by sensitivity, care, warmth, and responsiveness to others (Wiggins, 1992). Consequently, women are perceived to be better suited to the role of primary caretakers of children than are men, whereas men are seen as well matched to the competitive and goal-directed role of worker.

At the individual level, a variety of sex-specific skills and behavioral styles arise from adopting the typical gendered family and economic roles. Women and men proceed to adjust to sex-typical roles by adapting their social behavior and by acquiring the specific skills that will lead to successful role performance (Carli & Eagly, 1999). In families, greater power and status are usually associated with the male partner's roles, reflecting the higher esteem in which male roles are held in our society (Eagly, 1987). In the work domain, gender role acquisition influences the power and achievement motives of both women and men leading to career-related decisions and strategies for negotiating the challenges and pressures of work and family life in gendered ways.

Role Congruity Theory

Eagly and Karau (2002) recently articulated an extension of social role theory called role congruity theory. Like social role theory, role congruity theory is based on the premise that gender roles are normative in that they both describe expectations about the appropriate behaviors of members of each sex and prescribe what members of each group should ideally do. However, role congruity theory reaches further by examining the degree of congruity between gender-based roles and leadership roles, arguing that female leaders are at particular risk of prejudice because of their violation of gendered social roles. The theory posits that people are uncomfortable and may react with prejudice to women who occupy or aspire to leadership roles because of the "inconsistency between the predominantly communal qualities that perceivers associate with women and the predominantly agentic qualities they believe are required to succeed as a leader" (Eagly & Karau, 2002, p. 575).

We agree with Eagly and Karau's assertion that role congruity theory best describes the psychological process entailed in the derogation of women who defy the traditional female gender path by taking on leadership roles. In fact, we would argue that congruity theory could easily be extended to explain the challenges of many, perhaps most, working women. Although there is more diversity than ever in the workplace, organizations and the people within them continue to hold the implicit assumption that the ideal worker is a white man who is employed full-time. The idea persists that women should be responsible for housework, child care, and even care of elderly parents but that they should not be employed outside the home or, at the most, should be a secondary wage earner (Friedman & Greenhaus, 2000). We believe that all working women are violating the normative assumptions of the role of women to some degree simply by choosing to be employed.

The traditional gender norms that regulate women's lives conflict powerfully with the breadwinning role associated with employment, and the incongruity of these norms becomes progressively worse as women deviate further from their traditional expectations. Working part-time violates gender norms to an extent, and these norms are violated even more when a woman chooses to work full-time. Any additional hierarchical responsibility assumed by female workers, whether it is as a low-level manager or as CEO of a company, exacerbates this incongruity. Thus, we propose that most working women violate some level of social expectations and that the work they do gets increasingly questioned, judged, or negatively evaluated the more that they renounce expectations of their communal behavior by taking on agentic roles. For women, role incongruity creates additional pressures in two ways. First, it influences other people's views of the working woman— she might be defined as an imperfect worker, an unsuitable mother, or both. Second, role incongruity can affect women's own self-evaluation, leading them to feel as if they are inadequate in both spheres of their lives.

Role incongruity does not affect only women; we believe that men can also experience the negative ramifications of role incongruity but that the effects for them may be far less damaging. Men who choose to devote a great deal of their off-work time to childrearing and family care may feel the pressures of role incongruence, especially if the family pressures substantially reduce the amount of time and effort they can devote to paid work. The choice to increase one's caretaking responsibilities, a fundamentally communal act, clearly goes against the strong expectations regarding male agentic norms. Nevertheless, it is not as strong a violation of social norms as is women's decision to work. Furthermore, most men and those around them usually continue to perceive "work" as their primary role. Thus, the consequences of role incongruity may not be as harmful for men because men are less likely than women to experience negative consequences related to their decision in *both* spheres of their lives.

Connections Between Traditional Roles and Work Stress

Men historically had a clear definition of their role as provider, but this role has been challenged as a result of women's increasing entry into the workforce (Burke, 2002). As a result, many men are now confused about their contemporary roles (Burke & Nelson, 1998). Furthermore, because men are traditionally expected to be more invested in their work than in their family responsibilities (Bardwick, 1984; Stroh & Reilly, 1999), the realization that their expected domain of competence is being challenged is often distressing for many men. Unfortunately, gender-role socialization, along with available exemplars of masculine social roles, provide men with a highly restricted code of conduct such that they have few emotional and behavioral options available to them from their traditional repertoire to deal with the pressures of this role confusion (see Burke, 2002, for a recent review). Traditional norms inform men that they should be self-reliant, be physically tough, and have their emotions under control (Levant & Pollack, 1995; Pleck, 1981; Pollack, 1998; Real, 1997). Of course, there is variability among men in the way they adhere to masculinity norms, and it appears that difficulties are most pronounced for those who operate within a restricted masculine context or who adhere strongly with these norms (Addis & Mahalik, 2003). Negative effects on men's health associated with the masculine role (Courtenay, 2001) include lower life expectancy, gender role strain, increased health problems, higher levels of drug and alcohol abuse, higher levels of aggression (Burke, 2002), and lower likelihood of seeking professional help to cope with both physical and psychological health problems (Addis & Mahalik, 2003).

By contrast, Murphy (2003), in her paper "Being Born Female Is Dangerous to Your Health," suggests that there is a nearly universal pattern of gender inequality in most cultures wherein women form the disadvantaged group. Being a woman is associated with significant negative physical and psychological consequences such as unwanted pregnancy and unsafe abortions, higher rates of depression and psychosomatic symptoms, and high rates of experiencing violence (Murphy, 2003). In the context of work and family domains, women's normative social roles place them at risk for high rates of strain and stress. Indeed, women are subject to more stressors in both the parenting and employee roles (Barnett & Baruch, 1987), which results in more work-family conflict for women than men (see Greenhaus & Parasuraman, 1999, for a review).

Summary

The theories reviewed in this section suggest that being a man or a woman is associated with its own unique set of roles, each with its deleterious consequences. The effects of gender socialization in conjunction with the societal constraints arising from the gendered division of social roles act to create and reinforce women's and men's perceptions of how best to act and respond to social expectations. Men feel the pressure to meet their gender roles by being career-minded, promotion-driven primary wage earners whereas women try to live up to the expectations of homemaker, caretaker, and support giver. Thus, people who strongly adhere to traditional gender norms will feel more strongly the stress associated with work or family pressures when it is closely connected to their gendered sphere of activity—men feeling greater pressures from work and women responding most vigorously to home-based strain (Pleck, 1977). Moreover, when responding to stress, men and women are expected to act in accordance with their traditional roles, with women being more expressive, connecting with others, and focusing on the emotions associated with the stress and men showing independence, detachment, and focusing on the task at hand.

At this point, we switch our focus from theory to practice and begin our review of the research findings on gender and work stress. In the next section, we provide some background on the work environments and the kinds of stressors to which men and women must respond, paying special attention to the work stressors that are gendered in nature.

Review of Sources of Stress at Work

Work stressors are events or aspects of the workplace that have negative physical and psychological consequences for the people exposed to them (Kahn & Byosiere, 1992). Both women and men experience many of the most common types of work stressors, such as role ambiguity, job insecurity, downsizing, and time pressure (Nelson & Burke, 2002a), along with the contemporary pressures associated with the increased availability to employers that result from the introduction of new technologies (Fraenkel, 2003). Moreover, the pressures of work overload, described as having "too many multiple and conflicting expectations from others" (Nelson & Burke, 2002a, p. 5), are equally felt by men and women. However, studies have shown some gender differences in what types of events are perceived as stressful. For instance, a recent investigation identified interpersonal conflict as causing greater job stress for women than for men, whereas men reported time and effort wasters as the greatest source of stress (Narayanan, Menon, & Spector, 1999). Furthermore, it has been argued that gendered issues surrounding power, emotion, and politics may influence men's and women's perceptions of stressors (Narayanan et al., 1999). Even the expression of emotionality in organizations—emotions representing a highly stereotypical feminine quality—may result in increased stress for women (Narayanan et al., 1999; Parkin, 1993). We consider other gendered work realities in the next section.

Gender Segregation at Work

Today's workplace continues to be characterized by persistent gender segregation. There remain clear distinctions between men's and women's work (Burke & Nelson, 1998; Jacobs, 1999). Occupations associated with more career opportunities, greater compensation, and higher levels of career achievement such as finance, manufacturing, and the high-tech industry have traditionally had a high proportion of male employees and very few women (Stroh & Reilly, 1999). There are numerous consequences of this arrangement, the worst of which is the concentration of women in low-paying, female-dominated occupations, which inevitably contributes to the gender wage gap (Jacobs, 1999; see also Roos & Gatta, 1999, for a review of the gender wage gap).

Why do men and women work in different occupations? We believe that the most likely explanation for occupational gender segregation is one that is consistent with Eagly's (1987, 1997) social role theory in that men and women use cues about the current state of workplace segregation along gender lines to decide whether particular jobs are appropriate for them. Consistent with social role theory, Jacobs (1999) suggests that sex-role socialization provides only the early stages of the social controls that reinforce distinctions between men and women; "social pressures later in life, in school and at work, combine with socialization to form a lifelong system of social control" (p. 138). Other factors, such as discriminatory selection (see Graves, 1999), also play a role in accentuating the segregation pattern.

A recent review of occupational sex segregation patterns (Jacobs, 1999) suggests that the situation has changed over the past 20 years, with declines in sex segregation for every age-group considered. These findings hint that individuals are not adhering to sex-role attitudes as rigidly as they did in the past and that traditional sex-role behavior patterns are less entrenched for individuals (Jacobs, 1999). Still, it continues to be the case that much of the world of work remains segregated. The combination of gender socialization and gender segregation leads to different work realities for women and men and different exposures to work stress. For example, some aspects associated with the type of jobs done more often by men tend to be highly stressful. These stressors include long working hours, more required travel, more corporate politics, more competition at work, and more worries about performance

(Alvesson & Billing, 1997). On the home front, these pressures result in less available time for developing relationships with children (Nelson & Burke, 2002a).

Tokenism

Gender-segregated workplaces can result in other types of stressors that affect women primarily. Specifically, women may experience tokenism when they are the first of their gender to enter a particular position, for instance, in a traditionally masculine job or in management (Davidson & Cooper, 1992; Kanter, 1990). Tokens often feel isolated and excluded from informal networks (Davidson & Cooper, 1992) and often experience stereotyping and discrimination from the majority group (Kanter, 1990), which creates a more stressful workplace environment.

Sexual Harassment

Sexual harassment has been conceptualized as a workplace stressor (Glomb et al., 1997). Recent estimates suggest that sexual harassment, defined as "any behavior of a sexual nature that an individual subjectively perceives to be offensive and unwelcome" (Bowes-Sperry & Tata, 1999, p. 265), is experienced by 28 to 90% of women, which far exceeds the 14 to 19% reporting of similar experiences by men (see Bowes-Sperry & Tata, 1999; Stockdale, 1996, for reviews). Thus it seems appropriate to conceptualize sexual harassment as a stressor that is experienced disproportionately by women.

Sexual harassment is associated with many negative personal consequences, such as lowered job satisfaction (Morrow, McElroy, & Phillips, 1994; O'Farrell & Harlan, 1982), increased turnover intentions (Shaffer, Joplin, Bell, Lau, & Oguz, 2000), and increased stress (Crull, 1982; Shaffer et al., 2000), as well as physical symptoms such as nausea, headaches, and other psychological illnesses (Goldenhar, Swanson, Hurrell, Ruder, & Deddens, 1998). There are many perspectives about what causes sexual harassment (see Bowes-Sperry & Tata, 1999, for a review), with some researchers focusing on individual level characteristics or interpretations of the perpetrator and victim and others considering organizational or structural factors that increase the likelihood of harassment. From a structural perspective, the workplace is organized according to masculine and patriarchal values (Maier, 1999), which results in a far greater likelihood that men hold many of the positions of power at work, with increased opportunities to abuse it. By contrast, the most likely individual-level explanation for harassment is that the personal characteristics of harassers (usually men), such as adherence to traditional masculine gender norms and sex-role stereotypes, interact with the more global influence of sociocultural power associated with men's roles (see Prior, LaVite, & Stoller, 1993; Tangri, Burt, & Johnson, 1982). Furthermore, research suggests that men who are more likely to harass tend to closely link power and sexuality (Bargh, Raymond, Pryor, & Strack, 1995). This combination of structural and positional power in the hands of men, together with individual-level variables, places female workers in a potentially precarious situation. The gender-segregated nature of the workplace has a role to play here as well. The experience of sexual harassment is more frequent for women who work with large numbers of men in nontraditional settings (Fitzgerald, Drasgow, Hulin, Gelfand, & Magley, 1997) such as in the police force or in construction (Goldenhar et al., 1998). Regardless of the type of workplace setting, sexual harassment is a stressor that is experienced more frequently by women than by men.

One does not need to have direct experience of sexual harassment to suffer negative effects; sexual harassment may also distress employees who are not direct targets of harassment but who simply witness it (Glomb et al., 1997; Piotrkowski, 1997). The concept of "bystander stress" has been used to describe the stress that individual workers experience when observing or hearing about coworkers being sexually harassed (Schneider, 1995), whereas "ambient sexual harassment" refers to the frequency of sexually harassing behaviors perpetrated against others in a woman's working group, thus acting as a group-level measure of indirect exposure to sexual harassment (Glomb et al., 1997). Employees are often aware of the sexual harassment of their coworkers, and the negative outcomes of sexual harassment frequently disperse beyond the victim to include other women in the victim's working group (Glomb et al., 1997). Both direct and indirect (ambient) exposure to sexual harassment decreases job satisfaction and increases psychological distress resulting in work withdrawal behaviors like high levels of absenteeism, intention to quit, leaving work early, taking long breaks, and missing meetings (Glomb et al., 1997).

Impact of Family Status on Work Circumstances

For men, being family-oriented confers definite advantages in the workplace. Being a family man tends to upgrade perceived status, often resulting in higher financial rewards from work (Friedman & Greenhaus, 2000; Pfeffer & Ross, 1982). In addition, married men are more likely to occupy higher positions (Friedman & Greenhaus, 2000), and those who have children or anticipate having children are perceived to deserve more opportunities and even higher salaries than comparable single men, single women, or married women (Alksnis, 2000).

In contrast to the benefits that engagement in family life often bestows on male workers, women often find their career progression impeded by virtue of having a partner or children. Women in upper management are less likely to be married than men in similar positions (Parasuraman & Greenhaus, 1993). When compared with unmarried women, married women are more likely to hold low-status and part-time jobs (Rosin & Korabik, 1990; Valdez & Gutek, 1987). However, marriage does not seem to affect the career progression of women after they have gained access to managerial or professional positions (Friedman & Greenhaus, 2000).

Having children has also been shown to disadvantage women (see Greenhaus & Parasuraman, 1999). Working mothers have lower income and less work satisfaction than comparable women without children (Friedman & Greenhaus, 2000). Women also report experiencing the "maternal wall" in which they receive fewer opportunities and less desirable assignments or limited career opportunities once they have had children (Williams, 1999) or even as a result of being perceived as of the right age and in the right conditions to soon begin a family (Alksnis, 2000). Employers seem to assume that once a woman has a child, or even if she is perceived as likely to want children because of her circumstances, her commitment to her work will be reduced in comparison to her commitment to her family (Alksnis, 2000; Williams, 1999). Thus, working mothers are assumed to be uncommitted employees whereas fatherhood is perceived to improve one's status as an employee. This perception of working mothers reinforces the normative assumption that women generally lack the commitment and motivation needed to succeed in the workplace, especially in managerial positions (Fielden & Cooper, 2002). This faulty assumption is also used to "explain" women's presumed lack of interest in promotions, which in effect blames women for their own lack of advancement (Adler, 1993; Wahl, 1995).

That women have more obstacles to achievements in the workplace has been well documented since the concept of the "glass ceiling" was first discussed in the 1980s (Hymowitz & Schellhardt, 1986). By virtue of being in a position of greater power and status in our society, men tend to have more access to higher-paid work and better chances for promotions. Career progression can be difficult for women because the structure of organizations is essentially masculine with all the assumptions, expectations, and reward structures following masculine gender norms of how career paths unfold (see Maier, 1999, for a review). Studies have indicated that overt and covert biases become more evident as women begin to climb into positions of power and authority (Auster, 1993, 2001), which is consistent with role congruity theory (Eagly & Karau, 2002).

Total Workload Associated With Work and Family Responsibilities

Women report higher total workload when we add both vocational and domestic (paid and unpaid) responsibilities; women carry an average total workload of 78 hours whereas men carry 68 hours (Coltrane, 2000; Frankenhaeuser, 1991; Galinsky, Bond, & Friedman, 1993; Hochschild, 1989). Although men now spend more time with their children than they did 20 years ago (Barnett & Hyde, 2001), the gap in total workload remains (Bond et al., 1998) as women continue to do approximately three times more housework than men (Coltrane, 2000). Because of their higher workload, women are more threatened in terms of their physical and mental health and are particularly prone to role and work overload (Nelson & Burke, 2002a).

Midcareer women (the period approximately 15 to 20 years into one's professional career) in dual-career households are perhaps the group at highest risk of role and work overload (Friedman & Greenhaus, 2000). Women's responsibilities regarding their family-related roles have to be fulfilled despite interferences from work pressures, which frequently cannot be postponed either (Barnett & Shen, 1997). The midcareer period is the time during which work-life trade-offs pose the greatest struggle for women because of the difficulty of juggling child care and high performance expectations.

Summary

In the previous section, we highlighted the factors that expose women and men to a different set of circumstances at work and at home. Men feel the pressures to live up to expectations associated with traditional gender norms (see Eagly, 1987) by devoting more of their time and energy to paid employment and by internalizing the "masculine culture" of the workplace. The result is a combination of high workload, high demand, fear of low performance, worries about lack of recognition and advancement, and less involvement in the family aspects of their lives.

Women also experience a set of work stressors that are broadly associated with traditional gendered expectations; their work efforts, competence, and commitment are evaluated increasingly negatively the more they deviate from the traditional gender script for women. The pattern for both genders is consistent with predictions from both social role theory (Eagly, 1987, 1997) and role congruity theory (Eagly & Karau, 2002). Women are in the difficult position of balancing their home and work pressures while being exposed to highly stressful factors at work. Although the experience of occupational stress for men is related to their role in the power structure, a major component of women's work stress is associated with the conflict between job requirements and family relationships (Vagg, Spielberger, & Wasala, 2002). Other stressors that are more likely to be experienced by women include gender segregation (which often limits their promotion pattern and income), tokenism (which negates competence when achieving a promotion), sexual harassment, and lower evaluations on the basis of family status and childrearing responsibilities, all combined with role overload and higher total workload. We now turn our attention to the examination of the impacts of work stressors in men's and women's lives in order to ascertain whether gendered patterns exist.

Review of Effects of Work Stress

Some researchers have found little or no evidence of gender influences in perceptions of job stress and stress-strain relationships (Di Salvo, Lubbers,

Rossi, & Lewis, 1995; Martocchio & O'Leary, 1989; see also Westman, 2002). Others have argued that reactions to work stress are indeed gendered such that women report greater psychological distress than do men (Wade & Cairney, 1997; see also Vermeulen & Mustard, 2000). In this section we review the most commonly studied areas in which gender and work stress interface, including the perception and experience of stress by women and men. We also consider whether men and women differ in their response to the work-family balance dilemma and what factors contribute to these differences, if they exist.

Self-Reported Stress

There is some evidence that men and women experience acute stressors at the same rate, and some studies go even further in suggesting that there are no gender differences in reported levels of occupational stress (Miller et al., 2000; Spielberger & Reheiser, 1994) For instance, a meta-analysis of 15 studies (Martocchio & O'Leary, 1989) found no gender difference in perceived or experienced workplace stress. Similarly, in their study of public sector employees, Guppy and Rick (1996) also found no gender differences in the frequency of occurrence of workplace stressors.

Where there is some evidence of gender differences in work stress is in the experience, reporting, and reactions to chronic stressors. In a review of 19 studies, Jick and Mitz (1985) found that women experience more severe psychological distress in the workplace, whereas men experience more severe physical distress (see also Walters, 1993). Indeed it has been argued that one of the most consistent results in mental health research is that women report significantly more symptoms than do men (Tousignant, Brosseau, & Tremblay, 1987). Furthermore, recent studies suggest that women's reported level of depressive symptoms, in particular, continues to be higher than men's despite women's substantial gains in education and career opportunity (Mirowski & Ross, 1995). These psychological outcomes of work stress may be particularly pronounced for married working women (Cooper, Cooper, & Eaker, 1988).

Why do women report more psychological distress than do men? It is quite likely that gender differences in perceived stereotypical patterns of emotional expression greatly influence how women and men report work distress (see Brody & Hall, 1993, for a review). Women are assumed, even expected, to notice, acknowledge, and report negative feelings, even feelings in general, whereas men are believed to be more guarded about their feelings and to keep them inside, which has its negative consequences. It has been shown that men have more chronic health conditions, primarily heart problems, and that their work-related distress tends to be more precarious (Nelson & Burke, 2002a).

The other possible explanation for women's higher levels of reported work stress is that women are exposed to a greater amount of work stress than are men (Nelson & Quick, 1985) and that men are provided with some work circumstances that, if they were equally applied to women's work, would reduce or eliminate the gender difference in stress reporting (Roxburgh, 1996). The latter suggestion is quite convincing given that women on average have more work than men when we combine their paid and unpaid work responsibilities (Coltrane, 2000; Frankenhaeuser, 1991; Galinsky et al., 1993; Hochschild, 1989). Women are also exposed to many types of stressors arising from structural and normative factors that disproportionately affect their working conditions, including segregation, barriers to promotions, and sexual harassment.

A related but slightly different explanation for the gender difference in reported distress is provided by Vermeulen and Mustard (2000), who claim that women's role occupancy may be less important than the combination of their expected social roles in influencing the relationship between job strain and distress. From this perspective, work-family conflict is seen as affecting the quality of working life more for women than for men (Duxbury & Higgins, 1991) because of the multiple and equally pressing demands placed on women both at work and at home. The combination of the two sets of pressures results in greater stress for women. Thus, gender differences in psychological distress may be largely accounted for by the characteristics and demands of one's work and family roles as well as the experience of work-family conflict (Hughes & Galinsky, 1994). We turn our attention to work-family conflict issues in the next section.

Effects of Work-Family Conflict

In general, work-family conflict is associated with burnout (Bacharach, Bamberger, & Conley, 1991), negative mood (Williams & Alliger, 1994), decreased family and occupational well-being (Kinnunen & Mauno, 1998), psychological and physical complaints (Frone, Russell, & Cooper, 1992a), and job and life dissatisfaction (Netemeyer, Boles, & McMurrian, 1996). As conflict between family and work increases, satisfaction in both domains decreases (Kossek & Ozeki, 1998; see also Greenglass, 2002, for a review). Work-family conflict is a leading source of stress for working women in particular (Piltch, Walsh, Mangione, & Jennings, 1994; Spielberger & Reheiser, 1994), likely as a result of the total amount of time they invest in both spheres of activities (Duxbury & Higgins, 1991; Greenhaus & Parasuraman, 1999).

Gendered reactions to work-family conflict have been uncovered. For example, there are gender differences in the amount of exposure to work and family stress that are linked to marital status. Unmarried mothers report more parental strain than do unmarried fathers, but married mothers and fathers do not seem to differ in their exposure to stressors (Duxbury & Higgins, 1991). However, married men and women react differently to work-family stressors such that the psychological distress associated with work stress may be higher for married working women (Cooper et al., 1988). The presence of added pressures in the lives of married women who work, such as having the responsibility for children at home, has also been shown to affect their perceived stress level as well as their physiological responses to this stress. For instance, work-family pressures have been associated with an increase in cardiovascular disorders for working women with children (Haynes & Feinleib, 1980). It thus appears that as women's overall life demands increase, so does their overall level of stress.

Gender differences in vulnerability to stress are highly specific and seem to depend on the type of stressor and disorder involved. Wives are more depressed than husbands by parental and marital strains (Pearlin, 1975; Pearlin & Lieberman, 1979). These strains have implications for the nurturant role that is typically ascribed to mothers (Duxbury & Higgins, 1991). Husbands consume more alcohol than do wives when experiencing financial strain, likely because this type of strain is associated with the breadwinner role (Duxbury & Higgins, 1991; Simon, 1998). Men are more likely than are women to allow work conflict to spill over into the family domain (Duxbury & Higgins, 1991; Pleck, 1977), whereas women are more likely to allow family role demands to affect their work role (Pleck, 1981; Voydanoff, 1988).

High involvement in nontraditional roles creates increased time pressures for both men and women in dual-earner families, with greater repercussions for working women who try to balance the expected demands of their nurturant roles with the expectations of a career. Conversely, family involvement is associated with work-family conflict for men more than for women (Duxbury & Higgins, 1991). Whereas high work involvement may cause women anxiety and guilt regarding their performance in traditional family roles, high family involvement may cause men to be perceived by their coworkers and superiors as less committed to their jobs, thus creating work-family conflict for men (Duxbury & Higgins, 1991). Despite the negative perception of male workers who are highly involved in their family life, research suggests that multiple roles are actually associated with positive psychological effects on people's well-being and that the ill effects may be the result of people's adherence to traditional expectations about their roles (Barnett & Hyde, 2001). With gender role flexibility comes less pressure to meet the rigid expectations of one's normative gender norms. Of course, the positive effect of multiple roles is likely to be limited by the total extent of the demands on a person's life. Even with a flexible view of gender expectations, overcommitment to all the facets of one's life may result in overall increased stress levels.

Transfer of Stress From Work to Home and Home to Work

In a recent summary of the literature on work-family balance, including the transfer of stress from work to the family sphere and vice versa, Frone (2003) concluded that the bulk of the evidence pointed to men and women reporting similar levels of work-to-family conflict and family-to-work conflict. The findings were consistent regardless of the types of sample utilized, which included small convenience samples of employees from an organization (e.g., Eagle, Miles, & Icenogle, 1997; Grandey & Cropanzano, 1999) to regional probability samples (e.g., Frone, Russell, & Cooper, 1992b; Marks, 1998) and even to larger national probability samples (e.g., Frone, 2000; Grzywacz & Marks, 2000).

Frone's (2003) conclusion differs from those reached in other research reviews, which contend that there were important gender differences in the degree to which job stress transfers into negative family processes (see e.g., Larson & Almeida, 1999). This last review suggests that research on couples' and families' emotional transmission generally find that men's emotions affect women's emotions more reliably than the reverse (see Larson & Almeida, 1999, for a review). This pattern has been interpreted to reflect and reproduce the typical power difference between men and women, although others argue that it may reflect women's greater responsiveness and their deliberate attempts to elicit their male partners' emotions (Larson & Almeida, 1999). The opposite conclusions reached by these researchers likely result from the combination of their different research focus and methodology. Whereas the research reviewed by Frone (2003) was designed to examine the degree to which people report work-family conflict, usually using surveys, Larson and Almeida's (1999) approach centers mainly on the detailed assessment of interfamilial processes of emotional distress transmission, a more focused microlevel analysis. In all likelihood, both sets of results are accurate in that men and women may not differ in their global evaluations of work-family conflict, although they can identify different patterns when required to think about these issues more strategically. These contrary results do indicate the importance of a multimethod approach to study these complex interpersonal issues. In addition, Westman's (2002) point that the transfer of work or family stress from one partner to the other may depend more on the relative job status of the respondent than on his or her gender, and her recommendation that other variables should be taken into account when examining the pattern of stress crossover, is also worth heeding.

The stress spillover literature provides some indication that women may be more susceptible than men to the impact of stressors affecting their partners. For instance, Kessler and McLeod (1984) showed that events happening to significant others are more distressing for women than for men. They speculated that women's greater involvement in family affairs led them to become more sensitive not only to the stressful events that they experience themselves but also to those that affect their spouses. Similarly, Lambert (1990) suggested that gender is a potential moderator of the impact of one's stress on the spouse's strain because of differences in the traditional role demands and expectations for men and women.

It may be the case that women's apparent vulnerability to their partners' stress is simply the result of inadequate research. Westman (2002) identified a gap in the work-family conflict literature in that there has been no research focusing exclusively on the crossover of stress from wives to husbands. Some researchers have examined how women's employment status influences their husbands' well-being, but how a woman's job stress affects her partner has not been studied (see Westman, 2002, for a review). Several studies found that women's employment status had significant negative effects on the well-being of their male partners. For instance, Greenhaus and Parasuraman (1986) found that husbands of employed women displayed lower levels of satisfaction and quality of life than husbands of nonemployed women. A later study by Rosenfield (1992) found that it was not the wives' employment status per se that affected the husbands' well-being but rather the impact on the husbands' status in the family. A powerful illustration of this point is shown in a recent study of spousal abuse by Melzer (2002). Melzer showed that the men in the sample who held clerical occupations (female-dominated jobs) were the most likely to use physical violence against their intimate partners, and contrary to what many would assume, men in male-dominated occupations were not very likely to use violence against intimate partners. Similarly, men's unemployment was a better predictor of male violence against intimate partners than was female unemployment. And, shockingly, female partners who earned more of the overall income were 93% more likely to face violence from their partners than were women with incomes comparable to their partners'. Results suggest that female partners often suffer from men's occupational violence and stress spillover (Melzer, 2002).

Studies have shown that transmission of stress to family members other than spouses is also possible. Indeed, both men and women react to work stress in ways that affect family life, but they do it slightly differently. Fathers tend to transmit more job-related stress to their children than do employed mothers (Larson & Almeida, 1999), whereas mothers have been found to withdraw from their preschool children after stressful workdays (Repetti & Wood, 1997). In other words, men transmit the stress to their children and to the family as a whole (see Larson & Almeida, 1999), but women seem better able to contain their distress (Downey, Purdie, & Schaffer-Neitz, 1999). But the topic of emotional transmission from the workplace to home is not without its controversies, perhaps because of popular misconceptions about gender norms. Researchers have argued that there is an underlying discomfort with women in the workplace (Barnett & Rivers, 1996; Haddock, Zimmerman, Ziemba, & Current, 2001; Holcomb, 1998; Moen & Yu, 2000; Williams, 1999), one that persists despite studies that reveal that a mother's employment in and of itself does not negatively affect mother-child bonding (Harvey, 1999; National Institute of Child Health and Human Development [NICHD] Early Child Care Research Network, 1997). Some researchers have even shown the many positive mental and physical health and relational effects for both partners when both work (Barnett & Hyde, 2001), but this evidence is slow to change people's perspectives on men's and women's traditional spheres.

Summary

Our previous sections highlighted how gender influences perceptions of one's own stress level as well as how work and family stress interface for women and men. Consistent with the tenets of social role theory (Eagly, 1987, 1997), many researchers who study the interaction of work and family pressures (Burke, 1991; Frone, Russell, & Cooper, 1995; see also Greenhaus & Parasuraman, 2002) argue that much of the gendered reactions to work-family balance are associated with the pressures of gender-relevant social roles that would lead men and women to respond differently to work-family pressures by organizing their responses to such dilemmas in terms of the domain that is most central or salient to their identity (Thoits, 1991; see also Deaux & Major, 1987, and Deaux & Lafrance, 1998, for theoretical reviews). Similarly, women and men cope differently with the work and family pressures they experience. The next section reviews how gender influences how men and women cope with work stress.

Review of Strategies for Coping With Stress

Clearly, there are numerous strategies that people could use for coping with stress. The question is, do men and women use the same ones? Research findings on this point are quite mixed. Moreover, the means of classifying coping strategies can be quite different across studies. For example, some researchers make a distinction between problem-focused and emotion-focused strategies and have shown that men tend to use the more adaptive problem-focused coping mechanisms whereas women tend to use less adaptive emotion-focused methods (Trocki & Orilio, 1994; Vingerhoets & Van Heck, 1990). Men may be socialized to deal with stress instrumentally, whereas women may be socialized to express emotion (Burke, Weir, & DuWors, 1980; Mainiero, 1986). Given the same stressor, it is thought that men are more likely to be problem-focused whereas women are more likely to be emotion-focused (Burke & Belcourt, 1974; Ptacek, Smith, & Zanas, 1992). In a recent study (Narayanan et al., 1999), men reported using problem-solving coping (taking direct action or taking the problem up with their supervisor or head) more than did women, but this gender difference disappeared when the researchers examined how higher-level professionals (professors) coped with stress. For this group of workers, both men and women preferred problem-focused strategies (Narayanan et al., 1999).

Other researchers differentiate between "control" and "escape" coping mechanisms (see Van Emmerik, 2002) and have shown that men may use more control coping strategies (e.g., thinking about solutions, gathering information, or taking actions) than do women (Billings & Moos, 1980; Defares, Brandjes, Nass, & van der Ploeg, 1984; Ptacek, Smith, & Dodge, 1994; see also Van Emmerik, 2002). Women, on the other hand, tend to use more escape coping strategies (e.g., venting or expressing emotions, feeling more depressed, or avoiding stressful situations; Ptacek et al., 1994). One exception to this pattern is that men are more likely to engage in particular types of escape coping strategies, like alcohol and drug use (Davidson & Cooper, 1984; Carver, Scheier, & Weintraub, 1986). Gianakos (2002) found a similar pattern whereby men are more likely use strategies that may not be adaptive in the long run, such as coping with workplace stress using alcohol more often than do women, whereas women were more likely than men to cope by working longer and harder. In her conclusions, Gianakos (2002) argues that coping style may indeed be better predicted by gender role than by sex.

In her recent review, Greenglass (2002) goes even further. She argues that when demographic factors such as education, occupation, and position are controlled in statistical analyses, few gender differences emerge in coping strategies. In her view, coping strategies may, therefore, have less to do with gender than with other forms of resources usually associated with gender, such as status and power. This may help explain the mixed results in this area of research. For instance, a recent study by Christie and Shultz (1998) found only minimal support for the claim that men and women use different coping mechanisms. Contrary to their hypotheses, the authors found that women use control coping slightly more than do men but that they used escape coping to the same extent. Men also reported higher levels of exercise than did women, suggesting that men are more likely to use exercise to cope with stress than are women, whereas women reported receiving higher levels of emotional social support than did men (Christie & Shultz, 1998).

Social Support

Social support is generally defined as the amount of emotional and instrumental assistance received from another (Beehr, 1985). In general, social support is associated with lower reported levels of strain (Carlson & Perrewé, 1999; Eastburg, Williamson, Gorsuch, & Ridley, 1994). Social support has positive effects on mental and physical health (Bell, 1987; Cohen & Syme, 1985; Greenglass, Fiksenbaum, & Burke, 1996; Hobfoll, Dunahoo, Ben-Porath, & Monnier, 1984; Waldron & Jacobs, 1989).

Research to date is ambiguous about whether social support affects men and women differently (Greenhaus & Parasuraman, 1999; see Perrewé & Carlson, 2002, for a review). However, what is clear is that social support is rather specific in its effect, as support from the family has the greatest stress-reducing effects on family strain, and social support from work tends to be most effective in reducing work stress (Aryee & Luk, 1996; Frone, Yardley, & Markel, 1997; Parasuraman, Greenhaus, & Granrose, 1992).

For support with work-related stresses, men tend to use smaller, usually work-based support networks (Greenglass, 1993), whereas women tend to turn to family members and friends (Piltch et al., 1994). Although some studies have shown that men find work-based support networks to be more effective in reducing stress than do women (Geller & Hobfoll, 1994), women's broader social support strategies have also been associated with positive outcomes (Greenglass, 1993). Some research suggests that men receive more support in problem solving and in forming attachment for emotional support in the workplace than do women (Pugliesi & Shook, 1998), whereas other studies show that women are more likely to get support from their entire social network (Baruch, Biener, & Barnett, 1987) and especially from their coworkers (Parasuraman & Greenhaus, 1993). This last finding is consistent with a gender socialization perspective that suggests that because women seek social support such as advice, information, and assistance more often than do men (Ptacek et al., 1994; see Greenglass, 2002, for a review), they may also be more likely to receive the assistance and support they seek. But this gendered pattern has some negative effects too. Although social support in general increases satisfaction and well-being in dual-career couples (Parasuraman et al., 1992), women's reliance on family and friends may ultimately increase their stress by exacerbating work-family conflict. Because women tend to form extended networks of social support (Kessler & McLeod, 1984), they may also have to deal with the additional problems of their friends and family (Wethington & McLeod, 1987).

With respect to the types of support sought, women generally report higher emotional support from friends and coworkers, whereas men report receiving higher instrumental (e.g., providing money) and informational support (e.g., providing direction) from coworkers (Olson & Shultz, 1994). This pattern coincides with traditional gendered patterns of behavior whereby women tend to be more affectively oriented and more willing to inquire about upsetting situations whereas men are more instrumental (Kunkel & Burleson, 1998; see also Taylor et al., 2000). Men also report receiving more performance appraisal feedback from their spouses (see Christie & Shultz, 1998).

Summary and Conclusions

We began this chapter by challenging the view that work stress affects women and men in different ways or at least in ways that are fundamentally gendered. Instead, we argued in a manner consistent with the recent conceptualizations defined by Barnett and Hyde (2001) that there are far more commonalities than differences in the way men and women experience work stress and that by and large the differences that exist are associated with a rigid adherence to traditional views of gender best captured by the notion of separate spheres. Such rigid acceptance of traditional gender scripts creates deep conflicts for both men and women, especially because it often does not capture the full reality of people's lives. With women now fully engaged in the workplace and men greatly increasing their family involvement, members of both genders experience the difficulties of time management, multiple demands, conflicting role pressures, role overload, and ever increasing stress.

The "old" ways neither capture the current life-balancing act of women and men nor facilitate people's efforts to deal with their work and life pressures.

We believe that it is important for researchers to ask themselves this question: "Is comparing men's and women's experience of work stress really addressing the right issue?" Is this research question loaded with biological determinism, or does it truly help answer essential truths about work stress? We ask that researchers review their assumptions before they engage in this research—and the assumptions are many. The ramifications of this approach are well described in Deaux and Lafrance's (1998) thorough review of gender research in social psychology wherein the authors critique research on sex differences. They suggest that this approach to gender research is "often framed in such a way as to stress opposites rather than overlap, to emphasize the person rather than the setting and to highlight biology or prior socialization rather than current assignment of women and men to different and unequal positions in the social structure" (p. 789). Korabik (1999) makes a similar point in her review of gender and sex research, in which she argues that researchers have mainly failed in providing a theoretical framework to their research on sex and gender, and as a consequence, the literature is filled with accidental and incidental sex differences. Of course, highlighting gender similarities rather than differences has obvious methodological ramifications, but we believe that it may be time to consider whether focusing on gender differences in the connection between work and family stress is truly warranted, especially when the changes in the family and working lives of women and men are now beginning to show their impact (Barnett & Hyde, 2001).

References

Addis, M. E., & Mahalik, J. R. (2003). Men, masculinity, and the contexts of help seeking. *American Psychologist, 58*(1), 5–14.

Adler, N. J. (1993). Competitive frontiers: Women managers in the triad. *International Studies of Management and Organization, 23*(2), 3–23.

Alksnis, C. (2000). Sexism, stereotyping and the gender wage gap. *Dissertation Abstracts International, 6*(12), 6744B.

Alvesson, M., & Billing, Y. D. (1997). *Understanding gender and organizations.* London: Sage.

Aryee, S., & Luk, V. (1996). Work and nonwork influences on the career satisfaction of dual-earner couples. *Journal of Vocational Behavior, 49,* 38–52.

Auster, E. R. (1993). Demystifying the glass ceiling: Organizational and interpersonal dynamics of gender bias. *Business in the Contemporary World, 5*(3), 47–68.

Auster, E. R. (2001). Professional women's midcareer satisfaction: Toward an explanatory framework. *Sex Roles, 44*(11/12), 719–750.

Bacharach, S. B., Bamberger, P., & Conley, S. (1991). Work-home conflict among nurses and engineers: Mediating the impact of role stress on burnout and satisfaction at work. *Journal of Organizational Behavior, 12,* 39–53.

Bandura, A. (1986). *Social foundations of thought and action: A social cognitive theory*. Englewood Cliffs, NJ: Prentice Hall.

Bardwick, J. (1984). When ambition is no asset. *New Management, 1*, 22–28.

Bargh, J. A., Raymond, P., Pryor, J. B., & Strack, F. (1995). Attractiveness of the underling: An automatic power-sex association and its consequences for sexual harassment and aggression. *Journal of Personality and Social Psychology, 68*, 768–781.

Barnett, R. C., & Baruch, G. K. (1987). Social roles, gender, and psychological distress. In R. C. Barnett, L. Biener, & G. K. Baruch (Eds.), *Gender and stress* (pp. 122–143). New York: Free Press.

Barnett, R. C., Biener, L., & Baruch, G. K. (Eds.). (1987). *Gender and stress*. New York: Free Press.

Barnett, R. C., & Hyde, J. S. (2001). Women, men, and family: An expansionist theory. *American Psychologist, 56*(10), 781–796.

Barnett, R. C., & Rivers, C. (1996). *She works/he works: How two-income families are happier, healthier, and better off*. San Francisco: HarperCollins.

Barnett, R. C., & Shen, Y. C. (1997). Gender, high- and low-schedule-control housework tasks, and psychological distress: A study of dual-earner couples. *Journal of Family Issues, 18*, 403–428.

Baruch, G. K., Biener, L., & Barnett, R. C. (1987). Women and gender research on work and family stress. *American Psychologist, 42*, 130–136.

Beehr, T. A. (1985). The role of social support in coping with organizational stress. In T. A. Beehr & R. S. Bhagat (Eds.), *Human stress and cognition in organizations: An integrated perspective* (pp. 375–398). New York: Wiley.

Bell, D. (1987). Gender differences in the social moderators of stress. In R. C. Barnett, L. Biener, & G. K. Baruch (Eds.), *Gender and stress* (pp. 257–277). New York: Free Press.

Bem, S. L. (1981). Gender schema theory: A cognitive account of sex-typing. *Psychological Review, 88*, 354–364.

Bem, S. L. (1985). Androgyny and gender schema theory: A conceptual and empirical integration. In T. B. Sonderegger (Ed.), *Nebraska symposium on motivation, 1984: Psychology and gender* (pp. 179–226). Lincoln: University of Nebraska Press.

Berger, J., Fisek, M. H., Norman, R. Z., & Zelditch, M., Jr. (1977). *Status characteristics and social interactions: An expectation states approach*. New York: Elsevier Science.

Billings, A. G., & Moos, R. H. (1980). The role of coping responses and social resources in attenuating the stress of life events. *Journal of Behavioral Medicine, 4*, 435–447.

Bond, J. T., Galinsky, E., & Swanberg, J. E. (1998). *The 1997 national study of the changing workforce*. New York: Families and Work Institute.

Bowes-Sperry, L., & Tata, J. (1999). A multiperspective framework of sexual harassment: Reviewing two decades of research. In G. N. Powell (Ed.), *Handbook of gender and work* (pp. 263–280). Thousand Oaks, CA: Sage.

Brody, L. R., & Hall, J. A. (1993). Gender and emotion. In M. Lewis & J. M. Haviland (Eds.), *Handbook of emotions* (pp. 447–460). New York: Guilford Press.

Burke, P. J. (1991). Identity processes and social stress. *American Sociological Review, 56*, 836–849.

Burke, R. J. (2002). Men, masculinity, and health. In D. L. Nelson & R. J. Burke (Eds.), *Gender, work stress and health* (pp. 35–54). Washington, DC: American Psychological Association.

Burke, R. J., & Belcourt, M. L. (1974). Managerial role stress and coping responses. *Journal of Business Administration, 5,* 55–68.

Burke, R. J., & Nelson, D. L. (1998). Organizational men: Masculinity and its discontents. In C. L. Cooper & I. T. Robertson (Eds.), *International review of industrial and organizational psychology* (pp. 225–271). New York: Wiley.

Burke, R. J., Weir, T., & DuWors, R. E. (1980). Work demands on administrators and spouse well-being. *Human Relations, 33,* 253–278.

Carli, L. L. (1991). Gender, status, and influence. In E. J. Lawler, B. Markovsky, C. Ridgeway, & H. A. Walker (Eds.), *Advances in group processes* (Vol. 8, pp. 89–113). Greenwich, CT: JAI.

Carli, L. L., & Eagly, A. H. (1999). Gender effects on social influence and emergent leadership. In G. N. Powell (Ed.), *Handbook of gender and work* (pp. 203–222). Thousand Oaks, CA: Sage.

Carlson, D. S., & Perrewé, P. L. (1999). The role of social support in the stressor-strain relationship: An examination of work-family conflict. *Journal of Management, 25,* 513–540.

Carver, C. S., Scheier, M. F., & Weintraub, J. K. (1986). Assessing coping strategies: A theoretically based approach. *Journal of Personality and Social Psychology, 66,* 267–283.

Christie, M., & Shultz, K. S. (1998). Gender differences on coping with job stress and organizational outcomes. *Work & Stress, 12,* 351–361.

Cialdini, R. B., & Trost, M. R. (1998). Social influence: Social norms, conformity, and compliance. In D. T. Gilbert, S. T. Fiske, & G. Lindzey (Eds.), *The handbook of social psychology* (4th ed., Vol. 2, pp. 151–192). Boston: McGraw-Hill.

Cohen, L. L., & Swim, J. K. (1995). The differential impact of gender ratios on women and men: Tokenism, self-confidence, and expectations. *Personality and Social Psychology Bulletin, 21*(9), 876–884.

Cohen, S., & Syme, S. L. (1985). Issues in the study and application of social support. In S. Cohen & S. L. Syme (Eds.), *Social support and health* (pp. 3–22). San Diego, CA: Academic Press.

Coltrane, S. (2000). Research on household labor: Modeling and measuring the social embeddedness of routine family work. *Journal of Marriage and the Family, 62,* 1208–1233.

Cooper, C. L., Cooper, C. R., & Eaker, L. H. (1988). *Living with stress.* London: Penguin.

Courtenay, W. H. (2001). Constructions of masculinity and their influence on men's well-being: A theory of gender and health. *Social Science and Medicine, 51,* 203–217.

Crull, P. (1982). Stress effects of sexual harassment on the job: Implications for counseling. *American Journal of Orthopsychiatry, 52,* 539–544.

Davidson, M. J., & Burke, R. J. (2000). *Women in management: Vol. 2. Current research issues.* London: Sage.

Davidson, M. J., & Cooper, C. L. (1984). Occupational stress in female managers: A comparative study. *Journal of Management Studies, 21,* 185–205.

Davidson, M. J., & Cooper, C. L. (1992). *Shattering the glass ceiling: The woman manager.* London: Paul Chapman Publishing.

Deaux, K., & Lafrance, M. (1998). Gender. In D. T. Gilbert, S. T. Fiske, & G. Lindzey (Eds.), *The handbook of social psychology* (4th ed., Vol. 1, pp. 788–827). Boston: McGraw-Hill.

Deaux, K., & Major, B. (1987). Putting gender into context: An interactive model of gender-related behavior. *Psychological Review, 94,* 369–389.

Defares, P. B., Brandjes, M., Nass, C. H., & van der Ploeg, J. D. (1984). Coping styles and vulnerability of women at work in residential settings. *Ergonomics, 27(5),* 527–545.

Desmarais, S., & Curtis, J. E. (1999). Gender differences in employment and income experiences among young people. In J. Barling & E. K. Kelloway (Eds.), *Young workers: Varieties of experience* (pp. 59–88). Washington, DC: American Psychological Association.

Di Salvo, V., Lubbers, C., Rossi, A. M., & Lewis, J. (1995). Unstructured perceptions of work-related stress: An exploratory qualitative study. In C. Crandall & P. Perrewé (Eds.), *Occupational stress: A handbook* (pp. 53–68). Belmont, CA: Wadsworth.

Downey, G., Purdie, V., & Schaffer-Neitz, R. (1999). Anger transmission from mother to child: A comparison of mothers in chronic pain and well mothers. *Journal of Marriage and the Family, 61(1),* 62–73.

Duxbury, L. E., & Higgins, C. A. (1991). Gender differences in work-family conflict. *Journal of Applied Psychology, 76,* 60–74.

Eagle, B. W., Miles, E. W., & Icenogle, M. L. (1997). Interrole conflicts and the permeability of work and family domains: Are there gender differences? *Journal of Vocational Behavior, 50,* 168–184.

Eagly, A. H. (1987). *Sex differences in social behavior: A social-role interpretation.* Hillsdale, NJ: Lawrence Erlbaum.

Eagly, A. H. (1997). Comparing women and men: Methods, findings, and politics. In M. R. Walsh (Ed.), *Women, men, and gender: Ongoing debates* (pp. 24–31). New Haven, CT: Yale University Press.

Eagly, A. H., & Karau, S. J. (2002). Role congruity theory of prejudice toward female leaders. *Psychological Review, 109(3),* 573–598.

Eastburg, M. C., Williamson, M., Gorsuch, R., & Ridley, C. (1994). Social support, personality and burnout in nurses. *Journal of Applied Psychology, 24,* 1233–1250.

Fielden, S. L., & Cooper, C. L. (2002). Managerial stress: Are women more at risk? In D. L. Nelson & R. J. Burke (Eds.), *Gender, work stress and health* (pp. 19–34). Washington, DC: American Psychological Association.

Fitzgerald, L. F., Drasgow, F., Hulin, C. L., Gelfand, M. J., & Magley, V. J. (1997). Antecedents and consequences of sexual harassment in organizations: A test of an integrated model. *Journal of Applied Psychology, 82(4),* 578–589.

Fraenkel, P. (2003). Contemporary two-parent families: Navigating work and family challenges. In F. Walsh (Ed.), *Normal family practices* (3rd ed., pp. 61–95). New York: Guilford.

Frankenhaeuser, M. (1991). The psychophysiology of workload, stress, and health: Comparisons between the sexes. *Annals of Behavioral Medicine, 13,* 197–204.

Friedman, S. D., & Greenhaus, J. H. (2000). *Work and families—Allies or enemies?* New York: Oxford University Press.

Frone, M. R. (2000). Work-family conflict and employee psychiatric disorders: The national comorbidity survey. *Journal of Applied Psychology, 85,* 888–895.

Frone, M. R. (2003). Work-family balance. In J. C. Quick & L. E. Tetrick (Eds.), *Handbook of occupational health psychology* (pp. 143–162). Washington, DC: American Psychological Association.

Frone, M. R., Russell, M., & Cooper, M. L. (1992a). Antecedents and outcomes of work-family conflict. Testing a model of the work-family interface. *Journal of Applied Psychology, 77,* 65–78.

Frone, M. R., Russell, M., & Cooper, M. L. (1992b). Prevalence of work-family conflict: Are work and family boundaries asymmetrically permeable? *Journal of Organizational Behavior, 13,* 723–729.

Frone, M. R., Russell, M., & Cooper, M. L. (1995). Job stressors, job involvement and employee health: A test of identity theory. *Journal of Occupational and Organizational Psychology, 68,* 1–11.

Frone, M. R., Yardley, J. K., & Markel, K. (1997). Workplace family-supportive programmes: Predictors of employed parents' importance ratings. *Journal of Occupational and Organizational Psychology, 69,* 351–366.

Galinsky, E., Bond, J. T., & Friedman, D. E. (1993). *The changing workforce: Highlights of the national study.* New York: Families and Work Institute.

Galinsky, E., Kim, S., & Bond, J. T. (2001). *Feeling overworked: When work becomes too much.* New York: Families and Work Institute.

Geller, P. A., & Hobfoll, S. E. (1994). Gender differences in job stress, tedium, and social support in the workplace. *Journal of Social and Personal Relationships, 11,* 555–572.

Gianakos, I. (2002). Predictors of coping with work stress: The influences of sex, gender role, social desirability, and locus of control. *Sex Roles, 46*(5/6), 149–158.

Glomb, T. M., Richman, W. L., Hulin, C. L., Drasgow, F., Schneider, K. T., & Fitzgerald, L. F. (1997). Ambient sexual harassment: An integrated model of antecedents and consequences. *Organizational Behavior and Human Decision Processes, 71*(3), 309–328.

Goldenhar, L. M., Swanson, N. G., Hurrell, J. J., Ruder, A., & Deddens, K. (1998). Stressors and adverse outcomes for female construction workers. *Journal of Occupational Health Psychology, 3,* 19–32.

Grandey, A. A., & Cropanzano, R. (1999). The conservation of resources model applied to work-family conflict and strain. *Journal of Vocational Behavior, 54,* 350–370.

Graves, L. M. (1999). Gender bias in interviewers' evaluations of applicants: When and how does it occur? In G. N. Powell (Ed.), *Handbook of gender and work* (pp. 145–164). Thousand Oaks, CA: Sage.

Greenglass, E. R. (1993). The contribution of social support to coping strategies. *Applied Psychology: An International Review, 42,* 323–340.

Greenglass, E. R. (2002). Work stress, coping, and social support: Implications for women's occupational well-being. In D. L. Nelson & R. J. Burke (Eds.), *Gender, work stress and health* (pp. 85–96). Washington, DC: American Psychological Association.

Greenglass, E. R., Fiksenbaum, L., & Burke, R. J. (1996). Components of social support, buffering effects and burnout: Implications of psychological functioning. *Anxiety, Stress, and Coping, 9,* 185–197.

Greenhaus, J. H., & Parasuraman, S. (1986). A work-nonwork interactive perspective of stress and its consequences. *Journal of Organizational Behavior Management, 8,* 37–60.

Greenhaus, J. H., & Parasuraman, S. (1999). Research on work, family, and gender: Current status and future direction. In G. N. Powell (Ed.), *Handbook of gender and work* (pp. 391–412). Thousand Oaks, CA: Sage.

Greenhaus, J. H., & Parasuraman, S. (2002). The allocation of time to work and family roles. In D. L. Nelson & R. J. Burke (Eds.), *Gender, work stress and health* (pp. 115–128). Washington, DC: American Psychological Association.

Grzywacz, J. G., & Marks, N. F. (2000). Reconceptualizing the work-family interface: An ecological perspective on the correlates of positive and negative spillover between work and family. *Journal of Occupational Health Psychology, 5*, 111–126.

Guelzow, M. G., Bird, G. W., & Koball, E. H. (1991). An exploratory path analysis of the stress process for dual-career men and women. *Journal of Marriage and the Family, 53*, 141–164.

Guppy, A., & Rick, J. (1996). The influence of gender and grade on perceived work stress and job satisfaction in white collar employees. *Work & Stress, 10*(2), 154–164.

Haddock, S. A., Zimmerman, T. S., & Lyness, K. P. (2003). Changing gender norms: Transitional dilemmas. In F. Walsh (Ed.), *Normal family practices* (3rd ed., pp. 301–336). New York: Guilford Press.

Haddock, S. A., Zimmerman, T. S., Ziemba, S. J., & Current, L. R. (2001). Ten adaptive strategies for family and work balance: Advice from successful families. *Journal of Marital & Family Therapy, 27*(4), 445–458.

Harvey, E. (1999). Short-term and long-term effects of early parental employment on children of the National Longitudinal Survey of Youth. *Developmental Psychology, 35*, 445–459.

Haynes, S. G., & Feinleib, M. (1980). Women, work and coronary heart disease: Prospective findings from the Framingham heart study. *American Journal of Public Health, 70*, 133–141.

Hobfoll, S. E., Dunahoo, C. L., Ben-Porath, Y., & Monnier, J. (1984). Gender and coping: The dual-axis model of coping. *American Journal of Community Psychology, 22*, 49–82.

Hochschild, A. (1989). *The second shift.* New York: Avon.

Holcomb, L. W. (1998). *Not guilty: The good news about working mothers.* New York: Scribner.

Hughes, D. L., & Galinsky, E. (1994). Gender, job and family conditions, and psychological symptoms. *Psychology of Women Quarterly, 18*, 251–270.

Hymowitz, C., & Schellhardt, T. D. (1986, March 24). The glass ceiling. *Wall Street Journal*, p. 1.

International Labour Office. (1996). *Yearbook of labour statistics* (55th ed.). Geneva: Author.

Jacobs, J. A. (1999). The sex segregation of occupations: Prospects for the 21st century. In G. N. Powell (Ed.), *Handbook of gender and work* (pp. 125–144). Thousand Oaks, CA: Sage.

Jick, T. D., & Mitz, L. F. (1985). Sex differences in work stress. *Academy of Management Review, 10*, 408–420.

Kahn, R. L., & Byosiere, P. (1992). Stress in organizations. In M. D. Dunnette, D. Marvin, & L. M. Hough (Eds.), *Handbook of industrial and organizational psychology* (Vol. 3, 2nd ed., pp. 571–650). Palo Alto, CA: Consulting Psychologists Press.

Kanter, R. M. (1990). Token women in the corporation. In J. Heeren & M. Mason (Eds.), *Sociology: Windows on society* (pp. 186–294). Los Angeles: Roxbury.

Kessler, R. C., & McLeod, J. D. (1984). Sex differences in vulnerability to undesirable life events. *American Sociological Review, 49,* 620–631.

Kinnunen, U., & Mauno, S. (1998). Antecedents and outcomes of work-family conflict among employed women and men in Finland. *Human Relations, 51,* 157–177.

Korabik, K. (1999). Sex and gender in the new millennium. In G. N. Powell (Ed.), *Handbook of gender and work* (pp. 3–16). Thousand Oaks, CA: Sage.

Kossek, E. E., & Ozeki, C. (1998). Work-family conflict, policies, and the job-life satisfaction relationship: A review and directions for organizational behavior-human resources research. *Journal of Applied Psychology, 83,* 139–149.

Kunkel, A. W., & Burleson, B. R. (1998). Social support and emotional lives of men and women: An assessment of the different culture perspective. In D. Canary & K. Dindia (Eds.), *Sex differences and similarities in communication.* London: Erlbaum.

Lambert, S. J. (1990). Processes linking work and family: A critical review and research agenda. *Human Relations, 43,* 239–257.

Larson, R. W., & Almeida, D. M. (1999). Emotional transmission in the daily lives of families: A new paradigm for studying family process. *Journal of Marriage and the Family, 61,* 5–20.

Levant, R. F., & Pollack, W. S. (1995). *A new psychology of men.* New York: Basic Books.

Maier, M. (1999). On the gendered substructure of organization: Dimensions and dilemmas of corporate masculinity. In G. N. Powell (Ed.), *Handbook of gender and work* (pp. 69–94). Thousand Oaks, CA: Sage.

Mainiero, L. A. (1986). Coping with powerlessness: The relationship of gender and job dependency to empowerment-strategy usage. *Administrative Science Quarterly, 31,* 633–653.

Marks, N. F. (1998). Does it hurt to care? Caregiving, work-family conflict, and midlife well-being. *Journal of Marriage and the Family, 60,* 951–960.

Martocchio, J. J., & O'Leary, A. M. (1989). Sex differences in occupational stress: A meta-analytic review. *Journal of Applied Psychology, 74,* 495–501.

Meeker, B. F., & Wetzel-O'Neill, P. A. (1985). Sex roles and interpersonal behavior in task-oriented groups. In J. Berger & M. Zelditch, Jr. (Eds.), *Status, rewards, and influence: How expectations organize behavior* (pp. 379–405). San Francisco: Jossey-Bass.

Melamed, T. (1995). Career success: The moderating effect of gender. *Journal of Vocational Behavior, 47,* 35–60.

Melamed, T. (1996). An assessment of a gender-specific model. *Journal of Occupational and Organizational Psychology, 69,* 217–242.

Melzer, S. A. (2002). Gender, work, and intimate violence: Men's occupational violence spillover and compensatory violence. *Journal of Marriage and the Family, 64*(4), 820–832.

Miller, K., Greyling, M., Cooper, C., Luo, L., Sparks, K., & Spector, P. E. (2000). Occupational stress and gender: A cross cultural study. *Stress Medicine, 16*(5), 271–278.

Mirowski, J., & Ross, C. E. (1995). Sex differences in distress: Real or artifact? *American Sociological Review, 60,* 449–468.

Moen, P., & Yu, Y. (2000). Effective work/life strategies: Working couples, work conditions, gender, and life quality. *Social Problems, 47,* 291–326.

Morrow, P. C., McElroy, J. C., & Phillips, C. M. (1994). Sexual harassment behaviors and work related perceptions and attitudes. *Journal of Vocational Behavior, 45,* 295–309.

Murphy, E. M. (2003). Being born female is dangerous to your health. *American Psychologist, 58*(3), 205–210.

Narayanan, L., Menon, S., & Spector, P. E. (1999). Stress in the workplace: A comparison of gender and occupations. *Journal of Organizational Behavior, 20,* 63–73.

National Institute of Child Health and Human Development Early Child Care Research Network. (1997). The effects of infant child care on infant-mother attachment security: Results of the NICHD Study of Early Child Care. *Child Development, 68,* 860–879.

Nelson, D. L., & Burke, R. J. (2002a). A framework for examining gender, work stress, and health. In D. L. Nelson & R. J. Burke (Eds.), *Gender, work stress and health* (pp. 3–14). Washington, DC: American Psychological Association.

Nelson, D. L., & Burke, R. J. (Eds.). (2002b). *Gender, work stress and health.* Washington, DC: American Psychological Association.

Nelson, D. L., & Quick, J. C. (1985). Professional women: Are distress and disease inevitable? *Academy of Management Review, 10,* 206–218.

Netemeyer, R. G., Boles, J. S., & McMurrian, R. (1996). Development and validation of work-family conflict and family-work conflict scales. *Journal of Applied Psychology, 81,* 400–410.

O'Farrell, B., & Harlan, S. L. (1982). Craftworkers and clerks: The effects of male coworker hostility on women's satisfaction with nontraditional jobs. *Social Problems, 29,* 252–264.

Olson, D. A., & Shultz, K. S. (1994). Gender differences in the dimensionality of social support. *Journal of Applied Social Psychology, 24,* 1221–1232.

Paden, S. L., & Buehler, C. (1995). Coping with the dual-income lifestyle. *Journal of Marriage and the Family, 57,* 101–110.

Parasuraman, S., & Greenhaus, J. H. (1993). Personal portraits: The life-style of the woman manager. In E. A. Fagenson (Ed.), *Women in management: Trends, issues, and challenges in managerial diversity* (Vol. 4, pp. 186–211). Newbury Park, CA: Sage.

Parasuraman, S., Greenhaus, J. H., & Granrose, C. S. (1992). Role stressors, social support and well-being among two-career couples. *Journal of Organizational Behavior, 13,* 339–356.

Parkin, W. (1993). The public and the private: Gender, sexuality and emotion. In S. Fineman (Ed.), *Emotion in organizations* (pp. 167–189). London: Sage.

Pearlin, L. I. (1975). Status inequality and stress in marriage. *American Sociological Review, 40*(3), 344–357.

Pearlin, L. I., & Lieberman, M. A. (1979). Sources of emotional distress. In R. Simmons (Ed.), *Research in community and mental health* (pp. 217–248). Greenwich, CT: JAI.

Perrewé, P. L., & Carlson, D. S. (2002). Do men and women benefit from social support equally? Results from a field examination within the work and family context. In D. L. Nelson & R. J. Burke (Eds.), *Gender, work stress and health* (pp. 101–114). Washington, DC: American Psychological Association.

Perry-Jenkins, M., Repetti, R. L., & Crouter, A. C. (2000). Work and family in the 1990s. *Journal of Marriage and the Family, 62,* 981–998.

Pfeffer, J., & Ross, J. (1982). The effects of marriage and a working wife on occupational and wage attainment. *Administrative Science Quarterly, 27,* 66–80.

Piltch, C. A., Walsh, D. C., Mangione, T. W., & Jennings, S. E. (1994). Gender, work, and mental distress in an industrial labor force: An expansion of Karasek's job strain model. In G. P. Keita & J. J. Hurrell, Jr. (Eds.), *Job stress in a changing workforce: Investigating gender, diversity, and family issues* (pp. 39–54). Washington, DC: American Psychological Association.

Piotrkowski, C. S. (1997). Sexual harassment. In J. M. Stellman (Ed.), *ILO encyclopaedia of occupational health and safety* (pp. 34.28–34.29). Geneva, Switzerland: International Labor Office & Chicago: Rand McNally.

Pleck, J. H. (1977). The work-family role system. *Social Problems, 24*(4), 417–427.

Pleck, J. H. (1981). *The myth of masculinity.* Cambridge: MIT Press.

Pollack, W. S. (1998). *Real boys.* New York: Henry Holt.

Powell, G. N. (Ed.). (1999a). *Handbook of gender and work.* Thousand Oaks, CA: Sage.

Powell, G. N. (1999b). Introduction: Examining the intersection of gender and work. In G. N. Powell (Ed.), *Handbook of gender and work* (pp. ix–xx). Thousand Oaks, CA: Sage.

Prior, J. B., LaVite, C. M., & Stoller, L. M. (1993). A social psychological analysis of sexual harassment: The person/situation interaction. *Journal of Vocational Behavior, 42,* 68–83.

Ptacek, J. T., Smith, R. E., & Dodge, K. L. (1994). Gender differences in coping with stress: When stressor and appraisals do not differ. *Personality and Social Psychology Bulletin, 20,* 421–430.

Ptacek, J. T., Smith, R. E., & Zanas, J. (1992). Gender, appraisal, and coping: A longitudinal analysis. *Journal of Personality, 60,* 747–770.

Pugliesi, K., & Shook, S. L. (1998). Gender, ethnicity, and network characteristics: Variation in social support resources. *Sex Roles, 38,* 215–238.

Real, T. (1997). *I don't want to talk about it: Overcoming the legacy of male depression.* New York: Fireside.

Repetti, R. L., & Wood, J. (1997). Effects of daily stress at work on mothers' interactions with preschoolers. *Journal of Family Psychology, 11,* 90–108.

Reskin, B. F., & Padavic, I. (1994). *Women and men at work.* Newbury Park, CA: Pine Forge.

Ridgeway, C. L., & Diekema, D. (1992). Are gender differences status differences? In C. L. Ridgeway (Ed.), *Gender, interaction, and inequality* (pp. 157–180). New York: Springer-Verlag.

Roos, P. A., & Gatta, M. L. (1999). The gender gap in earning: Trends, explanations, and prospects. In G. N. Powell (Ed.), *Handbook of gender and work* (pp. 95–124). Thousand Oaks, CA: Sage.

Rosenfield, S. (1992). The cost of sharing: Wives' employment and husbands' mental health. *Journal of Health and Social Behavior, 33,* 213–225.

Rosin, H. M., & Korabik, K. (1990). Marital and family correlates of women managers' attrition from organizations. *Journal of Vocational Behavior, 37,* 104–120.

Roxburgh, S. (1996). Gender differences in work and well-being: Effects of exposure and vulnerability. *Journal of Health and Social Behavior, 37,* 265–277.

Schneider, K. T. (1995). Bystander stress: The effect of organizational tolerance of sexual harassment on victims' co-workers. *Dissertation Abstracts International, 57*(08), 5375B.

Shaffer, M. A., Joplin, J. R., Bell, M. P., Lau, T., & Oguz, C. (2000). Gender discrimination and job-related outcomes: A cross-cultural comparison of working women in the United States and China. *Journal of Vocational Behavior, 57,* 395–427.

Simon, R. W. (1998). Assessing sex differences in vulnerability among employed parents: The importance of marital status. *Journal of Health & Social Behavior, 39,* 38–54.

Spielberger, C. D., & Reheiser, E. C. (1994). The job stress survey: Measuring gender differences in occupation stress. *Journal of Social Behavior and Personality, 9,* 199–218.

Stockdale, M. S. (Ed.). (1996). *Sexual harassment in the workplace: Perspectives, frontiers, and response strategies.* Thousand Oaks, CA: Sage.

Stroh, L. K., & Reilly, A. H. (1999). Gender and careers: Present experiences and emerging trends. In G. N. Powell (Ed.), *Handbook of gender and work* (pp. 307–324). Thousand Oaks, CA: Sage.

Tangri, S., Burt, M., & Johnson, L. (1982). Sexual harassment at work: Three explanatory models. *Journal of Social Issues, 38,* 33–54.

Taylor, S. E., Klein, L. C., Lewis, B. P., Gruenewald, T. L., Gurung, R. A. R., & Updegraff, J. A. (2000). Biobehavioral responses to stress in females: Tend and befriend, not fight or flight. *Psychological Review, 107,* 411–429.

Thoits, P. A. (1991). On merging identity theory and stress research. *Social Psychology Quarterly, 54*(2), 101–112.

Tousignant, M., Brosseau, R., & Tremblay, L. (1987). Sex biases in mental health scales: Do women tend to report less serious symptoms and confide more than men? *Psychological Medicine, 17,* 203–215.

Trocki, K. F., & Orilio, E. M. (1994). Gender differences in stress symptoms, stress-producing contexts, and coping strategies. In G. P. Keita & J. J. Hurrell, Jr. (Eds.), *Job stress in a changing workforce: Investigating gender, diversity, and family issues* (pp. 7–22). Washington, DC: American Psychological Association.

Vagg, P. R., Spielberger, C. D., & Wasala, C. F. (2002). Effects of organisational level and gender on stress in the workplace. *International Journal of Stress Management, 9*(4), 243–261.

Valdez, R. L., & Gutek, B. A. (1987). Family roles: A help or a hindrance for working women? In B. A. Gutek & L. Larwood (Eds.), *Women's career development* (pp. 157–169). Newbury Park, CA: Sage.

Van Emmerik, H. (2002). Gender differences in the effects of coping assistance on the reduction of burnout in academic staff. *Work & Stress, 16*(3), 251–263.

Vermeulen, M., & Mustard, C. (2000). Gender differences in job strain, social support at work, and psychological distress. *Journal of Occupational Health Psychology, 5*(4), 428–440.

Vingerhoets, A. J. M., & Van Heck, G. L. (1990). Gender, coping and psychosomatic symptoms. *Psychological Medicine, 20,* 125–135.

Voydanoff, P. (1988). Work role characteristics, family structure demands, and work/family conflict. *Journal of Marriage and the Family, 50,* 749–761.

Wade, T. J., & Cairney, J. (1997). Age and depression in a nationally representative sample of Canadians: A preliminary look at the National Population Health Survey. *Canadian Journal of Public Health, 88,* 297–302.

Wagner, D. G., & Berger, J. B. (1997). Gender and interpersonal task behaviors: Status expectations accounts. *Sociological Perspectives, 40,* 1–32.

Wahl, A. (Ed.). (1995). *Men's perceptions of women in management*. Stockholm: Fritzers.

Waldron, I., & Jacobs, J. A. (1989). Effects of multiple roles on women's health: Evidence from a national longitudinal study. *Women & Health, 15*, 3–19.

Walters, V. (1993). Stress, anxiety and depression: Women's accounts of their health problems. *Social Science and Medicine, 36*(4), 393–402.

Westman, M. (2002). Gender asymmetry in crossover research. In D. L. Nelson & R. J. Burke (Eds.), *Gender, work stress and health* (pp. 129–149). Washington, DC: American Psychological Association.

Wethington, E., & McLeod, J. D. (1987). The importance of life events for explaining sex differences in psychological distress. In R. C. Barnett, L. Biener, & G. K. Baruch (Eds.), *Gender and stress* (pp. 144–158). New York: Free Press.

Wiggins, J. S. (1992). Agency and communion as conceptual coordinates for the understanding and measurement of interpersonal behavior. In W. M. Grove & C. Cicchetti (Eds.), *Thinking clearly about psychology* (pp. 89–113). Minneapolis: University of Minnesota Press.

Williams, J. (1999). *Unbending gender: Why work and family conflict and what to do about it*. New York: Oxford University Press.

Williams, K. J., & Alliger, G. M. (1994). Role stressors, mood spillover, and perceptions of work-family conflict in employed parents. *Academy of Management Journal, 37*, 837–868.

Witkowski, K., & Leicht, K. T. (1995). The effects of gender segregation, labor force participation, and family roles on the earnings of young adult workers. *Work and Occupations, 22*, 48–72.

20 International and Cross Cultural Issues

Cong Liu
Paul E. Spector

In recent years, job stress has become one of the major topics of interest among organizational researchers. Whereas most studies have been concerned with uncovering general principles, a stream of research has looked at international issues to ascertain the influence of both cultural and national differences. Cross-cultural/cross-national research on job stress is of growing importance. The globalization of business means that many organizations will increasingly operate in different cultures. Cross-cultural/cross-national job stress research is vital in such situations because we cannot assume that U.S.- and Western-developed job stress theories apply to other countries (e.g., Trompenaars & Hampden-Turner, 1998). For example, the nature of job stressors and job strains can be different among employees with differing cultural or national backgrounds (Liu, 2003; Narayanan, Menon, & Spector, 1999). Bae and Chung (1997) suggested that labor policies, labor market, industrialization condition, and culture influence perceptions of work. Many factors have direct effects on employees' work stress across cultures. Research is needed to define the nature and magnitude of job stress experienced by people with different cultural/national backgrounds in order to develop appropriate interventions (National Institute of Occupational Safety and Health [NIOSH], 2000).

Several factors affect the variability of employees' job stress in international contexts. First, national policy on employment is closely associated with job stress. For example, unlike the United States, most European countries have national or state-run institutions providing comprehensive "free-at-source" health services for their populations (Cooper & Payne, 1992). Through these institutions, the state wholly underwrites the health services for their people. In the United States, many employees do not have medical insurance coverage from their employers, and they have to pay for their own medical treatment. Thus, employees from the European countries would be more likely to seek treatment for stress-related illnesses (Sutherland & Cooper, 1990), which might reduce their severity and long-term impact.

Second, the national economy affects employees' perceptions of their jobs (Sadri, Marcoulides, Cooper, & Kirkcaldy, 1996). In countries with higher unemployment rates, employees will find job insecurity to be a more important stressor than in countries with low unemployment rates. Furthermore, level of economic development can influence the nature of stressors experienced. For example, in poor countries, organizational constraints due to insufficient resources is a greater problem (Liu, 2003).

Third, and the most important factor, culture within country will have substantial impacts on employees' job stress. Culture-specific job stressors and strains have been shown to exist (Liu, 2003; Narayanan et al., 1999). It is possible that some common job stressors/strains in one country will not be important in another. Some researchers have also reported cross-national coping strategy differences that are attributed to culture (Cohen, 1976; Etzion, Kafry, & Pines, 1982).

Theoretical Models of Culture Applicable to International Populations

The purpose of cross-cultural/cross-national job stress research is to understand the impact of culture on different aspects of job stress, including job stressors, job strains, coping strategies, and the job stress process. Such research will also help practitioners design culture-specific stress management programs.

The primary reason to study culture is to help researchers better understand the variations of job stress for people with different backgrounds. Existing cultural theories have been adopted to guide cross-cultural research on job stress (e.g., Liu, 2003). Cultural researchers have tried to define a full range of cultural values to group and compare cultures (e.g., Hofstede, 1980; Hofstede, 1984; Inglehart, 1997; Schwartz, 1994; Schwartz, 1999; Triandis, 1994). In this chapter, we review two popular cultural theories.

Hofstede's Cultural Theory

Hofstede's (1980, 1984, 2001) cultural theory contains four important cultural dimensions. *Individualism/collectivism* (I/C) describes the relation between the individual and the group. *Individualism* represents the subordination of group goals to personal goals, a sense of independence, and lack of concern for people other than one's immediate family. *Collectivism* reflects the subordination of personal goals to group goals, a sense of harmony and interdependence, and concern for others (Hui & Triandis, 1986).

In collectivistic cultures, people belong to in-groups, and the groups are supposed to look after them.

Power distance (PDI) is related to social inequality and the amount of authority of one person over others (Hofstede, 1980, 1984, 2001). It refers to the extent to which the less powerful members accept the fact that power is distributed unequally. In low PDI cultures, people do not accept unequally distributed power. Accordingly, consultation and participation are preferred. In high PDI cultures, low power groups accept unequally distributed power. Accordingly, people in authority are highly respected and obeyed.

Masculinity/femininity concerns emphasis on achievement and ambition versus nurturance and well-being (Hofstede, 1980, 1984, 2001). Members from masculine cultures value wealth, independence, recognition, and careers. They emphasize earnings, advancement, and ambition at work. Members from feminine cultures value "nurturance, affiliation, helpfulness, and humility" (Hofstede, 1984, p. 178). They emphasize social networks and participation at work. Achievement in life is related to one's (friendly) work and living environment and the quality of interpersonal relationships.

Finally, *uncertainty avoidance* (UAI) focuses on individuals' feeling of an uncertain environment. People in low UAI cultures value change, risk taking, and adventure. People in high UAI cultures are traditional and resistant to change. They prefer high security and have less tolerance of uncertainty.

Hofstede (1984) pointed out that countries are different on the levels of each cultural value. Using these cultural values, we can describe the cultural differences among countries. Table 20.1 presents such differences across 40 countries. Tables 20.1 and 20.2 were developed based on Hofstede's (1984) and Schwartz's (1999) original work. However, because neither of these authors clearly indicated the cultural values (in terms of high/low) for each country/cultural group, we redefined this by scrutinizing Hofstede's tables (Hofstede, 1984, p. 315) and Schwartz's co-plot (Schwartz, 1999, p 36). For example, for individualism, we gave a *high* to countries that received a score above the average score. For Schwartz's (1999) cultural value, we observed the co-plot and assigned *high* or *low* based on distance from the center.

Schwartz's Culture Model

Schwartz's (1994, 1999) cultural model has important implications for international job stress research. According to Schwartz (1999), there are three basic issues existing in all societies. Seven cultural values are structured along these three issues as three polar dimensions. Furthermore, Schwartz (1994, 1999) grouped countries in terms of the similarity and difference of these cultural values existing in each country.

The first dimension describes the relation between the individual and the group. This dimension is analogous to Hofstede's (1980, 1984, 2001) individualism/collectivism. One pole of this dimension describes cultures in which the members are viewed as autonomous individuals. In these cultures, people

Table 20.1   Hofstede's Cultural Value Differences Across 40 Countries

	Individualism/ Collectivism	Power Distance	Masculinity/ Femininity	Uncertainty Avoidance
Australia, Canada, Great Britain, Ireland, New Zealand, South Africa, Switzerland, USA	High Ind.	Low	High Masc.	Low
Austria, Germany, Italy,	High Ind.	Low	High Masc.	High
Brazil, Chile, Peru, Portugal, Taiwan, Thailand, Turkey, Yugoslavia	High Col.	High	High Fem.	High
Colombia, Greece, Japan, Mexico, Pakistan, Venezuela	High Col.	High	High Masc.	High
Denmark, Finland, Netherlands, Norway, Sweden	High Ind.	Low	High Fem.	Low
France, Spain	High Ind.	High	High Fem.	High
Hong Kong, India, Philippines	High Col.	High	High Masc.	Low
Iran, Singapore	High Col.	High	High Fem.	Low
Argentina	High Col.	Low	High Masc.	High
Belgium	High Ind.	High	High Masc.	High
Israel	High Ind.	Low	High Fem.	High

find their life meaning through their uniqueness and through seeking their own success and interests (*autonomy*). There are two types of autonomy. *Intellectual autonomy* emphasizes people's independent ideas and intellectual directions, whereas *affective autonomy* emphasizes people's independent feelings and emotions. The other pole of the dimension describes cultures in which the individual is embedded in the collectivity. In these cultures, people find the meaning of life mainly through social relationships and group interests (*conservatism*).

The second dimension describes how societies control responsible behavior. One way to ensure responsible social behaviors is through power differences based on legitimacy of an unequal distribution of power, authority, and resources. The value-type correspondent to this is *hierarchy*. The other way to ensure such behaviors is to educate members to cooperate voluntarily with others sharing the same basic interests as moral equals (*egalitarianism*). This dimension is similar to Hofstede's (1980, 1984, 2001) power distance.

The third dimension describes the relation between humankind and the natural and social world. One pole of this dimension encourages members to concur with the world and to get ahead with active self-assertion (*mastery*). On the opposite pole, members try to fit into nature and the social world rather than change them (*harmony*).

According to Schwartz (1994, 1999), countries are different in terms of the levels of these basic cultural values. Table 20.2 presents the differences of cultural values across countries.

Table 20.2 Schwartz's Cultural Value Differences Across 44 Countries

	Intellectual Autonomy	Affective Autonomy	Conservatism	Egalitarianism	Hierarchy	Mastery	Harmony
English-speaking[a]	moderate	high	low	moderate	moderate	high	low
West Europe[b]	high	high	low	high	low	low	high
East Europe[c]	moderate	low	high	low	low	low	high
Latin America[d]	moderate	moderate	high	moderate	high	moderate	moderate
Islam[e]	low	low	high	low	high	moderate	moderate
Far East[f]	low	low	high	low	high	moderate	low

a. Australia, Canada, New Zealand, United States
b. Germany, France, Italy, Netherlands, Spain, Switzerland
c. Bulgaria, Czech Republic, Hungary, Poland, Russia
d. Brazil, Mexico, Venezuela
e. Israel (Arab), Malaysia, Turkey
f. China, India, Singapore, Taiwan, Thailand

Cultural Groups Around the World

Because the cultural values proposed by the above cultural theories are "basic values" across societies, it is possible to compare national cultures in terms of the relative level of each value. Indeed, both Hofstede and Schwartz grouped countries based on the similarities and differences of culture values. As can be seen from Table 20.2, Schwartz's (1999) study revealed six cultural groups around the world: (a) English-speaking (e.g., Australia, Canada, New Zealand, and the United States), (b) West Europe (e.g., France, Germany, Italy, Netherlands, Spain, and Switzerland), (c) East Europe (e.g., Bulgaria, Czech Republic, Hungary, Poland, and Russia), (d) Latin America (e.g., Brazil, Mexico, and Venezuela), (e) Islam (e.g., Israel [Arab], Malaysia, and Turkey), and (f) Far East (e.g., China, India, Singapore, Taiwan, and Thailand). A graphic representation is available for these six meaningful cultural groups (see Schwartz, 1999, p. 36). The distances among the countries on the graph reflect the cultural similarities and the dissimilarities among the countries.

Such cultural groupings are related to geographical proximity and a number of factors such as shared history, religion, level of development, and cultural contact (see Schwartz & Bardi, 1997; Schwartz & Ros, 1995). Countries within the same cultural group share these basic values, other aspects of culture, and often language. For example, countries in the English-speaking group and the West Europe group have a high level of autonomy and low level of conservatism. On the other hand, countries in the Far East group and the Islam group, and some countries in the East Europe group, have a high level of conservatism and a low level of autonomy. Countries within cultural groups are considered more similar than countries between cultural groups (see Table 20.2).

Populations with different cultural values might perceive their jobs in different ways. Peterson et al. (1995) collected data for role conflict, role ambiguity, and role overload from middle managers from 21 nations. I/C and power distance at the country level were found to be the cultural dimensions that most closely related to the role stressors. Compared with personal and organizational characteristics, role stressors varied substantially more by country/culture. National characteristics other than values can also be related to job stressors (e.g., job control). Grob and Flammer (1999) investigated perceived control among adolescents from seven eastern European countries (Bulgaria, the Czech Republic, Hungary, Poland, Romania, Russia, and Transylvania), five western European countries (Finland, France, Germany, Norway, and Switzerland), and the United States. They concluded that national characteristics, such as the nations' GNP, country size, population, and population density, were significantly related to people's perceived control. People from countries with higher GNP, larger size, and larger population perceived higher levels of control. However, adolescents from countries with high population densities had lower levels of control.

Most of the cross-cultural/national research simply compares job stress across countries without studying the framework of cultural theories. A few studies used the cross-cultural theories to guide their comparisons of related basic cultural values with job stress variables. For example, in their 24-nation/territory study, Spector et al. (2001) related individualism to employees' well-being at the national level. Liu (2003) compared American with Chinese employees and Narayanan et al. (1999) compared American with Indian employees on their job stressors and job strains using Hofstede's (1980, 1984, 2001) cultural theory as a guide. Peterson et al. (1995) related Hofstede's (1980, 1984, 2001) cultural values (I/C and PDI) to role stressors in their 21-nation study. Clearly, there is a lack of cross-cultural job stress research with a theoretical basis.

Cultural Effects on Job Stress

Culture can have a substantial influence on employees' job stress. Culture is part of both the work environment and the individual. Because culture is part of the environment, it influences the types of job stressors that exist. Because culture is also part of the individual, it influences how the potential stressors are perceived and what kind of strains and coping strategies might be taken (Beehr & Glazer, 2001). People with different cultural backgrounds may experience unique sets of job stressors and job strains (Laungani, 1993). Basic cultural values perform an important role in explaining these differences.

Cultural Effects on Job Stressors

Individualism/collectivism (I/C). The value dimension that has received the most attention in job stress research is individualism/collectivism. I/C affects employees' perceptions about their work settings in many ways. First, I/C influences employees' perceptions about job control. Human beings desire control over their environment (Averill, 1973). Even simply having the illusion of control is comforting (Friedland, Keinan, & Regev, 1992). Prominent theories have listed lack of job control as one of the most important stressors, and as an important moderator of the effects of other stressors, and have linked it in various forms to employee health problems (e.g., Ganster & Fusilier, 1989; Hackman & Oldham, 1976; Karasek, 1979; Spector, 1986).

In a consideration of lack of job control as a stressor, culture is an essential factor. To some cultures, lack of job control is very stressful, whereas for other cultures it may not be. For example, members from individualistic countries are taught to value independence and control in life. They prefer to have direct control over various aspects of life including work. Accordingly, in work settings, members from individualistic cultures will tend to seek high levels of job control. Lack of such control will put the employee in an unpleasant situation. On the other hand, members from collectivistic countries value compliance and interdependence. Collectivistic members view the group as having legitimate control over their actions (Triandis, 1988). They do not expect to have as much job control as members of individualistic cultures (Ho & Chiu, 1994; Triandis, 1988). Thus, collectivists may not be as affected as individualists by not having job control. Narayanan et al. (1999) compared job stressors between individualistic Americans and collectivistic Indians in a study in which participants were asked to describe the most stressful event that occurred to them at work in the prior month. Although 22.6% of the American sample reported lack of job control as the stressor, none of the Indians reported it.

Research supports the idea that members of collectivistic cultures tend to be lower than members of individualistic cultures on perceived control (Hamid, 1994; Hui, 1982; Smith, Trompenaars, & Dugan, 1995). Lundberg and Peterson (1994) found that Japanese considered autonomy less important than did Americans. Bae and Chung (1997) reported that job autonomy in Korean industries was lower than it was in the United States. Analyzing Rotter's (1966) locus-of-control scale data provided by employees in business organizations in 43 countries, Smith et al. (1995) found that participants from individualistic Western countries more frequently endorsed indices for control than participants from collectivistic countries. In another study, American students scored higher on the need for autonomy than Indian and Chinese students (Singh, Huang, & Thompson, 1962). Furthermore, Oishi, Diener, Lucas, and Suh (1999) found that for American participants, autonomy positively correlated with life satisfaction; however, the correlation between autonomy and life satisfaction for Chinese participants was not significant. Thus, lack of autonomy might not be an important stressor to collectivists.

Second, I/C influences employees' perceptions about interpersonal relationships. Poor interpersonal relationships may have a negative impact on an individual's life (Berscheid & Reis, 1998). Individualists do not have as much concern for others beyond their immediate family as do collectivists (Hui & Triandis, 1986). Due to self-orientation and emotional independence, individualists believe that they have the right to take care of themselves and have a private life (Ho & Chiu, 1994). Going on one's own way and not paying attention to the views of others is acceptable. They make decisions more independently (Hui & Triandis, 1986). Individualistic members tend to keep interpersonal relationships with people beyond their immediate family more distant (Hui & Triandis, 1986).

On the other hand, members of collectivistic cultures are more susceptible to social influence because of the collectivity orientation and emotional dependency (Hui & Triandis, 1986). Private lives in these cultures are invaded by groups to which they belong. People share material benefits, nonmaterial resources (e.g., time, affection, and fun), and outcomes (Hui & Triandis, 1986). Collectivists have feelings of involvement in and contribution to the lives of others. Other people's experiences could have direct or indirect consequences for their own lives (Hui & Triandis, 1986). Interpersonal relations are more important, and interdependence is highly emphasized in collectivistic cultures. For example, interpersonal relationship is an essential part of the lives of Chinese and Japanese people. To be effective in such an environment, one must cultivate relationships with colleagues at all levels, and one must express a high level of social sensitivity. People may even attempt to influence powerful others through good relations in order to exert control (Kim, Triandis, Kagitçibasi, Choi, & Yoon, 1994). Accordingly, interpersonal relationships and conflicts in these cultures are more complicated than they are in individualistic cultures.

Empirical studies have supported these notions. Triandis, Bontempo, Villareal, and Asai (1988) pointed out that I/C is the key dimension in determining differences among cultures in social relationships. Gudykunst and Nishida (1986) presented a framework for theories of communication in interpersonal relationships in cross-cultural contexts. Investigating university students from Japan and the United States, they found strong support for the importance of I/C in understanding perceptions of interpersonal relationships as well as perceptions of the degree of personalization, synchrony, and difficulty of communication associated with relationships. In individualistic cultures, employees differentiated interpersonal relationships and task relationships, whereas in collectivistic cultures, interpersonal relationships were the basis for effective job performance.

Power distance (PDI). PDI is another cultural dimension affecting employees' job stressors (Cooper & Payne, 1992). Some unique job stressors are attached to high PDI cultures. For example, in high PDI cultures, it is unacceptable to question the decision of superiors, and subordinates are under pressure to meet demands of superiors. Thus, low control and high demands might be characteristic of such workplaces. Such a combination of working conditions has been noted as particularly stressful (Karasek, 1979). In high PDI cultures, lack of structure/clarity would likely be an important issue because employees will feel obligated to follow rules and directions (e.g., Kakar, 1978). Furthermore, in their cross-national study of stressful incidents, Narayanan et al. (1999) found that one of the most mentioned stressors by Indians was being given too little direction by supervisors. By comparison, not one of their American participants reported having too little direction.

Cultural Effects on Job Strains

Employees' job strains and well-being have been shown to relate to country and culture (e.g., Diener & Suh, 1999; Narayanan et al., 1999; Spector et al., 2001). I/C is an important cultural dimension that might be expected to influence employees' well-being. There are two competing tendencies of such influences. On one hand, individualistic cultures emphasize independence, freedom, rights, and one's own needs, whereas collectivistic cultures emphasize interdependence and harmony, acceptance of one's fate, and other people's needs. Collectivism represents the superordination of group goals over personal goals. Members from such cultures are expected to subordinate personal goals and interests to the interests of other people, especially the powerful authorities (Radhakrishnan & Chan, 1997). Accordingly, collectivists are educated to sacrifice personal well-being for group interests, harmony, and well-being, whereas individualists focus attention on their own well-being. Thus, individuals in an individualistic society will have greater individual well-being because they take actions to enhance that well-being (e.g., Reykowski, 1994). Further, it is more important for collectivists to follow cultural norms than to maximize one's own interests such as pleasure (Rozin, 1999; Suh, Diener, Oishi, & Triandis, 1998). Rozin (1999) found that far more American than Indian students consider a pleasant outcome (vs. an unpleasant outcome) as an important issue. For Americans, doing something pleasant is very important for one's successful life, whereas for Indians this is not always the case (Rozin, 1999). Job (dis)satisfaction, an important indicator of work adjustment and well-being, has received attention by cross-cultural researchers as an important psychological strain. Higher job satisfaction has generally been found in individualistic than in collectivistic countries. Thus, members of individualistic cultures have higher levels of well-being than members of collectivistic cultures (Diener & Suh, 1999; Veenhoven, 1993).

Contrary to the above function, I/C also influences employees' job strain in an opposite direction. To understand the second function of I/C, we must involve another important job stress concept—social support. There are two types of social support: structural support and functional support (Cohen & Wills, 1985). *Structural support* refers to the existence of supportive others. *Functional support* represents functions that the supportive others perform. Functional support includes emotional support and instrumental support (Caplan, Cobb, French, Harrison, & Pinneau, 1975). *Emotional support* will help the person experience positive emotions, whereas *instrumental support* will help the individual to solve problems. According to Beehr and Glazer (2001), if a person receives enough social support, the link between job stressors and job strains will be weakened. This is known as the buffering or moderating effect. Social support might also have a direct effect on job strains. Getting enough support from others may directly reduce job strains.

I/C influences social support. The type and the source of social support are different across countries. In collectivistic countries, people value close interpersonal relationships and provide a stronger social network, whereas in individualistic cultures, a relatively loose interpersonal network is manifested. Sinha (1988) has suggested that social support in collectivistic countries (e.g., India) serves to protect well-being and lower job stress, whereas in individualistic societies, a type of alienation may be a potential threat for emotional problems. Kamal, Phil, and Jain (1988) found that because collectivistic families (joint families) provided more social support, less work stress and mental illness were experienced by collectivistic family members than by single family members. They suggested that the family system in some collectivistic countries (e.g., India) could be a potential culture-based factor for reducing job stress. Studying the link between family support system and mental health, Teja (1978) concluded that, in general, the higher incidence of mental problems in the United States was related to the individualistic culture, whereas in collectivistic India, the interdependence and cohesiveness of the family support system resulted in a relatively lower incidence of such problems in Indian patients.

The two competing tendencies of cultural influence on employees' job strain and well-being complicate the process. We know of no study that has tried to disentangle the process of two tendencies in a cross-cultural context. Perhaps the social support of collectivism lowers certain types of strains and stressors, whereas individualism's greater focus on the individual helps with other aspects of well-being. More research needs to be done to better understand the process.

Other cultural/national characteristics may also play roles on the cross-cultural differences of employees' job strains and well-being. For example, financial satisfaction is more important for employees' well-being in wealthy countries than in poor countries (Veenhoven, 1991). Grob (2000) argued that people from Western countries (including west European countries and the United States) had better well-being than people from the former socialist countries. McCormick and Cooper (1988) found that employees' job strains were lower in economically developed countries than in developing countries.

Cultural Effects on Coping Strategies

In the past 20 years, most coping researchers have based their work on the research of Lazarus and his colleagues (e.g., Lazarus, 1991; Lazarus & Folkman, 1984). Two types of coping strategies for dealing with job stress have been studied: *emotion-focused strategies* and *problem-focused strategies* (Lazarus, 1991). Problem-focused strategies have been found to be more effective than emotion-focused strategies for enhancing well-being (Grob, 2000).

Employees' coping strategies are likely influenced by culture values. For example, in high PDI cultures, attempting to change the environment (including changing the behavior of one's supervisor) can be risky. Therefore, changing oneself (emotion-focused coping) is the more feasible method for people from high PDI cultures. Some psychological mechanisms are likely to be used by high PDI members to deal with job stress: for example, *projection, rationalization,* and *denial* (Cooper & Payne, 1992). By using projection, low power members can protect self-esteem by projecting the unreached standards placed by powerful authorities onto other people. Rationalization refers to the ability to view the unsatisfying fact as "this is what it ought to be." Finally, with denial, low power members simply deny the stressful incident happened at work.

An important form of coping is conflict management. In conflict situations, employees from different cultures will have different conflict management styles. I/C has been used to explain conflict style differences across cultures (Trubisky, Ting-Toomey, & Lin, 1991). Rahim's model of conflict management has identified five conflict-handling styles (e.g., Rahim, 1992; Rahim & Magner, 1995) reflecting different degrees of concern for parties involved in the conflict. First, the *integrating style* is concerned with collaboration between conflict parties. It involves high concern for both parties. Second, the *obliging style* focuses on the agreement but not the differences between parties. It involves low concern for both parties. Third, the *dominating style* is to force one's viewpoint at the expense of the other party. It involves a high concern for self and a low concern for others. Fourth, the *avoiding style* has been described as withdrawing from the conflict situation. It involves low concern for both parties. Fifth, the *compromising style* is described as searching for a middle-ground solution. It is associated with moderate concern for both parties. One important feature of individualistic cultures is the emphasis on individual goals, achievement, and autonomy; on the other hand, collectivistic cultures stress group goals. Collectivists value harmony and interdependence. Thus, members of individualistic and collectivistic cultures would prefer different conflict management styles when dealing with the interpersonal conflict (e.g., Trubisky et al., 1991; Elsayed- Ekhouly & Buda, 1996). Hall (1976) found that individualists tended to emphasize explicit and direct verbal interaction, linear logic patterns, and autonomous orientation whereas collectivists tended to emphasize implicit and indirect verbal interaction, spiral logic patterns, and group orientation. When dealing with interpersonal conflicts, individualistic Americans prefer a direct style of communication that emphasizes the values of autonomy and competitiveness and the need for control. On the other hand, collectivistic members prefer an indirect style of communication that emphasizes the value of passive compliance and maintaining relational harmony in conflict interactions (Chua & Gudykunst, 1987).

Empirical Comparisons of Stressors Across Countries

Cross-National Studies of Job Stressors

Many researchers have studied job stressors in a cross-national context. Many of these studies do not draw particular inferences to underlying cultural characteristics. Most of these studies have collected job stressor data with rating scales and compared the job stressor data across nations. Cooper and Hensman (1985), for example, compared job stressors among senior and chief executives from 10 countries including Brazil, Egypt, Germany, Japan, Nigeria, Singapore, South Africa, Sweden, the United Kingdom, and the United States. They found that the principal stressors for executives from developed countries were work overload (including time pressures, deadlines, and long working hours) and consequent interpersonal problems with colleagues and families, whereas for executives from developing countries, the principal stressors concerned lack of autonomy.

Harari, Jones, and Sek (1988) studied job stress in the United States and Poland. Their study showed that these two countries were different on the perceptions of job stress. Although Americans had more internal locus of control, Poles exhibited more external locus of control. For Americans, internal locus of control moderated the relationship between job stressors and strains. For the Poles, locus of control didn't moderate the stressor-strain relationship.

Hurrell and Lindstrom's (1992) studies revealed that Finnish managers had lower levels of job stressors (e.g., workload, lack of job clarity, intragroup and intergroup conflict, and limited promotion opportunities) than Americans. Kirkcaldy and Cooper (1992) found that German managers expressed higher levels of job stressors than British managers, particularly with organizational structure and climate, career and achievement, and home/work interface. A study of senior police officers from Berlin and Northern Ireland also showed that the German officers had higher levels of stressors, especially for the problems of work/family conflict and career and achievement (Kirkcaldy & Cooper, 1994).

Some researchers have studied job stressors between Eastern and Western countries. DeFrank, Ivancevich, and Schweiger (1988) examined global job stress (a global measure of perceived stress during the last month), specific stressors (e.g., role ambiguity, role conflict, and quantitative and qualitative overload), and job satisfaction among samples of lower-, middle-, and upper-level managers in the United States, India, and Japan. They found that Japanese reported the highest level on both global stress and specific job stressors, whereas Americans reported the lowest level on these stressors. Japanese employees were less satisfied with their jobs than American employees. Bae and Chung (1997) investigated work attitudes among American, Japanese, and Korean workers. Compared with American employees, Korean employees perceived job insecurity as a more important job stressor. Korean employees also had less autonomy at work than American employees. Interestingly, most Korean workers had good job satisfaction but didn't want to take the same jobs if they could decide all over again (Bae & Chung, 1997). Korean and Japanese workers were similar on teamwork, supervision style, and specific work values.

Spector, Sanchez, Siu, Salgado, & Ma (2004) studied job stressors among employed college students and university support personnel from mainland China, Hong Kong, and the United States. They found significant differences among employees from these three samples on role ambiguity, role conflict, job autonomy, and interpersonal conflict. Role ambiguity was significantly higher in those from Hong Kong than in those from the United States and China, but it was significantly higher in the United States than in mainland China. For role conflict, although there was no significant difference between Hong Kong and mainland China, Hong Kong and mainland

China were significantly higher than the United States. For perceived job autonomy, mainland China and the United States were significantly higher than Hong Kong. Finally, Hong Kong reported the highest level of interpersonal conflict, mainland China scored in the middle, and the United States was the lowest. Liu (2003) found that American employees perceived a higher level of job autonomy than Chinese employees.

Some researchers have used qualitative methods to study specific job stressors in different countries. For example, Narayanan et al. (1999) examined occupational stress for female clerical employees from an Eastern country, India, and a Western country, the United States. They used the open-ended methodology (stressful incident record [SIR]; Keenan & Newton, 1985) to let participants describe a concrete stressful event that happened at work. For Indian employees, the most mentioned job stressors were lack of structure/clarity, lack of reward and recognition, equipment problems and situational constraints, and interpersonal conflict. On the other hand, American employees reported work overload, lack of control/ autonomy, interpersonal conflict, and the perception that time/effort was wasted. Only interpersonal conflict was common to both samples.

Liu (2003) also used the SIR method (Keenan & Newton, 1985) to collect qualitative job stressor data in China and the United States. She found that employees from these two countries reported different types of stressful incidents. For both countries, frequently reported stressor incidents included organizational constraints (including physical employment conditions, lack of training, team problems, equipment problems, and lack of structure), interpersonal conflict, heavy workload, and time pressure. However, the Chinese sample also reported mistakes at work and job evaluations and exams as important job stressors, whereas Americans reported lack of control as an important job stressor. Chinese employees had more indirect interpersonal conflict, whereas American employees reported more direct interpersonal conflict.

Cross-National Studies of Job Strains

Psychological strains, physical strains, and employees' well-being have been studied in cross-national contexts. Comparing former socialist countries (the countries of eastern and central Europe, such as Bulgaria, the Czech Republic, Hungary, Poland, Romania, Russia, and Transylvania) to western European countries (Finland, France, Germany, Norway, French-speaking part of Switzerland, German-speaking part of Switzerland), and the United States, Grob (2000) concluded that former socialist countries had a lower level of subjective well-being than Western societies, perhaps due to the lower level of economic development in the socialist countries. This finding is consistent with Diener and Diener's (1995) assumption that people's subjective well-being is related to the wealth of the country, with a higher level of income related to better well-being.

Consistently, it has been noted that employees' job strains are higher in some developing countries than in more developed countries (e.g., McCormick & Cooper, 1988). Cooper and Hensman's (1985) 10-country (Brazil, Egypt, Germany, Japan, Nigeria, Singapore, South Africa, Sweden, the United Kingdom, and the United States) comparison of senior and chief executives showed that executives from countries undergoing large economic and social change (e.g., Brazil, Egypt, Nigeria, and Singapore) reported more mental health problems (e.g., anxiety, depression, and psychosomatic tendencies) and lower levels of job satisfaction than those from developed countries (e.g., Germany, Sweden, and the United States). McCormick and Cooper (1988) extended the above study by including executives from New Zealand. They found that New Zealand executives reported better mental health than did those from all other countries but Sweden. New Zealand executives had the highest level of job satisfaction.

Previous research has also shown that employees' well-being is better in individualistic than in collectivistic countries. DeFrank, Matteson, Schweiger, and Ivancevich (1985) investigated management practices of American and Japanese CEOs and found that Japanese CEOs experienced more strains at work and were less able to discharge tension. DeFrank et al. (1988) found that Japanese scored higher than Americans on tension and somatic symptoms. Iwata, Okuyama, Kawakami, and Saito (1989) reported a higher level of depressive symptoms in Japanese than in the United States. Spector et al. (2002) found in their 24-nation/territory study of job stress that those in collectivistic countries (e.g., China, Hong Kong, Japan, and Taiwan) had more overall psychological and physical strain than those in individualistic countries (e.g., Germany and the United States). Spector et al. (2004) examined employees' psychological strains and well-being, such as work anxiety and intent to quit, in mainland China, Hong Kong, and the United States. Hong Kong reported the highest work anxiety, followed by mainland China and the United States. For intent to quit, mainland China was the highest, Hong Kong was in the middle, and the United States was lowest. Liu (2003) found that Chinese employees reported significantly more physical symptoms than American employees. Perhaps this is because individualistic countries value high levels of independence and control. Grob's (2000) 14-nation study found that control expectancy positively correlated with participants' subjective well-being.

Other researchers have compared employees' job strains and well-being in individualistic countries. Cohen (1976) found that German employees had higher levels of psychological and physical anxiety than American employees. On the other hand, Kirkcaldy and Cooper (1992) found that even with higher levels of job-related pressure, German managers had significantly better mental health than British managers. They attributed this to better coping by the German mangers. Harari et al. (1988) found that Poles rated higher on anxiety and depression than Americans. Spector et al.'s (2001) study also indicated that Poles had higher psychological and physical strains than Americans.

Schaufeli and Janczur's (1994) study found that Polish nurses were significantly more burned out than Dutch nurses, reflected on all dimensions of the Maslach burnout inventory. Hurrell and Lindstrom (1992) described how managers in Finland and the United States differed on job strains. Although Finnish managers had more heart symptoms and stomach problems, the U.S. managers experienced more headaches and more sleep disturbance.

Many cross-cultural studies have been done for job satisfaction. Kirkcaldy and Cooper (1992), for example, found that German managers had lower job satisfaction than British managers. In Spector et al.'s (2002) 24-nation/territory study, the individualistic samples (e.g., Canada, Israel, and the United States) were among the highest for job satisfaction, whereas Japan, China, and Hong Kong scored the lowest (Taiwan was in the middle). For both job and life satisfaction, the United States was higher than mainland China (Spector et al., 2004). Liu (2003) found that American employees reported significantly higher levels of job satisfaction than their Chinese counterparts. American CEOs had a higher level of job satisfaction than their Japanese counterparts (DeFrank et al., 1985). DeFrank et al. further confirmed that American managers (including lower-, middle-, and upper-level managers) were more satisfied with their jobs than Japanese managers. In fact, many studies reported that Americans experience a higher level of job satisfaction than Japanese (Bae & Chung, 1997; Lincoln, Hanada, & Olson, 1981; McCormick & Cooper, 1988; Smith & Misumi, 1989).

Some qualitative studies have also reported that the frequency or level of strain is different and that people in different cultures tend to respond to stressors with different strains. Narayanan et al.'s (1999) qualitative study revealed that Indian and American employees were different in the type of psychological strains they reported in response to stressors. For Indian employees, the top three psychological strains reported were resignation/acceptance, disappointment, and disgust. For American employees, the top three psychological strains were frustration, annoyance, and anger. Liu (2003) found that employees from China and the United States also reported different psychological and physical strains. Whereas employees from both countries reported worried/pressured/nervous and angry/annoyed/mad, Chinese employees reported far more incidents of worry/pressured/nervous than their American counterparts. Helplessness was a unique strain for Chinese employees, whereas frustration was only reported by the American sample. Chinese and American employees also reported different physical strains. Both Chinese and Americans reported fatigue, but whereas Chinese reported sleep problems, Americans reported stomach disorders.

Cross-National Studies of Stress Coping Strategies

Stress coping strategies have been studied in cross-national contexts. Different populations tend to adopt different coping strategies for job stress. Kirkcaldy and Cooper (1992) found that German and British managers used different coping strategies. German managers scored higher than their

British counterparts on reorganizing work, making work more interesting, time management, and social support. British managers scored higher on home and work relations. Interestingly, Kirkcaldy and Cooper (1992) found that British managers tended to separate job and off-work domains whereas German managers exhibited compensation between these areas of life. Similarly, in another study, Kirkcaldy and Cooper (1994) found that a greater variety of coping strategies was reported by German than Northern Ireland police officers.

Finnish and American managers also reported different coping strategies (Hurrell & Lindstrom, 1992). Finnish managers' coping strategies included internalizing the problem and problem solving. On the other hand, American managers used more communicating with others and daydreaming.

Narayanan et al. (1999) found that Indian and American employees reported different coping strategies to mitigate stress. For Indian employees, the most frequently reported methods were talking to either family members or friends or doing nothing (acceptance), whereas the most frequently used method for American employees was talking to coworkers. Americans tended to take more direct action by talking to their coworkers (probably the source of the problem), whereas Indians talked to family members or friends who provided emotional comfort but couldn't help directly.

There are cross-national differences in people's conflict management styles as well. Trubisky et al. (1991) compared the conflict-handling style differences between the United States and Taiwan. Although Americans preferred the dominating style, Taiwanese scored higher on all other conflict-handling styles. Elsayed-Ekhouly and Buda (1996) investigated the conflict management styles of American and Arab Middle Eastern executives. Whereas American executives preferred dominating, compromising, and obliging styles, Arab Middle Eastern executives had significantly higher scores on both integrating and avoiding styles. Comparing American to Chinese university employees, Liu (2003) found that whereas Americans had more direct interpersonal conflict (e.g., yielding and being rude to other people), Chinese tended to engage in indirect and passive actions (e.g., doing nasty things behind people's backs).

Cross-National Studies of the Process of Job Stress

Not many job stress researchers have addressed the issue of the job stress process across countries/cultures. Agarwal (1993) compared salespeople's job stress process in the United States and India. He found that the effect of formalization on role stressors in these two countries was different. Generally speaking, organizational formalization, such as job codification and rule observation, had a greater dysfunctional influence on role stressors (e.g., role ambiguity and role conflict) for the American sample than for the Indian sample.

It seems likely that the underlying stress process (e.g., how stressors result in strain) is generalizable to different nations, although the specific stressors and strains might differ (Glazer, 1999). Comparing the stress process between German and British managers, Kirkcaldy and Cooper (1992) found that though the two samples showed significant mean differences on job stressors, strains, and coping strategies, respectively, the correlations among these variables were the same. Sadri et al. (1996) extended the above study by examining the generalizability of Sadri and Marcoulides's (1994) occupational stress model across Great Britain, the United States, and the Federal Republic of Germany. Using LISREL VIII (Jöreskog & Sörbom, 1993) to test the invariance of the proposed model across three countries, Sadri et al. (1996) found that the model fairly accurately reflected the observed variability in each sample. A large portion of variability in outcomes (e.g., psychological strains, physiological symptoms, and job satisfaction) can be accounted for by the other stress variables (e.g., job stressors and coping strategies) across each of the three countries, indicating the invariability of the occupational stress model.

Schaufeli and Janczur (1994) compared Poland with the Netherlands. Even though Polish nurses had a higher level of burnout than did Dutch nurses, subjective job stressors, personality variables, and physical working conditions related similarly to burnout in both countries. Uncertainty and imbalance of life were especially important to burnout in both samples. Glazer (1999) examined role ambiguity, role overload, role conflict, anxiety, affective and continuance commitment, and intention to quit among nurses in Hungary, Italy, the United Kingdom, and the United States. Results showed that whereas the means of stressors on strains differed, the relationships among the variables were quite similar.

Spector et al. (2001) investigated work locus of control (LOC), job satisfaction, psychological strain, and physical strain on managers from 24 nations/territories. Despite rather large differences in LOC across samples, they found that the relations of work LOC with employees' job satisfaction were similar across all samples with internality associated with greater job satisfaction. There was a little less consistency in results of LOC with psychological strain. Internality was associated with lower strain in all but two samples. The LOC-physical strain relation held in the United States was not found in a quarter of the other countries. Cross-cultural research on employees' job stress process is still in a developing stage. More studies need to be done in order to better understand the mechanism among job stressors, job strains, coping strategies, and other related variables.

Key Measurement Issues of Cross-Cultural/Cross-National Job Stress Research With Survey Methods

A great deal of job stress research relies on survey methods using self-report scales. A large number of measures used in cross-cultural research in this domain were developed in North America and other Western countries and exported. It would be ideal to find common stress measures that can be used across cultures and countries, but it cannot be automatically assumed that measures can be transported. In fact, one potential problem with these quantitative scales is the lack of equivalence of the scales used in different populations. Two major issues are involved. First, the translation may distort the meaning of the scale across countries (e.g., Hulin, 1987). Second, people with different cultural backgrounds may interpret the meaning of the scale in different ways (e.g., Riordan & Vandenberg, 1994). Given that culture can have a substantial influence on job stress, it might not be appropriate to simply translate the U.S.-based measurement and use it in other cultures, even if back translation is done. One approach often used by researchers is to conduct measurement equivalence analyses to demonstrate the success of the translation before interpreting results of cross-national studies.

Additional scale development work would seem worthwhile in order to provide scales that can be used cross-nationally, especially in different languages. Some researchers questioned whether sole reliance on North American and Western scales should be avoided and whether scales should also be developed in other countries (e.g., Cooper & Payne, 1992). One example of a multinational scale development effort is the secondary and socioinstrumental control scales of Spector et al. (2004). Colleagues from four countries/areas (Hong Kong, PR China, Spain, and the United States) wrote items that were combined into scales that were refined through administration in Hong Kong, PR China, and the United States at the same time.

Quantitative Approach and Its Weakness for Cross-Cultural/Cross-National Job Stress Research

Measurement equivalence (ME) is the prerequisite for cross-cultural job stress research using scales developed in one country. Unfortunately, many previous cross-cultural studies have failed to assess such equivalence and assumed that scales would be transportable. Commonly, researchers took a scale that had been developed and validated in country A and applied it in country B. Then they made a comparison of these two countries on the measured constructs. Observed differences or similarities may reflect true sample differences in the underlying constructs or may be due to measurement non-equivalence across the countries (Cheung & Rensvold, 2000). Examination of scale equivalence is desperately needed and is critical for cross-cultural job stress research.

Several methods have been developed for assessing ME in cross-cultural research. Roughly, they fall into two classes (Liu, Borg, & Spector, in press; Reise, Widaman, & Pugh, 1993). The first class refers to the factor analytic methods that are based on structural equation modeling (SEM). Confirmatory factor analysis (CFA) and mean and covariance structure analysis (MACS) belong to this category. The goal of CFA and MACS is to make comparisons of the item variance-covariance matrices for each sample of interest (e.g., Liu, Spector, Stark, Chernyshenko, & Borg, 2003).

Measurement equivalence is achieved when the comparisons indicate a good fit across samples. The second class refers to the item response theory methods (IRT) such as differential item functioning (DIF) and differential test functioning (DTF) approaches. Using IRT methods, one can detect biased items and assess the overall test equivalence by examining item functioning in terms of an appropriate model (e.g., Liu et al., 2003).

However, because factor analytic methods (e.g., CFA and MACS) and item response methods (e.g., DIF and DTF) are based on different assumptions and have different mechanisms for examining ME, different results might be expected. In practice, it is sometimes difficult to interpret the results in terms of ME (Liu et al., 2003). How to revise the nonequivalent questionnaire is another difficulty in this context.

Qualitative Approaches in Cross-Cultural/Cross-National Job Stress Research

In the past 20 years, researchers have developed qualitative methods to compensate for the weakness of the quantitative approach. Besides the ME problem related to the quantitative method, Narayanan et al. (1999) pointed out that such methods are not the best to study culture-specific job stress. Using the U.S.-developed scales to collect data in each specific culture may blur the difference between cultures and, thus, may not adequately capture stress-related experiences related to the unique features of each culture. The job stressors assumed to be common in the United States might not apply in other countries.

In order to better study job stress in cross-cultural/cross-national contexts, qualitative approaches can be applied. With qualitative approaches, participants can freely express their opinion on different aspects of their jobs. The uniqueness of their job stress process could be better captured (e.g., Keenan & Newton, 1985).

Qualitative approaches emphasize description, understanding, and interpretation of the stressful events by interviewing subjects or using open-ended questionnaires (Parkes, 1985). With qualitative approaches, respondents have more freedom to express their feelings, so cultural differences on job stress could be better captured. This method is particularly appropriate in cross-cultural contexts because of its emic (culture-specific) nature. The specific stressful events (stressors) generated by the participants with their specific culture backgrounds can provide detailed information about their experiences. This provides a clearer picture of specific stressors encountered in varying cultures. Therefore, the qualitative method will help us better understand the job stress process as well as uncovering cultural differences that are difficult to see from the quantitative data alone (Narayanan et al., 1999).

Keenan and Newton (1985) proposed the stress incident record (SIR) technique to collect qualitative data. Participants are asked to describe some concrete events that have been stressful for them in past 30 days. If there isn't a stressful incident during the time period specified, the subjects are instructed to say so. To acquire more detailed information about the incident(s), more specific questions can be included that might address context, history, or responses.

The qualitative data are categorized by content analysis (Kerlinger, 1964). The goal of content analysis is to develop an exhaustive set of job stressor, job strain, or coping strategy categories for each population and to assess the frequency of each job stressor and job strain (Parkes, 1985). With proper training of raters, good interrater agreement can be achieved. The SIR technique is qualitative in terms of data collection, but the materials are quantified with content analysis. There are other forms of qualitative analysis (e.g., personalogical accounts, discourse analysis), some of which do quantify the data or involve the calculation of interrater coefficients.

Implications for Practice, Policy, and Intervention

Job stress is an international problem. As the world's economies become more global, it is important to understand how culture and nationality might affect the mechanism of job stress. Business practice, policy, and intervention should be based on the specific features of different populations.

Job stress researchers need to understand what sorts of interventions might work or not work in different countries. Job stress interventions can be divided into three categories, and different countries may require different approaches in each. *Primary intervention* suggests that we intervene at the level of stressors (Cooper, Dewe, & O'Driscoll, 2003). With the fast growth of international business, it is more important than ever to understand country-specific job stressors, as this knowledge will help us to do different stressor-reduction interventions (Kirkcaldy & Cooper, 1992). For example, Narayanan et al. (1999) suggested that lack of job control was one important stressor for American employees. Accordingly, actions that are beneficial to improve employees' sense of control will be a useful strategy in countries such as the United States. Staff meetings that allow increased participation (Jackson, 1983) and flexible work scheduling exercise (Pierce & Newstrom, 1983) are two examples that can help American employees to exert control at work in order to reduce levels of job stress. On the other hand, Indian employees perceived lack of structure/clarity as an important job stressor (Narayanan et al., 1999). Therefore, training managers to provide more concrete direction and guidance could be an effective way to reduce Indians' job stress.

Secondary interventions help employees cope with stressors with approaches such as stress management training (Cooper et al., 2003). Such training typically includes some cognition-focused techniques, relaxation, medication, biofeedback, and so on (Murphy, 1984; McLeroy, Green, Mullen, & Foshee,

1984). Specific techniques might be effective in certain populations but not others. For example, in the relatively low power distance United States, we might provide assertiveness training to encourage American employees to speak up with management. This might not be effective in a high power distance country such as India, where speaking up might be seen as an inappropriate challenge to legitimate authority leading to increased rather than decreased stressors. For them, relaxation training might be more effective.

Tertiary interventions treat people who are suffering from stress-related disorders, both physical and psychological (Cooper et al., 2003). Issues of cultural differences in treatment approaches have been well-known in the field of clinical psychology, in which psychotherapy is one of the major interventions (Lo & Fung, 2003). Psychotherapy approaches developed in the United States may not be applicable in other countries. Therapists need to attain both *generic cultural competence* and *specific cultural competence* to provide more effective psychotherapy for people with different cultural backgrounds. General cultural competence requires therapists to acquire the knowledge and skills necessary to work effectively in cross-cultural settings, whereas specific cultural competence refers to the ability to work effectively in a specific cultural context. *Cultural analysis* (CA) provides a clinical tool to help therapists systematically study cultural effect on the patient's psychological world. Therapists need to employ culturally appropriate treatment in order to perform a successful therapy in cross-cultural settings (Lo & Fung, 2003).

There are also policy implications that depend on the social/political conditions of different countries. In some countries, as mentioned earlier, health care is more available. Thus, in the United States, we need policies to make treatment (tertiary intervention) more available, whereas in Scandinavia such treatment is readily provided.

Conclusions and Future Research _____

Cross-cultural job stress research has seen increased attention in recent years. Researchers have launched many important multinational projects to better understand employees' job stressors, job strains, coping strategies, and job stress process in cross-cultural and cross-national contexts (e.g., Cooper & Hensman, 1985; Smith et al., 1995; Peterson et al., 1995; Spector et al., 2001, 2002). Job stress theories developed in the United States or other Western societies are starting to be tested in other countries to determine whether or not they are appropriate.

Established culture theories have been used to inform job stress research in such contexts. However, there is a need for more theory-based studies. Most of the current cross-cultural/cross-national job stress studies are exploratory, merely providing comparisons of means or relations among variables. Some theories of culture values have been developed, as described earlier, and these could help inform theories of job stress. Furthermore, most cross-national studies made two- or three-country comparisons. To better understand the function of culture on employees' job stress, comparisons of a larger number of countries that vary in specified culture dimensions are needed.

In this review, all empirical studies are cross-national studies. People within a nation share the same politics, symbols, mass communications, official languages, and so on. Even so, there are subcultures within nations, despite the national culture, that may have a strong impact on the entire population. It is reasonable and realistic to conduct cross-cultural research based on the national boundaries, with recognition of the differences between the two (Schwartz, 1999).

Measurement issues are prominent in cross-cultural research. In order to reach accurate conclusions, measurement equivalence (ME) needs to be achieved before we interpret results of cross-national comparisons. What's more, quantitative methods have an inherent weakness for research on different populations. In such cases, qualitative studies are helpful for investigating culturally specific job stressors, job strains, and coping strategies.

Finally, the development and initiation of job stress interventions should be based on the unique cultural situations. Research has shown that certain interventions might only be effective for certain populations. More cross-cultural research needs to be done for stress interventions in order to accomplish the ultimate goal of improving employees' working conditions and psychological and physical well-being.

References

Agarwal, S. (1993). Influence of formalization on role stress, organizational commitment, and work alienation of salespersons: A cross-national comparative study. *Journal of International Business Studies, 24,* 715–739.

Averill, J. R. (1973). Personal control over aversive stimuli and its relationship to stress. *Psychological Bulletin, 80,* 286–303.

Bae, K., & Chung, C. (1997). Cultural values and work attitudes of Korean industrial workers in comparison with those of the United States and Japan. *Work and Occupations, 24,* 80–96.

Beehr, T. A., & Glazer, S. (2001). A cultural perspective of social support in relation to occupational stress. In P. L. Perrewé & D. C. Ganster (Eds.), *Exploring theoretical mechanisms and perspectives* (pp. 97–142). Kidlington, UK: Elsevier Science.

Berscheid, E., & Reis, H. T. (1998). Attraction and close relationships. In D. T. Gilbert, S. T. Fiske, & G. Lindzey (Eds.), *The handbook of social psychology* (4th ed., Vol. 2, pp. 193–281). New York: Oxford University Press.

Caplan, R. D., Cobb, S., French, J. R. P., Jr., Harrison, R. V., & Pinneau, S. R. (1975). *Job demands and worker health: Main effects and occupational differences.* Washington, DC: U.S. Government Printing Office.

Cheung, G. W., & Rensvold, R. B. (2000). Assessing extreme and acquiescence response sets in cross-cultural research using structural equations modeling. *Journal of Cross-Cultural Psychology, 31,* 188–213.

Chua, E., & Gudykunst, W. (1987). Conflict resolution style in low- and high-context cultures. *Communication Research Reports, 4,* 32–37.

Cohen, J. (1976). German and American workers: A comparative view of worker distress. *International Journal of Mental Health, 5,* 138–147.

Cohen, S., & Wills, T. A. (1985). Stress, social support, and the buffering hypothesis. *Psychological Bulletin, 98,* 310–357.

Cooper, C. L., Dewe, P., & O'Driscoll, M. (2003). Employee assistance programs. In J. C. Quick & L. E. Tetrick (Eds.), *Handbook of occupational health psychology* (pp. 289–304). Washington, DC: American Psychological Association.

Cooper, C. L., & Hensman, R. (1985). A comparative investigation of executive stress: A 10-nation study. *Stress Medicine, 1,* 295–301.

Cooper, C. L., & Payne, R. L. (1992). International perspectives on research into work, well-being, and stress management. In J. C. Quick, L. R. Murphy, & J. J. Hurrell, Jr. (Eds.), *Stress and well-being at work: Assessments and interventions for occupational mental health* (pp. 348–368). Washington, DC: American Psychological Association.

DeFrank, R. S., Ivancevich, J. M., & Schweiger, D. M. (1988). Job stress and psychological well-being: Similarities and differences among American, Japanese, and Indian managers. *Behavioral Medicine, 14,* 160–170.

DeFrank, R. S., Matteson, M. T., Schweiger, D. M., & Ivancevich, J. M. (1985). The impact of culture on the management practices of American and Japanese CEOs. *Organizational Dynamics, 13,* 62–76.

Diener, E., & Diener, M. (1995). Cross-cultural correlates of life-satisfaction and self-esteem. *Journal of Personality and Social Psychology, 68,* 653–663.

Diener, E., & Suh, E. M. (1999). National differences in subjective well-being. In D. Kahneman, E. Diener, & N. Schwarz (Eds.), *Well-being: The foundations of hedonic psychology* (pp. 434–450). New York: Russell Sage.

Elsayed-Ekhouly, S. M., & Buda, R. (1996). Organizational conflict: A comparative analysis of conflict styles across cultures. *The International Journal of Conflict Management, 7,* 71–81.

Etzion, D., Kafry, D., & Pines, A. (1982). Tedium among managers: A cross-cultural American-Israeli comparison. *Journal of Psychology and Judaism, 7,* 30–41.

Friedland, N., Keinan, G., & Regev, Y. (1992). Controlling the uncontrollable: Effects of stress on illusory perceptions of controllability. *Journal of Personality and Social Psychology, 63,* 923–931.

Ganster, D. C., & Fusilier, M. R. (1989). Control in the workplace. In C. L. Cooper & I. T. Robertson (Eds.), *International review of industrial and organizational psychology* (pp. 235–280). New York: Wiley.

Glazer, S. (1999). *A cross-cultural study of job stress among nurses.* Unpublished doctoral dissertation, Central Michigan University, Mount Pleasant, MI.

Grob, A. (2000). Perceived control and subjective well-being across nations and across the life span. In E. Diener & E. M. Suh (Eds.), *Culture and subjective well-being* (pp. 319–339). Cambridge: MIT Press.

Grob, A., & Flammer, A. (1999). Macrosocial context and adolescents' perceived control. In F. D. Alsaker & A. Flammer (Eds.), *The adolescent experience: European and American adolescents in the 1990s* (pp. 99–113). Hillsdale, NJ: Lawrence Erlbaum.

Gudykunst, W. B., & Nishida, T. (1986). Attributional confidence in low- and high-context cultures. *Human Communication Research, 12,* 525–549.

Hackman, J. R., & Oldham, G. R. (1976). Motivation through the design of work: Test of a theory. *Organizational Behavior and Human Decision Processes, 16*, 250–279.

Hall, E. T. (1976). *Beyond Culture.* Garden City, NY: Anchor Press.

Hamid, P. N. (1994). Self-monitoring, locus of control, and social encounters of Chinese and New Zealand students. *Journal of Cross-Cultural Psychology, 25*, 353–368.

Harari, H., Jones, C. A., & Sek, H. (1988). Stress syndromes and stress predictors in American and Polish college students. *Journal of Cross-Cultural Psychology, 19*, 243–255.

Ho, D. Y. F., & Chiu, C. Y. (1994). Component ideas of individualism, collectivism, and social organization: An application in the study of Chinese culture. In U. Kim, H. C. Triandis, Ç. Kagitçibasi, S. C. Choi, & G. Yoon (Eds.), *Individualism and collectivism: Theory, method, and applications* (pp. 137–156). Thousand Oaks, CA: Sage.

Hofstede, G. H. (1980). *Culture's consequences: International differences in work-related values.* Beverly Hills, CA: Sage.

Hofstede, G. H. (1984). *Culture's consequences: International differences in work-related values* (Abridged ed.). Beverly Hills, CA: Sage.

Hofstede, G. (2001). *Culture's consequences: Comparing values, behaviors, institutions, and organizations across nations* (2nd ed.). Thousand Oaks, CA: Sage.

Hui, C. H. (1982). Locus of control: A review of cross-cultural research. *International Journal of Intercultural Relations, 6*, 301–323.

Hui, C. H., & Triandis, H. C. (1986). Individualism-collectivism: A study of cross-cultural researchers. *Journal of Cross-Cultural Psychology, 17*, 225–248.

Hulin, C. L. (1987). A psychometric theory of evaluations of item and scale translations: Fidelity across languages. *Journal of Cross-Cultural Psychology, 18*, 115–142.

Hurrell, J. J., & Lindström, K. (1992). Comparison of job demands, control and psychosomatic complaints at different career stages of managers in Finland and the United States. *Scandinavian Journal of Work, Environment & Health, 18*, 11–13.

Inglehart, R. (1997). *Modernization and postmodernization: Cultural, economic and political change in 43 societies.* Princeton, NJ: Princeton University Press.

Iwata, N., Okuyama, Y., Kawakami, Y., & Saito, K. (1989). Prevalence of depressive symptoms in a Japanese occupational setting: A preliminary study. *American Journal of Public Health, 79*, 1486–1489.

Jackson, S. E. (1983). Participation in decision making as a strategy for reducing job-related strain. *Journal of Applied Psychology, 68*, 3–19.

Jöreskog, K., & Sörbom, D. (1993). *LISREL 8: Structural equation modeling with the SIMPLIS command language.* Chicago: Scientific Software.

Kakar, S. (1978). Authority patterns and subordinate behavior patterns in Indian organizations. *Administrative Science Quarterly, 16*, 298–307.

Kamal, P., Phil, M. A., & Jain, U. (1988). Perceived stress as a function of family support. *Indian Psychological Review, 33*, 4–10.

Karasek, R. (1979). Job demands, job decision latitude, and mental strain: Implications for job redesign. *Administrative Science Quarterly, 24*, 285–306.

Keenan, A., & Newton, T. J. (1985). Stressful events, stressors and psychological strains in young professional engineers. *Journal of Occupational Behavior, 6*, 151–156.

Kerlinger, F. N. (1964). *Foundations of behavioral research: Educational and psychological inquiry.* New York: Holt, Rhinehart and Winston.

Kim, U., Triandis, H. Ç., Kagitçibasi, C., Choi, S., & Yoon, G. (1994). Introduction. In U. Kim, H. C. Triandis, Ç. Kagitçibasi, S. Choi, & G. Yoon (Eds.), *Individualism and collectivism: Theory, method, and applications* (pp. 1–16). Thousand Oaks, CA: Sage.

Kirkcaldy, B. D., & Cooper, C. L. (1992). Cross-cultural differences in occupational stress among British and German managers. *Work & Stress, 6,* 177–190.

Kirkcaldy, B. D., & Cooper, C. L. (1994). Occupational stress profiles of senior police managers: Cross-cultural study of officers from Berlin and Northern Ireland. *Stress Medicine, 10,* 127–130.

Laungani, P. (1993). Cultural differences in stress and its management. *Stress Medicine, 9,* 37–43.

Lazarus, R. S. (1991). Psychological stress in the workplace. *Journal of Social Behavior and Personality, 6,* 1–13.

Lazarus, R. S., & Folkman, S. (1984). *Stress, coping and adaptation.* New York: Springer.

Lincoln, J. R., Hanada, M., & Olson, J. (1981). Cultural orientations and individual reactions to organizations: A study of employees of Japanese-owned firms. *Administrative Science Quarterly, 26,* 93–115.

Liu, C. (2003). *A comparison of job stressors and job strains among employees holding comparable jobs in Western and Eastern societies.* Unpublished doctoral dissertation, University of South Florida, Tampa.

Liu, C., Borg, I., & Spector, P. (in press). Measurement equivalence of a German job satisfaction survey used in a multinational organization: Implications of Schwartz's culture model. *Journal of Applied Psychology.*

Liu, C., Spector, P. S., Stark, S., Chernyshenko, O. S., & Borg, I. (2003). *A comparison of techniques for assessing measurement equivalence in cross-cultural research: Organizational research method.* Manuscript submitted for publication.

Lo, H. T., & Fung, K. P. (2003). Culturally competent psychotherapy. *Canadian Journal of Psychiatry, 48,* 161–170.

Lundberg, C. D., & Peterson, M. F. (1994). The meaning of working in U.S. and Japanese local governments at three hierarchical levels. *Human Relations, 47,* 1459–1487.

McCormick, I. A., & Cooper, C. L. (1988). Executive stress: Extending the international comparison. *Human Relations, 41,* 65–72.

McLeroy, K. R., Green, L. W., Mullen, K. D., & Foshee, V. (1984). Assessing the effects of health promotion in worksites: A review of the stress program evaluations. *Health Education Quarterly, 11,* 379–401.

Murphy, L. (1984). Occupational stress management: A review and appraisal. *Journal of Occupational Psychology, 57,* 1–15.

Narayanan, L., Menon, S., & Spector, P. E. (1999). A cross-cultural comparison of job stressors and reactions among employees holding comparable jobs in two countries. *International Journal of Stress Management, 6,* 197–212.

National Institute of Occupational Safety and Health (NIOSH). (2000). *Special populations at risk.* Retrieved August 2003 from www.cdc.gov/niosh/nrspop.html

Oishi, S., Diener, E. F., Lucas, R. E., & Suh, E. M. (1999). Cross-cultural variations in predictors of life satisfaction: Perspectives from needs and values. *Personality and Social Psychology Bulletin, 25,* 980–990.

Parkes, K. R. (1985). Stressful episodes reported by first-year student nurses: A descriptive account. *Social Science Medicine, 20,* 945–953.

Peterson, M. F., Smith, P. B., Akande, A., Ayestaran, S., Bochner, S., Callan, V., Cho, N. G., Jesuino, J. C., D'Amorim, M., Francois, P. H., Hofmann, K., Koopman, P. L., Leung, K., Lim, T. K., Mortazavi, S., Munene, J., Radford, M., Ropo, A., Savage, G., Setiadi, B., Sinha, T. N., Sorenson, R., & Viedge, C. (1995). Role conflict, ambiguity, and overload: A 21-nation study. *Academy of Management Journal, 38,* 429–452.

Pierce, J. L., & Newstrom, J. W. (1983). The design of flexible work schedules and employee responses. *Journal of Organisational Behaviour, 4,* 247–262.

Radhakrishnan, P., & Chan, D. K. S. (1997). Cultural differences in the relation between self-discrepancy and life satisfaction. *International Journal of Psychology, 32,* 387–398.

Rahim, M. A. (1992). *Managing conflict in organizations* (2nd ed.). Westport, CT: Praeger.

Rahim, M. A., & Magner, N. R. (1995). Confirmatory factor analysis of the styles of handling interpersonal conflict: First order factor model and its invariance across groups. *Journal of Applied Psychology, 80,* 122–132.

Reise, S. P., Widaman, K. F., & Pugh, R. H. (1993). Confirmatory factor analysis and item response theory: Two approaches for exploring measurement invariance. *Psychological Bulletin, 114,* 552–566.

Reykowski, J. (1994). Collectivism and individualism as dimensions of social change. In U. Kim, H. C. Triandis, Ç. Kagitçibasi, S. C. Choi, & G. Yoon (Eds.), *Individualism and collectivism: Theory, method, and applications* (pp. 276–292). Thousand Oaks, CA: Sage.

Riordan, D. M., & Vandenberg, R. J. (1994). A central question in cross-cultural research: Do employees of different cultures interpret work-related measures in an equivalent manner? *Journal of Management, 20,* 643–671.

Rotter, J. B. (1966). Generalized expectancies for internal versus external control of reinforcement. *Psychological Monographs, 80*(609).

Rozin, P. (1999). Preadaptation and the puzzles and properties of pleasure. In D. Kahneman, E. Diener, & N. Schwarz (Eds.), *Well-being: The foundations of hedonic psychology* (pp. 109–133). New York: Russell Sage.

Sadri, G., & Marcoulides, G. A. (1994). The dynamics of occupational stress: Proposing and testing a model. *Research and Practice in Human Resource Management, 2,* 1–19.

Sadri, G., Marcoulides, G. A., Cooper, C. L., & Kirkcaldy, B. (1996, Winter). Testing a model of occupational stress across different countries. *Journal of Business and Management,* 10–29.

Schaufeli, W. B., & Janczur, B. (1994). Burnout among nurses: A Polish and Dutch comparison. *Journal of Cross-Cultural Psychology, 25,* 95–113.

Schwartz, S. H. (1994). Are there universal aspects in the structure and contents of human values? *Journal of Social Issues, 50,* 19–45.

Schwartz, S. H. (1999). A theory of cultural values and some implications for work. *Applied Psychology: An International Review, 48,* 23–47.

Schwartz, S. H., & Bardi, A. (1997). Influences of adaptation to Communist rule on value priorities in Eastern Europe. *Political Psychology, 18,* 385–410.

Schwartz, S. H., & Ros, M. (1995). Values in the West: A theoretical and empirical challenge to the individualism-collectivism cultural dimension. *World Psychology, 1,* 99–122.

Singh, P. N., Huang, S. C., & Thompson, G. G. (1962). A comparative study of selected attitudes, values, and personality characteristics of American, Chinese, and Indian students. *Journal of Social Psychology, 57,* 123–132.

Sinha, J. B. P. (1988). Work-related value and climate factors. *International Review of Applied Psychology, 35,* 63–78.

Smith, P. B., & Misumi, J. (1989). Japanese management: A sun rising in the West? In C. L. Cooper & I. T. Robertson (Eds.), *International review of industrial and organizational psychology 1989* (pp. 329–369). Chichester, UK: Wiley.

Smith, P. B., Trompenaars, F., & Dugan, S. (1995). The Rotter Locus of Control Scale in 43 countries: A test of cultural relativity. *International Journal of Psychology, 30,* 377–400.

Spector, P. E. (1986). Perceived control by employees: A meta-analysis of studies concerning autonomy and participation at work. *Human Relations, 39,* 1005–1016.

Spector, P. E., Cooper, C. L., Sanchez, J. I., O'Driscoll, M., Sparks, K., Bernin, P., Büssing, A., Dewe, P., Hart, P., Lu, L., Miller, K., Renault de Moraes, L., Ostrognay, G. M., Pagon, M., Pitariu, H., Poelmans, S., Radhakrishnan, P., Russinova, V., Salamatov, V., Salgado, J., Shima, S., Siu, O. L., Stora, J. B., Teichmann, M., Theorell, T., Vlerick, P., Westman, M., Widerszal-Bazyl, M., Wong, P., & Yu, S. (2001). Do national levels of individualism and internal locus of control relate to well-being: An ecological level international study. *Journal of Organizational Behavior, 22,* 815–832.

Spector, P. E., Cooper, C. L., Sanchez, J. I., O'Driscoll, M., Sparks, K., Bernin, P., Büssing, A., Dewe, P., Hart, P., Lu, L., Miller, K., Renault de Moraes, L., Ostrognay, G. M., Pagon, M., Pitariu, H., Poelmans, S., Radhakrishnan, P., Russinova, V., Salamatov, V., Salgado, J., Shima, S., Siu, O. L., Stora, J. B., Teichmann, M., Theorell, T., Vlerick, P., Westman, M., Widerszal-Bazyl, M., Wong, P., & Yu, S. (2002). Locus of control and well-being at work: How generalizable are Western findings? *Academy of Management Journal, 45,* 453–466.

Spector, P. E., Sanchez, J. I., Siu, O. L., Salgado, J., & Ma, J. (2004). Eastern versus Western control beliefs at work: An investigation of secondary control, socioinstrumental control, and work locus of control in China and the U.S. *Applied Psychology: An International Review, 55,* 38–60.

Suh, M., Diener, E., Oishi, S., & Triandis, H. C. (1998). The shifting basis of life satisfaction judgments across cultures: Emotions versus norms. *Journal of Personality and Social Psychology, 74,* 482–493.

Sutherland, V., & Cooper, C. L. (1990). *Understanding stress: A psychological perspective for health professionals.* London: Chapman & Hall.

Teja, J. S. (1978). Mental illness and the family in America and India. *International Journal of Social Psychiatry, 24,* 225–231.

Triandis, H. (1988). Collectivism vs. individualism: A reconceptualization of a basic concept in cross-cultural social psychology. In G. K. Verma & C. Bagley (Eds.), *Personality, cognition, and values: Cross-cultural perspectives on childhood and adolescence* (pp. 60–95). London: Macmillan.

Triandis, H. (1994). Cross-cultural industrial and organizational psychology. In H. C. Triandis, M. D. Dunnete, & L. M. Hough (Eds.), *Handbook of industrial and organizational psychology* (2nd ed., Vol. 4, pp. 103–172). Palo Alto, CA: Consulting Psychologists Press.

Triandis, H. C., Bontempo, R., Villareal, M. J., & Asai, M. (1988). Individualism and collectivism: Cross-cultural perspectives on self-group relationships. *Journal of Personality and Social Psychology, 54,* 323–338.

Trompenaars, F., & Hampden-Turner, C. (1998). *Riding the waves of culture: Understanding cultural diversity in global business* (2nd ed.). New York: McGraw-Hill.

Trubisky, R., Ting-Toomey, S., & Lin, S. L. (1991). The influence of individualism-collectivism and self-monitoring on conflict styles. *International Journal of Intercultural Relations, 15,* 65–84.

Veenhoven, R. (1991). Is happiness relative? *Social Indicators Research, 24,* 1–34.

Veenhoven, R. (1993). *Happiness in nations: Subjective appreciation of life in 56 nations 1946–1992.* Rotterdam: Erasmus University Rotterdam.

21

Part-Time and Contingent Employment

Daniel G. Gallagher

Organizational researchers have had a long history of studying the nature and consequences of work and the employer-employee relationship. Efforts to understand the nature of the employment relationship have included a broad spectrum of topics such as individual worker attitudes, job design, motivation, leadership, group dynamics, and employee development, to name only a few. On the outcome side of the employment relationship, attention has been given to both the individual- and organization-based consequences of the employment experience. However, it is important to note that almost all academic efforts at theory building and model testing appear to be based on the underlying assumption that the structure of the employer-employee relationship involves a full-time and "ongoing" working arrangement (e.g., Beard & Edwards, 1995; Gallagher & McLean Parks, 2001; Pfeffer & Baron, 1988; Rotchford & Roberts, 1982). Alternatively stated, past research in most areas of behavioral research, including the study of work stress and employee well-being, have implicitly or explicitly focused on understanding the employment relationship in the context of the "standard" or "traditional" full-time and continuing employment contract. Research on the issues of work-related stress and worker well-being has also had predominate theoretical and empirical focus on standard employer-employee relationships.

Behavioral research that continues to entirely frame the study of work from the perspective of ongoing, full-time employment contracts will be ignoring the current and changing realities of employment in the twenty-first century. In Canada and the United States, more than one of every five jobs is currently being performed by a person on a part-time basis (Nollen, 1999; Zeytinoglu, 1999). In other countries, such as Australia, Japan, New Zealand, the Netherlands, Norway, Sweden, and the United Kingdom, part-time workers constitute between 18 and 25% of the total workforce (Delsen, 1999). In most industrialized countries, particularly those transitioning to a service sector orientation, the rate of part-time employment growth exceeds the rate of growth for the more standard or typical full-time job. Although no universal definition of part-time work exists, in most countries part-time workers are individuals who are employed less than 30 to 35 hours per week (Baffoe-Bonnie, 2001).

For many organizations, the regular use of part-time workers represents a form of "temporal" staffing flexibility (Feldman, 1990). In particular, part-time workers, along with full-time workers on "flextime" or compressed workweek schedules, are used to staff organizations during high customer demand hours or in lieu of the expense of hiring additional full-time workers (Pierce, Newstrom, Dunham, & Barber, 1989). The use of part-time workers is a cost savings strategy on the part of the employer, reducing the need to employ full-time workers whose labor would be underutilized during nonpeak service demand hours. As noted by Barling and Gallagher (1996), demographically, part-time workers are disproportionately young (16–24 years of age), married females (25–54 years of age), or older males (55 or more years of age). As the workforce in many industrialized countries becomes older, part-time work among retirement age workers probably will become an increasingly common means to transition out of full-time work yet maintain some form of continued employment (Kim & Feldman, 2000).

As part of the growing interest of employers wanting to minimize labor costs through human resource flexibility, there has been an extensive growth in what has become frequently referred to as "contingent" employment contracts (Belous, 1989; Cohany, 1998; Gallagher, 2002). Unlike most part-time work arrangements, the hiring of workers on the basis of contingent contracts exists as a means for organizations to attain "numerical flexibility" (Reilly, 1998). Numerical flexibility is characterized as the ability of the organization to easily adjust the size of the workforce to meet either cyclical changes or the unexpected short-term needs of the business. Contingent employment contracts have been operationalized in a variety of forms and for various types of occupational groups or professions. One of the most visible and commonly recognized forms of contingent employment is the hiring of workers through temporary help service firms (e.g., Manpower, Adecco, Randstad). Through the use of temporary help firms, an organization directly contracts workers for a fixed period of time or until the completion of a particular assignment (Connelly & Gallagher, 2004). Although such "dispatched" workers may be assigned full-time jobs within the client organization, the contractual arrangement is unlike the standard or traditional employment arrangement in that the employment contract is not ongoing in nature. Although the temporary help industry has historically focused on the short-term placement of clerical and manual laborers, there is a growing trend toward the assignment of professional workers (e.g., health care professionals, accountants, engineers, etc.).

A significantly larger number of temporary or contingent workers are actually hired through "direct-hire" or "in-house" arrangements with the employer organization. Direct-hire arrangements are normally characterized by systems in which the employer maintains a list of workers who are willing to accept short-term employment contracts when the employer organization has a need for additional staffing (Muhl, 2002). In practice, the direct-hire workers move in and out of the status of organizational employee. Direct-hire temporary contracts are variable in length and may normally range from daily to monthly. Direct-hire or in-house contingent arrangements are frequently found in educational, health care, and manufacturing sectors of most economies.

A third approach to numerical flexibility exists in an organization's use of independent contractors. In most countries, independent contractors, or freelance workers, are defined as self-employed individuals who contract or sell their services to a client organization on a fixed-term or project basis. An increasingly common illustration of professional independent contractors would be information technology specialists who perform short-term, project-based work that may be outside the specific skill set of the permanent employees of the organization. The duration of these contracts is normally tied explicitly to the completion of a specific task or project. The growing use of independent contractors as a contingent employment staffing strategy also fits into the realm that Reilly (1998) has referred to as an interest in "functional" flexibility. Unlike temporal and numerical flexibility, functional flexibility is less concerned with the number of hours and workers and more with how an organization internally assigns labor. The decision to utilize an independent contractor on a short-term basis could conceivably reflect the opinion of the organization that the skills of its permanent workforce would be more effectively allocated to existing or alternative tasks or that the transitory nature of the task does not justify the recruitment and retention of an employee in a standard or permanent position.

There is unquestionable evidence that contingent work arrangements, along with part-time jobs, are becoming a larger share of the new workforce. For example, in a study of 14 European countries, Brewster, Mayne, and Tregaskis (1997) found that nonpermanent or contingent work contracts ranged from a high of one third of the working population in Spain to a low of 7.5% in Belgium. In Canada and the United States, depending on definition, approximately 5 to 14% of the workforce could be characterized as contingent (Cohany, 1998; Muhl, 2002; Nollen, 1999; Zeytinoglu, 1999). Furthermore, it is interesting to note that at the organizational level, Brewster et al. (1997) found that 4 of every 5 employers in their European study used nonpermanent workers. An in-depth analysis of employment practices in Britain also indicated that close to one half of firms utilized workers on direct-hire, fixed-term contracts (Cully, Woodland, O'Reilly, & Dix, 1999). Similar to trends in the use of part-time workers, an increasing share of new job creations in the last decade have been in the form of contingent contract arrangements (Delsen, 1999; Nollen, 1999; Zeytinoglu, 1999).

Flexibility and Stress

In his research on the relationship between stress and job performance, Jex (1998) has suggested that the trend toward increased "flexibilization" of the workplace has created an interesting challenge for the study and understanding of occupational stress. Most notably, it is argued that organizations are becoming less focused on jobs and more focused on employee activities that are driven by participation in teams or the ability to accomplish changing objectives rather than simply fulfilling the requirements of an existing job description. This trend toward "dejobbing" has been driven by much of the aforementioned interest in flexible staffing as well as the realization that using jobs as the focal point for employee activities is not very effective (Jex, 1998). But more important, Jex notes that "role theory" has been the foundation for much of the past occupational stress research (e.g., Jackson & Schuler, 1985; Kahn, Wolfe, Quinn, Snoek, & Rosenthal, 1964). But if, as suggested by Jex, clearly defined jobs are being de-emphasized, then the underlying importance of role theory in the study of workplace stress may require reconsideration. Many comments pertaining to the relevance of role theory in the context of flexibilization are implicitly directed toward the changing structure of the work performed by the permanent or typical workforce within an organization. However, an even broader question can be raised concerning the applicability of existing occupational or workplace stress theories to the study of workers performing tasks for organizations on the basis of either contingent or part-time employment contracts. Alternatively stated, if the dejobbing of work within organizations presents a potential challenge to theories of workplace stress, then what impact do broader flexibilization efforts in the form of contingent and part-time work contracts have on existing models of work-related stress and worker well-being?

Objectives

The primary objective of this chapter will be to open the door to discussion of the applicability of some of the basic principles of work-related stress to growing numbers of workers who are employed through part-time and contingent employment contracts. In order to meet this objective, attention will be directed to three broad areas of inquiry and discussion.

First, in order to better understand the potential consequences that nonstandard jobs have in terms of work-related stress or well-being, it is necessary to more fully comprehend the nature of the employment contract that exists between the worker and the employing organization(s). This is a particularly important issue as it applies to the growing number of workers employed under contingent contracts. Focus will be directed to identifying how nonstandard employment contracts differ from traditional full-time employment contracts with respect to the structure of the worker-organization relationship, its duration, and the meaning of the term "job."

Second, drawing heavily from existing research on work-related stress, an illustrative listing of frequently cited "stressors" will be identified and discussed in the context of part-time and contingent employment contracts. Emphasis will be placed on evaluating the extent to which contingent or part-time workers may be less susceptible to certain work-related stressors. Conversely, attention will also be given to the question of whether or not contingent and part-time workers may be more sensitive to particular sources of stress than "standard" workers. In addition, consideration will be given to the identification of work-related stressors that may be more characteristic of contingent and part-time work relative to the typical work arrangement.

Finally, the chapter will conclude with some general observations pertaining to the importance of volition in the choice of employment arrangements as it may relate to occupational stress and well-being. In addition, a brief commentary will be offered pertaining to the overall status and future direction of research relevant to the understanding of work stress and well-being of workers outside the stereotypical full-time and ongoing employment relationship.

Nature of the Contracts

At one level, the nature of employment contracts can differ greatly in terms of the degree of explicitness. For many workers newly hired into an organization, the employment contract may consist of a simple verbal statement of the duties the worker is being hired to perform and the rate of pay and associated benefits. At the other extreme, the employer and employee may enter into a detailed statement of job duties, performance expectations, salary, and investiture rights (as well as the terms for contract continuation or termination, noncompetition agreements, and severance payments, etc.). Regardless of the terms of the agreement, the basic structure of the typical or standard employment contract involves an identifiable employer-employee relationship. Furthermore, as previously indicated, most typical or standard employment contracts from the start of the twentieth century were likely to assume that the employer-employee relationship was ongoing, subject primarily to satisfactory levels of individual and organizational performance (Cappelli, 1999).

Part-Time Workers

In reality, the contractual structure of most part-time jobs is not unlike their standard full-time counterparts. For most part-time jobs, there is a direct and identifiable employer-employee relationship. Again, the terms and explicitness of the contract may differ, but the relationship is typical in that there is a clear identification of the roles of the employer and employee. A further and important consideration is that most part-time work arrangements involve the assumption of an ongoing employment relationship that is also characteristic of standard employment (Barling & Gallagher, 1996). Of course, there may also be some experience-based assumptions made by employers that part-time jobholders are likely to be employed for a shorter duration than their full-time counterparts. The shorter duration of part-time employment is not a function of the nature of the contract but rather an issue of retention, with the choice being exercised by the employee or the employer. However, employer expectations concerning the actual duration of individual part-time work assignments, relative to full-time work, is likely to influence both the types of tasks provided to part-time workers and the level of support provided by the employer organization.

Temporary Help Workers

As previously noted, the use of temporary help service firms have become an internationally recognized means for employers to more effectively implement a practice of both numerical and functional flexibility in human resources staffing. However, as noted by a number of researchers, there is a fundamentally different structuring of the employment relationship for temporary help firm workers than is found in the standard employment contract (Gallagher & McLean Parks, 2001).

In many respects, the employment relationship associated with the use of temporary help firm workers has been characterized as being "triangular" in structure. The three principal parties to the relationship are the worker, the temporary help service firm, and the client organization to which the workers are dispatched by the temporary help firm. First, there exists a written contractual relationship between the temporary help firm and the client organization. Second, the individual worker is assigned to perform a job for the client organization. And third, the worker has a written contractual agreement with the temporary help service firm.

What is interesting about contingent employment, in the context of temporary help firm workers, is the fact that the worker is not an employee of the organization where the job is being performed. Hence, in the actual workplace there is no employer-employee relationship. Also, the worker-client organization relationship is by contract a fixed-term rather than ongoing relationship. In fact, in most countries the duration of fixed-term contract is limited by law. Further, complexity exists in the fact that if an employer-employee relationship exists, it is between the temporary worker and the temporary help service firm. However, within most countries, the temporary help firm often assumes an "arm's length" relationship with the temporary worker and contracts with the worker only for the duration of the assignment. Although in some countries (e.g., Sweden) temporary workers are ongoing employees of the temporary help service firm, the most common model is one in which workers contract with the temporary help firm to perform a particular job and are subsequently assigned to actually perform the job for the client organization. Once the assignment is completed, the worker holds no employment relationship with either the client or the temporary help service firm.

Direct-Hire Temporary Workers

Contractually, direct-hire temporary workers are similar to their standard full-time counterparts in that they have a direct and identifiable employer-employee relationship. However, the contingent nature of the arrangement is based on a series of fixed-term or spot contracts. In fact, direct-hire contracts could be viewed as multitiered. At the first tier is an agreement between the employer and a worker that specifies that the worker will be in a preferential hiring list or "pool" and will be hired on a fixed-term basis as the staffing needs require. Once work is available, the worker may then temporarily assume contractual status under a fixed-term employer-employee relationship.

Although direct-hire temporary workers have a more immediate employer-employee relationship compared with temporary help service firm workers, they still differ from the typical employment contract in that there exists an explicit understanding that the duration of the employment is not ongoing. However, there is an implicit understanding that a worker's status as an "on call" worker can be ongoing.

From the perspective of potential work stress implications, it is worthwhile to note that similar to workers hired through temporary help firms, the jobs that are assigned to direct hires by the employer organization may vary from contract to contract. Hence, there is no guarantee or clear expectation that a worker would move in and out of the same job when hired for a fixed-term assignment.

Independent Contractors

As noted by Gallagher and McLean Parks (2001), the status of self-employed or independent contractors represents one of the most serious challenges to the extension of existing employment-based theories to the study of contingent workers.

First, by definition, independent contractors are self-employed. As a result, the lines of demarcation found in the typical employer-employee relationship do not exist. By definition, independent contractors are their own employers and are more likely to operate in the environment of a contractor-client relationship. Also by definition, these contractor-client relationships, albeit renewable, are normally of fixed-term duration.

Second, independent contractors can, and frequently do, simultaneously hold multiple employment contracts. For example, entering into a contractor-client arrangement to provide a service does not preclude the same independent contractor from entering into separate agreements, with distinguishable contract terms, with other client organizations. The fact that independent contractors may contractually alter the nature of their tasks, duties, and responsibilities from one client to another results in a situation in which the job(s) to perform may vary and differ in scope at any particular point in time when multiple clients are involved.

Finally, understanding the nature of contingent work from the vantage point of independent contractors raises the possibility that independent contractors (i.e., the self-employed) may also assume the role of employer by virtue of the need to employ their own staff on a permanent or fixed-term basis. As a result, independent contractors can be viewed from the perspective of the roles of both contractor-client and an employer-employee.

Work Stress and Well-Being

In their framework for organizing and directing future theory, research, and practice regarding health and well-being in the workplace, Danna and Griffin (1999) suggest that research generally supports the presence of three broad groups of "antecedents" of well-being. The first broad group of antecedent factors consists of characteristics pertaining to the physical work setting, such as health and safety hazards. A second set of antecedent variables identified by Danna and Griffin consists of individual worker personality traits. Included within the realm of personality traits are variables such as behavior patterns (e.g., type A) and locus of control. The third and most comprehensive group of antecedent factors to worker well-being consists of occupational stress variables. Drawing heavily on prior research by Cooper and Marshall (1978), Danna and Griffin suggest that occupational stress variables include such considerations as factors intrinsic to the job, role in the organization, relationships at work, career development, organizational structure and climate, and the home/work interface.

In the following sections of this chapter, attention will be focused on examining well-being among part-time and contingent workers from the perspective of antecedent factors associated with occupational stress. For the purpose of organization and discussion, focus will be placed on work-related stress associated with five general occupation-based factors that may be of particular importance in understanding occupational stress among part-time and contingent workers. The five categories of occupational stress factors that will be examined are (a) factors intrinsic to the job, (b) role in the organization, (c) organizational integration-climate and support, (d) employment security and career development, and (e) volition.

Factors Intrinsic to the Job

As noted by Cartwright and Cooper (1997), as a starting point to understanding work stress and employee well-being, researchers have frequently studied those factors that may be intrinsic to the job itself, such as poor working conditions, shift work, long hours, work scheduling, risk and danger, the introduction of new technologies, work overload, and work "underload."

Within the context of this chapter, a simple phrasing of the research question might be "Do part-time or contingent workers confront stresses intrinsic to their jobs that clearly distinguish them from workers on standard, full-time employment contracts?" The search for an answer to what might appear a simple and straightforward question is, in fact, complicated by three immediate considerations.

First, for most workers, the term "job" is often associated with a position within an organization that is comprised of a fairly well-delineated set of tasks, duties, and responsibilities. For example, a person might consider himself or herself employed as a "salesperson," "accountant," or grocery store "cashier." For many people working on part-time schedules, there tends to be a clear and identifiable set of job-related tasks, duties, and responsibilities that the employee is charged to perform. However, among contingent workers the term "job" may be more nebulous. As noted by Gallagher and McLean Parks (2001), among some forms of contingent employment, workers may broadly self-define their jobs as that of temporary worker ("I'm a temp") or independent consultant. Analogous to the suggestion made by Jex (1998) that growth of project-based work has led to dejobbing with less precise job-related descriptions, contingent work may also be associated with less clearly defined or stable roles or jobs. From both theoretical and practical perspectives, understanding the extent to which previous research pertaining to factors extrinsic to the job extends to contingent employment arrangements requires that attention be given to how individual workers define the term "job."

Second, as previously implied, the question of the applicability of existing stress and well-being research to part-time and contingent workers requires consideration of the fact that not all forms of part-time work and contingent work are alike. As noted by Barling and Gallagher (1996) and Barling, Inness, and Gallagher (2002), the most notable differences between job-related attitudes are less likely to be found between part-time and full-time workers than they are among part-time workers based, in part, on the number of hours worked. Similarly, it can once again be suggested that contingent employment is not a unitary concept but one that involves fundamentally different types of contractual arrangements.

Third, many job-related tasks, duties, and responsibilities tend to be organizationally based. Among standard or traditional employment contracts, the "job" is defined within the context of the organization. Employees are assigned roles within the organization, and such roles are relatively fixed in content. Relatively stable job content may also be a characteristic of part-time work. However, for certain types of contingent workers, job content may regularly change, not so much as a result of how an organization has restructured the work but more reflective of the fact that many contingent workers frequently move between organizations. As a result, the nature of the tasks, duties, and responsibilities associated with a particular job are likely to change. It is important to note that some stressors, which are at times characterized as intrinsic to the job, may, in fact, be more intrinsic to the broader organization. For example, poor or unsafe working conditions may be less job specific than characteristic of the organization. For this reason, contingent workers whose contracts involve moving from organization to organization may be exposed to varying levels of particular stressors depending on the conditions under which they are employed at a particular point in time. This is not to suggest that poor working conditions are not related to stress but rather that stress and the resulting consequences could be more variable for contingent workers when their assignments involve exposure to different employer organizations with different employment environments that affect the nature of the work being performed.

Despite the above noted distinctions, which are particularly applicable to understanding some of the unique aspects of contingent employment, there does not appear to be any theoretical basis or empirical evidence to suggest that many of the stressors that are characterized as "intrinsic to the job" would not also be applicable to both part-time and contingent forms of employment. However, it is possible to hypothesize that the magnitude of job-based stressors may be more extensive for part-time and contingent employment than they may be in the case of workers on more standard, full-time working arrangements.

One job-based stressor that may create a particularly salient concern for part-time and contingent workers is associated with both the hours of employment and work scheduling. The hours of employment issue is not so much the extent to which an individual works an excessive number of hours but rather the extent to which the number of hours that an individual works is congruent with an individual worker's preference. Among studies of workers on part-time work schedules, considerable support exists for the finding that job-related satisfaction is strongly related to the closeness of the match between preferred and scheduled number of work hours (Barling & Gallagher, 1996). Given the ad hoc and fixed-term nature of most contingent work, a particularly salient potential stressor may be found in workers' concerns that they receive a sufficient number of assignments to meet the number hours of work that they deem necessary in their own situations. For example, contingent workers on direct-hire arrangements or working through temporary help service firms may experience anxiety when they encounter a reduction in the number of hours for which they are called in or dispatched to client organizations. In many respects, most contingent workers may experience unpredictable fluctuations in the number of hours that they are scheduled to work and subsequent unpredictability in income. Analogous to stress that may be experienced by traditional workers who experience periods of layoff from their jobs, contingent workers may actually experience stress from "partial layoffs" on a weekly basis. At the other end of the continuum, situations exist in which contingent workers may be called upon to work hours that greatly exceed their personal preferences. As noted by Rogers (1995, 2000), lower-skilled temporary workers may fear that a refusal to accept an assignment to a client organization may result in a loss of future assignments. Even higher-end independent contractors may be reluctant to take on an excessive number of contracts at one particular time for fear of losing future opportunities (Castaneda, 1999). In contrast to quantitative underemployment, contingent workers in high-demand occupations may, in fact, be exposed to high stress potential as a function of the size of their workload.

It is also worthwhile to note that unlike both standard full-time and part-time workers, contingent workers may also experience greater variability pertaining to which and how many hours a day they actually work. Even in the case of shift work, most workers have fairly predictable starting and finishing times within the workday. However, in the case of contingent workers employed through temporary-help agencies, the start and finish of the workday will vary by client organization. There is significant anecdotal evidence that the lack of clearly defined work hours can contribute to work-family conflict (Parasuraman & Simmers, 2001). For workers (primarily women) with young children, the task of securing dependable child care arrangements can be complicated by short-term notification of both the assignment itself and the designated starting and finishing times. This absence of a clearly defined and predicable work schedule for many contingent workers can create a form of home-work-based stress that is less problematic for workers who have more predictable schedules.

As noted by Xie and Johns (1995), jobs are experienced as stressful when they are either very low or very high in complexity. In the case of low-complexity jobs, the stress may result from boredom, whereas high complexity may lead to mental fatigue and exhaustion. This observation is also relevant to the understanding of work stress among part-time and contingent workers. At one end of the continuum, part-time and contingent workers are often hired to perform jobs that require limited, on-the-job training and involve fairly repetitive tasks. Such work is characteristic of tasks commonly assigned to day laborers and clerical temps (Rogers, 1995). However, the extent to which such work results in dysfunctional consequences, such as psychological distress (Melamed, Ben-Avi, Luz, & Green, 1995), may be more of a reflection of the extent to which part-time and contingent workers experience a mismatch between their capabilities and the specific tasks that they are assigned to perform (Feldman, Doerpinghaus, & Turnley, 1995). At the other end of the continuum, part-time workers employed in "job sharing arrangements" or as "specialized temps" (e.g., medical, accountants, engineers) or "independent contractors" may be more exposed to stress that results from the complexity of the tasks that they have been assigned to perform.

Within the context of contingent employment, consideration might also be given to the extent to which the complexity-stress relationship may be moderated by personal expectations and the work environment. For example, among temporary help firm workers, the potentially negative effects of monotonous work may be moderated by the expectation that the assignment is short-term in nature (Rogers, 1995). However, as the duration of the temporary assignment increases, the work monotony-stress relationship may become more pronounced. Conversely, for the segment of contingent workers performing more complex tasks, the complexity-stress relationship may be moderated by the extent to which contingent workers are provided social and intellectual support by permanent employees within the organization where the work is being performed (Danna & Griffin, 1999). Unlike workers employed in ongoing, part-time schedules, contingent workers may often lack access to informal support networks that develop within organizations that may help to minimize problems associated with both quantitative and qualitative work overload.

Role in the Organization

As noted by Danna and Griffin (1999), "role ambiguity," "role conflict," and the "degree of responsibility for others" are also major sources of potential stress. Again, among research studies that have predominately focused on workers employed in full-time and ongoing employment contracts, there is sufficient evidence to support a relationship between role ambiguity and role conflict with higher levels of negative affective and behavioral consequences (Jackson & Schuler, 1985).

To date, very limited empirical data exists to suggest that the levels of role ambiguity and role conflict differ between full-time and part-time workers. It is reasonable to suggest that role-related ambiguity may be less a function of employment status (full-time vs. part-time) than it is a function of organization- and task-related characteristics. As noted by Jex (1998), role ambiguity can be a partial result of such considerations as (a) poorly written job descriptions, (b) the reality that some jobs are simply difficult to define, and (c) the fact that within many organizations, environmental forces drive changes in role responsibilities and expectations.

Less empirically definitive is the question of whether or not workers employed on a contingent basis are more likely to experience role ambiguity than workers (both full- and part-time) with ongoing employment contracts. Among a number of studies, the research findings are, on the surface, rather indefinite. For example, research by Sverke, Gallagher, and Hellgren (2000) found that self-reported ambiguity among Swedish health care workers was significantly greater for contingent workers than for full- or part-time workers. In contrast, a study of Israeli clerical workers found no significant differences in role ambiguity (and role conflict) between permanent and temporary workers (Krausz, Brandwein, & Fox, 1995). Subsequent research by Krausz (2000) found that among temporary workers, levels of role ambiguity were significantly related to the extent to which temporary workers viewed their temporary jobs as means to finding permanent employment or had a desire to remain in the role of a "permanent" temporary. These results are interesting, albeit confusing because they suggest that ambiguity might not only be a function of the role itself but also the motivation for which workers have assumed the job.

From a theoretical perspective it is entirely possible to conceptualize that role ambiguity, and for that matter role conflict, may be influenced by the form of the contingent employment relationship. For example, among contingent workers dispatched by temporary help service firms, assignments to client firms are often of a short, fixed-term duration. Anecdotal evidence pertaining to the experience of temporary clerical workers has suggested that temporary workers may receive limited directions from the client organization concerning the nature of the jobs they have been assigned to perform. Job ambiguity may also develop as a result of miscommunication or lack of clarity between the client organization and the temporary help firm or between the temporary firm and the dispatched worker concerning the type of work to be performed. Such a mismatch may also create work-related stress as a result of qualitative work overload or underload.

Unlike direct-hire contingents, who are frequently assigned to the same or a small group of jobs within the organization, the ability of temporary help service workers to reduce initial levels of role ambiguity, through experience, is limited by the fact that such temporaries often move from job to job within different organizations (Buttram, 1996). In effect, the potential level of role ambiguity associated with contingent work assignments arranged through temporary firms is magnified by the extent to which workers are rotated into short-term assignments from one client organization to another.

Role ambiguity may also be created in the case of contingent workers employed as independent contractors as a result of a lack of congruence between the expectations of the client organization and the performance expectations of the contractor. Similar to the case of temporaries dispatched through temporary firms, the ability of an independent contractor to resolve role ambiguities may be offset by the fact that role- or task-related ambiguity may resurface as independent contractors move between client organizations or projects within the same organization. It is also possible to suggest that workers who voluntarily gravitate toward contingent employment, in particular independent contractors, may themselves have a high tolerance for ambiguity (Buttram, 1996; Castaneda, 1999).

As noted by Frone, Russell, and Cooper (1995), the relationship between job ambiguity and physical health and alcohol use is, in fact, moderated by job involvement. In particular, a high level of job involvement may actually exacerbate the negative health outcomes associated with job ambiguity. There is no reason to suggest that such a relationship would not also be applicable to part-time and contingent workers. The broader issue may be the extent to which part-time and contingent workers differ in their level of job involvement relative to workers in more traditional full-time jobs. However, as previously noted, for many temporary workers and independent contractors, the term "job" and subsequently "job involvement" may be nebulous. For example, independent contractors or temporary help service firm workers may hold high levels of job involvement as characterized by the type of work they perform but may periodically hold a low level of job involvement as it pertains to the work associated with a particular assignment. As a result, among some forms of contingent employment, understanding the moderating effect of job involvement among contingent workers may be complicated if the construct is defined in the context of each individual assignment or project (Gallagher & McLean Parks, 2001).

With regard to role conflict, there again is no particular reason to suggest that established findings pertaining to the linkage between role conflicts and well-being would not be applicable to both part-time and contingent workers (Cartwright & Cooper, 1997; Greenhaus & Parasuraman, 1986). However, different types of contingent employment arrangements may be confronted with differing forms and levels of role conflict. Among independent contractors, *intrarole* conflict may be minimal in those cases in which the contractors do, in fact, have control over the work process. In contrast, the unique structure of the employment relationship that exists for workers in the temporary help industry may hold the potential for increased levels of *interrole* conflict due to the feelings of responsibility that the worker may have to the unique interests of both the temporary firm and the client organization.

Organizational Integration—Climate and Support

To date, research on work-related stress has also placed a good deal of emphasis on the importance of interpersonal relationships and organizational climate as determinants of individual well-being (Cartwright & Cooper, 1997; Danna & Griffin, 1999). Within the realm of interpersonal relationships would be consideration of the extent to which interactions between an employee and others (e.g., supervisors, coworkers, subordinates and customers) contribute to feelings of conflict, unfair treatment, and work-related dissatisfaction (Jex, 1998). In addition, climate is often categorized in terms of organizationally based characteristics such as structure and situational constraints that facilitate or impede employee well-being (Danna & Griffin, 1999).

One salient aspect of the employment relationship, which manifests a blending of interpersonal relationships and organizational structure, is the extent to which workers employed under different types of employment contracts (full-time vs. part-time, contingent and noncontingent) are integrated into the organization. Although research on this issue is very limited, evidence suggests that part-time workers often see themselves as marginalized (Barker, 1993). This marginalization does not necessarily translate into expected negative consequences from an attitudinal perspective. In fact, research results generally suggest that part-time workers are more positive in their evaluation of the social aspects of the employment relationship than their full-time counterparts (Barling & Gallagher, 1996). In many organizations, part-time workers are employed side by side with their full-time workers (Olsen, 2003), or, in the case of many service-based organizations, part-time employment tends to be the predominate form of employment contract. However, the economic reality exists that part-time workers are less likely to be assigned managerial positions or have access to professional development opportunities within organizations (Zeytinoglu, 1999).

With regard to workers employed in varying types of contingent employment contracts, research by Rogers (1995, 2000) and Galup, Saunders, Nelson, and Cerveny (1997) tends to suggest that temporary workers are socially excluded by regular full- and part-time workers. Research by Sias, Kramer, and Jenkins (1997) also found that newly hired temporary workers are more communicatively isolated from current employees than newly hired permanent workers. Among studies of workers employed under traditional ongoing contracts, social exclusion has been found to be related to higher levels of workers' anxiety, depression, and loneliness (Baumeister & Leary, 1995). Whether such social isolation of temporary workers translates into increased levels of job-related stress is an empirical question that has not been fully investigated. But it is also important to recognize that isolation is not a universal characteristic of contingent employment. Among contingent workers employed in the role of independent contractors, the very nature of their job may require that they work in proximity to full-time employees of the organization. Within some sectors of the economy, there has also been a trend as part of organizational downsizing to reassign workers previously employed under traditional ongoing employment contracts to the status of independent contractor. Although these newly created independent contractors were extensively assimilated into the organization as a result of their prior work history, after downsizing, they are cast into a new employment arrangement that technically requires, in most countries, that the employer maintain an arm's length relationship. Such a shift in employment status within the same organization may be a unique source of individual worker stress associated with some forms of contingent employment.

As noted by Peters and O'Connor (1988), work-related stress may also be a result of inadequate resources to perform assigned tasks effectively. For both part-time and contingent workers, limited access to organizational resources could lead to performance-based frustration that, in turn, may negatively affect worker well-being. In contrast to both part-time and direct-hire temporaries, both temporary help service workers and independent contractors may be particularly disadvantaged because they are more "external" to the employing organization and, in fact, may have less access to organization resources.

It is also important to note that, in addition to the varying degrees of communicative and physical isolation that may occur between regular full-time and contingent workers, contingent workers may also be physically and socially isolated from each other. In the particular case of workers employed through the services of the temporary help firm, there tends to be very little, if any, interaction among temporary workers if they are not dispatched to the same workplace. With rare exception, there is very little social and support networking among temporary help firm workers. In contrast, for many independent contractors, particularly those in high-skill and technology-based occupations, professional networking is often a present and important aspect of their work (Castaneda, 1999). Networking with other independent contractors provides a level of professional affiliation that is not only part of a system of updating skills and locating employment opportunities but also provides a form of social support that independent contractors may not be able to develop within their client organizations. The presence of social support, in any form, may serve as a buffer between work-related stressors and well-being (Ganster, Fusilier, & Mayes, 1986).

Recent research by Lautsch (2002) suggests that organizations may undertake fundamentally different strategies concerning the extent to which they integrate contingent workers with the permanent workforce. Issues of integration pertain not only to questions of physical locations but also issues related to common or differential work practices and compensation. Based in part on case study research design, Lautsch's research suggests that, driven by both performance objectives and the technological context of the industry, treatment of contingent workers may include staffing models that keep temporary workers physically isolated from permanent workers as well as models in which temporaries are employed side by side with other employees with similar responsibilities and compensation (integration model) or similar work but dissimilar compensation and benefit treatment (two-tier). Lautsch's research also indicated that regular workers' reactions to the use of contingent work varied according to the type of system that the organization was attempting to put into place. The study indicated that resistance by regular workers was greatest in situations wherein contingent and regular workers had more similar jobs but pay inequity was the highest (i.e., two-tier systems).

Lautsch's (2002) research and that of other researchers suggest the need to consider the possible "spillover" effect that the employment and treatment of contingent workers may have on the employment-related attitudes of an organization's noncontingent workforce. For example, research by Pearce (1993) examining the use of independent contractors (engineers) in the aerospace industry found that the practice had the unanticipated negative consequence of being associated with decreased levels of organizational trustworthiness among regular staff engineers. A partial replication of Lautsch's framework in Japan by Morishima and Feuille (2000) found that within organizations where contingent workers were integrated with regular employees there was a significantly lower level of workplace morale and trust among regular employees than in organizations where contingents and noncontingents were kept physically isolated from each other. Along similar lines, Chattopadhyay and George (2001) found that noncontingent workers who were employed in work groups dominated by temporary workers had significantly lower levels of self-esteem and organizational trust than noncontingent workers who were more likely to be working side by side with other noncontingents. Data from two national surveys of U.S. workers also found that traditional workers who worked in organizations that regularly employed temporary workers were more likely to experience negative relationships with their managers and express a higher level of intent to leave the organization (Davis-Blake, Broschak, & George, 2003). Although there may be concerns associated with causality, this research does raise questions pertaining to the potential impact that the use of contingent workers has on the well-being of noncontingent or regular workers. In particular, it would appear that the use of contingent workers may create stress by negatively affecting perceived job security and increasing organizational distrust, which could, in turn, negatively affect their own well-being.

Employment Security and Career Development

It is well recognized that in an environment of organizational restructuring, firm acquisition and mergers, and limited economic growth, the resulting fear of job loss can have negative consequences for employee well-being (Hellgren & Sverke, 2003). As noted by Greenhalgh and Rosenblatt (1984), "job insecurity" is a complex subjective feeling composed of four different components: continuation of the job itself, continuation of the job conditions, the importance of those conditions to the worker, and the worker's sense of powerlessness about his or her insecurity. In more simplistic terms, job insecurity includes a fear not only of job loss (quantitative) but also of loss of tasks as a result of restructuring (qualitative) (Hellgren, Sverke, & Isaksson, 1999). But how individual workers perceive job insecurity and potential consequences is also influenced by the extent to which workers value the job they are performing and have some control over the preservation of their job.

On the surface, it would appear easy to hypothesize that workers performing contingent or temporary jobs are less likely to perceive their jobs as secure, relative to the perceptions of workers on full-time, ongoing employment contracts. Although there exists some research to support the finding that contingent workers perceive higher levels of job insecurity than more traditional full-time workers (e.g., Sverke et al., 2000), the findings are not necessary compelling.

It is very possible to argue that the extent to which workers perceive their jobs to be insecure and the potential impact on their personal well-being may be a function of both the form of the nonstandard work arrangement and the worker's motivation for undertaking a particular job or work assignment. An illustration of this point can be found in a recent study by Silla, Sora, and Gracia (2003) that investigated the relationship between job insecurity and health-related outcomes in a sample of permanent and nonpermanent workers. Not surprisingly, Silla et al. found that for the entire sample there was a significant negative relationship between measures of perceived job insecurity and worker well-being. However, utilizing a framework similar to that of Marler, Barringer, and Milkovich (2002), Silla et al. (2003) distinguished four main categories of contingent workers based on their preferences for temporary work and their skill level. *Boundaryless* temporaries consisted of high-skill workers (e.g., independent contractors) with a high preference for temporary work. Skilled workers with a strong desire to move into more traditional full-time jobs were classified as *transitional* workers. *Career* temporaries represented low-skilled workers with a strong preference for remaining as contingents, whereas the *traditional* temporaries were those contingent workers with low skills and a low preference for temporary work.

Silla et al.'s (2003) research found that self-reported job insecurity was most pronounced among the two categories of contingent workers (traditional and career) that were categorized as "low skill." Also interesting was the finding that transitional, temporary workers had significantly higher levels of job insecurity than permanent workers, whereas boundaryless workers were equivalent to permanent workers in terms of perceived job insecurity. However, despite an overall positive (albeit modest) relationship between self-reported job insecurity and well-being, the results indicated virtually no differences across categories of workers with the exception that traditional temporaries reported higher levels of personal well-being than permanent (noncontingent) workers.

These findings are particularly interesting because they may, in fact, suggest that, depending on skill levels and motivations, workers may differentially process the consequences of potential job loss. For example, among high-skill independent contractors or boundaryless workers, the perceived consequences of job loss might well be mitigated by their preference for project-based work. In addition, potential or actual job loss is of minimal concern to workers with skill levels that may be in high demand and a concurrent desire to remain employed on a contingent basis. Such a situation would, in many respects, be the antithesis of the job insecurity/well-being relationship that might be expected of a low-skilled worker facing the loss of a standard or permanent position or a worker of any skill level who is seeking to use the current position as a means of transitioning into a more permanent position. Research by Klein Hesselink and van Vuuren (1999) suggests that job insecurity may, in fact, be less of a concern for workers in flexible staffing positions because the difference between their level of expected and perceived job security is minimal. Collectively, this research implies that the potential consequences of job insecurity might very well be a function of the importance that workers place on maintaining or achieving a traditional full-time job. Along similar but unexplored lines, one could also apply this research to the job insecurity/well-being relationship that may exist among part-time workers. In particular, job insecurity might have greater negative consequences for part-time workers employed in relatively scarce, high-quality or "retention" part-time jobs (Tilly, 1992).

Volition

Theory and research have long contended that support for a particular course of action and related attitudes is a function of volition (Salancik, 1977). In a comprehensive review of the literature on the consequences of part-time employment, Barling and Gallagher (1996) point to the centrality of voluntary choice as a determent of employee attitudes and well-being. Workers who voluntarily choose to work part-time work schedules are more satisfied with their jobs and committed to their employer organizations than those who associate their employment arrangements with a lack of preferred alternatives.

Not unsurprisingly, one of the few but consistent themes in the contingent research literature relates to the conclusion that workers who voluntarily seek temporary or contingent employment contracts are more satisfied, experience more positive work-related attitudes, and have fewer psychological symptoms than workers who are employed under contingent contracts for reason of a lack of valuable alternatives (Ellingson, Gruys, & Sackett, 1998; Feldman et al., 1995; Isaksson & Bellagh, 2002; Krausz, 2000). In principle, the attitudes and associated well-being of part-time and contingent workers are closely tied to congruencies between their expectations and the reality of their employment status.

The term *volition* best expresses what it is that workers are seeking. Among direct-hire temporary workers, contingent work is primarily used as a means of gaining access to a standard full-time position within an organization. On the other side of the equation, employing workers on a temporary basis can provide organizations with a prolonged and minimal-risk job interview. For direct-hire workers, job insecurity may be equivalent to the concern over losing the opportunity to secure a full-time position and, as a result, carries a greater level of psychological stress. Conversely, among temporary help service workers and independent contractors, job insecurity may be equivalent to assignment termination, with minimal consequences if the expectation is that termination of one job or assignment will lead to subsequent work with a different client. This may also relate to the earlier observation that the term "job" may have an indeterminate meaning. For independent contractors or workers with a temporary career orientation, the threat and subsequent job loss may be less threatening to personal well-being than the potential loss of their career or occupation as a temporary or independent contractor. However, among independent contractors, it is important to recognize that some workers may be so reliant on work provided by a single client organization (perhaps a previous employer) that they may, in fact, be more appropriately characterized a "dependent contractor." Under these conditions, the prospect of job loss may be equivalent to the experience and well-being-related concerns of traditional or standard full-time employees (Marlin, 2000).

Epilogue

As suggested at the outset of this chapter, research on the topic of work stress and the broader issue of worker well-being has been based on the study of workers employed in a full-time and ongoing employer-employee relationship. Such research has been well focused and relevant for the simple reason that such employment relationships have been and will continue to be the prevailing form of employment in most nations. However, in addition to the ever present reliance of organizations, particularly those in the service sector, on the use of part-time workers, there is a gradual and increasing organizational use of contingent workers whose employment terms fall outside the prevailing model of employer-employee relationship. As indicated in this chapter, it is very important to recognize that contingent employment contracts can assume a wide variety of forms or contractual arrangements. There may also be substantial differences among both part-time and contingent workers pertaining to the reason why they work under such contractual conditions.

The most central and critical issues are questions concerning the applicability of work stress and employee well-being research, developed in the context of full-time employment, to workers employed in part-time and contingent work arrangements. In particular, it is entirely plausible to argue that existing theories of work stress and well-being and related empirical findings are entirely applicable to part-time and contingent workers. This argument of applicability might be most convincing in the situation of part-time employment in which the individual worker operates in the context of an ongoing and clearly identifiable employer-employee relationship. Even in the case in which differences may be found between the psychological well-being of full- and part-time workers, the issue is often a question of the magnitude or the relative impact of intervening variables (e.g., hours of work or volition) rather than the nonapplicability of the theoretical framework.

However, in the case of contingent employment arrangements, such factors as the frequent changing of the client organization, variable job-related tasks and responsibilities, and the absence of a clear employer-employee work relationship may cast some doubt on the extent to which existing role theory-based models of stress and well-being are fully relevant to contingent workers. Unfortunately, existing research pertaining to work stress and well-being among contingent workers is limited and extremely fragmented in terms of focus. As part of a future research agenda, greater attention should be given to the efforts to contrast the sources and outcomes of work-related stress and well-being for full-time and part-time workers in the same organization. Such research could also be extended to include intraorganization comparisons of contingent and noncontingent worker-related well-being. As in recent research by Lautsch, attention could be given to what effect, if any, organizational policies of workforce integration or separation have on the sources and magnitude of work-related stress. This type of comparative research could also provide the opportunity to more systematically explore the extent and implications of a possible spillover effect that the employment of contingent workers may have on the job security and related well-being of more traditional workers.

Within the realm of longitudinal research designs, future research should seek to address two particularly relevant issues related to work stress and well-being. With specific regard to the growing number of workers employed through temporary help service firms, it would be useful to determine the extent to which employee perceptions of work stress and associated well-being change as temporaries move from assignments at one client organization to another. Such research would be instructive in unraveling the extent to which work-related stress is specific to job assignments within client organizations or is more generally defined in terms of the stressors inherent to the job of a contingent worker. Along similar lines, it would be interesting to examine changes in job-based stress and well-being among direct-hire temporaries based on their underlying motivations for working temporary positions within an organization and the personal well-being-based consequences associated with the ability to successfully transition into a full-time, noncontingent employment contract.

Finally, as implied in the discussion of the existing research, much more attention needs to be given to personality-based characteristics of workers performing part-time and contingent work. Particularly among contingent workers, the absence of the apparent security of an ongoing employment contract may be more suitable to workers with certain personality traits than others. In addition, greater attention should also be directed to understanding how individual worker values and expectations affect workers' subjective evaluation of contingent work-related experiences.

In many respects, understanding the relationship between contingent work, stress, and well-being is an area of research that is not particularly well developed but will assume greater importance as the share of the workforce employed under contingent contract arrangements continues to grow.

References

Baffoe-Bonnie, J. (2001). The impact of income taxation on the labor supply of part-time and full-time workers. *International Review of Applied Economics, 15*, 107–128.

Barker, K. (1993). Changing assumptions and contingent solutions: The costs and benefits of women working full- and part-time. *Sex Roles, 28*, 47–71.

Barling, J., & Gallagher, D. G. (1996). Part-time employment. In C. L. Cooper & I. T. Robertson (Eds.), *International review of industrial and organizational psychology* (Vol. 2, pp. 241–277). Chichester, UK: Wiley.

Barling, J., Inness, M., & Gallagher, D. G. (2002). Alternative work arrangements and employee well being. In P. Perrewé & D. Ganster (Eds.), *Historical and current perspectives on stress and well being* (Vol. 2, pp. 183–216). Oxford, UK: Elsevier Science.

Baumeister, R. F., & Leary, M. R. (1995). The need to belong: Desire for interpersonal attachments as a fundamental human motivation. *Psychological Bulletin, 117,* 497–529.

Beard, K. M., & Edwards, J. R. (1995). Employees at risk: Contingent work and the experience of contingent workers. In C. L. Cooper & D. M. Rousseau (Eds.), *Trends in organizational behavior* (Vol. 2, pp. 109–126). Chichester, UK: Wiley.

Belous, R. S. (1989). *The contingent economy: The growth of the temporary, part-time and subcontracted workforce.* Washington, DC: National Planning Association.

Brewster, C., Mayne, L., & Tregaskis, O. (1997). Flexible working in Europe: A review of the evidence. *Management International Review, 37,* 85–103.

Buttram, R. T. (1996, August). *Working without a net: Predicting stress, strain, and satisfaction among temporary workers.* Paper presented at the annual meeting of the Academy of Management, Cincinnati, OH.

Cappelli, P. (1999). *The new deal at work.* Boston: Harvard Business School Press.

Cartwright, S., & Cooper, C. L. (1997). *Managing workplace stress.* Thousand Oaks, CA: Sage.

Castaneda, L. W. (1999, August). *Social networks in the open labor market: An exploration of independent contractors' careers.* Paper presented at the 1999 meeting of the Academy of Management, Chicago.

Chattopadhyay, P., & George, E. (2001). Examining the effects of work externalization through the lens of social identity theory. *Journal of Applied Psychology, 86,* 781–788.

Cohany, S. R. (1998). Workers in alternative employment arrangements: A second look. *Monthly Labor Review, 121,* 3–21.

Connelly, C. E., & Gallagher, D. G. (2004). Managing contingent workers: Adapting to new realities. In R. J. Burke & C. L. Cooper (Eds.), *Leading in turbulent times: Managing in the new world of work* (pp. 143–164). Oxford, UK: Blackwell.

Cooper, C. L., & Marshall, J. (1978). *Executives under pressure.* London: Macmillan.

Cully, M., Woodland, S., O'Reilly, A., & Dix, G. (1999). *Britain at work.* London: Routledge.

Danna, K., & Griffin, R. W. (1999). Health and well-being in the workplace: A review and synthesis of the literature. *Journal of Management, 25,* 357–384.

Davis-Blake, A., Broschak, J. P., & George, E. (2003). Happy together? How using nonstandard workers affects exit, voice, and loyalty among standard employees. *Academy of Management Journal, 46,* 475–485.

Delsen, L. (1999). Changing work relations in the European Union. In I. U. Zeytinoglu (Ed.), *Changing work relationships in industrialized economies* (pp. 99–114). Amsterdam: John Benjamins.

Ellingson, J. E., Gruys, M. L., & Sackett, P. R. (1998). Factors related to the satisfaction and performance of temporary employees. *Journal of Applied Psychology, 83,* 913–921.

Feldman, D. C. (1990). Reconceptualizing the nature and consequences of part-time work. *Academy of Management Review, 15,* 103–112.

Feldman, D.C., Doerpinghaus, H. I., & Turnley, W. H. (1995). Employee reactions to temporary jobs. *Journal of Management Issues, 7,* 127–141.

Frone, M. R., Russell, M., & Cooper, M. L. (1995). Job stress, job involvement, and employee health: A test of identity theory. *Journal of Occupational and Organizational Psychology, 68,* 1–11.

Gallagher, D. G. (2002). Contingent work contracts: Practice and theory. In C. Cooper & R. Burke (Eds.), *The new world of work: Challenges and opportunities.* (pp. 115–136). Oxford, UK: Blackwell.

Gallagher, D. G., & McLean Parks, J. (2001). I pledge thee my troth . . . contingently: Commitment and the contingent work relationship. *Human Resource Management Review, 11,* 181–208.

Galup, S., Saunders, C., Nelson, R. E., & Cerveny, R. (1997). The use of temporary staff and managers in a local government environment. *Communication Research, 24,* 698–730.

Ganster, D. C., Fusilier, M. R., & Mayes, B. T. (1986). Role of social support in the experience of stress at work. *Journal of Applied Psychology, 71,* 102–110.

Greenhalgh, L., & Rosenblatt, Z. (1984). Job insecurity: Toward conceptual clarity. *Academy of Management Review, 9,* 438–448.

Greenhaus, J. H., & Parasuraman, S. (1986). A work-nonwork interactive perspective of stress and its consequences. *Journal of Organizational Behavior Management, 8,* 37–60.

Hellgren, J., & Sverke, M. (2003). Does job insecurity lead to impaired well-being or vice versa? Estimation of cross-lagged effects using latent variable modeling. *Journal of Organizational Behavior, 24,* 215–236.

Hellgren, J., Sverke, M., & Isaksson, K. (1999). A two dimensional approach to job insecurity: Consequences for employee attitudes and well-being. *European Journal of Work and Organizational Psychology, 8,* 179–195.

Isaksson, K., & Bellagh, K. (2002). Health problems and quitting among female "temps." *European Journal of Work and Organizational Psychology, 11,* 27–45.

Jackson, S. E., & Schuler, R. S. (1985). A meta-analysis and conceptual critique of research on role ambiguity and role conflict in work settings. *Organizational Behavior and Human Decision Processes, 36,* 16–78.

Jex, S. M. (1998). *Stress and job performance.* Thousand Oaks, CA: Sage.

Kahn, R. L., Wolfe, D. M., Quinn, R. P., Snoek, J. D., & Rosenthal, R. A. (1964). *Organizational stress: Studies in role conflict and role ambiguity.* New York: Wiley.

Kim, S., & Feldman, D. C. (2000). Working in retirement: The antecedents of bridge employment and its consequences for quality of life in retirement. *Academy of Management Journal, 43,* 1195–1210.

Klein Hesselink, D. J., & van Vuuren, T. (1999). Job flexibility and job insecurity: The Dutch case. *European Journal of Work and Organizational Psychology, 8,* 273–294.

Krausz, M. (2000). Effects of short- and long-term preference for temporary work upon psychological outcomes. *International Journal of Manpower, 21,* 635–647.

Krausz, M., Brandwein, T., & Fox, S. (1995). Work attitudes and emotional responses of permanent, voluntary, and involuntary temporary-help employees: An exploratory study. *Applied Psychology: An International Review, 44,* 217–232.

Lautsch, B. A. (2002). Uncovering and explaining variance in the features and outcomes of contingent work. *Industrial and Labor Relations Review, 56,* 23–43.

Marler, J. H., Barringer, M. W., & Milkovich, G. T. (2002). Boundaryless and traditional contingent employees: Worlds apart. *Journal of Organizational Behavior, 23,* 425–453.

Marlin, E. (2000). The perspectives for a new and comprehensive vision of the protection of workers. *Proceedings of the Twelfth World Congress of the International Industrial Relations Research Association, 1,* 151–159 (Tokyo, Japan).

Melamed, S., Ben-Avi, I., Luz, J., & Green, M. S. (1995). Objective and subjective work monotony: Effects on job satisfaction, psychological distress, and absenteeism in blue collar workers. *Journal of Applied Psychology, 80,* 29–42.

Muhl, C. J. (2002, January). What is an employee? The answer depends on federal law. *Monthly Labor Review,* 3–11.

Morishima, M., & Feuille, P. (2000). *Effects of the use of contingent workers on regular status workers: A Japan-US comparison.* Paper presented at the World Congress of the International Industrial Relations Association, Tokyo, Japan.

Nollen, S. (1999). Flexible working arrangements: An overview of developments in the United States. In I. U. Zeytinoglu (Ed.), *Changing work relationships in industrialized economies* (pp. 21–39). Amsterdam: John Benjamins.

Olsen, K. M. (2003, August). *Contingency reversed: The role of agency temporaries and contractors in client-organizations.* Paper presented at the annual meeting of the Academy of Management, Seattle, WA.

Parasuraman, S., & Simmers, C. A. (2001). Type of employment, work-family conflict and well-being: A comparative study. *Journal of Organizational Behavior, 22,* 551–568.

Pearce, J. L. (1993). Toward an organizational behavior of contract laborers: Their psychological involvement and effects on employee co-workers. *Academy of Management Journal, 36,* 1086–1096.

Peters, L. H., & O'Connor, E. J. (1988). Measuring work obstacles: Procedures, issues, and implications. In F. D. Schoorman & B. Schneider (Eds.), *Facilitating work effectiveness* (pp. 105–123). Lexington, MA: Lexington Books.

Pfeffer, J., & Baron, N. (1988). Taking the work back out: Research trends in the structures of employment. In B. Staw & L. L. Cummings (Eds.), *Research in organizational behavior* (Vol. 10, pp. 257–303). Greenwich, CT: JAI.

Pierce, J. L., Newstrom, J. W., Dunham, R. B., & Barber, A. E. (1989). *Alternative work schedules.* Boston: Allyn & Bacon.

Reilly, P. A. (1998). Balancing flexibility: Meeting the interests of employer and employee. *European Journal of Work and Organizational Psychology, 7,* 7–22.

Rogers, J. K. (1995). Just a temp: Experience and structure of alienation in temporary clerical employment. *Work and Occupations, 22,* 137–166.

Rogers, J. K. (2000). *Temps: The many faces of the changing workplace.* Ithaca, NY: Cornell University Press.

Rotchford, N. L., & Roberts, R. H. (1982). Part-time workers as missing persons in organizational research. *Academy of Management Review, 7,* 228–234.

Salancik, G. (1977). Commitment and the control of organizational behavior and belief. In B. Staw & G. Salancik (Eds.), *New directions in organizational behavior* (pp. 1–54). Chicago: St. Clair Press.

Sias, P. M., Kramer, M. W., & Jenkins, E. (1997). A comparison of the communication behaviors of temporary employees and new hires. *Communication Research, 24,* 731–754.

Silla, I., Sora, B., & Gracia, F. (2003, April). *Job insecurity and health-related outcomes in permanent and non-permanent workers.* Paper presented at the 11th meeting of the European Association of Work and Organizational Psychology, Lisbon, Portugal.

Sverke, M., Gallagher, D. G., & Hellgren, J. (2000). Alternative work arrangements: Job stress, well-being and work attitudes among employees with different employment contracts. In K. Eriksson, C. Hogstedt, C. Eriksson, & T. Theorell (Eds.), *Health hazards in the new labour market* (pp. 145–167). London, UK: Kluwer Academic/Plenum.

Tilly, C. (1992). Dualism in part-time employment. *Industrial Relations, 31,* 330–347.

Xie, J. L., & Johns, G. (1995). Job scope and stress: Can scope be too high? *Academy of Management Journal, 38,* 1288–1309.

Zeytinoglu, I. U. (1999). Flexible work arrangements: An overview of developments in Canada. In I. U. Zeytinoglu (Ed.), *Changing work relationships in industrialized economies* (pp. 41–58). Amsterdam: John Benjamins.

PART III

Consequences of Work Stress

22

Editors' Overview: Consequences of Work Stress

The adverse consequences of work stress are manifold. Jex and Crossley (see Chapter 24) present a taxonomy of work stress–related outcomes by crossing two dimensions: outcome relevance (individual vs. organizational) and outcome type (psychological, physical, and behavioral). Adverse individual outcomes include poor psychological and mental health outcomes (e.g., anger, depression, anxiety, posttraumatic stress syndrome, burnout), impaired physiological processes (e.g., cardiovascular reactivity, elevated levels of various hormones, impaired immune function) and physical disease outcomes (e.g., hypertension, stroke, cancer, ulcers and gastrointestinal disorders, musculoskeletal disorders, migraine headaches), and detrimental behavioral outcomes (sleep disturbance; alcohol, tobacco, and illicit drug use; poor eating habits; intimate partner violence). Adverse organizational outcomes include poor psychological and emotional outcomes (e.g., job dissatisfaction, low organizational commitment), indicators of poor physical health (absence due to illness, workers' compensation claims), and work-related behavioral impairment (injuries, poor job performance, on-the-job substance use). Many of these outcomes, especially individual outcomes, have been discussed in the preceding chapters. However, in this section, two chapters provide a more detailed discussion of two specific types of outcomes related to exposure to stressors at work.

On the side of individual outcomes, Warr discusses employee psychological well-being and mental health in Chapter 23. When considering the individual psychological outcomes of work stress, most research has focused on various dimensions of mental illness. Warr points out that mental health is not merely the absence of mental illness. Thus, in contrast to past research, he primarily explores the positive states of mental health while also noting the interrelations between negative and positive states of mental health. He begins with a detailed discussion of the nature of mental health, which includes subjective well-being, positive self-regard, competence, aspiration, autonomy, and integrated functioning. Warr then defines 10 central dimensions of the work environment and examines their relation to employee mental health. Next, he discusses the relation of employee mental health to chronic personal characteristics such as personality and eight episodic or proactive personal features including social comparisons, comparisons with expectations, and counterfactual comparisons. He then considers the joint impact of work environment and personal characteristics on mental health. The relation of employee subjective well-being to behaviors at work also is considered. Finally, directions for future research are discussed.

In Chapter 24, Jex and Crossley review the organizational outcomes associated with stressor exposure at work. They begin by defining the various types of individual and organizational outcomes. They then review five theoretical models of occupational stress, focusing on their relevance for organizational outcomes. Methodological challenges and opportunities associated with measuring organizationally relevant outcomes are discussed. The literature linking job stressor exposure to adverse organizational outcomes is reviewed. This is followed by discussions of implications for managerial practice and public policy and directions for future research. Jex and Crossley conclude that although work stress has negative effects that extend beyond the health of employees to the health of organizations, relatively little research on work stress has explored organizationally relevant outcomes.

23

Work, Well-Being, and Mental Health

Peter Warr

Most constructs can be viewed at several levels of generality. Although research in a particular field tends to become located at a single level, it is important also to view central concepts in alternative terms. The notion of stress can usefully be examined within the broader constructs of well-being and health.

Health itself is defined by the World Health Organization in terms of three forms of well-being: physical, mental, and social. Physical reactions to job conditions can include muscular strains and injuries of many kinds as well as cardiovascular disorders and other conditions that have both physical and psychological aspects. They are not always apparent as immediate bodily changes, sometimes developing only across years or decades. The third element in the World Health Organization's definition (well-being that is social) concerns equitable and beneficial involvement in social communities. For example, Keyes (1998) identified five dimensions (*social integration, social contribution, social coherence, social actualization,* and *social acceptance*) that emerged from questionnaire responses as separable statistical factors.

This chapter will deal with employee health mainly in its psychological aspects, examining some characteristics, causes, and consequences and also reviewing research needs. Previous investigations will be grouped in terms of their primary focus: on the environment, on the person, or on both.

The Nature of Mental Health

There are many views about the components and processes of mental health. The concept is value-laden so that a universally agreed definition is not likely to be attained (e.g., Jahoda, 1958). However, "health" is not merely the absence of ill health, in an either-or manner. We need to think also in terms of gradations from poor to good health such that people can be described with respect to the degree to which they are or are not healthy. In that way, we can consider people in general, not merely those who are defined as "ill," beyond a threshold of disorder or disease.

One perspective on variations in mental health, as the concept is applied in Western societies, is through six principal dimensions. Those may be labeled as "subjective well-being," "positive self-regard," "competence," "aspiration," "autonomy," and "integrated functioning."

Subjective Well-Being

The first dimension, subjective well-being, is usually taken to be a principal indicator of poor or good mental health. It has been studied with a greater emphasis on either affective or cognitive reactions. Some researchers have focused on current feelings, moods, or emotions, whereas others have emphasized a more cognitive interpretation of oneself and one's position.

Several within-concept distinctions have been made. For instance, separable facets of job satisfaction have been studied in terms of people's reactions to their supervisor, coworkers, pay, and other job features (e.g., Kinicki, McKee-Ryan, Schriesheim, & Carson, 2002). In respect to affective states, an important distinction is between two kinds of positive feelings: of excitement and active pleasure or of contentment and relaxation.

That distinction is made more formally in research examining the notion of mental arousal as well as affective direction. The framework set out in Figure 23.1 has been supported in many investigations (e.g., Remington, Fabrigar, & Visser, 2000; Yik, Russell, & Feldman Barrett, 1999) that have pointed to the importance of two independent dimensions of feeling, here labeled as "pleasure" and "arousal."

We may describe a person's subjective well-being in terms of its location relative to those two dimensions (representing the content of feelings) and its distance from the midpoint of the figure (such that a more distant location indicates a greater intensity). A particular degree of pleasure or displeasure (the horizontal dimension) may be accompanied by high or low levels of mental arousal (the vertical dimension), and a particular quantity of mental arousal (sometimes referred to as "activation") may be either pleasurable or displeasurable to varying degrees.

Within this framework, three principal axes of measurement are illustrated in Figure 23.2. In view of the central importance of displeasure or pleasure, the first axis is in terms of the horizontal dimension alone. The other two axes take account of mental arousal as well as pleasure by running diagonally between opposite quadrants through the midpoint of the figure.

In thinking about subjective well-being, we may thus consider three main axes (Lucas, Diener, & Suh, 1996). First is a general valence axis from displeasure to pleasure, the positive pole of which reflects overall positive feelings. The second axis runs from anxiety to comfort. Feelings of anxiety combine low pleasure with high mental arousal whereas comfort is illustrated

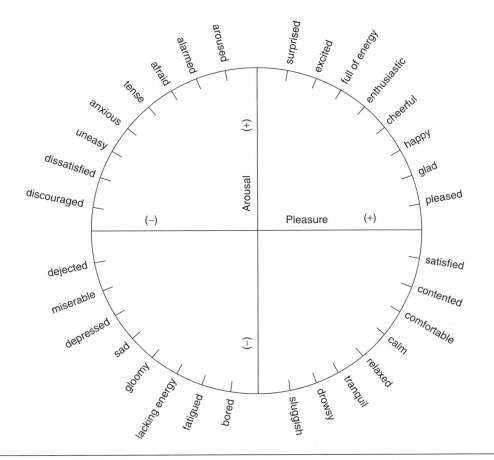

Figure 23.1   A Two-Dimensional View of Psychological Well-Being

as low-arousal pleasure. Third is the axis from depression to enthusiasm. Feelings of enthusiasm and positive motivation are in the top right quadrant, and depression and sadness (low pleasure and low mental arousal) are at

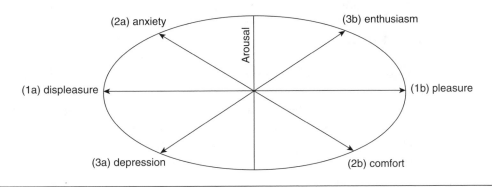

Figure 23.2   Three Axes for the Measurement of Well-Being

the other end of the axis. The three axes are intercorrelated through heavy loadings on pleasure, the horizontal dimension.

Despite that general intercorrelation, different associations exist with certain other variables. For example, a person's organizational level is linked in opposite ways with job-related anxiety and job-related depression. People in higher-level jobs report significantly *less* job-related depression than those in lower-level jobs but also significantly *more* job-related anxiety (Warr, 1990b). That differential pattern of subjective well-being (both better and worse at higher organizational levels) may be interpreted in terms of the dimension of mental arousal; people in higher-level positions experience greater arousal, on both the diagonal axes in Figure 23.2. A similar pattern also exists in relation to certain job characteristics; that will be reviewed later. More generally, those two axes may have different priorities in relation to either approach or avoidance goals: variations in depression-enthusiasm may be more dependent on approach processes, whereas anxiety-comfort may be more linked to avoidance activities (Carver, 2003).

In discussing subjective well-being (and other components of mental health), it is essential to distinguish between two different levels of abstractness. First, we can examine the concept in general, without restriction to a particular setting; let us call that "context-free" well-being. Or we can study "domain-specific" well-being in one limited situation such as the family environment or in respect to jobs. *Job-related* subjective well-being is the domain-specific form that is of particular interest in this chapter.

Well-being at the two levels is conceptually and empirically interrelated, although the two are influenced in part by different factors. For example, job-related well-being is more responsive to conditions and activities in employment, and context-free well-being is strongly influenced by health, family, and community factors (e.g., Warr, 1987). Both levels also reflect people's dispositional characteristics, with scores being somewhat stable across time and between situations (e.g., Dormann & Zapf, 2001; Heller, Judge, & Watson, 2002).

Instruments to measure employees' subjective well-being have varied in their level (context-free or domain-specific) and also in their coverage of the axes in Figure 23.2. Many questionnaires examine generalized distress by combining the two negative forms of well-being identified as 2a and 3a, as for example in the emotional exhaustion component of burnout (e.g., Maslach & Jackson, 1981). Others focus more specifically on either anxious (2a) or depressed (3a) forms, illustrated in studies by Netemeyer, Johnston, and Burton (1990) and Kehr (2003) respectively. A positive form of job-related well-being has often been examined as job satisfaction, along axis one of Figure 23.2, without regard to level of arousal. (In addition, both more aroused and less aroused forms of satisfaction can be envisaged toward either 3b or 2b in the figure. Research into job satisfaction of those different kinds would be of interest.)

Accurate estimates of the population prevalence of particular forms of well-being are difficult to obtain. Those require a large and representative sample of a population as well as validated indicators of well-being. Few studies meet those requirements.

In the United Kingdom, one survey of a single electoral district found that 3% of 4,044 workers viewed their job as "extremely stressful" and 16% as "very stressful" (Smith, 2001). However, no target period of time was specified, and definitions of "stressful" and its threshold were not provided. Another study obtained responses from a random sample of the British population, asking about a single day (*yesterday*) and about both negative and positive feelings: job-influenced forms of unpleasant emotional strain (defined in terms of 2a and 3a of Figure 23.2) and also job-influenced pleasure (specified in terms of 3b) (Warr & Payne, 1983). Four percent and 3% of full-time employed men and women respectively reported experiencing strain attributable to their job for *half or more of yesterday*; for *some time yesterday* those values were 15% and 10%. Corresponding responses for job-influenced pleasure were 16% and 15% for *half or more of yesterday*, and 21% and 16% for *some time yesterday*. Additional prevalence and comparative information would be of value.

Positive Self-Regard

In addition to subjective well-being, also important to mental health are feelings about oneself as a person. These feelings are less directed at features of the environment than is subjective well-being; they might be labeled as degree of positive self-regard. Such feelings have been examined in terms of self-esteem, self-acceptance, self-worth, and associated concepts, and it is clear that positive self-regard and subjective well-being overlap both conceptually and empirically (e.g., Ryff & Keyes, 1995). The factor analysis by Watson, Suls, and Haig (2002) indicated that low self-esteem was more associated with depressed (3a) forms of low well-being than with anxiety (2a).

Competence

A third dimension of mental health, here referred to as competence, was emphasized by many earlier writers (e.g., Bradburn, 1969; Jahoda, 1958). Terms have included "effective coping," "environmental mastery," "effectance motivation," and so on. This feature covers a person's ability to handle life's problems and act on the environment with at least a moderate amount of success. As with other aspects of mental health, competence may be viewed as either context-free (concerning life in general) or with a domain-specific (e.g., job-related) focus. Competence that is specific to particular activities has been viewed as self-efficacy, linked to a range of experiences, behaviors, and processes of self-regulation (e.g., Bandura, 1997).

Low competence is not always a sign of low mental health; everyone is incompetent in some respects. The key factor is a link with low subjective well-being and self-regard. Inability to cope with important environmental demands is often associated with negative feelings (e.g., Nezu, 1985), but that is not the case for all activities. For personally nonsalient activities, low competence is not normally a sign of low mental health.

Aspiration

The mentally healthy person has been viewed (perhaps in terms of "self-actualization" or "personal growth") as someone who establishes realistic goals and makes active efforts to attain them (e.g., Herzberg, 1966; Maslow, 1943; Schultz, 1977). Such people show an interest in the environment, engage in motivated activity, and seek to extend themselves in ways that are personally significant. On the other hand, low levels of aspiration are seen in apathy and acceptance of the status quo, no matter how unsatisfactory that is.

To characterize people in these terms in a context-free manner is difficult because a person's aspirations can have many different targets. However, a broad-ranging scale of goal directedness has been shown to be significantly related to employees' subjective well-being and positive self-regard (Payne, Robbins, & Dougherty, 1991). Examining the statistical structure of mental health questionnaires, Compton, Smith, Cornish, and Qualls (1996) reported that personal growth and subjective well-being emerged as separate factors. In occupational settings, where the interest may be in purely *job-related* aspiration, it is sometimes appropriate to examine intrinsic job motivation or growth-need strength. Those concern the degree to which a person desires challenging goals in his or her job, a feature that is central to job-related aspiration.

Autonomy

The fifth aspect of mental health, autonomy, has been emphasized more by Western than by Eastern writers. For example, in the United States, Angyal (1965) identified the tendency to strive for independence and self-regulation as a key aspect of mental health, and Loevinger (1980) included in her account of personal development a high-level "autonomous stage." Mentally healthy people are usually considered able to resist the influence of environmental features and to determine their own opinions and actions. However, too much as well as too little autonomy can be undesirable. We should thus think in terms of a continuum of personal autonomy ranging from extreme dependence on other people all the way to extreme counter-dependence with both interdependence and independence located between the extremes. It is a balance between interdependence and independence that reflects good mental health of this kind.

A factor analysis of questionnaire items by Kafka and Kozma (2001) identified an autonomy factor along the lines outlined above. Two other significant factors covered subjective well-being and a combination of environmental mastery and positive self-regard.

Integrated Functioning

A final aspect of mental health, here identified as integrated functioning, concerns the person as a whole and the relationships between other components. People who are mentally healthy exhibit several forms of balance, harmony, and inner relatedness. Different writers have their own preferred theoretical perspective on integrated functioning. For example, some psychoanalytic approaches include concepts of ego, id, and superego, and models of identity and the self may focus on coherence between goals and values or between cognitive and affective subsystems. One questionnaire investigation revealed a factor of integration as well as separate factors of subjective well-being and personal growth (Compton et al., 1996). However, current perspectives on integrated functioning rarely consider paid employment.

Certain aspects of this sixth component may be indexed in terms of behaviors that bring together several of the previous themes. For example, drug abuse or alcohol dependency reflects low mental health of several kinds in combination. Job-related examples will be cited later.

General Issues

Mentally healthy people experience to varying degrees positive states of the kinds illustrated above. Furthermore, they often experience anxiety in coping with their environment, and indeed they may *create* situations that are stressful as they identify and pursue difficult targets. For example, proactive, risk-taking people may be considered healthy in terms of competence, aspiration, and autonomy, but their difficult relations with the environment may make them anxious for a considerable proportion of time. High aspiration in those circumstances can be accompanied by low subjective well-being (Compton et al., 1996). Researchers have often given the impression that the presence of (for instance) anxiety is always a sign of low mental health. However, that is only the case if the anxiety is particularly severe or if it lasts for a long period of time. In other cases, anxiety can, in fact, be associated with a high overall level of mental health.

The intermittent experience of anxiety by people who are mentally healthy is linked to the fact that the separate components of mental health are not always positively intercorrelated. In examining the impact of work activities and conditions on employees, it is thus desirable to ask about more than one of the aspects of mental health considered here. Furthermore, we need to learn about patterns over time. For example, do negative work conditions affect people cumulatively so that their harmful consequences build up across a sustained period? Conversely, do employees adapt to stressors so that their impact becomes less harmful over time, perhaps through processes of learning and self-strengthening? Very few investigations have asked those longitudinal questions, and almost all research has been cross-sectional, examining job factors and employee reactions at about the same time.

Positive themes of the kind outlined above are not only important within discussions of mental health. For some commentators, they are central to a general perspective about people and society that differs in many ways from the position underlying conventional views of stress. For example, Wainwright and Calnan (2002) argue that stress researchers' dominating concern for negative outcomes reflects a diminished view of human potential with an overemphasis on people's frailty, powerlessness, and passivity and an inappropriately low expectation of their resilience, agency, courage, bravery, and capacity to overcome adversity. They urge a shift to investigate those more proactive behaviors and experiences.

In empirical terms, significant associations have been described in other chapters between negative job features and employee feelings of low subjective well-being. The direction of causality in those investigations is not always clear: jobs may influence well-being; well-being may affect perception of jobs; or characteristics of a respondent may determine well-being, entry into a job, or perception of a job. In many cases, several or all of those influences may be important. Nevertheless, a causal impact of job conditions has been shown by longitudinal studies in which changes in job conditions led to changes in well-being. For instance, Martin and Wall (1989) studied machine operators as they moved between roles with different levels of demand, finding predicted changes in job-related anxiety and depression. Similar posttransition changes in intrinsic job satisfaction and perceptions of pressure were reported by Wall, Corbett, Martin, Clegg, and Jackson (1990).

Most published research in the area of this book may be described as primarily "environment-centered," focusing on the nature of a job or organization and seeking links between environmental features and well-being. An alternative emphasis, that which is "person-centered," asks about ways in which individual differences and people's cognitive processes give rise to variations in their well-being. In addition, we might combine those approaches into models that adopt both environmental and personal perspectives. Principal issues will be addressed here in terms of those three approaches.

Job Features and Employee Mental Health

Warr (1987, 1999) has presented a general framework of jobs and other roles, classifying the key features of any environment that have been shown to be related to mental health. Settings and jobs differ between themselves in the presence of each feature, and those variations may give rise to differences in domain-specific or context-free mental health. For each category of the environment below, a principal label is accompanied by other terms that are commonly used. In three of the cases (5, 9, and 10), subcategories are suggested.

1. *Opportunity for personal control:* employee discretion, decision latitude, autonomy, absence of close supervision, self-determination, participation in decision making, freedom of choice

2. *Opportunity for skill use:* skill utilization, utilization of valued abilities, required skills

3. *Externally generated goals:* job demands, task demands, quantitative or qualitative workload, attentional demand, demands relative to resources, role responsibility, normative requirements, conflicting demands, role conflict, work-family conflict

4. *Variety:* variation in job content and location, nonrepetitive work, skill variety, task variety

5. *Environmental clarity:* (a) information about the consequences of behavior, task feedback; (b) information about the future, absence of job future ambiguity, absence of job insecurity; (c) information about required behavior, low role ambiguity

6. *Availability of money:* income level, amount of pay, wages, salary, financial resources

7. *Physical security:* absence of danger, low hazard level, good working conditions, ergonomically adequate equipment, safe levels of temperature and noise

8. *Supportive supervision:* leader consideration, boss support, supportive management, effective leadership

9. *Opportunity for interpersonal contact:* (a) quantity of interaction, contact with others, social density, adequate privacy; (b) quality of interaction, good relationships with others, good communications, social support, absence of interpersonal conflict, harassment, or bullying

10. *Valued social position:* (a) personal evaluations of task significance, valued role incumbency, contributions made to others, perceived meaningfulness of job; (b) wider evaluations of a job's status in society, social rank, occupational prestige

For example, the roles of employment, unemployment, and retirement typically differ in several of those features, and those environmental differences can account for much of the role-related variation in subjective well-being (Warr, 1987; Warr, Butcher, Robertson, & Callinan, 2004). In addition, there is considerable evidence that within the role of employment itself differences between jobs in each feature are accompanied by variations in job-related subjective well-being. (Dozens of studies are reviewed by Warr, 1987, 1999, or described throughout this book.) The 10 features are presented here in positive terms, but low values have been widely viewed as stressful.

Some job characteristics are more associated with one form of well-being than with others. For instance, the opportunity for personal control (1, above) is more closely associated with the well-being axis of job-related depression-enthusiasm than with anxiety-comfort, whereas job demands (3, above) are more strongly correlated with anxiety-comfort (Warr, 1990b). Correlations of control opportunity and job demands with overall job satisfaction (axis 1 in Figure 23.2) and job-related anxiety (axis 2) also show that differentiated pattern; control opportunity is more correlated with satisfaction, and demands are more associated with anxiety (Spector & O'Connell, 1994). Stronger associations with job-related depression-enthusiasm than with anxiety-comfort have been reported for features 1, 2, 4, 5, and 10 in the list above by Sevastos, Smith, and Cordery (1992). Conversely, job demands (3) are more associated with the emotional exhaustion component of job-related burnout than is social support (9b) (Lee & Ashforth, 1996). Research now needs to build on these differentiated patterns.

Most investigators have examined only linear associations between job features and well-being although it might be expected that too much (as well as too little) of a feature is often undesirable (Warr, 1987). In several cases, extremely high levels of a feature are likely to become unpleasantly coercive rather than provide opportunities for personal gain as is the case at moderate levels. Features of that potentially curvilinear kind are opportunity for personal control (1, above), opportunity for skill use (2), externally generated goals (3), variety (4), environmental clarity (5), and opportunity for interpersonal contact (9). All of those illustrate the possibility of having too much of a good thing. In addition, extremely high levels of one feature are often associated with other environmental characteristics that are themselves undesirable; for example, unremittingly very high control opportunities (1) tend also to result in relentless overload (3).

Based on considerations of that kind, Warr's (1987, 1994) "vitamin model" proposes that environmental characteristics and subjective well-being are related to each other in nonlinear fashion. Some features of a role or job (1, 2, 3, 4, 5, and 9, above) are likely to be beneficial up to a moderate level but increasingly harmful thereafter (analogous to vitamins A and D, referred to in the model as "additional decrement" features). Other environmental characteristics (6, 7, 8, and 10) (similar to vitamins C and E, with a "constant effect") appear likely to be beneficial up to a moderate level, with variations thereafter unrelated to well-being.

There is some evidence for nonlinear associations between certain job features and subjective well-being. Karasek (1979), Warr (1990a), and de Jonge and Schaufeli (1997) demonstrated significant curvilinearity for job demands: Job-related well-being scores were low with least demand ("underload"); they increased (cross-sectionally) with moderate demand; and then declined again at particularly high levels of demand ("overload"). The same pattern in respect to opportunity for personal control has been observed in laboratory situations by Burger (1989) and among employees by de Jonge and Schaufeli

(1997). Curvilinearity was also found by Xie and Johns (1995) for a general measure of features 1, 4, 5, and 10 (identified as "job scope") relative to employees' job-related emotional exhaustion. De Jonge, Reuvers, Houtman, Bongers, and Kompier (2000) observed nonlinear patterns more for feelings of depression or emotional exhaustion than for overall satisfaction.

Nonlinear associations of job features with well-being and health deserve more extensive investigation. Research in that area has typically examined inappropriately small samples of employees with little attention to spread of coverage across the possible range of job characteristic scores. For instance, there is now a need to focus on the poles of a job dimension (for instance, extremely high and extremely low control opportunity) rather than study jobs located in a possibly benign middle range.

Most research into work environments has examined job-related rather than context-free outcomes. However, a limited number of investigations have revealed significant links between job features and global distress, anxiety, or depression (e.g., Barnett & Brennan, 1997; Kalimo & Vuori, 1991). Is that association direct or indirect? Job characteristics might influence both job-related and context-free well-being directly; or a job might have its direct effect only on job-related feelings, and these might spill over into wider well-being. Research has supported the latter possibility, with job features linked indirectly to context-free well-being through job-related well-being (Kelloway & Barling, 1991; Pugliesi, 1995).

The other five dimensions of mental health (in addition to subjective well-being) have rarely been investigated in job settings. One study found that employees' increased opportunity for control (1, above) was followed by increased job knowledge and also job-related self-efficacy, a form of subjective competence (Leach, Wall, & Jackson, 2003).

Aspects of the sixth element, integrated functioning, have been studied in terms of alcohol or drug abuse. In both cases, research findings about linkages with job conditions have been inconsistent, in part because different indicators have been examined in different studies. Rospenda, Richman, Wislar, and Flaherty (2000) recorded several forms of problem drinking in a two-phase investigation across 12 months. They found that job characteristics in the form of decision latitude (1, above) and task demands (3) did not predict subsequent drinking. However, sexual harassment and a composite measure of generalized workplace abuse (including aggression, threats, and bribes) (within 9b here) were linked to more drinking in the later period. Martin, Roman, and Blum (1996) showed that over and above job features, problem and escapist drinking were more likely in the presence of job-based drinking networks.

Galaif, Newcomb, and Carmona (2001) found that "polydrug" problems (a combination of alcohol, marijuana, and cocaine abuse) were predicted by earlier employment instability and linked to later job dissatisfaction. However, results about drug abuse in relation to particular job features have not been consistently replicated between studies (Oldham & Gordon, 1999).

Personal Features and Employee Mental Health

In addition to the impact of environmental characteristics, there is considerable evidence that employees' mental health is also affected by aspects of themselves. Two research approaches have been taken, either seeking links with continuing personality dispositions or specifying the mental processes that might influence outcomes in a particular setting.

The first approach has included examination of dispositional appraisal bias. Some people are more likely than others to view the world in a despondent manner, and this general bias (or its opposite) is reflected in experiences in a particular setting. For example, the meta-analysis by DeNeve and Cooper (1998) showed that positive personality characteristics (e.g., extraversion) were generally related to positive well-being and that negative personality traits (e.g., neuroticism) were associated with more negative well-being. In employment settings, a meta-analysis by Judge, Heller, and Mount (2002) revealed average associations of job satisfaction with neuroticism and extraversion of −0.24 and +0.19 respectively. Connolly and Viswesvaran (2000) concluded from their meta-analysis that up to 25% of variance in job satisfaction scores was attributable to continuing individual differences in positive or negative affectivity.

A conceptually distinct but empirically related disposition is that of perfectionism, the tendency to seek unrealistically high achievements. Several chapters in the book edited by Flett and Hewitt (2002) summarize a pattern of negative associations with well-being.

Other aspects of mental health are undoubtedly also linked to employees' continuing characteristics. For example, drug abuse (here viewed as a form of poor integrated functioning) derives in part from patterns of social relationships (notably shyness and aggressiveness) established in childhood (Ensminger, Juan, & Fothergill, 2002). The role of dispositional consistencies in different aspects of workers' mental health deserves more extensive study.

In addition to those continuing individual differences, mental health is also affected by a second kind of personal feature of a more episodic kind. People can be active in shaping their own well-being, and person-specific processes of judgment can affect feelings. Eight such cognitive processes are important.

1. *Social comparisons.* First are judgmental comparisons with other people, assessing whether one's own situation is better or worse than that of others. In respect to context-free well-being, social comparison processes of this kind were illustrated by Wheeler and Miyake (1992). They asked students to record details of social comparisons made over a 2-week period, finding that downward comparisons (against people considered to be worse off than oneself) were associated with subsequent more positive feelings. This process has been shown to be important in employees' evaluation of

their pay equity (e.g., Walster, Walster, & Berscheid, 1978), and other studies of its influence on well-being in employment settings are desirable.

The targets of social comparison range in their specificity from individuals to groups or society in general. In respect to work groups, individuals have been found to experience feelings that are similar to their colleagues' (Totterdell, 2000). This process deserves further examination, for instance, to identify the particular comparisons and judgmental processes that give rise to between-colleague overlap. Similarly, research into strain in companies where job stressors have become central to employee-management negotiations may record negative feelings that have been amplified by cues from colleagues. Processes of social comparison and possible between-person contagion could usefully be investigated in those settings.

2. *Comparisons with expectations.* A second form of episodic judgment bearing on well-being is in relation to people's expectations for the situation in question. For example, it has been found in laboratory research that unexpected success yields positive feelings and unexpected failure gives rise to dissatisfaction (e.g., Feather, 1969). Similar comparisons of expectation against reality are likely to influence well-being in some job settings.

3. *Counterfactual comparisons.* Another judgment about alternative situations concerns those that might instead have developed. Subjective well-being can be affected by consideration of poorer or better counterfactual alternatives, those that are contrary to the facts. Upward counterfactual comparisons (relative to a more attractive possibility that might have occurred) tend to evoke unpleasant feelings, whereas downward comparisons (that present an alternative that is worse than reality) can yield better well-being (e.g., Roese, 1997). The process was illustrated by Medvec, Madey, and Gilovich (1995) in a study of Olympic medalists. Those receiving silver medals for achieving second place were less happy with their position than were bronze medalists in third place. Second-place winners appeared to base their feelings in part on upward counterfactual comparisons ("I failed to be the best"), whereas athletes in third place tended to make downward comparisons, being pleased to have reached the medal positions ("I did better than all the rest").

4. *Judgments in relation to a previous trend.* The fourth kind of episodic judgment affecting well-being is made relative to the past, appraising the direction and speed of change. There is some evidence from laboratory studies that perceived speed of movement toward a goal can in part determine well-being (e.g., Carver & Scheier, 1998). In everyday life this can be seen particularly clearly at times of abrupt change in velocity when sudden improvement or deterioration in goal progress can be followed by exhilaration or dismay respectively. Perceived distance from a goal has been shown to be important for well-being (in addition to speed of goal-discrepancy reduction) (e.g., Bandura & Locke, 2003), and judgments about those

two previous-trend reference standards should be included in research in this area.

5. *Judgments in relation to a likely future trend.* Expected future trend is also important to well-being, although during changes of consistent pace it may not be distinguished from movement in the past (4, above). Future trend has sometimes been examined as perceived probability of success with significant positive associations with well-being (e.g., Emmons, 1986). As part of these future estimates, perceived ambiguity can influence judgment. For instance, situations with a completely certain bad future can be less aversive than those in which the occurrence of a negative outcome remains merely possible (Frederick & Loewenstein, 1999).

6. *Judgments in relation to personal significance.* It has long been argued that occupational stressors are of greatest consequence when they are judged to threaten salient aspects of the self. In addition, the association between employees' subjective well-being and progress toward a goal has been found to be strongest for those goals that are personally more important (Harris, Daniels, & Briner, 2003). Judgments about this personal reference point deserve additional investigation in the area of this book.

7. *Judgments in relation to relevant self-efficacy.* A perceived ability to exercise some control over a situation can enhance current well-being even when that ability is in fact illusory (Bandura & Locke, 2003). Judgments of competence against one's benchmark level of self-efficacy are thus likely to contribute in some job settings to the experience of well-being. Of particular concern are retrospective assessments (in response to questions like "Have I coped well?" or "Have I made a mess of this?"). For example, an employee's perception that he or she has failed to prevent a controllable negative event may give rise to even lower well-being.

8. *Judgments in terms of novelty or familiarity.* Continued exposure to an environmental feature tends to reduce its affective potential, either negative or positive, so that more familiar inputs tend to generate feelings that are less extreme (e.g., Parducci, 1995). This process of adaptation reduces hedonic (and other) reactions to a constant or repeated stimulus so that feelings of pleasure or satisfaction can become reduced or even give way to indifference (e.g., Frederick & Loewenstein, 1999). Adaptation has typically been investigated in laboratory or other nonorganizational settings, but it is expected also to affect employees in their job activities.

In summary, employee well-being is likely to be influenced by the eight kinds of episodic judgment process summarized above. However, the traditional preference for environment-centered research rather than person-centered approaches has restricted the empirical evidence that is so far available. A change of emphasis is now required.

Both Environmental and Personal Features

The bias against person-centered investigation has also limited knowledge about employee well-being as a function of particular persons and situations together. In studying joint effects, the two approaches of the previous section might be followed. Person-situation research might either examine continuing personality dispositions in combination with particular job features, or it might study patterns of episodic judgments in different job settings.

Studies of continuing dispositions in conjunction with job features (e.g., Agho, Mueller, & Price, 1993) have found that both sets of factors contribute independently to job satisfaction. For example, Judge, Bono, and Locke (2000) showed that employees' neuroticism and also the complexity of their jobs were associated (negatively and positively respectively) with overall job satisfaction.

In addition to studying joint effects of that kind, other person-situation dispositional research has examined statistical interactions. Early investigations asked about interactions between growth-need strength (a preference for jobs with intrinsic rather than extrinsic rewards) and job features such as control opportunity and variety. A general finding is that such situational features (sometimes viewed as aspects of job complexity) are significantly more associated with job satisfaction for employees with higher growth-need strength than for those with a lower preference of that kind (e.g., Loher, Noe, Moeller, & Fitzgerald, 1985). Other research has examined managers' hardiness in terms of their commitment, experienced control, and liking for challenge. Kobasa, Maddi, and Kahn (1982) found that stressful life events were significantly more closely linked to (context-free) physical and mental symptoms among managers of low hardiness than among their more hardy colleagues.

Other health-related outcomes are also likely to be a function of both situational and personal characteristics. For example, Oldham and Gordon (1999) reported an interaction between job complexity and cognitive ability in relation to the abuse of marijuana and alcohol. Job complexity was associated with greater consumption for employees lower in ability, whereas the association was negative for higher-ability employees.

Possible combinations of job factors with episodic judgment processes bearing on employee well-being (the second person-centered approach) have yet to be investigated. For example, it seems likely that people will more often initiate social or counterfactual comparisons (judgments 1 or 3 above) in job conditions that are ambiguous, as for example in times of organizational change (Warr, 2004). Similarly, judgments about well-being as a function of a recent environmental trend (4 above) may be more common when the pattern of change is very clear. Research into those joint effects (of both situations and judgments) on the experience of well-being at work is much needed.

Subjective Well-Being and Work Behavior _____

What about the associations of well-being with behavior in a job? It is sometimes suggested that employees with higher job-related well-being behave differently from those with lower well-being. Several theoretical frameworks have considered this possibility. For example, the broaden and build theory develops themes about how positive emotions expand thought-action repertoires (Fredrickson, 2001), and the affect infusion model makes predictions about differences between situations (Forgas & George, 2001). Staw, Sutton, and Pelled (1994) suggested three possible processes: direct effects on personal goals and task activity, modified reactions by other people, and emotion-based responses to those others.

Even if behavioral associations with well-being were found, the direction of causality would usually remain unclear. It would not necessarily be the case that (say) high job satisfaction causes a particular form of behavior, for example good work performance. The opposite might be true: good performers might be more satisfied as a result of their effective performance. Alternatively, a third factor (or several of them) might bring about both high performance and high satisfaction. For instance, particular equipment characteristics, managerial styles, or personality attributes might enhance both performance and satisfaction. Note also that work behavior is determined by a range of different factors (for example, organizational policies, management practices, group pressures, individual abilities, and available options), so the maximum possible correlation with well-being alone is expected to be much less than +1.00.

Recognizing the causal ambiguity of such correlations, what is known about the behavioral correlates of job-related subjective well-being? Four variables will be considered: performance in the job, discretionary activities, absence from work, and staff turnover.

Performance in the Job

Iaffaldano and Muchinsky (1985) reported a meta-analysis of previous studies of job performance (usually indexed through supervisor ratings) as a function of job satisfaction. They found that overall job satisfaction (axis one in Figure 23.2) was on average associated +0.25 with performance. Petty, McGee, and Cavender (1984) reported similar findings (the average correlation was +0.23) and noted that the association of overall job satisfaction with rated performance was stronger for managerial and professional employees than for others (average correlations of +0.31 and +0.15 respectively). In a more recent examination of several hundred studies, Judge, Thoresen, Bono, and Patton (2001) observed a mean correlation of +0.18, with a stronger association (+0.27) when a person's work was of high complexity.

Ostroff (1992) examined this association at the level of organizations. Schools' academic performance, administrative efficiency, and student behavior were found to be significantly associated with their teachers' average job satisfaction score (an average coefficient of +0.28). Manufacturing companies were investigated by Patterson, Warr, and West (2004). The average of each company's employees' overall job satisfaction was found to predict the company's later productivity (net sales per employee), with a correlation of +0.44.

What about axis two in Figure 23.2, from feelings of job-related anxiety to comfort? Some employees who report high job anxiety might be experiencing difficulty in coping with job demands and thus perform relatively less effectively. Jamal (1984) found that job-related tension was on average associated −0.35 with supervisory ratings, and the average correlation in research by Cropanzano, Rupp, and Byrne (2003) was −0.21. (See also the perspective of Karasek and Theorell, 1990, outlined in the next section.)

An alternative hypothesis is in terms of a possible optimal amount of challenge, with lower performance occurring to either side of that optimum. It may be the case that the relationship between job tension and performance is one of an inverted U such that moderate demands are linked to raised but manageable job-related tension and also to high performance, but that both lower and higher levels of tension (and of job demands) are accompanied by lower performance. Anderson (1976) suggested that this was the case in data from a sample of small business owners, but the inverted U possibility has not been adequately tested. Muse, Harris, and Feild (2003) have pointed out that research in the area has been limited by a failure to examine in the same study a sufficiently wide range of job conditions, especially those that involve low levels of stress (one side of the inverted U).

The third axis of job-related well-being in Figure 23.2 ranges from depression to enthusiasm. It appears likely that employees with positive feelings of this activated kind will be among the more productive, but few studies have been reported. In respect to negative feelings, Motowidlo, Packard, and Manning (1986) examined the association between nurses' job-related depression and ratings of their effectiveness by supervisors and by coworkers, finding a significant negative association in both cases.

Discretionary Activities

Some work behaviors are discretionary rather than being prescribed as task requirements. It might be expected that employees' subjective well-being will be particularly associated with those voluntary behaviors. Three possibilities may be considered.

One form of discretionary behavior is seen in *voluntary overtime*. Many jobs offer the possibility to undertake some unpaid work outside the required hours, and employees' job-related well-being might be predictive of such behavior. This was found to be the case in a study of schoolteachers: overall job satisfaction was correlated +0.25 with the amount of additional (unpaid) time devoted to work-related activities (Gechman & Wiener, 1975).

Several investigators have examined a second form of discretionary behavior at work, sometimes referred to as "organizational citizenship behavior." Such behaviors include providing assistance to colleagues, being friendly, volunteering to undertake needed tasks, and making suggestions to improve effectiveness (e.g., Podsakoff, MacKenzie, Paine, & Bachrach, 2000). Overall job satisfaction is known to be associated with this type of discretionary behavior as rated by a boss or colleagues. Organ and Ryan's (1995) meta-analytic review revealed an average correlation of +0.25 with behavior ratings made by other people.

Finally, forms of *adaptive behavior* are increasingly valued in organizations facing market pressure and rapid technological change. Is subjective well-being likely to be associated with this type of discretionary activity, seen in a willingness to introduce change or to acquire new skills and knowledge? Karasek and Theorell (1990) suggested that anxiety in a stressful job inhibits new learning for two reasons: Employees under strain may become less able to handle a current situation, and they may be less likely to change their approach in the face of new requirements. A vicious cycle was thus thought to be created, with mutual augmentation between anxiety and ineffectiveness. On the other hand, high demands coupled with high discretion were suggested to enhance well-being, with discretion inhibiting the potential harmful impact of work overload and bringing about feelings of personal mastery together with an interest in facing new challenges and acquiring new skills and knowledge. There is at present no direct evidence for this longitudinal pattern, but the idea appears plausible.

Related information has been provided by Parker and Sprigg (1999). They found that job-related anxiety was significantly associated with less proactive behavior, measured in terms of self-reports of personal initiative and the tendency to persevere until success is attained. Birdi, Gardner, and Warr (1998) asked whether overall job satisfaction was greater for employees who are more active in work-based development activities (undertaking personal projects, serving on working groups, etc.). A significant positive association was found, but the nature of its underlying causality has yet to be determined.

Absence From Work

Another index of employee performance is in terms of absenteeism (or its converse, attendance at work). Such behavior is determined by a range of factors. In addition to sickness itself, social and family pressures can affect decisions to attend (e.g., Erickson, Nichols, & Ritter, 2000). Organizational influences can include specific policies to encourage attendance, support from a supervisor, and more broadly the "absence culture" in which a person works (Martocchio, 1994)—norms and sanctions (informal as well as formal) about reasonable levels of absence. Although employees' subjective well-being might be expected to be linked to absenteeism, other factors are clearly also important.

Absenteeism is conventionally measured in two different ways—through the Time-Lost Index or the Frequency Index. The Time-Lost Index is computed as the total duration of absence during a specified period, perhaps expressed as a proportion of the total time examined; and the Frequency Index is the number of separate incidents of absence in a specified period, regardless of their duration. The Time-Lost Index, which gives greater emphasis to long periods of absence, is considered primarily to represent involuntary responses to incapacitating sickness. On the other hand, the Frequency Index, in which a single day's absence is given the same weight as, say, a 3-month absence, is widely thought to describe more voluntary choices to take time off work for brief periods of time.

How do the three axes of job-related subjective well-being correlate with these two indexes of absenteeism? We might expect the Frequency Index (with its emphasis on possibly voluntary behavior) to be more linked to well-being, but as with other behaviors, the causes underlying any observed association would be complex and multidirectional.

The meta-analysis by Farrell and Stamm (1988) found that overall job satisfaction (the first axis in Figure 23.2) on average correlated only -0.10 with the Frequency Index and -0.13 with the Time-Lost Index. The average correlations of job-related anxiety (axis two) with the Frequency Index and the Time-Lost Index were found to be $+0.11$ and $+0.18$ respectively. Examining subsequent absences by medical staff, Hardy, Woods, and Wall (2003) found a correlation between the Time-Lost Index and overall job satisfaction of -0.29 and with job-related anxiety of $+0.22$.

The third axis of well-being ranges from feelings of depression to enthusiasm. George (1989) examined positive feelings of this kind and observed a correlation of -0.28 with the number of single-day absences. In the study by Hardy et al. (2003), job-related depression was correlated $+0.33$ with amount of subsequent absence. The review by Farrell and Stamm (1988) found that measures of job involvement (emphasizing active interest in one's role, as in positive forms of axis three) were on average correlated -0.28 with the Frequency Index of absenteeism.

Staff Turnover

A fourth behavioral measure likely to be related to job-related well-being is whether or not people remain in their position. The average correlation between absence (above) and subsequent turnover has been estimated at $+0.33$ (Mitra, Jenkins, & Gupta, 1992), and well-being precursors of the two forms of behavior no doubt overlap in many ways. The average correlation between overall job satisfaction and employee turnover was -0.17 in the meta-analysis by Griffeth, Hom, and Gaertner (2000). However, additional factors also influence staff turnover, especially the availability or otherwise of suitable alternative employment; job satisfaction better predicts actual turnover when local unemployment is lower (Carsten & Spector, 1987).

Two Missing Terms:
Ambivalence and Happiness

Some research needs have been suggested throughout the chapter. In addition, two broad themes will be raised in this section.

First, it is notable that the literature makes almost no mention of the term *ambivalence*. Yet work of all kinds, whether receiving pay in employment or undertaking tasks outside a paid job, is the source of feelings that are typically mixed. The concept implies labor, exertion, and effort, as well as possible gain. Research has, in effect, examined a mean value (e.g., of subjective well-being) without considering within-person variance around that mean or between it and other elements of mental health. For example, the establishment of personal work goals yields both negative feelings as their attainment is perceived to be problematic and also positive feelings as they provide an objective that is becoming attained. It is often impossible to have one without the other. There is a need to examine such ambivalence, both in its own right and also as a function of the environmental and personal features illustrated here.

A second omission from the research literature in this field is of the term *happiness*, which is widespread in daily speech and overlaps considerably with the more academic term *well-being*. Dictionary definitions of happiness identify its key elements as either pleasure or contentment, the two forms described by Freedman (1978, pp. 30–31) as "happiness as fun, excitement, pleasure" and "happiness as peace of mind and contentment." Those are poles 3b and 2b in the present (Figure 23.2) representation of subjective well-being. The opposite poles embrace many forms of strain examined in this book.

A conceptual and semantic shift to recognize our interest in happiness and unhappiness in work settings would introduce new themes from other literatures, potentially advancing our understanding of health and ill health. For example, the concept of happiness has been extensively analyzed by moral philosophers commencing with Aristotle and other early Greek writers. In examining the notion of a good life, Aristotle developed themes associated with *eudaemonia*. This is a matter of personal fulfillment through activities considered to be worth desiring or fit to be wanted; it is linked to notions of flourishing, living virtuously, and the attainment of goals that have intrinsic merit. Eudaemonic forms of happiness do not necessarily involve feelings of pleasure.

Happiness requires both the achievement of major wants and a freedom from major distresses. Telfer (1980) points out that people's wants may be hedonistic in the sense that their achievement brings about pleasure or enjoyment, or they may be eudaemonic in that their aims are desirable in more objective (rather than person-specific) terms. Eudaemonia may yield hedonistic satisfaction, but happiness does not necessarily imply the experience of affect.

Psychologists have recently emphasized hedonistic forms of happiness and unhappiness, with little interest in eudaemonic perspectives. The latter in practice tend to overlap with the behavioral aspects of mental health identified earlier in the chapter: competence, aspiration, and autonomy. Conceptual and empirical examination in those broader terms would now be helpful.

Epilogue: Well-Being and Stress

This chapter has set the notion of stress within the broader constructs of well-being and mental health. Attention has mainly been directed at a single outcome, subjective well-being because published research has concentrated on that variable. Similarly, the chapter's content reflects the fact that environment-centered research has been much more common than a primary focus on the characteristics of people and their mental processes or on combinations of personal variables and situational conditions.

The construct of stress covers only part of the conceptual space identified as well-being. Stressed employees are those above a threshold of harm, experiencing feelings that are both negative and extreme. Most people are located elsewhere in the space represented by Figure 23.1, and it is essential that researchers also examine that larger proportion of the population. In addition to a concern for harmful conditions and experiences, we need a shift in all the traditional areas of cognitive, affective, and conative functioning toward constructive thoughts, positive feelings, and motivated actions. Such a shift will bring into focus wider aspects of mental health.

In all cases, it is important to take a differentiated view, recognizing that the nature, causes, and consequences of a focal construct depend on which of its facets is under examination. For example, context-free well-being is not the same as domain-specific well-being, and within each of those, anxiety (for instance) is different from low satisfaction. There has sometimes been a tendency to treat different forms of employee stress as interchangeable, as though a finding about one indicator would be replicated for other forms. As argued by Spector, Chen, and O'Connell (2000, p. 216), research must move away from the widespread assumption "that job stressors in general lead to job strains in general."

In taking either a negative or a positive perspective, we should more often examine behavior as well as experience in the same study. Traditional research approaches have examined as outcomes either one or the other alone, yet they are of simultaneous interest and importance. In occupational settings, it would be particularly fruitful to study strain or other forms of well-being in conjunction with indicators of job performance. For example, the enhancement of either well-being or job performance on its own (without concern for the other) is considerably more straightforward than is their joint improvement. In both theoretical and pragmatic terms, understanding the conjunction is more important than a focus on strain alone.

References

Agho, A. O., Mueller, C. W., & Price, J. L. (1993). Determinants of employee job satisfaction: An empirical test of a causal model. *Human Relations, 46*, 1007–1027.

Anderson, C. R. (1976). Coping behaviors as intervening mechanisms in the inverted-U stress-performance relationship. *Journal of Applied Psychology, 61*, 30–34.

Angyal, A. (1965). *Neurosis and treatment: A holistic theory.* New York: Wiley.

Bandura, A. (1997). *Self-efficacy: The exercise of control.* New York: Freeman.

Bandura, A., & Locke, E. A. (2003). Negative self-efficacy and goal effects revisited. *Journal of Applied Psychology, 88*, 87–99.

Barnett, R. C., & Brennan, R. T. (1997). Change in job conditions, change in psychological distress, and gender: A longitudinal study of dual-earner couples. *Journal of Organizational Behavior, 18*, 253–274.

Birdi, K. S., Gardner, C. R., & Warr, P. B. (1998). Correlates and perceived outcomes of four types of employee development activity. *Journal of Applied Psychology, 82*, 845–857.

Bradburn, N. M. (1969). *The structure of psychological well-being.* Chicago: Aldine.

Burger, J. M. (1989). Negative reactions to increases in perceived personal control. *Journal of Personality and Social Psychology, 56*, 246–256.

Carsten, J. M., & Spector, P. E. (1987). Unemployment, job satisfaction, and employee turnover: A meta-analytic test of the Muchinsky model. *Journal of Applied Psychology, 72*, 374–381.

Carver, C. S. (2003). Pleasure as a sign you can attend to something else: Placing positive feelings within a general model of affect. *Cognition and Emotion, 17*, 241–261.

Carver, C. S., & Scheier, M. F. (1998). *On the self-regulation of behavior.* Cambridge, UK: Cambridge University Press.

Compton, W. C., Smith, M. L., Cornish, K. A., & Qualls, D. L. (1996). Factor structure of mental health measures. *Journal of Personality and Social Psychology, 71*, 406–413.

Connolly, J. J., & Viswesvaran, C. (2000). The role of affectivity in job satisfaction: A meta-analysis. *Personality and Individual Differences, 29*, 265–281.

Cropanzano, R., Rupp, D. E., & Byrne, Z. T. (2003). The relationship of emotional exhaustion to work attitudes, job performance, and organizational citizenship behaviors. *Journal of Applied Psychology, 88*, 160–169.

De Jonge, J., Reuvers, M. M. E. N., Houtman, I. L. D., Bongers, P. M., & Kompier, M. A. J. (2000). Linear and non-linear relations between psychosocial job characteristics, subjective outcomes, and sickness absence: Baseline results from SMASH. *Journal of Occupational Health Psychology, 5*, 256–268.

De Jonge, J., & Schaufeli. W. B. (1997). Job characteristics and employee well-being: A test of Warr's Vitamin Model in health-care workers using structural equation modeling. *Journal of Organizational Behavior, 19*, 387–407.

DeNeve, K. M., & Cooper, H. (1998). The happy personality: A meta-analysis of 137 personality traits and subjective well-being. *Psychological Bulletin, 124*, 197–229.

Dormann, C., & Zapf, D. (2001). Job satisfaction: A meta-analysis of stabilities. *Journal of Organizational Behavior, 22*, 483–504.

Emmons, R. A. (1986). Personal strivings: An approach to personality and subjective well-being. *Journal of Personality and Social Psychology, 51*, 1058–1068.

Ensminger, M. E., Juan, H. S., & Fothergill, K. E. (2002). Childhood and adolescent antecedents of substance use in adulthood. *Addiction, 97,* 833–844.

Erickson, R. J., Nichols, J., & Ritter, C. (2000). Family influences on absenteeism: Testing an expanded process model. *Journal of Vocational Behavior, 57,* 246–272.

Farrell, D., & Stamm, C. L. (1988). Meta-analysis of the correlates of employee absence. *Human Relations, 41,* 211–227.

Feather, N. T. (1969). Attribution of responsibility and valence of success and failure in relation to initial confidence and task performance. *Journal of Personality and Social Psychology, 13,* 129–144.

Flett, G. L., & Hewitt, P. L. (Eds.). (2002). *Perfectionism: Theory, research, and treatment.* Washington, DC: American Psychological Association.

Forgas, J. P., & George, J. M. (2001). Affective influences on judgments and behavior in organizations: An information processing perspective. *Organizational Behavior and Human Decision Processes, 86,* 3–34.

Frederick, S., & Loewenstein, G. (1999). Hedonic adaptation. In D. Kahneman, E. Diener, & N. Schwarz (Eds.), *Well-being: The foundations of hedonic psychology* (pp. 302–329). New York: Russell Sage Foundation.

Fredrickson, B. L. (2001). The role of positive emotions in positive psychology. *American Psychologist, 56,* 218–226.

Freedman, J. L. (1978). *Happy people: What happiness is, who has it, and why.* New York: Harcourt Brace Jovanovich.

Galaif, E. R., Newcomb, M. D., & Carmona, J. V. (2001). Prospective relationships between drug problems and work adjustment in a community sample of adults. *Journal of Applied Psychology, 86,* 337–350.

Gechman, A. S., & Wiener, Y. (1975). Job involvement and satisfaction as related to mental health and personal time devoted to work. *Journal of Applied Psychology, 60,* 521–523.

George, J. M. (1989). Mood and absence. *Journal of Applied Psychology, 74,* 317–324.

Griffeth, R. W., Hom, P. W., & Gaertner, S. (2000). A meta-analysis of antecedents and correlates of employee turnover: Update, moderator tests, and research implications for the next millennium. *Journal of Management, 26,* 463–488.

Hardy, G. E., Woods, D., & Wall, T. D. (2003). The impact of psychological distress on absence from work. *Journal of Applied Psychology, 88,* 306–314.

Harris, C., Daniels, K., & Briner, R. B. (2002). A daily diary study of goals and affective well-being at work. *Journal of Occupational and Organizational Psychology, 76,* 401–410.

Heller, D., Judge, T. A., & Watson, D. (2002). The confounding role of personality and trait affectivity in the relationship between job and life satisfaction. *Journal of Organizational Behavior, 23,* 815–835.

Herzberg, F. (1966). *Work and the nature of man.* Chicago: World.

Iaffaldano, M. T., & Muchinsky, P. M. (1985). Job satisfaction and job performance: A meta-analysis. *Psychological Bulletin, 97,* 251–273.

Jahoda, M. (1958). *Current concepts of positive mental health.* New York: Basic Books.

Jamal, M. (1984). Job stress and job performance controversy: An empirical assessment. *Organizational Behavior and Human Performance, 33,* 1–21.

Judge, T. A., Bono, J. E., & Locke, E. A. (2000). Personality and job satisfaction: The mediating role of job characteristics. *Journal of Applied Psychology, 85,* 237–249.

Judge, T. A., Heller, D., & Mount, M. K. (2002). Five-factor model of personality and job satisfaction: A meta-analysis. *Journal of Applied Psychology, 87,* 530–541.

Judge, T. A., Thoresen, C. J., Bono, J. E., & Patton, G. K. (2001). The job satisfaction-job performance relationship: A qualitative and quantitative review. *Psychological Bulletin, 127,* 376–407.

Kafka, G. J., & Kozma, A. (2001). The construct validity of Ryff's scales of psychological well-being (SPWB) and their relationship to measures of subjective well-being. *Social Indicators Research, 57,* 171–190.

Kalimo, R., & Vuori, J. (1991). Work factors and health: The predictive role of pre-employment experiences. *Journal of Occupational Psychology, 64,* 97–115.

Karasek, R. A. (1979). Job demands, job decision latitude, and mental strain: Implications for job design. *Administrative Science Quarterly, 24,* 285–308.

Karasek, R. A., & Theorell, T. (1990). *Healthy work.* New York: Basic Books.

Kehr, H. M. (2003). Goal conflicts, attainment of new goals, and well-being among managers. *Journal of Occupational Health Psychology, 8,* 195–208.

Kelloway, E. K., & Barling, J. (1991). Job characteristics, role stress and mental health. *Journal of Occupational Psychology, 64,* 291–304.

Keyes, C. L. M. (1998). Social well-being. *Social Psychological Quarterly, 61,* 121–140.

Kinicki, A. J., McKee-Ryan, F. M., Schriesheim, C. A., & Carson, K. P. (2002). Assessing the construct validity of the Job Descriptive Index: A review and meta-analysis. *Journal of Applied Psychology, 87,* 14–32.

Kobasa, S. C., Maddi, S. R., & Kahn, S. (1982). Hardiness and health: A prospective study. *Journal of Personality and Social Psychology, 42,* 168–177.

Leach, D. J., Wall, T. D., & Jackson, P. R. (2003). The effect of empowerment on job knowledge: An empirical test involving operators of complex technology. *Journal of Occupational and Organizational Psychology, 76,* 27–52.

Lee, R. T., & Ashforth, B. E. (1996). A meta-analytic examination of the correlates of the three dimensions of job burnout. *Journal of Applied Psychology, 81,* 123–133.

Loevinger, J. (1980). *Ego development: Conceptions and theories.* San Francisco: Jossey-Bass.

Loher, B. T., Noe, R. A., Moeller, N. L., & Fitzgerald, M. P. (1985). A meta-analysis of the relation of job characteristics to job satisfaction. *Journal of Applied Psychology, 70,* 280–289.

Lucas, R. E., Diener, E., & Suh, E. (1996). Discriminant validity of well-being measures. *Journal of Personality and Social Psychology, 71,* 616–628.

Martin, J. K., Roman, P. M., & Blum, T. C. (1996). Job stress, drinking networks, and social support at work. *Sociological Quarterly, 37,* 579–599.

Martin, R., & Wall, T. D. (1989). Attentional demand and cost responsibility as stressors in shopfloor jobs. *Academy of Management Journal, 32,* 69–86.

Martocchio, J. J. (1994). The effects of absence culture on individual absence. *Human Relations, 47,* 243–262.

Maslach, C., & Jackson, S. E. (1981). The measurement of experienced burnout. *Journal of Occupational Behavior, 2,* 99–113.

Maslow, A. H. (1943). A theory of human motivation. *Psychological Review, 50,* 370–396.

Medvec, V. H., Madey, S. F., & Gilovich, T. (1995). When less is more: Counterfactual thinking and satisfaction among Olympic athletes. *Journal of Personality and Social Psychology, 69,* 603–610.

Mitra, A., Jenkins, G. D., & Gupta, N. (1992). A meta-analytic review of the relationship between absence and turnover. *Journal of Applied Psychology, 77,* 879–889.

Motowidlo, S. J., Packard, J. S., & Manning, J. S. (1986). Occupational stress: Its causes and consequences for job performance. *Journal of Applied Psychology, 71,* 618–629.

Muse, L. A., Harris, S. G., & Feild, H. S. (2003). Has the inverted-U theory of stress and job performance had a fair test? *Human Performance, 16,* 349–364.

Netemeyer, R. G., Johnston, M. W., & Burton, S. (1990). Analysis of role conflict and role ambiguity in a structural equations framework. *Journal of Applied Psychology, 75,* 148–157.

Nezu, A. M. (1985). Differences in psychological distress between effective and ineffective problem solvers. *Journal of Counseling Psychology, 32,* 135–138.

Oldham, G. R., & Gordon, B. I. (1999). Job complexity and employee substance use: The moderating effects of cognitive ability. *Journal of Health and Social Behavior, 40,* 290–306.

Organ, D. W., & Ryan, K. (1995). A meta-analytic review of attitudinal and dispositional predictors of organizational citizenship behavior. *Personnel Psychology, 48,* 775–802.

Ostroff, C. (1992). The relationship between satisfaction, attitudes, and performance: An organizational level analysis. *Journal of Applied Psychology, 77,* 963–974.

Parducci, A. (1995). *Happiness, pleasure, and judgment.* Mahwah, NJ: Lawrence Erlbaum.

Parker, S. K., & Sprigg, C. (1999). Minimizing strain and maximizing learning: The role of job demands, job control, and proactive personality. *Journal of Applied Psychology, 84,* 925–939.

Patterson, M. J., Warr, P. B., & West, M. A. (2004). Organizational climate and company productivity: The role of employee affect and employee level. *Journal of Occupational and Organizational Psychology, 77,* 193–216.

Payne, E. C., Robbins, S. B., & Dougherty, L. (1991). Goal directedness and older-adult adjustment. *Journal of Counseling Psychology, 38,* 302–308.

Petty, M. M., McGee, G. W., & Cavender, J. W. (1984). A meta-analysis of the relationship between individual job satisfaction and individual performance. *Academy of Management Review, 9,* 712–721.

Podsakoff, P. M., MacKenzie, S. B., Paine, J. B., & Bachrach, D. G. (2000). Organizational citizenship behaviors: A critical review of the theoretical and empirical literature and suggestions for future research. *Journal of Management, 26,* 513–563.

Pugliesi, K. (1995). Work and well-being: Gender influences on the psychological consequences of employment. *Journal of Health and Social Behavior, 36,* 57–71.

Remington, N. A., Fabrigar, L. R., & Visser, P. S. (2000). Re-examining the circumplex model of affect. *Journal of Personality and Social Psychology, 79,* 286–300.

Roese, N. J. (1997). Counterfactual thinking. *Psychological Bulletin, 121,* 133–148.

Rospenda, K. M., Richman, J. A., Wislar, J. S., & Flaherty, J. A. (2000). Chronicity of sexual harassment and generalized work-place abuse: Effects on drinking outcomes. *Addiction, 95,* 1805–1820.

Ryff, C. D., & Keyes, C. L. M. (1995). The structure of psychological well-being revisited. *Journal of Personality and Social Psychology, 69,* 719–727.

Schultz, D. (1977). *Growth psychology: Models of the healthy personality.* Pacific Grove, CA: Brooks/Cole.

Sevastos, P., Smith, L., & Cordery, J. L. (1992). Evidence on the reliability and construct validity of Warr's (1990) well-being and mental health measures. *Journal of Occupational and Organizational Psychology, 65,* 33–49.

Smith, A. (2001). Perceptions of stress at work. *Human Resource Management Journal, 11,* 74–86.

Spector, P. E., Chen, P. Y., & O'Connell, B. J. (2000). A longitudinal study of relations between job stressors and job strains while controlling for prior negative affectivity and strains. *Journal of Applied Psychology, 85,* 211–218.

Spector, P. E., & O'Connell, B. J. (1994). The contribution of personality traits, negative affectivity, locus of control and type A to the subsequent reports of job stressors and job strains. *Journal of Occupational and Organizational Psychology, 67,* 1–11.

Staw, B. M., Sutton, R. I., & Pelled, L. H. (1994). Employee positive emotion and favorable outcomes in the workplace. *Organization Science, 5,* 51–71.

Telfer, E. (1980). *Happiness: An examination of a hedonistic and a eudaemonistic concept of happiness and of the relations between them.* London: Macmillan.

Totterdell, P. (2000). Catching moods and hitting runs: Mood linkage and subjective performance in professional sport teams. *Journal of Applied Psychology, 85,* 848–859.

Wainwright, D., & Calnan, M. (2002). *Work stress: The making of a modern epidemic.* Buckingham, UK: Open University Press.

Wall, T. D., Corbett, J. M., Martin, R., Clegg, C. W., & Jackson, P. R. (1990). Advanced manufacturing technology, work design, and performance: A change study. *Journal of Applied Psychology, 75,* 691–697.

Walster, E., Walster, G. W., & Berscheid, E. (1978). *Equity: Theory and research.* Boston: Allyn & Bacon.

Warr, P. B. (1987). *Work, unemployment, and mental health.* Oxford, UK: Oxford University Press.

Warr, P. B. (1990a). Decision latitude, job demands and employee well-being. *Work & Stress, 4,* 285–294.

Warr, P. B. (1990b). The measurement of well-being and other aspects of mental health. *Journal of Occupational Psychology, 63,* 193–210.

Warr, P. B. (1994). A conceptual framework for the study of work and mental health. *Work & Stress, 8,* 84–97.

Warr, P. B. (1999). Well-being and the workplace. In D. Kahneman, E. Diener, & N. Schwarz (Eds.), *Well-being: The foundations of hedonic psychology* (pp. 392–412). New York: Russell Sage Foundation.

Warr, P. B. (2004). *Multiple judgments in employee well-being.* Manuscript submitted for publication.

Warr, P. B., Butcher, V., Robertson, I. T., & Callinan, M. (2004). Older people's well-being as a function of employment, retirement, environmental characteristics and role preference. *British Journal of Psychology, 95,* 297–324.

Warr, P. B., & Payne, R. L. (1983). Affective outcomes of paid employment in a random sample of British workers. *Journal of Occupational Behaviour, 4,* 91–104.

Watson, D., Suls, J., & Haig, J. (2002). Global self-esteem in relation to structural models of personality and affectivity. *Journal of Personality and Social Psychology, 83,* 185–197.

Wheeler, L., & Miyake, K. (1992). Social comparison in everyday life. *Journal of Personality and Social Psychology, 62,* 760–773.

Xie, J. L., & Johns, G. (1995). Job scope and stress: Can job scope be too high? *Academy of Management Journal, 38,* 1288–1309.

Yik, M. S. M., Russell, J. A., & Feldman Barrett, L. (1999). Structure of self-reported current affect: Integration and beyond. *Journal of Personality and Social Psychology, 77,* 600–619.

24 Organizational Consequences

Steve M. Jex
Craig D. Crossley

O ccupational stress has become a topic of great interest to academic researchers, managers in organizations, and the general public as well. A clear indication of this interest is the sheer number of scientific studies as well as book chapters and reviews examining occupational stress (see Beehr, 1995; Tubre & Collins, 2000). Authors of these studies and reviews often attempt to "grab" the reader by describing the negative impact that employee stress has on organizations. For example, many authors cite the amount of money that stress costs organizations and drains from the economy in general. Although the negative impact of stress is often thought to be due to increases in health care costs, authors also claim that employee stress is costly to organizations in terms of reduced productivity, decreased quality of customer service, increased accident rates, and increased employee withdrawal, to name a few.

From a journalistic perspective, beginning a discussion of occupational stress by pointing out these adverse consequences to attract readers makes a great deal of sense. From a scientific perspective, however, such claims are problematic. Although conventional wisdom would suggest that negative consequences befall organizations when their employees are enduring high levels of stressors in their jobs, relatively little empirical evidence has been brought to bear on this issue. Similarly, very little has been done to specify the mechanism(s) whereby employee stress negatively affects organizational functioning. Does employee stress lead to more health problems, which in

Authors' Note: Correspondence regarding this chapter should be sent to Steve M. Jex, Department of Psychology, Bowling Green State University, Bowling Green, Ohio 43403. Electronic mail may be sent to sjex@bgnet.bgsu.edu turn lead to greater health care costs? Do employees under stress provide poor customer service, which in turn leads to fewer repeat customers? Are employees under stress involved in more accidents, which in turn increases workers' compensation premiums? Although these propositions seem reasonable, little empirical work has been done to validate such claims.

In this chapter, we examine the very important yet little understudied issue of organizational consequences of occupational stress. As a starting point, we first review the various outcomes that have been examined in occupational stress research as well as the relevance of these outcomes to organizational functioning. We then review theoretical models of occupational stress in an effort to examine the implications that these models provide in linking stressors to organizationally relevant outcomes. The focus of the chapter then shifts to methodological issues in the study of organizational consequences of stress. We then review empirical evidence linking employee stress with organizationally relevant outcomes. The chapter concludes with a discussion of practical implications and future research directions.

Stress Outcomes

Like many areas in the organizational sciences, the study of occupational stress is relatively new (Jex, 1998). In assessing the effects of job-related stressors over the years, however, a clear pattern has developed in terms of the various outcomes that researchers have investigated. Specifically, stress outcomes (called "strains") have typically been psychological, physical, and behavioral in nature. Common psychological outcomes that have been studied include anxiety, depression, and general psychological well-being. The study of physical outcomes has been popular due to the potential link between experiencing job-related stressors and ill health. Most researchers have opted to measure physical strain through self-reported physical symptoms, although some researchers have used more objective measures such as physiological indicators (e.g., blood pressure) or even health care utilization. Behavioral outcomes (e.g., job performance, absenteeism, and turnover) have been studied the least due largely to the practical difficulties associated with obtaining these indicators.

Given these three types of stress outcomes, questions have been raised about the degree to which various outcomes are relevant to organizational functioning. Feelings of anxiety, for example, do not necessarily have to occur in an organizational context and may have little if any effect on bottom-line organizational well-being. Conversely, decreased job performance occurs in an organizational context and may have a devastating impact on bottom-line profitability. Beehr and Newman (1978) were acutely aware of this issue as evidenced by the distinction made between "human consequences" and "organizational consequences" in their model of occupational stress (to be discussed later).

Exhibit 24.1 Outcome Type by Outcome Relevance

	Outcome Relevance	
Outcome Type	Individual	Organization
Psychological	(Cell 1) Anxiety Depression General Well-Being	(Cell 2) Job Dissatisfaction Low Organizational Commitment Low Job Involvement Job Frustration
Physical	(Cell 3) Psychosomatic Symptoms Diagnosed Health Problems Physiological Indices	(Cell 4) Health Care Utilization Sick Days Workers' Compensation Claims
Behavioral	(Cell 5) Decreased Positive Health Behavior Drug and Alcohol Use Risk Taking	(Cell 6) Decreased Job Performance Counterproductive Behaviors Accidents

Given these considerations, it is possible to classify stress outcomes as being primarily relevant to the *individual* or primarily relevant to the *organization*. Thus, the previously discussed stress outcomes (i.e., psychological, physiological, and behavioral) can be meaningfully crossed with the primary target of relevance (i.e., individual or organizational) to form the matrix shown in Exhibit 24.1.

The first row of this matrix contains stress-related outcomes that are primarily psychological in nature. Psychological outcomes that mainly affect the individual (Cell 1) may include anxiety, depression, and general well-being. Organizationally relevant psychological strains (Cell 2) include job dissatisfaction, low organizational commitment and job involvement, and feelings of job-related frustration, to name a few. Physical individual-relevant outcomes (Cell 3) may include psychosomatic symptoms, diagnosed health problems (e.g., coronary heart disease), and physiological indices (e.g., elevated blood pressure). Organizationally relevant physical outcomes (Cell 4) may include increased use of health care, sick days, and workers' compensation claims. The final row in the matrix contains outcomes that are primarily behavioral in nature. Individually relevant behavioral outcomes (Cell 5) may include increased drug and alcohol use, decreased positive health behaviors (e.g., exercise, adequate sleep), and higher levels of risk taking (e.g., unsafe driving). Organizationally relevant behavioral outcomes (Cell 6) may include decreased job performance, increased counterproductive behaviors such as aggression or theft, and increased accident rates.

In considering the outcomes listed in Exhibit 24.1, it is obvious that classifying a strain as being more relevant to the individual or to the organization is a subjective decision. Furthermore, many of the outcomes listed in Exhibit 24.1 are relevant to *both* individuals and organizations and could be placed into multiple cells. The choice to put an outcome exclusively under the Individual or the Organizational column is therefore based on the *degree* of relevance to the respective entity. As an example, employees' use of alcohol and drugs outside of work may affect their behavior in the work context and thus have some relevance to organizations. However, on balance we would argue that prolonged use of alcohol and drugs ultimately has a greater impact on the individual engaged in such behavior than on the organization in which he or she works.

Theoretical Models of Occupational Stress

Over the years, several theoretical models of the occupational stress process have been proposed, although relatively few have been rigorously tested. Reviewing the large number of models that have been proposed over the years is beyond the scope of this chapter. Nevertheless, in this section we review models that are considered to have had the greatest impact on the way that researchers conceptualize stress in the workplace and hence the way it has been studied.

ISR Model

This model came out of the seminal research program at the Institute for Social Research (ISR) at the University of Michigan in the 1960s. These researchers were among the first to view stress in the workplace from a psychosocial perspective and were particularly interested in the many sets of role demands that are placed on employees in organizational settings (Kahn, Wolfe, Quinn, Snoek, & Rosenthal, 1964). The model that guided this work is presented in Figure 24.1.

As can be seen, the steps in this model are general enough to explain outcomes that are relevant to individuals or to organizations. For example, behavioral and affective responses at Step 3 could be relevant to the well-being of employees as well as organizations. Although Step 4 appears to refer to outcomes that are primarily relevant to individuals, employees' mental and physical conditions have direct implications for organizational functioning. For example, depression and sleeplessness likely have a deleterious effect on job performance. Although the ISR model is quite generic and can be used to explain either individual or organizationally relevant outcomes, on balance the model seems to be more geared toward explaining health-related outcomes, which are typically more relevant to the individual than to the organization.

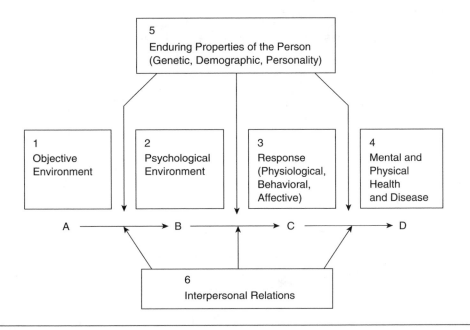

Figure 24.1 The ISR Model of Occupational Stress

McGrath's Process Model of Work Stress

McGrath (1976) proposed a model of occupational stress that focused largely on the impact of stress on performance-related behaviors. Given this focus, McGrath's model may be a bit more informative than the ISR model with respect to organizational consequences. As can be seen in Figure 24.2, the model begins with the objective situation (Box A). This situation is then perceived by the employee (Box B) and a choice is made regarding the most appropriate response to the given situation (Box C). Once a response is selected, the employee engages in the chosen behavior (Box D), which in turn affects the objective situation (Box A).

Unlike the ISR model, which was designed primarily to explain employee health, McGrath's process model appears to be focused on organizationally relevant outcomes. As such, this model can provide some guidance in understanding the impact of workplace stressors on organizational well-being. Many of the behaviors employees select when confronted with workplace stressors are highly relevant to organizations. Indeed, physical or psychological withdrawal from work as responses to stressors may cost an organization substantially in a number of ways (e.g., decreased productivity, staffing difficulties). In the same vein, employees who respond to stressors by being less helpful to fellow employees (Jex, Adams, Bachrach, & Sorenson, 2003) or to customers may create a more negative interpersonal environment among employees and may reduce the quality of services that an organization provides.

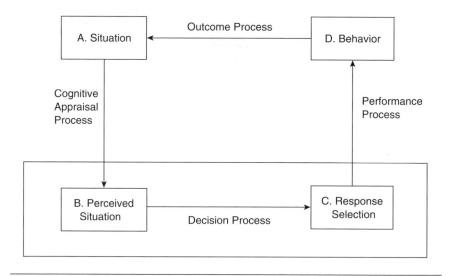

Figure 24.2   McGrath's Process Model of Occupational Stress

The Beehr and Newman Model

As part of their comprehensive review and facet analysis of the occupational stress literature, Beehr and Newman (1978) proposed a conceptual model of the stress process. The main purpose of this model was to organize their review of the literature, but this model has also proven to be a useful guide to many occupational stress researchers. The model is presented in Figure 24.3.

This model suggests that characteristics of the individual (person facet) and the situation (environmental facet) both influence peoples' cognitive appraisals and behavioral reactions to workplace stressors (process facet). This appraisal process affects employees (human consequences facet) as well as the organization (organizational consequences facet). This distinction between individual and organizational outcomes is noteworthy. Although other models may allude to both types of outcomes, Beehr and Newman's model is the most explicit in making this distinction. In the final portion of the model, Beehr and Newman proposed that adaptive responses may come about after the individual has experienced and reacted to organizational stressors (adaptive responses facet). Furthermore, this model includes a feedback loop, which acknowledges that adaptive responses may change the person (e.g., he or she may develop better coping skills) or the environment one works in (e.g., asking questions of one's supervisor may result in greater role clarity).

Although the Beehr and Newman model is more explicit in recognizing that stressors may result in organizationally relevant outcomes, this model does not describe the mechanisms by which these outcomes may occur. More specifically, there is no proposed mechanism linking stressors to organizational functioning. One would assume, for example, that stressors lead

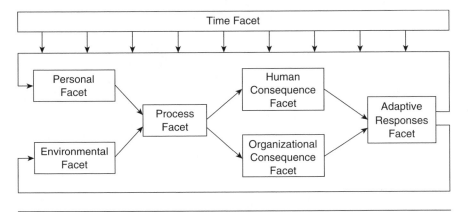

Figure 24.3   Beehr and Newman's (1978) Facet Model

to outcomes such as decreased performance, increased absenteeism, or decreased job satisfaction because of some intermediate link (e.g., general psychological distress), but this link is not specified. In fairness to Beehr and Newman, the model was developed simply to illustrate the conceptual domains of occupational stress research, yet the "organizational consequences" portion of the model is clearly underdeveloped.

The Demands-Control Model

Karasek (1979) proposed an interaction between work demands and job control whereby the most stressful situations are those in which high demands are placed on employees, yet employees have little discretion or control over decisions that affect their jobs. This model is illustrated in Figure 24.4.

Since its introduction in the late 1970s, considerable research has been done to directly test the demands-control model. Despite the intuitive appeal of the model, as well as its widespread use, empirical support has been somewhat equivocal. For example, many studies have supported an additive model whereby demands and control both contribute independently to strain (e.g., Spector, 1987). Although Karasek (1989) claimed that additive effects constitute support for the demands-control model, most studies have involved testing the *interaction* between demands and control (de Lange, Taris, Kompier, Houtman, & Bongers, 2003). It has also been shown that the demands-control interaction predicted by Karasek is most likely to occur in situations where there is high social support (see de Lange et al., 2003) and when employees have higher levels of self-efficacy (Schaubroeck & Merritt, 1997).

Like the ISR model, the demands-control model was designed largely to explain individual level health-related outcomes. Karasek's early work, for example, examined the relationship between high demands-low control work and the prevalence of cardiovascular disease (e.g., Karasek, Baker, Marxer, Ahlbom, & Theorell, 1981). Subsequent tests of the demands-control model

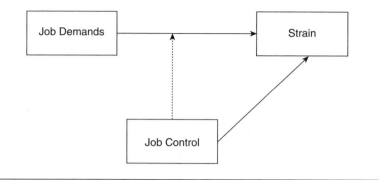

Figure 24.4   Karasek's (1979) Demands-Control Model

have also investigated cardiovascular morbidity (e.g., Schaubroeck, Ganster, & Kemmerer, 1994) as well as more indirect indicators of cardiovascular health (e.g., Schaubroeck & Merritt, 1997).

Given the focus of research on the demands-control model, it might be concluded that it was primarily designed to measure outcomes that are more relevant to individuals than to organizations. There is no inherent reason, however, that this model could not be used to predict more organizationally relevant outcomes as well. In fact, in the initial formulation and test of his model, Karasek (1979) examined both job dissatisfaction and sick days as outcomes. Thus, it is clear that Karasek intended for the model to explain outcomes that were relevant to both individuals and organizations.

Spector's Frustration Model

Based on the Dollard-Miller frustration-aggression theory (Dollard, Doob, Miller, Mowrer, & Sears, 1939), Spector (1975, 1997) proposed that frustrating job conditions (e.g., interruptions, lack of resources) may lead to a variety of forms of counterproductive behavior among employees. As can be seen in Figure 24.5, this model suggests that workplace stressors and frustrating conditions set the stage for counterproductive and often aggressive workplace behaviors. Whether environmental conditions cause an employee to actually experience frustration depends on how these conditions are appraised by the employee. The model proposes that frustration is most likely to be experienced when environmental conditions are seen as arbitrary (because of difficulty in predicting or adapting to conditions), block important goals, occur concurrently with other environmental frustrators, and when the frustrator is perceived as severe. Assuming that an employee experiences frustration, the next step in the model deals with the employee's behavioral reaction to such feelings. According to the model, whether feelings of frustration lead to antisocial behavior among employees depends on a number of factors, such as fear of being caught, hostility to rules, impulsiveness, sense of alienation, and social insensitivity.

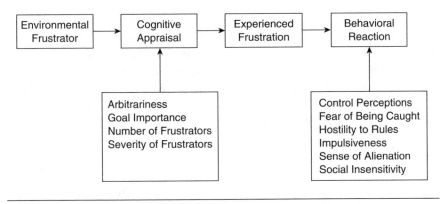

Figure 24.5   Spector's (1997) Organizational Frustration Model

Although not strictly designed to be an occupational stress model, Spector's frustration model is relevant to the present discussion for two reasons. First, many stressors in organizations are perceived by employees as frustrating conditions. An employee who has a heavy workload or experiences conflicting role demands, for example, is likely to perceive these stressors as getting in the way of task or goal accomplishment. The model is also relevant because many of the outcomes under the general rubric of "antisocial behavior" have important implications for organizational functioning. For example, when employees engage in behaviors such as sabotage, theft, violence, or even deliberately wasting time, an organization suffers financially (Murphy, 1993). More generally, such behaviors may also contribute to an organizational climate that is not conducive to effective work and may make an organization extremely unattractive to potential employees (Robinson & O'Leary-Kelly, 1998).

As was shown in this section, models of occupational stress have been developed to explain outcomes that are relevant to both individuals and organizations. Nevertheless, there is some difference between models in terms of how explicitly they distinguish between individual and organizational outcomes. Unfortunately, most occupational stress models lack explicit description, of the processes by which outcomes that are primarily relevant to individuals may affect organizational functioning. This is an issue we will return to later in the chapter.

_____ Methodological Challenges and Opportunities

As was shown in the previous section, many occupational stress models are general enough to explain outcomes that are relevant to individuals and to organizations and may be useful to researchers interested in documenting the organizational consequences of occupational stress. Despite this theoretical guidance, however, researchers seeking to establish links between stressors and organizationally relevant outcomes still face a number of difficult methodological challenges. Although many of these are similar to the challenges faced in all occupational stress research, assessing outcomes relevant to organizations presents some unique methodological challenges. At the same time, measuring such outcomes may also provide opportunities for methodological innovation. Next we discuss both methodological challenges and opportunities associated with measuring organizationally relevant outcomes.

Individual Level Indicators of Strain

Psychological strains. The most straightforward approach to measuring organizationally relevant psychological strains is through the use of self-report measures. Furthermore, instruments are readily available to measure psychological constructs such as job satisfaction (Ironson, Smith, Brannick, Gibson, & Paul, 1989), organizational commitment (Meyer & Allen, 1997), and job involvement (Lodahl & Kejnar, 1965). The primary advantage of using self-report methodology is that it is very efficient. Furthermore, because psychological strains are perceptual in nature, using self-report instruments makes intuitive sense. The major disadvantage of self-report methodology is that relationships between such measures and other self-reported variables may be inflated due to common method variance. This would be the case, for example, if one were interested in the correlation between self-reported role ambiguity and self-reported job satisfaction. Though there has been considerable debate about the *extent* to which common method variance is a problem in occupational stress research (e.g., Podsakoff, MacKenzie, Lee, & Podsakoff, 2003; Spector, 1994), it is still a potential problem when both stressors and strains are self-reported.

Although self-report is the method of choice for measuring psychological strain, there may be ways to decrease common method variance. One method that has been used is to augment self-report measures with "significant other" or coworker reports (e.g., Heinisch & Jex, 1998). For example, spouses or coworkers could provide job satisfaction ratings based on their knowledge of the respondent. This type of peer rating has been used to measure both stressors and psychological strains (e.g., Spector, Dwyer, & Jex, 1988), although it has not been used extensively.

When it is not possible to obtain peer ratings, another technique for reducing common method variance is to temporally separate measures of stressors and strains. This may be particularly important in the study of perceptions of stress and psychological outcomes. Introducing a time lag between measurements of stressors and strains reduces the respondents' ability and motivation to use previous responses to answer subsequent questions, thereby reducing demand characteristics and respondents' abilities to provide perceptually consistent answers (Podsakoff et al., 2003).

Physical strains. Whereas individually relevant physical strains have often been assessed by self-report measures of physical symptoms such as sleep loss and headaches, research has largely neglected to examine how physical strains may be measured in organizationally relevant terms (cf. Karasek, 1979). Because physical symptoms are important in their own right, and also because use of self-reports of physical strains are less susceptible to common method biases than are self-reports of psychological strain, some attention is devoted to discussing ways to assess organizationally relevant physical strain. Perhaps the easiest way to assess organizationally relevant physical strain is with the use of self-reports of the extent that employees experience physiological problems (e.g., sleep loss, headaches) that specifically affect performance or attendance. Coworkers or significant others could also be asked to indicate the extent to which the respondent suffers from health-related issues stemming from job stress that appear to hinder the respondent's task performance or attendance.

Perhaps the most objective way to assess organizationally relevant physiological strains is through assessing organizational records and archival data. Company reports such as the number of sick days used or workers' compensation claims may provide an estimate of how workplace stressors physiologically affect employees in ways that undermine the organization's success. Obviously, use of company records is not without concern. Indeed, even among companies that classify sick leave separately from vacation, researchers must rely on the integrity of employees who may use sick days to stay home with a sick child, for personal vacation, or for any number of other non-illness-related purposes. Workers' compensation claims may also have limited utility as strain indicators, due to low base rates as individual level phenomena.

Behavioral strains. In measuring the impact of stressors on organizations, behavioral strains are in some ways the most problematic to measure. Indeed, employees may not have good recall of their own behavior, and organizations may vary considerably in the extent and accuracy with which they keep records of employee behaviors (Dillman, 2000). Furthermore, many measures of employee behavior suffer from either criterion deficiency or criterion contamination. Nevertheless, several methods of assessing behavioral outcomes are available. Specifically, employee performance can be assessed by examining production reports (e.g., quality, quantity of output, etc.) or with supervisor ratings. Further, personnel records can be used to assess absenteeism, tardiness, and turnover, as well as accidents and insubordination or noncompliance. Because of their often covert nature, counterproductive workplace behaviors have most often been assessed by self-reports (e.g., Bennett & Robinson, 2000), although this has not been without criticism, most often dealing with social desirability of responses.

Organizational Level Indicators of Strain

In addition to organizationally relevant strain assessed at the individual level, data may also be aggregated or assessed at the group or organization level in an effort to examine the impact of workplace stressors on bottom-line indicators of organizational success. Perhaps the most straightforward approach to measuring organizational level strain is to aggregate measures of individual level strain (e.g., job dissatisfaction, physical symptoms, performance ratings). Aggregation of individual level responses, particularly with psychological strain measures, must be justified on theoretical, psychometric, and empirical grounds (Bliese & Jex, 2002). This is because the meaning of aggregate level variables may be very different from their individual level analogues and may thus be difficult to interpret.

Organizational level psychological strain. In addition to aggregating individual level responses, overall psychological strain in an organization can also be measured by using a "key informant" approach. This would involve, for example, asking key representatives (e.g., supervisors, executives) to rate the level of morale for the work group or organization. The obvious advantage of this approach is that there is no need to aggregate individual level responses and risk making inappropriate inferences across levels of analysis. The disadvantage of this approach, however, is that key informants may vary considerably in the extent to which they have a good handle on the "pulse" of employees in the organization. This is an issue that sociologists and anthropologists struggle with frequently (see Johnson, 1990).

Organizational level physical strain. As with psychological strain, physical strain represents outcomes that are indigenous to the individual. Thus, a certain degree of creativity must be used to develop indices of organizational level physical strain. One approach would simply be to aggregate individual level measures of physical strain. For example, a researcher could ask employees in an organization to complete a measure of physical symptoms (e.g., Spector & Jex, 1998) and aggregate the responses. This would allow a researcher to determine whether the average number of physical symptoms reported by employees in Company A was significantly larger than the average reported in Company B. As with psychological strain, a disadvantage to this approach is uncertainty regarding this aggregate level measure as a valid indicator of the overall health of employees in an organization.

Organizational level physical strain may also be measured using the key informant approach described earlier. This would involve, for example, asking someone in an organization who works in human resources or occupational health about the state of employee health. Such an approach could probably be made somewhat more systematic by asking such a key informant to consider objective data (e.g., number of sick days) when making such estimates.

The final, and in some respects the most preferable, approach to measuring physical strain involves the use of archival data. Some alternatives to be considered under this approach are number of recorded sick days, number of workers' compensation claims, number of visits to the organization's health clinic, or number of recorded visits to a physician for work-related problems. These individual level indices could then be aggregated to the broader organizational level. Another approach may be to measure an organization's cost of funding health insurance. This may be quite useful when an organization's health insurance premiums are strongly affected by the extent to which employees utilize health services, which is often the case.

The obvious advantage of using the archival measures described above is that they are at least potentially more objective than self-report indices. The disadvantage with archival measures, however, is that many of these have unknown or even questionable construct validity. For example, an employee may utilize the services of health professionals because of legitimate health conditions or simply because he or she has a tendency to be overly worried about health-related issues. It is also possible that such archival measures may be contaminated by health problems that have little to do with work-related issues. For example, an employee who is an avid runner may need to visit a physician frequently due to knee and ankle injuries—medical conditions that clearly have nothing to do with stressful job conditions.

Organizational level behavioral strain. Consistent with previously described approaches of assessing organizational level strains, one way of measuring behavior at the organizational level would be to aggregate individual level measures. For example, absences of individuals could be aggregated to develop an overall index of employee withdrawal. Supervisor performance ratings could also be aggregated to work group level performance. Further, the degree of accident involvement of individual employees could be aggregated to create an overall index of the level of safety within groups or the organization as a whole.

The key informant approach can also be used to measure organizational level indicators of employee behavior. This may involve, for example, asking a representative from an organization's human resources department to report the level of absenteeism, turnover, or productivity. This type of measurement approach can potentially be quite useful and efficient, as a great deal of data can be obtained very quickly (e.g., by mailing questionnaires to several organizations). The major problem, however, is that there is no guarantee that the information obtained is valid. Although it is certainly possible that a key informant would use organizational records to provide estimates of employee behavior, a researcher has no easy way of ensuring that this is the case.

Undoubtedly the most objective method of assessing the behavioral effects of stress on organizations is through organizational records. Many organizations keep records of a variety of employee behaviors that could be indicative of stress-related problems (e.g., absenteeism, turnover, production, sales, injuries, noncompliance reports, etc.). In some cases, data bearing on organizational outcomes are available in public domain sources. For example, publicly traded companies must report profits to the Securities and Exchange Commission (SEC), and these data are available to the general public through online databases. Although there are certainly clear advantages to using archival records kept by organizations, there are also some drawbacks as well. Perhaps the most important is that gaining access to organizational records can be quite difficult for researchers. This is particularly true for counterproductive behaviors such as accidents, workplace substance use, or incidents of violence or harassment (see Cortina & Magley, 2003). Further-more, even if a researcher were fortunate enough to gain access to organiza-tional records, the accuracy of those records is by no means guaranteed and may be questionable at best. For instance, workplace injuries often go unre-ported (Pransky, Snyder, Dembe, & Himmelstein, 1999) because, among other reasons, companies can be penalized with higher workers' compensa-tion and insurance premiums. Organizations are also likely to vary consider-ably in the accuracy of their record keeping (see Pransky et al., 1999), a phenomenon that cannot be easily verified or corrected by the researcher.

Empirical Evidence on Organizational Consequences

Most research linking stress to organizationally relevant outcomes has attempted to document the relationship between workplace stressors (e.g., role ambiguity) and individual level outcomes (e.g., job satisfaction). Because of the breadth of this literature, a thorough review is beyond the scope of this chapter. Indeed, several meta-analyses exist that conceptually and statistically summarize relations between stress and individual level organizationally relevant strains, including such job-related stressors as role conflict and ambiguity (see Jackson & Schuler, 1985; Tubre & Collins, 2000), work hours (Sparks, Cooper, Fried, & Shirom, 1997), job insecurity (Sverke, Hellgren, & Naeswall, 2002), and injustice (Cohen-Charash & Spector, 2001). Meta-analyses have also summarized empirical evidence related to strains such as burnout (Lee & Ashforth, 1996) as well as gender differences in occupational stress (Martocchio & O'Leary, 1989).

Despite the breadth of this literature, it is still possible to draw a number of conclusions. First, stressors have been shown to be strongly related to organizationally relevant psychological outcomes such as job satisfaction, organizational commitment, job involvement, job frustration, and burnout. Thus, it seems reasonably safe to conclude that stressors tend to induce negative affect in employees. Second, stressors have also been shown to be related to physical outcomes, but in most cases the physical outcomes exam-ined are more relevant to individuals than to organizations. For example, many studies have shown that stressors are related to psychosomatic symp-toms and even physiological indices. Far fewer studies have shown stressors to be related to outcomes such as health care utilization, sick days, and workers' compensation claims.

Finally, although there has been some investigation into the relationship between stressors and organizationally relevant behavioral outcomes, the relationships found in these studies tend to be considerably weaker than those between stressors and psychological outcomes. As an illustration of this, Jackson and Schuler (1985) found that the corrected correlations between role ambiguity and role conflict and job satisfaction were −.46 and −.48, respectively. In contrast, the correlations with performance were −.12 and −.11 and with absenteeism were .13 and −.02.

In addition to individual level outcomes of workplace stress, some empirical research has examined organizational level consequences of employee stressors and strains. A good example of this can be found in a study by Jones et al. (1988), in which these researchers examined the relationship between a composite index assessing employee feelings of stress from various aspects of their jobs and the number of malpractice claims in a sample of hospitals. As expected, higher stress among employees was associated with higher numbers of malpractice claims. Although not directly tested, the presumed mechanism by which this occurred was that employees who were experiencing a great deal of stress were more prone to errors when caring for patients due to a lack of concentration or being anxious on the job.

Research has also found that organizations where employees report high levels of stressors also tend to have higher rates of workers' compensation claims than organizations in which levels of stressors are lower (Moran, Wolff, & Green, 1995). This finding can be interpreted in one of two ways. For example, employees who are experiencing high levels of stressors may be more prone to suffer from work-related injuries and thus file more claims. As stated above, this may be due to a lack of focus or general distress. However, it also may be that employees experiencing high levels of stressors will be more likely to file fraudulent claims. In this case, filing a baseless workers' compensation claim may be viewed as a form of counterproductive behavior.

Although workers' compensation claims may represent a reasonable indication of organizational costs incurred by workplace stress, a more direct measure would be to assess the relationship between workplace stressors and actual health care costs. Manning, Jackson, and Fusilier (1996) used this approach in examining the relationship between stressful work *events* and a composite index of job tension, job dissatisfaction and negative affect, and subsequent health care costs among a sample of employees from a large chemical corporation. Five types of health care costs were assessed, including physician office visit costs, hospital outpatient costs, hospital inpatient costs, prescription drug costs, and other miscellaneous health care costs.

Although these researchers did not find stressful work *events* to be related to any of the five health care cost measures, they did find that the composite strain index was positively associated with doctor's office costs and outpatient hospital costs (.09 and .16, respectively). When a regression analysis was conducted and covariates such as age and gender were controlled, a slightly different picture emerged. Specifically, both work events and strain were positively related to doctors' office costs, but neither was related to hospital outpatient costs.

One important class of organizational outcomes that is very rarely examined is more "bottom-line" indicators (e.g., profits, production reports, customer satisfaction, etc.) of the performance of an organization. Although the causal chain linking workplace stress with these types of outcomes is admittedly long, the possibility that workplace stressors detract from bottom-line indicators of an organization's performance is both intriguing and undoubtedly of interest to organizations. This type of study was conducted by Ryan, Schmit, and Johnson (1996) in 142 branches of a large automotive finance company. These researchers examined aggregate level relationships between a workload stress index and multiple bottom-line measures of the performance of each branch (financial performance, customer service, and employee turnover). The results of this study showed that branches where employees reported higher levels of workload stress also had lower levels of customer satisfaction, higher numbers of delinquent accounts, and higher rates of employee turnover compared with branches with lower levels of workload stress. These findings again suggest that stressors experienced by employees, particularly due to workload, can have negative effects on organizations in very tangible ways. Unfortunately, this study did not explain *why* this might occur. It could be, for example, that employees who are overworked are simply unfriendly to customers. It could also be that a heavy workload leads to a great deal of absenteeism within branches, which ultimately causes staffing problems that make it difficult to provide high-quality customer service.

Bruner and Cooper (1991) examined the relationship between employees' feelings of stress from several aspects of their jobs and corporate financial performance among a sample of marketing managers in the electronics industry. The major purpose of their study was to examine the stressful effects of belonging to an organization that is doing poorly financially. The results of this study suggested that the relationship between stress and organizational performance might be reciprocal. These authors also found that the overall level of stress (the composite of stress felt from 61 different aspects of the job) among employees in financially unsuccessful organizations was equal to that in financially successful organizations. When examining specific sources of strain, however, employees in unsuccessful organizations reported higher levels of stress associated with the actions of top management compared with other potential stressors. This suggests that when financial performance is poor, employees may blame top management. It could also mean that employees may sense incompetence among top management prior to the effects of that incompetence being translated to poor financial performance.

Herried, Peterson, and Chang (1985) also examined the effects of stress on organizational performance, although their approach was somewhat different from that taken by Bruner and Cooper (1991). These researchers examined the relationship between stress-related physical symptoms (e.g., having trouble getting to sleep) and sales performance among real estate agents. The results of this study showed that symptoms were positively related to the number of real estate listings but unrelated to actual sales figures. The positive relationship between symptoms and listings was unexpected and, at first glance, counterintuitive. Nevertheless, real estate agents may have more control over the number of listings than the actual number or value of sales, and when under stress may thus increase listings but not sales. This finding, however, may also indicate that agents with many listings are suffering from overwork and hence tend to have higher numbers of physical symptoms. This same general finding has been shown in another study that utilized a sample of door-to-door salespeople (Beehr, Jex, Stacy, & Murray, 2000).

In a similar study, Nygaard and Dahlstrom (2002) investigated the relationship between role stressors (i.e., ambiguity and conflict) and perceived customer satisfaction and contribution to sales among a sample of managers in two Norwegian oil refineries. These researchers found that role ambiguity was negatively related to both performance measures whereas role conflict was not significantly related to either. This finding further suggests that stressors may have a direct impact on performance indices that are important to the overall success of an organization. The major limitation of this study was that all measures were perceptual in nature. Thus employees who perceived a great deal of role ambiguity might have rated the levels of sales and customer satisfaction lower than they actually were.

As was evident from the preceding section, few studies have directly examined relationships between stressors and indices of organizational well-being. Nevertheless, these small numbers of studies have generally found that indicators of employee stress have been related to a variety of indicators of organizational functioning. Unfortunately, a stronger statement regarding causality cannot be made because of the methodological limitations of these studies. Indeed, most studies have been cross-sectional and have used subjective measures of organizational outcomes. Further, many of these studies have failed to adequately control for potential confounding variables, thereby failing to rule out common-cause or third-variable explanations.

Another problem with much of the work reviewed is that it is somewhat *atheoretical*. As was argued earlier in this chapter, most occupational stress theories essentially end with the effects of stressors on *individual employees*. As a result, researchers attempting to show that employees' exposure to workplace stressors has a negative effect on whole organizations have little or no theory to go on. Although some may argue that there is nothing wrong with conducting atheoretical studies, in the long run it is problematic. This is because theory helps researchers to organize findings and ultimately leads to the advancement of knowledge. Ultimately, theoretical models must be developed that attempt to explain the mechanisms by which stress among individual employees negatively affects organizations at a more general level.

Implications for Managerial
Practice and Public Policy

Up to this point the focus has been primarily on theoretical and research issues associated with the organizational consequences of employee stress. The obvious next step is to review the more practical implications surrounding this issue. For example, what impact does this have on the way organizations are managed? How does this affect the types of stress management interventions organizations undertake? What impact does it have on public policy regarding work and working conditions? Each of these issues will be addressed in this section.

Managerial Practice

Research conducted on occupational stress over the years has undoubtedly influenced organizational functioning. Many organizations, for example, recognize the deleterious effects of stress and often provide employees access to stress management interventions (e.g., Beehr, Jex, & Ghosh, 2002) and employee assistance programs (Lindquist & Cooper, 1999). Although research has to some degree supported the effectiveness of these types of interventions (see Beehr et al., 2002; Cooper, Dewe, & O'Driscoll, 2003; Semmer, 2003), one may nevertheless think of them as being *reactive* ways of responding to workplace stressors.

By demonstrating the potential negative impact of employee stress on organizational profitability, it is certainly possible that organizations will take more *proactive* steps to prevent stressors in the first place (e.g., Hurrell, 1995). For example, a company may seek to become a "healthy organization," which has been defined as an organization that is financially successful and at the same time emphasizes employee health and well-being (Sauter, Lim, & Murphy, 1996). Research conducted by the National Institute for Occupational Safety and Health (NIOSH), as part of the healthy organizations initiative, has centered on three core characteristics: (a) an emphasis within the organization on strategic planning and continuous improvement and career development among employees; (b) an organizational climate/culture that emphasizes innovation, conflict resolution, and employee sense of belonging; and (c) organizational values that emphasize commitment to technology, employee growth and development, and valuing the individual employee. Although none of these characteristics is a stress intervention per se, they are proactive steps to preventing stress-related problems among employees.

Stress Management Interventions

Studies showing the negative outcomes associated with workplace stressors and work-related strains certainly have the potential to increase managerial awareness of stress in the workplace. Once managers are aware and concerned about stress, the next logical question is "What are we going to do about it?" For the most part, organizations have responded to this question by offering employees a variety of interventions (under the general rubric of "stress management training") designed to help employees cope more effectively with workplace stressors. The fundamental assumption behind stress management training programs is that employees are capable of modifying their *reactions* to stressors but that the stressors themselves are relatively unchangeable or that the cost of changing them would be prohibitive.

Given past responses to occupational stress, organizations in which managers realize the negative impact that stress can have on organizational functioning are likely to respond by increasing their reliance on stress management training interventions. Although the stress management literature is inconclusive about which interventions are most effective (Murphy, 1987), those such as relaxation training, biofeedback, and several forms of cognitive restructuring have been found to work well, at least in the short term (Beehr et al., 2002). Despite the value of stress management interventions aimed at helping employees cope more effectively with stress, the major drawback is that the organizational conditions causing stress remain unchanged. This has prompted concern that a focus on stress management interventions often leads organizations to ignore the root causes of strain among employees (Hurrell, 1995).

Organizations that are serious about stress reduction need to have a comprehensive strategy that includes reduction/management of symptoms as well as efforts aimed at reducing the sources of workplace stress. Given the variety of current stress management training programs and the vast number of stressors present in today's jobs and organizations, it is difficult to offer or model a prototypical example of what a comprehensive stress management strategy may look like. Nevertheless, it is certainly possible to speculate. At the very minimum, such a strategy should include some provision for stress management training interventions, as workplace stressors simply cannot all be eliminated or reduced. For example, police work carries with it some element of danger and probably always will.

A second component that a comprehensive stress management strategy should include is some form of monitoring workplace conditions and proactive efforts aimed at decreasing workplace stressors when possible. This may include assessment of the design and organization of work, interpersonal relationships among employees and between employees and customers, and the existence of constraints on performance that are frustrating to employees. By focusing on more than just management of symptoms, organizations can prevent many stress-related problems that may ultimately have bottom-line consequences. By doing so, organizations may ultimately be able to create a more cost-effective stress management strategy.

Public Policy

Occupational stress is not just an organizational problem but a societal problem as well. As a result, most countries devote at least some societal resources to understanding occupational stress and promoting health in the workplace. Notable examples are government-funded research organizations such as the National Institute for Occupational Safety and Health (NIOSH) in the United States, the Karolinska Institute in Sweden, the Canadian Centre for Occupational Health and Safety (CCOHS), and the Finnish Institute for Occupational Health. Although most countries do not allocate nearly as much financial support to occupational stress interventions as they do to other public health issues (e.g., AIDS, domestic violence, etc.), the fact that at least *some* resources are allocated toward improving employee health suggests that workplace stress is a concern to those who shape public policy.

Research documenting the impact of stressors and strains on organizationally relevant outcomes may lead to more legislative action regarding conditions such as work hours or job security. This is because such research drives home the realization that stressors affect not only individual health but also organizational functioning and ultimately economic prosperity. Beyond the impact of workplace stress on the economic well-being of organizations and society, some research has also demonstrated a relationship between workplace stress and other societal problems, such as domestic abuse (e.g., Barling & Rosenbaum, 1986). Thus, it is in the best interests of most industrialized countries to attempt to do something about workplace stress through both research and legislation regarding stressful working conditions.

Future Directions

To this point, we have examined several theoretical models that may be plausibly extended to incorporate organizationally relevant stress outcomes, we have summarized what is admittedly a relatively small empirical literature on organizational level outcomes of workplace stress, and we have described some implications of this body of research. In this final section, we discuss future directions for research on the relationship between stress and organizational outcomes.

Theoretical and Model Development

Perhaps the most pressing need for future research is the development of theoretical models to explain *how* employee stressors and strains affect organizations. As was made clear at the beginning of the chapter, occupational stress models were developed to explain the process by which workplace stressors affect individual employees. Although occupational stress research is beginning to address levels of analysis issues (e.g., Bliese & Jex, 2002), theories explaining how workplace stressors affect organizations are underdeveloped or nonexistent.

Measurement Issues

Measurement issues have, and always will be, important to occupational stress researchers. However, as is evident from this chapter, measurement issues become even more crucial when investigating the organizational consequences of employee stress. Perhaps the most important of these issues surrounds the development of reliable measures of organizational outcomes. Of those studies that have investigated the relationship between stressors and organizational outcomes, most have used measures that were readily accessible. Although many studies in the organizational literature are forced to rely on this type of measurement, it nevertheless raises the issue of whether such measures are the most appropriate.

In order to develop better measures of organizational outcomes, two things are necessary. First, researchers must have a clear idea of organizational outcomes that should be affected by employee stress. This point obviously ties in to the previous section on theory development. Well-developed and -articulated theories will help identify what organizational outcomes should and should *not* be affected by various types of workplace stressors.

Once researchers determine, at least at a conceptual level, which organizational outcomes should be affected by workplace stressors, the next step is to develop operational measures of these variables. In some cases, this may be as easy as obtaining current records from organizations or from other sources. In many cases, however, researchers will have to develop their own measures and in doing so will face a number of important choices. For example, researchers will often have to decide whether to aggregate individual employee responses or to obtain organizational level ratings from a single source. There may also be instances when researchers must choose between survey-based measures and the use of more qualitative strategies. Whatever choices researchers ultimately make, these choices will be better informed if they are based on solid theoretical development.

Interdisciplinary Research

An interdisciplinary approach may be necessary for high-quality research investigating the relationship between stress and organizational outcomes. Our current understanding of occupational stress has benefited from the contributions not only of psychologists but also of those trained in fields such as public health, occupational medicine, and human factors, to name a few. Collaborations among researchers in these areas are also necessary for a comprehensive understanding of organizational consequences of workplace stress.

Epilogue

The major conclusion to be drawn from this chapter is that the impact of employee stress extends beyond the individual to negatively affect organizational well-being. Unfortunately, this conclusion is based more on logic and conventional wisdom than on empirical evidence. Nevertheless, we have described a number of mechanisms by which stress may affect organizationally relevant outcomes and discussed several methodological issues that must be considered when investigating organizational consequences of workplace stress. Our hope is that the ideas expressed here will generate research in this neglected area and lead to healthier, more productive organizations.

References

Barling, J., & Rosenbaum, A. (1986). Work stressors and wife abuse. *Journal of Applied Psychology, 71,* 346–348.

Beehr, T. A. (1995). *Psychological stress in the workplace.* London: Routledge.

Beehr, T. A., Jex, S. M., & Ghosh, P. (2002). The management of occupational stress. In C. M. Johnson, W. K. Redmon, & T. C. Mawhinney (Eds.), *Handbook of organizational performance: Behavior analysis and management* (pp. 225–254). New York: Haworth Press.

Beehr, T. A., Jex, S. M., Stacy, B. A., & Murray, M. A. (2000). Work stressors and coworker support as predictors of individual strain and job performance. *Journal of Organizational Behavior, 21,* 391–405.

Beehr, T. A., & Newman, J. E. (1978). Job stress, employee health, and organizational effectiveness: A facet analysis, model, and literature review. *Personnel Psychology, 31,* 665–699.

Bennett, R. J., & Robinson, S. L. (2000). Development of a measure of workplace deviance. *Journal of Applied Psychology, 85,* 349–360.

Bliese, P. D., & Jex, S. M. (2002). Incorporating a multilevel perspective into occupational stress research: Theoretical, methodological, and practical implications. *Journal of Occupational Health Psychology, 7,* 265–276.

Bruner, B. M., & Cooper, C. L. (1991). Corporate financial performance and occupational stress. *Work & Stress, 5,* 267–287.

Cohen-Charash, Y., & Spector, P. E. (2001). The role of justice in organizations: A meta-analysis. *Organizational Behavior and Human Decision Processes, 86,* 278–321.

Cooper, C. L., Dewe, P., & O'Driscoll, M. (2003). Employee assistance programs. In J. C. Quick & L. E. Tetrick (Eds.), *Handbook of occupational health psychology* (pp. 289–304). Washington, DC: American Psychological Association.

Cortina, L. M., & Magley, V. J. (2003). Raising voice, risking retaliation: Events following interpersonal mistreatment in the workplace. *Journal of Occupational Health Psychology, 8,* 247–265.

De Lange, A. H., Taris, T. W., Kompier, M. A. J., Houtman, I. L. D., & Bongers, P. M. (2003). "The very best of the millennium": Longitudinal research and the demand-control-(support) model. *Journal of Occupational Health Psychology, 8,* 282–305.

Dillman, D. A. (2000). *Mail and internet surveys: The tailored design method* (2nd ed.). New York: Wiley.

Dollard, J., Doob, L. W., Miller, N. E., Mowrer, O. H., & Sears, R. R. (1939). *Frustration and aggression.* New Haven, CT: Yale University Press.

Heinisch, D., & Jex, S. M. (1998). Measurement of negative affectivity: A comparison of self-reports and observer ratings. *Work & Stress, 12,* 145–160.

Herried, C., Peterson, M., & Chang, D. (1985). Type A, occupational stress, and sales performance. *Journal of Small Business Management, 7,* 59–65.

Hurrell, J. J. (1995). Commentary: Police work, occupational stress, and individual coping. *Journal of Organizational Behavior, 16,* 27–28.

Ironson, G. H., Smith, P. C., Brannick, M. T., Gibson, W. M., & Paul, K. B. (1989). Construction of a Job in General Scale: A comparison of global, composite, and specific measures. *Journal of Applied Psychology, 74,* 193–200.

Jackson, S. E., & Schuler, R. S. (1985). A meta-analysis and conceptual critique of research on role ambiguity and role conflict in work settings. *Organizational Behavior and Human Decision Processes, 36,* 16–78.

Jex, S. M. (1998). *Stress and job performance: Theory, research, and implications for managerial practice.* Thousand Oaks, CA: Sage.

Jex, S. M., Adams, G. A., Bachrach, D. G., & Sorenson, S. (2003). The impact of situational constraints, role stressors, and commitment on employee altruism. *Journal of Occupational Health Psychology, 8,* 171–180.

Johnson, J. G. (1990). *Selecting ethnographic informants.* Newbury Park, CA: Sage.

Jones, J. W., Barge, B. N., Steffy, B. D., Fay, L. M., Kunz, L. K., & Wubeker, L. J. (1988). Stress and medical malpractice: Organizational risk assessment and intervention. *Journal of Applied Psychology, 73,* 727–735.

Kahn, R. L., Wolfe, D. M., Quinn, R. P., Snoek, D., & Rosenthal, R. A. (1964). *Organizational stress: Studies in role conflict and role ambiguity.* New York: Wiley.

Karasek, R. A. (1979). Job demands, job decision latitude, and mental strain: Implications for job redesign. *Administrative Science Quarterly, 24,* 285–308.

Karasek, R. A. (1989). Control in the workplace and its health-related aspects. In S. L. Sauter, J. J. Hurrell, & C. L. Cooper (Eds.), *Job control and work health* (pp. 129–159). New York: Wiley.

Karasek, R. A., Baker, D., Marxer, F., Ahlbom, A., & Theorell, T. (1981). Job decision latitude, job demands, and cardiovascular disease: A prospective study of Swedish men. *American Journal of Public Health, 71,* 694–705.

Lee, R. T., & Ashforth, B. E. (1996). A meta-analytic examination of the correlates of the three dimensions of job burnout. *Journal of Applied Psychology, 81,* 123–133.

Lindquist, T. L., & Cooper, C. L. (1999). Using lifestyle and coping to reduce job stress and improve health in "at risk" office workers. *Stress Medicine, 15,* 143–152.

Lodahl, T. M., & Kejnar, M. (1965). The definition and measurement of job involvement. *Journal of Applied Psychology, 49,* 24–33.

Manning, M. R., Jackson, C. N., & Fusilier, M. R. (1996). Occupational stress, social support, and the costs of health care. *Academy of Management Journal, 39,* 738–750.

Martocchio, J. J., & O'Leary, A. M. (1989). Sex differences in occupational stress: A meta-analytic review. *Journal of Applied Psychology, 74,* 495–501.

McGrath, J. E. (1976). Stress and behavior in organizations. In M. D. Dunnette (Ed.), *Handbook of industrial and organizational psychology* (pp. 1351–1395). Chicago: Rand McNally.

Meyer, J. P., & Allen, N. J. (1997). *Commitment in the workplace: Theory, research, and application.* Thousand Oaks, CA: Sage.

Moran, S. K., Wolff, S. C., & Green, J. E. (1995). Worker's compensation and occupational stress: Gaining control. In L. R. Murphy, J. J. Hurrell, Jr., & G. P. Keita (Eds.), *Job stress interventions* (pp. 355–368). Washington, DC: American Psychological Association.

Murphy, K. R. (1993). *Honesty in the workplace.* Belmont, CA: Brooks/Cole.

Murphy, L. R. (1987). A review of organizational stress management research: Methodological considerations. In J. M. Ivancevich & D. C. Ganster (Eds.), *Job stress: From theory to suggestion* (pp. 214–228). Binghamton, NY: Haworth Press.

Nygaard, A., & Dahlstrom, R. (2002). Role stress and effectiveness in horizontal alliances. *Journal of Marketing, 66,* 61–82.

Podsakoff, P. M., MacKenzie, S. B., Lee, J., & Podsakoff, N. P. (2003). Common method biases in behavioral research: A critical review of the literature and recommended remedies. *Journal of Applied Psychology, 88,* 879–903.

Pransky, G., Snyder, T., Dembe, A., & Himmelstein, J. (1999). Under-reporting of work-related disorders in the workplace: A case study and review of the literature. *Ergonomics, 42,* 171–182.

Robinson, S. L., & O'Leary-Kelly, A. M. (1998). Monkey see, monkey do: The influence of work groups on the antisocial behavior of employees. *Academy of Management Journal, 41,* 658–672.

Ryan, A. M., Schmit, M. J., & Johnson, R. (1996). Attitudes and effectiveness: Examining relations at an organizational level. *Personnel Psychology, 49,* 853–882.

Sauter, S. L., Lim, S., & Murphy, L. R. (1996). Organizational health: A new paradigm for occupational stress research at NIOSH. *Occupational Mental Health, 4,* 248–254.

Schaubroeck, J., Ganster, D. C., & Kemmerer, B. E. (1994). Job complexity, "Type A" behavior, and cardiovascular disorder: A prospective study. *Academy of Management Journal, 37,* 426–439.

Schaubroeck, J., & Merritt, D. E. (1997). Divergent effects of job control on coping with work stressors: The key role of self-efficacy. *Academy of Management Journal, 40,* 738–754.

Semmer, N. K. (2003). Job stress interventions and organization of work. In J. C. Quick & L. E. Tetrick (Eds.), *Handbook of occupational health psychology* (pp. 325–353). Washington, DC: American Psychological Association.

Sparks, K., Cooper, C., Fried, Y., & Shirom, A. (1997). The effects of hours of work on health: A meta-analytic review. *Journal of Occupational & Organizational Psychology, 70,* 391–408.

Spector, P. E. (1975). Relationships of organizational frustration with reported behavioral reactions of employees. *Journal of Applied Psychology, 60,* 635–637.

Spector, P. E. (1987). Interactive effects of perceived control and job stressors on affective reactions and health outcomes for clerical workers. *Work & Stress, 1,* 155–162.

Spector, P. E. (1994). Using self-report questionnaires in OB research: A comment on the use of a controversial method. *Journal of Organizational Behavior, 15,* 385–392.

Spector, P. E. (1997). The role of frustration in anti-social behavior at work. In R. A. Giacalone & J. Greenberg (Eds.), *Anti-social behavior in the workplace* (pp. 1–17). Thousand Oaks, CA: Sage.

Spector, P. E., Dwyer, D. J., & Jex, S. M. (1988). Relations of job stressors to affective, health, and performance outcomes: A comparison of multiple data sources. *Journal of Applied Psychology, 73,* 11–19.

Spector, P. E., & Jex, S. M. (1998). Development of four self-report measures of job stressors and strain: Interpersonal Conflict at Work Scale, Organizational Constraints Scale, Quantitative Workload Inventory, and Physical Symptoms Inventory. *Journal of Occupational Health Psychology, 3,* 356–367.

Sverke, M., Hellgren, J., & Naeswall, K. (2002). No security: A meta-analysis and review of job insecurity and its consequences. *Journal of Occupational Health Psychology, 7,* 242–264.

Tubre, T. C., & Collins, J. M. (2000). Jackson and Schuler (1985) revisited: A meta-analysis of the relationships between role ambiguity, role conflict, and job performance. *Journal of Management, 26,* 155–169.

PART IV

Interventions

25 Editors' Overview: Interventions

T he previous sections of this handbook have covered the major work stressors experienced by individuals in organizations, the major individual and organizational outcomes resulting from exposure to work stressors, and the experience of special populations of workers regarding the work stress process. Although the exploration of each of these issues is important for our understanding of work stress, we ultimately need to consider interventions aimed at managing exposure to work stressors and the resulting deleterious outcomes. As will be documented in the next two chapters, work stress interventions have received considerably less research attention compared with other aspects of the work stress process.

Work stress interventions can be conceptualized within the public health notion of prevention. As applied to the arena of work stress, prevention can be defined as the application of an intervention aimed at changing environmental, cultural, social, or personal factors in an effort to delay or avoid adverse outcomes resulting from exposure to work stressors. Traditionally, work stress interventions have been conceptualized as falling into one of three categories of prevention: primary, secondary, and tertiary. Primary and secondary prevention represent a classification scheme developed almost five decades ago (Commission on Chronic Illness, 1957). The concept of tertiary prevention came into vogue in public health after the report by the Commission on Chronic Illness (Gordon, 1983). For example, each of these three types of prevention was discussed by Caplan (1964). Within the context of work stress, primary prevention refers to intervention efforts that prevent exposure to work stressors. Secondary prevention refers to intervention efforts that prevent adverse outcomes despite exposure to work stressors. Tertiary prevention refers to intervention efforts aimed at the treatment and remediation of adverse outcomes that result from exposure to work stressors. These three types of prevention represent a single *temporal dimension* that focuses on *when* an intervention is attempted in the work stress process.

Prevention, however, is not a unidimensional construct. For example, Gordon (1983) proposed another dimension of prevention that focuses on the *inclusiveness of who* is in the population targeted for intervention. Universal interventions target all individuals in a workforce population (e.g., national workforce, regional workforce, or a specific work organization). Selective interventions target a subset of a specific workforce population who are thought to be at higher risk of an adverse outcome by virtue being a member of a specific subgroup defined by factors such as gender, age, occupation, or personality characteristics. Indicated interventions target specific individuals in a workforce population who are experiencing adverse outcomes.

Figure 25.1 presents a taxonomy of nine categories of work stress interventions based on crossing the temporal and population inclusiveness dimensions of prevention. Past research on work stress interventions has not considered the relevance and effectiveness of all nine categories of interventions. However, it is important to point out that although adverse outcomes experienced by some employees may not have their origin in the workplace, the work environment may act to worsen preexisting conditions. Thus, depending on the extant circumstances, all nine categories of interventions may have some potential to play a role in maintaining a healthy workforce and healthy organizations. Although new, we believe the broader taxonomy of work stress interventions presented in Figure 25.1 is useful to have in mind while reading the following two chapters on individually oriented and organizationally oriented work stress interventions.

Population Inclusiveness of Intervention

	Universal	Selective	Indicated
Primary	**Primary Universal** Minimize or eliminate stressor exposure among all employees	**Primary Selective** Minimize or eliminate stressor exposure among vulnerable subgroups	**Primary Indicated** Minimize or eliminate stressor exposure among specific individuals who are experiencing adverse outcomes
Secondary	**Secondary Universal** Improve resilience to stressor exposure among all employees	**Secondary Selective** Improve resilience to stressor exposure among vulnerable subgroups	**Secondary Indicated** Improve resilience to stressor exposure among individuals who are experiencing adverse outcomes
Tertiary	**Tertiary Universal** Provide treatment and employee assistance options for all employees	**Tertiary Selective** Provide treatment and employee assistance options for vulnerable subgroups	**Tertiary Indicated** Provide treatment and employee assistance options for individuals who have experienced adverse outcomes

Timing of Intervention (left axis label)

Figure 25.1   Taxonomy of Work Stress Interventions

In Chapter 26, Cartwright and Cooper review research on individually oriented interventions. Thus, they focus primarily on secondary and tertiary prevention efforts. It is pointed out that management prefers these types of prevention efforts because it tends to view adverse employee outcomes as the result of personality and lifestyle factors rather than the result of the work environment. This amounts to "blaming the victims" for their suffering. Also, management often views primary interventions aimed at the work environment to be too costly and disruptive. Cartwright and Cooper go on to review vulnerability factors that identify subgroups of workers who may be more vulnerable to adverse outcomes due to exposure to work stressors. This clearly is related to the aforementioned notion of selective intervention efforts aimed at vulnerable subgroups of workers. They then review the content and efficacy of individually targeted secondary and tertiary interventions that include health promotion activities, stress management training programs, relaxation and meditation techniques, exercise programs, cognitive behavioral therapy, and counseling. Limitations of individually targeted interventions are discussed next. Finally, they then conclude that prevention efforts should not be limited to secondary and tertiary prevention efforts alone; they must include primary prevention efforts as well.

In Chapter 27, Hurrell reviews research on organizationally oriented interventions. Thus, he focuses on primary intervention efforts. However, like Cartwright and Cooper in Chapter 26, he also explores tertiary prevention efforts because they are often made available by employing organizations. He begins with a review of "psychosocial" primary prevention interventions aimed at changing individuals' perceptions of the work environment. These psychosocial interventions include participatory action research, job redesign, changes in manager and supervisor behavior, and organizational communication. Hurrell then turns to "sociotechnical" primary prevention interventions aimed at changing the objective work environment. These sociotechnical interventions address workload, work schedules, and work processes and procedures. He then discusses tertiary interventions provided by organizations that include medical care, psychological counseling and therapy, and posttraumatic stress interventions. He then moves to a discussion of future research needs and implications for practice and policy. Finally, he concludes that despite our broad knowledge base regarding work stressors and the concomitant adverse outcomes, we know relatively little about how to effectively intervene in the work stress process at the organizational level.

References

Caplan, G. (1964). *Principles of preventive psychiatry*. New York: Basic Books.

Commission on Chronic Illness. (1957). *Chronic illness in the United States* (Vol. 1). Cambridge, MA: Harvard University Press.

Gordon, R. S., Jr. (1983). An operational classification of disease prevention. *Public Health Reports, 98*, 107–109.

26 Individually Targeted Interventions

Susan Cartwright

Cary Cooper

A consistent and continuing body of research evidence has identified stress as a major factor contributing to ill health, particularly psychological health (Cooper, Dewe, & O'Driscoll, 2001). Many workplace surveys (Cartwright & Cooper, 1997; Worrall & Cooper, 2001) have reported that stress at work significantly affects employee health and well-being and has an adverse impact on organizational productivity. In a study of changes in self-rated health among over 5,000 Danish workers over the period 1990 to 1995, Borg, Kristensen, and Burr (2000) found that health levels had deteriorated over the 5 years. A number of work-related factors, including repetitive work, high psychological job demands, and increased job insecurity, were found to be predictive of worsening health. As a consequence, many organizations are implementing a range of strategies in order to reduce stress levels, to help employees cope more effectively with experienced stress, and to reduce sickness absence and related organizational costs. At the same time, such activities are perceived to be effective in demonstrating a sense of organizational care and concern and a desire to improve employee morale (Sigman, 1992).

Stress has been variously defined (Burrows & McGrath, 2000; Cooper et al., 2001). Within the context of the transactional model of stress (Cox & Mackay, 1976), stress is considered to occur when there is a mismatch or discrepancy between the demands made on the individual and the individual's ability or perceived capacity to respond. Inherent in this view is the notion that stress is a highly individualistic process whereby personally significant events evoke a distressing psychological and/or physiological response (Burrows, Norman, & Stanley, 1999). Some theorists (Payne & Cooper, 2001), in emphasizing the role played by emotions, regard stress as the outcome of the overriding drive on the part of the individual to reduce

607

aversive emotional experiences and to maintain a sense of integrated self. Because of the subjective nature of stress, individual factors play a significant role in the appraisal and experience of stress as well as influence the way in which individuals subsequently cope to alleviate or reduce its potentially harmful effects. The focus of this chapter is on ways in which individuals can develop and improve their resilience, thus extending their capabilities to deal more effectively with stressful situations that they encounter both at work and in their personal lives (Dewe, 1989). These individually targeted interventions can take a variety of forms but typically concern stress management programs, lifestyle education, and health promotion activities as well as individual support and counseling.

In terms of the overall practice of stress prevention and intervention in the workplace, strategies can take the form of primary, secondary, and tertiary level interventions (Murphy, 1984). Primary level interventions are focused on modifying or eliminating the environmental sources of stress within the workplace that lead to stress in the first place. Typically, primary level interventions concern issues such as job redesign, structural changes in the organization, communication, and organizational processes and policies more generally. This type of intervention is the most proactive and preventative approach and so is argued by many researchers as likely to be the most effective, provided it is informed by a systematic and sound diagnosis of organizationally specific stressors (Burke, 1993; Ivancevich & Matteson, 1987). For example, Jackson (1983) conducted an evaluation of participative decision making in the outpatient department of a hospital and found that increased participation resulted in increased perceptions of influence and reduced emotional distress. Similarly, Cartwright, Cooper, and Whatmore (2000) found that an intervention designed to improve communication based on the results of a stress audit resulted in reduced stress levels and increased perceptions of control among U.K. government employees. However, although primary level interventions offer enormous potential as a means of stress reduction, Kompier and Cooper (1999) suggest that a disproportionate amount of organizational activity is concentrated on reducing the effects of stress rather than reducing the presence of stressors at work and so involves secondary and tertiary level interventions.

Whereas primary level interventions are job/organizational-oriented approaches, both secondary and tertiary level interventions are oriented toward the individual but address different stages in the stress process. Secondary level interventions (i.e., stress management programs and related activities) are directed at extending the personal resources of individuals so that they can cope better with experienced stress. Tertiary level interventions (i.e., counseling and employee assistance programs) are concerned with the treatment and rehabilitation of employees who have already developed serious stress-related health problems. Kompier, Gewts, Gründemann, Vink, and Smulders (1998) argue that organizations prefer "post hoc," individually targeted interventions over primary interventions because managers are often more inclined to attribute employee health problems to personality and lifestyle factors than job or organizational factors. McLeroy, Bibeau, Steckler, and Glanz (1988) warn that this kind of attribution results in the employee being regarded as "guilty" for his or her own health problems. Managerial attitudes are not the only drivers for increased reliance on and promotion of secondary and tertiary level interventions. Primary level interventions, because they often require organizational change, are often dismissed as being too costly or disruptive (Cartwright, Cooper, & Murphy, 1995) by organizational decision makers. Furthermore, health advisers, psychologists, and professionals traditionally tend to feel more comfortable dealing with stress as a subjective and individual phenomenon (Kompier & Cooper, 1999).

Individual Moderators in the Stress Response

As indicated in this handbook, the potential sources of stress in the workplace are many and various and differ between occupational groups and job status (also see Cooper & Cartwright, 1994). However, individuals exposed to the same stressors will respond and cope with those stressors in different ways: Some will display the symptoms of strain and will be at risk of developing health problems; others will not. Researchers have identified a wide range of individual and behavioral characteristics believed to be involved in the relationship between stressors and resultant strain (Parkes, 1994). For convenience, these variables are commonly grouped into three categories: (a) personality or dispositional factors, (b) situational, and (c) social (Cooper et al., 2001). However, these categorical distinctions are not always clear-cut. For example, the notion that coping is a stable dispositional characteristic is strongly debated (Lazarus, 1991). Similarly, the concept of locus of control (Rotter, 1966) is frequently classified as a dispositional variable, yet some research evidence (Cartwright et al., 2000) suggests that it may be situational (i.e., state rather than trait).

Gender

A number of research studies aimed at comparing gender differences in the way in which men and women experience and cope with stress (Jick & Mitz, 1985; Barling & Sorenson, 1997) have produced contradictory results (Miller et al., 2000). Recent research (Miller et al., 2000) investigated gender differences in work-related stress among over 800 managers across four countries. With the exception of stress emanating from the organizational climate, they found no differences in the levels and type of workplace stressors experienced between men and women. However, women were found to have poorer physical and psychological health than men. These findings were consistent with the results of Matuzek, Nelson, and Quick (1995) who found that females experience similar levels of stress to men but with more distress. It is suggested that this is because working women experience greater additive stress from the wider external environment (i.e., domestic and societal pressures).

Personality and Lifestyle

Many years ago, type A behavior pattern (Friedman & Rosenman, 1959) was identified as a cluster of personality characteristics and resultant behavioral style associated with increased risk of coronary artery disease. Type A individuals exhibit behaviors that reflect a strong sense of time urgency, impatience, competitive drive, and a sense of hostility. These behaviors manifest in the workplace as a tendency to work long hours, cut short holidays, report excessive work demands, feel misunderstood, and display frustration and irritability when dealing with colleagues (Davidson & Cooper, 1980). Over time, research has investigated the role of type A behavior pattern as both a direct predictor of strain and as a moderator in stress-strain relationship (Ivancevich, Matteson, & Preston, 1982; Sharpley, Dua, Reynolds, & Acosta, 1995). In a review, Parkes (1994) concluded that type A individuals create additional stress for themselves through their attitudes and actions compared with more relaxed and reflective type B individuals. In particular, the anger-hostility components of type A behavior pattern may account for increased stress levels and strain outcomes (Spector & O'Connell, 1994).

Sharpley et al. (1995) suggest that because type A behavior pattern is a psychological characteristic, it can be modified by awareness programs and that type A behavior pattern individuals can benefit from cognitive-behavioral and health promotion strategies. Friedman and Rosenman (1974) devised a number of behavioral drills individuals can follow to modify type A behavior based on positive/negative reinforcement theory. They have successfully used such techniques among clinical populations, particularly as part of the rehabilitation of patients recovering from heart disease. Given the potential importance of the anger-hostility component of type A behavior pattern, anger management programs may also be useful in helping type A individuals manage stress more effectively (Cartwright & Whatmore, 2003).

Locus of Control

Locus of control (LOC; Rotter, 1966) refers to the beliefs that individuals have over the amount of influence and control they have over events in their lives. Individuals with a high internal LOC perceive themselves as being able to influence what happens to them through their own actions and decisions. In contrast, individuals with high external LOC believe that they have little influence over events and situations and that what happens to them is largely due to luck, chance, fate, and other people. Consequently, LOC acts as a moderator between stress and strain. Individuals with an external LOC report higher levels of job stress and appear to experience less job satisfaction and more psychological ill effects than "internals" (Spector, 1982; Cummins, 1988). A study by Horner (1996) concluded that individuals with an external LOC were more vulnerable to illness and more likely to experience distressing emotions than internals. Compared with externals, they make fewer attempts to exert control over their experiences and are more likely to resort to self-blame tactics and avoidance behavior such as sleeping and watching television. It is suggested that externals can learn techniques to modify the way in which they appraise and subsequently cope with stressful events through cognitive-behavioral techniques such as rational-emotive therapy (Ellis, 1962). Such techniques enable individuals to challenge the irrationality of their beliefs and promote a greater sense of personal control and influence.

Emotional Intelligence

There is considerable controversy surrounding the concept of emotional intelligence (EI) as to whether it is a "true" form of intelligence, a set of behavioral competencies, or a cluster of personality traits (Davies, Stantov, & Roberts, 1998). However, it is accepted that the essence of what is regarded as EI is the capability of individuals to be aware, recognize, manage, and effectively integrate emotions with thoughts and behaviors. Importantly, individuals differ in their emotional aptitudes to do this (Bar-On, 1997). Slaski and Cartwright (2002, 2003) have provided research evidence to support the relationship between EI, stress, health, and performance. In a study of over 200 managers (Slaski & Cartwright, 2002), they found that high levels of EI were associated with lower stress levels, better health and well-being, and improved performance. Furthermore, they found that a program of developmental EI training raised EI levels and improved stress resilience (Slaski & Cartwright, 2003).

Other Individual Variables

Researchers have also considered other personality and dispositional variables such as negative affectivity (NA; Watson & Clark, 1984), hardiness (Kobasa, 1982), optimism, self-esteem, and self-efficacy (Cohen & Edwards, 1989), as well as aspects of situational control (Karasek, 1979), as factors explaining the differential response to and outcome of stress. Although in many cases research findings remain equivocal regarding the precise nature of their relationships in the stress process, it is clear that individual characteristics have implications for stress management (Cooper et al., 2001).

Coping Strategies

Individuals differ in terms of the number and variety of coping strategies they use to deal with stress. Some of the ways in which individuals cope with stress (e.g., smoking, alcohol, drug abuse, and binge eating) are maladaptive and increase the risk of ill health (Lindquist & Cooper, 1999). The problem with such strategies is that they are often habitual "quick fix" solutions that provide some temporary relief but have longer-term harmful effects. In contrast, adaptive coping strategies like exercising, seeking external social support, or organizing work time better have been shown to result in reduced stress and lower blood pressure (Lindquist & Cooper, 1999). Lazarus (1991) differentiates coping strategies between those that are "problem-focused" and are directed at dealing with the stressful encounter and those that are "emotion-focused" and directed at managing the resultant emotional disturbance of that encounter. Problem-focused strategies may involve gathering information, planning, seeking advice, or confronting others, whereas emotion-focused strategies may take the form of venting feelings, prayer, or distracting oneself. Although problem-focused coping is considered to be more effective, Cohen (1987) concludes that there is no single coping style that is more adaptive and effective across all situations. The effectiveness of problem-focused coping is limited to situations that present the individual with the opportunity to take control. When there is little or no opportunity to exert control, then emotion-focused coping is the only option. The important implication is that the individual needs to be able to implement ways of coping that are appropriate to the circumstances.

In the context of stress management, stress management training (SMT) can be useful in extending the individual's repertoire of coping behaviors. Lifestyle information and health promotion activities can also encourage the individual to abandon poor stress-related lifestyle habits, which account for almost half of all premature deaths in the United Kingdom alone (Cartwright & Whatmore, 2003).

The Content and Efficacy of Individually Targeted Interventions

Health Promotion Activities

In recent years, many large organizations have introduced broadbrush, companywide wellness programs and policies designed to detect the early symptoms of employee ill health and to promote the adoption of a healthier lifestyle (Ganster, 1995; Murphy & Cooper, 2000). The content of such programs typically incorporates periodic health assessment and screening activities, smoking cessation advice, the provision of exercise facilities and exercise programs, diet, nutrition, and general lifestyle information and advice. More extensive programs, such as that provided by the U.S. home improvement retailer Home Depot, include services dealing with health care benefit plans, child and elder care, family leave, and community activities (Schmidt, Welch, & Wilson, 2000). In a survey of stress prevention activities in the European Union (Kompier & Cooper, 1999), it was found that about half of the 6,157 companies surveyed provided periodic health screenings for all personnel. Nearly 40% had special policies on smoking and healthy diet, and about 30% had policies on alcohol. One in four organizations provided exercise facilities for their employees.

The evidence concerning the impact of health promotion activities in isolation has provided mixed support for their effectiveness as a means of stress reduction (Ivancevich & Matteson, 1987). Some organizational evaluations claim significant reductions in sickness absence and health care costs (Cooper & Cartwright, 1994) and high levels of employee support for such programs (Cooper & Williams, 1994). However, according to a review of studies conducted by Ivancevich and Matteson (1987), any health improvements are often short-lived, as after a couple of years 70% of individuals revert to their previous lifestyle habits. A more recent well-designed study conducted by Lindquist and Cooper (1999) evaluated the effectiveness of an intervention program targeting individual lifestyle and adaptive coping strategies in a government tax office. A 12-week postintervention follow-up showed significant improvement in job and home/work stress. Interestingly, the study found unhealthy eating patterns were predictive of stress levels and self-reported health outcomes as well as physiological measures (i.e., blood pressure). However, the intervention combined lifestyle education with specific coping skills training.

Stress Management Training (SMT) Programs

SMT is an umbrella term used to describe a wide range of activities designed to improve stress reliance. Consequently, SMT programs can vary considerably in terms of content, duration, and foci. Some programs focus on a single technique (e.g., relaxation training or the acquisition of a specific set of skills, e.g., time management). Other programs are multimodular in their approach, combining educational activities with a range of different cognitive and behavioral methods. SMT programs are often informed by employee attitude surveys or stress audits and embedded in a wider overall strategy addressing both individual and organizational factors (Griffen, Hart, & Wilson-Evered, 2000; Teasdale, Heron, & Tomenson, 2000). Typically, the content of SMT programs might include the following (Cartwright & Whatmore, 2003):

- Stress awareness and education
- Relaxation techniques
- Cognitive coping strategies (e.g., rational emotive behavior therapy [REBT])
- Biofeedback
- Meditation
- Exercise
- Lifestyle advice
- Interpersonal skills training such as time management and assertiveness training

One of the problems with multimodular programs is that it is difficult to isolate the effectiveness of specific modules, and the potential benefits of stress management training are largely accepted on faith rather than systematic evaluation studies (Cartwright & Whatmore, 2003).

Relaxation and Meditation Techniques

In a review of intervention studies (Giga, Faragher, & Cooper, 2003), relaxation was found to be one of the most popular techniques used in SMT, incorporated into a third of all programs reviewed. Wilholm, Arnetz, and Berg (2000) assessed the impact of relaxation training on computer-related skin problems among telecommunication system designers. The intervention group ($n = 66$) voluntarily chose to receive 25 hours of training over a 3-month period in one of three techniques—advanced relaxation, tai chi, or applied relaxation. Posttraining, all three methods were associated with a significant decrease in skin symptoms and serum levels of the stress hormone prolactic compared with the control group ($n = 50$). However, there were no residual benefit effects 6 months later. In a pilot study involving 21 student teachers, Winzelberg and Luskin (1999) assessed the effectiveness of meditation on stress levels, anxiety, and self-efficacy compared with a control group. The benefits of meditation, like other relaxation techniques, are founded on the somatic arousal-reduction hypothesis (Benson, Beary, & Carol, 1974). The practice of such techniques reduces the psychological effects of stress and also has potential cognitive-behavioral effects (Smith, 1986) in extending the individual's ability to tolerate and accept uncertain and unfamiliar experiences and so control and manage negative emotions. Measures were taken pretraining, 1 week posttraining, and 8 weeks posttraining. The training was found to be effective in the short term in reducing stress levels but did not improve anxiety levels or self-efficacy.

Bekker, Nijssen, and Hens (2001) assessed the outcome of a multimodular SMT program incorporating training in assertiveness, coping, relaxation, and realistic thinking on workers attending a series of courses organized by the Dutch Regional Institutions for Mental Health Care. Again, the results were compared with a nontraining group. Questionnaires were administered at three time intervals; T1, at the start of training; T2, immediately after training; and T3, 3 months posttraining. At T2, the 36 participants who completed the questionnaire reported significantly fewer psychological and somatic complaints, less stress, and a lower need for recovery after work. Furthermore, they made more use of active coping and social support seeking and reported an increased capability for managing new situations. These positive effects were not affected by gender and were maintained at T3, 3 months later. However, it is unclear as to the amount of training that was devoted to each element of the program and its influence on training outcomes.

Exercise

The role of exercise in improving health and stress resilience has received considerable support (Neck & Cooper, 2000; Flood & Long, 1996). Exercise strengthens the vital organs to allow the body to withstand higher levels of stress and distributes the impact of stress over a wider area. Through the release of endorphins, exercise relieves depression, diffuses anger and aggression, and increases energy (Brill & Cooper, 1993). In addition, regular exercisers report an improved sense of well-being and higher self-esteem (Geonie, 1988). It is claimed that an exercise program introduced at Tenneco Inc. (Gatty, 1985) more than halved the company's health care costs. Atchiler and Motta (1994) found that a single session of aerobic exercise reduced state anxiety levels. Exercise was found to result in significant physiological improvements and reduced muscle pain among insurance workers continuing up to 6 months after the initial program (Gronningsaeter, Hytten, Skauli, Christensen, & Ursin, 1992). However, the study did not incorporate any control group. In a study comparing the differential effects of three types of SMT programs, stress awareness, REBT, and exercise among government workers (Whatmore, Cartwright, & Cooper, 1999), exercise was found to be the most effective in stress reduction. The study included both a wait list and a control group. Three months posttraining, the exercise group showed significant improvements in physical health symptoms as well as anxiety, depression, and general mental health. These improvements in physical health and somatic anxiety were maintained 6 months posttraining. After 3 months, the group that received stress awareness education also showed significant improvements in depression and physical and mental health, but these were not maintained after 6 months. The group who received training in REBT reported no improvements on any of the variables. Whatmore et al. (1999) suggest that cognitive-behavioral strategies may be more effective when used on a one-to-one basis rather than delivered as a group method. Furthermore, they suggest that REBT may have been more effective if the training had been longer and more follow-up support had been available.

Cognitive Behavioral Therapy

The main aim of this technique is to attempt to reduce irrational and anxiety-provoking thoughts by improving cognitive skills (Kushnir & Malkinson, 1993). Cognitive behavioral therapy (CBT) has a successful history as a treatment method among clinical populations (Bond & Bunce, 2000). Giga et al. (2003) identified CBT as the most popular element of SMT programs, although it is frequently used in combination with other techniques. Freedy and Hobfoil (1994) assessed the effectiveness of CBT in isolation from other techniques in a study of nurses with some success. Kushnir and Malkinson (1993) similarly found that training in CBT alone resulted in significant short- and long-term (i.e., 18 months) reduction in physical and cognitive stress symptoms. Levels of assertiveness also increased in the short term. However, neither of these studies included control groups.

Other Techniques Used in SMT

Biofeedback is a technique usually involving the measurement of muscle and skin activity whereby individuals can monitor physiological changes in their bodies. It is commonly used in conjunction with other methods of stress reduction (e.g., relaxation) to inform individuals of the effectiveness of their efforts to reduce stress. Other elements of SMT programs focus on interpersonal skills training in areas such as assertiveness, emotional control, and time management. According to Giga et al. (2003), biofeedback is included in less than 5% of SMT programs, and time management training is covered in around 1 in 10 programs.

Counseling

Interventions at the tertiary level typically involve the provision of counseling services for employee problems in the work or personal domain. Such services may also involve procedures that identify and respond to personal issues that may be resulting in poor performance (Cooper et al., 2001). Such services are either provided by in-house counselors or outside agencies in the form of employee assistance programs (EAPs). EAPs provide counseling, information, and/or referral to specialist treatment and support services. Originally introduced in the United States to treat alcohol-related problems, the remit and usage of EAPs has extended dramatically in recent years (Davies & Gibson, 1994).

In a European survey, Geurts and Gründemann (1999) found that 30% of organizations provided counseling support. In the United Kingdom, over 1.75 million employees in 775 organizations are covered by EAPs (Arthur, 2002). Patterns of usage (Arthur, 2002) suggest that access to counseling is more frequently used by public sector employees and by men (70%) than by women (30%).

Because of the confidential nature of counseling, it is difficult to conduct studies to evaluate its effectiveness. However, the limited evidence that exists (Cooper & Sadri, 1991; Michie, 1992; Highley-Marchington & Cooper, 1998; Arthur, 2002) is consistent in demonstrating significant improvements in psychological well-being and reductions in sickness absence and health-related costs. Although earlier evidence (Cooper & Sadri, 1991; Highley-Marchington & Cooper, 1998) suggested that about one third of the problems presented to counseling were non-work-related, more recent evidence (Arthur, 2002) places personal issues as accounting for 70% of the caseload. The recent introduction of the Counseling and Life Management program (CALM) by AstraZeneca for its 6,000 U.K. employees to address health-related (in its widest sense) problems would seem to reflect the additional needs of employees to manage their "whole" lives (Teasdale et al., 2000).

However, evidence has also consistently shown that counseling has little, and in some cases negative, impact on job satisfaction, organizational commitment, and employee attitudes toward their work more generally (Highley-Marchington & Cooper, 1998).

Limitations of Individually Targeted Interventions

Because companywide programs are based on broadbrush, one-size-fits-all principles (Murphy & Cooper, 2000), little account has been taken of the differential effects of different types of training and individual characteristics that may affect individual responsiveness. For example, although exercise is argued to be an effective universal strategy for reducing stress (Whatmore et al., 1999), some forms of exercise, particularly those conducted in group settings, may actually increase the competitiveness and aggression of type A individuals (Cartwright & Whatmore, 2003). With certain exceptions, evaluation studies on the effectiveness of SMT have utilized relatively small sample sizes, which raises questions regarding external validity (Beehr & O'Hara, 1987). Hence, different organizational populations may benefit from different forms and types of SMT that are more tailored to their individual needs, characteristics, and preferences.

Attrition also seems to be a problem associated with SMT. Contrary to previous evidence (Conrad, 1987), volunteers for SMT, far from being the "worried well," have been shown to present higher levels of ill health symptoms than nonvolunteers, which may limit program effectiveness (Whatmore et al., 1999). Furthermore, as Whatmore et al. found, individuals with extremely elevated stress levels were more likely to "drop out" of programs than those whose stress levels were moderately high. This suggests that highly stressed individuals may benefit more from a one-to-one counseling/coaching approach than more generic group-training initiatives. More generally, techniques developed for use in a clinical setting may not easily transfer to a workplace environment (Saunders, Driskell, Johnston, & Salas, 1996).

In common with most training programs, there is a shortage of rigorous and systematic evaluation studies to assess the individual and organizational impact of such programs. Few studies incorporate control groups, and it is often difficult to assess which components of SMT programs account for any resultant beneficial outcomes. Niven and Johnson (1989) suggest that SMT programs are unlikely to prove successful because invariably they are too short in duration and do not allow sufficient practice time. Certainly there is considerable evidence to suggest that any measured benefits decay rapidly over time and are rarely maintained beyond 6 months posttraining (Reynolds & Shapiro, 1991; Bunce & West, 1996).

Epilogue

The aim of most individually targeted stress management programs is to help the individual assume responsibility for stress reduction and to take control over his or her circumstances and exercise greater personal influence. SMT programs have a role to play in an organization's strategy to reduce stress and improve employee health, but any benefits gained will rapidly disappear if the individual feels unable to transfer that learning into an unsupportive workplace. Both SMT and counseling do little to change environmental stressors or positively improve employee attitudes toward their jobs and their workplace. An effective strategy for stress prevention needs to incorporate both work-related and worker-related initiatives. Furthermore, potential solutions need to be developed through consultation with managers and employees to ensure the best use of resources.

References

Arthur, A. R. (2002). Mental health problems and British workers: A survey of mental health problems in employees who receive counselling from employee assistance programmes. *Stress and Health, 18*(2), 69–75.

Atchiler, L., & Motta, R. (1994). Effects of aerobic and non aerobic exercise on anxiety, absenteeism and job satisfaction. *Journal of Clinical Psychology, 50*(6), 829–840.

Barling, J., & Sorenson, D. (1997). Work and family: In search of a relevant research agenda. In C. L. Cooper & S. Jackson (Eds.), *Creating tomorrow's organisations.* London: Wiley.

Bar-On, R. (1997). *Bar-On Emotional Quotient Inventory: A measure of emotional intelligence technical manual.* Toronto: Multi Health Systems.

Beehr, T., & O'Hara, K. (1987). Methodological designs for the evaluation of occupational stress interventions. In S. Kasl & C. Cooper (Eds.), *Stress and health: Issues in research methodology.* New York: Wiley.

Bekker, M. H. J., Nijssen, A., & Hens, G. (2001). Stress prevention training: Sex differences in types of stressors, coping and training effects. *Stress and Health, 17*(4), 207–219.

Benson, H., Beary, J. F., & Carol, M. P. (1974). The relaxation response. *Psychiatry, 37,* 37–46.

Bond, F. W., & Bunce, D. (2000). Mediators of change in emotion-focused and problem-focused worksite stress management interventions. *Journal of Occupational and Health Psychology, 2*(3), 247–262.

Borg, V., Kristensen, T. S., & Burr, H. (2000). Work environment and changes in self-related health: A five year follow-up study. *Stress Medicine, 16*(1), 37–49.

Brill, P. A., & Cooper, K. H. (1993). Physical exercise and mental health. *National Forum, 73*(1), 44.

Bunce, D., & West, M. A. (1996). Stress management and innovation interventions at work. *Human Relations, 49*(2), 209–232.

Burke, R. (1993). Organizational level interventions to reduce occupational stressors. *Work & Stress, 7,* 77–87.

Burrows, G. D., & McGrath, C. (2000). Stress and mental health professionals. *Stress Medicine, 16*(5), 269–271.

Burrows, G. D., Norman, T. R., & Stanley, R. (1999). *Stress, anxiety and depression.* Frenchs Forest, UK: Aldis International.

Cartwright, S., & Cooper, C. L. (1997). *Managing workplace stress.* Thousand Oaks, CA: Sage.

Cartwright, S., Cooper, C. L., & Murphy, L. R. (1995). Diagnosing a healthy organization: A proactive approach to stress in the workplace. In G. P. Keita & S. Sauter (Eds.), *Job stress interventions: Current practice and future directions.* Washington, DC: APA/NIOSH.

Cartwright, S., Cooper, C. L., & Whatmore, L. (2000). Improving communications and health in a government department. In L. R. Murphy & C. L. Cooper (Eds.), *Healthy and productive work: An international perspective.* London: Taylor & Francis.

Cartwright, S., & Whatmore, L. (2003). Stress and individual differences: Implications for stress management. In A. Antoniou & C. L. Cooper (Eds.), *New perspectives in the area of occupational health.* London: Wiley.

Cohen, F. (1987). Measure of coping. In S. V. Kasl & C. L. Cooper (Eds.), *Stress and health: Issues in research methodology.* New York: Wiley.

Cohen, S., & Edwards, J. (1989). Personality characteristics as moderators of the relationship between stress and disorder. In W. Newfield (Ed.), *Advances in the investigation of psychological stress.* New York: Wiley.

Conrad, P. (1987). Who comes to worksite wellness programs? A preliminary review. *Journal of Occupational Medicine, 29*(4), 317–320.

Cooper, C. L., & Cartwright, S. (1994). Stress management interventions in the workplace: Stress counselling and stress audits. *British Journal of Guidance and Counselling, 22*(1), 65–73.

Cooper, C. L., Dewe, P. J., & O'Driscoll, M. P. (2001). *Organizational stress: A review and critique of theory, research and applications.* Thousand Oaks, CA; London: Sage.

Cooper, C. L., & Sadri, G. (1991). The impact of stress counselling at work. *Journal of Social Behaviour and Personality, 6,* 411–423.

Cooper, C. L., & Williams, S. (1994). *Creating healthy work organizations.* London: Wiley.

Cox, T., & Mackay, C. (1976). Transactional model of stress. In T. Cox (Ed.), *Stress.* Basingstoke, UK: MacMillan.

Cummins, R. C. (1988). Perceptions of social support, receipt of supportive behaviours and locus of control as moderators of the effects of chronic stress. *American Journal of Community Psychology, 16,* 685–699.

Davidson, M. J., & Cooper, C. L. (1980). Type A coronary-prone behaviour in the work environment. *Journal of Occupational Medicine, 22,* 375–383.

Davies, A., & Gibson, L. (1994). Designing employee welfare provision. *Personnel Review, 23,* 33–45.

Davies, M., Stantov, L., & Roberts, R. D. (1998). Emotional intelligence: In search of an elusive contract. *Journal of Personality and Social Psychology, 75,* 989–1015.

Dewe, P. (1989). Examining the nature of work stress: Individual evaluations of stressful experiences and coping. *Human Relations, 42,* 993–1013.

Ellis, A. (1962). *Reason and emotion in psychotherapy.* Secaucus, NJ: Citadel.

Flood, K. R., & Long, B. C. (1996). Understanding exercise as a method of stress management: A constructivist framework. In J. Kerr, A. Griffiths, & T. Cox (Eds.), *Workplace health: Employee fitness and exercise*. London: Taylor & Francis.

Freedy, J. R., & Hobfoil, S. E. (1994). Stress inoculation for reduction of burnout: A conservation of resources approach. *Anxiety, Stress and Coping, 6*, 311–325.

Friedman, M., & Rosenman, R. H. (1959). Associations of a specific behaviour pattern with increases in blood cholesterol, blood clotting time, incidence of arcus senilis and clinical coronary artery disease. *Journal of the American Medical Association, 169*, 1286–1296.

Friedman, M., & Rosenman, R. H. (1974). *Type A behaviour and your heart*. New York: Knopf.

Ganster, D. C. (1995). Interventions for building healthy organizations. In L. R. Murphy & J. J. Hurrell (Eds.), *Job stress interventions*. Washington, DC: American Psychological Association.

Gatty, B. (1985, July). How fitness works out: Helping employees keep fit improves both health and job performance. *Nation's Business*, 18.

Geonie, P. (1998, April 20). Wellness programs can help your company run the race. *Long Island Business News*, p. 31.

Geurts, S., & Gründemann, R. (1999). Workplace stress and stress prevention in Europe. In M. Kompier & C. Cooper (Eds.), *Preventing stress, improving productivity*. London: Routledge.

Giga, S. I., Faragher, B., & Cooper, C. L. (2003). Identification of good practice in stress prevention/management. In J. Jordan, E. Gurr, S. I. Giga, B. Faragher, & C. L. Cooper (Eds.), *Beacons of excellence in stress prevention* (Health and Safety Executive Contract Research Report No. 133). Sudbury, UK: HSE Books.

Griffen, M. A., Hart, P. M., & Wilson-Evered, E. (2000). Using employee opinion surveys to improve organizational health. In L. R. Murphy & C. L. Cooper (Eds.), *Health and productive work: An international perspective*. London: Taylor & Francis.

Gronningsaeter, H., Hytten, K., Skauli, G., Christensen, C. C., & Ursin, H. (1992). Improved health and coping by physical exercise or cognitive behavioural stress management training in a work environment. *Psychology and Health, 7*, 147–163.

Highley-Marchington, C., & Cooper, C. L. (1998). *An assessment of employee assistance and workplace counselling programmes in British organisations* (Health and Safety Executive Contract Research Report No. 167). Sudbury, UK: HSE Books.

Horner, K. L. (1996). Locus of control, neuroticism and stressors combined influences on reported physical illness. *Personality and Individual Differences, 12*(2), 195–204.

Ivancevich, J., & Matteson, M. T. (1987). Organizational level stress management interventions: A review of recommendations. *Journal of Organizational Behaviour Management, 8*, 229–248.

Ivancevich, J. M., Matteson, M. T., & Preston, C. (1982). Occupational stress, Type A behaviour and physical well being. *Academy of Management Journal, 25*(2), 373–391.

Jackson, S. (1983). Participation in decision making as a strategy for reducing job-related strain. *Journal of Applied Psychology, 68*, 3–19.

Jick, T. D., & Mitz, L. F. (1985). Sex differences in work stress. *Academy of Management Review, 10,* 408–420.

Karasek, R. (1979). Job demands, job decision latitude and mental strain: Implications for job redesign. *Administrative Science Quarterly, 24,* 285–308.

Kobasa, S. (1982). The hardy personality: Towards a social psychology of stress and health. In G. Sanders & J. Suls (Eds.), *Social psychology of health and illness,* Hillsdale, NJ: Lawrence Erlbaum.

Kompier, M., & Cooper, C. L. (1999). *Preventing stress, improving productivity: European case studies in the workplace.* London: Routledge.

Kompier, M. A., Gewts, S. A. E., Gründemann, R. W. M., Vink, P., & Smulders, P. G. W. (1998). Cases in stress prevention: The success of a participative and stepwise approach. *Stress Medicine, 14,* 155–168.

Kushnir, T., & Malkinson, R. (1993). A rational-emotive group intervention for preventing and coping with stress amongst safety officers. *Journal of Rational-Emotive Cognitive Behaviour Therapy, 11*(4), 195–206.

Kushnir, T., Malkinson, R., & Ribak, J. (1998). Rational thinking of stress management in healthworks. *International Journal of Stress Management, 5*(3), 169–178.

Lazarus, R. S. (1991). Psychological stress in the workplace. *Journal of Social Behaviour and Personality, 11,* 3–21.

Lindquist, T. L., & Cooper, C. L. (1999). Using lifestyle and coping to reduce job stress and improve health in "at risk" office workers. *Stress Medicine, 15*(3), 143–153.

Matuzek, P. A. Z., Nelson, D. L., & Quick, J. C. (1995). Gender differences in distress: Are we asking all the right questions. *Journal of Social Behaviour, 10*(6), 99–120.

McLeroy, K. R., Bibeau, D., Steckler, A., & Glanz, K. (1988). An ecological perspective on health promotion programs. *Health Education Quarterly, 15,* 351–377.

Michie, S. (1992). Evaluation of a stress management service. *Health Manpower Management, 18*(1), 15–17.

Miller, K., Greyling, M., Cooper, C. L., Lu, L., Sparks, K., & Spector, P. E. (2000). Occupational stress and gender: A cross cultural study. *Stress Medicine, 16*(5), 271–279.

Murphy, L. (1984). Occupational stress management: A review and appraisal. *Journal of Occupational Psychology, 57,* 1–15.

Murphy, L., & Cooper, C. L. (2000). *Healthy and productive work: An international perspective.* London: Taylor & Francis.

Neck, C. P., & Cooper, K. H. (2000). The fit executive: Exercise and diet guidelines for enhancing performance. *Academy of Management Executive, 14*(2), 72–84.

Niven, N., & Johnson, D. (1989). Taking the lid off stress management. *Industrial and Commercial Training, 21,* 8–11.

Parkes, K. R. (1994). Personality and coping as moderators of work stress processes: Models, methods and measures. *Work & Stress, 8*(2), 110–129.

Payne, R., & Cooper, C. L. (2001). *Emotions at work.* London: Wiley.

Reynolds, S., & Shapiro, D. A. (1991). Stress reduction in transition: Conceptional problems in the design, implementation and evaluation of worksite stress management interventions. *Human Relations, 44*(7), 717–733.

Rotter, J. B. (1966). Generalized expectations for internal versus external control of reinforcement. *Psychological Monographs, 30*(1), 1–26.

Saunders, T., Driskell, J. E., Johnston, J. H., & Salas, E. (1996). The effect of stress inoculation training on anxiety and performance. *Journal of Occupational Health Psychology, 1*(2), 170–186.

Schmidt, W. C., Welch, L., & Wilson, M. G. (2000). Individual and organizational activities to build better health. In L. R. Murphy & C. L. Cooper (Eds.), *Health and productive work: An international perspective*. London: Taylor & Francis.

Sharpley, C. F., Dua, J. K., Reynolds, R., & Acosta, A. (1995). The direct and relative efficacy of cognitive hardiness, Type A behaviour pattern, coping behaviour and social support as predictors of stress and ill health. *Scandinavian Journal of Behaviour Therapy, 24*, 15–29.

Sigman, A. (1992, February). The state of corporate healthcare. *Personnel Management*, 24–31.

Slaski, M., & Cartwright, S. (2002). Health performance and emotional intelligence: An exploratory study of retail managers. *Stress and Health, 18*(2), 63–69.

Slaski, M., & Cartwright, S. (2003). Emotional intelligence training and its implications for stress, health and performance. *Stress and Health, 19*, 233–239.

Smith, J. L. (1986). Meditation, biofeedback and the relaxation controversy: A cognitive behavioural perspective. *American Psychologist, 41*, 1007–1009.

Spector, P. E. (1982). Behaviour in organizations as a determinant of employee's locus of control. *Psychological Bulletin, 91*, 482–492.

Spector, P. E., & O'Connell, B. J. (1994). The contribution of personality traits, negative affectivity, locus of control and Type A to the subsequent reports of job stressors and job strain. *Journal of Occupational and Organizational Psychology, 67*(1), 1–12.

Teasdale, E., Heron, R. J. L., & Tomenson, J. H. (2000). Bringing health to life. In L. R. Murphy & C. L. Cooper (Eds.), *Healthy and productive work: An international perspective*. London: Taylor & Francis.

Watson, D., & Clark, L. (1984). Negative affectivity: The disposition to experience negative aversive emotional states. *Psychological Bulletin, 96*, 465–498.

Whatmore, L., Cartwright, S., & Cooper, C. L. (1999). United Kingdom: An evaluation of a stress management programme in the public sector. In M. Kompier & C. Cooper (Eds.), *Preventing stress, improving productivity: European case studies in the workplace*. London: Routledge.

Wilholm, C., Arnetz, B., & Berg, M. (2000). The impact of stress management on computer related skin problems. *Stress Medicine, 16*, 279–285.

Winzelberg, A. J., & Luskin, F. M. (1999). The effect of meditation on stress levels in secondary school teachers. *Stress Medicine, 15*(2), 69–79.

Worrall, L., & Cooper, C. L. (2001). *The quality of working life survey*. London: Institute of Management.

27

Organizational
Stress Intervention

Joseph J. Hurrell, Jr.

D uring the past 50 years, understanding of the causes of work-related illnesses and injuries has grown dramatically (Rom, 1998). In contrast, however, knowledge of how to utilize this understanding for prevention and intervention purposes remains limited (Schulte, Goldenhar, & Connally, 1996). This situation is especially troublesome when one considers not only the human toll of work-related illnesses and injuries but the massive drain on national economies that results from them. As mentioned over 30 years ago in *Work in America* (1973), a seminal report to the U.S. secretary of Health, Education, and Welfare, work represents an institutional tool that could be effectively used to improve the health of workers and thereby reduce the staggering costs of health care.

Nowhere in the field of occupational health is the gap between etiologic and intervention-related knowledge greater than in the realm of organizational (often called occupational or job) stress. Despite the ever burgeoning literature on the nature, causes, and physical and psychological consequences of organizational stress, surprisingly little is known regarding organizational stress intervention. The consequences of this gap may well be reflected in estimates of the enormous costs of stress to the U.S. economy, which have been estimated to be as high as $300 billion annually (American Institute of Stress, 2002).

Before discussing approaches to organizational stress intervention, it is important to have a common understanding of the organizational stress and the intervention-related terminology used in this chapter. Although various theoretical models of stress can be found in the job stress literature, nearly everyone would agree that "something" called organizational (job or occupational) stress results from an interaction between workers and the conditions of work (often called job stressors) to which they are exposed. Views differ, however, regarding the importance of worker characteristics versus working conditions as *the* major cause of organizational stress, and these viewpoints have in part led to the development and use of distinctly different intervention approaches for occupational stress. The approaches can be characterized using a public health prevention terminology as primary, secondary, and tertiary intervention (Hurrell & Murphy, 1996). The aim of primary prevention intervention is to reduce the risk factors or job stressors; the aim of secondary prevention intervention (often termed stress management) is to alter the ways that individuals respond to risks or job stressors; and finally, the aim of tertiary prevention intervention is to heal those who have been traumatized (Quick, Quick, Nelson, & Hurrell, 1997). As secondary organizational stress prevention has been the subject of extensive reviews (see, e.g., Murphy, 1988, 1996; van der Hek & Plomp, 1997) and is discussed in this handbook, it will not be considered here. Rather, this chapter will attempt to provide an understanding of the less scrutinized primary and tertiary organizational stress prevention intervention literature.

Primary Prevention Intervention

A major challenge to understanding and drawing conclusions from the job stress intervention literature in general involves the diverse and at times confusing terminology used by investigators and reviewers to characterize job stress interventions. For example, several recent review articles (van der Klink, Blonk, Schene, & van Dijk, 2001; and Reynolds, 2000) have compared the efficacy of various types of individual occupational stress interventions (secondary and in some cases tertiary intervention efforts) relative to organizational level and organizational-focused interventions. Their conclusions suggest that the effects on employee well-being of the latter type are insignificant or ineffective. Unfortunately, these reviews include only a small number of primary prevention studies and categorize a variety of different types of interventions under the rubric of "organizational." As a result, they draw conclusions that may be far too general in nature. Indeed, it is somewhat distressing that such conclusions are reported in journals targeted to public health practitioners who upon reading them may be tempted to "throw out the baby with the bathwater." Although primary prevention interventions can be thought of as organizationally focused, they clearly employ a diversity of approaches that may involve various elements of organizational change or job redesign.

Parkes and Sparkes (1998), in their careful and thoughtful review of organizational interventions to reduce job stress, characterized these approaches as being either psychosocial or socio-technical in nature. In general, psychosocial interventions focus *primarily* on human processes and psychosocial aspects of the work setting and aim to reduce stress by changing employees' perceptions of the work environment. Although they may include modifications of the objective working conditions, such changes are generally just one of several venues for bringing about changes. By contrast, socio-technical interventions focus *primarily* on changes to objective working conditions and are considered to have implications for work-related stress. Although all interventions don't fit neatly into these categories and, as just mentioned, some interventions involve elements of both approaches, it is nevertheless useful to consider them separately.

Psychosocial Interventions

Participatory action research interventions. The largest numbers of primary prevention intervention efforts described in the job stress literature appear to be psychosocial in nature and many are based on the principles of participatory action research (PAR) (Parkes & Sparkes, 1998). Although a number of definitions of PAR can be found (see Elden & Chisholm, 1993), the notion that employees are involved jointly with outside experts in an "empowering process" of defining problems, developing intervention strategies, introducing changes that benefit employees, and measuring outcomes is central to PAR (Landsbergis & Vivona-Vaughan, 1995). As described by Schurman and Israel (1995), PAR is a methodology in which researchers and workers collaborate in a process of data-guided problem solving for the dual purposes of improving the organization's ability to provide workers with desired outcomes and contributing to general scientific knowledge. An early step in this process is often the identification of major psychosocial stressors.

One of the earliest PAR approaches to job stress reduction (though not called PAR at the time) was conducted by Campbell (1973) and approached job stress from a person-environment fit theoretical perspective (French, Rodgers, & Cobb, 1974). This experimental intervention involved work teams at the Goddard Manned Space Flight Center in which group members received data on their person-environment fit with respect to a variety of measured job stressors. These data were used by work teams in a series of 10 weekly meetings to solve problems and improve person-environment fit. These meetings, it was felt, would also reduce the risk factors for coronary heart disease. A resource person (one of the researchers) was present to assist in leading the session. Unfortunately, this intervention effort could not be carried out completely as planned, and the results of the intervention did not show any effect on either organizational stressors or individual well-being. It was, however, one of the first attempts at a theory-driven psychosocial intervention specifically aimed at reducing job stress.

Heaney et al. (1993) implemented an extensive, multiyear, two-wave PAR intervention in two work settings in a manufacturing plant. The aims of the effort were to (a) change the working environment to reduce employee stress, (b) enhance factors that serve to buffer the impact of stressors (e.g., social support), and (c) promote employee mental and physical health. The process was conducted by a 26-member team and utilized 176 employee participants who served as the basis for the PAR evaluation. The intervention involved developing and conducting a job stress survey and a cyclical, participative problem-solving process. However, during the study, a major reorganization of the plant occurred that not only influenced the course of the study but likely influenced the study results. No improvements in either the social environment or employee well-being resulted from the intervention. There was, however, some limited evidence that the intervention improved coworker social support and decreased symptoms of depression (the only measure of worker well-being utilized) in one of the two work settings.

Landsbergis and Vivona-Vaughan (1995) report a PAR intervention based on the tenets of decision latitude theory (Karasek & Theorell, 1990) that involved employee problem-solving committees. The study design incorporated two pairs of matched departments and 113 employees at a public health agency. Data from 77 workers who completed both a pretest and a 1-year follow-up questionnaire were used to evaluate the intervention. Within the intervention departments, problem-solving committees were formed whose tasks were to identify and prioritize job stressors and develop action plans for their reduction. In general, it was felt that participation would lead to better communications, trust, supervisor and coworker support, improved skill utilization, participative decision making, and improved organizational climate. These improvements were expected to result in improved job satisfaction and lowered job stress. The study used only self-report measures, and the results were ambiguous at best. The authors suggest that methodological limitations such as the short duration of the study, limited sample size, and selection bias may have contributed to the disappointing findings.

Less ambiguous results involving another decision latitude–based PAR intervention were reported by Mikkelsen, Saksvik, and Landsbergis (2000). In this short-term intervention conducted at two different Norwegian community mental health care institutions, participants were randomly assigned to intervention and control groups. Sixty-four participants (including managers and supervisors) completed intervention assessments at baseline and at 1-week and 1-year follow-ups. The aim of the intervention, much like the aim of the Landsbergis and Vivona-Vaughan (1995) intervention, was to "set into motion a learning process on how to identify and solve work problems in order to improve workplace health and organizational performance continuously, on a long-term basis" (p. 159). In the intervention groups, participants identified job stressors and developed plans for their reduction. The intervention had a significant effect on self-reported work-related stress and psychological demands, but there were no significant effects on subjective health and anxiety. As commitment was lacking to continue the intervention, no follow-up data were collected, and it is difficult to conclude anything about the long-term effects of the intervention.

Job redesign interventions. A number of PAR interventions have specifically included or focused in large measure on efforts to redesign work or work processes. One of the first of these was conducted by Wall and Clegg (1981) in a department of a confectionary company with a long-standing employee morale problem characterized by high turnover rates among both workers and managers. In this 33-month study, the plant layout was redesigned so that two leaderless teams were given responsibility for production from raw materials to finished products. Although the study did not include a control group, improvements in self-reported job satisfaction, motivational variables, and mental health were evident after 18 months. During the last 10 months, researchers were not present, suggesting that the results were not due to a "Hawthorne effect."

Wall, Kemp, Jackson, and Clegg (1986) reported a somewhat similar intervention involving autonomous work groups. In this study, also at a U.K. confectionary company, the company took the opportunity when designing a new plant to establish new work methods. The researchers were not involved in the design or implementation of the intervention but evaluated the intervention for 3 years. The autonomous work groups were composed of 8 to 12 employees who met weekly and were given considerable responsibility for production. Study effects were evaluated in a quasi-experimental design with the principal hypothesis being that the implementation of autonomous work groups would have favorable effects. The results indicated very positive and long lasting effects on intrinsic job satisfaction but no effects on work motivation, organizational commitment, mental health, or performance. Moreover, labor turnover increased, and there were reports of increased stress among managers as a result of managing and maintaining the system.

Terra (1995) describes a PAR intervention in which consultants worked with management and workers in a Dutch metal can manufacturing company to introduce changes to the way work was organized and to improve the quality of some 430 production level jobs. These jobs generally involved repetitive, short-cycle work and were characterized by high levels of absenteeism. In the intervention, some 20 self-regulating production teams were created whose challenge was to design jobs that were complete (involving a whole task) and autonomous (maximizing task control), and that afforded the incumbent contact with coworkers. The teams were also afforded the opportunity to control organization level factors such as production control, work scheduling, and quality control. Unlike most PAR interventions, this intervention was evaluated entirely on organizational level outcomes. After 2 years, absenteeism was reduced by 50% and productivity increased by 66%, which resulted in considerable financial savings. The author attributed the remarkable success of the intervention to participation in the change process and control at work and distinguished three important types of participation: (a) strategic participation (involving general conditions of work and the employment relationship), (b) process participation (direct or indirect participation in the change process), and (c) operational participation (referring to participation inside of the transformation process).

Unfortunately, the study did not involve a comparison group; and as no employee perceptions of the changes were assessed, it is difficult to know the full effect of the intervention.

Wahlstedt and Edling (1997) describe an intervention in which postal employees involved in mail sorting contributed to the planning of organizational changes that ultimately involved work reorganization, the creation of small (4–5 worker) work groups, improved supervisory practices, an increased workforce, a new shift system, and better communications between workers and management. A longitudinal design was used in which self-reported measures of skill discretion, decision authority, sleep problems, gastrointestinal complaints, and sick leave were tracked from a baseline prior to the intervention and at 8-month and 12-month postintervention follow-ups. Perceptions of skill discretion and decision authority were significantly higher at the 12-month follow-up; but there were no differences in gastrointestinal complaints, and self-reported sleep problems were found to have increased. Rates of sick leave decreased over the course of the intervention. However, so many changes were implemented as a consequence of the intervention that it is difficult to know which if any particular changes may be associated with particular outcomes. This would be important to determine, as some changes may have had no effect on the outcomes measured.

Bond and Bunce (2001) conducted a job stress PAR intervention that involved developing and implementing work organization changes that were aimed at increasing workers' job control and thereby reducing job stress. Ninety-seven administrative employees of a U.K. central government department participated in the 2-year intervention that was quasi-experimental in nature. Work organization changes were developed and implemented by a 12-member steering committee in a series of five 2-hour meetings over a 3-month period. The results indicated that the intervention significantly improved mental health, sickness absence rates, and self-rated performance at a 1-year follow-up. Evidence was provided that these changes were mediated by increased job control.

As might be expected given the complexity and multifaceted nature of participatory interventions, it is difficult to determine which aspects of the intervention might be most responsible for the outcomes. Griffeth (1985), in an exceptionally well-designed field experiment, attempted to sort out the effects of the job redesign from those resulting from simply participating in the redesign process. In this 2×2 factorial study 2 months after the initial assessment, 57 part-time receptionist participants were randomly assigned to redesign versus no-redesign and participation versus no-participation groups. Participation involved brainstorming discussions, and their results were utilized to develop the redesign intervention that focused on job enrichment, increasing autonomy, and enhancing feedback. The job redesign was found to have significant and positive effects on overall job satisfaction and a number of affective outcomes but not on satisfaction with supervisors and coworkers or satisfaction with pay or job security. Effects for participation were found only on job satisfaction, and these results were less dramatic. Tests for interactions indicated that the effects of redesign and participation were additive and not multiplicative. Unfortunately, this study was of short duration (the follow-up was limited to 3 months) and the participants were part-time students where the intervention was conducted (raising questions regarding the degree to which they were affected by their jobs). Moreover, only limited changes could be redesigned into the job.

Taken as a whole, the studies described above provide very limited evidence of the efficacy of PAR and other participatory-type interventions. As Parkes and Sparkes (1998) have previously noted, the studies tend to be methodologically lacking, difficult to interpret, and causally ambiguous. When found, the effects of the interventions were often on job satisfaction and perceptions of the working environment, with fewer reported effects on outcomes that are more directly health-related. It is unclear whether the general lack of health effects are a result of ineffective interventions, the short duration of the studies (in which the change might not be expected to have an effect on health), or the nature of the health outcome variables studied. Moreover, which effects are attributable to the act of participating in the intervention and which are attributable to changes in working conditions or processes resulting from the intervention are unclear.

Interventions focusing on managers and supervisors. Schaubroeck, Ganster, Sime, and Ditman (1993) conducted a field experiment at a business services division at a large university that was aimed at reducing role ambiguity that had been deemed by management to be a significant stressor. In this effort, a supervisory role clarification process was conducted over a 2-year period. Conducted in 2-hour sessions, this process (facilitated by one of the investigators) involved the identification of overlapping responsibilities and gaps in responsibilities and corrected identified problems through a consensus process. Subsequent to conducting the process with top management, the role clarification process was conducted at progressively lower levels of the organization. The study involved a pretest and two posttests (spaced 6 months apart). A total of 27 workers in the experimental group and 25 in a control group provided data used to evaluate the intervention. The results of multivariate analyses provided suggestive evidence that supervisory role clarification resulted in reduced role ambiguity for subordinates. However, no effects on individual strain were evident. As with other studies, the sample size for this study was small, and the follow-up period was relatively short.

Several more recent intervention studies focusing on supervisors have provided evidence of more positive individual effects. Based on the premise that poor leadership skills contribute to job stress and employee burnout, Beaton, Johnson, Infield, Ollis, & Bond (2001) evaluated the effects of a brief leadership intervention provided to fire service supervisors in an urban fire department. A total of four separate 6-hour modules were presented to the supervisors over a 20-month time frame. Included in the modules were components on match leadership (Fiedler & Mahar, 1979), team building, and conflict management. Ratings by 51 line firefighters and 8 first-line supervisors documented improvements in their immediate supervisors' performance at 3 and 6 months postintervention. Self-reports by line firefighters also showed improvements in perceptions of their ability to attain career goals, which were also found at the 9-month, postintervention follow-up. The supervisors reported improvements on a number of stress-related symptom indices at both the 3- and 9-month follow-ups. No significant changes on any of the measures were found in a control sample of firefighters and their first-line supervisors in another untreated urban fire department.

In a similar fashion, Theorell, Emdad, Arnetz, and Weingarten (2001) report an intervention involving the training of 42 managers in a department of a Swedish insurance company. In this intervention, managers participated in a mandatory meeting every other week for approximately 1 year. At the start and end of the program, the managers spent the whole day discussing psychosocial work environment factors. During each session, there was a 30-minute lecture and 30 minutes for discussion of the lecture topic. The topics involved (a) "medical and psychological knowledge regarding the individual's function," (b) "social-psychological knowledge regarding the group," (c) social-psychological processes, and (d) psychosocial redesign. The 2-week period between programs was intended to be a time for reflection and discussion of the program with employees. A control group consisted of employees in another department of the company unaffected by the intervention. Morning blood samples were collected both at baseline and at a 1-year follow-up from 155 participants in the experimental department and 147 participants in the control department and analyzed for liver enzymes and lipids. Questionnaire data were also obtained from 119 experimental and 132 control department participants. Results of the study indicated that the intervention both lowered serum cortisol and improved self-reported decision authority among employees. Unfortunately, during the time of the study, there were three competing projects occurring at the insurance company that the authors acknowledge may have influenced their results. They also indicate that "in the modern world, it is impossible to find companies doing nothing in the field of work organization" (p. 729).

In general, the three psychosocial interventions described above provide some limited support for the efficacy of focusing psychosocial intervention efforts on supervisors and managers. Each of the three interventions resulted in positive organizationally relevant outcomes, and two of them found modest effects on individual well-being. An intriguing aspect is that the effects on well-being may extend beyond the supervisors and managers themselves. They may therefore represent a potentially effective and seemingly cost-efficient approach to primary prevention. However, as noted above, existent methodological challenges to conducting the studies inhibit any firm conclusions. Clearly, more research is needed that examines the efficacy of these types of interventions.

An intervention involving communications. Schweiger and DeNisi (1991) describe an intervention carried out in two plants (experimental and control) of a manufacturing company that was undergoing a merger, and as a consequence, the employees were threatened with either job loss and/or plant reorganization. The intervention involved a communications program designed to provide the 126 experimental plant employees with frequent information regarding the situation, to treat employees fairly, and to address questions and concerns. The intervention began with a letter from the company CEO informing individual employees of the merger and included a newsletter, a telephone hotline, and a list of weekly meetings between supervisors and employees. In the control plant (with approximately 146 employees), communications involved only an initial letter from the CEO informing employees of the merger. Measures of perceived uncertainty, stress, job satisfaction, organizational commitment, performance, absenteeism, and turnover were obtained 4 weeks prior to the announcement, 2 weeks following the announcement, 1 week prior to the implementation of the intervention, 3 days after the implementation, and 3 months later. The results of the study indicated a positive effect of the intervention on perceptions of uncertainty, job satisfaction, organizational commitment, and belief in the company's trustworthiness. The follow-up, however, was of a relatively short duration (3 months after the merger announcement), and the long-term benefits of the intervention are uncertain.

Psychosocial interventions: Summary. The psychosocial interventions reviewed above provide inconsistent evidence for the efficacy of the approach. In particular, the "global" PAR-type interventions are particularly unconvincing. Their effects, when found, appear to be largely on self-reported measures of affect (e.g., job satisfaction, job stress) and perceived job demands. By contrast, those PAR-type interventions that have focused more specifically on job design and redesign issues seem to have produced somewhat more consistent, though less than convincing, results. Clearly, the most consistent results have come from the three studies that focused on supervisors and managers. However, design and methodological limitations make it difficult to draw any reliable conclusions.

Socio-technical Interventions

As indicated at the beginning of this chapter, socio-technical interventions refer to primary prevention interventions aimed at eliminating job stressors by making changes to objective working conditions or to the objective work environment. In contrast to the psychosocial interventions described above, these changes are not generally a result of a collaborative employee-employer or employee-employer-researcher process. To date, socio-technical interventions described in the job stress literature have involved changing only a very limited variety of objective working conditions. In particular, these conditions have involved the modification of workload, work schedules, and work processes. Although the reasons for this are unclear, Parkes and Sparkes (1998) have suggested that this may be the case because not many objective conditions or situations easily lend themselves to change and rigorous evaluation.

Workload interventions. Workload is one of the most intuitively obvious of all job stressors and has been linked, in the job stress literature, to a plethora of both psychological and physical symptoms (e.g., Sutherland & Cooper, 1988). Evidence also points to a steady increase in workload over the last two decades (Bond, Galinsky, & Swanberg, 1997). Given these circumstances, it is somewhat surprising to see so few published intervention studies that have focused directly on workload. One of the first was reported by Parkes and her colleagues (Parkes et al., 1986; Parkes, 1995). The intervention was initiated in 1985 and investigated the effects of reducing objective workload for a large sample of driving examiners in 18 U.K. driving examination test centers. The normal workload for the participants involved conducting nine driving tests per day. In the intervention, examiners were randomly assigned to one period of normal workload and one period of either eight or seven tests per day. Each period lasted 12 weeks, with assessments occurring halfway through this period and again during the last week. Self-reports of perceived demands and discretion, affective symptoms, and objective data (cognitive performance, heart rate, and sickness absence) were collected in 1988 and used to evaluate the intervention. Reduced workload was found to be significantly associated with decreased anxiety and perceived demands as well as increased job satisfaction. Improved cognitive performance and heart rate parameters were also reported. As a result of the intervention, an eight-test-per-day work requirement was adopted on a permanent basis. This ultimately provided the investigators with the opportunity to conduct a follow-up survey of 285 of the original subjects. Contrary to expectation, the follow-up conducted in 1990 found a marginal increase in reported anxiety. However, covariance analyses suggested that the increase was not a function of the workload intervention and more likely the result of other working conditions.

Meijman, Mulder, & Cremer (1992) conducted a workload intervention that also involved driving examiners. In this study, 30 examiners were monitored at various times over the 3 weeks. Monitored variables included anxiety, mental efficiency (as measured by a standardized cognitive test), blood pressure, and adrenalin levels. No effects of the intervention could be found on either blood pressure or adrenalin levels. However, tension was significantly higher and mental efficiency was significantly lower in the 11 exams per day condition compared with the 9 and 10 exams per day conditions. Although this study was rigorous in design, it is nonetheless difficult to know whether these effects were in fact due to the workload reduction. As the authors note, they may have been mediated by increased social support and relaxation that were made available by the reduction in workload.

Work schedule interventions. Substantial evidence indicates that the temporal scheduling of work can have a significant impact on psychological, behavioral, social, and physical well-being (Sauter, Murphy, & Hurrell, 1990). Thus, a variety of interventions have been examined that involve changes to traditional work scheduling. In general, these interventions have involved alternative work schedules (e.g., compressed workweeks and flextime); however, at least one has examined changing rest break schedules.

Ivancevich and Lyon (1977), in a 25-month field experiment, examined the effects of a 4-day, 40-hour workweek by comparing 2 experimental groups (97 and 111 workers respectively) with a comparison group (94 workers). Participants were employees of a medium-size manufacturing company. Comparisons were made on measures of self-actualization, autonomy, personal growth, social affiliation, job security, pay, and overall job satisfaction, anxiety-stress, absenteeism, and performance over a 13- and 25-month period. The 13-month data indicated that the workers on the compressed workweek were more satisfied with autonomy, personal worth, job security, and pay. They also reported less anxiety-stress and showed greater productivity than those in the comparison groups. However, these improvements were not found at the 25-month follow-up, and no differences in absenteeism were observed at either the 13- or 25-month follow-up.

Kim and Campagna (1981) assessed the effects of a flextime program on 353 employees in a county welfare agency. In this effort, four units of the agency were randomly assigned to an experimental or a control group. In the experimental group, employees could start work anytime between 6:30 and 9:30 A.M. and finish the day anytime between 3:00 and 6:00 P.M. In the experimental group, employees continued to work their normal 8-hour, 8:00 A.M. to 4:30 P.M. schedules. All employees were required to work an 8-hour day and to be present during core hours (9:30 A.M. to 3:00 P.M.). Attendance and performance data were collected for the month prior to the intervention and in each of the 4 months of the study. An analysis of covariance results suggested that the flextime arrangement helped the participants to reduce their use of unpaid absence. However, there were no differences in paid absence between the two groups. Performance also tended to be higher under the flextime program.

Narayanan and Nath (1982, 1984) examined the effects of flextime using several approaches. Narayanan & Nath (1982) compared an experimental group of 173 employees in a large international company with a control group of 66 employees on dimensions of satisfaction, flexibility, work group relations, superior-subordinate relations, quality of supervision, job satisfaction, absenteeism, and productivity. Employees in both groups were required to be present during core hours (9 A.M. to 11:30 A.M. and 1:30 P.M. to 3:30 P.M.) but were otherwise given flexibility spanning a 12-hour period (7 A.M. to 7 P.M.). Results of the study indicated that employee flexibility, work group relations, and superior-subordinate relations improved and absenteeism (measured objectively) decreased. No changes in quality of supervision, job satisfaction, or productivity were found. In a subsequent moderator analysis, Narayanan and Nath (1984) found that work group cohesiveness moderated these relationships, with employees in highly cohesive groups reporting improved flexibility, backup, superior-subordinate relations, and productivity.

Dunham, Pierce, and Castaneda (1987) describe two quasi-experimental field studies that examined the effects of both a compressed workweek and the introduction of flextime. In the first experiment, 43 workers were changed from a 5/40 (day/hour) to a 4/40 workweek schedule for 4 months and then returned to a 5/40 schedule. These workers were compared with 41 workers who remained on the standard 5/40 schedule. In the second experiment, 55 workers were changed from a 5/40 schedule to a flextime arrangement, and 47 comparable workers served as controls. A set of some 28 different outcome variables was assessed in the first experiment with a similar set used in the second. The most powerful effect of both schedules was on measures directly related to the schedules (for example, worker attitudes toward the specific work schedule), with a less robust effect on measures of family and social life.

Although not interventions, a number of other studies (e.g., Pierce & Newstrom, 1983; Sharpe, Hermsen, & Billings, 2002) have examined the effects of compressed workweek and flextime schedules on various different individual and organizational outcomes. Baltes, Briggs, Huff, Wright, and Neuman (1999) used meta-analytic techniques to estimate the effects of flexible and compressed workweek schedules on productivity/performance, job satisfaction, absenteeism, and satisfaction with work schedule. The effects of both schedules were generally found to be positive, but the effects were different across the outcomes (for example, compressed workweek schedules did not affect absenteeism). Moreover, the degree of impact of either schedule was dependent on the outcome under consideration, and characteristics of the schedules seemed to serve as moderators. Highly flexible flextime, for example, was less effective in comparison to less flexible flextime. The positive benefits of flextime were also found to diminish over time. The attractiveness and potential effects of these schedules may also be a function of both interrole conflict (Rau & Hyland, 2002) and gender (Sharpe et al., 2002).

Not all reported work schedule interventions have dealt with workweek schedules. Galinsky, Swanson, Sauter, and Hurrell (2000) reported on a field study that examined the effects of providing supplementary rest breaks on mood, musculoskeletal discomfort, eyestrain, and performance in 42 data entry workers. Two rest break schedules were compared in a within-subject design. Workers alternated between a "conventional" and a "supplementary" schedule in 4-week intervals. In the conventional schedule, workers got a 15-minute break during the first half and second half of their work shift. In the supplementary schedule, workers got the two 15-minute breaks plus an extra 5-minute break during each hour that did not otherwise contain a break, for a total of 20 extra minutes of break time. The results were based on data from 42 workers and indicated that although there were no effects on mood (tension, cheerfulness, and energy), discomfort in several areas of the body and eyestrain were significantly lower under the supplementary schedule. These beneficial effects were obtained without reductions in data entry performance.

Work process and procedure interventions. A number of socio-technical interventions have involved changes in work processes and procedures that did not specifically involve making direct changes to work schedules or workload. The first of these was conducted by Jackson (1983). This effort sought to examine the effects of increased participation in decision making on perceived influence, role stressors, personal and job-related communications, social support, emotional strain, overall job satisfaction, absenteeism, and turnover intentions. Conducted at a hospital outpatient facility, the study involved the random assignment of 95 nursing and clerical workers to an increased participation or control condition and to a pretest or no-pretest condition. In the increased participation condition, staff meetings were increased from one to two per month. Outcomes were assessed after 3 and 6 months. At the 6-month follow-up, participation was shown to have a beneficial effect on role conflict, role ambiguity, and perceived influence. Both role stressors were found to be associated with emotional strain and job dissatisfaction. Job influence was found to have beneficial effects on job satisfaction and turnover intentions.

Wall, Corbett, Martin, Clegg, and Jackson (1990) report an intervention involving the redesign of work to increase the amount of control over work processes by assembly machine operators. The study was conducted in one department of a large electronics assembly company in the United Kingdom. The department employed 11 women and 8 men full-time across two shifts. In the intervention, responsibility for redesigning of operators' jobs was given to a working party comprising representatives from maintenance engineering, production planning, supervisors, managers, machine operators, and one of the researchers. The redesign involved a substantial enhancement of operator control over variances affecting production. The intervention was evaluated using a repeated measures design over some 120 days. The intervention resulted in reduced downtime and was associated with greater intrinsic job satisfaction and less perceived time pressure. However, there were no effects on extrinsic job satisfaction, general strain, or job-related strain.

Kawakami, Araki, Kawashima, Masumoto, and Hayashi (1997) describe a multifaceted intervention at a large Japanese electric company that principally involved changes to work processes and procedures. The intervention began with a job stress survey of the entire plant. Based on this survey, two sites were selected from those with high mean depression scores. Three matched reference/control sites were selected based on size, age of the workers, major products and occupations, and depression scores. Supervisors at the intervention sites identified problems (job stressors) at the sites that were targeted for change. Excess overtime, resulting from poor performance of production machines, was addressed by mechanically improving the machines and adjusting the machine speed. The machines also required many checks from workers before starting and stopping them (a source of excess demands). This problem was addressed by a reduction in the number of checkpoints. Finally, rapid technological changes in the production process made worker skills insufficient, which was addressed by on-the-job training and standardization of the production process. Effects of the intervention were assessed by comparing four outcomes (depressive symptoms, sick leave, and systolic and diastolic blood pressure) that were measured prior to the intervention and at 1- and 2-year follow-ups. After controlling for gender and age, depression scores were found to decrease for the intervention group and not the comparison group. Likewise, sick leave decreased in the last follow-up only in the intervention group. No intervention effects were found for blood pressure.

Considerable evidence (see Evans & Johansson, 1998) suggests that driving a bus in urban areas is extremely stressful and poses a variety of health risks. Evans, Johansson, and Rydstedt (1999) report an intervention conducted in Stockholm centered on physical design changes in the bus route and technological innovations to decrease traffic congestion, lessen passenger demands on bus operators, and generally ease bus operations. Ten drivers at the intervention route and 31 demographically matched comparison drivers participated in the study. Pre- and 9-month postintervention measures of perceived stress, blood pressure and heart rate, and on-the-job hassles (provided by outside observers) were recorded. The results indicated that there were significant pre-post decreases in systolic blood pressure, heart rate, perceived stress, and on-the-job hassles for the intervention route drivers. The control drivers experienced a decrease of systolic blood pressure but little or no changes on the other measured outcomes. The effects of the intervention on perceived stress, blood pressure, and heart rate were found to be mediated by job hassles.

Socio-technical interventions: Summary. Taken as a whole, the socio-technical intervention studies described above provide more consistent and "robust" evidence for the efficacy of the intervention than the psychosocial intervention studies reviewed earlier. In addition to incorporating self-report measures of affect (e.g., job satisfaction, anxiety, depression), most incorporated objective outcome measures (e.g., blood pressure, job performance, sickness absence). In general, these studies have also tended to be more rigorous, utilizing experimental and quasi-experimental designs.

Tertiary Prevention Interventions

As noted in the introduction to this chapter, tertiary organizational stress prevention is therapeutic and seeks to treat the physical, psychological, or behavioral consequences of exposures to job stressors. Perhaps because so many individual physical, psychological, and behavioral maladies are thought to be job stress–related, no truly comprehensive discussions of tertiary organizational stress prevention are found in the stress literature. Indeed, the task of developing such a discussion would be daunting. The following seeks to provide only an overview of tertiary stress intervention options that are often organizationally based.

Medical Care

Many large companies have medical departments that offer services that include urgent medical care, employee examinations, disability reviews, health promotion activities, and referral for medical treatment. In general, these departments are not structured to provide extensive or long-term care for stress-related illness or injury and must rely on making referrals to appropriate health care providers. Job stress–related mental health problems can present special challenges to occupational medicine departments, who may not be well equipped to deal with them or make referrals (Kahn, 1993).

Psychological Counseling and Therapy

Counseling and psychotherapy are commonly used methods to treat individuals suffering from work-related mental health problems. Common techniques of psychotherapy and counseling include behavior and cognitive therapy, supportive counseling, and insight-oriented psychotherapy (Kahn, 1993). Counseling and psychotherapy outcome research (e.g., Bower, Rowland, & Hardy, 2003; Lambert & Bergin, 1994; Seligman, 1995) clearly suggests that counseling and psychotherapy can have marked benefits on symptom reduction. Moreover, in a review of some 22 counseling programs, Jones and Vischi (1979) found that significant reductions in the use of general health services usually followed treatment for stress-related problems. However, a study by Reynolds (1997) suggests that such counseling may not have an impact on work performance as measured by absenteeism.

Many companies offer limited counseling at the workplace through employee assistance programs (EAPs) that often provide a variety of mental health–related services. Employees can refer themselves to the EAP or be referred by management. The goals of an EAP are to restore valuable employees to full productivity by (a) identifying employees with drug abuse, emotional, or behavioral problems resulting in deficient work performance, (b) motivate such individuals to seek help, (c) provide short-term professional counseling assistance and referral, (d) direct employees toward the best assistance available, and (e) providing continuing support and guidance throughout the problem-solving period (U.S. Department of Health and Human Services [HHS], 1986). Very few studies have addressed the cost-effectiveness of individual EAP programs. Indeed, some have questioned whether there should be an economic evaluation, and there is little agreement on evaluation methodology (Berridge & Cooper, 1993). However, reduced health claims, financial savings, and lower absenteeism rates were reported for EAP "graduates" in an analysis reported by Landy, Quick, and Kasl (1994), and a study by the Paul Revere Life Insurance Company (Intindola, 1991) reported a savings of $4.23 in claims expenses for every dollar of premium expenditure diverted into the EAP.

For many employees, a stigma continues to be associated with psychological treatment of any variety, and this fear, along with concerns regarding confidentiality, may limit the use of on-site mental health resources (Quick et al., 1997). Employees may also feel that the company has a vested interest in their productivity that is of greater importance than the employee's health (Stoline & Sharfstein, 1993). This concern may be exacerbated by the fact that EAPs are gatekeepers with a financial bias not to refer employees for more sophisticated and long-term care or to refer to providers with limited training who may be less costly (Stoline & Sharfstein, 1993). Indeed, who provides the care seems to be an important issue. Work by Seligman (1995), for example, suggested that psychologists, psychiatrists, and social workers seem to achieve equally positive results whereas results by other counseling professionals do not appear to be as positive. Bento (1997) describes a number of paradoxes imbedded in the very nature of EAPs that lead to the potential problems described above and lead to occupational stress for EAP employees. These include "employer versus employee assistance?" (referring to conflicting demands on EAP professionals) and "nature of the problem versus nature of the intervention" (referring to pressures to provide short-term individual solutions to what may be long-term structural problems).

Posttraumatic Stress Intervention

As the September 11, 2001, World Trade Center disaster made abundantly clear, exposure to traumatic events may result in various forms of recognized psychiatric morbidity (American Psychiatric Association, 1994). Although occupations such as law enforcement, emergency response, retail banking, and chemically intensive manufacturing carry higher-than-average risks for exposure to traumatic events, sudden death or injury, violence, or threat of violence can strike any workforce (Braverman, 1992). Unfortunately, psychological interventions to prevent the consequences of such traumatic events have only recently (and perhaps as a consequence of the September 11th disaster) been subject to rigorous evaluation. Recent systematic reviews (e.g., Ehlers & Clark, 2003) have concluded that single sessions of individual psychological debriefing after trauma are not effective in reducing symptoms or subsequent posttraumatic stress disorder (PTSD). Indeed, there appears to be no convincing evidence that debriefing (individual or group) reduces the incidence of PTSD, and a number of controlled studies have suggested that it may in fact impede natural recovery from trauma (McNally, Bryant, & Ehlers, 2003). Cognitive-behavioral therapy has been shown to reduce the symptoms of PTSD and appears to be more effective than either supportive counseling or no intervention (Ehlers & Clark, 2003; McNally, Bryant, & Ehlers, 2003). Unlike debriefing, cognitive-behavioral treatments are delivered weeks or months after the trauma and represent a form of psychotherapy.

There are strong indications that social support exerts important effects following workplace-based disasters. First, Chisholm, Kasl, and Mueller (1986) studied employees who were assigned to Three Mile Island on March 28, 1979, the date of the actual incident. Their results showed that emotional social support served as a main effect and as a buffer during the crisis. Second, Schat and Kelloway (2002) found that instrumental and informational support moderated the relationship between workplace aggression and violence and emotional well-being. Their findings on workplace aggression and violence may be especially salient in understanding the role of social support in coping with the violent nature of the terrorist incident. Last, the Corneil, Beaton, Murphy, Johnson, and Pike (1999) study of more than 800 firefighters in Canada and the United States showed that exposure to traumatic events does not necessarily predict PTSD and that the exposure outcome relationship may be mediated by both social support and chronic stress levels. A comprehensive workplace approach to PTSD should include the assessment of social support.

Future Research Needs

Primary Prevention Intervention

It is obvious that the primary prevention intervention research literature is fraught with various methodological problems. Especially glaring is the absence of strong study designs involving randomized trials, making evaluations and attributions of outcomes difficult. Yet as anyone who has attempted a job-related intervention will attest, strong designs are not always feasible because of both practical and legal constraints. Indeed, there are those who argue that job stress intervention research, particularly PAR-type intervention research, is not amenable to entirely empirical evaluation. A need exists for improved guidance and possibly a new paradigm for conducting research on primary job stress interventions. Approaches need to be articulated that build on the strengths and minimize the weaknesses of various methods.

Clearly, primary prevention intervention research in the job stress arena needs to be more theory-driven to learn why and under what circumstances interventions work. Well-designed, theory-driven intervention research increases the likelihood that a particular type of intervention will ultimately be effective because it leads to a better understanding of how the intervention works (or why it may have failed) and allows for generalization and tailoring of the intervention to diverse situations. For example, Israel, Baker, Goldenhar, and Heaney (1996) have offered a conceptual framework for job stress intervention that is based on a comprehensive model of stress and health and provides guidance for each step in the intervention process.

In addition to employee commitment, management commitment to the intervention process is critical. Given the very limited evidence currently available to support the economic utility of primary job stress intervention, more information is needed regarding what conditions motivate organizations to engage in them. Ethnographic study of organizations to better understand the processes that govern intervention decisions could lead to the development of ideas and products (e.g., casebooks on successful interventions, best-practice workshops on job stress and health).

Finally, a need exists to aggressively investigate the effects of primary organizational interventions that are already occurring in the workplace (i.e., natural experiments). For example, "family friendly" policies such as flextime and alternative work hours are becoming increasingly common in the modern workplace, presenting opportunities for research to investigate effects of these types of interventions. In Europe and the United Kingdom, opportunities exist to examine the effects of large-scale public policies geared toward protecting workers from job stress.

Tertiary Prevention Intervention

As alluded to above, very little is known regarding the efficacy of many tertiary occupational stress interventions. Moreover, their impact on organizationally relevant outcomes that affect profitability is unclear. Although some would argue that demonstrations of the cost-effectiveness of such interventions are immaterial if the interventions improve the health and well-being of workers, in the increasingly competitive global economy, organizations are scrutinizing these costs. Research in this area is critically needed.

Implications for Practice and Policy

As noted in the introduction, a tremendous gulf exists between our knowledge regarding job stress and the most efficacious and economical means to prevent it and treat its consequences at the work site. Although the primary prevention research is still sparse and provides only limited evidence that certain specific primary prevention efforts have worked, it is clear that some have "worked." Although it is as yet uncertain what made them work, there are some commonalities. This should provide encouragement to those researchers and practitioners who might be considering undertaking them. Although the literature does not provide a great deal of specific guidance, as shown above and as Parkes and Sparkes (1998) have noted, those primary prevention interventions that focus on a few stressors and those that don't try to introduce too many changes too quickly appear to have been most successful. It is also important to bear in mind that before primary prevention interventions are designed and implemented, the most prevalent and problematic stressors must be identified and prioritized with respect to their potency and amenability to meaningful change (Murphy & Hurrell, 1987; Hurrell & Murphy, 1996). Practitioners and researchers alike should also carefully choose objective and subjective outcomes (and valid and reliable measures of these outcomes) for use in evaluating the efficacy of their intervention efforts. In this regard, it is particularly important to include objective measures that are organizationally relevant (Hurrell & Murphy, 1996). Without evidence of effect on such outcomes, other organizations will be reluctant to engage in them.

It seems apparent that efforts to intervene for job stress, regardless of whether they are primary, secondary, or tertiary in nature, seem to happen in relative isolation within an organization. That is, depending on the circumstances, management, human resources, medical departments, and/or EAPs may be given the responsibility for the intervention, and there may be little mutual aid from other organizational structures. Clearly, primary, secondary, and tertiary job stress intervention efforts should be integrated within the organization as a whole (Quick et al., 1997).

Epilogue

In this chapter, I have attempted to provide a critical review of the primary and tertiary organizational stress intervention literature. After examining this literature, one cannot help concluding that despite our considerable knowledge of the etiologic relationships between stressful job conditions and various health and safety consequences, we know relatively little about how to effectively intervene at the organizational level to prevent or reduce the occurrence of stress-related maladies. The reasons discussed for this situation include, but are not limited to, the methodological challenges associated with conducting rigorous research in field settings, the use of inappropriate outcome criteria and measures for evaluating interventions, and the possibility that some types of interventions are truly ineffective. However, given the enormous human and financial costs associated with organizational stress, it is incumbent on both researchers and practitioners to begin to address this problem.

References

American Institute of Stress. (2002). *Job stress*. New York: Author.

American Psychiatric Association. (1994). *Diagnostic and statistical manual of mental disorders* (4th ed.). Washington, DC: Author.

Baltes, B. B., Briggs, T. E., Huff, J. W., Wright, J. A., & Neuman, G. A. (1999). Flexible and compressed workweek schedules: A meta-analysis of their effects on work-related criteria. *Journal of Applied Psychology, 84*(4), 496–513.

Beaton, R., Johnson, C. L., Infield, S., Ollis, T., & Bond, G. (2001). Outcomes of a leadership intervention for a metropolitan fire department. *Psychological Reports, 88,* 1049–1066.

Bento, R. F. (1997). On the other hand . . . The paradoxical nature of employee assistance programs. *Employee Assistance Quarterly, 13*(2), 83–91.

Berridge, J., & Cooper, C. L. (1993). Stress and coping in U.S. organizations: The role of employee assistance programme. *Work & Stress, 7*(1), 89–102.

Bond, F. W., & Bunce, D. (2001). Job control mediates changes in a work reorganization intervention for stress reduction. *Journal of Occupational Health Psychology, 6,* 290–302.

Bond, J. T., Galinsky, E., Swanberg, J. E. (1997). *The 1997 national study of the changing workforce.* New York: Families and Work Institute.

Bower, P., Rowland, N., & Hardy R. (2003). The clinical effectiveness of counseling in primary care: A systematic review and meta-analysis. *Psychological Medicine, 33*(2), 203–215.

Braverman, M. (1992). Posttraumatic crisis intervention in the workplace. In J. C. Quick, L. R. Murphy, & J. J. Hurrell, Jr. (Eds.), *Stress and well-being at work* (pp. 299–313). Washington, DC: American Psychological Association.

Campbell, D. (1973). *A program to reduce coronary heart disease risk by altering job stresses.* Unpublished doctoral dissertation, University of Michigan, Ann Arbor.

Chisholm, R. F., Kasl, S. V., & Mueller, L. (1986). The effects of social support on nuclear worker responses to the Three Mile Island incident. *Journal of Occupational Behavior, 7,* 179–193.

Corneil, W., Beaton, R., Murphy, S., Johnson, C., & Pike, K. (1999). Exposure to traumatic incidents and prevalence of posttraumatic stress symptomology in urban firefighters in two countries. *Journal of Occupational Health Psychology, 4,* 131–141.

Dunham, R. B., Pierce, J. L., & Castaneda, M. B. (1987). Alternative work schedules: Two field quasi-experiments. *Personnel Psychology, 40*(2), 215–242.

Ehlers, A., & Clark, D. M. (2003). Early psychological interventions for adult survivors of trauma: A review. *Biological Psychiatry, 53,* 817–826.

Elden, M., & Chisholm, R. (1993). Emerging varieties of action research: Introduction to the special issue. *Human Relations, 46*(2), 121–142.

Evans, G. W., & Johansson, G. (1998). Working on the hot seat: Urban bus driving: An international arena for the study of occupational health psychology. *Journal of Occupational Health Psychology, 3,* 99–108.

Evans, G. W., Johansson, G., & Rydstedt, L. (1999). Hassles on the job: A study of a job intervention with urban bus drivers. *Journal of Organizational Behavior, 20*(2), 199–208.

Fiedler, F. E., & Mahar, L. (1979). The effectiveness of contingency model training: A review of the validation of Leader Match. *Personnel Psychology, 32,* 45–62.

French, J. R. P., Jr., Rodgers, W., & Cobb, S. (1974). Adjustment as person-environment fit. In G. Coelho, D. Hamburg, & J. Adams (Eds.), *Coping and adaptation* (pp. 316–333). New York: Basic Books.

Galinsky, T., Swanson, N. G., Sauter, S. L., & Hurrell, J. J., Jr. (2000). A field study of supplementary rest breaks for data-entry operators. *Ergonomics, 43*(5), 622–638.

Griffeth, R. W. (1985). Moderation of the effects of job enrichment by participation: A longitudinal field experiment. *Organizational Behavior and Human Decision Making Processes, 35,* 73–93.

Heaney, C. A., Israel, B. A., Schurman, S. J., Baker, E. A., House, J. S., & Hugentoblerm, M. (1993). Industrial relations, worksite stress reduction, and employee well-being: A participatory action research investigation. *Journal of Organizational Behavior, 14,* 495–510.

Hurrell, J. J., Jr., & Murphy, L. R. (1996). Occupational stress intervention. *American Journal of Industrial Medicine, 29,* 338–341.

Intindola, B. (1991). EAP's still foreign to many small businesses. *National Underwriter, 95,* 21.

Israel, B. A., Baker, E. A., Goldenhar, L. M., & Heaney, C. A. (1996). Occupational stress, safety, and health: Conceptual framework and principles for effective prevention interventions. *Journal of Occupational Health Psychology, 1,* 261–286.

Ivancevich, J. M., & Lyon, H. L. (1977). The shortened workweek: A field experiment. *Journal of Applied Psychology, 62*(1), 34–37.

Jackson, S. E. (1983). Participation in decision making as a strategy for reducing job-related strain. *Journal of Applied Psychology, 68*(1), 3–19.

Jones, J. K., & Vischi, T. R. (1979). Impact of alcohol, drug abuse, and mental health treatment on medical care utilization: A review of the research literature. *Medical Care, 17*(12, Suppl.).

Kahn, J. P. (1993). *Mental health in the workplace: A practical psychiatric guide.* New York: Van Nostrand Reinhold.

Kim, J. S., & Campagna, A. F. (1981). Effects of flextime on employee attendance and performance. *Academy of Management Journal, 24*(4), 729–741.

Karasek, R. A., & Theorell, T. (1990). *Healthy work: Stress, productivity, and the reconstruction of working life.* New York: Basic Books.

Kawakami, N., Araki, S., Kawashima, M., Masumoto, T., & Hayashi, T. (1997). Effects of work-related stress reduction on depressive symptoms among Japanese blue-collar workers. *Scandinavian Journal of Work, Environment & Health, 23*(1), 54–59.

Lambert, M. J., & Bergin, A. E. (1994). The effectiveness of psychotherapy. In A. E. Bergin & S. L. Garfield (Eds.), *Handbook of psychotherapy and behavior change* (pp. 143–189). New York: Wiley.

Landsbergis, P. A., & Vivona-Vaughan, E. (1995). Evaluation of an occupational stress intervention in a public health agency. *Journal of Organizational Behavior, 16,* 29–49.

Landy, F., Quick, J. C., & Kasl, S. (1994). Work, stress, and well-being. *International Journal of Stress Management, 1*(1), 33–73.

McNally, R. J., Bryant, R. A., & Ehlers, A. (2003). Does psychological intervention promote recovery from post traumatic stress? *Psychological Science in the Public Interest, 4,* 45–79.

Meijman, T., Mulder, G., & Cremer, R. (1992). Workload of driving examiners: A psychosocial field study. In H. Kragt (Ed.), *Enhancing industrial performance: Experiences of integrating human factors.* London: Taylor & Francis.

Mikkelsen, A., Saksvik, P. O., & Landsbergis, P. (2000). The impact of a participatory organizational intervention on job stress in a community health care institution. *Work & Stress,* 14–170.

Murphy, L. R. (1988). Workplace interventions for stress reduction and prevention. In C. Cooper & R. Payne (Eds.), *Causes, coping and consequences of stress at work* (pp. 301–339). New York: Wiley.

Murphy, L. R. (1996). Stress management in work settings: A critical review of the health effects. *American Journal of Health Promotion, 11*, 112–135.

Murphy, L. R., & Hurrell, J. J., Jr. (1987). Stress management in the process of occupational stress reduction. *Journal of Managerial Psychology, 2*, 18–23.

Narayanan, V. K., & Nath, R. (1982). A field test of some attitudinal and behavioral consequences of flextime. *Journal of Applied Psychology, 67*(2), 214–218.

Narayanan, V. K., & Nath, R. (1984). The influence of group cohesiveness on changes induced by flextime: A quasi-experiment. *Journal of Applied Behavioral Science, 20*(3), 265–272.

Parkes, K. R. (1995). The effects of objective workload on cognitive performance in a field setting: A two-period cross-over trial. *Applied Cognitive Psychology, 9*, 153–157.

Parkes, K. R., Broadbent, D. E., Johnston, D., Rendall, D., Matthews, J., & Smith, A. P. (1986). *Occupational stress among driving examiners: A study of the effects of workload reduction. Final report and recommendations.* Prepared under HSE commission, 1/MS/126/158/79. Department of Experimental Psychology, University of Oxford, Oxford, UK.

Parkes, K. R., & Sparkes, T. J. (1998). *Organizational interventions to reduce work stress: Are they effective? A review of the literature* (Contract Report No. 193/198). Health and Safety Executive, University of Oxford, Oxford, UK.

Pierce, J. L., & Newstrom, J. W. (1983). The design of flexible work schedules and employee responses: Relationship and process. *Journal of Occupational Behavior, 4*, 247–262.

Quick, J. C., Quick, J. D., Nelson, D. L., & Hurrell, J. J., Jr. (1997). *Preventive stress management in organizations.* Washington, DC: American Psychological Association.

Rau, B. L., & Hyland, M. M. (2002). Role conflict and flexible work arrangements: The effects on applicant attraction. *Personnel Psychology, 55*(1), 111–136.

Reynolds, S. (1997). Psychological well-being at work: Is prevention better than cure. *Journal of Psychosomatic Research, 1*, 93–102.

Reynolds, S. (2000). Interventions: What works, what doesn't? *Occupational Medicine, 50*, 315–319.

Rom, W. N. (Ed.). (1998). *Environmental and occupational medicine* (3rd ed.). New York: Lippencott-Raven.

Sauter, S. L., Murphy, L. R., & Hurrell, J. J., Jr. (1990). Prevention of work-related psychological disorders: A national strategy proposed by the National Institute for Occupational Safety and Health (NIOSH). *American Psychologist, 45*, 1146–1158.

Schat, A. C. H., & Kelloway, E. K. (2002). Reducing the adverse consequences of workplace aggression and violence: The buffering effects of organizational support. *Journal of Occupational Health Psychology, 8*(2), 110–122.

Schaubroeck, J., Ganster D. C., Sime, W. E., & Ditman, D. (1993). A field experiment testing supervisory role clarification. *Personnel Psychology, 46*, 1–25.

Schulte, P. A., Goldenhar, L. M., & Connally, B. S. (1996). Intervention research: Science, skills, and strategies. *American Journal of Industrial Medicine, 29*, 285–288.

Schurman, S. J., & Israel, B. A. (1995). Redesigning work systems to reduce stress: A participatory action research approach to creating change. In L. R. Murphy, J. J. Hurrell, Jr., S. L. Sauter, & G. P. Keita (Eds.), *Job stress interventions* (pp. 235–263). Washington, DC: American Psychological Association.

Schweiger, D. M., & DeNisi, A. S. (1991). Communications with employees following a merger: A longitudinal field experiment. *Academy of Management Journal, 34*, 110–135.

Seligman, M. E. P. (1995). The effectiveness of psychotherapy: The *Consumer Reports* study. *American Psychologist, 50*, 965–974.

Sharpe, D. L., Hermsen, J. M., & Billings, J. (2002). Gender differences in use of alternative full-time work arrangements by married workers. *Family and Consumer Sciences Research Journal, 31*(1), 78–111.

Stoline, A., & Sharfstein, A. (1993). Mental health care: Providers, delivery systems, and cost containment. In J. P. Kahn (Ed.), *Mental health in the workplace* (pp. 26–53). New York: Van Nostrand Reinhold.

Sutherland, V. J., & Cooper, C. L. (1988). Sources of work stress. In J. J. Hurrell, Jr., L. R. Murphy, S. L. Sauter, & C. L. Cooper (Eds.), *Occupational stress: Issues and developments in research* (pp. 3–40). New York: Taylor & Francis.

Terra, N. (1995). The prevention of job stress by redesigning jobs and implementing self-regulating teams. In L. R. Murphy, J. J. Hurrell, Jr., S. L. Sauter, & G. P. Keita (Eds.), *Job stress interventions* (pp. 265–281). Washington, DC: American Psychological Association.

Theorell, T., Emdad, R., Arnetz, B., & Weingarten, A. (2001). Employee effects of an educational program for managers at an insurance company. *Psychosomatic Medicine, 63*, 724–733.

U.S. Department of Health and Human Services. (1986). *Standards and criteria for the development of and evaluation of a comprehensive employee assistance program.* Washington, DC: U.S. Government Printing Office.

Van der Hek, H., & Plomp, N. H. (1997). Occupational stress management programs: A practical overview of published studies. *Occupational Medicine, 47*, 133–141.

Van der Klink, J. J. L., Blonk, R. W. B., Schene, A. H., & van Dijk, F. J. (2001). Benefits of interventions for work-related stress. *American Journal of Public Health, 91*(2), 270–276.

Wahlstedt, K. G. I., & Edling, C. (1997). Organizational changes at a postal sorting terminal: Their effects upon work satisfaction, psychosomatic complaints, and sick leave. *Work & Stress, 11*, 279–291.

Wall, T. D., & Clegg, C. W. (1981). A longitudinal study of group work re-design. *Journal of Occupational Behavior, 2*, 31–49.

Wall, T. D., Corbett, J. M., Martin, R., Clegg, C. W., & Jackson, P. R. (1990). Advanced manufacturing technology, work design, and performance: A change study. *Journal of Applied Psychology, 75*(6), 691–697.

Wall, T. D., Kemp, N. J., Jackson, P. R., & Clegg, C. W. (1986). Outcomes of autonomous workgroups: A long-term field experiment. *Academy of Management Journal, 29*, 280–304.

Work in America. Report of a special task force to the secretary of Health, Education and Welfare. (1973). Cambridge: MIT Press.

Name Index

Edling, C., 628
Edstroem, M., 442
Edwards, J. E., 156, 157, 167, 170, 172, 174, 177, 611
Edwards, J. R., 72, 357, 517
Ehlers, A., 212, 638, 639
Ehmke, J. L. Z., 172
Ehrenreich, R., 151, 158
Ehrhart, M. G., 125, 126, 127
Eidelson, J. I., 381, 382
Eidelson, R. J., 381, 382
Einarsen, S., 91, 190
Eisenberg, W. M., 257
Eisenberger, R., 103, 386, 387
Ekerdt, D., 103, 445
Ekman, A., 317
Elacqua, T. C., 9
Elden, M., 625
Elder, G., 286
Elfering, A., 417
Elig, T. W., 16, 157, 167, 169, 170, 172, 174, 177
Elkins, T. J., 90
Elklit, A., 212
Ellingson, J. E., 535
Elliott, M. N., 381
Ellis, A., 611
Elmuti, D., 276
Elovainio, M., 47, 49, 68, 69, 90, 100, 327, 329, 330
Elsayed-Ekhouly, S. M., 498, 503
Emdad, R., 630
Emde, E., 39
Emery, G., 381
Emmelkamp, P. M. G., 212
Emmons, R. A., 560
Enander, A., 229
Engstrom, M., 234
Ensher, E. A., 159
Ensminger, M. E., 558
Enzmann, D., 78
Epstein, J. S., 421
Erickson, R. J., 564
Erikson, E. H., 408
Erikson, W., 229
Errera, P., 191
Erwin, P. J., 9, 250, 253, 258
Eskelinen, L., 444
Essed, P., 149
Estryn-Behar, M., 46
Ettner, S. L., 98
Etzion, D., 13, 119, 280, 488
Euwema, M., 78

Evans, G. W., 219, 220, 221, 225, 229, 230, 231, 233, 235, 236, 237, 238, 305, 636
Evans, O., 304
Everly, G. S., 390
Evers, G., 24
Ewart, C. K., 425
Eys, M. A., 383

Fabrigar, L. R., 548
Fahs, M., 247
Fain, R., 104, 389
Fain, T. C., 165
Falbe, C. M., 98
Faley, R. H., 168
Falsetti, S. A., 380
Fals-Stewart, W., 198, 203
Fandt, P. M., 354, 355, 356, 357, 360, 362, 366, 367, 368
Faragher, B., 614, 615, 616
Farmer, S. J., 17
Farr, J., 445
Farrell, D., 565
Farrell, M. P., 127, 128, 129
Fasenfest, D., 277
Fasolo, P., 103, 387
Fay, L. M., 589
Feather, N. T., 411, 559
Featherman, D. L., 115
Fedor, D. B., 355, 357, 358, 359, 360, 361, 363, 364, 366, 368
Feild, H. S., 563
Feinleib, M., 469
Feldman, D. C., 269, 270, 271, 274, 275, 277, 279, 280, 281, 288, 289, 518, 527, 535
Feldman Barrett, L., 548
Fendrich, M., 155, 164, 171, 172, 174, 190, 193, 203
Fenlason, K. J., 17
Fenwick, R., 46, 51
Ferrario, M., 237
Ferreira, M., Jr., 234, 309
Ferrie, J. E., 68, 327, 329, 330
Ferris, G. R., 100, 354, 355, 356, 357, 358, 359, 360, 361, 362, 363, 364, 365, 366, 367, 368, 369
Feuille, P., 532
Ficca, G., 54
Fiedler, F. E., 630
Fielden, S. L., 455, 465
Fieldman, G., 90
Fields, D., 120, 123, 125, 127, 128, 129

Subject Index

About the Editors

Julian Barling received his PhD from the University of the Witwatersrand and is currently the Associate Dean with responsibility for the PhD, MSc, and research programs in the School of Business. He is the author of several books, including *Employment, Stress and Family Functioning* (1990), *The Union and Its Members: A Psychological Approach* (with Clive Fullagar and Kevin Kelloway, 1992), *Changing Employment Relations: Behavioral and Social Perspectives* (with Lois Tetrick, 1995), *Young Workers* (with Kevin Kelloway, 1999), and *The Psychology of Workplace Safety* (with Mike Frone, 2004). He is the author or editor of well over 100 research articles and book chapters and the editor of the American Psychological Association's *Journal of Occupational Health Psychology*. He is on the editorial boards of the *Journal of Applied Psychology, Leadership and Organizational Development Journal,* and *Stress and Health.* He received the annual award for Excellence in Research from Queen's University in 1997, the *National Post*'s Leaders in Business Education award in 2001, and in 2002 he was named by Queen's University a Queen's Research Chair. In 2002, he was elected as a Fellow of the Royal Society of Canada.

Michael R. Frone, PhD, is a Senior Research Scientist at the Research Institute on Addictions and Research Associate Professor of Psychology, State University of New York at Buffalo. He has published extensively in leading journals on work-family dynamics, the work-related predictors and outcomes of employee mental health, physical health, and substance use, and the developmental outcomes of youth employment. He is coeditor, with Julian Barling, of *The Psychology of Workplace Safety* (2004). He is associate editor of the *Journal of Occupational Health Psychology* and serves or has served on the editorial boards of the *Journal of Applied Psychology, Journal of Occupational Health Psychology, Journal of Organizational Behavior, Organizational Behavior and Human Decision Processes,* and *Organizational Research Methods.* He has been principal investigator or coinvestigator on research grants totaling more than $5.5 million. He is currently the principal investigator on a grant from the National Institutes of Health to conduct a large national telephone survey of workplace health and safety.

E. Kevin Kelloway received his PhD in organizational psychology from Queen's University and is Professor of Management and Psychology, Faculty of Commerce at Saint Mary's University. He was the founding director of the PhD Program (Management) and is currently the Chair of the Department of Management. He founded and is Executive Director of the CN Centre for Occupational Health and Safety and is a Founding Principal of the Centre for Leadership Excellence (both research centers established at Saint Mary's University). His research interests include occupational health psychology, leadership, unionization, and the management of knowledge workers. He is coauthor of *The Union and Its Members: A Psychological Approach* (1992), *Using Flexible Work Arrangements to Combat Job Stress* (1998), and *Managing Occupational Health and Safety* (2002) and the author of *Using LISREL for Structural Equation Modeling: A Researcher's Guide* (Sage, 1998). With Julian Barling (Queen's University), he edited a book series, *Advanced Topics in Organizational Psychology* (Sage), and has coedited, with Kevin Kelloway, the volume *Young Workers: Varieties of Experience* (1999).

About the Contributors

Christine Alksnis received her PhD in applied social psychology from the University of Guelph and is currently an Assistant Professor of Psychology and Contemporary Studies at the Brantford Campus of Wilfrid Laurier University. Her academic research concentrates on issues affecting women, both in their work and personal lives. One line of research involves examining how gender stereotypes facilitate discriminatory sexist behaviour by employers, which in turn contributes to the persistence of the gender wage gap. A second line of research relates to stereotypes regarding sexual assault and their impact in the courtroom.

Leanne Barlow graduated with a master of business administration, specializing in management and organizational studies, from Simon Fraser University and is currently employed as a Human Capital Consultant with Watson Wyatt in Vancouver. She works in a variety of HR areas, including organizational measurement and performance management. She is actively involved with the Canadian Red Cross as a First Aid Instructor Trainer, she has an interest in the area of injury prevention.

Janet L. Barnes-Farrell is Associate Professor of Industrial/Organizational Psychology at the University of Connecticut. Her primary fields of expertise include aging and work, performance appraisal, and work-life balance. She has presented and published over 20 papers on the workplace concerns of older workers on topics ranging from age discrimination to retirement decision processes. Her research has appeared in a number of professional journals, including the *Journal of Applied Psychology, Personnel Psychology, Human Resource Management Review, Organizational Behavior and Human Decision Processes, Psychology and Aging*, and *Experimental Aging Research*. She is a member of the editorial board for the *Journal of Applied Psychology* and coeditor of a recent special issue on aging and work in *Experimental Aging Research*.

Terry A. Beehr earned his PhD in organizational psychology from the University of Michigan in 1974, subsequently worked at the Institute for Social Research and Illinois State University, and is currently Professor of Industrial and Organizational Psychology at the Central Michigan University Department of Psychology. He studies topics such as occupational stress, retirement, and careers, and some of his most current work involves the examination of social support in relation to occupational stress.

Gina M. Bellavia is a postdoctoral research associate at the Research Institute on Addictions, State University of New York at Buffalo. Her research interests include romantic relationships, families, work-family conflict, and flexible work policies. Her work has been published in journals such as the *Journal of Personality and Social Psychology, Personality and Social Psychology Bulletin,* and *Personal Relationships.* She also reviews articles for the *Journal of Occupational Health Psychology* and *Personal Relationships.* She is a member of the National Council on Family Relations, the Research Society on Alcoholism, and the Society for Personality and Social Psychology. She received her PhD in social psychology from SUNY–Buffalo.

Lehman Benson, III, is the McCoy/Fellow and Associate Professor of Management and Policy at the University of Arizona. He received his BA at the University of California, Davis; his MA at the University of California, San Diego; and his PhD in cognitive psychology at Lund University in Lund, Sweden. He completed his postgraduate education at the University of California at Berkeley, where he was awarded a Presidential Post-Doctoral Fellowship. His ongoing research examines the effect of time constraints on judgment and decision making. In addition to being a leading researcher in his field, he has won numerous teaching awards (including Professor of the Year); he taught at Georgetown University and Duke University.

Susan Cartwright is a Chartered Psychologist, Associate Fellow of the British Psychological Society, Director of the Centre for Organizational Psychology, and Professor of Organizational Psychology at the Manchester School of Management, U.K. She is currently vice chair of the British Academy of Management, associate editor of the *British Journal of Management,* and past editor of the *Leadership and Organizational Journal.* Susan has published widely in the area of occupational stress and was coauthor of a major report on stress interventions commissioned by the European Union.

Cary Cooper is Professor of Organizational Psychology and Health in the Lancaster University Management School at Lancaster University. He is the author of over 100 books (on occupational stress, women at work, and industrial and organizational psychology), has written over 400 scholarly articles for academic journals, and is a frequent contributor to national newspapers, TV, and radio. He is founding editor of the *Journal of Organizational Behavior* and coeditor of the medical journal *Stress & Health* (formerly *Stress Medicine*). He is the president of the British Academy of Management and one of the first U.K.-based fellows of the (American) Academy of Management. In 2001, he was awarded a CBE in the Queen's Birthday Honors List for his contribution to organizational health.

Michael D. Coovert is Professor of Psychology at the University of South Florida, where he is also the founding director of the Institute for Human

Performance, Decision Making, and Cybernetics. He earned his undergraduate degree in computer science and psychology and his PhD in psychology from the Ohio State University. He consults and publishes in the areas of performance measurement, teams, quantitative methods, human computer interaction, and computer-supported cooperative work.

J. Philip Craiger is an Associate Professor in the Department of Computer Science at the University of Nebraska at Omaha. He currently teaches and conducts applied research in the areas of computer and network forensics and information security. Philip is a GIAC-certified computer forensic analyst and provides computer forensics training and consulting services to the Department of Defense, DOD contractors, and law enforcement. He is also a member of the Computer Forensics Educators and Researchers Consortium, a small working group comprising academicians, FBI, NSA, and IRS agents whose goal is to create a robust computer forensics program for use by universities in the United States.

Russell Cropanzano is a Brien Lesk Professor of Organizational Behavior in the Department of Management and Policy at the University of Arizona. He serves on the editorial boards for the *Journal of Applied Psychology, Journal of Management, Organizational Behavior and Human Decision Processes,* and *Social Justice Research.* He has published roughly 70 scholarly articles and chapters. In addition, he is a coauthor of *Organizational Justice and Human Resources Management,* which won the 1998 Book Award from the International Association of Conflict Management.

Craig D. Crossley is a doctoral candidate in industrial/organizational psychology at Bowling Green State University. Prior to entering the program at Bowling Green, he completed his undergraduate degree at Weber State University. His primary research interests are in the areas of organizational deviance and employee turnover. He has also conducted research on job satisfaction and job search.

Serge Desmarais received his PhD in social psychology from the University of Waterloo and is currently an Associate Professor of Psychology at the University of Guelph, where he holds a Canada Research Chair in Applied Social Psychology. His research is broadly related to applied social psychology and focuses especially on issues of social justice, work and work expectations, pay entitlement, gender issues, and interpersonal relations. He has also been actively involved in consulting to both public and private organizations.

Gary W. Evans is Professor of Design and Environmental Analysis and of Human Development, Cornell University. He is an environmental and developmental psychologist interested in how the physical environment contributes to the development of human health and well-being among children and their families.

Lori Francis received her PhD in industrial/organizational psychology from the University of Guelph in 2002 and is currently an Assistant Professor in the Department of Psychology at Saint Mary's University in Halifax, Nova Scotia. She has broad research interests in organizational psychology including occupational health and safety, unions, and workplace fairness. She is a member of Saint Mary's University's Centre for Leadership Excellence as well as the CN Centre for Occupational Health and Safety.

Daniel G. Gallagher is the CSX Corporation Professor of Management at James Madison University in Harrisonburg, Virginia. He currently serves on the editorial boards of the *Journal of Organizational Behavior, Journal of Management, Industrial Relations* (Berkeley), and the *International Journal of Conflict Management*. His current research interests include the multi-disciplinary study of contingent employment and other forms of work outside of the traditional employer-employee relationship. He is also actively involved in the teaching of negotiation skills and conflict resolution strategies.

Sharon Glazer is an Assistant Professor in Industrial and Organizational Psychology at San Jose State University, Department of Psychology. She was a recipient of a Fulbright travel grant to Budapest, Hungary, and a doctoral research grant to northern Italy and London to collect data on occupational stress across cultures for her dissertation. She earned her PhD from Central Michigan University in 1999. Thereafter, she was a postdoctoral fellow at the National Institute of Occupational Safety and Health, where she studied social support across cultures. Research interests include cross-cultural issues in occupational stress, organizational commitment, values, social support, expatriation and repatriation, as well as safety climate and culture.

Barry M. Goldman is currently an Associate Professor at the University of Arizona. His research interests focus on organizational justice and investigating why employees file legal claims against their employers. He received his PhD and JD from the University of Maryland. He has been published in, among others, the *Academy of Management Journal, Personnel Psychology, Journal of Applied Psychology, Journal of Management,* and the *Journal of Organizational Behavior*. He teaches courses in human resource management, employment law, and conflict management and negotiations.

Ken Harris is currently a PhD candidate in organizational behavior/human resource management at Florida State University. His research interests include leader-member exchange processes, organizational politics, meta-perception, and employee turnover.

Joseph J. Hurrell, Jr., is currently the Associate Director for Science, Division of Surveillance, Hazard Evaluations and Field Studies, National Institute for Occupational Safety and Health. He received his PhD in psychology from Miami University in 1982 and has had a long-standing research interest in the health and safety consequences of occupational stress, publishing numerous scientific articles and six edited books on the topic. He is the recipient of numerous awards for his work, including the Health and Human Services Secretary's Award for Distinguished Service and the Alice Hamilton Award for Excellence in Occupational Safety and Health.

Michelle Inness is a doctoral candidate at Queen's University School of Business. Her main areas of research interest include workplace violence and aggression and various aspects of occupational health and safety. She is a member of a consortium of work and health. She is currently completing her doctoral dissertation on health, safety, and performance outcomes related to the work experiences of peacekeepers.

Roderick D. Iverson is Professor of Human Resource Management at the Faculty of Business Administration, Simon Fraser University. He received his PhD in industrial sociology from the University of Iowa. Rick's main research interests include the areas of employee withdrawal (absenteeism, voluntary turnover, and downsizing); psychological contracts; employee well-being; organizational, union, and dual commitment; organizational performance; occupational injury; and high-performance work systems. He currently serves on the editorial boards of the *Asia Pacific Journal of Human Resources, Human Resource Management Review, Journal of Occupational Health Psychology*, and *International Journal of Selection and Assessment*.

Steve M. Jex is currently an Associate Professor in the Department of Psychology at Bowling Green State University. He also holds a Guest Scientist appointment at the Walter Reed Army Institute of Research in Washington, DC. Prior to joining the faculty at Bowling Green, Dr. Jex held faculty appointments at Central Michigan University and the University of Wisconsin, Oshkosh. His research has focused primarily on job-related stress and has appeared in many journals, such as the *Journal of Applied Psychology, Journal of Organizational Behavior*, and *Journal of Occupational Health Psychology*.

K. Michele Kacmar is the Charles A. Rovetta Professor of Management and Director of the Center for Human Resource Management at Florida State University. She received her PhD from Texas A&M University. Her research interests include applying impression management and organizational politics to the field of HR. She has published over 50 articles in journals such as the *Journal of Applied Psychology, Organizational Behavior and Human Decision Processes*, and *Human Relations*. She served as editor of the *Journal of Management* from 2000 to 2002 and on the board of directors of the Society for Human Resource Management Foundation from 1993 to 2000. She is currently serving a 5-year term on the executive committee for the HR Division of the Academy of Management.

Katherine Lang is an Assistant Director of Admissions at Hampshire College in Amherst, MA. She is a recent graduate of the co-op management program at the University of Toronto. She specializes in the management of public institutions with a focus on higher education. Her past research projects include studying work stress in young workers and leadership in the Canadian military. She recently published a paper on the role of affirmative action in the admissions process at selective liberal arts colleges. She is currently teaching a workshop on the role of organizational behavior in everyday life.

Cong Liu received her PhD in industrial and organizational psychology from the University of South Florida in 2003. She is currently Assistant Professor in the Psychology Department at Illinois State University. Her research interests include cross-cultural job stress comparisons (e.g., common and cultural-specific job stressors and strains), methodology issues in job stress study, multinational job satisfaction surveys, cross-cultural psychology (e.g., the application of cultural theory to industrial and organizational psychology research), and measurement equivalence techniques in cross-cultural and comparative research.

Catherine Loughlin has a PhD in industrial/organizational psychology from Queen's University and teaches Organizational Behaviour in Management at the University of Toronto. She has consulted for private and public industry. Her research focuses on occupational health and safety (e.g., acute and chronic work stress; management's leadership role in workplace safety), leadership training and development, and the workforce of the future (e.g., young and nonstandard workers). She has published in the *Journal of Organizational Behavior* and the *Journal of Applied Psychology* and holds a grant from the Social Sciences and Humanities Research Council of Canada (SSHRC) to study young workers in the new economy.

Janetta Mitchell McCoy is Assistant Professor of Interior Design in the College of Architecture and Environmental Design, Arizona State University. She is an environment and behavior researcher interested in the relationship of the physical environment of work to the development of leadership, teamwork, and creativity.

Tahira M. Probst is an Associate Professor of Psychology at Washington State University, Vancouver. She received her PhD in industrial/organizational psychology in 1998 from the University of Illinois at Urbana-Champaign. Her current research focuses on occupational safety and health-related implications of organizational downsizing and employee job insecurity. In addition, she conducts research related to issues of workplace diversity. She currently serves on the editorial board of the *Journal of Occupational Health Psychology,* and her research has appeared in outlets such as the *Journal of Applied Psychology, Group and Organization Management, Journal of Occupational and Organizational Psychology, Organizational Behavior and Human Decision Processes,* and *Teaching of Psychology.*

Judith A. Richman, Professor of Epidemiology in Psychiatry at the University of Illinois at Chicago, received her doctorate from Columbia University in 1978. She is a sociologist who has conducted research on occupational stressors and workplace harassment since 1987 and is author of over 50 articles and book chapters on these and other topics. She is currently principal investigator of a longitudinal cohort study of workplace harassment and drinking outcomes funded by the National Institute on Alcohol Abuse and Alcoholism.

Kathleen M. Rospenda is Assistant Professor of Psychology in Psychiatry at the University of Illinois at Chicago. She received her doctorate in industrial/organizational psychology from DePaul University in 1998. Her primary research interests include harassment at work, job stress, gender issues, and alcohol use. Currently, she is principal investigator of a national study on workplace harassment, use of health and mental health services, and drinking outcomes funded by the National Institute on Alcohol Abuse and Alcoholism.

Aaron C. H. Schat received his PhD in industrial-organizational psychology in 2004 from the University of Guelph and is now an Assistant Professor of Organizational Behavior and Human Resource Management at the Michael G. DeGroote School of Business at McMaster University. His research interests include work-related stress and health and focus primarily on the measurement of workplace aggression, its antecedents and consequences, and moderators of these relationships. He is a member of the Academy of Management, the Canadian Psychological Association, the American Psychological Association, the Canadian Society for Industrial and Organizational Psychology, and the Society for Industrial and Organizational Psychology.

Niro Sivanathan is a PhD candidate in the Kellogg School of Management at Northwestern University. He received his BAH in psychology (2001) from Queen's University and his MSc in organizational behavior (2002) from the School of Business at Queen's University. His research interests include transformational leadership, well-being, trust, and behavioral decision making.

Paul E. Spector is Professor and Director of the Industrial/Organizational Psychology program at the University of South Florida. His interests include both content (counterproductive work behavior, occupational health psychology, occupational stress, and personality) and research methodology. He has published in many of the leading journals of the field and has served in editorial positions for several journals, including the *Journal of Occupational Health Psychology*. In 1991, the Institute for Scientific Information listed him as one of the 50 highest-impact contemporary researchers (of over 102,000) in psychology worldwide.

Lori Foster Thompson has recently joined the faculty of the Department of Psychology, North Carolina State University, having previously been a faculty member at East Carolina State University since 1999. She also works as a Senior Research Fellow at the Army Research Institute's Fort Bragg field office. She received her doctorate in industrial/organizational psychology from the University of South Florida in 1999, and her research primarily focuses on technology's effects on individuals, teams, and organizations. She has published her work in a variety of outlets and currently serves on the editorial board of the *Journal of Organizational Behavior*.

Peter Totterdell is a Senior Research Fellow in the Institute of Work Psychology, University of Sheffield, England, and a member of the U.K. Economic and Social Research Council's Centre for Organisation and Innovation. His PhD concerned the temporal aspects of well-being and his research interests include affect and well-being at work, diary methods, new forms of work, social networks, and work schedules. In relation to work schedules, he has conducted and published a variety of studies of public and private sector shift workers. He also pioneered the use of handheld computers in laboratory and field studies of shift workers and was part of the Sheffield Shiftwork Research Team that developed the Standard Shiftwork Index for surveying shift workers.

Peter Warr is Emeritus Professor in the Institute of Work Psychology at the University of Sheffield. He was previously director of the Social and Applied Psychology Unit at that university. The recipient of all three awards of the British Psychological Society for distinguished contributions to the development of the discipline, he is carrying out research into employee well-being and effectiveness, personality and work behavior, meeting processes, and aging in work settings.